# Software Engineering

# THE JOHNS HOPKINS UNIVERSITY
*Applied Physics Laboratory Series in Science and Engineering*

SERIES EDITOR: John Apel

Richard A. Henle and Boris W. Kuvshinoff.
*Desktop Computers in Perspective*

Bruce I. Blum. *Software Engineering: A Holistic View*

William H. Avery and Chih Wu. *Ocean Thermal Energy Conversion* (in press)

Vincent L. Pisacane (ed.). *Space Systems* (in press)

# Software Engineering
## *A Holistic View*

### BRUCE I. BLUM
*Applied Physics Laboratory*
*The Johns Hopkins University*

*New York    Oxford*
OXFORD UNIVERSITY PRESS
1992

## Oxford University Press

Oxford New York Toronto
Delhi Bombay Calcutta Madras Karachi
Petaling Jaya Singapore Hong Kong Tokyo
Nairobi Dar es Salaam Cape Town
Melbourne Auckland

and associated companies in
Berlin Ibadan

## Copyright © 1992 by Oxford University Press, Inc.

Published by Oxford University Press, Inc.
200 Madison Avenue, New York, New York 10016

Oxford is a registered trademark of Oxford University Press

Library of Congress Cataloging-in-Publication Data
Blum, Bruce I.
Software engineering: a holistic view / Bruce I. Blum
p. cm. (The Johns Hopkins University/Applied Physics
Laboratory series in science and technology)
Includes bibliographical references and index.
ISBN 0-19-507159-X
1. Software engineering. I. Title. II. Series.
QA76.758.B78 1992
005.1—dc20 91-31490

1 3 5 7 9 8 6 4 2

Printed in the United States of America
on acid-free paper

*To Harriet*

# PREFACE

This book provides a survey of software engineering as it is practiced after a quarter century of study. The book is intended for three audiences. First and foremost, it is a text for students in upper-level undergraduate and early graduate software engineering courses. As I explain in the Prologue, I was not satisfied with the texts available for teaching software engineering; consequently, I wrote my own. A quick review of the Prologue should help potential instructors decide if my approach improves on what now is available. The second target audience is that vast body of practitioners who, while earning their living by applying software engineering, are bombarded by new concepts, products, buzzwords, and panaceas. I hope to offer them a framework for understanding such diverse concepts as the entity relationship model, structured analysis, the various Jackson methods, formal techniques, abstract data types, and objected-oriented everything. Clearly, the practitioner must choose from among these competing alternatives, and I have tried to assist them in making intelligent choices. Finally, I am immodest enough to expect this book to be useful to teachers of software engineering (even if they do not use this book as a text). Few of them have practiced software engineering in a commercial setting. Indeed, most academic instructors are computer scientists. Therefore, my third goal is to provide a context to enrich their understanding of what they are teaching.

Now for some truth in labeling. What are my qualifications for writing a book on software engineering? To begin with, I have some 30 years of experience, mostly with the design, implementation, and maintenance of scientific information systems. That record is not as impressive as it might at first sound. I am 60 years old, and having worked for 30 years is not much of an accomplishment. Moreover, given that the half-life of our technical knowledge is only five years, I may not have much of an advantage over someone with half my work experience. To be specific, I was responsible for the development of the Ground Data Handling System for the first of the Landsat satellites, I worked on information systems for engineering and space science data, and I led the design and implementation of several clinical information systems at Johns Hopkins. Since 1985 I have been engaged in research that exploits my software development experience. The rationale for this grew out of the teaching of graduate courses in software engineering, which I have been doing for the past seven years.

Of course, the important question is, "Did I bring this book in on schedule, within cost, and with the expected functionality?" If I cannot manage my own, personal tasks, why should the reader take my advice in managing his[1] tasks? The long answer begins with, "Well, . . ." The short answer is that the book is a year later than I had planned, but I learned more doing it than I had expected. Regarding the book's contents, I think that this is a good book, and I am pleased with it. If I were planning the Great American Novel, I would consider this a first draft. If I were responding to a contract, perhaps I would have been able to defer other things and get the book out on time. But writing a book is hard work, and one should structure the work so it becomes enjoyable. Developing software is also hard work, and one also should structure that assignment to make it satisfying. That is what this book is about. The present paragraph suggests that the execution is more difficult than the explanation.

No one who writes a technical book can do so without the support and assistance of a great number of colleagues, friends, and associates. I owe a major debt to two institutions. First, the Johns Hopkins University has assisted me in my intellectual growth and provided me with productive avenues for pursuing my interests. I have been employed by the Applied Physics Laboratory for over 20 years; it took eight years in industry for me to appreciate the support and stimulation that the Laboratory provides. While at the Laboratory, I spent eight years on full-time assignment in the School of Medicine and seven years teaching part-time in the School of Engineering. Encouragement to write this book first came from Vince Sigillito, then Acting Dean of the Continuing Professional Programs in the School of Engineering. A Janney Fellowship, provided by the Applied Physics Laboratory, gave me the financial assistance to begin the task. The second organization whose assistance I wish to acknowledge is the United States Navy. My research in software engineering has been funded by Navy tasks. Some of these tasks are internal to the Laboratory, others are for the Office of Naval Research. I have been fortunate in being able to develop my insights and publish my results in the open literature. Although none

---

[1]Notice the masculine pronoun. There is an obvious gender limitation in the English language, which I have found difficult to accommodate. I would hope that half of the readers of this book are female, but I feel uncomfortable continually acknowledging that fact by employing "his or her" where just one word suffices. Consequently, I ask the reader to consider any masculine pronouns androgynous. In the words of Herbert Simon, "I believe that we should not abandon these pronouns but include women and men equally in their scope" [Simo69, p. 5].

of my Navy research support was used for the preparation of this text, it certainly has contributed significantly to my understanding of software engineering.

Many individuals helped me to bring this book to completion. I first thank Carl Bostrom, the Director of the Laboratory, Don Williams, the Director of the Research Center, and Vince Sigillito, my immediate supervisor, for making my environment secure and stimulating. I next acknowledge (with apology) the help of the students in my 1990 software engineering classes. They tolerated the preliminary drafts, the inappropriate assignments, and the lack of a complete text. I hope that their education did not suffer excessively; I am certain that the book benefitted from their feedback. I also was fortunate in having the following friends and colleagues review sections of book. Listed alphabetically, they are: Robert Arnold, Boris Beizer, Grady Booch, David Card, Peter Coad, James Coolahan, Robert Glass, Mars Gralia, David Gries, Watts Humphrey, Larrie Hutton, Michael Jackson, Harlan Mills, Jochen Moehr, David Parnas, and Ralph Semmel. They made many helpful comments and caught some embarrassing mistakes. I appreciate their time and interest; clearly, I am responsible for the errors and inaccuracies that remain.

Having written my first book with a fountain pen, I am proud to state that this one I typed myself. Still, I required the help of many others to get it into its final state. Joe Lew and his Graphics and Composition Section prepared the artwork and responded promptly to my many updates; Jane Scott got my all letters out on time; John Apel, who is coordinating the APL series with Oxford, made my job much easier; and Jeff Robbins, my editor at Oxford, Anita Lekhwani, his editorial assistant, and the production staff at Oxford also were most helpful and supportive. Thank you all.

The last paragraph belongs to Harriet. She showed patience when I was compulsive, interest when I was boring, and belief when I told her the book would be finished in "about one more month." She adds excitement to my life, and that helps me keep software engineering in perspective. Once again, thanks.

B. I. B.
Laurel, Md.
June 1991

# CONTENTS

## 6. MANAGING THE PROCESS, 425

## EPILOGUE, 503

# Software Engineering

# PROLOGUE

*Software Engineering: A Holistic View* is the third (and final) title for this book. Yet another book on software engineering? This prologue explains why I felt one more was required and why I had such trouble in selecting a title. To begin with, I find most software engineering texts less than satisfactory. They seem to start with a chapter that tells us why software is important and how poorly we have performed historically. Next, the text describes how to manage the software process, usually with references to the famous waterfall flow (which is criticized). The remaining chapters follow the waterfall development cycle.

These books make it easy to teach a software life-cycle model and identify the required documents. The texts also identify some methods and tools, but often the descriptions are not integrated. Many different examples are used, and it is difficult to contrast methods. Of course, one should not expect the students in a one-semester software engineering course to learn more than a few methods well. Still, most students come away with just an understanding of the software life cycle as it was designed for large projects in the mid-1970s. It is a clearly stated process that can be memorized and repeated. Unfortunately, the rest remains fuzzy. My early students seemed to accept software engineering methods as an adjunct to what they conceived to be their primary activity: writing program code.

After using these texts for several years, I decided that an alternative was necessary. The available books were based on a life-cycle orientation intended for large, complex systems that involved both hardware and software development. Most of my students, however, would work in project teams of 40 or fewer. I was not sure that the large-scale approach would scale down. I also had a second concern. Software engineering involves the creation of problem solutions using software, and code writing should be a relatively small part of that process. Yet with small class projects, the effort devoted to coding became so great that many students confused software engineering with good coding practices. (In fact, there are at least two books with software engineering in the title that are, in essence, language-specific programming texts.)

Thus, the first of my titles was *Software Engineering for Small and Large Projects*. Because most users of the book would work on small (more than half-an-effort-year) or large (up to 100-effort-year) projects, it seemed appropriate to focus on software engineering for activities of that size.   I intended to explain how software engineering improves productivity and quality in this class of project.  Moreover, because the problems to be addressed by the software were highly dependent on local considerations, I also wanted to introduce a variety of methods and tools and show how they differed.  Lacking a standard approach, I hoped to emphasize what we are doing and why.

I kept that orientation as I wrote, but I soon recognized that my title—while being descriptive—lacked pizazz.  I then toyed with *Software Engineering: A Problem-Solving Approach.*  The goal of the software product is to satisfy some need in the application domain.  There are problems to be solved in determining the need, specifying the solution, developing the software architecture, designing the software modules, certifying that the need is satisfied, and so on.  Although there is no cookbook for solving these problems, there are clear guidelines for ascertaining the problem, applying experience to arrive at a solution, and confirming that the goals have been achieved.

I retained that orientation as well, but I eventually abandoned the second title for the present one with its "holistic view."  As a researcher in software engineering, I have seen major changes during the past decade.  I believe that our approach to software engineering in the next millennium will be quite different from our current practice.  If this is true, then how should we now be teaching software engineering?  Although I reject some of the ideas of the 1970s, I nevertheless see them as the foundation of today's practices.  Most of our tools and methods have been a over decade in the making, and many represent a response to some older problem.  We need to acknowledge this and establish which beliefs remain valid and which must be reexamined.

Although I question some of our current perceptions, it is too early to identify the new approaches to software engineering that will prevail. I have my own views (which I present in the Epilogue), but I am not certain that they are shared by many in the software engineering community.   If this were a research monograph, I could allow my personal biases to dominate.  But this is a text for software engineering students and practitioners.  I am expected to explain what two decades of experience have taught us about the development and maintenance of software.  As my first title suggested, I am obliged to show how the combination of good engineering practices and today's technology can improve software in small and large projects.

Given these objectives, why a holistic view?  Two reasons.  First, if one accepts that software engineering (and, for that matter, computing) is in a period of transition, then one ought to understand current practices in the context of both the problems we are addressing and how we came to respond to them in this way.  That is, software engineering should be presented as a collection of evolving (but demonstrated) methods and practices.  I recognized the need for this orientation after

I taught software engineering for the first time. I had organized my presentation as a "revisionist" course, and the semester was half over before I realized that most students had no comprehension of the baseline methods that I was critiquing. Without this background, my discussion of process refinements had little meaning. Thus, in a fast-moving field we must both teach what is broadly accepted and anchor what we teach within some larger context.

The second reason that I favor the idea of a holistic view is that the software process really is holistic. We subdivide the process into smaller activities so we can manage it. Similarly, we improve our understanding of the target system by abstracting away details. But this decomposition is an artifact of the way in which we solve large problems; it does not necessarily reflect the inherent structure of either the problem or its solution. For example, as we specify a software solution to a problem, we implicitly make some design decisions. When we get to the level of coding, we often find that we must revise the design. The process is nonmonotonic with few discrete or independent activities. A holistic view recognizes that fact; tasks are broken off from the whole, but a sense of their unity is preserved.

In what follows, I have projected this holistic view onto six chapters. Chapter 1 presents an overview of software engineering and the software process. Its orientation may be considered philosophical. Certainly, it offers few facts or methods to memorize. My bias is that we ought to understand what it is we are doing as software engineers before we start learning how to do it. Moreover, if—as I suspect—software engineering is undergoing a major revision, then a firm conceptual foundation may be the most important benefit of reading this book. The next three chapters present various approaches to the development of a software product. Each chapter has modeling in its title. The chapter contents overlap, and the material within a chapter is grouped more by a methodological similarity than a concern for the topic suggested by the title.

Where the three modeling chapters focus on the forward-looking process of design, Chapter 5 looks backward. It examines the techniques for ensuring the quality of both the design and the finished product. Naturally, one designs and examines the quality of that design as part of a closed-loop process. Although I defer the quality examination until Chapter 5, this must not be taken as a suggestion that quality is reviewed after the design is complete. In the same way, I leave a discussion of management until Chapter 6. I do this because one should understand what is being managed before learning how to manage it. (In contrast, many software engineering texts begin with an introduction to project management.) Obviously, management is conducted in parallel with design and quality assessment.

These three activities are concurrent. Design is a problem-solving activity. It is poorly structured and opportunistic. Designers seldom channel their thoughts into a given level of detail. They examine the larger context of the problem as they explore the details to be refined in later stages. In time, however, the designers formalize their decisions, and an evaluation of the quality of those decisions immediately follows. In parallel with this, management controls the project. Using experience from previous projects, management assesses status, anticipates risk, and allocates resources. Although design is a continuous process, management must abstract it as a series of discrete events to be monitored and measured. With a holistic view, we can see that these three classes of activity are intertwined; with a traditional view, however, it is easy to confuse the conduct of a project with its management.

Let me restate this is a less holistic manner. There are three themes running through this book.

- The software process is a problem-solving activity. Because the process begins with the identification of a need and culminates with the implementation of an automated response to that need, the nature of the problems to be solved will change as the development progresses. Early in the process, application domain issues (e.g., specifying the requirements) will be critical; in time, the implementation concerns (e.g., modularization tradeoffs) will dominate. Clearly, different classes of problem imply a need for different solution methods, many of which may not be compatible.

- In software engineering, problem solving is accomplished by modeling. The implemented product (e.g., the program) is always a formal model, and it is the formality of that model that provides confidence in predicting its behavior. Software engineering also deals with models that are not formal (e.g., a user's vague request). The process, therefore, can be interpreted as a modeling activity that begins with informal (or conceptual) models and converts them into formal models. Until formal models exist, our reasoning remains imperfect.

- As a problem-solving, modeling discipline, software engineering is a human activity that is biased by previous experience. That is, unlike the modeling of physical phenomena, there are few confirmable answers bounded by invariant constraints. Lacking an external reality, we must conduct the process in ways that seem reasonable and work. Consequently, it is as important to understand why we do what we do as it is to learn how to do it.

Of course, these three points simply represent projections of my single, holistic understanding.

One final comment. This is a book about software engineering, and software engineering is a group activity. Writing computer programs is an individual activity, but that is not software engineering. It is difficult to learn software engineering in the abstract, just as it is difficult to understand group dynamics without being part of a group. The book describes many different methods. At a conceptual level, most methods can be understood just by reading about them. However, to appreciate the value of and difficulty in using a method, one should attempt the exercises in the appendix. Those flagged with an asterisk were designed for groups, and I believe that much can be learned when working in a group. Few of the exercises have anything to do with writing program code. Programming is an important part of software engineering, but it is not one of its central concerns.

I now have exposed enough of my prejudices regarding software engineering; it is time to examine what I have to say.

M. C. Escher, "Waterfall" Reproduction rights arranged courtesy of Vorpal Gallery, San Francisco and New York City.

# 1

## THE SOFTWARE PROCESS

Escher's "Waterfall" acts as a metaphor for what we hope to achieve from the software process. There is a well-conceived design with a careful architecture. The building is modular, and the interfaces all conform. There is only one problem. Escher's waterfall defies a three-dimensional realization. Of course, that is its charm.

Software engineering is somewhat like an art in that it begins with the identification of an objective and ends with a product that fulfills it. The artist's goal is to produce a work of aesthetic value; the software engineer's purpose is to solve a problem using software. The quality of the result will depend on the vision of the intent and what is learned during design and construction. The value of the artist's work will be determined by those who see it; the value of the software engineer's work will be measured by those who use it.

In this chapter I examine the software process: the collection of activities that begins with the identification of a need and concludes with the retirement of the software product that satisfies the need. I start by defining software engineering, first in an historical context, and then as others see it. My view is that software engineering is the conduct of the software process.

I next analyze the software process, which traditionally has been described as a waterfall. (Pun intended.) As it turns out, our waterfall model is about as satisfactory in the real world as Escher's. I explain why, discuss what the process really is, and then review some alternative process models.

Following this, I introduce a central theme: software engineering is problem solving. I summarize what we know about human problem solving and formal models. The objective is to provide a foundation for the material in the remaining chapters. The orientation is more philosophical than technical, but I find it interesting.

The chapter concludes with a brief review of what we have learned during two decades of software engineering. Some myths are debunked, some basic relationships are established, and some uncertainty is exposed. There is nothing in this chapter of a "how-to" nature, which suggests that its contents may remain valid beyond the end of this millennium.

## 1.1.   What is software engineering?

This is a book about software engineering, and it may seem unreasonable to begin with a basic question. The question suggests that the answer may not be obvious; in fact, there may be more than one answer. For this book, however, I have a particular answer in mind, and the text has been organized to support that answer. Yet, there are other ways of looking at software engineering, and the informed reader ought to understand these alternative viewpoints. That is what this section is about.

The short answer to my question is that software engineering is the application of tools, methods, and disciplines to produce and maintain an automated solution to a real-world problem. It requires the identification of a problem, a computer to execute a software product, and an environment (composed of people, equipment, computers, documentation, and so forth) in which the software product exists. Clearly, without computer programs there would be no software product and no software engineering. But this is only a necessary condition; it is not sufficient.

Without the identification of a problem and an environment in which the solution will operate, there would be no need for the software product. Thus, my view of software engineering is that it is the discipline of resolving problems with software solutions. As will be seen, there are many different kinds of problems that will challenge us. Consequently, we will require diverse methods and tools to help in our quest. What these methods and tools are and how to apply them is, of course, the topic of this book.

Notice that I refer to the computer program in the context of a response to a problem. For most computer science students, however, this is an unexpected orientation. Computer science education first teaches the mastery of programming languages and related software tools. The students are learning skills. To me, software engineering involves the application of those skills in a problem-solving situation; it is not a set of practices for using those skills. Good programming practices may be good software engineering practices as well, but good software engineering is not the same as good programming.

Stating this in another way, programming is to software engineering as the mastery of the English language is to literature. It is one of many tools used to achieve a goal. I assume the reader has the skills to produce effective programs. I am concerned with the much more difficult task of showing how those skills aid in the solution of problems. But enough of my short answer, on to the long answer.

*1.1.1.  The origins of software engineering*

Software engineering first emerged as a popular term in the title of a 1968 NATO conference held in Garmisch, Germany [NaRa69]. The juxtaposition of software and engineering was intended to be provocative. The digital computer was less than a quarter of a century old, and already we were facing a "software crisis." First we had invented computer programming, and then we taught people to write programs. The next task was the development of large systems that were reliable, delivered on schedule, and within budget. As with every technological advancement, our aspirations were at the boundary of what we could do successfully. As it turned out, we were not very good at building large systems on time and without overruns. Consequently, software engineering emerged as the organizing force to overcome the barriers that threatened our progress.

The successes of computing up to the mid-1960s were quite remarkable. Although the origins of computing machines can be traced back to the abacus and earlier, it was not until the 1940s that the architecture of the modern computer was established. Prior to that time there were attempts to build mechanical calculators, but the technology of the time could not sustain their extended operation. Thus Pascal produced an Arithmetic Engine and Babbage developed an Analytical Engine, but neither had much impact in its time. Later electro-mechanical devices offered a foundation for the more rapid and reliable calculators developed by Stibitz and Aiken. During the early 1940s, as Aiken worked on his Automatic Sequence Controlled Calculator (or Mark I), he discovered Babbage's writing and stated that he had learned more about computing from that work than he had from any other individual. In fact, he declared that the Mark I was "Babbage's dream come true." The road to the modern computer, however, followed the path of the vacuum tube. Electromechanical computing would not provide the answer, and Babbage would have to be rediscovered once more.

Stibitz and Aiken had independently rejected the use of the faster vacuum tube because of its unreliability. The war effort of the early 1940s fostered improvements in electronics that made the electronic computer possible. Radar required vacuum tube circuits of 100 or more tubes; it also handled discrete circuits and interfaced with a memory containing stored radar pulses. Writing about that period, Buchholz observed, "the availability of cheap, mass-produced components and of engineers trained to use them made it possible to experiment on a greater scale and at a lower capital investment than before" [Buch53, p. 1220].

The field was ready to find new uses for the improved technology. As the historian Ceruzzi put it, "Electronic computing was held up now by the need for a consensus on what a digital computer ought to look like.  This bottleneck was broken in 1945, with the emergence of the concept of the stored program principle" detailed by von Neumann in his "First Draft of a Report on the EDVAC" [Ceru89, p. 260].  Wilkes, whose EDSAC of 1949 was one of the very early computers,[1] recalled

> In [the EDVAC Report], clearly laid out, were the principles on which the development of the modern digital computer was to be based: the stored program with the same store for numbers and instructions, the serial execution of instructions, and the use of binary switching circuits for computation and control.  I recognized this at once as the real thing, and from that time on never had any doubt as to the way computer development would go.  [Wilk85, p. 109]

By 1955 the architecture was understood, and the model that was to dominate computing through the 1990s had been defined.  In fact, this may explain the phenomenal advances that we have seen in computer hardware.  For almost half a century we have been refining a basic design and miniaturizing its components.  The result has been reduced costs, increased functionality, and the identification of new, but related, applications, (e.g., networks and communications).  By way of contrast, progress is much slower in those areas in which we have poorer models (such as with highly parallel computing).

The computer had emerged; now it was to be used.  The first applications were obvious.  The machine was called a calculator, and the person who used it was the computer.  The immediate need was for a calculator to aid the "computer" in performing repeated computations.  The initial outputs were numerical tables used for ballistic computations, statistical evaluations, and so on.  Soon it was recognized that the computer (as it now had become known) could manage any symbolic information, and development of tools that facilitated programming followed.  In the mid-1950s Fortran proved that high-level languages (HLL) could produce efficient object code.  By 1961 Algol, Cobol, and Lisp were operational.  Thus, by the second decade of digital computing, all of the principal HLLs (other than Prolog) were in existence.  Of course, Algol has undergone numerous name changes; current versions include Pascal and Ada.

---

[1]The ENIAC, developed by Mauchly and Eckert in 1945, was the first implementation of a large scale vacuum tube computer.  It was developed in parallel with von Neumann's design efforts.  An early modification to the ENIAC replaced its plugboard memory with a stored program memory.

To understand the impact that the HLL had on computing, consider the following evaluation presented by Backus at a 1957 Western Joint Computer Conference.

A brief case history of one job done with a system seldom gives a good measure of its usefulness, particularly when the selection is made by the authors of the system. Nevertheless, here are the facts about a rather simple but sizable job. The programmer attended a one-day course on FORTRAN and spent some more time referring to the manual. He then programmed the job in four hours, using 47 FORTRAN statements. These were compiled by the 704 in six minutes, producing about 1000 instructions. He ran the program and found the output incorrect. He studied the output and was able to localize his error in a FORTRAN statement he had written. He rewrote the offending statement, recompiled, and found that the resulting program was correct. He estimated that it might have taken three days to code the job by hand, plus an unknown time to debug it, and that no appreciable improvement in speed of execution would have been achieved thereby. [Back57]

Here we see that the HLL allows the programmer to move from a description of the computation to be performed by the computer to an explanation of the calculation that is desired. That is, the 47-line statement defines *what* is to be done whereas the 1000 instructions detail *how* the calculation is to be carried out. The former is an expression of the problem to be solved; it is more compact than and just as efficient as its 1000-line expansion.

The 1950s also saw the commercialization of the computer. Eckert and Mauchly formed their own company and produced the UNIVersal Automatic Computer (UNIVAC I), which was installed in the Census Bureau in 1951. Eventually, they were bought out by Remington Rand, a company that had assembled an impressive array of technological skills. It was IBM, however, that was able to recognize the industry needs and ultimately dominate the field. Until 1959, when the transistorized 7090 was released, their offerings were still vacuum-tube based. Yet, after a somewhat shaky start, the 7090/7094 emerged as the most common platform for large-scale computing. The success of their early computers became obvious when, in 1964, IBM offered its third generation: the 360 family. The new systems corrected the limitations of the earlier generation. For example, character codes were expanded to 8 rather than 6 bits thereby supporting both uppercase and lowercase characters. These improvements meant that the keypunch machines, tape drives, and some old programs had to be changed. In a very short period of time, a new but obsolescent technology had entrenched itself, and the users who had committed themselves to the early systems objected to the changes. Consequently, the industry resolved to make future hardware transitions transparent to the users. Thus, while there is a fifth-generation computer, no computers are labeled fourth generation.

This was the background leading to the 1968 Garmisch NATO Science Committee conference on software engineering. Computers were in widespread use, integrated circuits had made them more powerful and smaller, the new operating systems supported man-machine interaction, and the HLLs had shown the way to improved productivity and reliability. Yet, progress was slower than one would have hoped. Large projects were difficult to manage and coordinate. Many computer professionals had learned their skills on the job, and few were aware of the techniques that a century of engineering had refined. As a result, 50 people from a dozen countries were invited to participate in this first conference to address the problems of building software applications. The attendees came from the ranks of academia and industry; each was involved in the application of computers in a large problem.

The Garmisch conference was a resounding success. A sense of euphoria arose from the fact that so many people had a common view of the problem and a belief that a solution was possible. A second conference, to meet near Rome, was called for the following year. The following is taken from the Rome report.

> The Garmisch conference was notable for the range of interests and experience represented among its participants. . . [They] found commonality in a widespread belief as to the extent and seriousness of the problems facing . . . "software engineering." This enabled a very productive series of discussions . . . [whose] goal was to identify, classify, and discuss the problems, both technical and managerial, up to and including the type of projects that can only be measured in man-millennia. . . .
>
> [The Rome] conference bore little resemblance to its predecessor. The sense of urgency in the face of common problems was not so apparent as at Garmisch. Instead, a lack of communication between different sections of the participants became, in the editors' opinions at least, a dominant feature. Eventually the seriousness of this communication gap, and the realization that it was but a reflection of the situation in the real world, caused the gap itself to become a major topic of discussion. [BuRa70, p. 7]

The NATO conferences had established the concept of software engineering, even if they could not determine how its goals could be met. The terms they chose, such as "software engineering" and "software manufacturing," were intended to provoke thought. They hoped that large software projects could benefit from experience with engineering control methods or extensions of the HLL's abstractions. Naturally, it would have been unreasonable for this diverse collection of individuals to resolve a knotty problem that has resisted unraveling for another 20 years. Nevertheless, they identified a set of issues and provided a foundation for the investigation of potential and partial solutions.

There was progress. In 1976, the *IEEE Transactions on Computers* celebrated its twenty-fifth anniversary, and Boehm contributed a paper that defined the field for the next decade and more. The contents remain timely; the paper certainly is recommended reading. In his conclusion, he describes the state of software engineering and hardware engineering and comments:

> It is clear . . . that software engineering is in a very primitive state as compared to hardware engineering, with respect to its range of scientific foundations. Those scientific principles available to support software engineering address problems in an area we shall call *Area 1: detailed design and coding* of *systems software* by *experts* in a relatively *economics-independent* context. Unfortunately, the most pressing software development problems are in an area we shall call *Area 2: requirements analysis, design, test, and maintenance* of *application software* by *technicians* in an *economics-driven* context. And in Area 2, our scientific foundations are so slight that one can seriously question whether our current techniques deserve to be called "software engineering."
> [Boeh76, pp. 1239-1240]

Although I disagree with the characterization suggested by Boehm's use of the word "technician," I believe that his description of the problem is accurate. This book is concerned with Area 2, and—as we will see—considerable advances have been made in building a scientific base to resolve the Area 2 problems.

Today, software engineering is recognized as an academic discipline. The first International Conference on Software Engineering was held in 1973, and the *IEEE Transactions on Software Engineering* was begun in 1975. Several academic institutions now offer a Master of Software Engineering degree [FoGi89]. Yet, to many the software engineering community remains closer to the temper characterized by the Rome than the Garmisch conference. There still are conflicts between those who seek to build a scientific foundation and those who look to address immediate problems. The historian Mahoney believes that software engineering "has developed more as a set of techniques than as a body of learning. Except for a few university centers . . . it remains primarily a concern of military and industrial R&D aimed at the design and implementation of large, complex systems, and the driving forces are cost and reliability" [Maho88, p. 117].

Of course, in my short answer to the question of what software engineering is, I offered an alternative view. I defined it as the discipline of producing software solutions to real problems. (These solutions are the application software of Area 2.) Moreover, I do not concentrate on the techniques required to implement large, complex systems. The problems of interest here have solutions that require from ½ to 100 effort years for development. This excludes very small projects (which tend to be dominated by the personal methods of the developer) and very large projects (which must already have established practices before they can win very large contracts). Naturally, everyone can benefit from the wisdom that I am about to impart. But if I have to choose one audience, let it be the software engineers who work on small to large projects. They constitute the vast majority of the practitioners, and often their problems are ignored. Because, this book's viewpoint breaks with the large-system tradition, I feel obligated to provide a review of how others view software engineering. This I do in the next section.

### 1.1.2. Some modern views of software engineering

In the previous section I referred to a "software crisis" when I introduced the early NATO conferences. Those words soon became a rallying cry for the advocates of software engineering. Indeed, most textbooks introduced software engineering with a section or chapter with that title. The software crisis label symbolized our failures to produce reliable software on time and within budget, to approach the productivity improvements seen in hardware, and to meet the ever-expanding demands for software products. Software engineering was seen as the key to crisis resolution.

Bauer, one of the early leaders in this new field, stated that software engineering involves the

> establishment and use of sound engineering principles (methods) in order to obtain economically software that is reliable and works on real machines. [Baue72]

With this definition, few would admit that they did not apply software engineering on their projects. Indeed, Bauer later remarked in 1972:

> In 1967 and 1968, the word "Software Engineering" had been

used in a provocative way, in order to demonstrate that something was wrong in the existing design, production and servicing of software. The situation has considerably changed since then; many people show concern about the problems of software engineering and some of the manufacturers, to which the provocation was mainly addressed, claim that they already obey the principles of software engineering, whatever they may mean. Soon "software engineering" will turn up in advertisements. [Baue73, p. 2]

For many, software engineering was interpreted as the institution of engineering discipline in the manufacture of computer software. There already were established models for equipment manufacture, standards for documentation control and progress reporting, and a heritage of formal review and testing. Engineers were trained in their technology, had resources for resolving questions prior to committing to a design decision, and had a tradition of problem solving within their domain of expertise. As Boehm pointed out in his 1976 paper, such resources did not exist for the software specialist. Most programmers learned their skills on the job. To some, programming was an act of personal creativity that resisted external control. An engineering discipline, it was believed, would resolve many of these problems. Analysts would document the design before the coding started; all software products would be inspected and tested systematically; and schedule and costs would be tracked and managed. This management orientation is the basis for Mahoney's earlier comment on the evolution of software engineering since 1969.

The definition that Boehm offered in his 1976 paper is more complete than that of Bauer. To him, software engineering is:

The practical application of scientific knowledge in the design and construction of computer programs and the associated documentation required to develop, operate, and maintain them. [Boeh76, p. 1226]

Here the emphasis shifts to a scientific knowledge base that will guide in making and evaluating decisions. For systems software (Area 1), Boehm believed that a scientific base, founded on logical formalisms and refined empirically, already existed. Engineering discipline was desirable in the context of a predictable process to be managed. By way of contrast, Dijkstra approached the problem from the perspective of computer science. His discipline of programming was mathematically motivated. These are two different categories of discipline, two approaches to the problem.

Belady and Leavenworth describe this tension between the management of the process and the discovery of its scientific underpinnings as follows:

> *Software engineering* is polarized around *two subcultures*: the speculators and the doers. The former invent but do not go beyond publishing novelty, hence never learn about the idea's usefulness—or lack of it. The latter, not funded for experimentation but for efficient product development, must use proven, however antiquated, methods. [BeLe80, p. 34]

The conferences and journals are the domain of the first subculture. This is how it should be; academicians are expected to identify solutions to general problems that may not impact the state of practice for five or more years. Much has trickled down, and the second subculture has benefitted from this knowledge. Still, at any point in time, each subculture will be facing different sets of problems, and often it is the differences that stand out. The author is a researcher who hopes to discover ways in which we can advance the state of the art. But this is a book for practitioners; it builds on what experience has shown us. Only in a very limited way does it report on experiments or speculate about what the future may bring.

Freeman suggests an alternative way of dividing the two cultures: according to their computer science orientation. He points out that

> it is important to keep in mind that computer science and software engineering have different objectives that should not be confused. . . . Computer science is concerned with the scientific study and description of algorithms, programs, the devices that interpret them, and the phenomena surrounding their creation and usage. Software engineering focuses on the application of this scientific knowledge to achieve stated technical, economic, and social goals. [Free80, p. 131]

Much of the research in software engineering, in reality, consists of computer science investigations into phenomena that affect the properties of a software product. It really does not matter how we characterize that research, as long as we distinguish between the discovery of scientific principles and their application. After all, engineers in other disciplines have been doing just that for quite some time.

Jensen and Tonies present this idea from a different perspective.

> The basic difference between the scientist and the engineer lies in their goals. A scientist strives to gain new knowledge about

the workings of our universe while the engineer puts that knowledge to work for the needs of mankind. Engineers may not have or need to have total knowledge of the concept they are applying to solve a problem. . . .

It is also important to note that the scientist's training concentrates on the application of the *scientific method* while the engineer's training concentrates on the use of the engineering design process. [JeTo79, p. 11-12]

They describe engineers as

basically problem solvers. They are practical people, pragmatists who tackle mundane problems and solve them efficiently and economically. Their solution to a problem may appear complex or seem to be a trivial bit of inventiveness; however, the solution's simplicity often masks a true work of inspiration and perseverance. [JeTo79, p. 11]

The last paragraph echoes Boehm's choice of the word "technician" in his definition of Area 2. It also seems to suggest a hierarchy in which engineers rank below scientists (and software engineers below computer scientists), but I think that would be a misinterpretation. There are distinctions between nuclear engineering and nuclear physics that are well differentiated. Thus, the engineering student is taught by the engineering faculty and not the physics faculty. Yet, it is still too early for separate software engineering and computer science departments. Consequently, there generally is but one faculty, and it is easy to confuse the two (overlapping) orientations. Nevertheless, there are clear differences in their objectives, and this is what the practitioners of each discipline should keep in sight.

I conclude this discussion with another of Freeman's observations.[2]

[T]he term "software engineering" must be kept in perspective. In reality, we must be concerned with the "engineering of information systems" that contain as components hardware, software, people, and other artifacts. Because computer engineering, systems engineering, information systems develop-

---

[2]In the Freeman quotation there is a reference to "information systems." It is common in the United States to equate this term with management information systems and commercial database applications. This is a very narrow view. In much of the world information technology (IT) includes electronic systems, telecommunications, computing, artificial intelligence, etc. [MaBu87, p. 2] In that sense, all computer applications are indeed information systems.

ment, and other disciplines have not addressed the software development question entirely successfully, it is useful to focus on software at this time in order to make progress. But, we must remember that software engineering exists only in a larger environment of entire systems, involving many different technical, economic, and social factors. [Free80, p. 131]

Paraphrasing this, software engineering is a subset of systems engineering. To produce a software solution to a problem, one first must understand the problem and how software solutions might mitigate it. That is the focus of this book. Moreover, I believe that we know enough about software development to insist on a system orientation for large and small projects.

The long answer to the question "What is software engineering?" is now complete. It is not very different from the short answer already given:

Software engineering is the application of tools, methods, and disciplines to produce and maintain an automated solution to a real-world problem.

In this longer answer I have examined the history of software engineering and explained how others view this topic. My perspective is not unique, and I offer no special "scientific foundation" to illustrate how software engineering principles should be applied. Neither do I offer this book as an overview of computer science research in software engineering topics. This is a book about how to resolve problems with software solutions. Problem solving, by definition, is not easy, and finding solutions to very complex problems is going to be extremely difficult. We have gained considerable knowledge about the design, construction, and maintenance of software products, and in what follows I shall try to explain how to adapt this experience "to obtain economically software that is reliable and works on real machines."

## 1.2.    Models of the software process

When Boehm presented the definition of software engineering quoted in the previous section, he added that the definition covered the software life cycle, which includes the redesigns and modifications that are considered "software maintenance." Recently, the term software process has come to be used instead of life cycle. This represents a shift from the study of the products being developed and maintained to an investigation of the processes that create and maintain those products.

By historical necessity, the first concern of software engineering had to be the computer program—the technology used to solve the problem. In the early days, the domain of problems that could be addressed was severely circumscribed by the limitations of the technology. For example, although artificial intelligence can be traced back to the Dartmouth conference of 1964, it was not until the advances in computing of the 1980s that it achieved wider acceptance and exploitation.

As the technology improved, the complexity of the projects grew. Still, the computer program remained a central focus for the field. People were taught to write computer programs, and proficiency in programming defined a profession. The title Knuth chose for his planned seven-volume series clearly indicated his orientation; it was called *The Art of Computer Programming*. In recent years there has been a move away from that view. Gries called his book *The Science of Programming*. In it, he states:

> Programming began as an art, and even today most people learn only by watching others perform. . . . In the past 10 years, however, research has uncovered some useful theory and principles, and we are reaching the point where we can begin to teach . . . this just-emerging science of programming. [Grie81, p. vii]

The science of programming is a direct result of computer science's concern for the algorithm. The principles that Gries alludes to are important in software engineering, and they are discussed at some length in this book. Yet, the computer program is limited to issues of fine granularity. We sometimes describe it as programming-in-the-small, whereas programming-in-the-large is reserved for higher level (coarser-grained) design decisions. Of course, we know the most about programming-in-the-small, and there always is comfort in teaching what we know well. But the greatest challenges, and the highest potential yields, reside in the other phases of the software life cycle.

The software life cycle begins with the recognition of some need that leads to the design and implementation of a software product, and it continues until that product is retired. In an ecological sense, the retired program does not die; it affects its users' perceptions and adds to our experience base. Future generations of the program are biased by what we have learned from it. We reuse our experience as we identify solutions to related problems. (Of course, the greatest distortions sometimes come from negative experiences.)

Many of our software tools formalize what already has been learned. For example, the Xerox Star popularized the use of windows and icons [JRVS89]. This concept was first replicated with custom-crafted programs; later software tools generalized the windowing functions, and now it is possible to develop products with environments that automatically include the window features. This extension of our technology is simply a replication of the process described in Backus's 1957 paper. We find ways to express in 47 statements what previously required 1000; we describe what we intend to do without having to provide all the implementation details.

This is the orientation that I like to use for the software process. It implies that we are more concerned with the process of solving a real-world problem (perhaps using many program generations to do so) than we are with the product itself. Naturally, most of our effort will be devoted to the creation and maintenance of the product. But that activity is only a means to an end. We expect computer science and software engineering research to make our jobs easier. We assume that new tools will emerge that allow us to ignore some of the housekeeping details that absorb so much of our time. We recognize that our experiences in a particular application domain[3] will add to the knowledge that we can reuse in subsequent projects (in that domain).

Thus, we see that the software process reflects how we use our experience with software technology and apply it in the target domain. It is the software life cycle viewed from the outside, the structure within which we, as software engineers, must operate.

### 1.2.1. A traditional waterfall model

Although I use the term software process, many still refer to it as the software life cycle. Frequently, what they mean is a sequence of phases in the development and use of a software product that is described with the "waterfall model." This section discusses that waterfall model and identifies its strengths and weaknesses. The reader should be aware that many in the software engineering community feel that this model has been discredited, whereas others believe it is a basic extension of the problem-solving paradigm.[4] In any case, it is currently in widespread use, and most of our empirical data have been derived from projects

---

[3]In mathematics, functions map from a set (called its domain) onto a set (called its range). Using this concept, the term application domain denotes the "field of use." Examples of application domains are business systems, embedded military systems, and operating systems. Domain is used without a qualifier when the context is obvious.

[4]A paradigm (pronounced para-dime) is simply a model. It usually is reserved for situations in which the word "model" seems inadequate. Common uses are computational paradigm and software process paradigm.

using this model.

Figure 1.1 presents a basic problem-solving paradigm that offers a high level representation of the software process. The first step is to decide *what* is to be done. Once the objectives have been determined, we next must decide *how* to achieve them. This is followed by a step in which we *do it*, whatever "it" was determined to be. We then must *test* the result to see if we have accomplished our objectives. Finally, we *use* what we have done.

We use this basic flow for virtually all our activities. In science the *what* is called the hypothesis, the *how* is the experiment design, the *do it* is the conduct of the experiment, the *test* is the evaluation of the experiment's data, and the *use* is the publication of the results or the redefinition of the hypothesis. The same process is used in building a bridge. First we decide where the bridge should be built, how many lanes it should have, and so on. Next we design the bridge and detail how it should be built. The bridge is then built, tested, and used. How is the bridge tested? Because we have considerable knowledge about bridges, most of the testing is done during the design stage using models. We must test our concepts and think through the design implications very carefully. Once the bridge is built, it is very difficult to correct any mistakes. Thus, the *test* that comes between *do it* and *use* is really a final inspection; when constructing a bridge, we expect the design to have zero defects.

When we start out to build a bridge, the assumption is that we have a proper design. (I use the word "proper" where the reader might expect to see "correct." I do this because I want to define correct and then use it only within the context of that definition. I consider a design to be proper if it does what is desired and does it without error.) We expect the design to be proper because, over the centuries, we have built

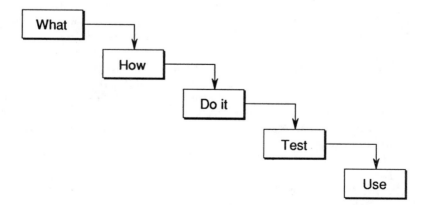

Fig. 1.1.  A simple problem-solving paradigm.

many bridges. Some failed, and we learned from our mistakes. As we gain confidence, we tend to lower the margin of safety, and failures appear again. Through this process, which is described very well by Petroski [Petr82], we learn to improve the reliability of the objects we build. In this bridge example, the process begins with a statement of need (the *what*) that is constrained only by a general understanding of what bridges can do. The next (*how*) step converts the need to a design based on both the requirements and our bridge-building experience. The activity can be viewed as an iteration of the Figure 1.1 flow: The objective is to produce a design (what), and the first design concept (how) is described and documented (do it). The design is analyzed, simulated, and reviewed (test). The more knowledge that we have to test the design concepts, the greater our confidence that the design is proper. Following the review, we either refine the design to correct for deficiencies identified by the analysis or we accept the design and proceed to the next step (use). This is a natural process, and all problem solving can be viewed as the recursive application of this basic five-step paradigm.

Christensen describes the phases in the systems development process as an extension of this simple model [Chri84]. The steps are as follows:

- *System requirements phase.* The product is a set of goals or objectives that represent a response to a need. The major decisions relate to the feasibility of responding at this time to the need.

- *Concept formulation phase.* The product is a feasibility report that considers advantages, disadvantages, alternatives, and a plan. The major decisions revolve around the concepts to be pursued.

- *System definition phase.* The product is a specification that defines what the system is to do. The major decision is whether or not to continue once the specification is complete.

- *Engineering design phase.* The product is a design that details how the specification should be implemented. In most hardware situations there is a prototype built to test the design uncertainties. In fact, there may be several prototypes or series of prototypes. The major decision is whether to release the design for production.

- *Design verification (test) phase.* As noted in the bridge example, it would be inappropriate to delay testing until the products were available. In this description of the process, the products of this phase are reports on the operability, safety, maintainability, and supportability of the designed product. The major decision is whether to produce the product in quantity.

- *Production and installation phase.* The products now are operationally qualified systems. Each unit undergoes quality tests to certify that it conforms to the standards established by the design, and the assembled units must demonstrate that they satisfy the objectives laid out in the specifications. The only decision at this point is whether to deploy the systems.

- *Operations phase.* During the period of use features are identified for improvement; modifications are made and new concepts are catalogued. The decisions relate to changes in utilization, equipment modification, and system retirement.

- *Retirement phase.* The product is retired, and the by-products here are limited to reusable parts and the decisions related to their disposition.

The context of Christensen's description is human factors, but the presentation is sufficiently general to include all systems including hardware and software. It consists of a sequence of phases with each phase containing an activity and a decision. Based on the outcome of that decision, control is sent to the next or some previous phase. In software engineering this flow is labeled the waterfall model.

When, in the early days of software engineering, it was agreed that an engineering discipline was needed, a natural first step was to structure software development in accordance with the flow used elsewhere in the system development process. Royce is credited with recognizing the need for this orientation in 1970 [Royc70]. Figure 1.2

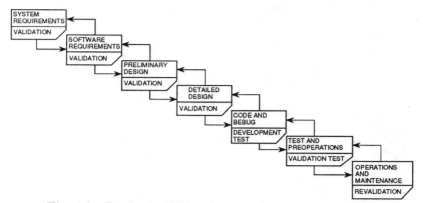

Fig. 1.2. Boehm's 1976 software life cycle model.
(Reprinted from [Boeh76] with permission, ©1976, IEEE.)

contains the waterfall diagram as it appeared in Boehm's 1976 paper [Boeh76]. Notice how, after the initial *system requirements* phase, the steps in this diagram parallel those of the hardware life cycle shown in Table 1.1. The major difference between the software and hardware phases is that code and debug replaces fabricate. Obviously, this similarity facilitates the management of large projects that include major hardware and software components. And it was in such large projects that the need for software engineering first was identified.

Each phase in the Boehm diagram has two properties. First, every step includes the complete problem-solving paradigm shown in Figure 1.1. The *what* is defined as the input to each step (except the first, which must define the requirements for the system). The *how* and *do it* activities are named in the upper box, and the type of *test* is named in the pentagon below the box. The output of each step is used as the input to the next step (except, of course, for the last step, which leads to retirement). The second property of the Boehm diagram is that it assumes that there will be lessons learned from later steps that will modify earlier decisions. Consequently, feedback is shown with backward-pointing arrows. To reduce the diagram's complexity, feedback is usually shown only to the previous level, but feedback to any previous phase is always permitted.

The waterfall life cycle of Figure 1.2 has the following beneficial properties:

- Phases are organized in a logical fashion. Steps that cannot proceed until higher level decisions have been made must await those decisions. Thus, *detailed design* awaits *preliminary design*, and *code and debug* is delayed until *detailed design* is complete.

- Each phase includes some review process, and product acceptance is required before the output can be used. In this way, the process is organized to reduce the number of errors passed on from one step to the next.

Table 1.1. Comparison of the hardware and software life cycles.

| Hardware | Software |
|---|---|
| Hardware requirements | Software requirements |
| Preliminary design | Preliminary design |
| Detailed design | Detailed design |
| Fabricate | Code and debug |
| Test and preoperations | Test and preoperations |
| Operations and maintenance | Operations and maintenance |

- The process is iterative. Although the basic flow is top down, it is recognized that problems encountered at lower level steps will affect decisions made at a higher level. One goal of management is to limit the iteration to the lowest active levels by ensuring that the highest level decisions have been thoroughly analyzed.

Figure 1.3 presents an alternative view of the waterfall flow that emphasizes the manufacture of the system. One begins with a single document, the system requirements,[5] and decomposes that into parts, which in turn are further decomposed. Thus, there are hardware and software requirements. The software requirements lead to the preliminary design of multiple functions, each of which spawns many detailed designs, which in turn evolve into even more program units. Product assembly follows a reverse flow. First the individual programs are accepted. These then are grouped into modules that are accepted. The modules are grouped to certify that they include the desired functionality. The software is then integrated with the hardware until, finally, there is one system that is certified to meet the system requirements.

The waterfall diagram of Figure 1.2 emphasizes the flow of the decomposition activities; all the composition activities are subsumed in the *test and preoperations* phase. Figure 1.3 emphasizes what goes on in that later phase by removing the end-of-phase certification and feedback arrows. In Figure 1.2 the outputs are shown as inputs to only the following phase, whereas in Figure 1.3 they are shown as going to both the next decomposition phase and the matching composition phase. That is, the output from one phase not only determines what the next phase is to do, but it also establishes the criteria for determining if the composed assembly satisfies the goals. In other words, the process is structured so that, at each step, we define what the next decomposition step is to do and document the criteria for determining if the resulting product satisfies the design intent.

There are limitations to diagrammatic representations, and no single representation can present all concepts. Figure 1.3 simply details another way in which the flow expressed in Figure 1.2 insists on closure. Every specification must make it possible to determine if a detailed expression satisfies its objectives. Moreover, the detailing or use of a component does not begin until there is a high confidence that the component (or its description) is essentially defect free. This waterfall flow is based on such sound logic and good engineering judgment, it is hard to see why anyone would object to it. Let us look at its faults.

---

[5]Some diagrams display the parallel development of the hardware and software plus the integration that produces a final system. The figures in this book show only the software-related activities.

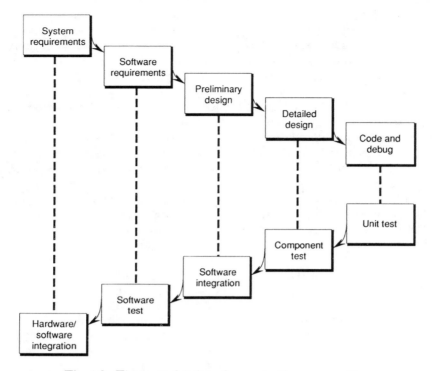

Fig. 1.3. The waterfall flow from a testing perspective.

The major difficulties found in using the waterfall model for software can all be traced back to the differences between hardware and software.

- Hardware requires manufacture, whereas software does not. Much of the hardware design process is concerned with the creation of instructions to the product's fabricators. Once hardware production begins, its is expensive to make modifications or correct errors. Therefore, the drawings used by the builders of the system ought to be error free and very precise. Consequently, documentation is the designers' end product. Software, on the other hand, requires no manufacture. The computer effortlessly transforms the code into the operational product. Thus, in the waterfall diagrams there is a major difference between *fabrication* and *code and debug*. The code is actually another level of design documentation. We speak of "program text," and perhaps we should relabel *code and debug* as *very detailed design*; that is really what is being done. Clearly, one must demonstrate that the design is proper before starting integration or installation, but the cost of establishing this fact is not analogous to the cost of manufacturing hardware.

- Hardware has physical models to use in evaluating design decisions, whereas software does not. Recall in the bridge example given earlier, most of the testing was done before the design was complete. The final test step was more of a pro forma acceptance certification. This could be done because there was a vast body of experience to draw on in bridge construction (e.g., strength of materials.) The bridge design is clearly the result of problem solving. Each bridge is unique, and there is no cata-logue of standard bridges to select from. But there are hand-books, formulas, and simulation programs that can be used to test design decisions. Software, on the other hand, lacks the historic collection of experience that we find in many other fields. There are few formulas that can be used to determine if a software design is proper, and most of those that exist are domain specific. Thus, much of the software design evaluation rests on judgment and intuition.

- Hardware, because of its physical limitations, has a practical bound on complexity, whereas software does not. Every hardware design must be realized as a physical implementation. To limit complexity and maximize the reuse of existing designs, most complex systems are decomposed into separate components or modules with well-understood interfaces. In part this is a good design principle; in part it is a reaction to the near impossibility of integrating two separate components by combining their individual designs. Software, on the other hand, does not have this constraint. Software is simply an implementable design, and it can be made to conform to almost any set of needs. In fact, many system implementors expect the software to compensate for deficiencies in the hardware design.

- Hardware is composed of parts that wear out, whereas software does not degrade from use. Reliability for hardware is a proba-bility measure for the failure of parts and components. Because there will be variations among the individual units produced from a common design, hardware designers must establish criteria for unit acceptance that will deliver the predicted reliability. Software, on the other hand, never shows wear. Its reliability is a measure of the number of defects (errors) remaining in the delivered product.

Thus, there ought to be major differences between the management of a hardware and a software project. The roles of design documentation are quite dissimilar. Therefore, emphasis on the traditional controls for hardware documentation may be counterproductive in a software setting. The end products also are not alike. Reporting software percent complete in terms of lines of code is like reporting the completeness of a hardware design in terms of the number of completed drawings. Because software requires no manufacture, there is a perception that software is easy to change. This is true only in a very special sense. If the code is viewed as *very detailed design*, then software design changes are as easy (or difficult) to make as hardware design changes; once the designs have been certified, however, software realization is always easier than hardware manufacture. One of the dangers of the waterfall flow, therefore, is that managers may attempt to control software projects as if they were analogous to hardware projects. Obviously, such an error invites an emphasis of the wrong characteristics of the process.

The biggest problem with the waterfall model, however, is not that it implies a hardware view of software project management. Rather, it is the fact that the flow is optimized for hardware, thereby neglecting the essential characteristics of software. The waterfall model presents a top-down flow that can be described with an architecture metaphor. One begins with a near-complete understanding of the need and produces a set of drawings and models. Once these are accepted, construction begins, and changes are restricted to minor or cosmetic changes. Of course, this is how one builds a house; it cannot be done any other way. Software, however, involves no fabrication. Once the drawings and models (programs) are complete, the final product exists. Consequently, the process should be optimized for producing proper designs and error-free models, (i.e., making them reliable in the software sense of the word). Here a sculpture metaphor may be more appropriate. One uses analytic techniques to sketch out what is needed and then constructs a product, which is iteratively refined until it is aesthetically pleasing. (Lacking objective criteria for establishing the soundness of many of our software designs, we must recognize that our judgment is essentially an aesthetic decision.)

In later sections I will show how some computer scientists are modifying the software process to bring it closer to this sculpture metaphor. Still, the architecture metaphor must not be dismissed out of hand. For very large projects (which are not a central concern of this book) the architecture approach may be the only way to manage the project. It also is the best way to manage a project with a well-understood product. For example, if a company has experience in building accounting systems, I/O controllers, or compilers, then building another such product based on the existing designs is best managed with the waterfall model as it has been described. Where there is uncertainty regarding *what* is required or *how* it can be built, the waterfall fails. It assumes that the requirements are known before the design begins. But one may need experience with the product before the requirements can be understood. (Prototypes offer one way to gain experience.) It also assumes that the requirements will remain static over the development cycle and that a product delivered years after it was specified will meet delivery-time needs. (Incremental development is one way to avoid this problem.) Finally, even when there is a clear specification, it assumes that there will be sufficient design knowledge to build the product. (Experimentation with prototypes can reduce the uncertainty.) More on these techniques later.

In summary, for some projects the waterfall model remains the most efficient approach. Clearly, it is based on well-established engineering principles. It certainly is the most appropriate way to integrate tasks in a hardware-software project. Its failures can be traced to its inability to accommodate software's special properties and its inappropriateness for resolving partially understood issues.

### 1.2.2. The essential software process

Before describing the different approaches to modeling the software process, it will be helpful first to examine its essence. I use "essence" in the sense that Brooks used it ([Broo87], see Section 1.3.2.). He categorized the difficulties in software production as the *essence* (i.e., those difficulties inherent in the nature of software) and the *accidents* (i.e., those difficulties that presently attend its production but that are not inherent) I follow his method in identifying the essence of the software process. That is, the object of concern here is the inherent nature of producing a software solution in response to a need independent of any accidental difficulties imposed by the available technology, training, project-specific experience, etc. The idea is that if we can describe what is inherent in, *all* software process implementations, then we will have a context within which to address the accidental problems that currently limit our productivity.

I begin by abstracting the previously described waterfall model. Figure 1.4 reduces its essence to three basic transformations:

- From the need in the real world to a problem statement that identifies a software solution for that need. This is the definition of what is to be done (i.e., the requirements specification).

- From the problem statement to a detailed implementation statement that can be transformed into an operational system.

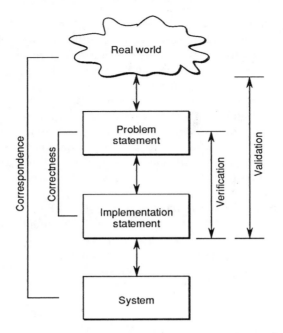

Fig. 1.4. The essence of the waterfall model.

This transformation includes the bulk of the waterfall activity. It encompasses the definition of how to build the software, its building, and its testing. The implementation statement includes the design descriptions, the source code, and the testing materials.

■ From the implementation statement to a system that will satisfy the real-world need. This requires equipment, procedures, people, etc. It represents the embedding of the software product within its operational environment.

The composite transformation is one from a need to a software product that satisfies that need. Naturally, after the system is installed in the real world, the environment is modified, thereby altering the accuracy of the problem statement and consequently generating new software requirements. Thus, the figure represents only the trace of one path in an iterative process.

The figure also displays two quality measures for the system and the processes used to evaluate them. *Correspondence* measures how well the delivered system corresponds to the needs of the operational environment. *Validation* is an activity used to predict correspondence; true correspondence cannot be determined until the system is in place.

(Moreover, as those experienced in system evaluation know, the determination of correspondence for an operational system can be difficult and controversial.)

Unlike correspondence, *correctness* can be established formally. Correctness measures the consistency of a product with respect to its specification. *Verification* is the exercise of determining correctness. Notice that correctness is always objective. Given a specification and a product, it should be possible to determine if the product precisely satisfies the requirements of the specification. Validation, however, is always subjective; if the evaluation criteria could be detailed, they would have been included in the specification. As Boehm puts it, these quality activities answer the following questions [Boeh84]:

- *Verification.* "Am I building the product right?"

- *Validation.* "Am I building the right product?"

Validation begins as soon as the project starts, but verification can begin only after a specification has been accepted. Verification and validation are independent of each other. It is possible to have a product that corresponds but is incorrect (for example, a necessary report is part of the delivered product but not included in the specification). A product also may be correct but not correspond (for example, after years of waiting, a system is delivered that satisfies the initial design statement but no longer reflects current operating practices). Finally, observe that when the specification is informal, it is difficult to separate verification from validation.

The process model in Figure 1.4 reduces the number of phases in the waterfall flow to just two: decide what is needed and implement it. The implementation steps are not specified, the quality functions are shown in the context of the full process rather than with each step, and the implication is that this is one cycle in an iterative process. This description abstracts different properties of the waterfall model and, in this sense, complements Figures 1.2 and 1.3. The next level of abstraction, shown in Figure 1.5, shows the software process as a single undifferentiated activity to be presented as just one box. I call this the

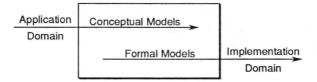

Fig. 1.5.  The essential software process

essential software process model, and I assert that all software process models are specializations of it.[6]

Like the previous model, the essential software process consists of three transformations, which when composed represent a transformation from a need to a software solution. In this case the three transformations are as follows.

- From a need recognized in an application domain into a conceptual model that describes the solution in terms of the domain vocabulary.

- From the solution as expressed in the conceptual model into some formal model that defines what the software is to do. The model is considered formal in that it defines what the product is to do and can determine if an implementation satisfies its definition.

- From the formal model into a software product that is correct with respect to that model.

Relating this back to the model shown in Figure 1.4, here the first two transformations are concerned with the definition of the problem statement and the third represents the process of detailing the implementation statement; Figure 1.5 does not show the activity of converting a set of programs into a system.

What new insights does this essential model provide? First, it points out that the process takes place in (at least) two different domains. The development team must know about the domain in which the application will be used; this is the basis for the validation decisions. Obviously, the team also must understand the software environment and tools that they are to use in the implementation. Computer science teaches only the second domain, and many applications are in that domain, (e.g., software tools, operating systems). But application domain experience is equally as important. Because there are so many application domains, most of that domain knowledge is acquired on the job. In fact, this is why software development companies are asked to detail their previous experience when bidding on a contract. An accounting system is relatively easy for a company that has built many such systems but quite difficult for a company that has built only compilers.

Next, it is clear that two kinds of modeling technique are required. Conceptual modeling relies on the formalisms of the application domain

---

[6]In this sense, Figure 1.5 presents a metamodel of the software process, i.e., a model of the operational software process models.

to establish and validate a solution that can be understood by domain specialists. There are no rules or conventions for guaranteeing that this model is proper.[7] One cannot, in general, use the conceptual models to establish how the software product must perform. That is, the vocabulary of the conceptual model is not specific enough to detail unambiguously what the software is to do. Therefore the conceptual model must be translated into a formal model that relies on the formalisms of computer science, i.e., those based on mathematics and logic. Thus, the problem statement of Figure 1.4 actually has two forms: a conceptual model in some application domain vocabulary and a formal model that acts as the specification for the software.

In addition to displaying two kinds of models, the essential software process also indicates their scope. Conceptual modeling always begins in the application domain, and it can never extend into the implementation domain. Formal modeling, on the other hand, can never extend into the application domain; the formal model must be defined from a conceptual model. The formal model always ends in the implementation domain, and conversion of the lowest level formal model into the software product is always managed by automation, (e.g., the source code is compiled into the object code). Verification can begin only after the formal model exists; validation must refer back to the conceptual model. There are no objective criteria for deciding which conceptual model is best or if the formal model is an accurate representation of it. However, there are objective criteria for determining if the design components and implemented product are correct with respect to the formal model. Consequently, if we are concerned with the correctness of an implementation, we must look to formalisms for help.

In summary, the essential waterfall model suggests how the quality factors of correspondence and correctness relate to the process, and the essential model indicates why the software process is so difficult: it requires experience in two domains, depends on two classes of modeling tools, and relies on the analysts' judgments for all decisions prior to formal modeling. No tools, no management orientation, and no process flow will change these facts. They are the essence of the software process.

---

[7]As mentioned earlier, I have been careful to avoid the word correct. Correctness is a property that must be with respect to some agreed statement. For example, a program is correct with respect to its design specification. If a design specification has an error, then a correct program will have that error. Validity, on the other hand, relates to the ability of the software product to satisfy the application need. I have been using the word "proper" to suggest that the design or model is both valid (i.e., the specification establishes exactly what is desired) and correct (i.e., the product is error free with respect to its specification). A proper design should result in an error-free product. Perhaps I should not have left this point to a footnote, but I will make it again.

## 1.2.3.  Some alternative models

There are three basic approaches to revising the software process model. The first is to adjust the management of the waterfall model so that it will be less sensitive to the need for a complete requirements specification at the start of the project, the second is to integrate software experimentation with the process, and the third is to extend the scope of formalism.  The three approaches are not mutually exclusive.  Each is intended to reduce uncertainty regarding the application need and the associated solution, improve the reliability of the product by the early elimination of errors, and provide tools that can take advantage of software's special properties.  As we shall see, most modifications to the waterfall model tend to move it away from the architecture metaphor and closer to the sculpture metaphor.

All process models recognize the fact that small problems are easier to solve than large ones.  In the waterfall model the large project is broken into smaller problems by decomposition.  The specification is subdivided into components, which in turn are subdivided into modules, and so on.  The result is a set of program units that must be designed, implemented, and then integrated.  An alternative partitioning of the system divides the requirements specification into a family of layered specifications.  Each higher level implementation, usually called a *build*, depends on the functions provided by earlier (or lower level) implementations.  The first builds to be constructed are those that are the best understood or will provide the most service for subsequent builds. Builds scheduled for later integration are only sketchily defined until they are ready for implementation.  We call this incremental or evolutionary development [MiLD80, Gilb88].

There are many advantages to this incremental approach.  First, because a larger problem is decomposed into a sequence of smaller problems, each implementation task will be relatively small.  There are many short schedules, which makes progress easy to track.  Construction of a build normally is managed using a waterfall model.  However, because there are many small deliverables being produced on a semimonthly schedule, there can be rapid feedback for the evaluation process.  Team members will not be faced with an extended period of speculation about the utility and completeness of their designs; there will be a sense of immediacy to their actions.

A second advantage of incremental design is that the development team has an opportunity to learn about the problem as the design progresses.  The process may be characterized as one of doing what is understood best, learning from that activity, identifying the next build, and then iterating.  Historically, this is how information systems were developed to assist in patient care [Lind79].  In the beginning, the needs were not well understood because the designers lacked domain experience and the users had no conceptual framework to articulate their requirements. One had to build some smaller systems, learn about their use in an operational setting, anticipate where the technology could improve the process, and then build the next increment. The results sometimes were surprising; in the end, the developers became specialists in the field, and the users became sensitized to the benefits of computers. In time, both developers and users grew adept at recognizing potential computer applications, and holistic clinical information systems could be built. (For an interesting case study, see [EnLB89].)

Brooks describes this approach as one of growing, not building, systems. Gilb uses the term evolutionary delivery, and he establishes the following principles for operation and management [Gilb88]. He believes that one must begin with an open architecture in which there is freedom to accommodate change. Obviously, this requirement limits the range of applications that can be constructed with this technique. Given the right type of problem, however, the design team should decompose the project into many useful partial result steps and establish a sequence for their implementation. The focus should be on the immediate build, with emphasis on the delivery of the result; little effort should be spent on the management of intermediate activities (such as monitoring program construction) or distant tasks (such as the design of later builds). The open architecture provides considerable freedom for altering plans to adjust for revised understandings. Thus, only limited effort is expended on tasks with high uncertainty.

A second technique for reducing uncertainty is to experiment with prototypes before committing to a design. In the hardware environment, the use of prototypes is very common. Automobile manufacturers build prototypes to experiment with advanced concepts; they also build prototypes to certify design concepts before committing to a production run. In settings where an incremental plan is not practical, the prototype may be the only approach to gaining an understanding of the problem to be solved.

The idea of a prototype is as old as software engineering. Royce, in his 1970 description of the software development process, described preliminary program design in a section labeled "Do It Twice." He wrote:

> After documentation, the second most important criterion for success revolves around whether the product is totally original. If the computer program in question is being developed for the first time, arrange matters so that the version finally delivered to the customer for operational deployment is actually the second version insofar as critical design/operations areas are concerned. [Royc70, p. 7]

Because of the technology available at the time, a simulation is used for the prototype. Royce continues,

> the point of all this . . . is that questions of timing, storage, etc. which are otherwise matters of judgment, can now be studied with precision. Without the simulation the project manager is at the mercy of human judgment. With the simulation he can at least perform experimental tests of some key hypotheses and scope down what remains for human judgment, which in the area of computer program design (as in the estimation of takeoff gross weight, costs to complete, or the daily double) is invariably and seriously optimistic. [Royc70, p. 7]

In his book *The Mythical Man-Month*, Brooks echoes these sentiments. In a chapter called "Plan to Throw One Away," he writes,

> In most projects, the first system built is barely usable. It may be too slow, too big, awkward to use, or all three. There is no alternative but to start again, smarting but smarter, and build a redesigned version in which these problems are solved. . . .
>
> The management question, therefore, is not *whether* to build a pilot system and throw it away. You *will* do that. The only question is whether to plan in advance to build a throwaway, or to promise to deliver the throwaway to the customer. Seen this way, the answer is much clearer. [Broo75, p. 116]

Both references recognize that when the systems are new, the first implementations are contaminated by artifacts of the learning process. Either they are not as good as the increased understanding would allow them to be, or they contain a residue of false starts and rejected approaches. In either event, the programs do not offer an effective base for a robust and maintainable system. Thus, the suggestion that the first system should be treated as a learning experience. Of course, this simply reflects good engineering practice. Before building a missile, for example, there is extensive analysis, computer simulations are run, individual units are constructed and tested, prototypes are built and evaluated, and then—and only then—does the missile go into production. The building of two generations of a software product may seem like a very expensive learning technique, but prototypes allow us to increase our understanding selectively in a more targeted and less expensive manner.

Although rapid prototyping was a topic of discussion in the 1970s, it received renewed attention in 1981 when Gomaa and Scott presented their experience at the International Conference on Software Engineering [GoSc81]. Their goal was to specify the user requirements for a computer system to manage a semiconductor processing facility; they selected the prototype method because of shortcomings in the traditional requirements analysis methods. An interpretive tool with a report generator was used to build an incomplete demonstration prototype (SHARP APL). The prototype was shown to the potential users, and feedback from the exercise resulted in a refinement of both the developers' and users' understanding of the system needs. After the prototype was experimented with and the report formats were established, a requirements document was drawn up and a waterfall flow was followed. The prototype then was discarded. The total cost of the prototype exercise was 10% of the total project cost.

This is the typical use of a rapid prototype: to increase our understanding of the requirements. It is called "rapid" because it addresses only the issues of immediate concern; the resultant product is in no sense complete or intended for permanent use. The prototype represents knowledge pertaining to the problem's solution. This knowledge will be incorporated into the requirements document, and the prototype always is discarded. (Notice that any attempt to retain the prototype code and convert it into a deliverable product is best characterized as hacking; it is not an approach recommended by software engineering.)

Recently Boehm introduced a spiral model of software development that integrates the prototype with the waterfall flow. As shown in Figure 1.6, the spiral model consists of a series of learning cycles in which one begins with a risk assessment to identify those areas of greatest uncertainty that may affect the project. Prototypes are defined that will offer insight into the problems, thereby reducing risk. This cycle of risk assessment, prototype construction, evaluation, and formalization of lessons learned continues until a low-risk requirements document exists. In Figure 1.6 four prototypes are constructed, but the number of cycles is not fixed. It is a function of the developers' uncertainty, and it is possible to experiment with more than one prototype concurrently. Once the requirements are defined, Boehm uses a traditional waterfall flow to manage system implementation. Incremental development also could follow the initial prototyping activity.

There is another class of prototype that is usually associated with artificial intelligence (AI) applications. The process of developing an expert system using a shell, for example, has been described as one of modeling in the application domain without concern for the implementation activity [WeKe89]. That is, the expert system shell provides the inference mechanism and knowledge-structuring facilities, and the knowledge engineer focuses on the representation of domain knowledge. This knowledge is formalized, modified, and tested in the shell environment. During the early stages of this process, the system with an incomplete knowledge base is considered a prototype. Once the

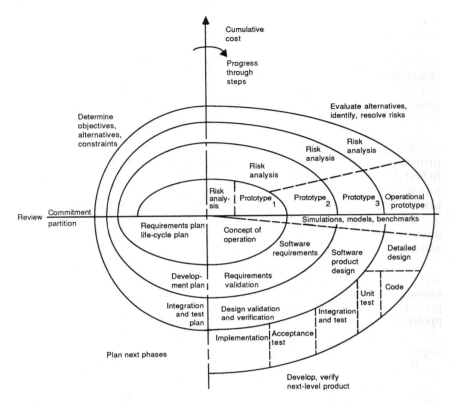

Fig. 1.6. The spiral model of software development and enhancement.
(Reprinted from [Boeh88] with permission, ©1988, IEEE.)

knowledge base is rich enough to support an operational function, the development shell is replaced by a delivery shell, and the prototype label is removed. The knowledge base grows from a prototype to an operational tool. To a limited extent, the commercial Fourth Generation Languages (4GL) provide a similar, but less complete, facility for database applications.

The third, and final, approach to improving the software process involves the use of formalism. In Figure 1.5 two modeling lines were drawn. The formal modeling activity provides objective criteria for establishing the correctness of the software product with respect to its specification. In most current environments, the initial specification is textual, and the determination of correctness is seldom unambiguous. However, if that specification could be defined with the same precision as, say, the computer program, then we could be as certain of the correctness of the source program with respect to its specification as we are of the correctness of the object program with respect to the source program.

At present, most formal methods are research topics. Nevertheless, some techniques have been used successfully on commercial products. For example, there is over 10 years of operational experience with the Vienna Development Method (VDM), and both quality and productivity are quite good with this method [Jone80, CoHJ86]. Many other formal methods (some supported by automated environments) are emerging. Although these tools still have limited acceptance, it seems reasonably certain that many will evolve into the system-level HLLs that some of the NATO conference organizers envisioned. Although I provide a simple illustration of VDM in Chapter 2, this is essentially a book for today's practitioners. Consequently, I concentrate on the methods and tools used most widely. In time, I am certain, software developers will come to rely on formal methods. For now, however, I shall limit my discussion to the concept of a prototype in a formal system.

Two types of prototype already have been defined: the throwaway prototype and the evolutionary knowledge-based prototype. The availability of formal specifications enables the use of a third class of prototype: the executable specification. A specification differs from a program in that the specification defines the behavior for *all* implementations while the program defines *an efficient implementation for a particular target operating system and machine.* If the specification is formal and if there is a translator such that the specification is operational (i.e., it can be used to determine if the specification defines the desired behavior for arbitrary test cases), then this operational specification can be viewed as a prototype of the intended system [Zave84]. Of course, the operational specification does not offer the efficiency of the end product, but it does provide a test bed for experimenting with the statement of requirements.

Balzer points out that implementing a system mixes two very difficult tasks: describing what the software is to do (i.e., its behavior) and optimizing the performance to produce an acceptable implementation [Balz85]. The operational approach allows the developers to separate these two concerns. The goal of this type of development can be thought of as using a CAD/CAM system to deliver a design that is transmitted automatically to tooling machines and robots that produce finished products. We do not yet have enough knowledge to do this with either software or hardware manufacture, but it is a worthwhile objective and one that will soon be feasible for specialized domains. When such tools become available, the role of the computer professional (as well as the design engineer) will change. There will be less concern for how to construct a solution (after all, much of that process will be automated) and more regard for what the product is to do and how it will be used.

Restating this in terms of the essential software process, we will have shifted our problem-solving activities from the implementation domain to the application domain. Naturally, the application domain for computer science tools is also the implementation domain; because this domain has well-understood, formal models, we can expect the software process in this domain to become increasingly formal. Unfortunately, it will be some time before the computer scientists can provide us with effective tools for other domains. Until they are available, we will continue to rely on variations of the waterfall model. However, this reliance on the waterfall model is not an obstacle as long as we understand our objectives, the problems that we are trying to solve, and the limitations of the methods that we must use.

## 1.3.    Software engineering as problem solving

The previous two sections discussed the meaning of software engineering and described the software process. The presentation may have seemed excessive, particularly for readers who are anxious to get on with finding out how software engineering is done. What methods and tools do software engineers use and how do they apply them? There is a reason for my leisurely beginning. I believe that there can be no cookbook approach to software engineering, that the computer field is dynamic and currently undergoing a major change, and that the methods we will use at the end of this century will differ significantly from those currently in practice. Perhaps, if I could anticipate which methods and tools were going to succeed, I would present them in some cookbook fashion. However, I cannot predict the future. This is a research issue, and more factors than just technical superiority will determine which concepts prevail.

Even if I could guess the winners in this technological evolution, it would be wrong to orient this book toward those potentially dominant methods. This is a book for current practice, and the state of practice will always lag behind the state of the art. There is an educational investment in the technology we use, and we cannot alter our organizational infrastructures as rapidly as we can install new equipment. Consequently, I believe our most immediate need is for an understanding of what software engineering is about and how our methods and tools contribute to its objectives. If the reader comprehends that, then this conceptual foundation can be adapted to most professional environments; it also can evolve as better methods are disseminated.

In the previous sections I pointed out that one cannot describe how to solve a problem until the problem is understood. Much of the discussion so far has been concerned with how we identify and resolve problems. Certainly, the orientation of the next three chapters is one of methods for problem solving. In this sense, the theme of this book may be characterized as a problem-solving approach to software engineering. What is the application need to be satisfied by a software product? How do we design a product that meets that need? How do we detail the design to meet the desired performance characteristics? Each question is a response to an identified problem, and we rely on software engineering to provide the methods and tools for arriving at a proper solution to each. The problems bridge several domains; they begin in the application domain and evolve to more detailed problems in the implementation domain.

Now, if I intend to present software engineering from the perspective of problem solving, then I should examine how software engineers solve problems. I do this at three levels. First, I present an overview of how people solve problems. One may view the next section as interesting psychology but irrelevant software engineering; nevertheless, it is important for problem solvers to understand how the human information processor works and what its strengths and weaknesses are. We should be sensitive to the kinds of mistakes that humans are prone to make and how they may be avoided. Following the section on problem solving there is one on modeling concepts. Again, the discussion may be rejected as irrelevant—this time for being too philosophical. The point made by the discussion is that we use models to guide use in certain types of problem solving. The presentation identifies the power and limitation of our formal models. In a sense, not only am I telling readers that there is no cookbook, but I am also telling them that it is impossible to write one. The final unit in this section on software engineering as problem solving examines how software tools and environments can improve the process. The bottom line is that software design is a human, conceptual activity, and no silver bullet can solve all our problems. Once we accept these constraints as our "software engineering solution space," we can then consider how to produce software that is valid, correct, and delivered on schedule and within cost.

### 1.3.1. Problem solving

There are several ways to review how people solve problems. First, I might examine the psychology literature of that topic to summarize what has been learned. For example, consider Dunker's candle problem, which has been studied for over 50 years. The subject is given a candle, a book of matches, and a box of tacks and is instructed to attach the candle to a wooden door so that there will be light for reading. Think about solving this problem. Most people try to find some way of embedding the tack into the candle so that the candle can be tacked to the door.  As it turns out, the "best" (but not the most obvious) solution is to tack the box to the door and use the box as a holder for the candle.  Not only does this solution hold the candle so that damage to the door is minimal, but it also catches the dripping wax.  The resolution of this problem involves the use of materials in unintended ways.  Interesting, but how does this relate to the kind of problems that a software engineer encounters?  Let me continue.

A second approach to problem solving is to teach a general method or a heuristic.[8]  Bransford and Stein call their method the IDEAL problem solver [BrSt84].  Here the acronym stands for the following sequence of activities:

I     Identify the problem.
D     Define and represent the problem.
E     Explore possible strategies.
A     Act on the strategies.
L     Look back and evaluate the effects of your activities.

It can be seen that their method is not very different from the sequence:

Decide *what* to do.
Decide *how* to do it.
Do it.
Test the result.
Use the result.

This, of course, is the basic structure of the waterfall model.  Thus, at a macro level, the waterfall flow incorporates the IDEAL method.  Unfortunately, most problems come at the micro and not the macro level.  The IDEAL problem solving method certainly helps, but it is not sufficient.  Domain knowledge is required.

Given both domain knowledge and a general heuristic method, the problem solver still must operate within the constraints of his own ability.  Some of these limitations are personal; others are common to all people.  We know, of course, that people are excellent problem

---

[8]A heuristic is an informal rule of thumb that generally provides a good solution.  By way of contrast, an algorithm is precise and always arrives at a solution for the domain in which it is valid.  When dealing with uncertainty, algorithms are not available, and we must fall back to heuristics.  Normally, as understanding grows, heuristics are replaced by algorithms.  In a sense, one may think of a heuristic as a formalization of intuition.  Of course, intuition matures with experience, and we replace trial-by-error approaches with proven methods.  An obvious goal of education is to make the student aware of those methods so that they do not use heuristics when algorithms are available.

solvers; the scientific advances of this century are a testament to this fact. But there are physiological and psychological factors that affect how we think, plan, and decide. In what follows I review some of the findings about information processing and rationality in decision making. The presentation is incomplete and biased by its brevity. Nevertheless, it does identify some of the pitfalls that we, as human problem solvers, must avoid.

Although theories of thought and problem solving have been in existence for some time, the new discipline of cognitive science has had a profound effect on our understanding [Gard85]. Newell and Simon, in their 1972 book on human problem solving, interpreted this transition as follows.

> Within the last dozen years a general change in scientific outlook has occurred, consonant with the point of view represented here. One can date the change roughly from 1956: in psychology, by the appearance of Bruner, Goodnow, and Austin's *Study of Thinking* and George Miller's "The magical number seven"; in linguistics, by Noam Chomsky's "Three models of language"; and in computer science, by our own paper on the Logic Theory Machine.
>
> As these titles show, the common new emphasis was not the investigation of problem solving, but rather the exploration of complex processes and the acceptance of the need to be explicit about internal, symbolic systems. [NeSi72, p. 4]

Restating their conclusion, there was a move from observing behavior to developing models that explained how humans processed information. As it turned out, these models were extensible to artificial processing environments such as the computer. This new "cognitive perspective" not only altered psychology, but it also had an impact on computer science (with the introduction of artificial intelligence) and philosophy (with the ontological issue of *an* artificial intelligence).

When we create a model, we expect it to predict and explain. That is, we want the model to serve as an analogue to the phenomena being investigated. In biological systems, size adds complexity. Thus, we know more about constrained, repeatable tasks that occur in a relatively brief time span than we do about tasks that extend over days and weeks. In other words, we have effective models that explain the mechanics of processing information, but we have few models to explain why one person solves the candle problem and another does not.

Because there is greater certainty about precisely measured physical events, I begin from the bottom up. Card, Moran, and Newell have developed a model to understand and evaluate human-computer interactions, which builds on much of what has been learned from cognitive science [CaMN83]. They describe a Model Human Processor, shown in Figure 1.7, which consists of three systems. The Perceptual Processor receives visual and auditory inputs and enters them into a partitioned store; the Motor Processor takes commands and translates them into motor actions; and the Cognitive Processor operates on working memory (including the visual and auditory image stores) and generates commands for the Motor Processor. The duration of most actions is a fraction of a second, and the major use of the model is in the analysis of short-term actions such as keystroke entry or response to a visual alert. However, the model of the Cognitive Processor also provides insight into the actions of longer term activities.

The model displays two classes of memory.

- *Working or Short-Term Memory (STM).* This holds the information under current consideration; it is the working memory that interacts with the Cognitive Processor. A limited number of STM processes can be active at one time. The figure shows a capacity ($\mu_{WM}$) of 3 and an effective capacity ($\mu_{WM*}$) of 7 chunks. The contents of a process are shown to have a mean half-life ($\delta_{WM}$) of 73 seconds for 1 chunk and 7 seconds for 3 chunks. Processor cycle time ($\tau_C$) is 70 msec.

- *Long Term-Memory (LTM).* This stores the knowledge for future use. LTM is considered to be nonerasable and unlimited in size. Retrieval from LTM is instantaneous, but the storage of new information with its associated (semantic) links takes several seconds.

The units managed by memory are called *chunks*. A chunk is a symbolic entity (or pattern) that generally is expressed in terms of other chunks. Because STM is relatively small, the Cognitive Processor continually activates chunks from LTM (which replace chunks in STM) or refreshes chunks already in STM (a process called rehearsal). The result is that there are bounds on what can be retained in STM during a short period. For example, when one is asked to listen to and then repeat a string of random digits, the ceiling on a correct response is seven plus or minus two digits.[9] This is not a function of intelligence; rather, it is related to the number of STM chunks available and the time it takes to activate LTM.

Of course, it is possible to repeat longer strings when the strings are expressed as chunks. For example, the string

---

[9]The value 7 ± 2 is taken from the title of Miller's seminal paper, "The magical number seven plus or minus two: Some limits on our capacity for processing information" [Mill56].

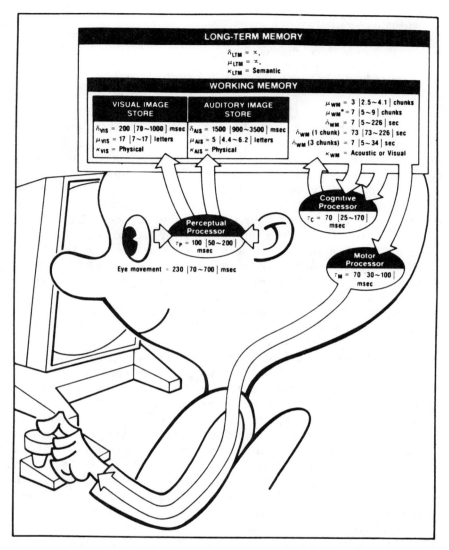

Sensory information flows into Working Memory through the Perceptual Processor. Working Memory consists of activated chunks in Long-Term Memory. The basic principle of operation of the Model Human Processor is the *Recognize-Act Cycle of the Cognitive Processor* (P0 in Figure 2.2). The Motor Processor is set in motion through activation of chunks in Working Memory.

Fig. 1.7. The Model Human Processor—memories and processors.
(Reprinted from [CaMN83] with permission, ©1983, Lawrence Erlbaum Assoc.)

47

C B S I B M R C A

is in reality only three chunks,

CBS IBM RCA.

In this illustration, the chunks were identified symbolically (e.g., CBS), and each chunk has associated with it many other chunks; moreover, the associations will differ among individuals. We may think of LTM as a network of related chunks (and their semantic links) that can be accessed via links to chunks currently in STM. A chunk may be thought of as a symbolic representation of some pattern match. Chunks contain facts, procedures, history, etc.; chunks may be composed of chunks. We can retrieve chunks from LTM only if they are "closely related" to the STM contents. We navigate through LTM by following such relationships. For example, in one scenario CBS makes one think of a television network, which makes one think of a TV set, which makes one think of the room in which the TV set is located, and so forth. This is a common association game for children. In actual problem solving, the chain of reasoning occurs quite rapidly, and it is very difficult to reconstruct the symbolic sequences applied. That is why retrospective analyses of the problem solving process are so unreliable.

Because STM is small and the processing cycle time is significant, the number of LTM retrievals in a fixed period is bounded. To reduce the cognitive load and improve response times, skills are developed for frequently repeated tasks. For example, the unskilled typist must look for each key, whereas key selection is a motor skill for the experienced typist. Training eliminates the need for explicit thinking about the keys. Once a skill is learned, it is difficult to manage it consciously; one may stumble when trying to concentrate on how to walk up a flight of stairs. One can think of learned skills as patterns (chunks) that abstract the processes of many (lower level) chunks. By speeding the processing of learned tasks, skills bypass the need for conscious information processing. Skill learning also applies to thinking tasks. For example, in school one learns to add by first manipulating physical objects. The concept is then abstracted, and the addition relationships and methods are memorized. Because this skill is over taught, one produces sums without returning to the concrete models. Thus, in a sense, skills represent the learned patterns that let us operate with abstractions without requiring recourse to first principles.

We may think of learning as the process of increasing the number of available patterns (chunks) in LTM. Consider de Groot's experiments of the 1960s. Chess masters first were shown chess boards with situations taken from actual games, and then they were asked to reconstruct the boards. As might be expected, their performance was significantly better than that of novice players. When shown chess boards with random placements, however, the masters' ability to recall proved to be no better than that of the novices. To explain this difference, it subsequently was determined that experienced chess masters had built up a library of 10,000 to 100,000 patterns that they used in identifying the most promising moves (i.e., retrievals from LTM that helped determine the best move). Further, when a player was shown a board and asked to select a move, he spent the first 15-30 seconds gathering information about the situation in order to build up an internal representation of the position. Therefore, it was postulated, real game boards generated perceptions that could be reduced to a small number of previously stored patterns. These patterns (with their semantic links) were compact enough to be processed effectively in STM, and so the masters could reconstruct the boards accurately. With the random placement boards, on the other hand, there were no abstracting patterns available. The chess master was limited by the same $7 \pm 2$ chunks as the novice, and performances were comparable. Similar experiments have been repeated with programmers using real and scrambled programs; they produce similar results [Shne80].

The structure in which the learned patterns are stored in LTM is called a *schema* (plural, schemata). The schemata provide the organization for retrieving and recognizing patterns. Studies of how students learn science, for example, show that learners look for meaning and try to construct order even in the absence of complete information [Resn83, KuAO88]; they seek to find a way to append the new information onto their existing schemata. When links are not available, *naive theories* are constructed to connect the new information to what is already known. Naive theories are always part of the learning process, and understanding always relies on relationships to established knowledge in the schema. Information isolated from these structures will be lost or forgotten. Thus, all learning is carried out in the context of current perceptions. In the words of the physicist Sir Harold Jeffries, "I wouldn't have seen it if I hadn't believed it."

We use the term *mental model* to describe how an individual understands a domain of knowledge [John83, GeSt83]. As will be shown in the next chapter, matching a system to a user's mental model is an important task in the design of an effective interactive system. Shneiderman observes that, for computer interactions, there are two distinct categories of knowledge [Shne87]. Syntactic knowledge is varied, device dependent, and acquired by rote memorization (e.g., the symbol used by a programming language as a statement terminator). Semantic knowledge, on the other hand, is structured, device independent, and acquired by meaningful learning (e.g., the concept of loop recursion). Syntactic knowledge is easily forgotten—it requires over-learning or mnemonics for retention. Semantic knowledge, on the other hand, is stable in memory—it can be organized in the form of a coherent mental model.

Having described the basic operations of the human information processor, it is time to examine some higher level models of problem solving. One of the earliest of these was introduced by Wallas in 1926. By means of a retrospective analysis of thought, he produced a four-stage model.

- *Preparation*. Here the problem is investigated "in all directions."

- *Incubation*. During this stage there is no conscious thinking of the problem.

- *Illumination*. This is the appearance of the "happy idea," i.e., the "Aha!"

- *Verification*. The idea is verified using knowledge of the initial problem.

In this model, an unconscious mechanism produces the solution. Indeed, Wallas even recommended not reading during incubation so as to avoid interfering with that unconscious operation. Subsequent studies suggest that all thought, creative and otherwise, follows the same process, but that the role of the unconscious is minimal [Weis86]. Olton uses the term "creative worrying" for what Wallas called incubation; it may be characterized as persistence combined with breaks that relieve fatigue [OlJo76]. Apparently, the same kind of information processing is carried out during creative worrying as is used during conscious thought. The effectiveness of the problem-solving activity improves with the richness of domain understanding. The more patterns available during Wallas's stages of preparation and verification, the more constructive the problem solver.

Many modern studies of problem solving and decision making make use of verbal protocols. The subjects speak aloud during the task, and their utterances and actions are used as data that offer clues to the information being processed [ErSi84]. (Notice how this differs from retrospective analysis, in which the subject tries to reconstruct his activities after the event.) This technique has been used extensively to study how clinicians make decisions. One broadly accepted model has been constructed by Elstein and his colleagues [ElSS78]. Called the hypothetico-deductive model, it consists of the following four steps:

- *Cue acquisition*. Taking a history, performing a physical examination, reviewing test results, etc.

- *Hypothesis generation.* Retrieving alternative hypotheses of the diagnosis from long-term memory.

- *Cue interpretation.* Considering the data in the context of the hypotheses previously generated.

- *Hypothesis evaluation.* Weighing and combining the data to determine which hypotheses are supported or ruled out.

The process is iterative. It may result in a decision that more data are required (i.e., that a test should be ordered), that a probable diagnosis (and associated therapy) is indicated, or both.

In analyzing the model, researchers found that the generation of early hypotheses had considerable natural force; medical students generated early hypotheses even when asked to withhold judgment. The number of hypotheses was usually around four or five and appeared to have an upper bound of six or seven. The generation of hypotheses was based more consistently on single salient cues rather than on combinations of clues. Very few cues seemed to be used, and hypothesis selection was biased by recent experience. Also, cue interpretation tended to use three measures: confirm, disconfirm, and noncontributory; the use of a seven-point scale had no greater explanatory power. Finally, researchers noted that lack of thoroughness was not as important a cause of error in diagnosis as were problems in integrating and combining information. Interpreting these results in the context of the information-processing model already presented, one might observe that simple pattern matches are preferred, that the magical number 7 ± 2 holds, and that retrieval from LTM in response to a problem is quite spontaneous.

In an unrelated study, McDonald tried to measure the impact of reminders on physician behavior [McDo76]. Here, the physicians were assisted by a computer system that reviewed a patient's history and made recommendations for the current visit. For example, if the patient was a woman who had not had a Pap smear in the last 12 months, then the program would recommend that one be ordered. Previous studies had shown that these reminders affected the physician's behavior. McDonald now wanted to learn something about the long-term effect of this type of system. He designed a crossover study divided into two phases. In the first phase, half the clinicians received the reminders and the other half worked without them. During the second phase, the reminder group worked without the reminders and vice versa. An analysis of the physicians' actions again indicated positive changes whenever they had the reminders. McDonald also expected to find a learning effect; he thought that the group that first used the reminders would better conform to the standards of care after the reminders were withdrawn.

But this was not the case. Neither order in the experiment nor the physicians' experience affected their behavior. The only factor that seemed to impact behavior was the presence of a reminder. McDonald concluded that the physicians were confronted by too many standards of care and, consequently, suffered from information overload. He titled his paper, "Computer reminders, the quality of care, and the nonperfectability of man."

Fortunately, the software engineer seldom has to make decisions with the time pressures found in medical situations. Accuracy and quality are far more important than speed to solution; one can indulge in extensive creative worrying before being satisfied that the proposed solution is sound. This, then, raises another question. If we think about a problem long enough and hard enough, will we be able to solve it? It would be nice to postulate that, when a problem is solvable, we always use rational means to solve it. Unfortunately, papers with titles such as

"Can human irrationality be experimentally demonstrated" [Cohe81], and
"Under what conditions does theory obstruct research progress" [GrLP86],

suggest that this may not be possible. This raises the issue of bias in human reasoning [Evan89]. How rational are we when we approach a problem?

There have been many studies of how people interpret syllogisms. In the 1920s, Wilkins found that people were better able to evaluate the validity of concrete arguments, such as

All mammals have backbones.
All dogs are mammals.
Therefore, all dogs have backbones.

than they were at evaluating abstractions, such as:

All Q's are S's.
All P's are Q's.
Therefore, all P's are S's.

Subsequent research has shown that the use of quantifiers (some or all) or the introduction of ambiguity into the syllogism adds to the difficulty in comprehending argument validity. For example,

It is important to talk about things that are on our minds.
We spend so much of our time in the kitchen that household problems are on our minds.

Therefore, it is important to talk about household problems.

has logical validity but lacks factual truth. Many subjects allow their evaluation of the factual truth to bias their interpretation of the logical validity; they examine the problem in the context of their mental model rather than as a logical abstraction. (See [Gilh88], from which the last syllogism was taken, for a more complete discussion of this and other classic experiments in directed thinking.)

Another type of reasoning bias was uncovered by Wason in the mid-1960s. In the *selection task*, a subject is given a deck of cards with letters on one side and numbers on the other. The rule is that if there is an A on one side of a card, then there is a 3 on the other side. The following cards are shown:

Which cards must be turned over to see if the rule is true or false?

We must turn over the A card to see if a 3 is on the other side and the 7 card to see if an A is on the other side. Most people select the A card for turning to see if the cards are consistent with the rule:

One side **A** ⇒ Other side **3**, [i.e., $(p \wedge (p \rightarrow q)) \Rightarrow q$, or *modus ponens*].[10]

Most people do not select the **7** card even though it is required to test the complementary rule

One side not **3** ⇒ Other side not **A**, [i.e., $(\neg q \wedge (p \rightarrow q)) \Rightarrow \neg p$, or *modus tollens*].

---

[10]A philosophical footnote. One cannot prove that for every card with an **A** on one side there is a **3** on the other unless *every* **A** card can be inspected. However, just one **A** card with something other than a **3** on the other side *proves* the rule to be false. This is the source of the expression "the exception that proves the rule." (It does not mean, as it is commonly used, that finding a counterexample adds to our confidence in the rule's correctness.) To take this a step further, much of science is empirical in that one begins with a hypothesis, and then collects data to confirm that hypothesis empirically. Popper pointed out that, unless all possible cases could be tested, this approach proved nothing. Proof, in the logical sense, could only refute the hypothesis—not support it [Popp59]. Thus, he suggested that experiments should be defined to falsify the hypothesis so that if they failed we would have greater confidence in an unprovable hypothesis. It was over a decade before Popper published his observations; he assumed that it was so obvious that everyone recognized this fact. Now read on about confirmation bias and the hesitancy to refute favored hypotheses.

This is called confirmation bias. We seek to test our theories by examining the data that confirm them, but we seldom try to refute them. Confirmation bias seems to be universal. Mahoney has conducted extensive studies to show that it is present in the reasoning of most scientists [Maho76]. Some suggest that confirmation bias is a mechanism to reduce cognitive load; we ought not feel obliged to disprove what we already believe. Subsequent studies have shown that when the selection experiment is carried out with concrete materials, confirmation bias diminishes. For example, at one time postage was 3¢ for a sealed envelope and only 2¢ for an unsealed envelope. Subjects, who understood this rule, were shown two stamp-up envelopes, with 2¢ and 3¢ postage, and two stamp-down envelopes, sealed and unsealed. They were asked to decide which envelopes had the incorrect postage, and they had little difficulty with this form of the selection task. They turned over the envelope with the 2¢ stamp to be certain that it was not sealed and the sealed envelope to establish that it had 3¢ postage. Thus, when confronted with a less abstract problem, people exhibit less difficulty in identifying cases that might otherwise be considered disconfirmatory.

Tversky and Kahneman have done considerable research into the heuristics of thinking under uncertainty. In one paper they identified three categories of bias [TvKa74]:

- *Representativeness.* In many probabilistic questions people do not question how representative the sample is of the population. This leads them to ignore prior probabilities, sample size, the nature of chance, etc. For example, the flipping of a true coin will produce a head 50 percent of the time. After a sequence of H-H-H-H-H, what is the probability that the coin will come up heads? The answer, of course, is .5; most people confuse this question with that of computing the probability of a H-H-H-H-H-H sequence in six flips.

- *Availability.* In many situations people access the frequency of a class according to the ease with which instances are brought to mind. For example, which is more frequent, words that begin with an **r** (road) or those that have an **r** in the third position (car). Because most people can access more examples of the former, they assume that there will be more words that begin with an **r**. They are wrong.

- *Adjustments and anchoring.* People frequently make estimates by starting from an initial value that is adjusted to yield the final answer. Subjects tend to anchor the outcome based on that initial estimate. For example, one group was asked to estimate the product of

$$8 \times 7 \times 6 \times 5 \times 4 \times 3 \times 2 \times 1,$$

and another group was asked to estimate the product of

$$1 \times 2 \times 3 \times 4 \times 5 \times 6 \times 7 \times 8.$$

To provide a rapid response, people tend to multiply the first few terms and then adjust from that partial product (the anchor). Thus, the mean estimates were 512 for the ascending sequence and 2250 for the descending sequence. The correct answer, by the way, is 40,320.

Notice that in these examples of bias there is a tension between the formalisms of logic and the subject's intuition. I will explore this further in the next section.

So far, the discussion has focused on biases that can be represented in a written form, but the Perceptual Processor also processes nonverbal sources. We know, for example, that the two brain hemispheres process information differently [SpDe81]. The left hemisphere is more adept at generating rapidly changing motor patterns, processing rapidly changing auditory patterns, and other forms of sequential processing. The right hemisphere, by contrast, is more effective in simultaneously processing the type of information required to perceive spatial patterns and relationships. An obvious question, then, is whether we can use these other dimensions to reduce biases. Unfortunately, we shall see that mental imagery is no more reliable than text.

Norman observes that when we are asked to answer a question, we use our memory in different ways [Norm82]. For some questions, such as what is the capital of Maryland, we search for facts. For other questions, such as is Lincoln's profile facing left or right on the penny, we rely on a mental image. Finally, there are questions, such as does an elephant eat more than a lion, that we can answer only by inference. One of the powers of human reasoning is that the inference mechanism allows us to infer more than we factually know. But this can be dangerous. For example, when asked about the capital of Maryland, many will infer the capital is the state's largest city and respond with Baltimore rather than Annapolis. If the person can visualize a penny, there is no difficulty in stating that Lincoln is looking to the right. But where visualization fails, inference takes over. Figure 1.8 shows some results of an experiment by Stevens and Coupe in which subjects were asked to indicate the direction between two well-known geographic locations [StCo78]. The figure contains maps with the correct answer; the bars outside the circles indicate the subjects' responses. Notice the effect of inference. Lacking an internal representation for the map, the subjects were forced to infer global facts (e.g., the direction from San

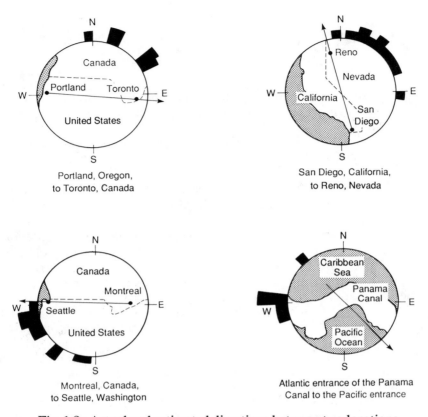

Portland, Oregon,
to Toronto, Canada

San Diego, California,
to Reno, Nevada

Montreal, Canada,
to Seattle, Washington

Atlantic entrance of the Panama
Canal to the Pacific entrance

Fig. 1.8. Actual and estimated directions between two locations.
(After [StCo78] with permission, ©1978, Academic Press.)

Diego to Reno) from local facts (e.g., Nevada borders on the east of
California), and they were wrong. The conclusion that I would like to
leave with the reader is that images (and diagrams) can be of enormous
help in problem solving and visualizing potential solutions. Nevertheless, such devices are not free of bias.

It is now time to summarize what has just been presented in the
context of software engineering. Starting with the physical characteristics, we note that the human information processor has a small working
memory capacity. The working (or short-term) memory processes
symbolic chunks. Its contents decay rapidly, and they must be either
rehearsed or activated from long-term memory. (Like an airplane in
flight, it can never stop.) Activation is associative and is guided by the
current context (goal). The hypothetico-deductive model indicates that

very few cues are processed in combinations and that a three-point evaluation scale is satisfactory. This suggests that the reasoning in short-term memory relies on surface pattern matches. Overstating the conclusion, we reason using abstractions and seldom rely on first principles. The power of the human information processor lies in its vast store of long-term memory, its many links for recall, and its ability to infer information rapidly. The weakness in this mechanism is that the subject's mental model (or schema) always directs the thinking, and that model may be inappropriate (i.e., a naive theory) or biased.

Fortunately, the software engineer normally will have time to reflect on the quality of his decisions. The merit of his work will depend on his experience (i.e., the number of patterns available for recognizing approaches and barriers to the solution), the effort expended to identify and remove errors in the solution (e.g., confirmation bias), and his persistence. Simon estimates that it takes about 10 years to achieve expert status in a field. Consequently, the student should be prepared for an extended apprenticeship. During that period he will be both a builder and user of software tools. If we, as tool builders, can be sensitive to the strengths and weaknesses of the human problem solver, then our products should both meet the users' needs and help him master his natural limitations.

By way of a closing comment, the reader will observe that this discussion of human problem solving has not referenced any literature regarding the psychology of computer programming. I have avoided those references because I am most concerned with how people solve problems. The specifics of how programmers learn and perform is a specialization of this larger field. Inasmuch as most software engineering does not involve programming, I have not addressed the particulars of programming. For studies of this topic see [Shne80], [Curt85], [SoJo85], [SoIy86], [OISS87], and [BaBu87]. Some of these references also contain papers that address issues in the management of human-computer interactions, which is considered in Chapter 2. Finally, I note that there is an emerging literature on the psychology of design. Guindon has performed a protocol analysis of two designers in a laboratory setting, and she has found that their approach to an ill-structured design problem tends to be opportunistic rather than top down [Guin90]. Rosson and Alpert have examined object-oriented design from the perspective of its cognitive consequences as part of a general effort to have the design and mental models overlap [RoAl90]. But this experimental work is not of general concern to the practicing software engineer. I believe that Kim's guide to tackling difficult problems [Kim90] will prove to be more helpful than any programmer-oriented study.

### 1.3.2.  Modeling concepts

The previous section used models of the human information processor to help explain how people solve problems.  The use of models is quite common in the physical sciences.  Our understanding of motion, for example, is expressed in terms of a formula that is, in reality, a model.  It both explains and predicts.  Of course, there is a distinction between the mathematics that the formula must satisfy and the actual motion of an object in the universe.  For very small, or very large, or very distant objects, a particular formula may cease to be an effective model.  Nevertheless, the formula, as a mathematical entity, will always satisfy the laws of mathematics independent of its utility.

This differentiation between the model and the object modeled has been of concern to applied mathematicians for some time.  Barwise puts it as follows:

> The axiomatic method says that our theorems are true *if* our axioms are.  The modeling method says that our theorems model facts in the domain modeled *if* there is a close enough fit between the model and the domain modeled. . . .  [A]s a philosopher might say, applied mathematics may not guarantee knowledge of facts about the physical world, but it can lead to the next best thing—justified true belief.  [Barw89, p. 847]

That is, if we accept the validity of our axioms, then we can have confidence in all that follows (i.e., justified true belief).  But we can have confidence in these axioms only from experimental, empirical evidence.  Barwise defines the *Fallacy of Identification* as the failure to distinguish between some mathematical model and the thing it is a model of.

So, what does that have to do with software engineering?  Everything.  When I defined the essence of the software process, I described it as a three step process:

- The formulation of a conceptual model that describes a solution to the problem.

- The translation of that conceptual model into a formal model that prescribes the implemented solution.

- The construction of an implementation that satisfies that formal model.

The conceptual model describes an automated solution, but it lacks the rigor and precision of a formal model.  With a complete and consistent formal model, on the other hand, every decision, operation, or interpretation can be verified as being either correct or incorrect. Because the final implementation is always a formal model of the program's behavior, the software process always involves a transformation from informal mental models (which describe *what* we want to do) to a formal implementation (which details *how* the intended solution will operate). We must avoid thinking that, if a program is correct, it will correspond to the environment's needs, and vice versa.

Recall that in the diagram of the essential software process (Fig. 1.5) the conceptual modeling line was shown as starting in the application domain and extending into the process, while the formal modeling line began somewhere in the process and culminated in the formal model that we call the implementation. The science of computer science is, to a very large extent, the study of the formal modeling activity, its logical foundations, representations, and invariants. Thus, most computer scientists look to extend the formal modeling line to the left and to identify formalisms for expressing portions of the conceptual model. This book examines the formal tools that support this activity and shows how to use them. However, this is only part of the problem. Systems analysts (or other domain specialists) must determine the validity of each formal model. Without this validation obligation, the Fallacy of Identification is inevitable.

Let me extend this argument in a more precise fashion. The software process begins with some real need called the application (**A**), whose solution we describe in a specification (**S**). Our goal is to produce a product (**P**) that satisfies the needs identified in **A**. Thus, the essential software process reduces to the transformation **A** ⇒ **P**. However, this transformation is difficult to work with because it combines both subjective (conceptual) and objective (formal) evaluations. Consequently, it is more convenient to decompose the process into two transformations: **A** ⇒ **S** and **S** ⇒ **P**.

Lehman, Stenning, and Turski have described the software process in these terms [LeST84]. In their model (LST), they call the transformation **A** ⇒ **S** *abstraction* and the transformation **S** ⇒ **P** *reification*. In a later work, Turski opts for the terms *abstraction* and *satisfaction* [TuMa87]. Others use the terms *analysis* and *detailing* for these activities. In almost all cases, however, the researchers offer little insight regarding what happens before **S** exists. The emphasis is on the construction of a product **P** that satisfies its specification **S**. This, of course, is the domain in which the tools of computer science can be of the most benefit.

Because the LST model provides one of the clearest statements of the reification process, it is worth describing it in some detail here. Reification is represented as follows:

$$S \Rightarrow S_1 \Rightarrow S_2 \Rightarrow \ldots \Rightarrow S_n \Rightarrow P$$

It begins with some specification S. For a given problem, there are many potentially valid specifications that could be selected. Reification is not concerned with why S was selected. In the LST model the primary concern is that P be correct with respect to S. The specification S acts as a set of axioms, and the central issue is how to preserve correctness with respect to S.

In the LST model, the specification S is considered a theory. Given a theory, the designers derive a model in a linguistic form that is closer to that of the desired product P. The result is a model of the theory. Many correct models for the theory exist, and the designers must select the one they consider to be the best. If the model is not derived by use of behavior-preserving transformations, then it must be verified. (That is, one must test to see if the model is correct with respect to its theory.) Following this there is a validation obligation to ensure that no inappropriate behaviors have been introduced. (That is, that the defined solution still does what is intended.) Once accepted, the model is elevated to the status of a theory for another iteration of this canonical step. Notice that this process can proceed only if there is a formal theory that will allow the developers to establish the model's correctness unambiguously.

Expressed in this fashion, it is clear that reification must be a sequential process. The model $S_{i+1}$ cannot be built until the model $S_i$ is accepted as a theory. Once $S_j$ has been accepted as a theory, any changes to the theory $S_k$, $k < j$, will invalidate the chain of logic from $S_k$ forward. Clearly, the goal is to maintain a logically correct trail until some model ($S_n$) exists that is isomorphic to the desired product P. The $S_n$ represents a program that will be correctly transformed into the product.

Because it is unlikely that a single linguistic representation is appropriate for each level of modeling, LST presents the canonical steps in terms of different linguistic levels.[11] One may think of going from a top-level design to a detailed design to a program design language (PDL) to code. Of course, these are all informal models, and it is difficult to prove that one (model) is correct with respect to its parent (theory). To guarantee rigor, one must have formalisms to express the descriptive theories of the application domain in ways that can be transformed correctly. For example, to the extent that FORTRAN expresses the scientist's intent, the FORTRAN program can be

---

[11]Some computer scientists have developed representation schemes that are broad enough to support formal modeling from the preliminary (and incomplete) initial specification through the final implementation. These are called *wide spectrum languages*.

considered a descriptive theory. The compiled code will be a correct model of that theory. (Different compilers might produce alternative, but equally correct, models.)

At one level, the discussion of reification offers a neat and logical approach to system development. It reduces the activity to a clear sequence of steps that has the potential for formal definition and automated support. But it is not that straightforward. First, S cannot capture everything about the product to be delivered; that is why there is always a validation obligation at each step of the process. Subjective domain knowledge must be applied to be certain that the right system is being built. This is further confounded by the inherent incompleteness of S. Maibaum and Turski observe that there are two reasons why the specification will not be complete [MaTu84]. To begin with, the sponsors seldom know enough about the application to define it fully at the start. Moreover, even if we could make S complete, it would be undesirable to do so. There are many behaviors in the product P that are not important to the sponsor; they represent design choices of no consequence to the system user. Thus, if the specification S were complete, S would have to identify all those design choices. Consequently, S would be isomorphic to P, and the problem would be overspecified. What is necessary is that S contain only the essential behaviors. The behaviors added by some $S_i$ are *permissive* as long as they do not violate the essential behavior of S.

We now see that what began as a clean logical process has turned out not to be so neat at all. The LST model assumed that S contains all the essential behaviors of the desired P. But we have just observed that the sponsor may not know what those behaviors are. Therefore, during reification it may be necessary to augment S as the problem becomes better understood. Changes to the theory S, naturally, may invalidate the models that were derived from it. Consequently, the software process is not simply one of the logical derivation of a product from a fixed specification. Rather, it is best understood as one of problem solving in two domains using both subjective and objective criteria. Of course, that is what makes software development so difficult.

This is summarized in Figure 1.9, which decomposes the software process activities by phase (abstraction and reification) and evaluation criteria (objective and subjective). The figure suggests the following interpretation of the LST model. Abstraction consists of a judgment-based requirements analysis activity that relies on formalisms and heuristics derived from domain experience. Where domain formalisms exist, they describe properties and behaviors in the application domain, but they may offer little insight into what the software should do. The outcome of the abstraction step is the specification S. The reification that follows is best described as an iteration of canonical steps, $S_i \Rightarrow S_{i+1}$, each of which culminates with (objective) verification followed by

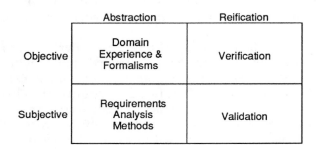

|  | Abstraction | Reification |
|---|---|---|
| Objective | Domain Experience & Formalisms | Verification |
| Subjective | Requirements Analysis Methods | Validation |

Fig. 1.9. Objectivity and subjectivity in the software process.

(subjective) validation. Much of the objective domain knowledge will be represented in S; it is the goal of the validation obligation to ensure that none of the introduced permissive behaviors is inconsistent with the domain experience. Naturally, the boundary between the objective and subjective criteria is fuzzy. Nevertheless, the figure clearly shows the important role of subjective and domain-specific (i.e., extralogical) decision making in the process.

It should be clear from this discussion that it is not possible to treat software engineering as only a formal activity. Recently, there was an extended debate regarding the limits of program verification [Fetz88, Edit89]. Central to the argument was the Fallacy of Identification. Some participants in the debate discussed how well the model represents reality; others considered how accurately the implementation reflects the behaviors identified by the model. As we have seen, these are two different questions, and both are important. In the previous section it was shown that people have difficulty in reasoning logically. The biases in interpreting syllogisms and ignoring refutation suggest that our natural thinking processes are not those of formal logic. The problems that people have with representativeness, availability, and in anchoring also indicate that our inference mechanisms for dealing with statistical and mathematical problems are inadequate. Fortunately, much of our universe can be modeled with logic and mathematics, and therefore we must use formal tools if we are to avoid errors. Yet, although the formalisms are necessary, they are not sufficient. Consequently, we need ways of applying the knowledge and experience that have not been (or cannot be) formalized.

Clearly, the software engineer must use a variety of modeling tools; let us now examine how they may be classified. In decision making, models are divided into two categories:

- *Descriptive models* define and describe a process and its parameters. Descriptive models, such as those of statistics, can be used to account for differences among groups.

- *Normative or prescriptive models* define a normative behavior that details "what ought to be." For example, operations research methods may define an optimal solution to some problem even though individuals do not behave that way.

Obviously, there is uncertainty in decision making, and we use these two types of models to decide how people behave and how, in principle, they should behave. Because there are so many complexities, people are limited by the number of facts that they can manage in making a decision. Simon calls decision making within this constraint *bounded rationality*; most normative econometric models assume rational behavior in that context. Unfortunately, bounded rationality is of little help to the software engineer. He can gain no comfort from the law of large numbers in his modeling. He produces a single product, and it must be both correct and valid. For him, a more formal view of modeling helps.

In logic, a prescriptive model also describes "what ought to be," but it does so in a universe that allows only outcomes that can be verified. In this sense, the source code of the delivered implementation is a prescriptive model. Higher level prescriptive models offer higher degrees of abstraction and provide powerful mechanisms for proving (or refuting) assumptions. The value of the prescriptive model is that it removes most of the semantic information that confuses us in our evaluations (but aids us in our concept formulation). The benefit of the complementary descriptive model is that it facilitates the processing of the semantic information. As the discussion of the LST model has shown, there is no clear division between the descriptive and formal models, and the software engineer must learn to work with both types.

In summary, formal modeling complements intuitive human problem solving. We have seen that short-term memory is small and that facts and procedures cannot be accessed from long-term memory unless the necessary semantic links are available in the schema. The objective of software engineering is to work in the formal modeling domain as early as possible, for it is only in that domain that tools are available to ascertain correctness. But there is also the parallel responsibility of constructing valid models. Here, there is no concept of correctness. The software engineer must learn enough about the domain of application to have confidence in his model. And learning can be difficult, indeed. In 1938, the psychologist Woodworth described the learning process in four steps: chaos, analysis, synthesis, and automatization. It is during the chaotic period that the naive theories are formed. Analysis refines and corrects these theories, and here formal modeling helps.

Still, the discovery process is essentially a cognitive one. For older problems, where solutions exist, they can be learned and adapted. For new problems, creative solutions are required, and the software engineer must be innovative.

This is how Weisberg analyzes creative problem solving in tasks such as the candle problem.

> subjects first attempted to solve the problems directly, based on their knowledge of the problem situation or situation like it. Creative solutions developed as the problem solvers acquired information indicating that their initial solutions were inadequate. In attempting to overcome these inadequacies, subjects were led to try things they had not tried before.
>
> . . .Changes in the way the person approaches the problem (that is, "restructurings") occur in response to information that becomes available as the person works on the problem. . . . [N]ovel solutions to problems also arise in response to information that becomes available as the person works on the problem. [Weis86, p. 90]

In short, one learns by doing and then reacting to the observed mistakes. Fortunately, there are methods and tools that can help the software engineer in "creative" problem solving. Most are designed to structure what is known in the form of a model that (1) offers a clear expression of what has been agreed to, (2) aids in the identification of what remains unknown, and/or (3) facilitates the recognition of contradictions. Some of the models will be descriptive, and others prescriptive. The final model, (i.e., the delivered program), is always prescriptive, and thus the software engineer is, in essence, a builder of models.

### 1.3.3. Methods, tools, and environments

This section has described software engineering as problem solving. First, I examined how people solve problems, and then I considered how models assist them in this activity. I concluded with the observation that, in the end, the software engineer is basically a model builder, and his tools must aid him in this activity. In this final segment of that discussion I provide a taxonomy for the tools and methods[12] and identify their fundamental limitations. I begin by describing the software engineering hierarchy shown in Figure 1.10 [Musa83]. It presents a

---

[12]*Methodology* is the study of methods. Because the word is impressive, some use it instead of the more accurate word, *method*.

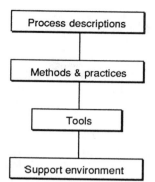

Fig. 1.10. The Software Engineering Hierarchy.

four-level structure that implies that methods and practices are designed to support a particular process description, and that tools are designed to carry out the tasks defined by methods and practices. The lowest level in this hierarchy is the environment, which is defined as an integrated collection of tools that supports the overriding process description (or model). There are several contradictions in this hierarchy. The most glaring of these is that it is not a hierarchy; the same tool can be used with many methods, and the same methods can be used with many process descriptions. Nevertheless, the diagram does offer an effective definition for an environment, and it does display the relationships among process models, methods, and tools.

In what follows, I assume that the process model will be some variation of the waterfall model. This is not an endorsement; rather, it is a recognition that virtually all commercial development conforms to that model. Because this book is intended for practitioners, it would be foolhardy to expend much time on alternative paradigms that are not widely used. The discussion of the methods and practices is presented in the form of approaches to modeling. A quick review of the table of contents shows that the material is grouped into the following three types of activity:

- *Requirements modeling*, where models describe what is to be done without prescribing how it is to be done. During this activity, the software engineers use models to guide them in clarifying their understanding of the problem and its solution, (i.e., in going from the chaos through the completion of the analysis).

- *Modeling-in-the-large*, where one begins with a statement of what the system is to do and translates it into a design that satisfies the initial intent. The emphasis is on architectural issues and not implementation details. Of course, for small student projects there really is no modeling-in-the-large.

- *Modeling-in-the-small*, where the components identified in the previous activity are transformed into efficient, executable entities. Traditional programming is an example of modeling-in-the-small.

The emphasis in the following chapters will be on defining the objectives of each type of model, identifying the methods and tools that aid in meeting those objectives, and showing how the methods and tools are used.

Of course, there is the hope that, as we learn to build better tools, they will be able to do much of the work for us. The compiler eliminated our reliance on assembly language programming. In the Backus example, FORTRAN produced a 20:1 reduction in problem size. Will Computer-Assisted Software Engineering (CASE) and its related Integrated Project Support Environment (IPSE) have similar effects? Or will the next generation of automated tool simply improve the existing process? Rather than answer these questions directly, let me turn to one of the most important conceptual papers of the 1980s: "No Silver Bullet" [Broo87].

In this paper, Brooks predicts the rate of progress for software technology by examining its difficulties. Following Aristotle, he divides the difficulties into *essence*, those that are by nature inherent in software, and *accidents*, which currently attend its production but which are not inherent. He then identifies four essential difficulties.

- *Complexity*. Software is more complex for its size than any other human construct. Because no two parts are alike, software systems contain more details than most manufactured systems in which repeated elements abound.

- *Conformity*. Software lacks the existence of underlying principles that assist the physicist; much of its complexity is determined by the external interfaces with which it must conform.

- *Changeability*. Software is under constant pressure for change. The functions it provides are dynamic and require modification; moreover, in an integrated system the software is the easiest component to change.

- *Invisibility*. Software is invisible and unvisualizable; its reality is not inherently embedded in space.

Brooks continues with a review of past breakthroughs that solved accidental difficulties. In this category he examines high-level languages, time-sharing, and unified programming environments. He first shows how each removed some accidental difficulties and then explains why it is unable to resolve any essential difficulties. He then lists an array of "hopes for the silver bullet:" Ada and other high-level languages, object-oriented programming, artificial intelligence, expert systems, "automatic" programming, graphical programming, program verification, environments and tools, and workstations. His discussion shows why each hope is bound to be frustrated. Nevertheless, Brooks does offer some promising attacks on what he calls the "conceptual essence." These are

- Buy versus build.

- Requirements refinement and rapid prototyping.

- Incremental development—grow, don't build software.

- Encourage the development of great designers.

His first recommendation represents the ultimate success in reuse. The next two suggestions are modifications to the waterfall model designed to improve our understanding of what software is to do. The final attack on the problem recognizes that software construction is a creative process; the key to effective designs is the training, experience, and excellence of the designers who must create them.

In this paper, Brooks states,

> The essence of a software entity is a conceptual construct of interlocking concepts: data sets, relationships among data items, algorithms, and invocations of functions. This essence is abstract in that such a conceptual construct is the same under many different representations. It is nonetheless highly precise and richly detailed.
>
> *I believe the hard part of building software to be the specification, design, and testing of this conceptual construct, not the labor of representing it and testing the fidelity of the representation.* We still make syntax errors, to be sure; but they are fuzz compared with the conceptual errors in most systems. [Broo87, p.11]

Keep this observation in mind. The essence of software engineering problem solving is problem identification, and the "No Silver Bullet" paper offers clues for recognizing the important problems and provides insights into solving them. Certainly, Brooks's analysis suggests that the role of the human problem solver (i.e., the designer) is central and that the hope for purely technological solutions is limited.

## 1.4.    Facts, myths, and perceptions

This chapter began with a definition of software engineering in the context of its history and the views of computer scientists and other software engineers.  The orientation of this book was clearly stated: *Software engineering is the application of tools, methods, and disciplines to produce and maintain an automated solution to a real-world problem.* The next two sections addressed the process of supporting this activity from two different perspectives: management of the process and problem solving during the process.  This final section reviews what we have discovered empirically as the result of several decades' experience.  As the section title suggests, the results include facts (repeatable and undisputed findings), myths (beliefs that are accepted without recourse to extensive justification), and perceptions (underlying structures that systematize and unify the findings).  Because we normally associate myths with concepts that we no longer can justify, there is the assumption that myths represent misinterpretations and errors.  Of course, this is a post hoc interpretation, and believers find it impossible to separate their convictions into (false) myths and (true) perceptions.[13]

What are the myths in software engineering?  Here are a few.

- System development is primarily concerned with programming. I will show that a relatively small part of the development process is devoted to the coding activity and that most errors are failures in design and not coding.  Thus, even though coding is a labor-intensive activity and we make mistakes when doing it, coding is a task that we have learned to do reasonably well.

- Software tools and development methods can solve the problem. I will show that most errors (and associated costs for repair) can be traced back to failures in the initial requirements.  As the

---

[13]For an interesting and very readable examination of scientific change see Kuhn, *The Structure of Scientific Revolution* [Kuhn70]. Kuhn calls the set of perceptions that guides the understanding in some scientific field a paradigm. All problems are interpreted in the context of this paradigm. When the paradigm fails to explain or predict observed events, there is a *paradigm shift*. Older scientists, whose perceptions are rooted in the old paradigm, resist this change. Thus, in the sense of this section, refuted scientific perceptions are viewed as myths.

previous section emphasized, there are no mechanical means to avoid these errors. When used properly, tools and methods help, but they cannot substitute for effective designers.

- The difficulty of implementing a system is essentially a function of its complexity. I will show that individual productivity depends on project size, and that productivity is roughly the same for all languages. Thus, there are factors unrelated to project complexity that have a major effect on productivity.

- Once a program is delivered, the job is finished. A corollary myth is that maintenance is just fixing errors. I will show that about two-thirds of the lifetime cost for a system comes after installation and that only one-fifth of that effort involves error correction. Thus, structuring the process to optimize for development is shortsighted.

- Errors are an unavoidable side effect of software development. I will show that there are development techniques and testing methods that can eliminate errors in the delivered product. Thus, while to err may be human, the delivery of those errors is just poor software engineering.

There are more myths. Some are tied to management's perception that software production can be managed as if it were hardware. Others reflect a consumer's naive theory that software will magically (and effortlessly) solve his problems. Finally, some myths achieve fame simply by the memorability of their assertions. Section 1.4.1 examines one such myth.

### 1.4.1. The famous GAO report

In 1979 the General Accounting Office (GAO) issued a report that stated [GAO79]:

50% + of contracts had cost overruns.
60% + of contracts had schedule overruns.
45% + of software contracted for could not be used.
29% + of software was never delivered.
19% + of software contracted for had to be reworked to be used.
 3% - of software contracted for had to be modified to be used.
 2% - of software contracted for was usable as delivered.

This list is reproduced in its entirety from a 1984 paper in the *IEEE Transactions on Software Engineering*. The data are correct, but we can gain a better understanding of the problem by returning to the source.

The GAO report reviewed contracts for the development of custom-built business and administrative systems. The projects studied represented the state of the practice in the mid-1970s. The analysis was divided into two activities. First, there was a pair of surveys, one of 163 contractors, and the other of 113 Federal data processing personnel with contracting experience. The first survey was never printed, but the results of the second survey are shown in Figure 1.11. These data appear to contradict the results just presented.

The second task, which led to the report's most dramatic findings, was an analysis of nine software contracts. These projects were brought to the reviewers' attention because they were problem cases; in fact, some were the subject of extended litigation. One small contract was included as an exemplar of good practice. In all, the nine contracts had a total value of $6.8 million. The value of the exemplar contract was $119,800. The distributions were computed on the basis of contract cost. Consequently, what might have been reported as "one contract out of nine" became even more striking as "less than 2% of the software contracted for was usable as delivered."

Figure 1.12 summarizes the causes for failure in the eight contracts. (Case 5 obviously was the exemplar.) Notice that only the last item in the list involves technical issues. In fact, the primary causes for failure were an inability to: identify what was needed, specify a valid product, select an appropriate contracting mechanism, and/or control the process. There is little evidence to suggest that the projects failed because of shoddy workmanship. Of course, in a chaotic environment, poor performance usually follows.

| | Very Common | Fairly Common | Not Very Common | Very Rare | Never Occurs | Don't Know |
|---|---|---|---|---|---|---|
| Software development has dollar overrun | 21.2 | 29.2 | 25.7 | 9.7 | 6.2 | 8.0 |
| Software development has calendar overrun | 30.1 | 31.9 | 25.7 | 8.0 | 1.8 | 2.7 |
| The delivered software must be corrected or modified by in-house programmers before it is usable | 8.8 | 34.5 | 35.4 | 13.3 | 6.2 | 1.8 |
| The software is paid for but never used | * | 3.6 | 16.1 | 57.1 | 20.5 | 2.7 |
| The delivered software is difficult to modify | 5.3 | 37.2 | 38.1 | 11.5 | 4.4 | 3.5 |
| The contractor's programming practices are such that the software is easily understood by agency programs | 14.2 | 62.8 | 15.0 | 6.2 | * | 1.8 |

Fig. 1.11.  GAO responses from Federal data processing personnel.

| Cause | Case Number | | | | | | | | |
|---|---|---|---|---|---|---|---|---|---|
| | 1 | 2 | 3 | 4 | 5 | 6 | 7 | 8 | 9 |
| Agency overestimated its own state of progress when it let the contract | X | X | | | | X | | X | |
| Incorrect agency management action, such as using inappropriate contract | | | X | X | | X | | X | |
| Agency failed to specify requirements adequately | X | X | | X | | X | X | X | X |
| Agency overcommitted itself | | | | | | | X | | X |
| Agency failed to manage during execution, including excessive changes | X | X | | | | X | X | | X |
| Agency failed to adequately inspect and test | X | X | X | | | X | | X | |

Fig. 1.12.  Causes of case study problems.

What are the lessons to be learned?  First, there is a difference between data (i.e., what is supplied to the analyst) and information (i.e., groupings of data with an interpretation).  We should be suspect of data unless we understand the context in which they were collected. Fortunately, more than 2% of the Federal Government's contracts produce software that is usable as delivered.  The report also presents some clues into why projects fail.  The first insight was contained in the report subtitle, "Serious problems require management attention to avoid wasting additional millions."  Their recommendations focused on procurement guidelines and the development of standards; the latter were intended to ensure that the project manager received a quality product that did what was specified.  Returning to the language of the previous section, the report confirmed that establishing the necessary "conceptual construct" (with the appropriate contracting mechanism) was the source of more difficulty than carrying out the implementation.

And so we have demystified the ubiquitous GAO report.  The problem was not in GAO Report FGMSD-80-4 itself, but in the persistence of its misinterpretation.  Actually, the report made some provocative comments, and I close this section with one about software development on the mid-1970s.  I leave the reader to decide how valid these remarks are today.

Several factors contributed to the situation [of having software development problems].  First, the invisible nature of both the work process and its product made software projects very difficult to manage and predict.  Second, the explosive growth of the use of computers created a great demand for new programmers, most of whom were self-taught on the job; and frequently, low productivity and poor quality resulted.  Third, there was little idea then of how to train programmers properly. Fourth, a tradition grew that programmers were secretive craftspersons whose products, during development, were their own property. [GAO79, p. 6]

### 1.4.2. Software engineering findings

Having just invited skepticism, I now report on what we know about the software process. I rely on reports from a variety of projects (ranging from commercial applications to embedded systems, from assembly language to high-level language programs) collected over several decades, and interpreted with an assortment of analytic methods. Naturally, this diversity ensures imprecision. The objective is to present broadly held beliefs that are founded on empirical evidence. Gross measures will suffice to characterize the software process. In Chapter 6 I return to this topic with an examination of how these measures may be refined to aid managers improve software quality, productivity, and predictability. For that goal, more refined measures are necessary.

I begin with the classic distribution of cost trends shown in Figure 1.13. This figure is taken from Boehm's 1976 paper, and it shows both the relative decrease in hardware costs and an increasing commitment to software maintenance. It should be pointed out that the software costs include the software (and documentation) associated with the hardware; that is, the figure does not necessarily represent a ratio for new developments. Nevertheless, it is clear that equipment cost is now a secondary factor, and that about half the software activity is devoted to maintaining systems already in operation. Surveys typically report that, in an internal data processing organization, less than half the staff are available for new projects; the rest are engaged in system support and software maintenance. This results in backlogs of two or more years from problem identification to solution delivery. Indeed, Martin talks of an invisible backlog because, when faced with such delays, clients see no purpose in making a request [Mart82].

If, as the figure demonstrates, software is the critical commodity in automated systems, it does not follow that most of this investment is in programming. In project planning, it is common to allocate effort according to a *40-20-40 rule*. Forty percent of the effort is expended on analysis and design, 20% on coding and debugging, and 40% on testing. Boehm uses a 40-30-30 distribution with his cost projection model, where the first 30% is for programming and testing and the second 30% is considered integration [Boeh81]. All of these rules are based on the analysis of effort distributions from many projects. It is clear that more effort is devoted to deciding what the software is to do, how it is to do it, and determining what is done than is expended on the programming.

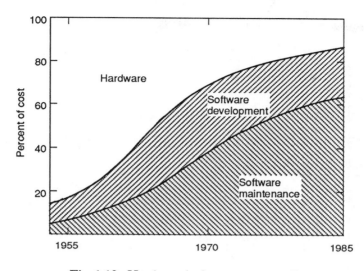

Fig. 1.13. Hardware/software cost trends.
(Reprinted from [Boeh76] with permission, ©1976, IEEE.)

When analyzing the errors found in programs, most faults cannot be corrected by modifying only the code. Studies of TRW command and control projects and IBM operating system projects have shown that the ratio of design to coding errors generally exceeds 60:40 [Boeh76]. Those data were collected in the late 1960s and early 1970s before the use of high-level languages, structured programming, and program design languages (PDL) became standard practice. Consequently, one might expect the ratios from today's projects to have an even lower proportion of coding errors.

There have been numerous studies of the errors found in programs. Fagan routinely collects and categorizes the errors encountered during program inspection [Faga76]. In one study 40% were labeled logic errors and 17% were labeled prologue/prose errors; none of the other categories accounted for more than 7% of the total errors encountered. Of greater interest, the data showed that 57% of the errors involved missing code and 11% of the errors were associated with extra code; in only 32% of the errors was the code found to be wrong. Similar results were reported by Glass [Glas81]. Of 200 errors examined, 50 were for omitted logic, 23 for failure to reset data, and 16 for incorrect documentation (with correct code). These findings further validate the argument that, relative to establishing the correct design, coding need not be an error-prone activity.

The correction of errors is most efficient when they are detected early. Figure 1.14 presents data from several projects confirming that

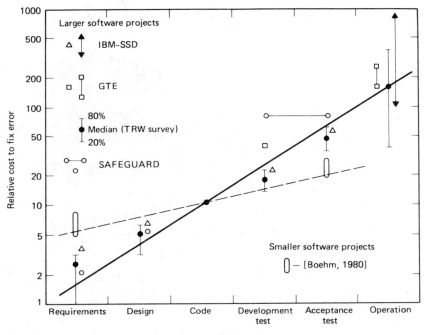

Fig. 1.14. Cost to fix or change software throughout the lifecycle.
(Reprinted from [Boeh81] with permission, ©1981, Prentice Hall, Inc.)

the later a defect is found, the more expensive it will be to correct it
[Boeh81]. Two slopes are shown in the figure. The solid line indicates
the relative costs for large projects, and the dashed line is for smaller
projects. As the figure illustrates, if one unit of effort is required to fix
a problem early in the requirements phase, then as many as 100 units
may be expended to correct the error if it is not discovered until the
operations phase. The reason for this is obvious. When an error
remains undetected, it propagates errors; it serves as an invalid assertion
that spawns many correct assumptions that must later be removed.
Thus, the early detection of errors is essential. Incidently, consistent
with the results of the GAO study, most errors can be traced back to the
initial requirements. One source stated that 56% of the bugs and 82%
of the correction effort resulted from improper requirements.

The data presented so far indicate that failure to define a set of
valid requirements is the greatest cause for errors, that the longer an
error remains undetected the more expensive its correction becomes, and
that—even though programming is labor intensive—it tends to be less
error prone than design. I now consider some factors that affect

productivity: the size of the project, the compactness of the representations used, and the skills and experience of the staff.

Jones has studied the productivity of individuals as a function of project size [Jone79]. In calculating the average effort to produce 1000 lines of assembly code in commercial applications, he found the following relationships:

| Project size (LOC) | Average effort/K lines |
|---|---|
| < 4K | 1.5 |
| 4K -- 16K | 2.5 |
| 16K -- 64K | 4 |
| 64K -- 512K | 6 |
| 512K > | 14 |

The reason that individual productivity is inversely proportional to project size seems to stem from difficulties in communication.

People work effectively in groups of up to five; they can share information informally and remain aware of what others in the group are doing as long as the group remains small. Projects requiring 25 people will tend to be organized as 5 groups, each with a leader responsible for communicating among groups. The 5 leaders constitute a group, which must have a leader who reports to another authority. In this way, 125 developers require three group levels. Communications among the lowest level groups may require decisions at each level in the hierarchy. To retain stability in the lowest level groups, changes are resisted and elaborate documentation schemes are relied on. Also, because the lowest level groups have a limited understanding of the total project, there is a higher likelihood that their members will misinterpret requirements or designs. Thus, size adds complexity independent of the inherent complexity of the project.

For some projects, the work may be well understood and easily segmented. Where there is an experienced staff and the assignments have clear interfaces, the communication difficulties just described may not be a factor. However, in general, smaller is better. In particular, for a project under pressure, adding more staff will be counterproductive. This, of course, is Brooks's Law,

*Adding manpower to a late software project makes it later* [Broo75, p. 25]

The reason for this is that the added staff requires training, which just adds to the burden of the already overworked, behind-schedule staff.

There are several ways for projects to improve their performance efficiency (which can be translated into smaller, more effective groups). The proper use of methods eliminates unnecessary work and avoids the errors that lead to rework. There also is a broad consensus that the number of program lines produced per unit of time is independent of the language used [Broo75, WaGa82, Blum90]. Consequently, the use of compact representations will improve productivity. As will be shown in the following chapters, this principle can be applied with higher level languages, encapsulation, and reuse. Here I limit the discussion to the effects associated with the choice of programming language. For example, recall that the Backus FORTRAN example reduced a 1000 line assembly language project to one of only 47 lines; what might have taken days was reduced to an afternoon's work.

There are some formal measures for the expressiveness of languages, such as the language level of software science [Hals77]. It will suffice, however, to provide an illustration of the phenomenon without a more general discussion. In the late 1970s, Albrecht introduced a method for estimating the size of a project according to the amount of function that the resulting product would deliver; he called its unit of measure the function point [Albr79]. Albrecht and Gaffney then analyzed several projects and showed that productivity (as measured by the number of lines of code required to produce one unit of functionality) was related to the language used [AlGa83]. They reported the following:

| Language | Lines/Function Point |
| --- | --- |
| COBOL | 110 |
| PL/1 | 65 |
| DMS/VS | 25 |

Thus, with more expressive languages, fewer lines of code were required to program the equivalent functionality, and effort was reduced.

Another factor affecting productivity is the experience and capability of the development staff. Much of the thrust of the previous section is that software engineering involves problem solving, and that the more expert the software engineers, the better the solutions. Do the data support this view? There have been studies of individual differences going back to the late 1960s. In one small, but frequently cited study, it was found that there were performance differences of up to 28:1 [SaEG68]. A later study by Curtis found differences on the order of

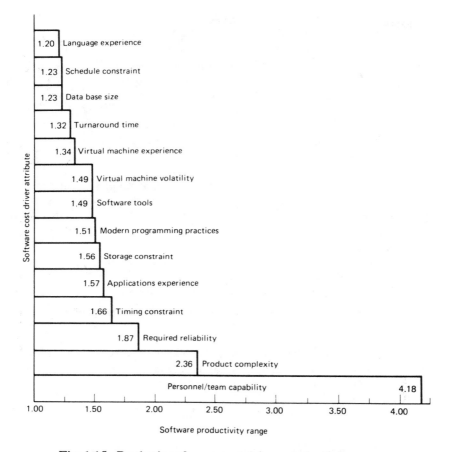

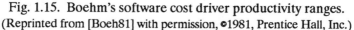

Fig. 1.15. Boehm's software cost driver productivity ranges.
(Reprinted from [Boeh81] with permission, ©1981, Prentice Hall, Inc.)

23:1 [Curt81]. Boehm analyzed the factors that effect software project costs and classified them as the set of cost drivers shown in Figure 1.15. This chart shows that the element with the largest range is "personnel/team capability" (i.e., the skills, experience, and talent of the personnel assigned to the project). Again, this confirms that there are great differences among individuals. Fortunately, some of my data suggest that much of this difference reflects a training deficit rather than an inherent, uncorrectable difference [Blum90]. Thus, Brooks's advice to grow great designers (and implementers) implies a productivity bonus.

The initial design, however, represents only a small part of the total effort devoted to software development. Figure 1.13 showed that half the software cost is for maintenance. Estimates for the proportion of the life-cycle cost devoted to maintenance range from 50 to 80%. In any case, it is broadly recognized that this is the most expensive, and longest living part of the process. To gain an understanding of the problem, Lientz and Swanson surveyed 1000 Data Processing Management Association (DPMA) members who considered themselves "managers." They received 486 17-page returns, which led them to the following categorization of maintenance [LiSw80]:

- *Corrective maintenance.* This is maintenance to correct errors. About 20% of the surveyed resources were devoted to this class of activity.

- *Adaptive maintenance.* This maintenance results from external changes to which the system must respond, e.g., changes in the hardware or operating system. This accounts for about 25% of the maintenance work.

- *Perfective maintenance.* This represents all other changes to an operational system. As a percentage of the total maintenance effort, user enhancements account for 42%, documentation changes 6%, and efficiency improvements 4%. In all, 55% of the maintenance effort is perfective.

Lientz and Wegner followed the DPMA survey with one of embedded Navy systems, and they found substantially the same results. The five most severe problems identified by both surveys were

- Quality of application software documentation.

- User demand for enhancements and extensions.

- Competing demands for maintenance-programmer personnel time.

- Difficulty in meeting scheduled commitments.

- Turnover in user organizations. [Lien83, p. 276]

Clearly, user demand is a positive problem; it implies that the system is used. Poor documentation quality, like any quality deficit, will make maintenance more difficult. The remaining three concerns are common in development projects as well. As a result, some computer scientists now consider software development to be a special case of maintenance. The process does not end with product delivery, and new projects should borrow from old projects just as existing systems are extended with new programs.

Lehman and Belady also carried out a series of studies of software maintenance in the 1970s [BeLe76, Lehm80]. Here the objects of study were operating systems, and certain patterns emerged. Lehman associated these changes with what he called *E-programs*, which become embedded in the world that they model. That is, the requirements for the program are based on conditions that are changed when the E-program is installed. Thus, the program modifies its requirements, and must be modified in turn. This evolution process continues until the program is retired or replaced. This analysis led Lehman to identify five *Laws of Program Evolution*. The first three of these follow; the remaining two are corollaries and will not be listed.

I. *Continuing change.* A program that is used and that . . . reflects some other reality, undergoes continual change or becomes progressively less useful. The change or decay process continues until it is judged more cost effective to replace the system with a recreated version.

II. *Increasing complexity.* As an evolving program is continually changed, its complexity, reflecting deteriorating structure, increases unless work is done to maintain or reduce it.

III. *The fundamental law of program evolution.* Program evolution is subject to a dynamics which makes the programming process, and hence measures of global project and system attributes, self-regulating with statistically determinable trends and invariants. [Lehm80, p. 1066]

The laws of continuing change and increasing complexity are broadly accepted. The fundamental law, however, has not been demonstrated. It suggests that the evolution process can be modeled statistically, and that such data can be used for planning and control. As will be discussed in Chapter 6, local variations will have a major impact on the prediction of maintenance activity.

In summary, what are the quantifiable universal statements about the software process? Unfortunately, I know of none. The data that we use for determining schedules and staffing are based on previous experience. Where that earlier effort is efficient and based on good practice, reliable estimates will follow. When we catalogue and classify the errors encountered in our products, we do this to help eliminate similar errors in subsequent systems. The data just presented offer only a gross outline of how software is constructed at the beginning of the 1990s. I have been imprecise with good reason. There is no fundamental law of software engineering. Local variability is large, and—as the GAO report has shown—some of our data must be interpreted carefully.

In fact, most sets of software engineering data are not comparable, and citations of unreliable data are common. For example, many carefully analyzed student exercises produce unusable software. If the outcome of a project is unacceptable, how interested should we be in the process that created it? I have avoided using such results even though they are often referenced. Also, I have not tried to separate the factors that affect the process. For example, in the early 1970s Weinberg and Schulman conducted an experiment in which five groups were given the same project but asked to optimize for a specific factor: completion time, program size, data space used, program clarity, and user-friendly output. Each group ranked highest on its target attribute; naturally they did less well on the other attributes [WeSc74]. The software process is holistic. As with any engineering activity, we want to do "well enough" in every important category. Achieving one of the local maxima at the expense of other important properties may have little value.

Finally, it must be observed that all of the data presented in this section were taken from projects organized in the waterfall flow. Consequently, the data actually characterize the *waterfall process* and not the *essential software process*. As we change paradigms, we may find that many of our fundamental assumptions are questioned.[14] Moreover, even within existing paradigms, new data become available that force us to reexamine old assumptions. For instance, we have long accepted the fact that program errors were a regrettable, but unavoidable part of the process. But now we have data that show that this is not the case. Work with the Cleanroom environment, which will be discussed in some detail in Chapter 5, has demonstrated that it is possible to deliver software with zero defects. Even though I defer the description of how to do this, here is an important fact with which to close this section:

> *It is possible to deliver software from which virtually all errors have been removed.*

Knowing that this is possible changes our mindset. After all, if bridge engineers can deliver bridges that require no postconstruction testing, it is reasonable for us, as software engineers, to expect similar standards.


## 1.5.   Some final comments

Earlier I stated that programming is to software engineering as the mastery of the English language is to the production of literature. Continuing with this analogy, novelists are taught that there is just one way to learn to write: they must write. But software engineering is not

---

[14]For example, see the final chapter in *TEDIUM and the Software Process* [Blum90].

a solitary task. It is a team activity that involves users, designers, implementors, testers, and so on. Unlike writing (and programming, which, after all, is just the production of program text), it is difficult to teach software engineering as an individual activity. Interactions are required. Answers are seldom right or wrong. Much depends on the problem being solved and the tools available in the software engineer's environment. Also, there is no consensus regarding which are the best tools and methods.

To help provide this context for software engineering, I have identified a central problem to be solved and organized all examples and exercises around that problem. Thus, in one sense, this book may be considered a treatise on the solution of that problem. Of course, only an incomplete solution is offered. As they say in the mathematics texts, we leave the proof to the reader. Nevertheless, when the reader is finished with this book, he should have solid understanding of the problem being solved.

I already have mentioned that there is no consensus regarding the best methods and tools. Moreover, I have suggested that our perceptions of what is best evolve over time. Therefore, I have a responsibility to present both the most popular and the most promising techniques. In many cases these techniques are not complementary. Thus, I must offer alternative, and often mutually exclusive, solutions to a single problem. Because this book exists in a universe of pedantry, this is not a concern. Obviously, the approach presented here should not be considered a real-world strategy. Selection of and commitment to a consistent, unified approach are prerequisites to success in a commercial-grade project.

As with most software engineering books, the volume is organized according to the phases in the development cycle. The design activities are divided into two levels: modeling-in-the-large and modeling-in-the-small. Each of these, in turn, is divided into two approaches: decomposition and composition. I think that it is important to understand both approaches, but if time is a factor, it probably is better to understand one technique well than both superficially.

Finally, I conclude the book with a chapter on management of the software process. Many texts begin with this topic. My feeling is that we first should understand the process that we are managing. Then we can examine what we know about project management and decide how to apply that experience in this particular domain. Too often software engineering is interpreted as a management discipline, and I personally do not find that perspective very informative.

Well, my introduction is complete. I have laid down a foundation for viewing software engineering as problem solving, I have outlined some models for problem solving, and I have described the software process. It is now time to start solving problems.

*"Are you sure about this, Stan? It seems odd that a pointy head and long beak is what makes them fly."*

# 2

## REQUIREMENTS ANALYSIS AND MODELING

Stan has completed his analysis and is about to plunge headlong into the hypothesis testing stage. There are some uncontrovertible facts that support his theory, and he shall receive immediate feedback. Fortunately, cartoon characters always survive their mistakes, and Stan's lesson will be that more analysis is required.

It usually takes longer for software engineers to get feedback, and often their projects cannot survive major failures. So let us learn from Stan and finish our analysis before we rush to code our solutions.

Requirements analysis is a very difficult task. It involves understanding a problem in some application domain and then defining a solution that can be implemented with software. The methods that we use will depend on the kind of problem that we are solving and our experience with this type of problem.

Experience is often the best teacher, and prototypes provide an opportunity to learn. Of course, the prototypes will reflect the errors of our way, and they should be discarded. As Brooks has told us, "Plan to throw one away, you will anyway." Ask Stan.

There also are ways to learn without doing. In what follows I show how to model what we know about the data, the processes that transform the data, and the underlying formalisms that specify the target system. There are many methods, and few will be used in any one project.

As a result of this analysis, we will come to understand the problem we are to resolve and the solution that we intend to implement. We will document that solution in a software requirements specification, or SRS. Naturally, the SRS will not detail everything about the intended product; it will define only its essential properties. Not included in the SRS are the implicit requirements (necessary for all applications of this class) and the derived requirements (expressed as design responses to the essential requirements).

Once we have established *what* we want, we can proceed to the next level of modeling and define *how* to implement it. Unfortunately, separating this what from the how is not as simple as it may seem, and we will continue doing requirements analysis and modeling through the end of Chapter 4.

## 2.1.    Approaching requirements analysis

We now begin the process of creating a software product. As explained in the previous chapter, the process begins with a need and ends with a product that meets that need. Traditionally, we refer to the need as a set of requirements and call the formal requirements statement the specification. Recall the argument from Chapter 1 that our understanding of the requirements depends on our knowledge of the application domain. We begin with general concepts in the application domain, which may be stated in terms of domain formalisms such as mathematical formulas or report layouts. Our goal is to produce a specification that prescribes the software solution. Unfortunately, our development methods are not sufficiently mature to allow us to verify that the delivered program is correct in the same sense that we have confidence that our compiled object code is correct with respect to its source code. Therefore, we must be satisfied with a specification that details what we consider to be essential and also provides enough information to establish that a delivered product conforms to the intent detailed in that specification.

Notice how I am avoiding a rigid definition of the requirements specification in the context of the waterfall flow. In that flow, one begins with a step that isolates the need from the potential solutions and culminates with a document that determines *what* is to be done. Clearly, this is a desirable objective, but there are some problems. First, as will be discussed in the following section, it is not always possible to separate *what* we need from *how* we will meet that need. Second, without a formal specification language, a specification cannot detail all the essential properties of the desired product unambiguously. Finally, we know that the specification represents an understanding of the need at one point in time based on some level of experience. As observed in Chapter 1, software evolves during both its development and operational lifetime. Fixed requirements are rare.

What are we to make of this? Obviously, we ought not begin building something until we know what it is we want to build. Many of the problems that the software engineering discipline first responded to could be traced back to the attitude that, because the requirements were going to change, one might just as well begin by coding. The resulting code was viewed as a product, and it was never discarded. Consequently, the system was built around the first units of code that were perceived to do something useful—a philosophy best suited for very small applications to be used only by their developers. We now recognize that the process must always begin with an analysis of what it is we expect the software to do. At the same time, however, we ought not to lose sight of the purpose and limitations of the specification. It is only the first step in a rather long and complicated journey; requirements analysis does not always produce a complete definition of the product to be constructed.

The title of this chapter identifies two activities: analysis and modeling. The analysis activity will vary from one domain to the next. For example, one would not expect to use the same analytic tools for a computer operating system, a weather prediction simulation, and a medical diagnostic device. In each case, very different domain knowledge is required, and there will be little crossover among the domains. Yet, the analysts may use the same modeling tools. This is because the analysis activity includes two overlapping tasks. First, the application domain knowledge must be organized to provide a meaningful solution. Of course, that solution must be described in a fashion that can be realized with procedures, data structures, human interactions, and computer equipment. Although software engineering cannot provide the desired application analysis models (except, of course, for products such as the computer operating system), there are models that we can use to present application concepts in a computer-implementation context. As will be shown, these models are powerful tools for evaluating possible solutions and identifying potential failures and errors. Naturally, familiarity with the use of the models will not substitute for domain experience.

One final issue needs to be discussed before proceeding to the technical discussion. It is universally accepted that one needs a good understanding of what is to be done before the solution can be constructed. It is also undisputed that the only way to reduce ambiguity when communicating among individuals is to rely on written records. Therefore, there is no way of avoiding the preparation of a written requirements specification. Brainstorming notes on the back of an envelope are satisfactory for only the smallest of projects. However, one should not be deluded into thinking that all requirements documents are the same and that each must contain all the information detailed in some standard. In Chapter 6 I will address some of the techniques for managing different types of projects. This chapter examines only the underlying concepts of requirements analysis. Not all methods are valid (or even necessary) for all projects. I stress pragmatism and not conformity, but I also warn that pragmatism can be used as a shield for intellectual sloppiness.

In closing this introduction to requirements analysis, I observe that this is the most important step in the entire software process. Most projects fail or exceed costs because this initial activity is not carried out properly. Requirements analysis demands an understanding of the problem to be solved and a background in computer applications; both are necessary, and neither is sufficient. The result is a "contract" between the sponsor and the developer. If the sponsoring and developing organization are the same, some of the formalities of the requirements specification may be mitigated; in other situations the specification becomes a legal document and must be composed with rigor. In all cases, however, the specification must be complete with regard to the essential characteristics of the intended product. One cannot begin to implement a project before determining what is to be built. If the uncertainties are too many, then the project must be managed to limit the risks; methods for doing this are examined in Chapter 6. For the next four chapters, however, we shall assume that there is sufficient knowledge available to discover and specify the requirements for a product. The immediate task addressed in this chapter is the preparation of that requirements specification.

### 2.1.1.  *Distinguishing between the what and how*

There is a difference between stating *what* we want and *how* we realize our objectives. We can, for instance, describe processes that we cannot realize. Formal specifications can define behaviors without regard to how they will be implemented. For example, I can specify what a chess-playing program should do without concern for how well the program will play, or even if I can build one at all. The specification need only define the chess board, the pieces with their legal moves, and the condition for winning. Every chess-playing program will satisfy these requirements independent of its ability to beat other programs, novices, or masters. Here the description of what should be done acts as a predicate for all possible chess-playing programs. If a program fails to satisfy these basic conditions, it will violate the rules of chess. It is an uncluttered description of what a program must do.

In Chapter 1 I mentioned executable specifications. Continuing with this illustration, if the chess-playing moves and heuristics were written in the form of an executable specification, then it would be possible to determine how that specification operates, that is, what valid output results from a valid input. One would then be able to "play" the specification just as if it were a program, and it would behave just as the program would in the sense that any legal input move would result in a legal output move. Of course, the specification's play might be disappointing. First, it might be very slow; a game could take years to play. Second, it may be a very poor player and always lose.

We might address the responsiveness of the specification by adding *nonfunctional* requirements. To now, everything in the specification describes the *behavior* of the target programs: the functions they should perform. We now might introduce a requirement to establish operational characteristics. For example, "After every input the program shall produce a valid output within 30 seconds." The ability to produce a valid output is one of the behaviors already prescribed by the specification; we know that two pieces cannot occupy the same space at the same time and that the queen cannot move like a knight. This is true for every program, on every machine, in every language, in every operating environment. But the requirement to respond in 30 seconds is quite different. A particular program in a particular computer with a controlled number of users might satisfy this requirement. Yet, when another person logs onto that computer, the response time may degrade so that it fails to meet the specification. The queens still move like queens, but the moves may take longer.

Thus we see that there are two types of requirements:

- *Functional requirements* that establish the essential behaviors for all correct implementations (e.g., valid moves, ability to display a chess board on a bitmapped display, automatic retention of a log of moves).

- *Nonfunctional requirements* that establish operational properties for the delivered implementation (e.g., response time, storage constraints, ease of use).

Notice that I just introduced two new items in the above list of functional requirements: use of a bitmapped display and maintenance of a move log. Not all chess-playing programs need to satisfy these two additional requirements, but a particular developer may find these two requirements essential for any program he builds. The specification augmented by these two functional requirements still describes the behaviors for all programs (independent of their implementation characteristics or operating environment). These behaviors can be verified as logical properties of all implementations, and that is why I referred to them as a predicate earlier. The nonfunctional requirements, on the other hand, are a property of the implementation, and they cannot be described logically. In the context of the specification, they represent descriptive information that can be verified only after the product is complete.

Thus, the description of what the product is to do can be divided into two categories: the functional requirements define behaviors that may be logically tested throughout the development process, and the nonfunctional requirements represent operating characteristics of the product that can be demonstrated only after the product is available. Our challenge as software engineers, therefore, is (1) to identify the functional requirements clearly and verify that no decisions violate them and (2) to document the nonfunctional requirements and choose design alternatives that have the highest probability of being able to meet them.

In summary, we see that there are some attributes of the desired system that we cannot describe logically. That is, our definition of *what* it should do must include some requirements concerning *how* it operates. It also turns out that the requirements may imply *how* the program should be designed. Continuing with the chess-playing program example, notice that we have added a requirement that it present a board with piece positions on a bitmapped display. The designer still is free to choose any mechanism to implement this. However, suppose next that we specify the use of a specific searching algorithm that we know from experience will improve responsiveness. Now we are on the threshold between the what and how. Using a particular searching algorithm rules out the use of certain data structures and control algorithms. Thus, elevating a helpful suggestion to the mandatory level constrains the solution space. In fact, knowing of the algorithm, the analyst may assume that his implementation will use it whether or not it is part of the requirements. Restating this, when we are asked to specify a product that must operate effectively, we necessarily bias our definition of the requirements by our knowledge and experience with similar implementations. Consequently, the separation of the requirements from the design is an abstract goal and not a human reality.

Even though the what and how are intertwined, we still must try to separate them. If we do not, there will be the danger that we will specify a program that we know how to build rather than the product that the sponsor needs. I will return to this in the next section, but here I would like to address another reason why it is difficult to isolate the statement of needs from the preliminary design of its solution. Recall the essential software process of Chapter 1. It was defined as a transition from a conceptual model to a formal model, with no sharp transition from one model category to the other. Unlike the waterfall flow, the essential model was expressed as a smooth flow rather than a sequence of discrete modeling steps. As it turns out, the essential model provides a more accurate picture of what goes on during the software process. Our most useful models are those that help us in the transition from one form of representation to another. We begin with mental models, transform them to conceptual models, which eventually evolve into formal models of computation. If these models are disjoint, then it will be difficult to transition from one to another; when they are well integrated, however, it will be impossible to map the modeling tools onto exclusive development phases.

In the waterfall flow, which I use in this and the next three chapters, there is a clear demarcation between the end of the requirements analysis and the beginning of the design. As the result of the requirements analysis activity, a specification is produced and validated. Only after this validation can the design begin. But this is really just a management device. Many of the tools and methods used to establish the requirements are also used in the first stages of design. Unless the development team changes after the requirements are approved, there seldom will be a sharp transition from requirements analysis to preliminary design.    The understandings developed during the requirements analysis are used as a guide in the design, and the general structure and orientation is carried forward from one phase to the next. The models evolve and grow richer in detail, and—as impasses are reached—backtracking to requirements analysis may result.    There are very valid reasons for controlling the process as distinct phases.   From the perspective of human problem solving, however, a sequence of smooth transitions is the most appropriate flow.

So here is another tension in the software process: between solving the problem and managing the activity.  We know that there are some things that are definitely wrong that must be avoided at all times: for example, starting to design before the requirements have been identified. But we also understand that we seldom will be able to produce an essentially complete specification that will remain static and valid. Moreover, we recognize that one of the powers of our modeling tools is the way they help us move from phase to phase.   Thus, we must constantly exercise judgment in balancing the conflicting demands of management control and technical creativity.

In this book I have chosen to group integrated methods as units. Thus, in the design chapters I include requirements analysis methods, and in this chapter I include methods that imply a design.  Of course, I know the difference between defining what is required and describing how it should be done.   Nevertheless, I mix these methods and phases to reinforce the ideas that (1) it is very difficult to purge design considerations from the requirements analysis, (2) many methods provide a smooth transition from one phase to another and thus they are best described in that continuum, and (3) the phase orientation results from a need to maintain control, whereas the development actually follows a much steadier path.

### 2.1.2.  The role of prototypes

In the previous section I spoke of the danger that our designs may reflect what we know how to build rather than what the sponsor needs. The section on human problem solving in the previous chapter suggested that we approach a problem with a particular mental model, that we organize all new information to be consistent with that model (frequently constructing naive theories), and that our reasoning mechanisms are imperfect and biased.   I also referenced Simon's observation that "even the most talented people require approximately a decade to reach top professional proficiency" [Simo69, p. 108].  Thus, unless there is considerable experience with a particular class of application, invalid requirements may result. Fortunately, the technique of prototyping offers a benign method for gaining experience.

Many texts on software engineering describe rapid prototyping as a special development orientation and often present a "prototyping flow chart" as an alternative to the waterfall model. I do not subscribe to that view; instead, I see the prototype simply as a tool to gain understanding about some problem to be solved or implementation technique to be used. In Chapter 1 I cited Royce's advice to do it twice and Brooks's warning that we should plan to throw one away. Both were suggesting that we can learn from our experience and that we ought to remove the learning artifacts from the finished system that we deliver and maintain. The advantage of the rapid prototype is that it can be built quickly, that it is designed to deliver information where there is uncertainty, and that it is intended *not* to become a part of the finished system. The prototype is one of many tools available to the software engineer; it does not represent a new way of developing systems.[1]

The following remarks from a recent study of software and knowledge engineering help to put the role of the prototype in perspective.

> The vast literature on software engineering discusses, almost exclusively, the production and maintenance of software as an industrial process. Predictable in its outcome, repeatable in its execution, and portable in its independence on particular individuals. Many conditions must be met for the managerial and technical processes advocated in software engineering to work. The principal requirement is that the designer knows fairly well what end product can be achieved (so it can be specified), what resources are required (so the product can be sized up), and how to build the product (so the production process can be planned). The source of all this knowledge is experience based on previous production of similar products. Conventional software engineering works best when producing the $(n+1)$st version of a compiler, text processor, or other well known software systems component or applications package.
>
> A small but important class of software development projects meets none of the conditions above. For good reasons, such

---

[1]Some forms of prototyping, as discussed in Chapter 1, do provide alternatives to the waterfall process model [Zave84], but for the purposes of this book they are considered to be preoperational research systems. Other approaches to prototyping, for example the spiral model [Boeh88], are really management techniques, and they will be considered in further detail in Chapter 6.

first-of-a-kind projects are typically conducted in a manner diametrically opposite to traditional software engineering practice. . . . Thus it behooves the software engineering community to recognize that exploratory software development is an activity of long-term importance worth studying. [KiCN90, p. 152]

Here the authors contrast traditional and exploratory software development.   In science it is common to distinguish between exploratory and exploitative research.  In exploratory work, the goals are poorly defined, and the emphasis is on the discovery of new knowledge and insight.  Exploitative research, on the other hand, builds on what is known to extend our understanding; it clearly must be goal directed.  In the above paragraphs, the authors suggest that software engineering is best suited to the exploitation of our previous experience; hence the $n+1$ reference.  But the line separating the two approaches is not as clearly drawn as the citation suggests.  The $(n+1)$st version has much in common with the $n$th; nevertheless, each variation must identify and resolve new differences.  In some cases, analytical tools may suffice.  For other situations, experimentation with operational software may be the most appropriate mechanism for establishing a solution.  I call this form of exploratory development prototyping, and I assert that it is a useful device in all project environments.

The goal of every prototype should be the reduction of uncertainty. That is, one builds a prototype to shed light on some aspect of a larger problem.  The end products are knowledge and insight, *not* computer programs.  Here are some areas in which prototyping may be helpful.

- *Process flow design*.  Many interactive systems will support a processing activity, and it is necessary for the analyst to discover how the system will be used.  The user normally finds it difficult to describe his actions except in the context of a standard operation.  Exception processing and alternative flows are more easily identified in a scenario than in an interview.  For such applications, it may be useful to prepare a set of mock screens with the proposed control flows so that the user can test and evaluate the proposed system design.  While reviewing the flow, the user will also confirm that the screens are clear, the vocabulary is understandable, and the desired information is accessible.  (Often, a PC-based tool can generate this form of prototype.)

  Following the user trials, a formal set of requirements can be prepared; the prototype will then be discarded.  (In actual practice, the tools used for prototyping are not practical for implementation purposes.)  One of the major dangers of this type of prototype is that the user will read too much into his interactions, and the delivered product will not match his expectations.

- *User interface design.* Prototypes and user interface management tools offer a means to establish how the interface should be constructed (e.g., the use of color, the section of a pointing device, and the modes of use). This kind of prototype can be tested in a laboratory setting to validate the best interface approach for the target product. Items that can be measured include ease of learning, clarity of presentation, and responsiveness in operational situations. Where the prototype is supported by a set of implementation-independent tools, the prototype is actually a simulation.

- *Performance modeling.* Prototypes may implement one or more algorithms to determine how well they perform with a given set of data structures, operating environments, or external constraints. Strictly speaking, such prototypes might be thought of as investigating design trade-offs; I include them here because they also are useful in establishing feasibility. The prototypes are treated as exploratory development, but the resulting product is used and subsequently discarded. Hacking is sanctioned, but refinement of the prototype code for operational use is discouraged.

This list is far from complete. Throughout the text I shall suggest problems that can benefit from experience with prototypes. The point that I wish to make here, however, is simply that prototyping is not a new and foolproof way of developing systems; rather it is as old as exploratory experimentation and computer simulation.

## 2.2.    The configuration management case study

I have frequently made the point that the software process involves the transition from a need to a product that satisfies that need, and that one cannot apply the process without an understanding of the need being addressed. That is, because software engineering is a problem-solving activity, one must know something about the problem being solved to study the process. For this reason I shall use a common case study for all the examples in this book. The idea is that if the reader understands the problem being solved, it will be much easier to follow the methods used to produce the solution. Moreover, by choosing a problem from the domain of software engineering, I expect the reader to become sensitive to that problem and the nuances of automating a solution to it.

Here is the case study. Ho-Hum Industries (HHI) is a software development company that produces commercial products that they sell and maintain for a broad range of platforms including PCs, minicomputers, and mainframe computers. Sometimes their customers hire HHI to produce custom products that HHI maintains; in other cases, products with complete documentation are delivered for the customer to maintain. The organization has grown from 5 to 50 employees, and further growth is expected. Some of the products that they have marketed are now 10 years old, and the company expects to maintain operational products for at least 20 years. HHI recognizes its need for help in configuration management. The vice president of development has looked at the available products and finds that they do not meet his company's needs. Therefore, he has decided that HHI will design and build their own configuration management system. If it works well, HHI may add it to their catalogue of commercial products.

Ho-Hum's vice president decided to implement a configuration management system because the company's name describes the prevailing corporate policy in every area other than software design. As a small company that gained prominence by providing a casual atmosphere in which bright designers could develop advanced products, HHI now was faced with the complications of dealing with success. Customers were sending in "problem reports" about both problems and misconceptions, the staff was filled with new ideas and improvements to existing systems, the vice president of marketing was continually identifying new platforms for company products, and the maintenance programmers (mostly new hires) found it difficult to determine what source code went with an installed product and which products were affected by a trouble report. If HHI were to survive through the next decade, configuration management was required.

Configuration management has long been a standard practice in hardware manufacture. Recall from Chapter 1 that the design of equipment to be fabricated in quantity requires a series of design steps that culminates with a set of drawings and instructions that are thoroughly tested before fabrication begins. The costs of making changes after manufacturing starts are very high, and great care is taken to verify the design at each step in the process. Once a design decision has been made, it must be preserved for future reference. Each document or drawing is called a *configuration item* (CI), and it is the responsibility of the configuration management system to preserve these items and control any changes to them. Without the ability to reference correct CIs, it would be impossible to modify or maintain a product. For example, how would one maintain an aircraft's electrical system without a reliable wiring diagram for that aircraft? If new electronics were added to an airplane, it would be necessary to use the configuration drawings for the installation. Moreover, there is the need to maintain complete sets of drawings for every aircraft class with a different electrical configuration.

Software development faces the same challenges as hardware plus some additional complications. First, the products are more complex (with respect to the number of components and details that can be modified), the fabrication process (e.g., compilation) is automated and almost instantaneous, and the products (i.e., software code) are text and can be managed as a document. Thus, a *software configuration management* (SCM) system must both manage changes throughout the life-cycle and also control the software once it has been accepted. Consequently, SCM is composed of two major units: a procedure for managing acceptance and change and a set of tools to maintain the accepted software products. Both benefit from automated assistance, and the case study to be used in this book involves the definition and construction of these two complementary units within an integrated system.

I first examine the procedures for controlling accepted products and managing change. Recall that the waterfall flow consists of a series of steps in which each step is complete only after an acceptance process; furthermore, no step can begin before its parent step is complete. That is, the accepted output from one step is used as the input to the next step. Each output/input product represents a CI to be preserved; without this preservation, there can be no certainty that the proper input is being used in any step. A second characteristic of the waterfall flow is that lessons will be learned that result in changes to the outputs of earlier steps (i.e., there is feedback). Mechanisms are required to review proposed modifications to CIs and maintain the approved changes. Every CM system must manage these changes. In a hardware setting, documents and drawings are stored in their hardcopy form, and automated records keep track of the document identifiers and status. Although advances in computer-based publishing now enable the storage of many documents in electronic form, we shall assume that all CIs not in the form of code will be preserved as hardcopy documents and represented in the automated database by surrogate records.

Because every project has its own special characteristics, the SCM approach to be followed may vary from project to project. Therefore, the definition of the SCM procedures normally is established in a CM planning activity and published as a CM Plan, which itself is placed under configuration control. This plan describes the CM organization (including the boards that approve changes, the kinds of CIs to be managed, and the auditing and accounting procedures), the CM tools (for identification and labeling, control, and auditing), the CM procedures (during design, development, deployment, and operations/maintenance), and the CM resources (budget and staffing). Naturally, the CM plan addresses all hardware, software, and system concerns. In what follows, I present an overview of this level of CM. The standard texts on the topic are by Bersoff, Henderson, and Siegel [BeHS80] and Babich [Babi85]; IEEE also has published a *Guide to Software Configuration Management* (ANSI/IEEE Standard 1042).

Management of the configuration is the responsibility of a *configuration control board* (CCB) that approves all changes to the existing *baseline* (i.e., accepted design or product). Several baselines will be created during the product's life-cycle (e.g., the functional baseline documents the system requirements, the allocated and design baselines define two levels of design detail, and the product baseline contains the operational software). There also may be more than one CCB (e.g., one for hardware and one for software). To be certain that the baseline is complete, each CI must be *audited* prior to entry under CM. CIs are entered into the baseline once they have been accepted at the conclusion of a waterfall step or after an approved change has been verified. Before entry into a baseline, the analyst or designer is free to make changes to his assigned CI. After a CI has been entered under CM, however, no changes can be made unless they are authorized by the CCB.

Requests for change are initiated in one of two ways. A problem may be identified and reported on a *software incident report* (SIR, also known as a trouble report, discrepancy report, error report, etc.). The SIR may be submitted as the result of a failure at the customer's site; SIRs also may be used to record errors in requirements or implementation and violations of standards. In each case the SIR must be analyzed to determine if the incident was caused by a previously undetected defect in the product. Alternatively, the review might conclude that no action is required (e.g., a fix to the problem is underway, the reporter misunderstood the incident). Once it is decided that an action is required, a priority must be established so that emergency actions can be taken at once. Following analysis, a recommended correction is proposed and forwarded to the CCB for approval. Of course, not all changes are initiated in response to an error. The second way that a proposed change comes to the CCB for review is through the submission of a *change request* (CR, also called a request for change, etc.). Here, the CR identifies a proposed change to the accepted requirements. Examples might be the revision of an unimplementable requirement or the addition of a new feature or enhancement. Figures 2.1 and 2.2 contain sample SIR and CR forms.

In reviewing a proposal for change, the CCB takes into account the importance of the change, its cost, potential conflicts with other changes in progress, the possibility of combining several proposed changes into a more integrated revision, etc. The responsibility of the CCB is to maintain configuration stability, control costs, and foster orderly change.

**SOFTWARE INCIDENT REPORT**

Product Name: _____          Report Number: _____

| Submitted by: | Priority: | Software identification |
|---|---|---|
| Name: | ☐ Routine | Name/acronym |
| Organization: | ☐ Urgent | |
| Address: | ☐ Emergency | Module/subroutine |
| | **Occurred:** | Software function |
| Telephone:          E-mail: | Date: | |
| Date: | Time: | ☐ Document          ☐ Executable code |

| Description: | Analysis: |
|---|---|
| | |

**TO BE COMPLETED BY CM MANAGER:**

| Received by: | Title: | Date: |
|---|---|---|

| Corrective action | Disposition |
|---|---|
| | ☐ NAR    ☐ DTF    ☐ SCN# ____    ☐ CR# ____ |
| | Documents affected: |

| | Effort estimate: | QA: |
|---|---|---|
| | Programmer _____ | Monitor: |
| | Computer _____ | |
| | Other _____ | V&V: |
| | Total _____ | Implementor: |

Fig. 2.1. Sample software incident (SIR) form.

In general, all SIRs not classified as *no action required* (NAR) are acted on in an expeditious manner. Proposals from SIRs and CRs deemed worthy of further consideration are documented as an *engineering change proposal* (ECP), which is ultimately accepted or rejected by the project sponsor. If an ECP is approved, then the affected CIs are copied from the baseline for modification. The baseline remains unchanged until the approved changes are made, the amended CIs have been audited, and the revisions are available for baseline update. Naturally, the baseline will retain both the version prior to the update and the new version. (Both versions may be in operational use; alternatively, errors may be found in the changed baseline that require the reversion to an earlier baseline.)

**CHANGE REQUEST**

Product Name: ——————————————  Request Number: ——————————————

| Submitted by:<br>Name:<br>Organization:<br>Address:<br><br>Telephone:          E-mail:<br>Date:               Need by: | Priority:<br>☐ Routine<br>☐ Urgent<br>☐ Emergency | Cls affected:<br><br>Documents affected: |
|---|---|---|
| Narrative:<br>Description of change:<br><br><br>Need for change: | | Estimated effects as other components<br><br><br>Alternatives: |

| TO BE COMPLETED BY CM MANAGER: |
|---|

| Received by:          Title:          Date: |
|---|

| Active summary:<br>☐ NAR          ☐ Ecp requests<br>Comments | Description of change: | |
|---|---|---|
| | Effort summary:<br>Programmer ————<br>Computer ————<br>Other ————<br>Total ———— | QA:<br>Monitor:<br>V&V:<br>Implementor: |

Fig. 2.2.  Sample change request (CR) form.

By way of summary, Bersoff, Henderson, and Siegel [BeHS79] point out that every SCM system will be composed of three basic ingredients:

1.  Documentation (such as administrative forms and supporting technical and administrative material) for formally precipitating and defining proposed changes.

2.  An organizational body for formally evaluating and approving or disapproving proposed changes.

3.  Procedures for controlling changes.

In particular, every SCM system (whether or not it is automated) must be concerned with

- *Identification.* What is my system configuration? Am I working on the latest version? Is this the version with the reported error? Does this documentation go with the software I am working with?

- *Control.* How do I control changes to a dynamic product? Does this version include the changes made in response to an emergency SIR? This change seems too obvious, has it already been tried? Who is responsible for making this approved change?

- *Status accounting.* What changes have been made to the system? What are the outstanding SIRs? How long have the SIRs with a routine authority been pending?

- *Auditing.* Does the system satisfy the stated objectives? Do the baseline CIs conform to the agreed standards? Do the CIs in this baseline conform to the stated intent of the CIs in the parent baseline?

Of course, everything in this list is true for all CM systems.

Unlike hardware CM systems, the SCM system can control its CIs in a form that can be modified, built, tested, and accepted. Earlier, I ruled out electronic publishing and suggested that documents would be managed as hardcopy CIs. Programs and test data, however, should be controlled in their electronic form. Consequently, a comprehensive SCM system ought to support both the standard CM functions plus those special functions associated with the management and control of computer-stored CIs. Thus, when a machine-processable CI (such as a source code file, object file, or test data file) is available for entry into the baseline, both the transfer and the storage of the CI should be managed by the SCM system. Further, when a decision is made to release a CI for modification, the SCM system ought to (1) make a copy for alteration, (2) note in the current baseline that a change is pending, and (3) create a new baseline version once the change has been accepted and electronically transferred.

Tools that manage the machine-processable CIs generally are called code or revision management systems; examples include the Revision Control System (RCS, [Tich85]), the Source Code Control System (SCCS, [Roch75]), and Digital's Code Management System (CMS, [CMS82]). Each is designed to preserve an inviolate baseline, release files for read-only or update use, accept the modified files, and update the version identifiers. To illustrate, a typical code management system would support the following types of commands:

- *checkin*. This checks in a file to establish a baseline or update the baseline after a revision. The command prompts for a descriptive header and version log comment. The first entry is assigned the initial revision number of 1.1. As will be discussed below, subsequent revisions may alter the revision number in different ways. In normal use, the checked-in revision is deleted from the designer's workspace and flagged as read-only in the baseline workspace.

- *checkout*. This checks out a file for modification by copying it from the baseline workspace to the designer's workspace with a read-write access. The copy in the baseline workspace is normally locked so that read-write access will not be permitted in more than one workspace at a time. The command also identifies to whom and when the CI was checked-out.

- *compare*. This compares two revisions to see if they are identical or where there are changes. It is a useful tool for learning about changes as a revision evolves.

- *merge*. This merges two sets of nonoverlapping changes to produce a composite revision. Obviously, the use of such a tool is rife with danger. The fact that it exists suggests that the system requires options to permit concurrent modifications to the same programs. The merge also may be used to combine successive revisions thereby eliminating a version and saving space.

- *list*. This produces various lists from the commentary in the code management system, for example, a summary of change logs or a list of checked-out files by version or designer.

- *editcom*. This allows the user to edit commentary fields that describe the changes or processes associated with a revision.

- *clean*. This cleans up the baseline by deleting checked-out files that have not been changed.

- *admin*. This manages the many administrative functions including access rights, workspace identification, version renumbering, and default states.

- *delete*. This deletes checked-in changes that were improperly accepted.

Finally, one would expect a code management system to have help facilities and links with the host operating system.

System version numbers are normally written in the form *r.v* where *r* is a release number and *v* is a version within that release. Releases usually constitute major changes to the system whereas versions represent improvements within the context of the release. Thus, DOS 3.2 adds some features to and corrects some deficiencies in DOS 3.1, but DOS 4.0 makes significant changes to all the DOS 3 releases. When working at the CI level, unfortunately, this numbering convention is of too coarse a granularity. For example, there may be a program in DOS 3.1 that is in error. Numbering its correction 3.2 would imply that it belonged to the DOS 3.2 version, which might not be the case. Therefore, most code management systems provide more complex numbering schemes. In the target code management system, we shall assume that all version numbers are of the form *p.r.v* where *p* is a prefix (defaulted to null), and *r.v* is initialized as *1.1*. Each check-in will increment the *v* value by one or, on explicit command, increment the *r* by one and reset the *v* to *1*. The prefix *p* is set by command to indicate that a branch has been created that allows the parallel development of two variants of the same programs. For example, Figure 2.3 illustrates a revision flow in which the initial version (*1.1*) has been modified twice producing revision *1.3*. Now it is decided that this program is to be used on two different platforms (e.g., a PC and a mainframe), and each platform will require its own version. The revision number of the main line is updated with the next change to *2.1* and the prefix *p* for the variation is set to *1.3* thereby producing revision numbers *1.3.1.1*, *1.3.1.2*, .... Clearly, variants to the variants will make the numbering system complex [Wink87, Katz90], but we will defer solutions to these problems until release 1.2 of our code management system.

Because HHI produces products for a range of platforms, their version management process may be very complicated. For example, one tool that operates on both a PC and a mainframe may share one set of programs and use variants of other programs, while two PC-based tools with very different functions may share many of the same platform-specific programs. Obviously, one would want the SCM system to facilitate program reuse and avoid unnecessary rework. For instance, if changes were made in the PC-specific programs and the changes were compiled for one product line, then one would not want to recompile these programs for each different product line. Moreover, when building the most recent version of a system for test or distribution, one would hope that the code management system would include all appropriate accepted changes implicitly. The ability to perform this function is

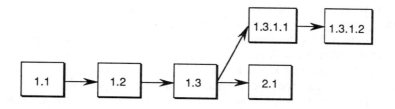

Fig. 2.3. Sample revision numbering for revisions and variants.

called *program manufacture*, and many code management systems provide this facility either directly or through the host environment [Tich86]. (For example, this is the function of the Unix make program [Feld79].)

Finally, the designers of the SCM system should keep in mind some implementation experience gained from the earlier code management systems. Each revision in the baseline can be defined as a function of the previous (parent) revision expressed as a *delta* change. To save storage space, it is possible to retain one parent and all deltas that have the parent as an ancestor. When the latest version is required, the system can extract the root version and successively apply the deltas until the desired version exists. Alternatively, the design could maintain only the most recent versions and construct the deltas so that they produce earlier versions on demand. Empirical studies have shown that the use of deltas can reduce the storage space requirements by 90%. The obvious danger in implementing a system with deltas is that errors in the delta-construction or version-reconstruction programs could be catastrophic. Unlike a report program in which formatting errors represent a simple annoyance, the delta-management programs of a code management system must have zero defects.

Here then is the case study that will be used throughout this book. Of course, our advice to the vice president for development is that he really ought to buy rather than build. Even if he cannot get exactly what he wants, he ought to purchase the best he can find and then augment it with special, locally developed tools. But the vice president is adamant. (Frankly, I think that he sees software development as just being fun.) So in what follows, we shall let him watch us build the one we plan to throw away.

## 2.3. Modeling techniques

Each paragraph in the above description of the configuration management system seems straightforward enough. Nevertheless, it is difficult to get one's arms around the whole thing. Perhaps this is because the system was defined in two parts. The first focused on the control activities of the CCB, and the second concentrated on the management of the computer programs. These two functions are interrelated, but the connections are not always obvious. Even in this short description of a relatively simple system, it is not clear what we expect the system to do or how it should function as a system. Each reader will feel most comfortable with descriptions that match his experience base. A hardware engineer will understand the CCB process and the preparation of ECPs, and the computer programmer may even have decided how to code the *checkin* command. But if we begin by chipping away at what we understand, we will be like the blind men describing the elephant. Locally each begins with a valid analogy, but globally each is wrong. What we need to do in the requirements analysis activity is construct a holistic model of what we intend to build. We must be careful, and we should avoid undue haste to start building. Remember, every undetected error at this early stage will propagate; the subsequent costs to repair can grow by orders of magnitude.

Because the SCM system is to be developed internally, there is some freedom in choosing the form for the specification. Normally, HHI uses the requirement document to define what they will deliver to a customer. It is a legal document, and any discrepancies between what was contracted for and installed may have major legal ramifications. Moreover, by starting with a formal requirement, HHI can control changes to the system once it is under development. Recall that every change is formalized as an ECP that is either approved or disapproved. Many ECPs do not affect the behavior of the product with respect to its specification, and the ECP can be reviewed on a no-cost basis. Other ECPs, however, do imply a *change of scope*, and here the sponsor must pay for the modification. In this context, the precision and formality of a requirements specification are very important to HHI.

When the contractual dimension is removed from the specification, the need for formality is reduced. However, one must be careful to distinguish between informality and laziness. The objective of the requirements analysis activity is to produce a clear understanding of what the target software is to do. In a sense, this has already been given in Section 2.2. But that discussion (let me claim by design) is something of a jumble. It described how people have been responding to the configuration management problem, and how some of the existing solutions work. It is not clear if major (implicit) functions have been omitted or if contradictory alternatives have been suggested. The employees of HHI already have a way to manage their software configuration, and they do it badly. We want to make sure that, if HHI invests in new tools and training, improvements will result. At this point in the process, the last thing that we want to consider is what programs we want to write. Section 2.2 provided a veneer of domain understanding; our task now is to build an SCM system model that is realistic in the context of our domain understanding and realizable based on our experience with automated systems. Because this is an internally developed product, we can avoid statements that begin, "The vendor shall . . . ." But we still need clear and reasoned statements about what we intend to deliver.

The remainder of this section describes techniques for gaining the insight necessary to produce an effective requirements specification. Many of the techniques overlap, and only pedants would attempt to apply all methods to a single problem. In what follows, I ignore management issues; these will be addressed in Chapter 6. The focus is on deciding *what* the SCM system is to do. There is an old saying that when one is in a swamp with alligators and water up to one's neck, it may be difficult to remember that one is there to drain the swamp. So keep this in mind: we will be building models to help us understand the requirements. Although the temptations will be great, we must avoid concentrating so much on the modeling tool that we forget why we are using it.

### 2.3.1.  Data models

The software configuration management (SCM) system, which we are about to specify, must interact with a database containing software incident reports (SIRs), change requests (CRs), engineering change proposals (ECPs), and files with programs and test data (i.e., configuration items or CIs). Perhaps if we begin by modeling the data to be processed, we will deepen our insight into what the system must do. The goal is to understand *what* the SCM system should do, and it is reasonable to approach this objective by considering *how* the system might operate. The concern here, of course, is how the SCM system will be used and not how it will be implemented. However, the modeling tools that I will describe were developed for both requirements analysis and design. Therefore, in some cases I will extend the discussion to show how the scope of a method or tool progresses from one role to another. Nevertheless, the emphasis of this section will be on the requirements identification activities.

Warnier proposes a method, called the logical construction of systems, that begins with this premise: if one can model the data that the organization requires and uses, then the structure of the system will follow. He starts with the following axiom and continues with his basic hypothesis:

**Any collection of data constitutes a set in the sense defined and utilized in mathematical theory.**

Once this axiom is accepted, every set of data in a system should be precisely defined.

Then, the various sets related to a particular problem can be manipulated through classical logical operations in order to comply with the needs that arise during the data organization. [Warn81, p. 1]

Warnier's method proceeds to identify the sets of data, decompose them hierarchically, identify the functions that act on them, group those functions according to their data interactions, and then lay out the system.

I cite Warnier's introduction to the logical construction of systems because it is one of the strongest statements regarding the central role of data in a system. The origins of the Jackson method, to be described in Chapter 3, also stem from this premise. The idea is that, for some classes of system, the principal activity is the transformation and use of computer-stored data. This use of data is intended to serve the organization's needs in all their operations. Thus, if we can discover what data the organization uses and how they are used, the system can be defined in terms of user interactions and data transformations. (Alternatively, one could make a list of the functions to be supported, and then define the data according to the needs of the functions. I present some approaches for doing this in Section 2.3.2. As I will show, the two techniques complement each other, and both are recommended.)

What can be learned about the SCM system through data modeling? One might begin by looking at the SIR in Figure 2.1 and conclude that the data model must contain a file with SIR surrogates composed of the date, submitter, problem title, priority, etc. Unfortunately, this level of detail immediately gets us into design decisions (and also trouble). We do not yet know how we expect to use the SIR data; therefore, it is premature to define what it should contain. Fortunately, there are some data modeling tools that help us gain an understanding at the appropriate level of detail. In what follows, we will use the entity-relationship model (ERM) to learn about the SCM system. I begin with a brief introduction to the ERM, then construct an ERM for the SCM, and conclude with an examination of semantic data models (of which the ERM is an instance).

The ERM evolved as a means to model the universe of interest for a database application; it was seen as a tool that would lead to an implementable data model for the target system [Chen76]. Although the concepts were intended for projects to be constructed using a *database management system* (DBMS), subsequent work has led to extensions, which, in turn, have contributed to object-oriented programming, design, and databases. Thus, even though the discussion may detour from our immediate objective, some of the material in this section provides a foundation for concepts to be developed further in later chapters.

By way of background, in the 1970s, as the storage technology matured, methods were devised for structuring databases so that they could be managed as unified sets rather than as collections of independent files. Perhaps the most important contribution of this effort was the use of a *scheme* (or schema) to define the logical model of the database separate from that of the physical model (i.e., the low-level implementation). In other words, how the data were organized for comprehension and use was separated from how they were structured for access. With this two-level model, a *data base administrator* (DBA) could improve performance by manipulating the physical data model without altering the logical data model (and the programs that reference it). *Views* also were introduced; these restricted the scheme to only that portion of the database of interest to a particular application (and by extension, developer or user). In this way the DBMS was able to distinguish between what the database represented from how it was stored. (For a more comprehensive treatment of databases see [Date86], [Ullm88], and [ElNa89].)

While the concept of the logical data model, with its scheme and views, was clearly an improvement over the traditional management of independent files, the first DBMSs remained highly procedural. The programmer wrote code that would *navigate* through the logical data model. In 1970 Codd proposed a mathematically based relational model, which could be manipulated with an algebra (with operators) or a calculus (declaratively) [Codd70]. It took a decade before the theory was refined and efficient relational DBMS implementations made the concept commercially viable; today, most commercial database products are based on this relational model. The relation can be described as a table in which the rows are called *tuples* and the columns are called *attributes*. Figure 2.4 lists a relation for the SIRs. The SIR attributes in this example are SIR-No, SIR-Receipt-Date, SIR-Status, and SIR-Close-Date. Because the relation is a set, there are assumed to be no duplicate tuples in the relation set.[2]

To ensure that tuples can be retrieved and updated, the relation must have a unique set of attributes that serves as a key. In the standard notation, the key is underlined, and the relation SIR is described as

SIR(SIR-No, SIR-Receipt-Date, SIR-Status, SIR-Close-Date).

---

[2]In actual practice, most relational DBMS implementations allow duplicate tuples. This is a performance compromise and not always a desirable system property.

| SIR-No | SIR-Receipt-Date | SIR-Status | SIR-Close-Date |
|--------|------------------|------------|----------------|
| 123456 | 1/17/90 | Validated | 1/19/90 |
| 123467 | 1/20/90 | Not appoved | 3/17/90 |
| 123490 | 1/20/90 | Waiting | |

Fig. 2.4. Sample data from the Software Incident Report relation.

This relation definition is shown in the heading of the Figure 2.4; it is part of the scheme. The information in the figure represents tuples in the SIR relation taken from an *instance* of the database. (The column headings, and therefore the data model, can also be referred to as *metadata*; it represents data about the data stored in the database.) By defining the relational model only in terms of relations, attributes, and keys, it is possible to define operators that act on these elements independent of the real-world objects that they represent. That, of course, is the power of the relational model, and modern relational DBMSs are very effective in manipulating data organized in this fashion.

The problem we have, however, is one of understanding the real-world requirements so that we can produce an ERM, which in turn can lead to a relational data model. Of course, we could produce our data model from the bottom up, as we did with the above definition of the SIR relation. But this might create problems. For example, SIR-No seems like a good choice for a key; one would not expect to find two SIRs with the same number. But the choice of attributes for the SIR relation may leave something to be desired. How could the SIR relation be used to answer a question concerning the change requests submitted by a particular organization? In its present form, SIR cannot answer this question. There are two issues here. First, is that an important question? Second, are there other relations that could be used to answer the question? We will construct an ERM to help us uncover the answers.

In the ERM an *entity* is some item in the universe being modeled that may be described by attributes. In effect, the entity may be thought of as a type. (In some nomenclatures one speaks of an entity type. The set of valid values is then called the entity set and the individual instances are the entities. I will be less precise and more intuitive in this discussion.) Examples of entities are the SIR, ECP, and files in the code management system; examples of potential attributes for the code management system files are the revision number, the file type (e.g., source code, object code, test data), lock status, original author, last modifier, etc. The *relationship* (not relation) is an association that links two or more (not necessarily distinct) entities. For example, there is the relationship "produces" between SIR and ECP that states that an SIR can produce an ECP. The ERM is a graphic model. The entities are drawn in boxes and the relationships are shown in diamonds. Normally the relationship names are verbs, and the entity names are nouns. Figure 2.5 presents an ER diagram for this simple relationship. There are no arrows in this diagram to suggest the flow in which instances are created. The diagram may be read from left to right as the declarative statement, "SIRs produce ECPs," and from right to left as, "ECPs are produced by SIRs."

Of course not every SIR will result in the production of an ECP; the configuration control board (CCB) may determine that the change is inappropriate or unnecessary. Thus, the relationship is optional with respect to the ECP (i.e., if an ECP exists, then an SIR must exist, but if an SIR exists, it does not follow that an associated ECP has been produced). Also, a single SIR may produce more than one ECP. We say that the relationship is one to many from SIR to ECP. Many ERM notations use symbols on the line between the entities and the relationship to indicate if the relationship is optional or mandatory as well as the *cardinality*. Figure 2.6 illustrates three such notations; unfortunately, there is no standard. The first depicts the 1:n relationship with one solid symbol on the SIR side and two open symbols on the ECP side; solid implies mandatory and open optional. The second example denotes the cardinality with (1:1) and (0:N) meaning that each Produces relationship has exactly one SIR and from zero to an arbitrary number of ECPs. Variations of this form sometimes omit the *participation constraint* and use only a 1 along the line near the SIR box and N along the line near the ECP box; other formats combine all the information into a single notation, such as 1:(0,n), written anywhere in the area. The third example uses a circle to indicate optional, cross lines for a cardinality of one, and a fan-out triangle to express many. (Not shown is the optional one, which is indicated by a single cross line and a circle.) In any case, the meaning should be clear. Every SIR may produce several ECPs, or none; but every ECP is produced by exactly one SIR.

The important thing about the ERM and the definition of cardinality is that it forces the analysts to think about the universe being modeled. If the 1:(0,n) relationship is true, then it follows that an ECP may not be prepared in response to more than one SIR. Does this make sense? In the abstract, one could argue with equal conviction that the relation-

Fig. 2.5. ER diagram for the Produces relationship.

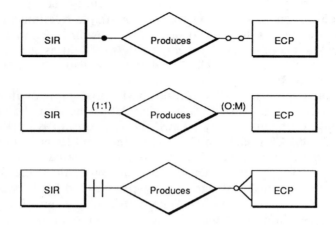

Fig. 2.6. The Produces relationship with cardinality expressed.

ship ought to be 1:n or m:n.   The advantage of the ERM is that it presents a graphic model that forces the analyst to document his assumptions and, at the same time, provides an understandable diagram for resolving uncertainties with the sponsor.   In this case, the vice president for development must decide what is desired.   If the SCM system is to be used internally by HHI, then he should base his decision on how the ECPs currently are prepared at HHI.  If, on the other hand, this is to be a marketable product for other organizations, then some market research is required to establish the appropriate relationship cardinality.  What is important about the ERM, therefore, is the role it plays in formalizing, communicating, and resolving issues concerning the universe in which the new system will operate and how it is expected to act.   The form used for representing cardinality is a detail; there are many easily learned, equivalent alternatives for expressing what has been agreed on.  What is important is that every member of the team use the same form.

Every entity has attributes that describe it.  In the SIR example we have identified the SIR-No (a unique identification number), SIR-Receipt-Date (the date that the SIR was logged into the system), SIR-Status (a code that indicates the current status of the SIR), and SIR-Close-Date (the date that all actions on the SIR are completed). Attributes are depicted by circles or ovals attached to the entity.  (In some notations, where it is clear that the items are attributes, they are simply listed alongside the entity.)  Associated with the attributes are their validation properties (i.e., typing information) called *value sets*.

For SIR-No the value set contains numbers that can be assigned at the time of SIR receipt, the value set for both SIR-Receipt-Date and SIR-Close-Date is a set of dates in the form month/day/year, and the value set for SIR-Status is {Analysis, Review, Pending acceptance, Not approved (closed), Waiting assignment, Change authorized, Validated change (closed)}. Figure 2.7 uses the notation of [FuNe86] to illustrate the associations among these items for the data shown in Figure 2.4.

Again, our interest is not in the notation but in the concepts expressed. Is the value set of SIR-Status complete? Is it too detailed? Is this concern for SIR status important at this stage of analysis? None of these questions has an answer outside the context of the application to be developed. How the system will be used and what reports are required will establish what status codes are necessary. In some cases, the status code may be linked to some other action, and thus it must be defined explicitly. For example, we may state that the code management component will permit release of CIs only if they are identified with an ECP whose parent SIR has the status "W". Alternatively, the sponsors may decide that the SIR status will be used only in reports, and that control over the release of CIs with be enforced manually. In this way, questions about the value set codes can precipitate an analysis of fundamental behavioral issues.

In the SIR entity there still is no way of determining who initiated the SIR. One could add an attribute to the SIR entity called SIR-Submitter. Another approach would be to identify two more entities, Developers and Customers and the relationship Submits between them and the SIR entity. Developers also create CIs, receive CIs for revision, and submit revised CIs for auditing and entry under SCM. From the perspective of procedural actions, each of these tasks has a different operational flow. From the point of view of the data being modeled, however, perhaps one abstract data representation can manage all three processes. This represents a trade-off that has no single correct answer; there are only poor or wrong answers that ought to be avoided through careful, up-front analysis. Figure 2.8 contains an ERM that proposes a model for this part of the SCM system. Before examining it, one last notational detail must be explained: the *weak relationship*.

|  | Primary Key |  |  |  |
|---|---|---|---|---|
| Attributes | SIR-No | SIR-Receipt-Date | SIR-Status | SIR-Close-Date |
| Value Sets | SIR-No | Dates | {A, R, P, N, W, C, V} | Dates |
| Entities | 123456 | 1/17/90 | V | 1/19/90 |
|  | 123467 | 1/20/90 | N | 3/17/90 |
|  | 123490 | 1/20/90 | W |  |

Fig. 2.7. The entity relation Software Incident Report.

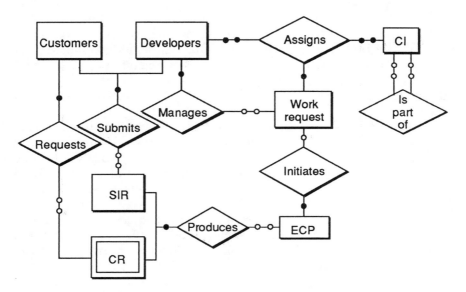

Fig. 2.8. Entity-Relationship Model for SCM system.

The weak relationship, depicted by a double box, is used to express a dependency among entities. The most commonly used textbook example is the Has Dependent relationship between the Employee and Dependent entities. Here, the name of a dependent is of little interest except in the context of a known employee. If the employee leaves the organization and his record is deleted from the database, one would expect all those entities weakly related to the employee instance to be deleted as well (i.e., one would not want to preserve the names of dependents for employees whose records are no longer in the database). To illustrate this here, assume that change request could come only from a customer. We might then model CR as a weak entity related to Customer if the CR could only be processed when knowing the Customer key. Thus, if a customer ceased to do business with HHI and data about him were deleted from the Customer entity, then all CRs initiated by that customer also should be deleted.

The ERM shown in Figure 2.8 is not complete. During the early stages, the ERM provides a mechanism for identifying and resolving questions about the system to be specified. We would be overwhelmed by details if we attempted to consider everything at once. (Remember the magical number $7 \pm 2$.) Like design, requirements analysis is an iterative process. To see how the ERM can help us get closer to the specification that we are working to produce, let us examine Figure 2.8 in some detail.

Starting with the upper left corner, the diagram shows that both customers and developers can submit an SIR. Some special notation is used to indicate that every submission of an SIR comes from either a customer or a developer, but never both (i.e., the Submitter Submits an SIR where Submitter is composed of the nonintersecting sets: Customers and Developers). In this diagram, a weak relationship is shown for the CR entity to indicate that only Customers Request a CR. Either an SIR and CR can Produce an ECP. In this notation, it is not clear that CR *is not* weakly related to the relationship Produces. Some notations avoid this ambiguity by using a double-line diamond for the weak relationship (i.e., Requests). The diagram now establishes relationships among customers, designers, CRs, and SIRs. Does this set of relationships conform to reality? Recall that some change requests may be submitted by the developers (e.g., if there is no reasonable way for a requirement to be met, the developers may submit a CR requesting that the requirement be amended). This ERM does not permit this. I leave the modification of the ERM to allow designer-submitted CRs as an exercise, but I shall use this deficiency to make an important point. When we draw the ERM, our intent is to have a valid model of the desired SCM system and not just a syntactically correct ERM diagram. In this case, even though the ERM is correct, it is not valid. The goal of requirements analysis is to establish validity; correctness can follow only after the specification exists. As with the draining-the-swamps example, it is important to remember why we are drawing the ERM.

Figure 2.8 also helps to identify other issues that require clarification. Consider the relationships among CRs, SIRs, and ECPs. Should we be able to trace an ECP back to more than one CR or SIR? If so, then are attributes for the Produces relationship necessary to indicate status changes when the ECP is rejected, aborted, or completed? What do we want the system to keep track of at the customer level, and is it the same as for the developers? Do we want to link information about Customers in the SCM system with information about Customers in the Accounts Receivable or Marketing systems? (This concerns the boundary of the automated SCM.) There are many more questions. Because we cannot answer them without input from the sponsor, it is best to move on with the diagram review. Nevertheless, it is important to notice how we begin with a reasonable approximation and use that baseline to improve our understanding of the problem. Too often books present only a diagram containing some accepted solution. But the diagram is most valuable when it guides us to that solution. Most of the time our diagrams will be either invalid or incomplete, and the process of requirements analysis is one of completing and validating the model.

Reading down from the middle of Figure 2.8 we see that Work Requests are Initiated by an ECP. The figure shows that Work Requests and ECP are in 1:1 correspondence, but that the initiation of a Work Request is optional (i.e., not all ECPs are approved). Up to this point, I have been describing the ERM in the context of a procedural flow: a Customer Submits a CR, which Produces an ECP that Initiates a Work Request. That is a misrepresentation of the ERM. It depicts the static associations among data; it should not be interpreted as suggesting a sequential flow. For example, consider the Assigns relationship. It relates Work Requests with the CIs that must be changed and the Developers that must make the changes. Here one relationship links three entities, and that relationship can be used to identify the Developers working on a particular requests, the CIs assigned to a Developer or Work Request, etc. A second relationship shows that Developers both are Assigned Work Requests and Manage them. This is an example of two entities joined by more than one relationship. Finally, CI illustrates another kind of relationship. Is Part Of is a recursive relationship on CI. We defined CIs to be any files that could be preserved in machine-sensible form, and we included source code, object code, test data, manufacture instructions, etc. One could treat the organization of the CI entities as independent objects whose type would be determined at the time of release for processing. One also could establish a structure for the CI entities like a parts list in which parts may be composed of parts and each part may be a component in many composite parts.

To reduce the clutter in this diagram I have not identified any of the attributes. For the entities Customers and Developers, the attributes might simply be Customer-No and Developer-No, respectively. In that case the system would not have much information about customers and developers, and (in practice) the entities could be reduced to attributes of the relationship Submits. Let us assume that the attributes for the Customer entity include a name and address and for the Developers entity the attributes include a name and job title. Then, with the ERM as shown, we might wish to add an attribute to Submits called Source with the value set {Customer, Developer}, which indicates the type of source. In the same way, we may find it useful to add attributes to the relationship Assigns to indicate when a task was started (AT-Start-Date), its current status (AT-Status), and the date it was completed (AT-Close-Date). I will not obscure the clarity of Figure 2.8 by adding these details; rather I leave that exercise to the reader. The point is that relationships can have attributes.

The objective of building an ERM is twofold. From the perspective of this chapter, the modeling activity provides a method and viewpoint that support a systematic examination of the product being specified. What we have found in the ERM we will see again in many different modeling methods. As with most methods to be examined, the ERM provides tools and techniques to achieve the following goals:

- *Abstraction.* The ERM reduces the system to a single facet: in this case the data to be operated on. The model abstracts away details about how the data are to be used, and it concentrates on those items in the external universe that will be served by the target product. In effect, the ERM projects the system to be specified into the domain of data structures. It obscures some important information (such as that an ECP must be approved before a Work Request can exist) while exploring the features of other, equally vital characteristics. The abstraction process reduces a complex problem to one of manageable size.

- *Communication.* The ERM provides an easily learned mechanism for the exchange of ideas among the analysts, sponsors, and users. It is best used as a graphic device for explaining and questioning, and it should never be treated as a substitute for a more complete specification. The diagrams represent effective tools for showing concepts and eliciting feedback and discussion. Because of the critical importance of a valid specification, this use of the ERM to gain domain understanding cannot be too strongly emphasized.

- *Documentation.* Some see documentation as a passive exercise that produces "read-only" artifacts best suited for a sponsor's bookshelves. To me, documentation is a tool that binds our understanding and thereby facilitates critical examination. In Chapter 1 I presented some information about how the human mind works and how naive theories are formed. Only discipline, experience, and intellectual integrity can reduce uncertainty; documentation (be it in the form of text, diagrams, or formal expressions) is the only mechanism that I know of that enables the necessary rigor and also maintains a persistent record.

- *Integration.* Because the ERM obscures details considered irrelevant to its primary objectives (e.g., temporal relationships), it is important that the modeling results be linked to the conclusions produced by methods addressing other concerns (e.g., flow analysis). Thus, the analysts must be able to map items from the ERM model onto items defined using other modeling methods, and vice versa. By way of analogy, this is similar to the essential integration of the architect's use of electrical, plumbing, and construction drawings.

Building the ERM is not an abstract task to be completed in isolation; rather it is one of many overlapping discovery activities directed at learning enough about the product to produce a valid specification.

Although the ERM provides a useful technique for nondatabase applications, it is most commonly employed when defining information systems that use a database. In fact, the ERM can be used to construct a DBMS scheme. Though this is clearly a design activity, it will be instructive to carry this discussion forward to show how a modeling technique provides continuing support throughout the software process. I begin with a short description of the relational data model and normalization; I then will show how the ERM of Figure 2.8 can be mapped into a relational data model.

Earlier the relational model was described in terms of relations (tables) that are defined as sets of tuples where the tuple positions (columns) are called attributes. Because the relations are sets, there are some well-understood algebraic operators on them: *union, set difference,* and the *Cartesian product.* There are also some very useful specialized operators as well. The *projection* operator acts on the attributes and can create a relation with only some of the attributes of a given relation. The *selection* operator takes a formula and a relation and creates a relation with tuples whose attributes satisfy the formula. For example, to produce a relation containing only the SIR-No and SIR-Receipt-Date values for SIRs that are waiting action, one could define the relation

Project SIR-No, SIR-Receipt-Date(Select SIR-Status="W"(SIR)).

Each of the operators is a function from the set of relations to the set of relations. Select produces a relation from SIR that satisfies the formula SIR-Status="W", and Project transforms that relation into a relation with just the two named attributes.

By combining the five primitive operators, one can produce additional operators. The *natural join* operator takes two relations that share one or more attributes and produces a relation in which the tuples contain all attributes of the independent relations (without repetition of the shared attributes); tuples are included in the new relation if and only if the tuples of the original relations share identical values for the specified attribute(s). For example, assume that we wanted a list of ECP identifiers (ECP-No) whose source SIR still was waiting assignment. The relationship between SIR and ECP is the relationship Produces, and it can be expressed as the relation

PRODUCES(ECP-No,SIR-No).

Because the relationship Produces is one to many, it is sufficient to have a single key attribute for PRODUCES. (If the relationship were n:m, then the key would be ECP-No + SIR-No.) In any case, the following (natural) join can be used to produce a relation containing only ECP-No values where SIR-Status is Waiting assignment:

Project ECP-No(Select SIR-Status="W"(SIR) Join PRODUCES).

In this nonstandard notation, Select is a unary operator that acts on SIR to produce the unnamed relation (Select SIR-Status="W"(SIR)), which has all the same attributes as SIR but includes only tuples with a status of "W". The Join is a binary operator that acts on two relations within the parentheses. Tuples in the resulting relation will have all the attributes of SIR plus the PRODUCES attribute ECP-No; a tuple is included in this new relation if and only if the values for SIR-No were identical for the two tuples from which it was created. Finally, the unary operator Project transforms the resulting relation into one with a single attribute: the list of ECP numbers that we sought.

What is important here is not the notation that I have used or even the features of the operators that I have described. I have included this overview for two reasons. First, I wanted to point out that if we can identify meaningful mathematical isomorphisms for the concepts that we abstract, then we can interpret the implications of conceptual extensions with greater confidence. In the above join example, all reference to the meaning of the relations and attributes has been obscured. Unlike the ERM, in which the emphasis was placed on arriving at the correct interpretation of the associations (which concerns the *semantics* of the problem statement), in the relational model the semantics are embedded in the structure of the items, and the modeling is specified using abstract, well-defined forms (which involve the *syntax* of the solution description). Reverting back to the Chapter 1 discussion of the essential software process, the goal of conceptual modeling is the capture and organization of the semantics of the problem to be solved, and the objective of formal modeling is the application of syntactic transformations that result in an implementation. In that sense, the ERM is a conceptual model and the logical data model and associated physical model are formal models. Indeed, there is a broadly accepted three-level framework that describes this modeling flow in terms of a sequence of conceptual, logical, and physical data models [TsKl78]. Although this nomenclature is restricted to database applications, it offers a useful rubric for all categories of software applications and modeling methods.[3]

The second reason that I introduced the details of the relational model here was to point out that, once the modeling enters into the formal domain, some additional obligations emerge. These obligations are beneficial; they preserve correctness and ensure predictable

---

[3]In the field of database design, the term conceptual model implies a model in the context of this framework. In this book, however, I use the term to represent a much broader concept.

outcomes. To illustrate, consider the join example in which a select, join, and projection were used to create a list of ECP numbers. Would the same list be produced if these operators were used in some other order? (For example, if we first joined SIR and PRODUCES and then performed the Select.) Moreover, if we applied another sequence of operators to the list just produced, could we get back to a selection of the original relations? Obviously, the utility of the relational operators depends on our ability to use them in any order and to be able to use them without the danger of losing information as the operators are applied. The relational model can be shown to be a closed system. Moreover, there are normalization techniques to ensure that the reconstruction of joins will not introduce spurious tuples (i.e., the joins are *lossless*). The proofs of these facts are contained in the database texts already referenced; in what follows I provide an overview of normalization and how the ERM contributes to the construction of a normalized data model.

The *first normal form* for a relation is its reduction to atomic attributes with no repeating groups (i.e., as a relation). The remaining normal forms are concerned with *dependencies* (i.e., relationships among attributes within a relation typically used to define a key). In many cases, a relation will have more than one attribute (or set of attributes) that can be used to identify each tuple uniquely. For example, assume that the SIRs are so rare that no more than one SIR is ever processed on a single day. If this unlikely assumption were true, then there would be two *candidate keys* for the relation SIR: SIR-No and SIR-Receipt-Date. Either would identify the tuple uniquely, and the selection of SIR-No as the key is a design decision based on the understanding (semantics) of the universe being modeled. Once the key is selected, however, the semantics of its selection are of secondary concern, and the focus shifts to the implications of key dependencies in the given syntax.

Let us now consider the weak relationship REQUESTS, which we might want to define as the following relation:

REQUESTS(<u>Customer-No + CR-No</u>, Customer-Name)

where CR-No identifies the CR. Clearly, this structure may seem to offer efficiency if we always expect to list out the customer name with the CR-No. However, Customer-Name would also appear in the relation CUSTOMER, and replicating the name can cause problems. For example, consider the potential for error if we insist on the consistent spelling of customer names. For a relation to be in *second normal form*, all nonkey attributes that are dependent on a proper subset of the key must be removed. In this case, one would delete Customer-Name from the REQUESTS. Given that the name already existed in CUSTOMER, access to Customer-Name would be available by joining REQUESTS with CUSTOMER on Customer-No.

A relation in *third normal form* has no dependencies among nonkey attributes. To illustrate, assume that each customer is assigned just one salesman; the relation

CUSTOMER(Customer-No, Customer-Name, Customer-Address, Salesman-No, Salesman-Name)

violates third normal form because Salesman-Name is functionally dependent on Salesman-No. It should be removed from CUSTOMER, and another relation SALESMAN should be added to the scheme.

SALESMAN(Salesman-No, Salesman-Name)

There are other normal forms that deal only with multiple keys (*multivalued dependencies*), and it can be shown that third normal form can produce a scheme that guarantees lossless joins and the preservation of dependencies. Thus, I will close out the discussion of normal forms here by simply observing that once the ERM exists it must be transformed into a set of relations that satisfies some normalization conditions. All entities and relationships in the ERM must be expressed in the form of a relation. (I have assumed that a relational DBMS will be used; the REM is not restricted to the relational model.) If the ERM properly defines the entities, then the derived scheme generally will be in third normal form. Thus, an awareness of normal forms will help in the creation of the ERM. For a simple guide to normal forms see [Kent83], and for a discussion of the transformation of the ERM into a data model or scheme see [Chen85].

Figure 2.9 contains a partial scheme (in third normal form) derived from Figure 2.8; it omits the structure for the CI entity, which I discuss below. The first five relations need no explanation. Notice that SUBMITS has one key term, and REQUESTS has two key terms. This reflects the fact that the latter is a weak dependency. PRODUCES, which was referenced in the join example, is not shown here. In Figure 2.8 we see that for every ECP there is exactly one SIR or CR, and we have stored the identifier as an attribute and added the attribute Source to indicate whether SIR-No or CR-No was to be used. SIR-No and CR-No are called *foreign keys* because they are keys to other relations (i.e., SIR and CR). Notice that one of the keys will always be null, and Source is used to identify which is not null. Managed-By (which is of the type Developer-No) serves as another foreign key that eliminates the need for a "manages" relation. Notice that the attributes of SUBMITS could be appended to those of SIR. Thus, the only relationships that

CUSTOMER(Customer-No, Customer-Name,
   Customer-Address, Salesman-No)
DEVELOPER(Developer-No, Developer-Name)
SALESMAN(Salesman-No, Salesman-Name)

SIR(SIR-No, SIR-Receipt-Date, SIR-Status, SIR-Close-Date)
CR(CR-No, CR-Receipt-Date, CR-Status, CR-Close-Date)

SUBMITS(SIR-No, Source, Customer-No, Developer-No)
REQUESTS(Customer-No + CR-No)

ECP(ECP-No, ECP-Title, ECP-Submit-Date, ECP-Status,
   ECP-Cost, ECP-Close-Date, SIR-No, CR-No)

WORK-REQUEST(Task-No, ECP-No, Task-Title,
   Source, Customer-No, Developer-No, Managed-By)

ASSIGNMENTS(Task-No + CI-No + Developer-No,
   Asgn-Start-Date, Asgn-Status, Asgn-Complete-Date)

Fig. 2.9. Partial scheme of an SCM system.

require separate relations are those with more than one key term. Unfortunately, not all DBMS products support null foreign keys and types.

Now that we have examined the bark of a few neighboring trees, let us return to our task of mapping the forest. By way of retracing our steps, we began by saying that we could learn about the system we were about to specify by abstracting away all the details save for those that described the data that the system would use. We adopted the ERM as the tool to guide us in this odyssey, and the early discussions of the validity of our ERM pivoted on our understanding of what the system was to do and how the environment in which it would operate behaved. Because this is only an exercise, we feigned satisfaction with our understanding as expressed in Figure 2.8, and we moved on to see how this conceptual model could be transformed into a more formal model. This involved some backtracking and a whirlwind description of some relational database theory. The critical observation was that a formalism offers a rigid, beneficial structure that must be understood to be used. That is, whereas a wave of the hand can be used to communicate or clarify a semantic concern, such informality is worthless when dealing with syntactic issues. And, as I hope I made abundantly clear in Chapter 1, software engineering is the process of managing the transition from a valid conceptual model to an efficient implementation (expressed as a formal model).

In a sense, the modeling of data relationships serves as a microcosm for the entire software process. Therefore, it will be instructive to close out this section with a discussion of a data-structuring problem in which the ERM was not very helpful. I refer to the CI entity, which is structurally much more complicated than any of the other entities modeled in Figure 2.9. The CI consists of identification (e.g., CI-No, CI-Revision-No, CI-Name), CI history (e.g., CI-Log-Date-Out, CI-Log-Date-In), CI objects (e.g., source code files, object code files, test data files), etc. The relationships among these items are far more complex than the diagram in Figure 2.8 suggests. Moreover, I have introduced types (such as the text for a source code file) not available in a traditional relational DBMS. I now examine some of the implications of dealing with these more involved constructs. The perspective here focuses on the abstraction of structures; the review of object-oriented design in Chapter 4 will examine similar issues in terms of behavioral abstractions. (See [KiLo89] and especially [King89].)

In the previous paragraph I used the word *object*. I have avoided use of that word because it implies *object-oriented*, and I would like to describe that concept in the context of *abstract data types*. As a very brief introduction, observe that both the relational model and the value sets define types that can be used to validate inputs and operations. Examples are number, character string, date and the enumeration type SIR-Status (i.e., {A, C, N, P, R, V, W}). For each type there are validity tests and operators such as add and subtract for numbers and concatenate for character strings. When we introduce new types, such as the date type, we can also introduce new operators. For example, we could define the sum of a date and a number as a date advanced by the given number of days from that date. Doing this enriches the programming language and hides a level of detail of no concern to the immediate task.

To extend this concept, observe that each of the types just named has a very simple structure that can be managed by most programming languages. The CI entity, however, is far more complicated. Source code text, for example, can be treated as a file to be copied or deleted. Alternatively, it can be viewed as a type (object) that has some special operators associated with it including edit, compile, copy, and delete. Generalizing this idea, consider how we could extend the CI type to include documents. We would need a model that would also manage objects of type figure, photograph, and engineering drawing, and each of these types would have a set of valid operators associated to it. Whereas an *object-oriented DBMS* can support the definition of types and operators and then facilitate the execution of the operations, *semantic data models* (of which the ERM is an example) are intended primarily to define the types and their interrelationships. That is why I discuss semantic data modeling in the chapter on requirements analysis and object-oriented concepts in the chapter on modeling-in-the-small.

The origins of semantic data modeling can be traced back to AI work in knowledge representation. Because the relational model lacked the power to express all the semantics necessary to describe a complex application, semantic data modeling sought richer representations by building on the results of AI research. The emphasis of semantic data modeling continues to focus on the design of record-oriented systems, but there also are some systems that can produce operational applications [HuKi87, PeMa88]. In what follows, I briefly examine how a semantic data model assists in clarifying relationships among data model types. I begin by defining two terms, aggregation and generalization, first introduced by Smith and Smith [SmSm77]. We will apply these concepts in other contexts throughout this book.

- *Aggregation* is the means by which relationships between low-level types (entities) can be considered a higher level type. The ERM emphasizes aggregation using the type constructor *relationship*.

- *Generalization* is a means by which differences among similar objects are ignored to produce a higher order type (entity). For example, we might choose to ignore the differences between customers and developers and form a type called submitter. With respect to the action of submitting an SIR or CR, we would assume that there are no differences between customers or developers. (This, of course, might be an invalid assumption.)

The inverse of generalization is *specialization*. Assume that the CIs were to be divided into source items and object items. If a type were defined for CI, it could be specialized as CI-Source and CI-Object. Specialization is sometimes defined as an *ISA* (pronounced *is a*) relation (e.g., CI-Source ISA CI). Obviously, if only CI-Source and CI-Object existed, the type CI could be created by means of generalization. Note that generalization and specialization create a type hierarchy that enables *inheritance*. If a CI-Source ISA CI, then the attributes of CI would also be valid for CI-Source (e.g., CI-Source would inherit CI-Name from CI). Specialization may involve disjoint types (e.g., a Submitter is either a Customer or a Developer but not both), or overlapping types (e.g., CI source code may be categorized according to both size and language, thus we might have the overlapping types CI-Source-Large, CI-Source-Ada, and CI-Source-C).

The point to be taken away from this discussion is that, as the data types (and associated structures) become more complex, more powerful tools are required to model and manipulate them. In Figure 2.8 I have presented an entity-relationship model that I admit is incomplete. I have deferred a careful examination of the configuration items. (In fact, throughout the discussion I used the word "file," which is a physical storage descriptor, rather than one that defines a logical object such as "source text.") The ERM is not a rich enough representation scheme to model the CIs effectively. There are extended entity-relationship models (EERM) that are more powerful (see, for example [ElNa89]), and work on other semantic data models continues. I will pursue this topic in further detail when I take up object-oriented concepts in Chapter 4. But the reader should observe that I am closing this section on a note of failure. The immediate task is to gain an understanding of CIs so that we can specify what we want the SCM system to do with them. We did not finish this task; moreover, we must examine some implementation issues so that we will not specify a product that will be difficult (or impossible) to deliver. The benefit of the semantic data model is that it allows us to experiment with concepts when the cost for change is very low: just paper and erasers. If this were a real project, it would be inexcusable to stop here with the observation that this is very complicated, and I'll think about it tomorrow. Fortunately, we are building the one that HHI will throw away, and so it is permissible to allow pedagogy to triumph over practicality. At least until Chapter 4.

### 2.3.2. Process descriptions

The previous section described some modeling tools designed to uncover the structure of the data used by the target system. By concentrating on the data and how they would be used, it was possible to gain a better understanding of what we expect the system to do. In this section we shall abstract away our concern for how the data are structured and concentrate on the processes we want the system to support. Of course, we could do this by creating a "wish list" such as follows:

- The system shall record and display every software incident report (SIR) and change request (CR) received.

- The system shall display the status of SIRs and CRs including dates of receipt, source, and status.

- The system shall maintain links between the engineering change proposals (ECPs) and the SIRs and/or CRs that initiated them.

- The system shall maintain all configuration items (CIs) in a permanent archive and release them only when authorized.

- The system shall . . . .

Unfortunately, if we follow this path, we will soon discover that the system is quite large, our list is quite haphazard, and we are quite bored. The advantage of a method is that it provides both a structure to guide the modeling activity and an orientation to assist in deferring unnecessary details for later resolution.

There are many different methods available for process modeling, and I shall examine a few in this section. I begin with what Orr calls the *entity diagram*. It is also referred to as the *context diagram* (or sometimes as the *level-one diagram*) in *structured analysis*. To avoid confusion with the entity-relationship model, I will use the term context diagram and continue with the discussion of structured analysis in Chapter 3. First, let us understand the problem we are trying to solve. We know that HHI needs a software configuration management (SCM) system and even what such a system should do. But at this very early stage of the requirements analysis it is easy to become overwhelmed. We do not know what to include in the system and what to exclude. For example, in Section 2.3.1 we talked about customer addresses and even salesmen's names and identifiers. Do we need to know the salesmen, and, if we do, how else should the system use this salesman information? Clearly, we must establish a boundary for what we propose to build. We must identify what automated functions are going to be the responsibility of our system and what tasks will be supported outside the system. Orr describes the diagram that we are about to construct as a device to move from "fuzzy thinking" to "clear thinking" [Orr81]. Because the diagram is helpful only to the extent that it clarifies our thought, its usefulness lies in the *process* of its creation. Orr suggests that after the *product* (i.e., diagram) is accepted, it need not be maintained. By way of contrast, in structured analysis the context diagram is the highest level of abstraction, and it is maintained. So in what follows we use Orr's method and the structured analysis terminology. Our concern is with what we learn as we draw this simple diagram. When we are finished we may discard the picture but retain the knowledge gained. (Sounds like a low-cost prototype.)

We begin by identifying a key user of the system and placing his name in the center of the diagram in an oval. We will repeat this process for each user of the system, so it does not matter with whom we begin. Let me start with the configuration control board (CCB). The CCB must interact with customers, developers, and management. I also enter these items in ovals on the page. This is shown in Figure 2.10. I now identify the interactions and transactions between the central oval and the outside ovals. I am not at all concerned about any interactions among the outside ovals. That is, I am interested only in what the central oval does and who or what interfaces with it. Some obvious

Fig. 2.10. A context diagram at step 1.

interactions are the SIRs, CRs, ECPs, and CIs. SIRs and CRs come from both customers and developers,[4] somehow ECPs are reviewed by management and get to the customers (who, after all, may have to pay for the changes), and eventually the developers get CIs to change and then submit as updated revisions for SCM. This is a fuzzy, stream-of-consciousness examination of the SCM flow. But it does not seem to fit into the framework suggested by the initial diagram because Figure 2.10 is not a good start. So consider the next few paragraphs a scenario rather than an instruction in context diagramming. Problem solving always involves backtracking.

One reason that Figure 2.10 is poor is that its choice of CCB as the central oval is too restrictive. The CCB makes decisions about changes to the configuration based on the analysis of SIRs and CRs. The CCB will have to use the SCM system to help them manage their activities and review the status of outstanding activity. I could concentrate on how the CCB works and what they need from a SCM system, but this would be the wrong tool for that purpose. My goal now is to establish a boundary for the system I am about to specify. More formally, I wish to restrict the solution space for this application. (For example, does the SCM solution space include concerns about salesmen, and, if so, what are they?) Putting the CCB in the center of the diagram may have been a reasonable start, but now I recognize that the choice was too fine grained. Therefore, let me change the central oval to a more generic "CM Group" that includes the CCB plus the people charged with maintaining the CIs, conducting the CI auditing, tracking the status of

---

[4]The entity-relationship diagram in Figure 2.8 contradicts this fact. The ERM diagram, therefore, is invalid; it is syntactically correct but nevertheless wrong. As an exercise, the reader ought to produce a modified diagram. In what follows I will ignore the misconceptions previously explained away for pedagogical purposes and continue by modeling only the real world as I see it.

the ECPs, managing the company's other CM activities, and so on.  For the boundary problem that I am trying to solve here, I do not need more than a general definition of what organizational entities constitute the CM group.  When I look at the management oval, on the other hand, I find exactly the opposite fault.  If I lump all management together into a single oval, I end up with a bureaucratic tangle that seems to interact with everything.  For our immediate concerns, it is best to separate the developers' managers, who will control the technical decisions, from the upper-level management, which interacts with the customers and makes the financial decisions.

This revised set of ovals is shown in Figure 2.11 along with the key interactions between the central oval and the outside ovals.  Let me trace the sequence of operations for a SIR submitted by a customer.  As shown in the diagram, the SIR is sent from Customers to the CM Group, which logs it and prepares an Analysis Request that is sent to the Developers who prepare and return an Analysis Recommendation to the CM Group.  The recommendation is structured by the CM Group as an ECP for Costing, and it is sent to the Development Managers for action.  The completed ECP is sent to Upper Management for approval, and if approved it is forwarded to Customers for action.  If the customer is willing to authorize (and possibly pay for) the ECP, that fact is transmitted to Upper Management, which in turn transmits a Task Authorization to the Development Managers.  The Development Managers assign Developers to the project and send a Task Authorization to the CM Group, which causes them to send (perhaps electronically) the CIs for Modification already identified in the ECP.  After the Developers complete the changes, they inform the Development Managers and submit the CIs for Auditing and reentry under SCM as revisions.  The Development Managers coordinate the completion of the task with Upper Management and the Customers, and eventually the CM Group sends the modified product to all Customers who have paid for the change (either by contracting for it directly or by way of a maintenance or warranty agreement).  Of course, these organizations can also Request and Receive Status Reports while all this is happening.

Did Figure 2.11 say all that?  No, some of the details were purposely excluded.  The transactions among the Development Managers, Management, and the Customers are of no immediate concern to the CM Group, therefore they do not belong on this diagram.  We will draw separate step-2[5] diagrams for Upper Management, Development

---

[5]The step numbers are informal references to the steps in this particular scenario, and they should not be mistaken for a standard nomenclature.

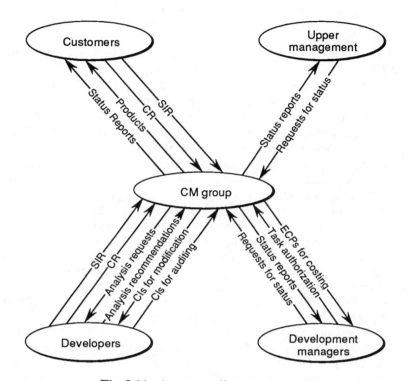

Fig. 2.11.  A context diagram at step 2.

**Managers, and Developers.** There is no need for a step-2 diagram for customers; we never expect them to be internal users of our SCM system. Perhaps, as we go along, we will recognize how important the salesmen are to this SCM system and even prepare a step-2 diagram for the Marketing Department. Still, even with this explanation for why some of the activities have been removed, it is obvious that there is much less information in Figure 2.11 than in the paragraph that explained it. This is both a strength and weakness of any diagramming and abstracting technique. To emphasize some characteristics of the item being modeled we must obscure other, equally important properties. Here we want to find out who will use the SCM system and how. To avoid confusion, we examine the users one at a time. Our goal is to go from fuzzy thinking to clear thinking. Already, Figure 2.11 is much better than Figure 2.10; there is nothing in it that contradicts the flow that we have just described. So we will accept Figure 2.11 as good enough and go on to draw the remaining step-2 diagrams. Naturally, as we work on the other diagrams we may uncover defects in what we had hoped was finished. Now is the time to make changes; everything that we do during context diagram creation is part of a larger discovery activity. At this early stage, what we find out is more important than how we represent it.

To simplify the scenario, assume that we have drawn all the other step-2 diagrams and then combined them into one composite diagram, which Orr calls a *combined user-level entity diagram*. This is shown in Figure 2.12. The only thing in this diagram not already discussed is the fact that Development Managers provide Product Review information for the Customers to review, and the Customers return their Review Evaluations. We now have all the information about SCM interactions *relevant to the system we are about to specify*. Development Managers rank Developers for promotions, Upper Management sets budgets for Development Managers, and Upper Management responds to telephone calls from important Customers. But these activities have nothing to do with the SCM system, and they need not be modeled here. If we are satisfied that this little diagram captures the essence of the system that we are to specify, we now must draw a boundary around what transfers we wish to have internal to the system. As in most requirements analysis work, major decisions should be made with the sponsor's involvement. This diagram is easy to understand, and it offers an excellent catalyst for arriving at an informed agreement.

I now assume that, following an examination of the alternatives, it has be determined that the SCM system boundary will include both the CM Group and the Development Managers. The next step in the sequence is the transformation of the combined user-level diagram into one with an SCM system in the center oval and ovals for the interacting units on the outside. This is shown in Figure 2.13. Here the CM Group and the Development Managers are not shown; they are part of the SCM System. That is, any SCM-related interactions with other units will be managed through the SCM System. Obviously, Development Managers still manage the Developers, but all of their SCM obligations will be controlled by the SCM System. Because this diagram projects only the SCM activities, none of the other developer-manager relationships need be shown. In drawing Figure 2.13, some details were eliminated. Because the SCM System will treat SIRs and CRs as almost the same kind of input, they are joined as one input to reduce the detail. In the same way, we can combine the Developers' Task Assignments and CIs for Modification into a single Assignments package. Finally, notice that the review exchanges between the Development Managers and the Customers are not in the final context diagram. The fact that we included Development Managers within the system boundary did not obligate us to incorporate all their CM-related functions into the system.

We now have achieved our objective. There is a system boundary that establishes what the system is to do and with whom it must interact.

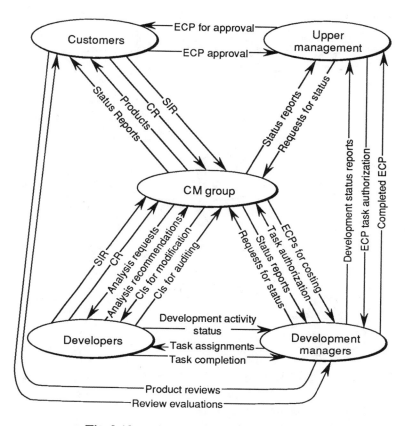

Fig. 2.12. A combined user-level diagram.

In fact, we know much more than is shown in this simple diagram. The diagram's concise presentation acts as a framework for retrieving that knowledge as we explore the system's complexity. We can stop at this point, or we can use Orr's methods to continue beyond requirements analysis and begin the design. By way of illustration, I will outline the next few steps in Orr's approach. The method is called *Data Structured System Development* (DSSD), and it is described in [Orr81] and [Hans83]. The principal tool used by DSSD is the *Warnier/Orr diagram*. These names suggest that I should have described this method in the section on data modeling. Soon, I will rationalize my discussing DSSD in a section on process models; for now I simply acknowledge that the astute reader is correct in assuming we are about to determine the underlying real-world structures and then fit the system's processes to them.

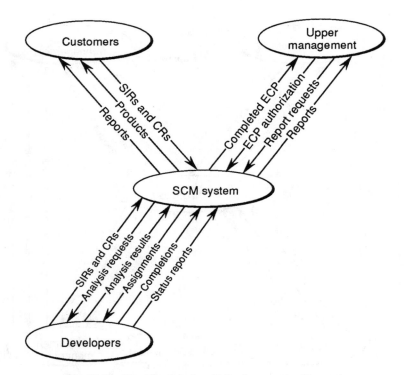

Fig. 2.13. The final form of Orr's context diagram.

Briefly, the next step in Orr's method is to organize the interactions of Figure 2.13 into sets of sequential processes. For example, one such sequential flow might be:

SIR leads to
Analysis Request, which leads to
Analysis Result, which leads to
Completed ECP, which leads to
ECP Authorization, which leads to
Assignments, which leads to
Completions, which leads to
Products.

Orr represents this sequence of activities in a *main line functional flow* as shown in Figure 2.14. Here each action in the flow is associated with the preconditions (i.e., what must already exist and what data must be added) necessary to trigger and carry out that action. There will be more than one such functional flow in a system, and each must be identified and diagrammed. Figure 2.14 is an example of a Warnier/Orr

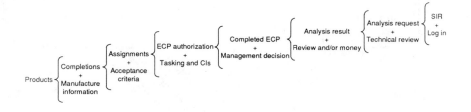

Fig. 2.14. Main line functional flow for SIR processing.

diagram. The same diagramming technique can be used to show data structures. For example, Figure 2.15 contains a Warnier/Orr diagram for an ECP data structure. Each Warnier/Orr diagram is used to establish the dependencies among events or the structure of the data required to advance from event to event. DSSD provides methods for systematically transforming the high-level diagrams that I have just described into lower level diagrams that ultimately reduce to implementable units. As the name implies, the data structure provides the principal abstraction in the design analysis.

I now have some explaining to do. Why did I describe DSSD here and not in the data modeling section, and why did I insist on calling the entity diagram a context diagram? I begin by admitting that Orr's entity diagram does not look like a context diagram. Figure 2.16 displays a context diagram. It shows the SCM system inside a circle (or bubble) and its external interfaces in boxes on the outside. As I suggested earlier, one does not build a context diagram using Orr's method; moreover, the diagram displayed in Figure 2.16 presents a very different view of the system than the one shown in Figure 2.13. It abstracts the system as a single process that transforms inputs into outputs. The goal of structured analysis (or *structured analysis/structured design*, SA/SD) is to decompose this single bubble into a manageable number of bubbles, which in turn can be decomposed, until we have bubbles that can be described as algorithms. I illustrate how this is done in Chapter 3. For now, however, it should be obvious that the form of the diagram in

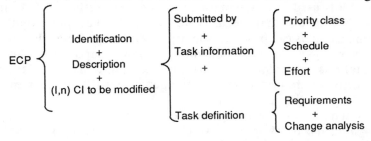

Fig. 2.15. A Warnier/Orr diagram for the ECP.

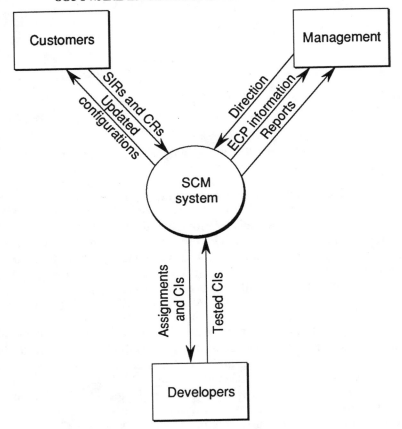

Fig. 2.16. A typical context diagram.

Figure 2.16 would be of limited help in constructing the functional flow in Figure 2.14. Knowledge about the SCM system that is essential to DSSD is of no concern to SA/SD; therefore, it is abstracted away. The lesson to be learned from this (and the reason I organized the discussion in this fashion) is that the diagrams have little meaning by themselves. They are tools used in a systematic process of converting a need into a product that meets that need. We see here that philosophically conflicting methods can produce isomorphic diagrams. Thus, the process by which we gain an understanding is more important than the representations with which we record our learning. This obvious fact can be lost in an era of "methodology-independent CASE diagramming tools."

Although I devote a major portion of Chapter 3 to the use of SA/SD for designing the SCM system, structured analysis really is a tool for requirements analysis. To show how it can be so applied, I explain the structured analysis method developed by Ross here; in Chapter 3 I will present a more comprehensive description of the methods associated with DeMarco, Yourdon, et al. I begin by reviewing the problem to which Ross was responding. Writing in 1977, Ross and Schoman stated that requirements definition must deal with three subjects [RoSc77]:

- *Context analysis*, which explains *why* the system is to be developed.

- *Functional specification*, which describes *what* the system is to do.

- *Design constraints*, which specify *how* the system is to be constructed and implemented (i.e., the boundary conditions for deciding which things will be in the system).

They proposed a concept, called the *functional architecture*, that could express these three overlapping subjects in a manner that was (1) consistent with the systems to be developed, (2) easily constructed, and (3) economically beneficial (i.e., technically, operationally, and economically feasible). To construct the functional architecture precisely, Ross proposed as the primary structural relationship the recursive use of "parts and wholes." That is, he applied a top-down decomposition technique in which the system was divided into parts, each of which was then viewed as a whole to be divided into parts. He recognized that the definition of the functional architecture needed an effective communication medium, and he modeled his diagrams after blueprints. By organizing the diagrams in a decomposition hierarchy, the analysts could maintain their orientation throughout the requirements analysis activity.

Ross called his system *Structured Analysis and Design Technique* (SADT®, a registered trademark of SofTech). As the name implies, it is intended to do much more than just requirements analysis, but I shall describe it only in this context. In the following illustration, the problem to be addressed is one of understanding the procedural flow from the time of an SIR submission to the distribution of the modified product. This flow has just been described using Orr's method, and we should now be familiar with the process. Consequently, the discussion concentrates on how the method and tools help us gain an understanding of the process being modeled (and the functions that the SCM system must support). SADT is a very effective tool for describing this kind of process flow, and Freeman has used it to define a software development system [Free87b]. While SADT is a proprietary tool belonging to SofTech, details on the method's use are described in [Ross77] and [MaMc88].

Like DSSD, SADT is part of a comprehensive approach that begins with a fuzzy understanding and systematically proceeds to a design. By describing only the form of an SADT diagram I run the danger of implying that the strength of the method is in the representation it uses. That is not true. Modeling in SADT begins by first bounding the system to be modeled and then determining a purpose and viewpoint for the model to be constructed. The model is built by analysts and reviewed by domain experts, and the diagram that I am about to describe is one part of the model's documentation. SADT uses other documentation forms as well. In Chapter 3 I will focus on two methods and present all the tools they use; there the emphasis will be the method's ability to support design activities across the software process phases. In this chapter, however, I am surveying the alternative (sometimes complementary, sometimes conflicting) methods available to understand the system we are about to build. Keep this in mind as we learn how to draw SADT diagrams.

The purpose of the diagram we are about to discuss is to establish a general flow for both the manual procedures and automated support in processing changes to an existing software system; its point of view is that of the CM unit. The diagram displays the flow of data and control into boxes that represent processes. The basic diagrammatic unit, the SA box, is shown in Figure 2.17. It shows the transformation of a horizontal stream of data from an input to an output, controls from above, and underlying mechanisms from below; outputs from one box may include controls or mechanisms to other boxes. The diagram represents a model, which Ross defines as

**M** *models* **A** *if* **M** *answers questions* about **A**.  [Ross88, p. xii]

Each diagram is limited to three to six SA boxes, where each box models a subject (process) described in the form: under control, input is transformed into output by the mechanism. Because every box is a

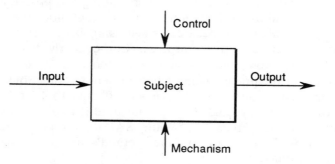

Fig. 2.17.  The SADT diagrammatic unit.

process, it too can be explained (modeled) by means of an SADT diagram. This decomposition of the system continues until the process represented by a box is so well understood that further decomposition will have little value. Even though this exercise will be limited to a single diagram, the strength of this diagrammatic approach rests in its ability to produce a network of diagrams. Naturally, each diagram will denote its place in the network.

The SADT diagram in Figure 2.18 depicts the processing flow from the receipt of an SIR or CR through the delivery of a revised version. First we will go through the diagram to understand its syntax, then we will examine the information that it contains. There are five SA boxes, which represent the activities of logging and evaluating requests, proposing modifications, initiating and completing tasks, and updating the software configuration. The overall flow can be thought of as a process that takes two inputs (SIR and CR) and produces one output (the revised version). Diagram flow goes from left to right. The SA boxes normally are presented in a cascading sequence except where feedback or interbox relationships can be clarified by changing the placement of the boxes. In this diagram, there are two controls that act on the five subjects: **CM Practices** and **Management**. The diagram does not indicate which **CM Practices** control a particular subject; the reader

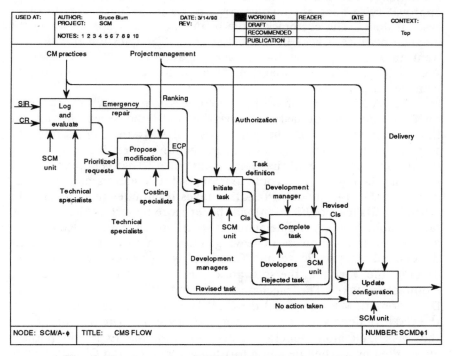

Fig. 2.18. A top-level SADT diagram for SCM flow.

is assumed to know. Because there are so many management controls, however, it is necessary to indicate the specific controls for each subject. At this stage of the modeling activity, we still are concerned with procedures that are essentially manual. Consequently, the model shows only nonautomated mechanisms.

A description of the inputs, outputs, and subjects is best done in the context of an explanation such as an analyst might present to a domain expert. It might go as follows. SIRs and CRs are submitted to the system where they are subject to a Log and Evaluate activity. The logging is performed by the SCM Unit according to the CM Practice. Technical Specialists are on hand to review the reports and assign priorities. If the specialists determine that a change requires an Emergency Repair, then it is immediately forwarded for correction. All other Prioritized Requests are subjected to further analysis by Technical Specialists and Costing Specialists during a Propose Modification activity. Here control is exercised using CM Practices with Management assuming the responsibility for Ranking the ECP preparation assignments. As a result of this activity, all SIR and CR inputs result in either an ECP or a No Action Taken notification that is used to close out the initial request. Management is responsible for Authorizing the work proposed by the ECP. (In some cases, the approval cycle does not involve costs or customer decisions; in other cases it does. The customer's role in this process is not shown in the diagram because it is of little interest here. The question that we now want answered is, "How does a task get authorized?" The answer is succinctly given in the diagram, "Except for emergency repairs, by management.")

The SADT diagram shows just two processes for everything that goes on from the time of task authorization until the acceptance of the finished change. From the perspective of software engineering and software maintenance, this is where the action is. Yet it is hard to find in this diagram where all that work takes place. That is because we are modeling the control of a configuration, not its creation, enhancement, or repair. For this model, a task that takes 10 minutes (e.g., release the following CIs for modification) may be far more important than one that takes months (e.g., implement a specified change). Remember, abstraction is the process of leaving things out so that we can better understand what we leave in. Thus, just two processes will suffice to describe the work that the software engineers will do: Initiate Task and Complete Task. The mechanism for Initiate Task consists of the Development Managers and the SCM Unit acting under the control of the CM Practices and Management Authorization. The outputs are (1) the Task Definition, generally extracted from the ECP and perhaps augmented by a schedule and effort budget, and (2) the CIs released to the developer for modification. Notice that the ECP is shown as a controlling factor for Initiate Task and not an input; this orientation suggests that the Task Definition output is constrained by the ECP.

Somehow the developers work within their schedule and budget and do one of two things: either they decide that the task was not properly defined, or they finish the task. There are three ways to finish a task. It may be completed as planned, aborted because it was subsequently decided that the change should not be installed as initially assigned, or the change may be rejected and submitted for rework. These three options are shown in the Complete Task box, which is controlled by Development Managers and CM Practices. (Here the level of management control is so well defined that Management has delegated its authority; only status reports are necessary, and these are not considered important enough to show on this diagram.) The mechanisms for task completion are the Developers who make the determination that the task is complete and the CM Unit, which in this scenario is responsible for auditing the change. The outputs from Complete Task are Revised CIs if the change was made as proposed, a No Action Taken finding if the task was aborted, and feedback to the Complete Task box if it is a Rejected Task. For tasks that cannot be completed without revisions to the task definition, there is the Revised Task feedback to Initiate Task. To avoid clutter, I have not shown that there also might be feedback to the Propose Modification box as well. The goal of this level of the diagram is to communicate what is known; nuances can be deferred.

The final SA box is Update Configuration, which processes the CIs and No Action Taken reports, updates the logs, and communicates with the change requestors. When given a Delivery instruction for Management to forward a Revised Version, the CM Unit does so. This completes the flow analysis displayed in this SADT diagram. It seems to convey more information about how the SCM system works than any of the diagrams that we have produced before. On the other hand, the diagram says little about the interactions among the data used by the system or the interfaces with entities outside the system. Of course, I have only gone through the first step in a rigorous process. The diagram's blueprint-like format is intended to imply an engineer's discipline. At the top of the diagram are sign-off boxes for the readers (experts and managers) who must review and approve it. Naturally, if someone is to sign off, he must be able to read and understand the implications of the diagram. As it turns out, reading the SADT is much easier than drawing one. Diagram creation requires thought and organization; diagram review demands only a willingness to extract the expression of that effort as it is represented in the diagram.

The engineering-drawing format also suggests that there will be many drawings. Figure 2.18 presented the top level diagram, and that is indicated in the upper right hand corner. At the bottom of the diagram are a number (node) and title; the author, project, date, and off-page references are shown at the top. Each box can be expanded as an SADT diagram. The parent node will be shown in the upper right hand corner, and the node number of the expanded diagram will be given just below the box that is being detailed. The expanded diagrams must have the same inputs and outputs as the higher level parent box. The set of diagrams produces a network as shown in Figure 2.19, whose title is taken from the 1977 Ross and Schoman paper [RoSc77]. Here the emphasis is on decomposition. Each box can be detailed at a lower level, and each diagram can be abstracted at a higher level. Indeed, some diagrams can be shared by more than one higher level diagram. The strength of this method is that it provides a model to answer questions about how processes interact.

Notice in the upper left of Figure 2.19 there is the legend:

MORE GENERAL
↕
MORE DETAILED

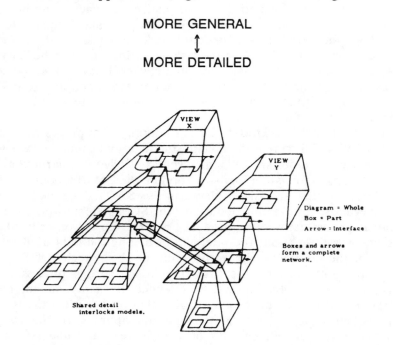

Fig. 2.19. "SADT provides practical, rigorous decomposition."
(Reprinted from [RoSc77] with permission, ©1977, IEEE.)

Is this an analogue of the generalization and specialization concepts presented in Section 2.3.1? Does this imply some form of inheritance? At first glance, the diagram might suggest a parallel. But the analogy does not hold. Data and process are distinctly different items. Although both may be represented with the same notation, the underlying differences in their composition require that they be considered independent views of a holistic system. Data structures require processes to transform them, and processes can be defined in terms of their inputs and outputs. What we have done so far in this requirements analysis chapter is to examine how the data and processes can be modeled to gain insight into the product that we will build. I am using a fragmented approach that obscures how we preserve the links among these differing views. I do this here to emphasize that we are now engaged in a discovery activity in which many tools can be of help. I will close out this section by discussing two more process modeling methods. In Sections 2.3.3 and 2.3.4, which follow, I will consider how we can structure the knowledge we have accumulated.

Because the computer can be abstracted as a mechanism that moves from one state to another, one can model a system (or program) as a series of events that cause the computer to proceed from one state to another. The most common form for displaying this kind of model is the *state-transition diagram* (STD). To begin with, let me provide some background. The concept of the STD is derived from the mathematical discipline called *automata theory*, which in turn evolved from Turing's early work with what we now call a *Turing machine*. The Turing machine is an abstract computing device, invented in 1936, that consists of (1) a control unit that assumes one of a finite number of possible states, (2) a tape divided into discrete units, each containing a single symbol taken from a finite alphabet, and (3) a read/write head that moves along the tape and transmits information to or from the control unit. Computation is performed by reading from or writing to the tape, moving it one position to the left or right, and changing the control unit state; each operation is determined by the current state and what is read from the tape.

The STD extends this model by abstracting the computing system as a set of states and inputs (generally called *events*) and identifying the valid events for each state together with the transition triggered by that event. In other words, we will model the system as a set of states S and events E such that

$$s_i, e \rightarrow s_j \quad (s_i, s_j \in S, e \in E),$$

and $i$ may be equal to $j$. The state[6] may be viewed as the holding (or definition) of a set of conditions, and the transition may be interpreted as the termination of some conditions and the beginning of other conditions. An event may be thought of as either the state change or the external activity associated with the transition. The effect of the state transition may be observed as an action or output. The granularity of these events, transitions, and actions will define the detail of the model being constructed. This may seem like a very abstract way to model a system, but there is a very natural isomorphism. One may speak only of events, transitions, and actions. Thus, we can list the events of interest for the process being modeled and identify how they affect the state and what actions they produce. Once the list exists, we can use an STD to represent the system.

In the SCM system requirements analysis, the major emphasis has been on the processing of requests for change. Let us now focus on what happens to the SCM system as CIs are checked in and out. The following events and actions seem obvious, and they provide an excellent start for the event list.

- *Initial.* The initial state assumes that the CI is checked into the SCM workspace and locked.

- *Check-out.* The action is to copy the CI to the developer's workspace in the unlocked state. In the SCM workspace the CI is flagged as out, but it remains locked.

- *Modify.* The action is to modify the contents of the developer's workspace.

- *Check-in.* The action is to copy the modified CI to the SCM workspace, remove the flag in the SCM workspace, and delete the CI from the developer's workspace.

The STD in Figure 2.20 displays the relationships among these events (i.e., state transitions). There are several diagramming conventions that one could use. Here the states are shown in boxes, and squared lines are used for the transitions. The line to the side of the transition line signals the event; above it is the event (or condition) and below it is the action. (Another common diagram format uses circles for the states and curved arcs for the transitions; to avoid confusion with the notation used with SA/SD, I have used this straight-line form.)

---

[6]In Chapter 4 I will return to the subject of state when I discuss object-oriented techniques.

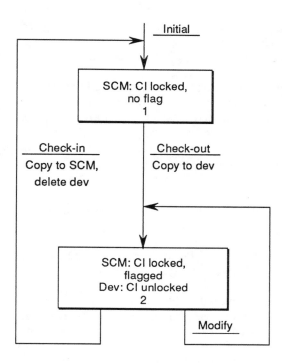

Fig. 2.20.  A state-transition diagram.

In this figure there are just two states.  Initial sets the first state, and Check-out moves to the second state.  Modify does not change state, and Check-in returns the system to the initial state.  The lines to the side of the transitions identify the events and, where considered important, the key actions implied by the state change.  As with an SADT diagram, each of the state boxes can be decomposed into a more detailed STD. At first sight, this STD does not seem to help us understand the problem better.  This type of diagram is most useful in process control, real-time, and man-machine interaction problems.  Nevertheless, even here we can use it to examine what we know about our problem.  First, we should observe that the four different events reduce to just two states.  Is this too high a level of modeling, and if so where should we add details?  For example, we know that we want to use the latest configuration to prepare an updated release, a process I called manufacture.  Therefore, we should be able to add a Manufacture event as a transition from the first state back to itself with the action of creating a new version.  This would imply that we can manufacture products only if the CIs are not flagged.  This STD is for a single CI, and adding **Manufacture** as just suggested would imply that we could build a new version only when no changes were in progress. Clearly, this is too restrictive a condition because such a quiescent state might never be reached. Again we see how using a diagram can help us uncover details about the SCM system that we might otherwise have overlooked.

The example in Figure 2.20 is quite shallow; its intent was simply to show what a diagram looks like. When STDs are drawn, one normally begins by creating an exhaustive list of events, with all events having the same level of importance. (Obviously, we can define events to the level of byte transfers to and from computer registers, but that would not help very much in requirements analysis.) Yourdon suggests that there are two approaches to building a list of events [Your89]

- Identify all events without concern for the states first and then go back to make meaningful connections.

- Begin with the initial state and methodically trace through the system identifying all state changes as you go.

In actual practice, one will probably alternate between methods until the list is reasonably complete. Once the events have been identified, they should be associated with transitions (i.e, from one state to another) and actions. This could be organized in the form of a list (as shown above), or it could be represented as a table. For example, event data could be displayed with the states in the first column, the events that cause the system to enter the given state in the next column, and the events that cause the system to exit from that state (perhaps back to itself) in the last column. For the present example, the table would be as shown in Table 2.1. This information also could be organized by state alone as shown in Table 2.2.

By presenting the same information in different formats, one can test the data for completeness and closure. One can ask:

Table 2.1. Sample list of states with enter and exit events.

| State | Event to Enter | Event to Exit |
|-------|----------------|---------------|
| State 1 | Initial<br>Check-in | Check-out |
| State 2 | Check-out | Modify<br>Check-in |

Table 2.2. Sample list of state transitions with events.

| State | Exit to | Entered from |
|-------|---------|--------------|
| State 1 | State 2 | Initialization |
| State 2 | State 1 | State 1 |
|         | State 2 |  |

- Have all states (of an appropriate level) been defined?

- Can all states be reached?

- Are there exits from each state?

- In each state, does the system respond properly to all possible conditions?

One can even restructure the information into the form of a *decision table* as presented in Figure 2.21. In this table we are concerned with identifying invalid conditions. Above the double line we identify state conditions that are of interest to us, and below we list what transitions are enabled (i.e., valid). Each column in the decision table represents a rule. The first rule reads that if the CI is flagged in the SCM workspace and the Dev workspace is empty, then for any value for the Dev workspace locked status (represented by a dash) this is an invalid state. The second rule reads that a CI flagged in the SCM workspace and locked in a nonempty Dev workspace is also invalid. The last column gives the rule that if the CI in the SCM workspace is not flagged and the Dev workspace is empty, then check-out is enabled. One can test this decision table to verify that all possible combinations have been

| SCM W/S flagged | Y | Y | Y | N | N |
|-----------------|---|---|---|---|---|
| Dev W/S empty | Y | N | N | N | Y |
| Dev W/S locked | — | Y | N | — | — |
| Enable check-out |  |  |  |  | X |
| Enable check-in or modify |  |  | X |  |  |
| Invalid state | X | X |  | X |  |

Fig. 2.21. Decision table for enabled transitions.

tested (in this case $2^3$ combinations are shown) and that each combination above the double lines produces exactly one outcome below the double lines.

In the discussion of state-transition diagrams I have presented four or five equivalent representations for the same information. Although the example is trivial, it should be clear how an event orientation contributes a different perspective for examining the system being specified. Peters has an example illustrating how event analysis can be combined with the ERM and SA/SD [Pete87], and (as will be discussed in more detail in Chapter 3) Yourdon shows how the states in a STD can map onto process definitions [Your89]. In the remainder of this section I will show how the STD can be extended to model concurrent operations using a *Petri net* [Ager79, Pete81, Mura89]. Before describing the Petri net, I will outline the process to be modeled with one. Assume that the software product that we maintain in the SCM system consists of two software components with the following rule for distributing new versions. One component, the operating system (OS), is externally supplied, and updates are periodically delivered to the SCM system. The other component is developed internally and is kept under configuration management; changes to it are made only in response to the receipt of an SIR. When an OS change is made, it is tested and released only if no authorized changes to the internally developed component are in

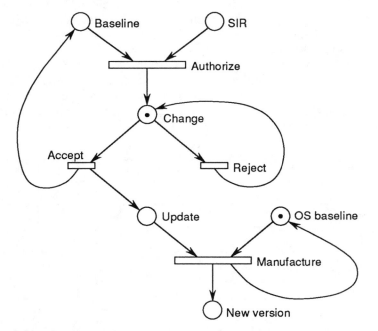

Fig. 2.22.  Petri net for SIR processing and product manufacturing.

progress. When an SIR-initiated change is complete, it is distributed immediately. Figure 2.22 contains a Petri net that models a part of this process.

Disregarding the two dots within the circles (called *tokens*), it will be immediately recognized that the Petri net looks very much like the STD. In fact, State 1 of Figure 2.20 is represented by the Baseline node (a Petri net place) in Figure 2.22, and State 2 corresponds to Change. Reading the graph from the top down, we see the process is initiated by the submission of an SIR, which joins with the Baseline and the Authorize event (a Petri net transition) to move into the Change state. That is, the Authorize event cannot take place unless the system state includes both a current Baseline and a new SIR; as a result of the Authorize event, the system will enter the Change state. The Change state, like State 2, is exited by either an Accept or Reject. So far, except for the identification of the SIR and the change in notation and diagrammatic symbols, the STD and Petri net are essentially the same. The Petri net in Figure 2.22, however, is extended to include the release of a new version of the system. Thus, it shows that after Accept, the Baseline is updated, *and* the component is placed in the Update state. To Manufacture a New Version we need to have both the OS Baseline and the Update. To reduce complexity, I have not included the management of the updates to OS Baseline.

One of the key features of a Petri net is its use of tokens to show state and identify constraints. The token in the OS Baseline node, for example, indicates that a stable release is available. The token in the Change node indicates that the system (i.e., process) state shown in this diagram is one during which time a change is underway. Therefore, the diagram not only displays the possible state transitions, but it also indicates the model's current state. For the present, assume that each node can hold only one token, and that all state changes pass only single tokens. A transition can *fire* only when it has a token in each of its input places; the result of that firing will be the removal of the input tokens and the placement of a token in each of its output places. Thus, we can gain insight into the state changes by examining the token positions necessary to move from one state to the next. Given the state shown in the diagram, we cannot Manufacture a New Version because there is no token in the Update node. Also, if an SIR is received (which would place a token in the SIR node), we cannot Authorize a change because there is no token in Baseline. Once the Change completes the Accept event (i.e., it fires), the token in Change is removed, and tokens are passed to both Baseline and Update. In this state it will be possible to respond to new SIR submissions and to Manufacture a New Version. Notice that Manufacture replaces the token in OS Baseline so that Manufacture can be fired with each new

**Update.** Admittedly, this was a poor example to use for a demonstration of the power of Petri nets, but it does make clear how they can help us gain insight into concurrent operations.

Actually, what I have shown can be generalized. The Petri net can be defined as a 6-tuple $N = (P, T, E, M_0, K, W)$ where the sets $\{P, T, E\}$ define the places (nodes or states), transitions (elongated rectangles or events) and edges (connecting lines) of the static graph structure. $M_0$ is the initial distribution of tokens (also called the *initial marking*), and it is a function from the set of places to the set of nonnegative integers $N$ ($M_0: P \rightarrow N$). $M_0(p)$ denotes the number of tokens at place $p$, $K(p)$ denotes the maximum number of tokens that $p$ may hold (i.e., capacity of place $p$), and $W(e)$ denotes the number of parallel edges represented by the single edge drawn in the graph (i.e., the weight or multiplicity assigned to the edge $e$). The graph can be augmented to include timing requirements for time-driven systems [CoRo83]. Models can be constructed to explore concepts (as in Fig. 2.22), to examine the behavior of concurrent programs, or to analyze abstract features such as reachability, liveness, boundedness, and coverability. For example, Figure 2.23 displays a Petri net in a deadlock state; $T_1$ cannot fire until $P_2$ receives a token, but that can happen only after $T_2$ fires, which is dependent on $P_3$ receiving a token by having $T_1$ fire.

That is a lot to absorb in one paragraph. The point that I am making is that the diagram of Figure 2.22 is a simple expression of a rich, mathematically defined concept. My illustration may have trivialized the use of Petri nets; nevertheless, I hope that the reader will interpret this simple exercise in the context of the following remark.

Petri nets and similar formalisms offer some promise in the modeling of *asynchronous, concurrent* execution of cooperating processes. Thus, these nets provide an ideal means of learning from each other; that is, practitioners can learn from theoreticians ways to make their models more methodical, and

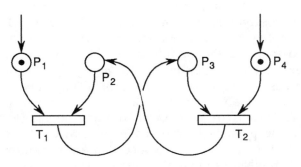

Fig. 2.23.  A deadlocked Petri net.

theoreticians can learn from practitioners ways to make their models more realistic. [Mura84, p. 39]

The idea is that we need to know about both the specific application being developed and what has been discovered for all applications of this class. Not understanding the practical constraints may doom us to unrealistic solutions; not being aware of the underlying theory may lead to suboptimal (or even unworkable) solutions.

We have now completed a survey of modeling tools that can enhance our understanding of the problem to be solved; I now turn to the task of transforming that hard-found knowledge into representations that will guide the design and implementation activities.

### 2.3.3 Formal methods

In Sections 2.3.1 and 2.3.2 the emphasis was placed on learning about the problem to be solved and constructing possible solutions. I suggested that this was a process of going from fuzzy to clear thinking, and I showed a variety of methods that could be used to structure our understanding. Some of these methods were informal, and others were based on rigorously defined mathematical formalisms. For example, the descriptions in the SADT boxes captured concepts informally; details would be added later. The Petri net models, on the other hand, were pictorial equivalents of a mathematically precise abstraction. In each case, we used the modeling device to refine our understanding by transforming partial solutions into a concrete, abstract form that could be reviewed by our colleagues and sponsors. I now consider how we can represent what we have discovered during the requirements analysis.

First, we must note that people communicate through words and text, and some explanatory text is always required. That is discussed in Section 2.3.4. What I outline here is not a substitute for a written requirements document; rather, it supplements the written text *for those system attributes that can be expressed formally*. Recall that the software process begins with conceptual models that are eventually transformed into formal models. In some cases, the conceptual and formal models are essentially the same. For example, if one were building a compiler, the programming language would be defined formally; if one were developing a communication protocol, one might want first to define an abstract model of that protocol. In both these instances, the output of the requirements analysis process could be a model that prescribes reification (i.e., a formal model).

As it turns out, we also can be taught to recognize formality as we carry out requirements analysis. That is, we can learn to express our conceptual models formally (as we do when we translate a computational problem into an algebraic statement). Once we have the necessary skills, we can represent the behaviors of the target product prescriptively rather than just descriptively. The obvious advantage of a formal representation is that it has the potential for automating the preservation of behaviors and the identification of errors. Of course, that is precisely why we insist on formal definitions for high-level languages. To illustrate this, consider how FORTRAN II processed its subscripts in the late 1950s and early 1960s. At the time, the concept of the high-level language was new, and extensions to the basic constructs were treated on an ad hoc basis. In FORTRAN II, therefore, all array subscripts were expected to match the pattern $[a*]b[+c]$. Thus, $X(3*I+2)$ was a valid term, but $X(2+I*3)$ was not. FORTRAN IV corrected this deficiency by defining the subscript to be an expression, and then both representations were allowed. The point is, without the underlying abstractions and formalisms, languages exhibit anomalous behaviors. Moreover, lacking an unambiguous definition, different compilers produce different responses to identical inputs.

Today we expect formal definitions for our programming languages. But can we have formal definitions for the systems that we are to program? The answer is a qualified "yes," and this brief section suggests how this is being done. The reader should be aware that some formal systems have been in production use for a decade, and they are proving to be effective. Nevertheless, considerable training is required before one can apply a formal method, and most work in formal specifications still is carried out in research settings. Because an example would extend this chapter to a truly unmanageable size, I shall do little more than describe the general intent of the formal methods. Cohen, Harwood, and Jackson have written a brief and very readable introduction to formal specifications, and they illustrate three different methods with a unified case study [CoHJ86].

Figure 2.24 provides a framework for understanding the different approaches to software specifications. At the left there is a scale for languages that goes from natural (e.g., the spoken languages) to artificial (e.g., musical and mathematical notations). The figure on the right represents specification categories. At the top is the natural language (i.e., text-only) form, and at the bottom are two classes of formal specification. The operational specification concentrates on establishing a representation for the software behavior so that responses to system inputs can be demonstrated. Often there is an interpreter for the operational (or executable) specification that permits one to experiment with the prototype design [Zave84]. The mathematical specifications, on the other hand, focus more on the properties and constraints that the product must preserve. (This is the orientation of the Cohen, Harwood, and Jackson book.) In reality, the distinctions between these two classes are less dramatic than the diagram might suggest.

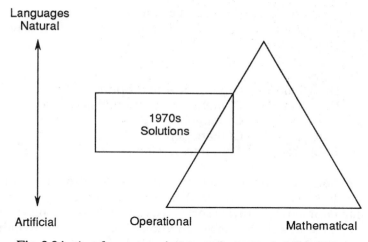

Fig. 2.24. A software requirements framework (after Zave).

The box in the middle of the specification triangle represents the solutions of the 1970s. These, of course, are the practices of the 1980s described in this book. These practices were a reaction to the difficulties of working with textual requirements. The written documents were too long, full of inconsistencies, and ineffective in communicating concepts. The result was a requirements document that was both inherently flawed (e.g., it lacked important definitions and contained contradictions) and invalid (i.e., it failed to express what the sponsor truly needed). There were two distinct responses to this need to improve the specifications. One was the use of diagrammatic techniques to clarify analysis decisions and facilitate exchanges with the sponsors and users. Several of the methods described in Section 2.3.2 belong to this category; others will be presented in more detail in Chapter 3. Each of these methods began as a manual process; automation (normally in the form of a computer-aided software engineering, or CASE, tool) was introduced later to facilitate the drafting functions and to perform some of the consistency testing. Nevertheless, the thrust of these solutions was to create systematic procedures and associated representations to reduce the textual overhead, thereby improving comprehension and communication.

The second reaction to this difficulty of working with textual documents was an attempt to embody parts of the requirement in a form amenable to automated analysis. The Problem Statement Language/Problem Statement Analyzer (PSL/PSA), developed by Teichroew, is one of the best known exemplars of this approach [TeHe77]. PSL provided the analyst with a mechanism for identifying the processes, their characteristics, and principal interactions. It supported a very simple syntax that could be used to specify the essential objects in a system along with their relationships. For example, one might define

Check-in
    Description:    Logs in new and updated CIs
    Receives:    CI-materials, Version-instructions
    Derives:    CI-version
    Part of:    CI-manager
    Subparts:    Compute-version,...

CI-materials, Version-instructions, etc. would also be defined in a similar fashion. PSA would then analyze the database to identify missing information, provide sorted lists and pictorial displays, and print the available descriptive documentation. The Software Requirements Engineering Methodology (SREM) of TRW is an extension of this same approach [Alfo77]. It has a Requirements Statement Language (RSL), a requirements network modeling tool (R-Nets), and a Requirements Engineering Modeling System (REMS). Like PSA/PSL, it can produce error checks and documentation summaries.

Each of these "1970s solutions" was designed to counter the ambiguity, inconsistency, and incompleteness of the textual requirements document. Yet *none* was formal in the sense that this section uses the term. Each represented a nonintegrated adjunct to the requirements document and the system derived from it. By nonintegrated I mean that one could make changes to the requirements document without having those changes reflected in the associated diagrams and automated representations, and vice versa. These new tools proved to be valuable as a means for analyzing, understanding, and explaining. But they simply augment the written specification, and their formality is limited. In fact, the automated tools just cited (e.g., PSL/PSA, SREM, and the CASE drafting tools) plus the techniques described in Sections 2.3.1 and 2.3.2 are really just refinements in the textual (i.e., descriptive) requirements specification. Moreover, there is no way in which they can be extended to serve as formal (i.e., prescriptive) specifications. And that is why it is so difficult to shift from the current tradition of program design with informal specifications to the rigorous development of programs that satisfy a formal specification. In our present paradigm, formality is delayed until the coding stage; consequently, we rely on judgment and heuristics to ensure that the products satisfy their requirements.

Now that I have told you what a formal method is *not*, I next observe that there are several different categories of formal method. In the *axiomatic* (or algebraic) approach, the specifications are given in terms of axioms that define relationships and operators. The system is then specified in terms of these operations. This is the underlying strategy used with the *abstract data type* to be discussed in Chapter 4. Other methods are intended to manage concurrency in a system. The *Communicating Sequential Process* (CSP) technique of Hoare is one such example, and his book provides an excellent introduction to his view of formal development [Hoar85]. Finally, there are a variety of model-based specification techniques in which the specification provides an explicit model of the target system in terms of either abstract or concrete primitives. I will illustrate this with the *Vienna Development Method* (VDM), which has been used in real projects for over a decade. Other model-based formalisms include *Z* (given the European pronunciation of "zed") [MoSu84, Haye87, Spiv89] and *GIST* (which specifies systems using the operational approach) [Wile82].[7]

VDM was developed at the IBM Vienna Research Laboratories during the 1970s, and the method has since been extended to support the entire process from specification to implementation. The method has been described by Jones and Bjørner in [Jone80], [BjJo82], and [Jone86b], and there are reports on projects in which it was used in [CoHJ86], [Bjør87], and [HeIn88]. Briefly, the VDM specification consists of two major parts.

- The definition of the internal state of the system as a number of abstract variables and types.

- The definition of the operations and functions that act on that state.

I shall sketch out a VDM specification informally without first introducing the notation or conventions. The goal simply is to offer an intuitively acceptable introduction to the topic. I shall model (a part of) the configuration item control software.

I begin with a state definition in which the only things of concern are the configuration items and, for those undergoing modification, the persons to whom they were assigned. The state model is shown in figure 2.25. Notice the convention that the sets use uppercase only, and the type names have an initial uppercase letter followed by lowercase letters. In this state we define the set of configuration items CIS to be of type Config, which is composed of two variables, CI-ID and CI-BODY. CI-ID is of type Cid which, as is shown at the bottom, is of the primitive type

---

[7]Special issues of *Software* and *Computer* were devoted to software development using formal methods. In these companion issues, Gerhart provides a general introduction to the theme [Gerh90], and Wing contributes a more formal overview [Wing90]. Each paper in these collections either reviews the role of formal methods in development or provides an example of their use.

```
State ::    CIS          :Config /* The configuration items */
            ASSIGN       :Assign /* CI-developer assignments */

            Config ::    CI-ID        :Cid
                         CI-BODY      :P-file

            Assign     = Cid → Developer
            Cid        = Text
            Developer  = /* a set of authorized developer ids */
```

Fig. 2.25. VDM state model for SCM example.

Text. The type of CI-BODY is also of a primitive type, in this case the type that defines a program file (P-file, assumed here to be a system-wide definition). ASSIGN, the second state variable, is of type Assign, which is defined as a mapping from one type to another. That is, we have defined the state so that the assignments are preserved as maps from an item of type Cid to one of type Developer, which is defined as a set of authorized identifiers. Because a mapping is a function, no CI can be assigned to more than one developer in this model.

In a certain sense, the state model just described is similar to the data models that were presented in Section 2.3.1. The major difference is that the earlier models were intended first to gain an understanding of the target system and then to establish a foundation for the design. Here, the formal definition establishes the exact relationships to be implemented. Methods such as ERM are intended to accommodate some fuzziness in their descriptions of large systems. Formal methods such as VDM, on the other hand, require precision and completeness; often the price that they pay for this is a loss of succinctness. Thus, what we are doing in this section is recording what we already have decided about the application to be implemented. (In fact, the conclusions used here may have been arrived at by using the techniques described earlier.) The objective now is to have a precise definition that will allow us to recognize inconsistencies and preserve correctness.

To continue with the illustration, all systems must have a set of invariant state conditions that is always true. In this example we might establish the restriction that the domain of Assign must be a subset of that of Config (i.e., no CIs can be assigned to a developer unless they are already in the system). This state invariant would be described in the VDM notation. Once the state has been specified, operations on it may be defined. For example, there must be an operator that establishes the state for a new configuration management system. Naturally, we would want that operator to be available only to authorized developers.

INIT (MANAGER: Developer)

/* Initializes CM system */

**ext** CIS          :**wr** Config
       ASSIGN     :**wr** Assign

**pre**     has-privilege (manager)

**post**    config' = [] $\wedge$ assign' = []

has-privilege:   Developer $\rightarrow$ Bool
has-privilege $\triangleq$ /* defined as a system-wide function */

Fig. 2.26. The INIT operator.

Figure 2.26 defines the INIT operator that tests for authorization and initializes the variables CIS and ASSIGN as empty.

In this definition the variable MANAGER of type Developer is supplied. The **ext** indicates that the definitions for CIS and ASSIGN are external to this operation. The **wr**, however, indicates that the operation may alter the state of (i.e., write to) the identified variables. The actual operation is defined in terms of a precondition (**pre**), which must be true if the operator is to become active, and a postcondition (**post**), which must be true after the operator is complete. Here the precondition is that the value for manager be that of a developer with the manager privilege. The function that determines this, has-privilege, is defined in the specification's last two lines. The first line indicates the domain and range, and the second line establishes transformation. In this example, I have used a comment to indicate that some external system-level function will be required. The post condition is that the state for both the variables after the operation (as signified by the prime) be empty (i.e., =[]). Observe how this specification models what the INIT operation does without in any way indicating how it should do it.

Finally, consider a slightly more interesting operation: one that checks out a CI and assigns it to a developer as shown in Figure 2.27. In the CHECKOUT operation, a CI and developer are provided. (I assume that only authorized users have access to this operation.) The general structure is the same as for INIT. Here only read access is required to CIS. The precondition is that the CI not already be assigned. The postcondition indicates that after the operation the state of ASSIGN

CHECKOUT (C: Cid, D: Developer)

/* Checks out a CI by assigning it to a developer */

| **ext** | CIS | :**rd** Config |
| | ASSIGN | :**wr** Assign |

**pre**     c $\notin$ **dom** assign

**post**    assign' = assign † [c → d]

Fig. 2.27. The CHECKOUT operator.

(with the prime) is the state before the operation (without the prime) with the mapping c → d added (actually, overloaded).

Now that the state and operations have been defined, we have an obligation to prove that the state invariant cannot be violated as the result of the system invoking any of its operations. We do this in a *rigorous* rather than fully formal manner. That is, we do not attempt to produce a mathematically exact proof; instead we go through the rigorous process of establishing that such a proof could be produced. For example, to verify the CHECKOUT operation, we would need to show

**pre**-CHECKOUT ∧ invariant-state(s) ∧ **post**-CHECKOUT → invariant-state(s').

Once we have carried out this proof, we are confident that our model of the CM system preserves the correctness of the initial definitions. The specification and design process then is repeated at successively lower levels of detail until a complete implementation results.

It should be obvious from even this watered-down description of VDM that the use of a formal modeling method is quite different from the techniques with which most developers are familiar. Because software engineering always involves groups of people working together, no general textbook can provide more than an introduction to the concepts involved. Learning how to use VDM (or Z or GIST, etc.) usually involves working with experienced leaders. The orientation is so different that competence requires training with an informed feedback. Nevertheless, the approach is very important, and it is reasonably certain that its use will advance over time. Therefore, it is instructive to examine what these formal techniques contribute and to survey their strengths and weaknesses.

Recall that there are two dimensions to quality: validation (is this the right system) and verification (is the system right). The formal specification extends the level of the formal models so that we begin with a reference point that defines what the system must do (rather than just what the programs do). There are methods and tools (such as the rigorous proofs of VDM) to verify that no decisions violate the conditions designated in that formal model. Consequently, the implementation will be correct with respect to its requirements specification. In other words, *the system will always be right.* Conditions that might lead to a failure in verification include massive specification definitions that make rigor unwieldy, improperly trained developers, etc. Such problems, however, can be resolved by means of automated support and more experience with the methods. From a theoretical perspective, formal methods are the only way to guarantee correctness, and there now is an emphasis on rectifying the deficiencies of the present support environments. Once this is accomplished, dissemination of the formal approach should accelerate.

The problem of validation, however, is more persistent. When I started this section, I observed that this was an appropriate technique for certain domains. Moreover, I gave several citations to show that VDM has indeed been used outside a research setting. But the issue remains, how do the formalisms help us go from fuzzy to clear thinking? For some applications, forcing us to think about the problem in new, and abstract terms forces us into a better understanding. In other areas, such as security and concurrency, we can reason about behaviors only in the abstract; we lack "natural insights" and can understand the problem only by reference to formal models. Still, the fact remains that many formal systems sacrifice our intuitive insights in order to achieve an unambiguous and complete specification. As a result, they increase the risk of delivering a correct, but invalid product. Of course, this tension between verification and validation is not unique to the formal methods; it is simply that the abstractness of the formalisms can make it more difficult to recognize whether this is the right system.

In summary, the development of formal methods and support environments is an active area of research, and software engineers are certain to have increasing exposure to them. As every proponent of a formal method will testify, the methods are not complete unto themselves. Designers still will need to use many of the tools and techniques that are described in this book. And that is my justification for asking you to read on.

## 2.3.4. Textual specifications

This section describes the form and contents of a written requirements specification. In the documentation chain, this is probably the most important document.  It serves as a "contract" between the purchaser and the developer and defines *exactly* what the delivered software product should do.  Exactly is the critical word here; it implies that if the software product is to have some property, then the specification must contain the criteria to determine whether that property is provided.  Terms such as "user friendly," "reliable," and "responsive" are imprecise descriptors with little value.

There are many standards for a software requirements specification (SRS) document, and I shall review one.  However, before starting on the SRS, it is important to determine why one is necessary.  (In other words, how will it be used?  It follows that if it will not be used, it is not necessary.)  To begin with, observe that there is a spectrum of project types (ranging from well defined and highly constrained to poorly understood and unconstrained) and a variety of development settings (including internal development, personal assignments, and contracted work).  For example, if the sponsor requires a programming system that can be developed by an individual familiar with the project over a six-month period (something that I have called a small project), then it may be appropriate for the sponsor to call in the developer, explain what is required, and conclude the conversation with, "You know what I want, don't you?"  Here it may be practical to limit the SRS to a small (5 page) document that describes the developer's understanding of the problem and outlines the particular approach to be taken in its solution.  The designer subsequently may implement some rapid prototypes that help explain how the software product will work; using the feedback from those prototypes, he will extend his description of what the system is to do (and how it will be implemented).

This approach, however, would be unacceptable with a large (say 100 effort-year) embedded application.  Here, it is necessary to understand all the interfaces with precision and understand the obligations that the resulting software must satisfy.  It is highly unlikely that any one individual will "know what the sponsor wants," and the cost for error repair can be very high.  Considerable effort must be expended before one can produce an SRS that defines *what* is to be built; obviously, design decisions should be deferred until the SRS is complete.

Two different projects involve two contrasting views of the SRS.  In preparing an SRS (or any software documentation for that matter), the following questions ought to be asked:

- What is the *function* of the document?  In the first example, the function was twofold.  First, it was an exercise for the developer to formalize his concepts and express them effectively and succinctly.  The second objective was to communicate this understanding to the sponsor and validate that the initial understandings were the same.  In the second case, the SRS is a "build-to" document that describes what should be delivered, how it must behave, and how it must interface with the devices external to the software. With 100 effort-years devoted to this project, it is important to resolve the details of what is to be built before that building begins.

- What is the *uncertainty* in the project? Clearly, one would not expect to prepare a very detailed SRS for a project that was poorly understood. Remember, the software product is expected to provide a valid solution to a real problem; the product should not simply be an implementation that is correct with respect to the SRS. In general, the SRS should describe only the *essential features* of the target system. In an underconstrained application, such as the SCM system that we are using as the case study, it will be sufficient to detail *what* the system must do and allow the designers to determine *how* the system works. With well-defined or overconstrained applications, however, it is essential that the SRS contain everything that is fixed, known, and agreed to.

- What is the *management view* of the document? Management has responsibility for resources such as designer effort, contracts, computer equipment, software products, and operational expenses. The SRS may be an important factor in making a decision about committing resources. For example, in the small project, the management decision may have been made to commit six months of effort on this task before it was assigned to the developer. Consequently, the SRS and subsequent documents ought to focus on clarifying the technical issues. In the large-project example, the SRS should reflect a complete and careful analysis that improves management confidence prior to contract commitment.

- Who are the *readers* of the document? The formality of a document will depend in part on how it is used and who will read it. If an SRS is to be read by sponsors, it should use a vocabulary that the sponsors understand. Obviously, the objective is to communicate with the readers, and not to dazzle them with buzz words and esoteric observations. If the document is intended for other computer specialists, then it should define the sponsor's vocabulary and thereby establish a standard that all can follow. If this is a small project, then the most important reader will be the SRS author. As development continues, it is common to lose sight of the agreed-on objectives. A review of the SRS will reorient the reader and identify areas that require discussion with the sponsor.

- What are the *local conventions* that the document should follow? In most organizations there are established standards or conventions for document preparation. Unfortunately, in many instances these standards are too informal (actually bordering on nonexistent); in other cases they may be very exact (and sometimes even excessive). The software engineer has an obligation to work within his organization to achieve an appropriate level of documentation for the range of tasks that the organization undertakes. Too little documentation is unprofessional and invites disaster; too much documentation transfers energy from the problem-solving task to a mechanical and unrewarding activity. Each organization must determine what is best for it, and each software engineer is expected to respond to that definition and its refinement.

The underlying message of what I have just written is that we require flexibility in deciding what to include in an SRS. The discussion should not be taken to suggest that we do not always need to have an SRS (or some other document). Documentation is the most important product that a software engineer produces. In fact, the program that represents the product's implementation is only a special kind of document. (That is why it is referred to as program text.) Most of software engineering involves communication with domain specialists, among designers, and with oneself over time. The document forces one to express one's concepts clearly, and it provides a permanent record. Both the process and the product (i.e., both the act of producing a document and the document itself) are important. Thus, these comments should be interpreted as a recognition that we require flexibility in determining the kind of documentation that we produce, but we do need documentation.

There are several standards for software documentation. The Department of Defense has different standards for the documents to be delivered with various classes of product. If the software engineer is working on such a project, then he will be aware of those requirements. In this book I will use the standards developed by the Institute of Electrical and Electronics Engineers (IEEE). As with most standards developed by the IEEE, committees of volunteers are set up to establish the standard. After many reviews, both among committee members and interested outsiders, a standard is adopted. The objective is to formalize a consensus to which all will conform. In some highly technical areas, proprietary interests may favor the inclusion or exclusion of certain features. (For example, the standard for an operating system will meet considerable resistance if it favors the architecture of one vendor while omitting the capabilities of another vendor's product.) Of course, documentation standards, such as IEEE 830 for a Software

Requirements Specification, are not subject to such problems.

Documentation standards are not "standards" in the sense of one for an electronic interface connector. Actually, they are guidelines that justify the need for the document, describe the process of its creation and use, and offer formats for its contents. It is assumed, consistent with the previous discussion of this section, that the document will be adjusted to meet the project's needs. Before describing the formats suggested for the SRS, let me point out that the SRS is but one document in a much larger document chain. Thus, it ought to be considered in the context of those other documents and not in isolation. Among the most common of these documents are

- *Plans*. Plans are necessary before a project (or one of its phases) begins. The objective of a plan is to lay out the activity in some preliminary detail and to establish the standards that will be followed. One of the greatest benefits of a plan is the thought that goes into it. We plan in order to anticipate problems and make mistakes when correcting them is still inexpensive. In that sense, the SRS is a kind of plan for the project. In a large project there will be a project plan, staffing plans, a configuration management plan, a testing plan, and so on. Some plans will simply be a pro forma adaptation of plans used for previous projects; other plans will be the result of intensive analysis and risk trade-off. All are important.

- *Software Requirements Specification*. This, of course, is the topic of the present section. Depending on the product, it may be considered a refinement of some larger system requirements specification. As described here, it is the single source for determining what the delivered software product will do. In effect, the software designer has the freedom to interpret these requirements any way he desires as long as the finished product delivers everything that is explicitly specified and does not include any explicitly forbidden features. Fortunately, the designers temper their freedom with common sense.

- *Software Design Specification*. This is the highest level specification that details how the product will be organized to satisfy the requirements. As will be described in the next chapter, there are several methods for doing the design, and the design specifications should be organized to reflect the way in which the design actually is derived. Although it may not be immediately apparent, all document standards provide sufficient flexibility to describe the design in a meaningful fashion. Again, documentation is both a helpful and useful product; if its format or organization does not satisfy pragmatic objectives, then it should be changed. Developing software is difficult enough without burdening it with abstract exercises of undetermined value.

- *Detailed Design Specifications.* Whereas the previous specifications were organized around the project, these specifications are linked to the individual products to be developed. Again, the form of the design documents should match the methods chosen for establishing the design. In general, the two levels of design specification share two common objectives. First, during the design activity, they serve as a mechanism to record (and have others review) the design decisions as they are being formulated. Second, after the design is complete and the product has been installed, the design specifications describe the product. Recall that twice as much money will be spent on maintaining the software product than was spent on its initial design; therefore, the design specifications are a very important part of the delivered product. This longer term use should be kept in mind as design specifications are being written. They should describe effectively, provide "road maps" as needed, and not burden the reader with excessive details that are available from other documents (or code).

- *Testing Plans and Specifications.* The process of testing was described in Chapter 1 as being the inverse of the design process. During design, one begins with a single product (whose requirements are detailed in the SRS), and breaks it down into many smaller parts until, ultimately, the programs are created. Testing involves the certification of these individual programs and their integration as successively larger units (which also must be certified) until only the system exists. For each of these tests there must be a test plan that states what is to be tested and how, a test set to be used during the test, and a report that certifies that the test was successful so the next testing step can begin. Because the SRS is the only document that specifies what the delivered software product must do, it is the single source for preparing the final acceptance (or system) test.

Returning to the Software Requirements Specification, the format defined in IEEE 830 suggests it be organized in five sections. The first of these contains the introduction, which includes

- *Purpose.* This describes the general purpose of the software product. It should be a brief description intended to convey the general functionality to be provided in the context of its use.

- *Scope.* This describes the scope of the product with respect to the larger environment in which it is used.

- *Definitions, Acronyms, and Abbreviations.* This establishes the vocabulary to be used throughout this document. Where ambiguity exists, even common terms can be included. The material presented here can be augmented by an appended glossary.

- *References.* This is a list of other documents that either provide definitions or contribute to the understanding of the specification.

- *Overview.* This is a brief but informative overview of the software to be developed. It represents the most important concise source for understanding what the software product does.

Although many persons naively think of the Introduction Section of the SRS as being "boilerplate" to be copied from other sources as rapidly as possible, it is perhaps one of the most useful parts of the specification. It establishes a framework for all that follows; it helps sponsors, designers, testers, users, and maintainers organize their mental models about the product. An organization may restructure or combine the introduction segments, but the topics covered must present an effective preamble that informs and communicates.

The second section of the SRS provides a more detailed introduction to the product in each of a number of specific categories. Naturally, the categories may vary with the product, but IEEE 830 suggests the following organization for this section.

    2  General Description
      2.1  Product Perspective
      2.2  Product Functions
      2.3  User Characteristics
      2.4  General Constraints
      2.5  Assumptions and Dependencies

The third section, Specific Requirements, represents the details of the specification. The standard proposes two alternative formats. The first format is most effective for projects in which there are relatively few system interfaces and they are not associated with specific functions. In this case, the specification uses the following format.

3   Specific Requirements
3.1 Functional Requirements
    3.1.1   Functional Requirement 1
       3.1.1.1 Introduction
       3.1.1.2 Inputs
       3.1.1.3 Processing
       3.1.1.4 Outputs
    3.1.2   Functional Requirement 2

    ...
    3.1.$n$   Functional Requirement $n$
3.2 External Interface Requirements
    3.2.1   User Interfaces
    3.2.2   Hardware Interfaces
    3.2.3   Software Interfaces
    3.2.4   Communication Interfaces
3.3 Performance Requirements
3.4 Design Constraints
    3.4.1   Standards Compliance
    3.4.2   Hardware Limitations

    ...
3.5 Attributes
    3.5.1   Security
    3.5.2   Maintainability

    ...
3.6 Other Requirements
    3.6.1   Database
    3.6.2   Operations
    3.6.3   Site Adaption

    ...

The alternative format is used for applications in which the interfaces tend to be associated with functions. Here, the interfaces become part of the functional requirements as follows:

3.1.1   Functional Requirement 1
    3.1.1.1 Specification
       3.1.1.1.1   Introduction
       3.1.1.1.2   Inputs
       3.1.1.1.3   Processing
       3.1.1.1.4   Outputs
    3.1.1.2 External Interfaces
       3.1.1.2.1   User Interfaces
       3.1.1.2.2   Hardware Interfaces
       3.1.1.2.3   Software Interfaces
       3.1.1.2.4   Communication Interfaces
3.1.2  Functional Requirement 2
...

The final two sections of the SRS are the appendices and an index.

To illustrate how the SRS for the SCM might look, Sections 1 and 2 would provide an overview of the SCM software system. Notice that much of the analysis in the earlier part of this chapter has been concerned with something much broader than just the SCM software system. To understand the system, we first needed to model the host environment. Thus, for example, the SADT flow described in Figure 2.18 depicted the processing of a CI; it did not concentrate on what the automated portions of the SCM would do. Now that we have established a model for the environment in which the SCM software system will operate, we can narrow in on what occurs within that system boundary. Consequently, the SRS will specify only the features of the software product that we intend to build. When we talk of product functions in Section 2.2 of the SRS, we detail only the *software product* functions; we do not describe how the entire SCM operates. In the same way, SRS Section 2.3 defines the characteristics of the SCM software users. In this case, there are casual users (the CCB), dedicated users (the data entry clerks), and programmer users (who receive and submit CIs for update); this characterization of the users' needs will help the designers. We should not include descriptions of persons who interact with the SCM system but not the software (e.g., the customers who submit CRs). They are outside the system boundary as we have defined it, and we want the SRS to focus on only the system to be implemented.

Most of the information in the SRS is documented in Section 3. Section 3.1 might identify the following six functional requirements:

- *Preliminary processing.* This involves the initial processing of the change requests and their disposition. The inputs are changes and priority information, the processing is data entry support, and the outputs are file updates and messages.

- *Detailed analysis.* This involves the identification of the actions required and the CIs affected. The inputs are messages, the processing is the recording of decisions, and the outputs are file updates and messages.

- *Release for change.* This involves the release of CIs for modification. The inputs are authorizations, the processes include releasing and flagging, and the outputs are copies of CIs.

- *Audit change.* This involves the return of changed CIs for version update. The inputs are requests to update and authorizations for update, the process include update and flagging, and the output is an updated configuration.

- *Management review.* This involves the reporting of SCM status. The inputs are requests, the processes consist of report preparations and retrievals, and the outputs are status reports and information.

- *Configuration manufacture.* This involves the manufacture of a configuration from an existing configuration. Inputs are messages, processing entails the preparation of configuration building instructions and their execution, and the outputs are new configurations.

Having identified the major functional requirements, the analyst must next provide the details. The introduction section would be descriptive, and each of the following sections would be precise and independently numbered. For example, the inputs might be identified as

3.1.1.2.1  Change Requests. (A description of the form and its principal contents.)

3.1.1.2.2  Software Incident Report.

3.1.1.2.3  Emergency Priority Statement.

. . . .

Processing would be defined similarly. For example, Section 3.1.1.3.1 might detail the requirements for entering a CR. It would specify only what is essential; it would not describe how the interface operated *unless it was necessary that the SCM software system interface operated in that manner.* Care must be taken to avoid specifying implementation details. For example, the CR contents have been defined external to the software system as shown in Figure 2.2. Section 3.1.1.2.1 will reference that form and identify the data items that are important from the perspective of the SCM software system. It should identify which elements are to be processed, and a subsequent output section (e.g., 3.1.1.4.1) would specify which data elements are to be saved in a file. But the SRS must not define the format for that file. We know, for example, that there is a requirement for the software system to associate a three-valued priority with each active CR. The internal formats of the priority codes and the CR file structure, however, are design decisions; they do not belong in an SRS. Notice too that each paragraph is directed to a very specific topic. This makes the SRS a little difficult to read, but it does facilitate modification and the association of SRS requirements with the software units that detail or realize them (i.e., tracing).

Section 3.2 of the SRS defines the interfaces between the SCM software system and its operational setting. In the HHI example, we will be using an off-the-shelf computer system. If we know what it is and which of its facilities that we expect to use (e.g., its logon security control), then we ought to specify that here. If HHI plans to have the SCM system ported to other platforms, then that too should be spelled out. But if the promotion of the SCM system as a commercial product is only a pipe dream, then the SRS should not discuss the possibility. Although there should be no secrets from the designers, we must also avoid the opposite extreme of providing vague or irrelevant information. Section 3.3, on performance requirements, must be specific and verifiable; otherwise it will suffice to state, "The system must respond." The design constraints section (3.4) normally will augment or reference internal standards documents or a project-specific plan. Section 3.5.1, security, could simply indicate that vendor-supplied logon facilities shall suffice. If the specifier asked for more, there would be an obligation to demonstrate that the finished product delivered what was specified. (Although it might be reasonable to request an extra level of security for a highly sensitive, potentially hostile software setting, such a requirement would be inappropriate for an internal SCM system.) Finally, there always will be some category called "other." In this case it identifies features such as an external database that the system requires (e.g., a file identifying the authorized designers may be made available to the SCM system by some external system). Operations and site adaption would probably not apply to an SCM system that is to be installed on existing equipment.

Returning to the general discussion of IEEE 830, let me again emphasize the significance of the descriptive text. Earlier I pointed out the importance of the communications role of the introduction. Of course, this is not restricted to just the first section; it is equally important throughout the document. The fragmentation of the SRS into highly specialized paragraphs tends to obscure the holistic nature of the product being specified. Lucid commentary is needed to orient the reader. After all, of what value is an unambiguous specification when it is misinterpreted in the context of a naive theory? I also have indicated that the document format includes alternatives and ellipses. Clearly, the SRS contents must be adjusted to the needs of the project. It is useful to have a standard that offers a guideline and provides a checklist for essential topics; we should not have to reinvent the wheel. Nevertheless, it would be foolish to use any standard as a rigid template for entering a series of "not applicable" entries (or even worse, paragraphs of meaningless text). Finally, it important to restate that, although the SRS is intended to specify *what* is to be done, its very format may suggest *how* the product will be implemented. That is, the Functional Requirements sections may be interpreted as modules with inputs, processes, outputs, and external interfaces. *However, that is not the intent of the SRS.* The SRS should not be seen as (or written as if it were) a Software Design Specification. The analyst must avoid presenting the requirements as implying a design.

The SRS instructions help isolate the statement of needs from those descriptions that might suggest how the needs can be met. IEEE 830, for example, offers the following guidance for emphasizing the requirements objectives rather than the design implications (as adapted from [Post85]).

- *Unambiguous.* Every statement should have only one interpretation. This implies that every characteristic of the final product is described with a single term. Where the meaning of the term can vary in different contexts, its alternative uses must be described in the glossary.

- *Complete.* Here completeness is defined as possessing the following attributes: All significant requirements are included, whether relating to functionality, performance, design constraints, interfaces, etc. Software responses are defined for all realizable classes of input (including invalid inputs). The document conforms to all standards it references. All paragraphs, figures, and tables are properly labeled and consistently referenced; in particular, there are no TBDs (i.e., "to be defined").

- *Verifiable.* The specification is verifiable if and only if all its requirements are verifiable in the sense that there is a cost-effective mechanism to determine if the software product meets that requirement. This implies quantifiable characteristics that can be verified. The requirement, "The CM shall implement the version control identification scheme detailed in Reference *n*" can be verified if the referenced document is explicit. "User response time shall not exceed 2 seconds" may be very difficult to verify, but "User response shall be demonstrated to be less than 2 seconds for 95% of the interactions measured over a four-hour period" can be verified more easily. The fundamental rule for verification is: If there is no subjective test to confirm that a desired feature was delivered, it should not have been asked for in the first place.

- *Consistent.* This is defined as the absence of conflicts or contradictions. Examples can be as simple as the use of different terms for the same action or item (e.g., calling a CI the "program text" in one section and the "source program" in another) or as basic as having two requirements contradict each other (e.g., the requirements for processing CRs state that only customers can submit changes and also that designers can submit CRs for no-cost changes).

- *Modifiable.* This property implies the ability to make changes that are complete, verifiable, and consistent. To do this, the SRS must have a clear structure with a table of contents and index. The contents should avoid redundancy; redundancy, while not an error, makes modification more difficult and error prone.

- *Traceable.* The SRS is traceable if each referenced requirement is uniquely identified so that one may map properties of the delivered product into requirements of the SRS, and vice versa. Traceability and verifiability are the key determinants of the contents of the software test plan. There are two types of traceability. Backward traceability refers to requirements identified in a referenced document (e.g., how CI version numbers are defined), and forward traceability indicates links to design specifications that will implement the requirement (e.g., module X implements the function described in SRS paragraph *x*, which references specific features regarding how CI version numbers are defined).

- *Usable during the operation and maintenance phase.* Although the SRS is being described in the context of starting a project, it is important to recognize that its value does not diminish once the design is complete. The SRS is the most complete and concise description of the software product. Its life extends well beyond that of the development cycle, and it should be written (and updated) with that in mind.

To ensure that the SRS contains these properties, the analysts (and their managers) must systematically review it for completeness. The document should include or reference the models described earlier in this chapter, and the models must be checked to ensure that the requirements they imply are properly expressed in the text. The documentation style should facilitate both understanding and traceability. In general, the requirements of Section 3 are best expressed in paragraphs composed of lists of simple sentences. The vocabulary should be limited to verbs and nouns that are understood in the context of the SRS, and the vocabulary should avoid terms that are not readily understood by the users (e.g., avoid programming terms). Finally, the specifications should describe actions and items that are external to the product; internal actions, of course, are to be established during the design.

Figure 2.28 provides a different description of the properties of a satisfactory software specification. Prepared by Boehm, this taxonomy augments the properties of completeness, consistency, and testability (verifiability) with the issue of feasibility: have we specified all the necessary characteristics, and are we satisfied that the product can be

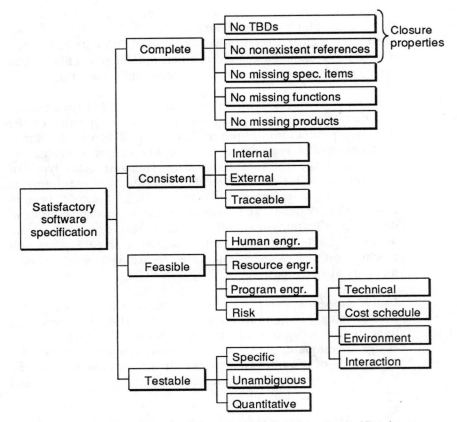

Fig. 2.28. Taxonomy of a satisfactory software specification.
(Reprinted from [Boeh84] with permission, ©1984, IEEE.)

developed as specified? Finally, Meyer identifies "The seven sins of the specifier" (obviously to be avoided), and I close this discussion by sharing his classification scheme [Meye85, p. 7].

- *Noise.* The presence in the text of an element that does not carry information relevant to any feature of the problem. Variants: *redundancy; remorse.*

- *Silence.* The existence of a feature of the problem that is not covered by any element in the text.

- *Overspecification.* The presence in the text of an element that corresponds not to a feature of the problem but to features of a possible solution.

- *Contradiction.* The presence in the text of two or more elements that define a feature of the system in an incompatible way.

- *Ambiguity.* The presence in the text of an element that makes it possible to interpret a feature of the problem in at least two ways.

- *Forward reference.* The presence in the text of an element that uses features of the problem not defined until later in the text.

- *Wishful thinking.* The presence in the text of an element that defines a feature of the problem in such a way that a candidate solution cannot realistically be validated with respect to this feature.

## 2.4.    Implicit requirements

Section 2.3 focused on modeling techniques that help us establish and document what we expect the product to do.  In effect, it was concerned with *a particular product* (as distinct from all other products).   Of course, the requirements specification did not detail every function to be supported by the product.   To do so would have been considered overspecification.   We only specified what was *essential* to the system. Decisions about many features were deferred as design considerations. For example, in the Software Requirements Specification (SRS) we indicated that the software configuration management (SCM) system must allow for version updates to the configuration items (CIs), and there was a reference to a report that detailed the version numbering convention to be used.  That was important to the SCM system, and so it was included in the SRS.  We would expect every SCM built to those specifications to follow that convention.  The method used to enter a CI version change, however, was not considered important.  Therefore, it was not included in the SRS.  In effect, it was left to the designer to decide how the user would interact with this part of the system.  Of course, the SRS could have constrained how changes should be entered. For example, it might have specified that all software shall interface using a mouse and windows.  This would have restricted the number of possible designs (i.e., the design or solution space); nevertheless, many different interfaces still would satisfy that requirement.

The point is that the SRS identifies only those characteristics to be included in every delivered product that meets its specifications.  The fewer the stated requirements, the more flexibility the designers have, and, consequently, the more likely that they will be able to produce a satisfactory product.  Naturally, with too much freedom, the designers may misunderstand the problem and deliver a product that meets the specification but does not correspond to the environment's needs (i.e., not enough of the essential requirements were identified and delivered). Thus, the analysts must learn to specify enough for the designers to understand both what is to be delivered and how broad their design latitude is.

There is also a second dimension to what the SRS does not state; it consists of the requirements that are assumed to be included according to the conventional standards of practice. In effect, they represent those requirements that all applications of this class are expected to meet, *even if the SRS does not call them out explicitly*. For instance, one would be very disappointed to receive a software product in which all the variable names were in the form Xnnnnnnn, where n is a decimal digit. However, one would feel quite silly explicitly specifying that the developers shall not use such mnemonics (even though the designers might find them meaningful).

Thus, on closer examination we see that there really are three categories of requirement.

- *Essential*. These are the requirements considered necessary for this product. They may define functions that the software must support (i.e., its behavior), nonfunctional properties of the finished system (e.g., responsiveness or sizing constraints), or external interfaces or restrictions (e.g., the use of a mouse or communication with a special device).

- *Derived*. These are product features that are derived by way of design decisions to implement the essential requirements. The division between essential and derived requirements is determined during the requirements analysis phase and is based on the experience and judgment of the analysts.

- *Implicit*. These are features to be included in all products of this general category of application, even if they are not explicitly stated. In some cases, an implicit requirement may be considered essential and explicitly presented in that category instead.

Restating this informally, the essential requirements are those that the sponsor needs to see in the requirements document, the derived requirements represent details added by the designers, and the implicit requirements are the standards followed by the design team for all products of this category. (The concept of application class is important; different categories will have different implicit requirements. For example, one would not expect the same implicit features for a real-time embedded system as for an ECP Reporting System.)

Most software engineers learn about the implicit requirements from the workplace. It usually is presented in the form of, "We always do such and such with this type of product." In time all software engineers in the organization recognize the importance of those conventions and techniques, and they become implicitly included in all the products they develop. For example, implementors with experience in interactive information systems recognize that all inputs must be tested for validity, that responses to help requests are required for all interactive transactions, etc. To the experienced developer, such features need not be called out explicitly; they are as natural as the selection of reasonable mnemonics for variable names. Of course, to inexperienced developers, this type of requirement is something to be recognized and learned.

Because the set of implicit requirements varies with the application class, it would be impossible to catalog all of them in one place. In the remainder of this section, therefore, I review two sets of generally accepted conventions that ought to be considered part of every specification. These are the practices for managing a human-computer dialogue and the factors that measure product quality.

### 2.4.1.  The user interface

Prior to the personal computer (PC) revolution, computer scientists studied the command structures of text editors. The text was interpreted on a line-by-line basis, and the concern was for the best command structure for searching, replacing, deleting, and so on. The hardware limitations had forced the user to model a document as a collection of numbered lines; consequently, the editor was visualized as a program for manipulating text lines. The mechanics of editing these lines was an extra step in the task of identifying a change and then reviewing the resulting modification. Such distractions are referred to as a *break* [Bødk89]. For example, when driving a nail with a hammer, one uses one's arm and the hammer as a tool; the focus is on the task of driving the nail. If, however, the hammer's head is not well seated and one is aware of this fact, then there is a break: the tool has become the focus rather than the task [Ehn88].[8]

After the PC became common, perceptions about the man-machine (or human-computer) interface changed. Some of this can be traced to the highly competitive market for PC software; other advances were the

---

[8]This idea of a break is derived from Heidegger's concept of a *breakdown*, in which some event forces an individual to become aware of aspects of his environment. For a very interesting discussion of this topic in the context of computers and design see [WiFl86].

result of research with personal workstations [Gold88]. In any event, hardware now is inexpensive enough to replace line editors with full-screen editors, and research in text-editing commands has been discontinued. Many tools employ "what you see is what you get," or *wysiwyg*, and Shneiderman has popularized the term *direct manipulation* for this linking of objects with their actions [Shne83]. Now, when editing a document, one simply moves the cursor to the character to be deleted and presses the delete key; the command language is implicit in the action. There are no breaks, and the model of a document as numbered lines has atrophied.

Not every application can benefit from direct manipulation, and few projects can afford to develop a direct manipulation environment if one is not already available. Thus, the message is not that all interfaces must be wysiwyg; rather, my point is that the best interfaces are those that are *natural for the task*. The technology may not be available to provide that natural interface, or the project resources may not support the development of one. Nevertheless, there are some general rules for managing the user interface so that we can minimize the number of breaks. In that sense, such rules clearly qualify as implicit requirements.

Shneiderman reduces the principles of interface design to "Eight Golden Rules" [Shne87]. These are

- *Strive for consistency.* Use consistent sequences and patterns for similar situations and actions. Use a consistent vocabulary; the same terms should be used for inputs, menus, listings, and help screens. Exceptions should be few and comprehensible (e.g., always echo inputs *except* for passwords).

- *Enable frequent users to use shortcuts.* Systems will have a range of users, and it would be short-sighted to optimize the interface for any one group. Plan an easy-to-use interface for casual (or learning) users plus abbreviations, commands, hidden keys, or macros for experienced users. Notice that, whereas naive users may view a helpful interface as an intermediary between their task and goal, experienced users may interpret that same helpfulness as a break.

- *Offer informative feedback.* For every operator there should be some system feedback. For infrequent or major actions, substantial feedback is required (e.g., a two-step delete-file process with confirmation). Naturally, the messages (or visual effects) should be informative and clear. Coded references to error message lists went out even before the line editor!

- *Design dialogues to yield closure.* Each process should be organized as a sequence with a start, middle, and end. The completion should inform the user of the action taken (or aborted); in this way, the user can move on to the next task without having to remember to complete actions from some earlier task.

- *Offer simple error handling.* To the extent possible, design the system to anticipate serious user errors. When an error is encountered, make its correction easy. For example, include tests that check for numbers in a person's name, but if a number is detected, do not force the user to reenter the entire name. Whatever the user's actions, allow for recovery to some earlier, safe state, and explain the outcome to the user.

- *Permit easy reversal of actions.* To the extent possible, allow the user to reverse (or "undo") his actions. The ability to ignore faulty actions reduces the user's fear of the consequences of an error (which represents a break). The reversal may be at the level of a single action, command, or group of actions.

- *Support internal locus of control.* By this Shneiderman means that the user should feel that he is in charge, and not the system. Avoid surprising system actions, tedious processes, or difficulty in getting the desired results. Users should be the initiators of the actions, not the responders.

- *Reduce short-term memory load.* Remember the magical number 7 ± 2, and do not expect the user to manage complex sequences. Limit what must be remembered in multiscreen scenarios by displaying context information on each screen; use clear mnemonics and sequences of action.

Notice that these rules are really guidelines. It is very difficult to specify how a human-computer interface should operate; it is much easier to establish conventions for what should be avoided. In fact, there even are dangers in the slavish conformance to any guideline. Grudin, for example, points out that there are occasions in which user interface consistency is bad; the goal of the system is to support the user in some range of activities, and the interface conventions should be varied to accommodate different tasks [Grud89]. Like most design decisions, the selection of the "best" design or interface depends on judgment and aesthetics. Even the identification of potential problems in a dialogue design can be difficult [MoNi90]. For this reason, there is interest in transferring this facet of the problem to a user-interface management system (UIMS) that allows design specialists to treat the user interface in a layered approach [HaHi89, January, 1989 special issue of *Software*].

Even though many of the properties of the user interface cannot be included as essential features in the requirements specification, there are some human factors properties of the product that can be quantified and specified explicitly. These are

- *Time to learn.* How long does it take typical target users to learn to use the product for a set of relevant tasks? To quantify this one must identify the users (e.g., secretaries, data-entry clerks, nurses) and the generic tasks (e.g., format a letter, enter a category of data, review medical orders).

- *Retention over time.* How well do the users retain their knowledge or skills over time? The periods may be hours, weeks, or months, and retention usually is of concern for tasks that are not part of the users' routine daily activity.

- *Speed of performance.* How long does it take to carry out a set of benchmark tasks? The tasks must be identified, and the measurement includes the effects of the interface, the designers' implementation of the support software, and the users' understanding of the task.

- *Rate of errors by users.* How well does the product support the benchmark tasks as measured by the users' errors? The same benchmarks should be used for this, the previous, and the next quantifier.

- *Subjective satisfaction.* How well does the product support the benchmark tasks as measured by the users' perceptions of satisfaction? Unlike the other measures in this list, this can be ascertained only by a subjective interview or survey.

In this list, the first two factors relate to the ability of the user to build (and retain) an effective model of the tasks supported by the system. For some tasks (e.g., developing the interface for an automatic teller machine), it is necessary to have the system map onto the users' mental models and be very easy to learn. For other activities, however, the product may reorient the existing task structure, and a much longer training period may be necessary (e.g., many consultants suggest that at least a week of training is necessary for a CASE tool to be integrated into the process). Here, time to learn includes both an understanding of the context of the new product plus its use. The remaining three measures also combine the general design and user interface factors. Of course, that is not a problem because we are developing a system that will be used to meet previously identified needs. We do not want the user interface to detract from our overall objective, but neither can we expect a spectacular interface to compensate for a poor design.

The fact that there are some measurable human-factors goals suggests that we can quantify some implicit properties of the target system and specify them as essential requirements. Requirements based on these five measures are categorized as *usability*. Sample requirements in the SCM case study might be the following:

- An experienced designer, given one hour of instruction plus a manual for the SCM system with 4 hours to review it, shall be able to set up the manufacturing instructions for the target application described in Section $x$ and manufacture a product with no major errors and no more than one minor error, where the error categories are defined in Section $y$.

- A member of the CCB shall be able to access all functions of module X following a 15-minute orientation. Satisfaction, as measured on a five-point scale, shall be at least 3.5 with no subjects rating the system unsatisfactory (i.e., 1). After a period of one week, the subjects shall be able to repeat the same functions without requesting help from others.

- Data-entry staff shall be able to enter SIR and CR forms at a rate of 20 per hour over a two-hour period with no detectable errors and a satisfaction measure, using a five-point-scale, of 3.5.

These usability requirements clearly show how the essential and implicit requirements differ. The former are explicit and testable. The designer has an obligation to meet them, and there are unambiguous criteria for seeing that they have been met. The latter represent good practices that one expects the designers to use in producing an implementation. Experienced designers will know what these implicit characteristics are and when to modify them. Unfortunately, because these requirements are subjective, we have no choice but to treat them as design decisions.

### 2.4.2. The ilities

A second class of implicit requirements that I will discuss is the so-called "ilities," such as reliability, portability, maintainability, and so on. These are, of course, quality attributes for the intended product. I refer to them here because most cannot be characterized with unambiguous standard measures.[9] The following list, which is adapted from Shooman [Shoo83, p. 432], identifies some of the key quality factors. Shooman labeled his list "Quality metrics and their definition," but the reader will observe that few metrics can be computed at the time of requirements analysis. (Gilb, however, is a firm believer that all of these properties can be so quantified [Gilb77].)   As technical measures, Shooman identified

- *Maintainability.* He defines this measure to be how difficult and costly it will be to correct errors found in the field (i.e., corrective maintenance).

- *Adaptability (changeability).* This is defined as the difficulty and cost to introduce new features after release (i.e., adaptive and perfective maintenance).

- *Utility (usability).* This measures how well the program satisfies its intended function. This is a much broader concept than the usability criteria defined in the previous section.

- *System security (privacy).* This relates to how difficult it is for unauthorized persons to gain access to information in or control of the system. In general, this should be treated as an essential requirement. (For example, in the SCM system one might state explicitly that the system shall operate using the security tools available with the operating system. If one requires more, then one also has the obligation to verify that the identified features have been delivered.)

- *Installability.* This is a measure of the effort required to customize the product for a specific environment as would be done with a SYSGEN, for example.

- *Simplicity.* This attempts to answer the question, "Is the design straightforward and direct, or is it sophisticated and complex?" There are a variety of complexity measures, and I consider them and their use in Chapter 6.

- *Portability.* This relates to the ease in transferring a software system to a different computer and/or operating system. One can

---

[9]In Chapter 6 I will consider management approaches to establishing quality measures. As I will point out, such measures are local to the environment and mission of the organization; there are few "gold standards."

measure portability after the fact as the ratio of the cost to develop and the cost to modify. If portability is a concern, however, target environments or desirable properties of the implementation ought to be called out as essential requirements.

- *Understandability*. This is a subjective measure of how easy it is to understand and use the software. The usability measures of the previous section suggest some added dimensions to this factor.

Shooman also identifies three managerial measures, but I will defer the discussion of these considerations until Chapter 6.

This list does not exhaust the set of quality metrics. Figure 2.29 displays a frequently cited illustration of the principal quality concerns and the metrics available to measure them. On the left are the quality components of a model developed by Boehm et al. [BoBK78], and on the right is a comparable model described by McCall et al. [McRW77]. Both models begin with a few high-level quality concerns, which are decomposed into key factors, which in turn are reduced into measurable criteria. The Boehm model defines general utility in terms of how the product supports its objectives (i.e., as-is utility, which includes reliability, efficiency, and human engineering), how easily the product can be modified (i.e., maintainability, which includes testability, understandability, and modifiability), and (at a slightly lower level of importance) the product's portability. These, in turn, can be described by primitive constructs. The McCall quality model also addresses roughly the same three concerns. These have been summarized as follows [CaMc78]:

- *Product operation*, which measures how the system satisfies its goals in terms of usability (can I run it?), integrity (is it secure?), efficiency (will it run on my hardware as well as it can?), correctness (does it do what I want?), and reliability (does it do it accurately all of the time?).

- *Product revision*, which measures how easily the system can be altered to meet new demands in terms of maintainability (can I fix it?), testability (can I test it?), and flexibility (can I change it?).

- *Product transition*, which measures how well the system can accommodate external changes in terms of reusability (will I be able to reuse some of the software?), portability (will I be able to use it on another machine?), and interoperability (will I be able to interface it with another system?)

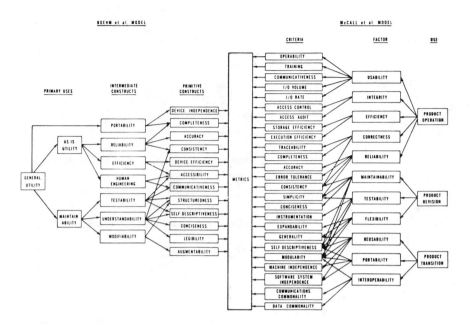

Fig. 2.29.  Two software quality models as described by Curtis.
(Reprinted from [Curt80] with permission, © 1980, IEEE.)

Frequently, this figure is used to illustrate that software quality has many dimensions with associated metrics that can be used to evaluate it. However, the astute reader will observe that there are some contradictions among the definitions and that most quality models are based on the analysis of historic data.  Thus, these models do not prescribe the quality for a new product; they describe the quality of existing products.  Of course, the latter is important, but its domain is management (Chapter 6) and not requirements specification (Chapter 2).  What we need for the purposes of specification are well-understood models of software phenomena that can lead to predictable, reliable measures that we can use to describe attributes of a product to be constructed.  The usability of the previous section is an example of such a quantifiable criteria, but the contents of Figure 2.29 confound as much as they explain.  In fact, although the figure is often used to point out how much we know about quality measures, it was prepared for a very different message.

Curtis presented the figure in a paper on measurement and experimentation in software engineering.  Here is some of the text that accompanied the illustration.

There have been several attempts to quantify the elusive concept of software quality by developing an arsenal of metrics which quantify numerous factors underlying the concept. . . .

No software project can stay within a reasonable budget and maximize all the quality factors. The nature of the system under development will determine the proper weighting of quality factors to be achieved in the delivered software. . . .

The omnibus approach to metric development had its birth in the need for measures of software quality, particularly during system acquisition. However, the development of these metrics has not spawned explanatory theory concerning the processes affected by software characteristics. The value of these metrics in focusing attention on quality issues is substantial. However, there is still a greater need for quantitative measures which emerge from the modeling of software phenomena. Much of the modeling of software characteristics has been performed in an attempt to understand software complexity. [Curt80, pp. 1146-1147]

Here complexity (actually, unnecessary complexity) is used as a marker for potentially poor quality, and consequently a trait to be avoided.

Throughout this book I have pointed out the tension between what we can measure objectively (e.g., verification and product acceptance criteria) and what we can describe only subjectively (e.g., validation and quality attributes). The essential requirements must all be objective, and we must establish that they have been delivered. The equally important implicit requirements are the responsibility of the software engineers and their managers; it is a matter of professionalism. Naturally, the level of quality to be delivered will vary with the product. If the SCM system is to be developed only for internal use with a single operating system, then the product transition factors may not be of much importance and little effort should be allocated for the features that support transition. If, on the other hand, the SCM system is to run on a number of different platforms, then this fact is considered essential. The difficulty comes in deciding if the product satisfies this requirement *before it is accepted*. (Naturally, after the product has been accepted it will be easy to measure the cost to port the system to another platform, but then it may be too late.)

In closing this section on implicit requirements, let me observe that there is an historic trend that begins with the identification of some property of a system and leads to either a model for its measure or an environment for its automatic satisfaction. For example, there is a requirement that no variables of type integer accept a value containing alphabetics. At one time, we specified this as an essential test, then we assumed that the programmer would make the appropriate test, and finally we used HLL typing to automate this test. I do not think that we will ever be able to automate quality, but we can extend our environments to exclude many of the common faults that degrade quality. Also, as we gain experience, we can build formal models for selected quality attributes to ensure that we achieve the required level without expending effort on a degree of performance that exceeds our needs. The usability of the previous section is one illustration of such a model; examples taken from the ilities include reliability [Shoo83, Musa80, MuIO87] and efficiency (performance) [Ferr78].

## 2.5.    The next steps

It is perhaps fitting that the longest chapter in this book is the one on requirements analysis.    This is the most difficult task in system development; it also is the most error-prone activity.    We begin requirements analysis with a perceived need, and we must end with a specification for the automated product that will address that need. Of course, this is the same kind of engineering problem that we face when we build a bridge, or a ship, or an electronic device.    If we have constructed solutions to this type of problem before, then our task reduces to one of detailing a solution tailored to the present conditions. There is always a margin for error, and we must be careful to test every decision and assertion.    But that is no different for software than for hardware.

Naturally, the first time a problem is addressed (either because the technology is moving to a new area or because the developers have no previous experience), the analysts need to discover what the intended product must do.    There is seldom a single correct (or even best) answer, and one typically learns only by making (and rectifying) errors. In Chapter 6 I present several ways in which projects can be structured to facilitate this discovery process.    Here I have described a variety of modeling tools that foster communications with domain specialists and provide a better understanding of the problems to be solved.    I have been careful to deemphasize methodology considerations.    The reader should be aware that many believe the consistent use of a fixed set of methods to be critical; therefore, they begin by teaching the methods. Although I certainly agree that each organization must commit itself to a limited number of tools and methods, I have not endorsed any specific approaches.    Each organization must choose based on its problem domain, operational culture, and customer demands.

Like this chapter, requirements analysis must come to an end. One can never discover all the requirements; neither will the requirements remain stable.    Thus, at some point the development team must document the requirements for the new product and begin the task of constructing it. Up to this point, the analysts have been concerned with the environment in which the product will operate, and their descriptions have conveyed how that product will interact with that larger universe. Naturally, their judgments have been tempered by their knowledge of how to build software, and their specifications are intended to be read by software implementors as well as sponsors and users. Nevertheless, the primary interest in requirements analysis has been on *what* the product should do. It is a view of the software as a *black box*; a perspective from the software to the *outside*.

In the next steps we change this orientation. We assume that we begin with a specification that (1) prescribes the behavior of the target software, (2) details the essential properties of the product, and (3) offers sufficient descriptive information to guide in all the design choices. We now redirect our gaze and look *inside* to *how* we can realize a solution to the problem described in the specification. Rather than being treated as a black box, the details of the software are revealed to us through a *glass box* (also called a *white box*). We must consider domain knowledge as we validate, but most of the problem solving will center around implementation issues. We will have to revisit many of the same issues encountered during requirements analysis.

- How do we break the problem down so that it can be managed? For design we do this in two (overlapping) steps. Modeling-in-the-large (Chapter 3) is concerned with the structure of the total solution, and modeling-in-the-small (Chapter 4) deals with the implementation units.

- How do we know that we have it right? Of course this is a problem for the requirements as well. All of this falls under the heading of verification and validation (Chapter 5), which is usually treated as a separate topic even though it is an integral aspect of every analysis and design task.

- How do we coordinate the activities of many people working together? As we move closer to the implementation stage, the number of participants increases. Each is challenged by an assignment that requires insight and innovation, but each must operate in an environment that demands conformity and restricts change. Chapter 6 considers techniques to manage that inherent tension.

We are ready to move on. Developing software products is the natural arena for software engineers. We have learned what we can by looking outside the software; it is time to redirect our attention and determine how that box works.

*Paulson found that the Naciremas were simple hunter/gatherers, although they sometimes confused the two concepts.*

# 3

## MODELING-IN-THE-LARGE

The Naciremas, as Poulson has discovered, have confused their tools and goals. For now, the damage will be limited to some bruised vegetables. Nevertheless, they had better get their act together before they go off on a lion hunt, or the results may be catastrophic.

This chapter describes modeling-in-the-large in the context of two philosophically opposed approaches. Like the tools of the hunter/ gatherer, the methods are not interchangeable. Therefore, the software engineer should learn from the Naciremas' example. He must be careful to match his tools to his goals.

The two orientations are called decomposition and composition. Oversimplifying, decomposition starts with a model of the entire system as a single black box. This is then decomposed into a set of interfacing functions, each of which also is viewed as a black box. The interfaces among the functions are identified and defined, and the process is repeated until the granularity of the black-box contents is so fine that their operations can described.

In contrast, composition begins by modeling what is known about portions of the system. Each smaller model is completed, and the set of all smaller models is combined to form the system. Where decomposition is top down, composition is outside in. Where decomposition works with an incomplete model of the entire system, composition deals with complete models within an incomplete system model. Thus, it should be obvious that a recipe consisting of two parts decomposition and two parts composition will be unsatisfactory.

I use structured analysis and structured design to illustrate decomposition. Structured analysis began as a method for requirements analysis, and structured design originated as a technique for effective modularization (i.e., what I call modeling-in-the-small). For composition I describe two Jackson methods. The first was developed for program design (clearly modeling-in-the-small) and the second for system design (modeling-in-the-large).

The following text justifies what may seem a strange choice for a chapter with the present title. One obvious explanation is that we are taking a holistic view of software engineering, and boundaries implied by labels may have little meaning.

## 3.1.    Decomposition and composition

In this chapter we make the transition from determining how a need can be met with a software system to describing how that target system should be constructed.   In the requirements analysis of the previous chapter, we were concerned only with decisions regarding what the product must do.   We developed an understanding of the application domain, and we used modeling tools to establish how a software product could be used.   Based on the results of that analysis, we were able to document a set of requirements that identified all of the essential features of the target product.

In our software configuration management (SCM) case study, we first examined how the environment dealt with the issues of change control and configuration integrity.   We constructed a model for an idealized flow, and then we identified how a software system could support this flow.   Using this model, we then defined the essential features of the desired system:  it must manage the storage and update of configuration items (CIs), it must log and report on the status of change requests and software incident reports, etc.   Exactly what the product must provide was documented in a Software Requirements Specification (SRS).   This SRS, naturally, did not detail all the features of the system to be delivered; we deferred many of the particulars as design decisions.   Thus, for example, the SRS stated that we must be able to update CI version numbers, but it did not specify how the interface should operate.

Throughout the requirements analysis phase, we directed our thinking to how the software would be used in the application domain. We addressed implementation issues only from the perspective of feasibility.   That is, could a software system reasonably be expected to support some feature within the given constraints?   Once we answered all these questions, we had a descriptive model that contained

- *Acceptance criteria* as explicit descriptions of what the finished product must do.   These criteria might be functional (e.g., manage CI version updates as prescribed) or nonfunctional (e.g., operate on the specified computer configuration within the given response times).

- *Validation criteria* as a basis for deciding if a design decision violates some system convention or intent.   For example, although the SRS did not specify the CI update interface, there will be many interfaces (each of which might seem logical) that would be incompatible with the system's intended use.

All of the acceptance criteria must be in the SRS; in fact, acceptance criteria not in the SRS will be ignored. Much of the validation criteria, on the other hand, will not be available in an unambiguous form. Consequently, the design team must make decisions involving application issues throughout the design process. That is, even though the designers have an implementation task, they also are expected to have an understanding of the application domain.

In what follows I assume we have an SRS, which details what the product must deliver, plus sufficient knowledge of the application domain to validate the design decisions.[1] In other words, there exist both a document that specifies exactly *what* the system must do and an experience base for determining if the design corresponds to the requirements' intent. With this prerequisite satisfied, we now address *how* to construct a software product that satisfies the stated objectives. Restating this in terms of problem solving, during requirements analysis we sought a solution to this problem: How can a software product meet the needs of the application domain? Now, during design, we shift our attention to a different problem: How can we construct a software product that satisfies the given criteria?

Notice that I have made a simplifying assumption. Often we do not know the requirements with any precision, and we may have to begin the design before they are understood fully. To reduce the risk, we can experiment with prototypes that enrich our understanding of what is desired or how the software operates. Alternatively, we can organize the project as a sequence of incremental deliveries; each build is specified precisely, but there may be no SRS for the full set of builds. Finally, for small, internal products we may elect to rely on some informality in the SRS; for example, it might not be efficient for HHI to document the SCM system SRS as if it were a customer product. I touched on some of these issues in Chapter 1, and I shall address them in further detail in Chapter 6. For now, however, I shall make the unlikely assertion that our requirements are well defined and stable. This will allow us to concentrate on developing an effective design for our software product.

The term modeling-in-the-large is derived from programming-in-the-large. I have avoided the word "programming" for a reason. Too often programming is viewed as a code-creation activity. From a software engineering perspective, coding is a minor (but essential) aspect of the process. When we emphasize the task of coding, there is a tendency to interpret analysis and design as preliminary steps that lead to program-

---

[1]Recall the distinction between verification and validation. Verification refers to correctness with respect to the acceptance criteria (i.e., the system is right). Validation addresses how well the product meets the environment's needs (i.e., this is the right system).

ming. Yet, if we consider the code an executable model that completes a sequence of modeling activities, then code writing will be seen to be just one more modeling step. This is the orientation I would like the reader to adopt. Do not think of the code as the product to be delivered, view it as the most detailed of a set of models.

Although modeling-in-the-large and programming-in-the-large sound similar, they address different concepts. Programming-in-the-large was introduced in the mid-1970s as a way to combine modules written in programming languages (i.e., programming-in-the-small). It involved the development of a module interconnection language "for knitting those modules together into an integrated whole and for providing an overview that formally records the intent of the programmer(s) and that can be checked for consistency by a compiler" [DeRK76, p. 80]. Modeling-in-the-large, on the other hand, offers a framework and architecture for constructing the computational units (i.e., the models-in-the-small). That is, with the modeling orientation one begins by analyzing the target environment to establish what the product is to do, then establishes the structure of a solution to achieve those ends, and finally produces executable models that realize the solution. This modeling view establishes a top-down orientation in which each model elaborates on the antecedent models. Programming, as the writing and debugging of code, is simply the final step in this process.[2]

In what follows I examine two different techniques for modeling-in-the-large. As the name implies, we will model our solution at a level that emphasizes structural features and obscures implementation details. That is, we shall concentrate on the functions that the software supports, how they can be grouped, and the structure of the data that they must access. We introduce this modeling step because the transformation from a requirements document to code involves too many decisions. We

---

[2]This key lesson of software engineering is probably the most difficult to teach. Because students begin by learning how to write code (i.e., programming-in-the-small), there is a tendency to focus on the complexities of that task. Further, when students are given exercises, they often are of a scale that demands only superficial modeling-in-the-large. The result is that the problem solution can be understood in terms of program units. To resolve uncertainty, code is experimented with through a process called "hacking," and "commercial-grade" software is seldom expected. Obviously, there are solid pedagogical foundations for this approach to teaching. But in the world of software engineering, it is assumed that the development staff already has the prerequisite coding skills. Here the emphasis ought to be placed on establishing what the product is to do and how it should be constructed. Experimentation with software should be limited to prototypes where only the lessons learned are preserved in the delivered product. Once the specification for a program has been established, its coding and verification should become routine.

need intermediate steps to create an orderly process for determining the structure and details that ultimately will produce the desired software product. There is always the danger that the path will meander and introduce inefficiencies. But our 7 ± 2 ceiling offers us no alternative; we can proceed incrementally only by dividing a large problem into smaller problems to be attacked independently.

There are two basic ways to subdivide a problem. *Decomposition* uses a top-down approach to organize a system as a set of interconnected subsystems. For example, in the SCM system one might divide the total system into a reporting function, change control function, a CI management function, and a task-assignment function. This phase is sometimes called "allocation of functions." Naturally, these functions are not independent of each other; therefore, one also must identify the interfaces among the functions and describe the structure of the data that they share. There are many possible allocations, and some will be better than others. (By way of illustration, one might consider separate change request and software incident report functions, each of which included its own reporting and control tasks.) Once the system is decomposed into subsystems, the subsystems in turn will be decomposed. This process continues until the components are small enough to be subjected to modeling-in-the-small.

A second approach to abstracting away the unnecessary detail is to concentrate on only selected aspects of the problem. In *composition* one models portions of the system completely; after enough portions have been modeled the entire system emerges. In the SCM application one might build separate models for the management of change requests, the control of the CIs, and the control of the changes. Unlike the decomposition example, there is no separate reports function; each report is defined in the context of the flow that it supports. In contrast to decomposition, composition is not a top-down technique. Perhaps it is best described as being outside-in.

There is something artificial in this distinction between decomposition and composition, and most designers will revert to both techniques in the process of design. With decomposition one always has an incomplete model of the complete system; the model is complete only when all the details are filled in. This approach facilitates the tracing of requirements and is very effective for applications in which there is sufficient experience to anticipate effective functional groupings. Composition, on the other hand, begins with complete models of portions of the system; the complete system model is not available until all portions have been composed into a unified whole. This approach is very effective for applications in which there is either uncertainty or change. Because the designers structure the software to capture what is known about the application objects, the software will be easier to maintain as those objects evolve.

I use structured analysis/structured design to illustrate decomposition. This is one of the most widely used methods; consequently, many people are familiar with its diagramming conventions. To demonstrate the composition approach I use the two Jackson methods: JSP and JSD. In each case I demonstrate the method with examples from the SCM case study. The illustrations begin with a requirements analysis flavor and end with a modeling-in-the-small flavor. I do this for several reasons. First, it is important to recognize that the software process does not involve distinct and separate steps; only *the management of the process* requires identifiable phases. Next, the reader should be aware that most methods provide continuous support throughout major segments of the process. The designers should not let arbitrary phase labels obscure this continuity. Finally, by taking a broader view of the methods we gain better insight into how we shift our problem solving from the application to its implementation.

Although I have selected just two methods, many others exist. It is better to understand two methods well than to be able to recognize the diagrams of many methods. In fact, it may be best to know just one method and understand it very well. Each method is intended to structure the problem-solving activity and generate information for communication. When we have too many formats, communication suffers; if we have too many tools to choose from, our skills degrade. I have chosen two different techniques for modeling-in-the-large because I believe that students of software engineering should understand their underlying philosophies. As software professionals, we ought to know about both decomposition and composition. The former represents the predominant approach since the mid-1970s, and there is reason to believe that the popularity of the latter will increase in the 1990s.

## 3.2.    Structured analysis and structured design

The word "analysis" generally is associated with the process of requirements determination. Therefore, it may seem strange to find a section on structured analysis in this chapter on design. Structured analysis is concerned with establishing what the product is to do. As a by-product of the method, however, one also describes the architecture of the solution. Structured design then may be used to transform that organization into a framework for the implementation. The examples in the next sections will clarify this; for now it will suffice to note that I illustrate decomposition with two related methods that span the software process from requirements analysis to program specification.

Both structured analysis and structured design belong to the "1970s solutions" that I referenced in the box of Figure 2.24. Recall that in the late 1960s and early 1970s Dijkstra (and others) introduced the concepts of structured programming and a discipline of programming. Although many misinterpreted his intent, the field was ready for improvements. Text documents were too verbose, and more systematic methods would encourage discipline and improve a system's structure. As a result, the 1970s witnessed changes in both coding style (e.g., readable code using block structures and white space, the avoidance of the goto, the restriction of procedure size to what could fit on a single page) and program design (e.g., the substitution of standardized diagrammatic notations for descriptive text, a concern for how program modules could be combined, the development of theories concerning the structure of very large systems).

The tools of the 1970s (which we rely on today) were a response to the success that we had with high level languages and the difficulties we encountered with building systems. We knew how to write instructions for the computer, but we had trouble developing large programs. This is how Constantine and Yourdon characterized the state of practice in the mid-1970s.

> Concepts like "modular design" and "top-down design" have been circulating through the industry for more than a decade. Yet, if one watches what an average programmer actually *does* (as compared to what he *says* he does), it is apparent that the process of designing a program or system is still art, characterized by large doses of folklore (e.g., "Every program has to have an initialization module, right?"), black magic, and occasional flashes of intuition. To say that the average programmer's design process is organized, or *structured*, would be charitable. [YoCo79, pp. xv-xvi].

Their book on structured design was "an attempt to provide elements of a discipline of program and systems design. . . . Our concern is with the architecture of programs and systems. How should a large system be broken into modules? *Which* modules?"

Restating this in terms of my chapter titles, modeling-in-the-small seemed to be understood in the early 1970s, and the concern now was for an underlying theory for modeling-in-the-large. Constantine started working on such theories in the late 1960s. He later joined IBM where he began to teach courses in what he called "composite design." In 1974 he and his students published their methods in the *IBM Systems Journal* under the title "Structured Design" [StMC74]. Myers, a student of Constantine, retained the composite design title and published two books on that topic [Myer75, Myer78]. Finally, in 1975, Yourdon collaborated with Constantine to publish *Structured Design: Fundamentals of a Discipline of Computer Program and System Design*, from which the above quotation was taken [YoCo79].

Whereas structured design was concerned with how the program modules should be combined into an efficient and adaptable system, the goal of structured analysis was to provide a systematic approach for establishing the requirements for an application.    In Chapter 2 I described Ross's interpretation of structured analysis [Ross77].  Others were working on alternative methods, and the technique that has gained the greatest acceptance was that developed somewhat independently by DeMarco [DeMa78] and Gane and Sarson [GaSa79].  Here diagramming techniques were used to identify the proposed application's functions with their interfaces, data structures, and algorithms.  Yourdon and DeMarco, who played a major role in the dissemination of these methods, subsequently showed how the output of the structured analysis process could be transformed by the structured design methods.

The key point of this historical summary is that there were many pragmatic attempts to improve the software design process in the mid-1970s.   Some focused on the implementation objects, and others concentrated on the application domain and the structure of a system to satisfy the identified needs.  There also was considerable diversity under the label of structured analysis/structured design (SA/SD).  Although the various techniques lacked a consistent unifying theory, each included

- A systematic method to guide the process.  The method contained heuristics for a good design plus rules for identifying faults in the design or its specification.

- A set of diagrammatic tools that improved comprehension, reduced documentation, and offered a readily understood format for communication among designers and users.

- An orientation that deferred coding decisions until the higher level architecture had been established.

As one would expect, these methods evolved over time.  SA/SD was initially developed for data processing applications, and the 1980s saw extensions to the basic SA diagrams for use in real-time applications.  Individuals modified their methods as the underlying technology changed.  DeMarco continually points out that his views are evolving and his books should not be read too literally; Yourdon recently has written a book to correct some of his earlier teachings [Your89].  Thus, when we speak of SA/SD we are talking of a set of tools that guide us in problem solving.  The problems that we confront in SA are different from those we find when performing SD; consequently, the tools and methods also change.  We should not expect a comprehensive, formal approach to system design.  However, we will find a flexible framework that guides us in our efforts.

The following section illustrates SA using the orientation that DeMarco presented in 1978. DeMarco's diagrams were drawn by hand, and they had an aesthetic quality that is hard to capture with a CASE product.[3] My handwriting cannot recreate the boldness of DeMarco's figures, and so I have elected to use pictures prepared by an artist. For a real application, however, I would use hand-drawn diagrams. The benefit of the diagrams is in their role of clarifying thought and conveying information to others. An excessive emphasis on the diagrams as end products detracts from their usefulness. Illustrations for a textbook, on the other hand, ought to be attractive.

### 3.2.1. Structured analysis and the SCM case study

When SA was introduced as an analysis tool, the first task in the method was the definition of four models:

- *Current Physical Model.* This is a model of the actual system that is currently in use. Recall that most applications were for data processing, and consequently the first objective was to gain an understanding of the application domain by studying the environment in which the data processing system would operate.

- *Current Logical Model.* This is a model of what the current system actually does once the implementation details are removed. For example, if change requests (CRs) are stamped with a receipt date and time by one clerk and then forwarded to another clerk for entry into a log, the logical model would ignore the fact that two clerks were involved in the process and identify a single logical task, Log and Time-Stamp CRs.

- *New Logical Model.* The new logical model describes the essential features that the sponsor wants the new system to provide. The New Logical Model will be the same as the Current Logical Model if the sponsor does not expect the automation to provide any new functionality (i.e., the benefits of

---

[3]Computer-Aided Software Engineering (CASE) is the generic name for a range of automated tools used to support aspects of the software process. There are many CASE tools that manage the creation and maintenance of SA/SD diagrams and their associated documentation. These tools also perform some of the consistency tests described below. The interface for many CASE tools is such that the creation of a computer-stored diagram is no more difficult than drawing it manually.

the automation will be derived from the efficiencies that it introduces.)

- *New Physical Model.* This model incorporates the implementation constraints imposed by the sponsor. Note that the above three models describe the sponsor's operational environment and not the proposed software system. The target system will be a component in the New Logical Model that includes processes external to the proposed system. The New Physical Model establishes a boundary between the new software product and the operational processes (and, perhaps, existing automated tools) that interact with it.

These four models are constructed using *data flow diagrams* (DFD), which I will describe below.

The New Physical Model, once it has been constructed, is redrawn as a *context diagram* that consists of a single bubble (circle) with the key external interfaces identified. In Chapter 2 I used Orr's method to establish the system boundary, and there is no need to repeat that process with the above four models. Figure 2.16 (which has been copied here as Figure 3.1) is a context diagram for the SCM system. It represents the culmination of the above analysis process and the beginning of what I call modeling-in-the-large. The context diagram describes what the system is to do; our task now is to decide how the software can provide the desired functionality. In doing this, we refer

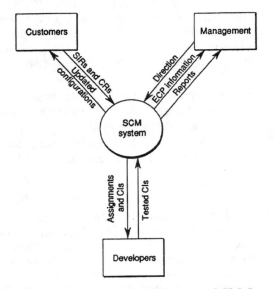

Fig. 3.1. A context diagram for the SCM System.

back to the Software Requirements Specification (SRS) for guidance, and we also make decisions that affect the product's functionality. Thus, even though we are engaged in a design activity, an understanding of the users' domain is essential.

Once we have a context diagram, the next step is to create a DFD that explains what happens in that single bubble. The DFD is a network composed of four symbol types.

- *Processes*. These are the nodes in the network that represent processes (or transformations). The nodes are depicted as circles, and sometimes the processes are referred to as bubbles. In fact, the DFD is sometimes called a bubble chart.

- *Data flows*. These are the directed arcs of the network. They represent the data transfers to or from a process. In effect, the data flows define the process interfaces. The data flows are drawn as directed lines between nodes in the network.

- *Stores*. These are special nodes in the network that define a source or sink for a data flow. The stores are implemented as some form of an automated database or manual filing system. Stores are indicated by writing the name between parallel lines, in a narrow box open on the right, or in some other long and narrow enclosure-189.

- *Terminators*. These are special nodes in the network used to identify external entities (i.e., those processes that are external to the system). Terminators normally are drawn as boxes.

Each DFD is the functional decomposition of one bubble from a higher level DFD. By this I mean that the DFD details the functions carried out within a higher level bubble; it displays the data flows among the processes as an expanded network. The context diagram defines the entire system as a single bubble. (It may be thought of as a one-bubble DFD.) This level-1 DFD can be expanded as a level-2 DFD, which represents the highest level view of the processing that takes place within the system. To maintain readability, DFDs generally contain 7 ± 2 bubbles. Each of these bubbles, in turn, can be expanded as a DFD. This iteration continues until a process identified by a bubble is well enough understood to be described in a *minispec* or process description. The *data dictionary* completes the DFD documentation set; it describes the structure and contents of the data flows. (Recall that we are engaged in modeling-in-the-large, and therefore this data dictionary need not contain the details required for an implementation.) As I will now show, the DFD creation process is quite simple. Once mastered, it is very easy to create descriptive materials that are easily understood. The DFDs display system functions in arbitrary levels of detail, the data dictionary describes the essential characteristics of the data flows, and the minispecs contain the processing details.[4] The result is a collection of documents that, in combination, can resolve all design concerns.

The context diagram in Figure 3.1 delineates the domain of our system. The SCM system is shown to interface with three external entities (terminators) with three major inputs and four major outputs. Obviously, the diagram reduces system complexity considerably. We make simplifying assumptions so that we can concentrate on what is of primary importance in our current analysis. For example, we see that Developers receive Assignments and CIs from the SCM System and return Tested CIs to it. That high-level statement has an almost comical obviousness to it. Our next objective is to clarify what the statement implies. We will add details as we proceed, but we will always defer some of the particulars until the final step. Figure 3.2 represents the first step in this expansion of the context diagram. As a refinement of the bubble in the context diagram, the level-2 DFD must have exactly three terminators with four output and three input flows. And the names of these items must be the same. We are treating the bubble as a black box and detailing its internal workings; viewing it as a black box implies that we cannot violate its interfaces.

The SCM System displayed in Figure 3.2 has been decomposed into six major functions, which bear a remarkable similarity to the system functions defined in the SRS of Section 2.3.4.

- Preliminary Processing. This involves the processing of the software incident reports (SIRs) and change requests (CRs), their entry into a Change Status File, and the flagging of the Prioritized Requests for subsequent processing. To avoid unnecessary delays, Emergency Repairs are routed for immediate processing.

- Detailed Analysis. Here the Prioritized Requests are received and analyzed. The affected CIs are identified. For changes that require customer or management approval, an engineering change proposal (ECP) is required. In such cases, the technical information necessary to prepare an ECP is forwarded to Management. The results of all actions are recorded in the

---

[4]Most SA documents prefer to use the term "process description" or "process specification." The word minispec has the obvious advantage of not being confused with concepts associated with other methods, and I shall use it here for the SA process descriptions.

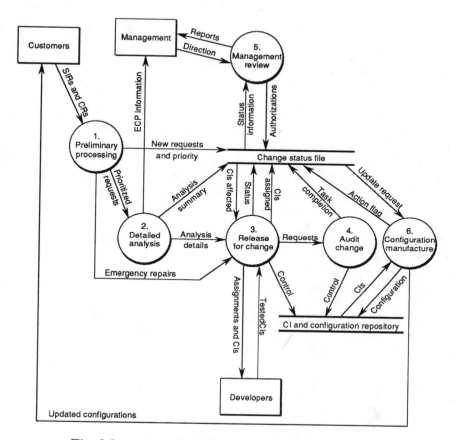

Fig. 3.2.  A level-2 DFD for the SCM System.

Change Status File, and the Analysis Details messages are produced.

- **Release for Change.**  This process initiates the change task.  It determines which changes are authorized from the **Change Status File** and sets the **CI and Configuration Repository** so that the assigned developers can have access to the necessary **CIs**. Assignments are recorded in the **Change Status File**, and **Requests** for auditing are generated.

- **Audit Change.**  The process begins with a **Request** to enter **Tested CIs** into the **CI and Configuration Repository**.  The audit is performed, the status is updated in the **Change Status**

File, and the Control is set in the repository to inhibit further changes to the Tested CIs.

- Management Review. This sends Reports to and receives Direction from Management. It relies on the contents of the Change Status File and enters Authorizations into it.

- Configuration Manufacture. This is diagrammed as a fully automated activity. It is initiated by an Update Request in the Change Status File, it extracts CIs from the CI and Configuration Repository, and it returns a New Configuration to the repository. Updated Configurations are sent to Customers. The results of the activity are indicated by an Action Flag set in the Change Status File.

These six functions describe the interface between the SCM software system and its users. Both manual and computer supported procedures are implied. We still are modeling the SCM System we intend to build. Although our present goal is to design the software, we have begun by modeling the software in the context of its use. One could argue that this is requirements analysis, and that the discussion belongs in Chapter 2. But we really are making *design decisions*. Notice that we have structured the SCM System around two central data stores:

- Change Status File, which collects all information about the changes in process and communicates the actions to be taken within the system.

- CI and Configuration Repository, which retains all the CIs and configurations managed by the system.

There was no requirement to have these two data stores. We also have allocated our functions in a very specific way. We set Management outside the processing flow and allowed it to control activities only by placing Authorizations in the Change Status File. We identified four functions in the processing flow, and assumed that Configuration Manufacture operates asynchronously with respect to the change tasks. In one sense, this allocation could be presented as a convenient mechanism for describing *what* the SCM system does. But it really represents a commitment to *how* the implemented system will operate (and by implication, how it will be built). Given our holistic view, we should not feel uncomfortable in using an analysis tool for design.

To illustrate the departure that we have taken, compare Orr's approach with the SA method shown here. Both begin with the identical context diagram (Figs. 2.13 and 3.1). The DSSD "entity diagram," however, was elaborated to identify sequences of actions as shown in the main line functional flow of Figure 2.14. The DFD of Figure 3.2, on the other hand, obscures these sequential associations. For example, the DFD does not make it clear that the **Release for Change** can begin for **Emergency Repairs** without receiving any inputs from the **Detailed Analysis** process. In fact, there is nothing in this DFD to suggest that **Audit Change** does not always occur *before* **Release for Change**. Thus, to clarify the interfaces, SA hides the sequential processing highlighted by DSSD.

The DFD also differs from the SADT diagram in Figure 2.18. The SADT diagram in that illustration was really the "new logical model." It included management as a control and did not explicitly show data stores. As a logical model, the SADT diagram concentrated on the flow within the total system. Naturally, one could make the two types of SA diagrams seem more alike by changing the names of the processes (e.g., calling "Preliminary Processing" "Log and Evaluate"). But that would provide only superficial conformance. Both the diagrams and the analysis processes differ fundamentally. In the SA that we are using in this section, the system is represented as a set of functions (or processes). We display those functions as bubbles and link them with other nodes via data flows. Our objective is to decompose the entire system into a set of discrete processing units. The DFDs provide a picture of how the system operates, but little information about what goes on inside a process or the temporal dependencies among processes. Naturally, by the end of the SA process—when the data dictionary is complete and we have the minispecs—we will have discovered and recorded everything that we need to know to implement the system.

The SA method is iterative. To understand how a process (represented by a bubble) operates, one must either expand it as a next-level DFD or describe it in a minispec. Figure 3.3 details bubble 1, Preliminary Processing. Notice that each bubble has been numbered with a prefix that indicates parentage. In Figure 3.2 Preliminary Processing has one input, one update to the Change Status File, and two outputs. These same interfaces are shown in Figure 3.3; the file update information, however, has been elaborated. Before describing the DFD, let me review the concept of Preliminary Processing that this DFD represents. Recall that Customers submit SIRs and CRs. Although Developers also can submit SIRs, this was not shown in the context diagram. It could be argued with some justification that this fact was omitted to eliminate a minor detail that would clutter the diagram and thereby inhibit comprehension. In any event, the SCM unit receives the SIRs and CRs along with special information for emergency repairs. (This is the "Emergency Priority Statement" identified in the SRS discussion of Section 2.3.4.) Obviously, there will be two processing flows. For

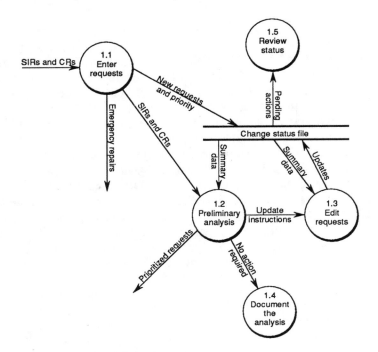

Fig. 3.3. DFD for Preliminary Processing.

routine and urgent repairs, the staff will enter the initial information and send the paper report for review and preliminary processing. That processing may determine that no action is required, and the request will be closed out. Alternatively, it may be determined that a more detailed analysis is necessary; in this case, the status will be so set, and the prioritized requests will be forwarded. For emergency repairs, one would expect some action to be taken even before the paperwork is processed. In those situations, the request may be entered after it has been completed, or the emergency may have been resolved with a quick fix combined with a lower priority change request. Obviously, there is a need to edit the change data in the Change Status File and review the status of pending actions.

The flow supporting the above view of Preliminary Processing is shown in Figure 3.3. Is this how we actually expect the SCM system to work? Would it be better to combine the Preliminary Analysis process identified here with the larger Detailed Analysis process of bubble 2? There are still many open questions, a fact that reenforces my observation that the requirements analysis of the previous chapter and the design of this chapter overlap. In part, the difference is a mater of focus and orientation. We are using the DFD here to identify the functions that the software will support. We recognize that one person may conduct both the preliminary and the detailed analysis. The present concern is for the software-supported tools that he will use in each of those tasks. Naturally, if the tools will not conform to the flow that the SCM organization uses, then those tools will not be effective. Thus, when we wear our analyst's hat, we must consider what the environment expects the software to support, and when we wear our designer's hat, we need to concentrate on how to decompose the software into the units that will provide the desired services. In the context of this discussion, we begin with an essential requirement to process new requests of various priorities. We must validate the subsequent design decisions to ensure that the finished product will indeed do what was specified. The fact that validation continues throughout implementation indicates that the requirements analysis task is never really finished.

Now for a more detailed examination of the level-3 DFD. There are five functions:

- Enter Requests. This process enters the new requests into the Change Status File and forwards the (hardcopy) SIRs and CRs for Preliminary Analysis. Emergency Repairs are shown here as being routed directly for action; further discussion with the users may revise this part of the flow, but a change should have little impact on the overall processing.

- Preliminary Analysis. This process reviews the information in the Change Status File and on the request forms. It is important to have the change logged into the system promptly, but it is recognized that the change form may not always be complete and ready for detailed analysis. Additional information may be required, and this may affect the disposition or priority. Clearly, one does not want to initiate Detailed Analysis before the basic information is available. The output of his process is either the fact that no action is required or a Prioritized Request for further processing.

- Edit Requests. This process updates the Change Status File based on Update Instructions. From the perspective of the software, this process is described as a set of screen layouts and validity tests. Notice that the same description would be valid if (1) the analyst did the updates as he was performing the analysis or (2) the analyst wrote the update instructions on a form for subsequent entry by a clerk. The point is that we now are describing what the software does and not who uses it. Naturally, if the software would have to behave differently for different modes of use, then the design would have to take this requirement into consideration.

- **Document the Analysis.** This process documents the analysis for requests that require no action. In this flow there is no indication of what happens to the documentation; it never emerges from the bubble. At an early stage it is reasonable to use a bubble to indicate that some special activity is needed for requests that require no action. As we continue the modeling we will either find some source for the document (e.g., the terminator NAR Report) or delete the bubble. (As a general rule, DFD bubbles are transformations, and none should be without at least one input and one output data flow.)

- **Review Status.** This process is shown as a control activity that reviews the pending tasks by examining Pending Actions in the Change Status File. Notice that, unlike the SADT diagram, the DFD does not indicate who exercises control over this function.

Having expanded Preliminary Processing one level, I now consider if I need to repeat the process and draw level-4 DFDs. Document the Analysis is sort of a place holder to remind me that something has to be done, but I need not spend any more time on that bubble for now. I cannot describe Review Status without some further thought. What reports are required? How will they be displayed? Who will have access to them? I need some of those answers before I can decompose that bubble. (Of course, I hope that the SRS will provide the necessary answers; I also assume that I can go back to the users to validate my understanding.) I do have enough information, however, to decompose the Enter Requests process. Based on some earlier analysis, here is the flow that the system must support. Requests are received in hardcopy (by hand, electronically, by mail or by fax). They are immediately logged into the system with a unique computer-assigned identifier (which is copied onto the paper form). There are separate entry programs for SIRs and CRs. It is assumed that the identification of a request is done as close to the time of receipt as possible, and that the remaining data entry is batched for more efficient processing. Following data entry, each new entry is subjected to a quality review; based on the outcome of that review, a status flag is set to indicate if further information is required before processing can begin. All request entries must have two elements: an identification number and a source. To maintain the integrity of the database, we insist that all source identifiers be taken from a standard dictionary of customer and developer identifiers. When a request is submitted that does not use an identifier known to the

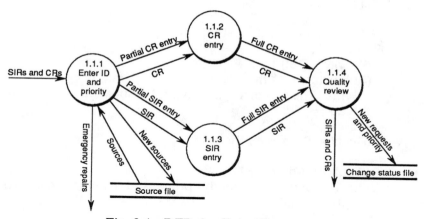

Fig. 3.4. DFD for Enter Requests.

system, the source dictionary must be updated. Figure 3.4 contains a level-4 DFD that depicts a system organization to support this flow.

Returning to the level-3 DFD for Preliminary Processing (Fig. 3.3), we note that Preliminary Analysis seems to be quite straightforward. It simply involves the display of a request entry followed by an analysis of its completeness. Therefore, I need not expand that process into a level-4 DFD; I can define it as a minispec.

Enter change identification number.
    If invalid, EXIT.
Display partial change entry in format shown in Figure X.
Perform the following validity tests:
    If Priority = Emergency, OK.
    If Submitter = null, HOLD.
    If Receipt-Date = null, HOLD.
    . . . .

This minispec identifies all the validation criteria that must be satisfied before a request is forwarded to Detailed Analysis; Emergency Repairs, of course, receive special handling.

The format for this minispec has emphasized the ability to communicate. The display of the change entry is shown in a figure (i.e., the Figure X appended to the minispec). The testing associates with each acceptance criterium a value of OK or HOLD. The objective is to document what the algorithm will do and not how the algorithm will be implemented. For example, the above minispec might be coded (in part) as

Preliminary_Analysis begin;

  . . . .

(Get the values to be tested)
Flag := "Y";
If (Priority = "E") then RETURN;
If (Submitter = "") then do
    Write "The Submitter field must be supplied";
    Flag := "N";
    end;
If (Receipt_Date = "") then do

  . . . .

If (Flag ="Y") then RETURN;
Write "The change cannot be processed, its status has been
    set to HOLD";

  . . . .

Preliminary_Analysis end;

Notice how the implementation details, even in this relatively simple example, obscure the intent of the process. In the minispec we wish to document how we expect the system to meet its requirements in a clear an concise manner; there will be ample time to add the implementation refinements.[5]

In this minispec I have made reference to some data by name. Therefore, in parallel with the definition of the DFDs and the minispecs, I also must define the structure of the data represented by the flows. As with the DFDs, I may elect to document the data definitions in increasing levels of detail. For example, I may begin by stating that New Requests and Priority is defined as either an SIR Entry or a CR Entry, written,

New Requests and Priority = [SIR Entry | CR Entry].

The data dictionary will not be complete until I have provided definitions for SIR Entry and CR Entry, but it will remind me of what has not yet been defined. Observe that most of the time our design will be incomplete; in fact, the design will be complete only when it is finished. Thus, we want our methods to help us deal with the incompleteness we

---

[5]Observe that some of the validation criteria defined in the minispec for 1.2 Preliminary Analysis are the same as those that will be used in 1.1.4 Quality Review. This suggests that we might want to define some common subroutines to be used for both processes. Unfortunately, the SA method that we are using will not remind us of that fact; we will need to recognize and remember this efficiency on our own.

face during design. We expect a method to allow us to work on different parts of the holistic problem concurrently and to identify what has not yet been specified.

Continuing with the data dictionary example, in time a definition for SIR Entry must be supplied, for instance as

SIR Entry = SIR-No + Product-ID + Submitter + SIR-Status
Submitter = [Customer-ID | Developer-ID]
SIR-Status = Priority + Receipt-Date + (Assign-Date) + Close-Date
Emergency-Repair = [Y | N]
Priority = [R | U]
Receipt-Date = *Date type, ≤ Assign-Date, mandatory*

In this notation the equal sign establishes the definition, the plus sign is an "and," the square brackets and bars represent a selection ("or"), the parentheses indicate an optional term, and the asterisks set off comments. Thus the SIR Entry consists of an identifier (SIR-No), the product name (Product-ID), information about the source of the SIR (Submitter, defined on the next line), and the status (SIR-Status, also defined below). Submitter is defined to be one of two terms, neither of which is defined in this part of the data dictionary. This implies that there must be files that identify the customers and developers, a fact that is not obvious from the first two DFDs. Of course, this fact will be clear when the data diction is complete. SIR-Status is defined as the priority flag (defined below as either R for routine, U for urgent, or E for emergency), the receipt date, the optional assign date (unnecessary for requests that require no actions), and the close date. Finally, the definition of Receipt-Date uses a comment to indicate its type, range and the fact that it is required.

This segment of the data dictionary defines everything about an SIR that we want our automated SCM system to maintain in the Change Status File. Let us return to the SIR form in Figure 2.1 to consider what is *not* in the Change Status File. None of the information in the software identification block (upper right corner) is included. Observe from the level-2 DFD that if we expect the Change Status File to contain enough information to identify the CIs Affected for the Release for Change process, then this information must be entered. However, there is a reasonable chance for errors in this information at the time of Preliminary Processing, and it would be best to defer the entry of this information as part of the Analysis Summary after the Detailed Analysis is complete. Returning to the SIR form, the description and analysis boxes contain text that might be costly to enter. If the text were created using the same computer that stored the Change Status File, then its automatic capture should be considered. Yet, if the SIR forms were filled out manually at a customer site, then there would be little justification for including it as part of the SIR entry. Finally, what should be entered in the SCM System database from the section labeled "To be completed by SCM manager?" That answer requires some discussion with the SCM manager. What is available? What is necessary? How will it be used? Who will enter it and when? And so on.

The modeling process involves asking questions of ourselves and others and then recording the answers in the representation scheme we have selected. In SA we use DFDs to show interactions among the processes (functions), minispecs to describe a process after it cannot be decomposed further, and the data dictionary to establish the contents and structure of the interfaces. The activity involves iteration, and few functions are neatly isolated. Nevertheless, the tools of SA provide a natural media for recording a design model and critiquing it with others. After all, this section has provided only a very sketchy definition of the DFD, minispec, and data dictionary, yet I am confident that the reader understands the examples. In fact, their intuitive clarity is one reason for the widespread acceptance of the SA analysis tools. Naturally, learning to create these documents is not as easy as learning to read them. It takes time to develop new skills, and one needs the experience gained from the feedback of error identification and correction.

As we already have seen, the minispecs for computer programs explain the functions to be supported without providing the implementation details. When do we express the processing of a bubble as a minispec? DeMarco offers the following guidelines [DeMa78].

- The processing carried out in a bubble is normally described as a verb phrase with an object. When the name takes the form of a strong action verb with a single object (e.g., **Preliminary Analysis [of New Request and Priority entry]**), a minispec should be considered.

- Each bubble is a transformation. When the bubble has been reduced so that there is a single input and a single output, the transformation may be specific enough for documentation as a minispec.

- Expanding on the previous criterium, there should be no structure clash; each input should eventually cause one output.

- The processing to be described in the minispec should be simple enough to be detailed in a page or less.

The format of the minispec should be based on the function it describes, how it will be implemented (or documented), and the best manner to convey the information to those who must reference it. Some standard minispec formats include

- *Structured English.* This is a simple form of natural text that avoids unspecific qualifiers, compound sentence structures, and expressive punctuation. It relies on a limited set of conditional and logical statements, uses imperative verbs, and limits references to the terms defined in the data dictionary. All the constructs are closed-end. The **Preliminary Analysis** minispec is written in Structured English.

- *Pseudocode.* This is a type of Structured English that is limited to the constructs of a block structured programming language. The notation is intended to convey information about an algorithm to one who will implement it. Whereas Structured English is most effective for resolving application issues with the users, a pseudocode form can be more expressive for describing algorithms.

- *Decision tables.* The decision table (or decision tree) is a very convenient method for displaying a set of choices. For example the conditions used in the **Preliminary Analysis** tests might be presented as a decision tree (e.g., divide if emergency request or not; if not emergency request, divide if mandatory identifier or submitter present or not; and so on). In fact, there is no reason why a minispec cannot be written using both a decision tree and Structured English.

- *Other formats.* Some suggest diagrams such as flow charts to describe the process, but I personally do not recommend that approach. Still, one should be free to select what seems to be the most expressive form for conveying what the process does. For example, the minispec for **Enter Requests** might be in the form of a screen layout together with branching or input validation instructions. The format for a partial change entry in the **Preliminary Analysis** minispec was given in a report layout.

Clearly, the minispec is not a specification in the context of the formalisms described in Section 2.3.3. It is a communication device intended to convey information and reduce ambiguity. The data dictionary also relies on an informal syntax. We have already seen all but one of the principal conventions. More precisely stated, they are as follows:

= means IS EQUIVALENT TO
+ means AND
[] means SELECT ONE from the items separated by |
() means OPTIONAL
{} means ITERATIONS OF
** are used to set off comments
@ is sometimes used to identify a key field for a store (e.g., @SIR-No)

Only the iteration symbol requires further elaboration. When there are cardinality constraints, the minimum number of iterations is written to the left of the bracket and the maximum number to the right (e.g., 1{CIs} for at least one CI identifier and 0{Developer-ID}5 for an optional field that can contain up to a maximum of five Developer-ID values). Obviously, the various data dictionary entries for the lists of CIs and developer assignments will utilize iteration symbols.

There also are conventions for the DFD, and I shall illustrate them with Figure 3.5, which is the highest-level DFD for the Configuration Manufacture function. I begin with some observations about the particular process that I have selected as an exemplar. As noted in Section 2.2, there are software tools that support this function [Feld79], but a complete manufacturing system remains a research topic. Thus, although there are models for configuration manufacture, it is far from a simple task. We lack a sound conceptual model for describing how it should be implemented, and we ought to be prepared for feedback, learning, and revision. (In Brooks's words, we should plan to throw one away.) In fact, we have here an excellent candidate for a prototype. Unlike a prototype for a user interface (e.g., Enter Requests), this prototype would address implementation concerns: Does the data structure express all the necessary configurations? Are there conflicts in processing sequences? Is there a potential for deadlock? And so on. It can be argued that neither the prototype nor the SA method is appropriate for this type of problem, but I will not participate in that debate. I simply use the current example to show (1) that DFDs can be used for other than data processing applications and (2) any analysis or design method depends on iteration to resolve questions when new problems are being addressed.

The DFD in Figure 3.5 conforms to the basic rules for all DFDs:

- Every bubble is numbered, and the prefix for these numbers is the number of the parent bubble (here the prefix is 6).

- Every data flow to or from the parent bubble (or a terminator)

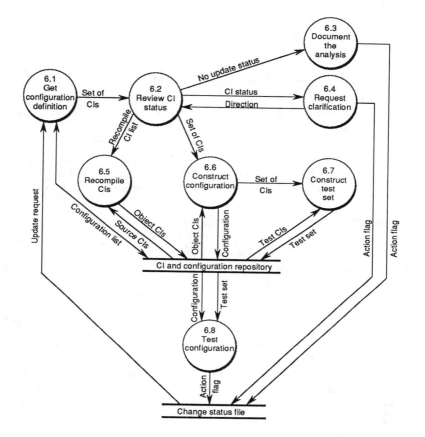

Fig. 3.5. DFD of Configuration Manufacture.

is shown as an input to or output of this lower-level DFD. The
names of the data flows are identical in both DFDs. In this case
there are no such interfaces.

- Every data flow to or from a store is included in the lower level
  DFD. When the same data flows are implied, data flow names
  must be identical. It also is allowable to refine the data flows to
  a store as subsets of the flow used in the parent DFD.

- Every item in a DFD should have a meaningful name. Processes
  usually will use verbs, data flows and terminators will use nouns,
  and stores will use implementation-type names.

- The level of detail implied by each bubble in a DFD should be approximately the same. That is, each bubble should require approximately the same number of levels before it is reduced to minispecs.[6]

- When a store has no interfaces outside a DFD, it should not be shown in the higher level DFDs. (That is, because the store is not accessed by the higher level functions, it should be hidden from them.)

- Because the bubbles represent transformations, every data flow must either originate or terminate in a bubble (e.g., flows between a file and terminator are invalid).

It can be seen by a quick inspection that the DFD in Figure 3.5 is syntactically correct, but what does it show? I begin by considering how it fits into its parent DFD. There **Configuration Manufacture** begins when an **Update Request** is entered in the **Change Status File**. This implies that all configurations are defined somewhere in the SCM System. (Perhaps there is another file that has not yet been shown.) We need to know what the configuration contains, how it differs from similar configurations, and what modules it shares. Recall that HHI, for whom we are developing this system, produces versions of the same product for different computers and operating systems. Changes to one functional system may affect many different configurations. Moreover, some customers may use products that do not access the changed function, and therefore their configurations need not be updated (i.e., manufactured). Somewhere in our SCM System, all this information must be recorded. For the purposes of this discussion, we can assume that all the necessary information is in the **Change Status File** and the **CI and Configuration Repository**. As the contents of the data dictionary are defined, these stores may be reorganized and extended as families of files.

Looking inside the level-3 DFD, we observe that configuration manufacture begins once an **Update Request** is made. (Of course, there is nothing in the DFD that makes this fact obvious; actually, we knew this even before we started looking.) The DFD in Figure 3.5 also does not make it clear if this is a fully automated process or one that requires

---

[6]This is the number of levels for a DFD, and the level of a system is given as the number of levels for the context diagram. Yourdon suggests, "In a simple system, one would probably find two or three levels; a medium-size system will typically have three to six levels; and a large system will have five to eight levels" [Your89, p. 168].

human control. Still, the figure does identify the following processes and their interfaces:

- **Get Configuration Definition.** This involves the identification of the CIs that make up the given configuration. The figure shows a **Configuration List** that is stored in the **CI and Configuration Repository.** This implies that the repository must contain both the CIs and lists to show how they are combined to produce configurations. The output of the process is a **Set of CIs** to be reviewed.

- **Review CI Status.** There are some questions to be answered before a configuration is updated. Are changes pending for some modules in the configuration? Will this configuration be identical to the previous one? Is all the documentation available for distribution with the new configuration? And so on. Although this may be an automated process, the process name suggests a manual activity.

  Where do the data come from to support the **Review CI Status** process? The DFD shows only the **Set of CIs** input, which implies that the data contain all the information to make the necessary decisions. That is probably a poor assumption, and one will gain a better understanding as the 6.2 DFD is diagrammed and the data dictionary is augmented. For now, it suffices to identify the need to perform this function and the processes that interface with it.

- **Document the Analysis.** This is the documentation of an analysis that indicates no changes to the CIs comprising this configuration; therefore, its manufacture is not required. The input to the process is a **No Update Status** message. The output is a value for the **Action Flag** to be stored in the **Change Status File.** Notice that, although the process title suggests that a document will be prepared, no document is shown as an output. We will have to clean this up when we decide how to manage the **Document the Analysis** process of Figure 3.3.

- **Request Clarification.** This involves some human action to resolve the problems identified in **CI Status.** From this level bubble it is not clear if this is a manual process or the preparation of a report that is sent to **Management** for them to provide direction. This will be clarified in the 6.4 level-4 DFD (or minispec). In any case, at this level we note that the function seems to receive **CI Status** data from and to return **Direction** to the Review CI Status process. I say "seems" because the DFD does not rule out the possibility that Request Clarification sends Direction to Review CI Status and receives CI Status in return; only an understanding of the next level of specification can clarify this ambiguity. Request Clarification also sends a value for the Action Flag to the Change Status File.

- Recompile CIs. From the level-2 DFD in Figure 3.2 we know that Tested CIs are deposited in the CI and Configuration Repository, but is not clear if they have been compiled. Thus, it is necessary to identify any Source CIs that must be compiled and generate Object CIs from them. As shown in the figure, the Recompile CI List is an input from Review CI Status.

- Construct Configuration. The manufacture of a configuration implies the building of a configuration from a set of object modules and then testing it with an appropriate set of test data. Here the Construct Configuration process receives a Set of CIs that defines the configuration, retrieves the necessary Object CIs, creates and stores the Configuration, and sends the Set of CIs to Construct Test Set to begin that process.

   Some questions: How does Construct Configuration know that all the necessary Object CIs have been compiled by Recompile CIs? Is a data flow missing? Is this a detail that would only add clutter to the DFD? Perhaps this is a problem that will be recognized and resolved at the next level of analysis.

- Construct Test Set. This process receives a Set of CIs and uses it to construct a Test Set, which is stored in the CI and Configuration Repository. This is a deceptively simple process description. It implies that we keep test sets under configuration control, that we update them when we modify the program CIs, and that we know how to combine them into a system (i.e., configuration) test.

- Test Configuration. Before the configuration can be released, it must be tested. Both the Configuration and the Test Set are available in the CI and Configuration Repository. The results of the test are indicated as an Action Flag value to be stored in the Change Status File. We assume that Management will provide direction if the Action Flag indicates that the configuration failed this test.

In this description of Figure 3.5 I used considerable information that would be available only as the result of further analysis. A system design (i.e., a model-in-the-large) in SA requires a complete set of DFDs and minispecs with a data dictionary. The context diagram establishes the system boundary, the level-2 DFD provides an overview of the architecture, and the remaining DFDs and minispecs define what occurs within each bubble. The data dictionary defines the contents and structure of each data flow. Thus, we end up with a complete description of the model. We can use a CASE tool to draw the diagrams and check that all the data flows are defined, that the dictionary is complete, that all process bubbles have been decomposed, that the numbering conventions are adhered to, etc. In this section I have used the DFD in Figure 3.5 to explain how **Configuration Manufacture** might work and what some of the potential design pitfalls might be. The creation of the DFD was an exercise in formalizing how I saw the SCM System carrying out the functions identified in Chapter 2. In explaining its contents, I was able to identify problems that I have deferred for later resolution. Thus, the SA products were not examples taken from a complete design; rather they are working documents from a design in process. The specifications (and most particularly the DFD) facilitate communication and comprehension. That is why they have proven to be so effective for walkthroughs with users and designers.

However, the DFD can be misinterpreted. DeMarco points out

> . . .that trying to understand the system by following items serially through the DFD is using it imperfectly. It is this serial means of absorbing the subject matter that has hampered us in the past. With a DFD, you have the opportunity to absorb the information in parallel; not to *read it*, but to *see it*. [DeMa78, p. 95]

This is a very important point. What we are doing when modeling-in-the-large is determining the structure of the product we are about to build. To *see* certain attributes of that structure we must *ignore* other properties. The DFD provides a view that obscures sequential dependencies but emphasizes functions and their interfaces. Each bubble represents an abstraction that we can understand only by referencing what has been defined elsewhere in the SA specification. We are restricted to our $7 \pm 2$ chunks, and the SA tools represent a reasonable way to overcome our limitations. The method does not offer us the precision of a formal specification, and there are other ways to suppress the details that can confuse us. Nevertheless, more people probably know how to read a DFD than almost any other systems analysis diagram, and the SA method described here offers a proven and effective technique for modeling-in-the-large. Therefore, every software engineer ought to be familiar with this method and its tools.


### 3.2.2.  Structured design

In the previous section, SA was used for modeling-in-the-large. We started with an understanding of what the product should do, and we developed a model of the product's software. There may be some confusion regarding the difference between "requirements analysis" and "design" because the same modeling tools were used for both. As I have tried to suggest, the end of requirements analysis is determined by project management; it generally is the completion of a document or specification. Few requirements specifications are complete enough to define precisely what is to be delivered. Therefore, they simply establish the essential properties of the target product along with the acceptance criteria. Moreover, the requirements are seldom stable; they are subject to constant change, and any design approach that ignores this fact will have limited success. Thus, once design begins, the development team will make design decisions that affect the functionality to be delivered. In fact, the freedom of design is constrained only by the need for the delivered product to satisfy the acceptance criteria.

Therefore, we must face the fact that in an operational setting many design decisions involve requirements analysis conducted within the scope of the project charter. Consequently, it will be almost impossible to divorce requirements analysis from design. The delineation of the project phases, the definition of the milestones, and the identification of the project's goals are important factors that are essential to the success of a project, but they are the responsibility of management. I will discuss some of management's options in Chapter 6, and in Chapter 5 I will examine how to know if a design satisfies its specifications. Both these issues are crucial to the success of a project. The delay of their discussion until later chapters does not suggest that they are post-design activities. It is just that here I want to focus on how to construct the architecture of a software solution to a specified problem. Software engineering, like design, is a holistic process; we can manage the details by temporarily obscuring other (perhaps critical) factors. In time, each problem will be addressed with the thoroughness it deserves; we call this the *separation of concerns.*

Although SA can be used for requirements analysis, the SA specification that we have just described (i.e., the collection of DFDs, minispecs, and data dictionary entries) represents a high-level design of the target system. The stores and functions are identified; sometimes even the formats of data elements are given. We have augmented the initial requirements with a set of decisions that affects how the SCM

System will serve its users. For example, when a need for management reports was identified in Chapter 2, there was no reference to a Change Status File. We made a design decision that affects the implementation; indeed, as a result of the SA method we have established both the file contents and the functions that reference it.[7] The obvious questions now are, Is the design complete? Can we begin to code? As one might guess from the chapter heading, the answer to both questions is "No." So far we have been modeling how the system must be decomposed into functions. The result is the identification of a set of functions and their interfaces. The primary orientation throughout this process was the concern for how the requirements could be expressed and decomposed as functions. Although we made implementation (i.e., design) decisions, we were motivated by the need to define how the system would support its objectives and not how it would be implemented.

It is now time to consider how the system should be implemented. Not as program code (which would be modeling-in-the-small) but as an organization of modules. Structured Design (SD) is a method for composing systems in a way that improves reuse, reliability, and maintainability. Some SD techniques show how to convert a data flow graph (such a DFD) into a *structure chart* that displays the relationships among the modules. In fact, many commercial training organizations teach SA and SD as complementary techniques. (Sometimes the combined approach is called Structured Analysis and Logical Design, SALD.) Thus, the output of SA can be used as the input to SD; both SA and SD also can be used independently. Although many of the concepts developed with SD have broad acceptance, SD does not enjoy the same popularity as SA. Nevertheless, a brief introduction to its principles will be instructive.

The origins of both SA and SD can be traced back to the *IBM System Journal* paper prepared by Constantine and his students. In it, the authors defined the problem as follows:

> It is possible to divide the design process into general program design and detailed design as follows. General program design

---

[7]Actually, we would know this only if we had completed the SA analysis process. As previously noted, I am on the horns of a dilemma. If I chose an application simple enough to produce a complete solution in a textbook, then I would be guilty of using my design tools in excess. On the other hand, when I jump around and produce only parts of the solution, I invite a casual approach. For readers interested in SA, [DeMa78] has a simple but rather complete example, [GaSa79] illustrate their method with a central case study, [Your89] includes a case study as an appendix, and other books on SA (such as [Kowa88]) include examples that they cover in some depth.

is deciding *what* functions are needed for the program (or programming system). Detailed design is *how* to implement the functions. . . . [Structured Design results] in an identification of the functions, calling parameters, and the call relationships for a structure of functionally bound, simply connected modules. The information thus generated makes it easier for each module to then be separately designed, implemented, and tested. [StMC74, p. 127]

The concern of SD was not on how the modules were implemented (i.e., how the code was written) but on how the system's functions could be realized as a set of communicating modules. The prevalent modeling tool of the time was the flowchart, which detailed the order of and conditions for the execution of blocks of code. SD raised the level of abstraction from code processes (as would be expressed in a flowchart symbol) to modules, and the structure chart provided a tool for modeling module connections and their calling parameters.

In SD the module is defined as an identifiable set of contiguous program statements such as a subroutine. (While the size of a module was not defined, the conventions of structured programming limited a program unit to what could be printed on a single page: about 50 lines with comments.) The central issues that SD faced were

- How should modules interact with each other? *Coupling* was the term adopted to identify and rank the alternative techniques.

- How should the desired functions be converted into modules? *Cohesion* was the word chosen to classify the organizational categories.

- What simple system structures are characteristic of modular systems? Two major design structures were identified: *transaction-centered* and *transform-centered*.

SD began by identifying the properties of a good design. It then developed the methods and heuristics to a convert a functional description (usually expressed as a data flow graph) into a design. I discuss these issues in turn.

Although coupling deals with the connections among modules, its motivation was derived from the question, How much of one module must be known in order to understand another module? Obviously, the more independent the modules, the more localized the decision making and the less danger that unanticipated interactions will materialize. Constantine defined coupling as the *strength* of module interconnection. "Highly coupled" modules are joined by strong interconnections, and "weakly coupled" modules are joined by weak interconnections. "Uncoupled" or "decoupled" modules have no interconnections and are independent of each other. Obviously, the goal is to reduce the coupling strength. Yourdon and Constantine identified some factors that influence coupling [YoCo79].[8]

- *Type of connection between modules*, which ranges from minimally connected to pathological connections. Modules with a single entry and exit point avoid the pathological connections that were common with assembly language routines.

- *Complexity of the interface*, which was defined as the number of distinct parameters passed.

- *Type of information flow along the connection*, which favored data-coupled over control-coupled systems.

- *Binding time of the connection*, which favored run-time table lookups to decisions made at earlier binding times.

A scale of coupling strengths then was identified that begins with no direct coupling, continues through data coupling (by passing parameters), control coupling (by passing control flags), and common coupling (by accessing shared data), and terminates with content coupling (whereby one module takes advantage of knowledge about the internal workings of another module). The terms are imprecise and subjective. Clearly, content coupling should be avoided, but there is no need to insist on no direct coupling. The process of *decoupling* is used to reduce coupling strength; decoupling permits the use of stronger coupling as an explicit design decision.

Cohesion, the second property of modules, is concerned with the complementary problem of deciding which functions should be combined *within* a module. Yourdon and Constantine defined seven levels of cohesion [YoCo79].

- *Coincidental cohesion*, which implies little or no constructive relationship among elements in a module (e.g., several unrelated functions are joined in one module to share some common segments of code).

---

[8]This topic is closely related to the issue of information hiding introduced by Parnas [Parn72b]. I discuss Parnas's work in the context of the abstract data type in Chapter 4.

- *Logical cohesion*, which collects elements that are logically associated by class (e.g., a collection of all "input" processing elements).

- *Temporal cohesion*, which collects elements that take place at one time (e.g., start-up processes).

- *Procedural cohesion*, where the module separation decision was based on flowchart structure rather than the processing it implied. (The authors had difficulty in offering examples; see sequential cohesion.)

- *Communication cohesion*, which is the lowest level at which there is a relationship among processing elements that is intrinsically problem dependent (e.g., one module processes the input of a record and a second its output).

- *Sequential cohesion*, in which a function is decomposed into a sequence of transformations with each implemented as a module. (Compare this with procedural cohesion in which the module divisions are based on the flowchart topology rather than the flow of the functions performed; as will be seen, the structure chart provides an effective tool for identifying sequential cohesion.)

- *Functional cohesion*, where every element in the module is an integral part of, and essential to, the performance of a single function. (Yourdon and Constantine also defined it as any cohesion not otherwise defined.)

Cohesion measures how well the elements in a module belong together, and here (unlike coupling) stronger is better.

The concepts of coupling and cohesion offered guidelines to help SD achieve a system design that was simple, reusable, and maintainable. Other design heuristics for module connections also were offered. The *span of control* was defined as the number of immediate subordinates of a module; it should seldom exceed 10. *Fan-in* represents the number of sources of reference to a module. Whereas fan-in is a modularization goal (i.e., a module ought to be called by many others), high fan-in values can be a sign of low cohesion. The *scope of control* identifies the modules subordinate to a module, and the *scope of effect* represents the modules affected by the processing of that module. One should keep the scope of effect within the scope of control. The structure chart was introduced as a diagrammatic device for presenting the module organization and interfaces. It is depicted as a directed graph containing *modules* (drawn in boxes) and *connections* between modules (drawn as lines with an arrow to the subordinate module). The chart also may include *information flows* (drawn as straight lines with an arrow head to indicate the direction of flow and a circle at the base to indicate the type of information). Two categories of information are identified. *Data flow* is denoted by a white circle and *control flow* by a black dot.

To illustrate the structure chart, consider the functional flow shown in Figure 3.6 and the associated chart in Figure 3.7. The process described is a simple sequence for producing a report. First the dates for the report are entered; then the data required for the report are extracted from the database; next the data are transformed into the summary information required for the report; and finally the report is printed. Figure 3.6 contains a data flow graph similar to a DFD. In the examples in this section, the level of detail for the graphs may be lower than what one would expect of a DFD. Nevertheless, the same techniques can be used to transform a DFD into a structure chart. Figure 3.7 displays a structure chart in which the entire process is represented by a control module called Report. It has three modules immediately subordinate to it, one of which, Transform Data, has two subordinate modules. At the first level, Input Date reads an input and returns a data flow, Dates, and a control flow, Valid. The first contains the date range and the second is a flag to indicate if the user has entered a valid input. The Dates data flow is input to the Transform Data module. Here the input is sent to Retrieve Data, which returns the data flow Data. The data flow Data is input to the module Process Report, which returns the data flow Summary. Once the data have been transformed, the data flow Summary is input to the module Print Report to produce the desired output. (As with the DFD, one can use a data dictionary to describe the flows and module specs to define a module's internal operations.)

The structure shown in Figure 3.7 represents a transform-centered design, and the method for producing it is called *transform analysis*. Essentially, the design model is an Input → Process → Output construct. The input module (Input Date) is called the *afferent module* because it receives the external stimuli for processing. The module that receives

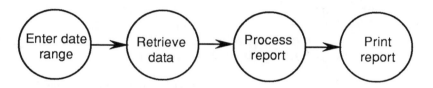

Fig. 3.6.   Model of a process to produce a report.

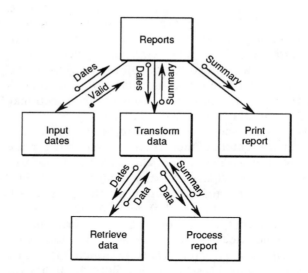

Fig. 3.7. Structure chart for the process model in Figure 3.6.

one set of input data flows and returns another (Transform Data) is called a *transform module*. Print Report, the module that receives only input data flows (i.e., produce outputs), is called an *efferent module*. (Not shown in the figure is a *coordinate module* that receives control flows from one module and sends control flows to another module.) The structure in this example is almost trivially simple. Of course, that is its advantage. The goal is to reduce a complex system into uncomplicated structures that are easy to code and maintain.

Transform analysis defines a four-step process for modeling a function as the transformation of an input into an output. The steps are as follows:

1. *Restate the problem as a data flow graph.* When working with SA/SD, one begins with a data flow graph; however, it may be necessary to extend the level of detail.

2. *Identify the afferent and efferent data elements.* This can be done only by understanding the processing represented by each bubble in the data flow graph. For example, the structure of the graph in Figure 3.6 does not rule out the possibility that the first two bubbles represent a two-step afferent process.

3. *Perform first level factoring.* *Factoring* is defined as the process of decomposing a system into a hierarchy of modules. The result

is the Input → Process → Output flow of the first level of
subordinates.

4. *Factoring of afferent, efferent, and transformation branches.* The
process is iterated until all the modules can be implemented as
page-sized modules with high cohesion. Here the structure of
Transform Data has been factored as a control and two subordinate modules; the assumption is that this structure was determined by the processing characteristics of the resulting modules.

The structure chart in Figure 3.7 uses three levels to illustrate the
concept of repeated factoring. Naturally, the number of levels required
depends on the complexity of the functions that they implement. That
must be a problem-specific consideration; the rules for structuring a
transform-centered design, on the other hand, are always problem
independent.

A second form of analysis is called *transaction analysis.* Here some
data value or event is used to determine the actions of the system. The
transaction center for this kind of system must get the transaction in its
raw form, analyze it to determine its type, dispatch it according to its
type, and complete the processing of each transaction. Figure 3.8
illustrates transaction processing in a data flow graph for the actions
taken after a new configuration is tested and the Action Flag is entered.
It shows that, depending on the value of the Action Flag, reports will be
sent to management, the testers, and/or the SCM team. The structure
chart for this flow is given in Figure 3.9. On the left the flag is received
and the analysis retrieves information about the configuration. This has
been factored as a transform-centered design. The module structure on
the right illustrates a transaction-centered design. The transaction
processing is detailed on the right. It shows the module connections in
which the processed disposition information (Flag) is used to direct the
configuration information (Summary) to one or more reporting
modules. The diamond represents a selection. Because Flag controls
the processing flow, it is shown with a black dot. Again, the result is a
very simple structure.

Figure 3.10 contains a more complex data flow graph and its
structure chart is shown in Figure 3.11. The overall structure is
determined by transform analysis, and the factoring indicates that each
process in the graph can be implemented as a single module in the
chart. Notice that, even though we speak of a hierarchy, we do not
insist that the structure chart depict a hierarchy. Process F sends data
to both processes A and E. Consequently, module F must be processed
before either A or E can complete; that is, F is subordinate to both
modules A and E. In constructing the structure chart, we expect the
module structure to reflect the organization of the graph (e.g., because

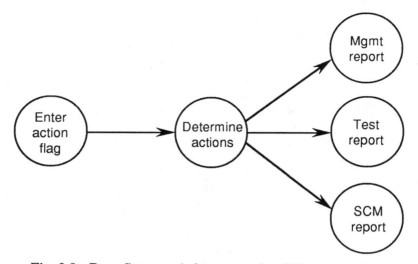

Fig. 3.8.  Data flow graph for processing SCM test results.

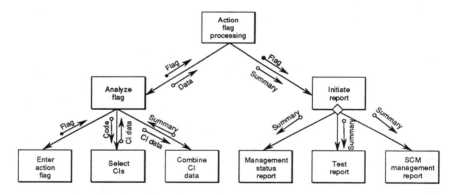

Fig. 3.9.  Structure diagram for the process model in Figure 3.8.

process A provides an input to process B, module A must be subordinate to module B).  Yet we do not expect the order of the modules in the chart to convey any meaning other than that implied by the afferent-transform-efferent convention.  Thus, no relationships among the modules C, B, and D are implied by this chart.  Module B may always be called before module D, or it may always be called after module D is called, or it may be called only as the result of certain conditions.  What we are modeling with structure charts is *only* the relationships among modules and not their order of execution.  In Section 3.3, when I describe the Jackson methods, I will present a modeling technique that defines the order in which the processes are executed.  Naturally, to

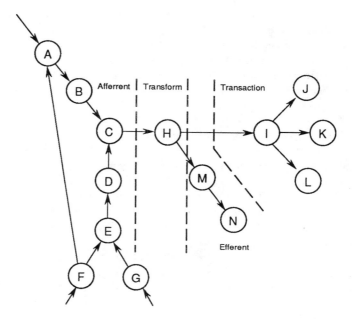

Fig. 3.10.  Data flow graph for an arbitrary process.

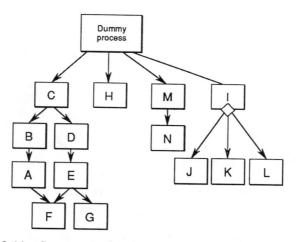

Fig. 3.11.  Structure diagram for the model in Figure 3.10.

show that characteristic of the model, some of the module features presented here will be obscured.

By way of conclusion, I believe that the major contribution of SD is the emphasis it has placed on the heuristics of modularization.  The concepts of coupling and cohesion make us think about how we organize our modules. Transform analysis and transaction analysis provide useful generic design templates. When we reduce the design to very elementary constructs, we lose some elegance, but we gain clarity and avoid errors. This, of course, should be the goal of our modeling activity. We want simple, efficient structures for our users and not elaborate monuments to our ingenuity.

### 3.2.3.  *Variations on structured analysis*

When describing the background of SA, I pointed out that its origins were in data processing. The basic principles of SA, however, are not limited to that application class. SA provides a systematic approach to the definition of requirements and the decomposition of functions once a system boundary has been established. For data processing applications, communications among the functions (i.e., processes or bubbles) are quite straightforward, and they can be modeled with the four symbols of the DFD. For other types of application, however, more complex interfunction communications must be supported, and the symbology of the DFD must be enhanced. In what follows I illustrate how SA has been extended to support the modeling of real-time applications. I also show how that experience, in turn, has affected SA.

All computer systems operate in real time. To my knowledge, only the British Museum algorithm ignores time constraints. (It solves problems, such as theorem proving, by an exhaustive and unsystematic search for correct results.) What characterizes a real-time system, then, is not its concern for performance but

- The presence of many well-defined computational processes, several of which may be active at any one time.

- The existence of external devices that request (and may compete for) processes and/or their computational results.

- The asynchronous (and often nondeterministic) nature of the processing.

- The perishability of the data in the sense that process outputs have no value after a specified period.

- The frequent need for unique hardware, which implies the need for parallel development of hardware and software.

The study of real-time systems has an extensive literature (e.g., [Glas83, Mell83, StRa88, NiSh88]). Several researchers have shown how SA can be adapted to support the analysis and implementation of such systems (e.g., [Goma84, Goma86, HaPi87, Kowa88]). In what follows I limit the discussion to the techniques introduced by Ward and Mellor [WaMe85], the most widely referenced application of SA to real-time systems. My emphasis is on the modeling methods and tools and not the constraints of this particular domain.

The three-volume Ward and Mellor book, *Structured Development for Real-Time Systems*, considers both analysis and design. The authors begin by identifying three activities in the evolution of a system:

- *Build the essential model*, which describes the required behavior of the system.

- *Build the implementation model*, which describes the organization of the automated technology that embodies the required behavior.

- *Build the system*, which embodies the implementation in hardware and software.

At this level of generalization, these three activities are common for virtually all software development projects. The details of the modeling processes, however, will reflect the kind of application to be constructed.

Ward and Mellor decompose the essential model into two more specialized models.

- *Environmental model*, which describes the environment in which the system operates. It consists of a
  - *Context diagram*, which defines the boundary that separates the system from its environment, and an
  - *Event list*, which establishes the external events in the environment to which the system must respond.

- *Behavioral model*, which describes the system's behavior responses to events in the environment. It consists of
  - *Transformation schema and specifics*, which describe the transformations the system makes in response to environmental events, and
  - *Data schema and specifics*, which describe the information the system must have in order to respond.

Notice how this essential model reflects the type of application under consideration. In the SA model prepared for the SCM system, our concern was for an application to be used in an operational setting. Thus, we began by modeling that setting. In Chapter 2 we explored the use of modeling tools to understand how change requests were managed, how configurations were defined, etc. This was also the motivation for the physical and logical models described at the beginning of Section 3.2.1. Once we modeled the environment (i.e., established how the system would be used), we then could model a system to provide the required functionality (i.e., behavior). That is, our goal was to implement a product to be used in an operational setting, and our method was first to model that setting and then to define the product in the context of that setting model. The target product was underconstrained, and many different designs could (in theory) satisfy the need for a SCM System. The most effective systems would be those with no seams between the system and the environment it supported (i.e., there would be no breaks in the sense they were discussed in Section 2.4.1). But even if we were unable to create a seamless design, learning about the domain of application remained a prerequisite to success. Defining this kind of application without knowing how it would be used is a clear invitation to failure; there is a high probability that the product will not correspond to the environment's needs (i.e., it would be invalid). Consequently, for information-oriented applications the design process begins by defining the environment and its needs.

With a real-time system, on the other hand, we face a different modeling challenge. Here the environment already has a formal definition (which, perhaps, has even been overconstrained). As the result of a *systems engineering* allocation of functions process, we know how the system environment behaves and exactly what responses are expected from the software component.[9] Viewing the software system from the perspective of its external interfaces, we can establish its boundary (in a context diagram) and define its interactions (as a list of events). Then, turning to how the software system should respond to these external stimuli, we can model its behavior as transformations (which are an extension of the DFD and minispec) and states (which is an extension of the data dictionary). The outcome of this process is an implementation-independent design of the essential features of the software. (Again, I observe that the process includes some design

---

[9]This statement implies that the hardware design is available prior to the specification of the software. Unfortunately, this is seldom the case. With the parallel development of hardware and software, the designers often must work with partial requirements and test environments. Because of the physical difficulty in implementing hardware changes, there is a tendency to rely on software modifications to compensate for system-level design inadequacies. This is the essential difficulty of *conformity* to which Brooks referred [Broo87]. It is a management-determined response to an unanticipated problem, and no design method can circumvent its effects.

decisions, such as the distribution of functions among processors, but it does not make any decisions that affect modeling-in-the-small.)

After the essential model has been accepted, Ward and Mellor begin the definition of the implementation model. It is constructed in three layers. First a *processor model* identifies a set of concurrent processors to carry out the activities and store the data declared in the essential model. Next, a *task model* expands on this and identifies the tasks that can be scheduled and the storage units that they share. Finally, a *module model* adds the details on how the module is to be implemented. Both the processor and task models use transform and data schemata with their specifics to describe the processors, tasks, and interfaces; the module model is described using structure charts. Once the implementation model is complete, coding follows.

From this brief overview, it is clear that there are many similarities between SA for information and real-time applications. Because the behaviors of the latter are more complex, the DFD notation must be extended to express the new concepts. Figure 3.12 contains a DFD for a process control device that monitors two process variables, temperature and current, and feeds back current changes to stabilize the process. A walkthrough of this diagram will introduce the reader to most of the symbols used in the Ward and Mellor books. The first, and most obvious difference between the DFD in Figure 3.12 and those of Figures 3.2-3.5 is the presence of symbols drawn with dashed lines. These represent control functions and flows. For example, the Process Control function responds to the events (i.e., control flows) Start and Stop and sends the control flow Enable/Disable to the process Compute Current Change. Similarly, the control function System Control processes the events On and Off and sends the control flows Power-up and Power-down to the process Power Source. Power Source sends Current as an output data flow and receives Correction as an input data flow. Notice that the Current data flow has a split, which indicates that the same data flow (in this case electrical current) is sent to two destinations. Also observe that both Current flows terminate with a double arrow. This symbol is used to distinguish between continuous and discrete flows. Here, current is always flowing, thus it is shown as a continuous flow with the double arrow. Correction, the input flow to Power Source, is discrete, and it has a single arrow.

Process is actually not just one process but a number of similar independent processes. This is indicated by the multiple circles stacked on each other. One can indicate parallel control processes with a similar construct using dashed-line circles. In this DFD, one common Current flow is input into each of the processes, and each sends out a continuous Temperature flow to be processed by both Compute Current Change and Emergency Shutdown. Compute Current Change

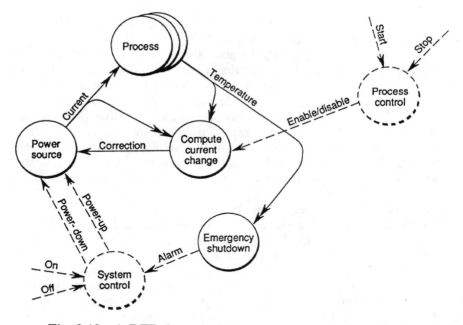

Fig. 3.12. A DFD for a real-time process-control application.

processes the Current, which is input to all the Process functions and the Temperature flows that each of them report. From this information it computes a Correction flow that is sent to Power Source. Here there is just one Compute Current Change for all the Process transformations. To show one Compute Current Change for each Process, Compute Current Change would be drawn as a stack of bubbles. Finally, the figure shows that all Temperature flows are sent to Emergency Shutdown, which can send the control flow Alarm to System Control. There are some symbols not included in this DFD. For example, there is a notation to show that a flow combines the flows from more than one process. Other SA tools for real-time systems expand further on this notation to include symbols for loosely coupled (queued) and closely coupled (synchronized) messages [Goma84, Goma86].

Once the DFD notation has been expanded to model the concepts essential to a real-time system, Ward and Mellor devote the remainder of Volume 1 to describing the modeling tools used in their method.

- *Transformations* are modeled using the solid symbols in the extended DFDs.

- *Control transformations* are modeled using the dashed symbols in the extended DFDs.

- *Data transformations* (i.e., the processing represented by a bubble that transforms data) are depicted as minispecs as described in Section 3.2.1. A state-transition diagram (see Section 2.3.2) also is suggested as an alternative for some processes; fully half their examples are defined in this way.

- *Executing the transformation schema* (i.e., the dynamics or *executability* of the transformation schema) is modeled as a Petri net (see Section 2.3.2).

- *Stored data* are modeled with an entity-relationship model (see Section 2.3.1).

- *Data specification* uses a form of the SA data dictionary described in Section 3.2.1 extended to include some entity-relationship concepts.

Ward and Mellor use Volume 2 to describe the essential modeling techniques, and there are two case studies that illustrate the context schema, event lists, and the modeling of the above objects. Volume 3 concentrates on implementation modeling techniques. It has chapters on modeling processes, tasks, interfaces, and system services; the case studies of the previous book are continued. Each volume is relatively short, clearly written, and well illustrated; together, they provide a useful introduction to real-time system development.

In discussing the application of SA to real-time systems, the emphasis was on methodology; I described how the SA methods and tools were extended for that domain. I now consider the effect of those extensions on SA's evolution. Recall that this chapter began by identifying two contrasting modeling approaches: decomposition and composition. Decomposition begins with a black-box model of a complete system. This model is decomposed into functions, which are further decomposed until they can be defined as implementation units. This is the traditional approach to system design; it is the foundation of stepwise refinement [Wirt71]. In SA/SD, modeling-in-the-large begins after the complete system is represented as one bubble in a context diagram. DFDs are constructed to define each level of decomposition; minispecs, structure charts, and data dictionaries fill in the details. As described in Section 3.2.1, each DFD bubble is expanded as a lower level DFD until its processing is simple enough to be presented in a minispec. SD then converts the system's data flow graph description into an implementation-oriented model that incorporates the heuristics of good module design. By way of contrast, composition was described as a method in which one first models those aspects of the system that were well understood. The complete system is composed by combining those smaller (but well-defined) models.

The distinction between these approaches is clear. With decomposition one starts from the top and works down. The system is divided into $7 \pm 2$ functions to be analyzed in further detail, and the process is iterated for each function until all the issues are resolved. Composition, on the other hand, begins with specific features of the target system (perhaps events and responses to them), models those processes, and continues until all processes are defined. It was described as an outside-in process. But, from the very brief discussion of the real-time modeling tools, one sees that SA can also be interpreted as a constructive process. The entity-relationship model captures knowledge about the data that cannot be expressed in the DFD; the event list invites a description of the system as separate processes from which the whole is composed. Does this imply that recent changes to SA have moved it away from its underling decomposition philosophy?

Yourdon, who has been one of the leaders in the dissemination of the SA approach, presents his current views in *Modern Structured Analysis* [Your89]. He observes that the field of systems analysis is dynamic, and the way in which it will be conducted in the mid-1990s will differ from how we do it today. Thus, he continues, the software engineer needs to know both the methods in use and how they evolved. After an historical survey that justifies the orientation described in Section 3.2.1, Yourdon identifies the following changes to "classical structured analysis."

- The emphasis on the building of "current physical" and "current logical" models has been dropped. "The project team often spent so much time . . . studying the user's *old* system, . . . that the project was canceled by an impatient user" [p. 125]. Moreover, the "system analyst gets carried away with the task of modeling the current system and begins to think of it as an end in itself" [p. 322].

- The distinctions between physical and logical models were ambiguous. Building on the contributions of McMenamin and Palmer [McMP84] (and applied by Ward and Mellor), the terminology has been changed to essential and implementation models.

- Methods have been extended to support real-time applications.

- "Classical structured analysis concentrated almost entirely on the modeling of the *functions* to be carried out in a system; the modeling of data was done in a primitive way" [p. 126]. State-transition diagrams and entity-relationship models have been integrated into the method.

- "The *process* of structured analysis has changed dramatically. Classical structured analysis assumed that the systems analyst would begin by drawing a context diagram . . . and then partition the system into several functions and data stores in a strictly top-down fashion. Unfortunately, this has not worked well [and] a new approach known as *event partitioning* has been added" [p. 126].

Modern structured analysis, as described by Yourdon, expands the collection of tools to include entity-relationship diagrams and state-transition diagrams in addition to the standard data flow diagrams, data dictionary, and process specifications (i.e., minispecs). Its environment model is defined with an event list, and this list is used to build the behavioral model. The process "is substantially different from the top-down approach described in such classical textbooks as DeMarco and Gane and Sarson" [p. 359]. Yourdon observes that he is not opposed to a top-down approach

> . . . *if it works.* However, you should be aware that many systems analysts encounter the following problems when attempting to follow the top-down approach:
>
> *Analysis paralysis.* In many large, complex systems, there simply isn't a clue to guide the systems analyst in drawing an appropriate Figure 0 from the context diagram. So the analyst sits at her desk, staring at the context diagram, waiting for divine inspiration, . . .
>
> *The six-analyst phenomenon.* In a large, complex system, . . . in order to divide up the work equally . . . they arbitrarily create a Figure 0 with one bubble for each analyst. Thus, if there are six analysts, Figure 0 will consist of six bubbles. . . .
>
> *An arbitrary physical partitioning.* In many cases . . . the top-level partitioning of the current system . . . is often used as the rationale for developing the partitioning of the new system . . . [even though this might not be the best partitioning] of the system. [Your89, p. 360]

The event partitioning that Yourdon proposes as an alternative begins after the environment model has been defined. This model consists of a textual statement of purpose, a context diagram, and an event list. These data then are used to establish the behavioral model as follows.

- *Identify event responses.* First, a bubble is drawn for each event in the event list. The bubble is named to reflect the system's response to the event, and the appropriate input and output flows are drawn. Finally, these first-cut DFDs are tested against the context diagram and event list for consistency.

- *Develop the initial data model.* This is done by identifying the data stores necessary to connect the events. The data model is developed from "the initial version of the entity-relationship diagram [which is being worked on] *as an independent activity, in parallel with the development of the initial DFD*" [p. 365].

- *Level the DFDs.* This is a process similar to that used in classical SA to produce a model in which all bubbles within a DFD represent roughly the same complexity.

- *Finish the behavioral model.* Finally, the details are supplied in the data model and process specifications using the tools of classical systems analysis plus entity-relationship diagrams and state-transition diagrams.

The resulting behavioral model is combined with the environmental model to complete the essential model definition. A user implementation model may be constructed to resolve implementation issues such as the automation boundary or the formats of inputs and outputs. Design follows using three models similar to those described by Ward and Mellor: the processor model, the task model, and the program implementation (or module) model.

What conclusions can we draw from this review of "modern structured analysis?" First, all methods evolve as we learn to use and extend them. Second, there may be major variations among proponents of a common method, and labels can be misleading. Finally, and perhaps most important, there is a tension between the conceptual neatness of a method and its effectiveness in solving problems. When SA introduced new modeling tools it also complicated the process of integrating the various models into a unified model. The advantage of a top-down approach is that it defines an order for the decisions. Unfortunately, problem solving (such as creating a Figure 0 from a context diagram) may be inhibited by the wealth of detail available at the top. We may solve problems unsystematically, but we must always present the results systematically.[10]   Jackson observes that we do not prove mathematical theorems in a top-down fashion, but we report our results as if we did.   Thus, we must strike a balance between how we organize the design activity and how we carry it out.   We expect our modeling tools to aid in both comprehension (i.e., problem resolution) and presentation (i.e., communication to others); we want our methods to establish clear procedures for the systematic use of these tools. Unfortunately, however, as we enrich our tool set for one objective, it complicates our achieving the other; as we expand the tool set, we dilute the method's guidance.

Stepping back to examine the big picture, our goal is the design of a system to meet a specified set of needs.   We should be free to use any tools that help us in this process.   We should select methods that guide the use of these tools in the context of the overall problem-solving activity.   Consequently, we may use many tools but only a few methods. And the tools we select must complement each other with respect to the coordinating method.   In this section I have described a family of methods that structures the process as a decomposition activity.   Each method models the system as a hierarchy of functions.   Some use tools to augment the top-down orientation of the method; nevertheless, the result is a top-down description of the system design.   In the next section I will introduce an approach with a very different design philosophy and set of supporting tools.

### 3.3.    Jackson System Development and programming

If one were to group the design methods as they emerged in the 1970s, one would not choose the decomposition-composition rubric I am using. Rather, one would organize the methods into those that concentrated on the flow of data among processes (i.e., *data-flow* methods) and those that focused on the structure of the data (i.e., *data-structure* methods).   As its name implies, the data flow diagram (DFD) of structured analysis was developed for a data-flow approach.   One builds a model of the system by first establishing how the data move within the system and then by defining the transformations that affect the data flows.   The transformations are represented as bubbles (processes) in the DFD, and structured analysis provides a systematic method for detailing the process descriptions.

The data-structure proponents, on the other hand, believe that the best way to understand an organization is to model the data that it uses. This model, it is asserted, reflects the structure of the universe in which

---

[10]For an enjoyable commentary on this subject see [PaCl86].

the organization operates. That is, because the organization uses the data as surrogates for the real-world entities with which it interacts, the data structures represent the organization's richest understanding of its universe. How the organization uses (transforms) the data (i.e., its processes) is subject to more change than the data's underlying structure. The same analogy can be made for programs; if one understands the structure of the input and output data, then the structure of the program should follow.

Both sides in this debate recognized that there was such a philosophic difference that compromise was impossible. One could use either a data-flow or a data-structure method, but not a combination of the two. In Section 3.2, the early history of some of the data-flow methods was summarized. For the data-structure methods, there were three principal method developers: Warnier (referenced in Section 2.3.1), Orr (whose requirements analysis methods are described in Section 2.3.2), and Jackson (whose program design method can be characterized as data-structure driven).

As its name implies, the Jackson Program Design Methodology (called JSP for reasons too complicated to get into) is a method for program design and not for modeling-in-the-large. It begins by defining the structure of the data on which a program is to operate and then uses a rigorous approach to ensure that the program and data structures match. Because of its algorithmic base, it is possible for different designers using this method to produce identical program solutions. That is, for some types of problem, two programmers given the same assignment will produce near-identical solutions. This achievement is not common to many design methods.

Jackson described his method in 1975 [Jack75] and went on to address issues in the design of systems. The result was a second method, called Jackson System Development (JSD), that was presented in [Jack82]. As one would expect, there is a great deal of commonality between JSP and JSD, but the former is not a subset of the latter. These are two different methods; as with structured analysis and structured design, they can be used either separately or in combination.

Naturally, the Jackson methods continued to evolve. Cameron, who works for Michael Jackson Systems, Ltd., has written a frequently cited overview of JSD [Came86] and has edited an excellent IEEE tutorial on JSP and JSD [Came89]. Among the other books on these methods are one by King on JSP [King88] and one by Sutcliffe on JSD [Sutc88]. In what follows I defy the logic of the book's top-down organization. Rather than starting with the modeling-in-the-large method of JSD, I begin by describing JSP. JSP is easy to understand, and by presenting it first I can lay the foundation for a discussion of JSD, which is often explained in ways that are difficult to comprehend.

### 3.3.1. Jackson Program Design (JSP)

JSP relies on just one diagrammatic convention, and it is used to model both data and processes (programs). Actually, the diagrams are simply an alternative form of the three constructs that comprise structured programming:

- *Sequence (seq)*. This is a sequence of items (i.e., data elements or program actions). A sequence is indicated by a row of boxes with nothing in the upper right corner.

- *Iteration (iter)*. This is the repetition of an item for zero or more times (e.g., do while). Iteration is indicated by a single box with an asterisk in the upper right corner.

- *Selection (sel ... alt)*. This is the selection of one item among alternatives (e.g., case). Selection is indicated by a row of boxes with a small circle in the upper right corner.

Thus, the notation reduces to rows of boxes with possible symbols in the upper right corner. A JSP diagram labels the boxes and connects them with lines. Because the JSP diagram is a graphic representation of a structured program, each diagram is in the form of a hierarchy. The two equivalent forms of the JSP notation are shown in Figure 3.13.

Although the notations are similar, there is a fundamental difference between a Jackson diagram[11] and a structured program. In structured programming, each item may be elaborated in the form of other structures. It is good practice to design programs using stepwise refinement [Wirt71], and one often removes unnecessary detail by replacing a complex structure with a simple abstraction (e.g., substituting for a complex process the name of a procedure that carries out that process). In JSP, however, our goal is to create a complete model, and its notation does not rely on symbols that capture an abstracted concept to be elaborated. Thus, unlike a DFD, which displays a portion of the model as a node in a nested representation scheme, each JSP diagram must be complete. Naturally, the designers cannot work on all aspects of the problem concurrently; they will have to separate their concerns and defer independent segments of the design, but the diagrammatic notation is not intended to manage their incomplete designs.

---

[11]Although Jackson refers to the diagrams as structure diagrams, I shall call them Jackson diagrams to avoid confusion with other notations such as structure charts.

Sequence: A consists of one B, followed by one C, followed by one D.

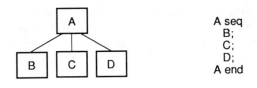

A seq
B;
C;
D;
A end

Iteration:    A consists of zero or more whole Bs.

A iter
B;
A end

Selection:    A consists of either one B, one C, or one D.

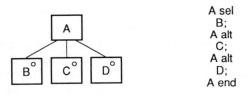

A sel
B;
A alt
C;
A alt
D;
A end

Fig. 3.13.  The Jackson notation.

An example will help.  Figure 3.14 presents a Jackson diagram for the data structure that might be extracted from the Change Request form shown in Figure 2.2.  (That is, the diagram shows the information that might be extracted from the form for entry into the database.) Reading across the top, it indicates that a change request (CR) consists of one Identification, followed by one Description, followed by one Status.  Reading on, we find that the Identification consists of one Number, followed by one Source, followed by one Priority, and the Priority consists of either a routine (R), urgent (U), or emergency (E) entry.  The Description is a sequence of a Summary followed by an Affected Items, and the Affected Items consists of a sequence of CIs (which in turn consists of an iteration of CI) and Docs (which also consists of an iteration, this time of Doc).  Finally, Status is seen to be a selection from either Active or Complete.

Observe that in this diagram the rows of boxes (with a common parent) represent sequences, iterations, or selections.  By their very nature, iterations must be in a row with exactly one box, and selections in rows of two or more boxes.  Also notice that the structure is hierarchical and includes the structure for every item.  Items at the

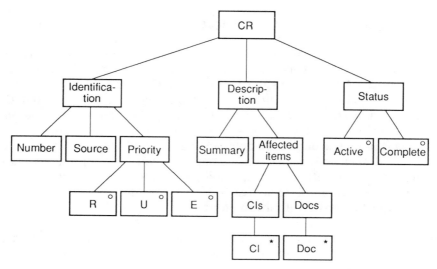

Fig. 3.14. Jackson diagram for a change request.

lowest level are assumed to represent the primitives (in this case, the fields in the data structure). Finally, note that some of the boxes are necessary to produce a valid structure. For example, **Affected items** is a list of the CIs and documents that will be affected by the proposed change. One might be tempted to write this as a sequence of two iterations, but that diagram could not be expressed in the formal notation of structured programming (i.e., one cannot write structured code for a sequence of two iterations, but one can write structured code for a sequence of two items, each of which is an iteration). Thus, one of the main advantages of the Jackson notation it that is enforces formality on a diagram that is easy to comprehend. The naming of the nonleaf nodes in the tree also has the advantage of providing labels for things (such as the set of all CIs) that ought to be named.

In this example we have taken the notation of structured programming, which was designed to model dynamic structures, and we used it to model data, which is static. Jackson believes that programmers often focus on the dynamics of the program, thereby becoming distracted by details. They ask questions such as, "What should the program do here?" when they might better consider, "How often should this operation be executed?" For example, if the programmer began to write code for the entry of **Affected items**, he might have difficulty in managing the special cases of both CIs and documents, neither CIs nor documents, and only CIs or only documents. Naturally, if the programmer happened to stumble onto the solution of a sequence of two items, each of which was an iteration, he would have no trouble. But it certainly would have been better to start with a good (formal) understanding of the structure rather than hope that a good structure may present itself.

JSP avoids the bad program designs that result from an undirected approach. One begins (as would be expected with a data-structure method) by diagramming the inputs to and outputs from the desired program. These two groups of structures then are merged, and the result is a program structure for transforming the input into the output. After the program structure has been established, the operations carried out within that structure are detailed and assigned. Up to this point, all of the design activity has been concerned with the program's static properties; it is left to the final step, in which the structure is copied over into textual form, to address any remaining dynamic concerns. This can be restated as the following four steps:

1   Draw Jackson diagrams to describe each of the data streams input to or output from the system.

2   Merge these data diagrams into a single Jackson diagram, which is the program diagram.

3   Make a suitable list of programming language operations, and then allocate them to the program diagram.

4   Convert the program diagram from its diagrammatic form to an equivalent textual form.

To illustrate the method, consider the following simple example, which has only one input and one output. We want a report that will list out, by priority, the number of active change requests by their source. We want a new page for each priority, and within a priority we want to list each source followed by the number of changes requested by the source. A final summary page will display the total number of active CRs by priority. As an input to this report we have a file containing all the active CRs sorted by Priority, Source, and CR-No. This file has a header containing its date of creation, and we want that date to be included in the heading of the report.

The structures of the sorted input file and the output file containing the report are shown in Figure 3.15. The sorted input is a Header followed by a Body followed by an End of File. The Body consists of iterations of Priority, which in turn consists of iterations of Source, which in turn consists of iterations of CR-No. The report, shown on the right, has a similar structure. It is a Header, Body, and Summary totals. (The names are intended to be descriptive in the context of the structure and do not imply, for instance, that the input Header is the same as the output Header.) The report Body is defined as iterations

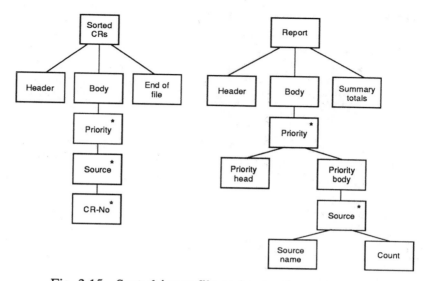

Fig. 3.15. Sorted input file and output report structures.

of Priority, which is a Priority Head followed by a Priority Body. The latter consists of iterations of Source lines, which is a Source Name followed by a Count. When there is only one input and one output, it is useful to draw the two Jackson diagrams next to each other so that we can compare structures. In this example we see that the input has an iteration of CR-No that has no equivalent in the output, and the output has some items, such as Priority Head and Count, that do not match equivalent items in the input. The process of merging these two structures will produce the structure of a program that accounts for all inputs necessary to produce the desired outputs.

The technique for creating a program structure involves three steps. First the corresponding components are merged, then the noncorresponding input components are added, and finally the noncorresponding output components are added. The complete merged program structure is shown in Figure 3.16. It most closely follows the structure of the report to be produced. The merging of the structures produces one that looks like the input file without the CR-No iteration. It is appended, and the noncorresponding outputs are added. The Print Header and Process Priority sequences fit in naturally, and the final level of the report is expanded to include the sequence Initialize Counter, Compute Count, List Count, and Update Totals. Finally, the CR-No iteration is represented as Total Number. So far, the program design process has not been difficult; it is really quite mechanical (i.e., algorithmic). The next step, listing and assigning the operations, is equally methodical.

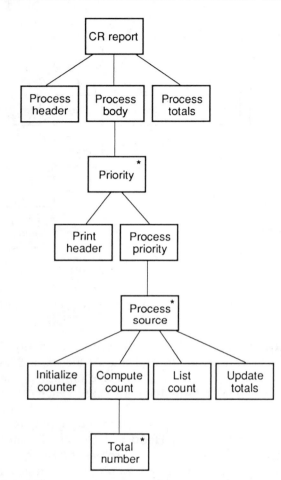

Fig. 3.16. Jackson diagram for the report program.

Figure 3.16 displays the structure of the desired program; we now must identify the processes carried out in that structure. For example, in **Process Header** we know that we must open the input and output files, read records, get the date from the input file, and print a report heading including that heading. We might be tempted to treat the box as a minispec and specify a little program to do that, but that would be a bad approach. The Jackson diagram contains the structure for the *entire program*, and it would be foolish to go off inventing new substructures. Also, the nonleaf boxes in the diagram are there simply to enforce the structure; only the elementary boxes can have operations or do anything. JSP uses a two-step approach to identifying the operations. First the programmer produces a list of all the operations that will be used in the program, and then he associates them with the boxes in the diagram. (As with the program that is being modeled, the same operation may be used in more than one place.)

The numbered list of operations for the report program is produced by starting at the output side of an imaginary data-flow graph and working toward the input side. By listing the operations in this order the developer becomes aware of the need for interior nodes in the data-flow graph whenever an output value cannot be copied directly from an input value. Here is one such list.

1.   Open Output
2.   Close Output
3.   Head new page
4.   Print Source and Count
5.   Print Total, all priorities
6.   Total(Priority)=Total(Priority)+Count
7.   Total=0, all priorities
8.   Count=0
9.   Count=Count+1
10.  Get Priority
11.  Set page header
12.  Get Source Name
13.  Read record
14.  Get Date
15.  Open Input
16.  Close Input

In Figure 3.17 these operations are appended to the Jackson diagram as sequences of operations. (All constructs other than the sequence are already in the diagram.) Step 3 is now complete, but it should be observed that some JSP users extend this step by augmenting the diagram with the iteration conditions, bounds on the number of allowed iterations, and so on.

The fourth and final step in JSP is the transformation of the diagrammatic form into a textual form that serves as the *pseudocode*[12]

---

[12]There are many forms of pseudocode. One type is the minispec described in Section 3.2.2, which is intended to convey a process using the precise constructs of programming. In most cases, however, there is no obligation to implement the program using the structure implied by the minispec. In this section, the pseudocode is intended to convey how the program will operate. It eliminates details to aid comprehension, but it is assumed that the final program will be a refinement of the pseudocode structure. In JSP, the pseudocode serves as a *program design language* (PDL), which will be discussed in Chapter 4.

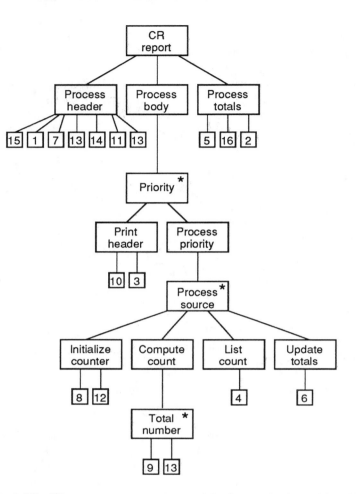

Fig. 3.17. The program structure with the operations identified.

for the executable program. Figure 3.18 contains the result of step 4; it should not be difficult to translate this pseudocode into an operational program in any of a number of programming languages. Depending on the language chosen, one might have to augment the structure to deal with dynamic issues such as tests for invalid files, end-of-file processing, and so on.

This example illustrates the power of JSP with a very simple program. If the reader has been doing the exercises, it would be interesting to compare the above pseudocode with the minispec produced as the result of exercise 3.10. Also, if this book is being used as a textbook, it would be interesting to compare the results of the

```
CR-Report seq
    Process-Header    seq
        Open Input
        Open Output
        Total=0, all priorities
        Read record
        Get Date
        Set page header
        Read record
    Process-Header    end
    Process-Body seq
        Priority iter until EOF
            Print-Header    seq
                Get Priority
                Head new page
            Print-Header    end
            Process-Priority    seq
                Process-Source iter    while (not EOF)
                    Initialize-Counter    seq
                        Count=0
                        Get Source Name
                    Initialize-Counter    end
                    Compute-Count    seq
                        Total-Number    iter    while ((not
                                                EOF) and (priority =
                                                last group priority))
                            Count=Count+1
                            Read record
                        Total-Number    end
                    Compute-Count    end
                    List-Count seq
                        Print Name and Count
                    List-Count end
                    Update-Totals    seq
                        Total(Priority)=Total(Priority)+Count
                    Update-Totals    end
                Process-Source end
            Process-Priority end
        Priority end
    Process-Body    end
    Process-Totals    seq
        Print Total, all priorities
        Close Input
        Close Output
    Process-Totals    end
CR-Report end
```

Fig. 3.18.  Pseudocode for report program.

various answers to exercise 3.22 using JSP.  How similar are the designs?  Do they differ because people were solving different problems?  Were the different solutions to the same problem all free of errors?  Was any correct solution noticeably superior to the others?  Clearly, the above program structure is uninspiring and lacks any creative flair.  As Jackson puts it, it is easier to make a good program fast than to make a fast program good.   Of course, this just confirms the goal of software engineering.  Inspiration and creative flair should be reserved for the problems that merit them; they should not be dissipated on problems for which a complete solution can be obtained through the application of a standard technique.

Naturally, not all programs are as simple as the one just shown.  JSP has compiled methods for collating data streams, handling recognition difficulties (e.g., knowing when to end the Process-Source iteration in the above example), and error handling.  A major concern in JSP is the problem of the *structure clash*, or what to do when the structure of the input does not match that of the output.  There are three categories of structure clash: boundary clashes, ordering clashes, and interleaving clashes.  In the CR-Report program I eliminated an ordering clash by starting with a sorted input file, which could be constructed from iterations of the CR data structure shown in Figure 3.14.  However, if I were asked to prepare the report whose structure is shown on the right of Figure 3.15 from an input file with iterations of the CR structure in Figure 3.14, then I would have a structure clash.  These two structures cannot be merged into one without producing an excessively complex structure that would prove difficult to maintain.

One approach to dealing with an ordering clash is to divide the program into two parts.  The first part produces data in a structure that the second part can use to produce the output.  In the above example, one program (Sort) produces Sort File from the structure in Figure 3.14, and the CR-Report program uses Sort File to produce the desired report.  Figure 3.19 illustrates this processing flow.  In some cases this is the most natural way to organize the processing, but in many cases the result can be inefficient.  An implementation solution offered by JSP is called *inversion*, and because inversion is also an important tool in JSD, I shall describe it here.   Briefly, inversion is defined as a transformation technique that introduces a suspend-and-resume mechanism into a process thus implementing it as a variable-state subprogram.  Again, an example will help.

Assume that we would like to remove the intermediate file shown in Figure 3.19.  One way to do this would be to structure the first program so that it could provide the second program with the data it needed when it was needed.   Then, instead of getting its inputs from the intermediate file, the second program could invoke the first program as a subroutine.  In this example, the CR-Report would change its

Fig. 3.19.  Removing a structure clash with an intermediate file.

**Read record**

statements with

**Invoke program Sort to get record**

statements.  In this particular instance it is difficult to see how the Sort program could be more efficient as a subroutine than as a file-building program, so I shall make the example more general.   Figure 3.20 substitutes P1 and P2 for Sort and CR-Report as the program names and shows the inversion of program P1 with respect to the sorted file, which now has been eliminated.

The impact of inversion on P2 is not very great; P2 simply must substitute invocations for reads.  Because we assume that the structure of P1 is such that the desired data will be available for each invocation, inversion should not impact the *structure* of P1.  But it may affect its *operation*.   When P1 executes as a stand-alone program whose sole mission is to create the intermediate file to be read by P2, it is in control from start to finish.  But, if P1 is to be called as a subroutine to deliver the results of some processing increment, then each time it is invoked it must begin processing at the position immediately following where it stopped at the end of the previous invocation.  P1 must "remember" where it stopped processing at the end of each invocation, and JSP uses a *state variable* to provide that memory.  That is, we must augment P1 with a state in the sense that the term is used in a state-transition diagram.  To show how this is done, consider the pseudocode in Figure 3.21 for a version of P1 that creates an intermediate file (i.e.,

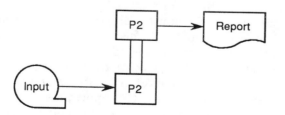

Fig. 3.20.  Inversion of P1.

```
P1 seq
    Setup seq
        Get header stuff from input
        Write header stuff to output file
    Setup end
    Body seq
        Process    iter    until finished
            Do what's needed
            Write processing stuff to output file
        Process    end
    Body end
    Finish seq
        Write final stuff to output file
    Finish end
```

Fig. 3.21.  A program that creates an intermediate file.

P1 before inversion).

In this code there are three places that stuff is written to the output file. We would like to access the three different categories of output immediately, rather than wait until the last of the stuff has been entered in the intermediate file. Thus, we would like the first invocation of the inverted P1 to return the header stuff, subsequent invocations to return the processing stuff, and the last invocation to return the final stuff. Moreover, we do not want to change the structure of P1. We can do this by introducing the variable QX, which is part of the state of P1 that remains persistent for all invocations during a single execution of P2. In other words, execution always begins at the start of P1, and QX provides a computed go to the appropriate segment of code. Figure 3.22 shows the structure of the inverted form of P1; added or changed lines are underlined and are in bold. The final label of Q4 causes any invocations after what is expected to be the last invocation to return the final stuff. Notice that the suspend-and-resume has not removed the structure clash, but it has provided an acceptable implementation of its solution.

In summary, for simple examples such as the production of a CR report, JSP is easy to use. Obviously, for more complex problems, more experience with JSP is required. The discussion has not shown how JSP manages the problems of error testing, identifying changes in the input data, collating, and so on. The issue of structure clash, however, was addressed, and two solutions were offered: the use of intermediate files (which made sense in the case of the CR report program), and program inversion (which can be used to extract transaction processing routines from a much larger program). The orientation of JSP is clearly data-

**Declare QX value, initialize to Q1**
**GO TO Q1 or Q2 or Q3 or Q4 depending on the value of**
**QX**
**Q1:**    P1**(Buffer)** *seq*
          Setup  *seq*
              Get stuff from input
              **Reset QX=Q2**
              **Return header stuff in Buffer**
          Setup  *end*
          Body  *seq*
**Q2:**          Process  *iter*    until finished
              Do what's needed
              **Reset QX=Q3**
              **Return processing stuff in Buffer**
**Q3:**          Process  *end*
          Body  *end*
          Finish  *seq*
              **Reset QX=Q4**
**Q4:**              **Return final stuff in Buffer**
          Finish  *end*

Fig. 3.22. Program with suspend-and-resume implementation.

structure oriented. The CR report program was not concerned with what is to be done as much as what it is doing it to. In creating the program, we began with an analysis of static representations, and we ignored the dynamic flows that guided us when we learned to write program code (e.g., "What happens after this statement?"). Chapter 4 will discuss these two different views of the computer program in more detail. However, it now is time to abandon modeling-in-the-small and return to the topic of this chapter, modeling-in-the-large.

### 3.3.2.  *Jackson System Development (JSD)*

In the section on JSP I introduced the Jackson diagram and showed how it could be used to represent the structure of either data or a program. Because I defined the diagrammatic notation in the context of the three structured-programming constructs [BoJa66], it should be clear the notation can be used to represent anything that can be displayed as a flow diagram.[13] In JSD we will use the notation to diagram models of

---

[13]The Warnier notation also has the ability to represent these three basic constructs.

sequential processes (i.e., processes that have a start, a sequence of next steps, and a conclusion). We then will develop a network that links these processes, and finally we will convert the network into a hierarchy of programs.

First, let me clarify how the Jackson diagrams can be used to model processes. Consider a CI from the perspective of the SCM system. We put it under configuration control, we release it for modification, we test the changes and audit the CI, we update the CI, and eventually we delete it. These actions are ordered in a very specific way; we cannot, for example, update the CI unless it passes the audit. This is the life history of a CI, and if we are to build an SCM system to manage CIs, then that system must be able to support that sequence of activities (i.e., that process model). In the sense of the JSP discussion, the structure of the SCM system should reflect the structure of the behaviors, life histories, and/or traces of the objects with which it is concerned; in this case, processing within the SCM system must not clash with the natural processing flow for a CI.

Figure 3.23 contains a Jackson diagram model for the life of a CI. It depicts a CI as having three phases. First it is designed, then it is maintained, and finally it is retired. Design begins with an Assignment followed by a Test and then Enter the accepted CI under configuration control. From the perspective of SCM, we do not care how the CI is assigned or even what the designer does to produce it, but we do care about its quality before it can be accepted. Therefore, Test is shown as an iteration of Audit processes, each consisting of a Review followed by a Decide. Decide is a selection of Pass or Fail. If the decision is to fail, the CI is returned to the designer, and another audit will be required. If the audit is passed, the CI is entered under configuration control. Notice that what we are modeling here is the *process* of controlling the CI and not the *physical routing* of the CI itself. If the CI fails, it is returned to its designer, but this is quite different from restarting the Assignment process. The Jackson diagram describes an irreversible sequence of actions; we cannot "back up" just as our programs cannot run backward in their normal operational setting. In effect, we have returned to the analysis activities of Chapter 2. We are modeling real-world processes that the software product is to support. It is our obligation to be sure that the model is valid; if it is not, the software may not correspond to the needs it was intended to meet.

Continuing with the diagram, Maintain is an iteration of Update processes. (Obviously, we need the Maintain process to avoid the mixed structure that would result if we raised the Update iteration up one level.) Each update consists of a sequence of three steps, Release, Test Change, and Revise. From the designer's perspective, what follows Release is most interesting, but this process model is intended to reflect an SCM system view, which is much narrower. The SCM system comes

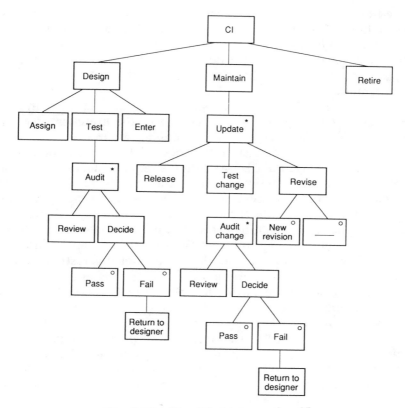

Fig. 3.23. The life history of a CI.

into action with the return of the CI for testing. **Test Change** is an iteration of **Audit Change**, and, as one would expect, the **Audit Change** process is isomorphic to the **Audit** process of **Design**. The process repeats until either the change is certified or abandoned. The next process, **Revise**, is a selection: enter a **New Revision** or, as indicated by the dash, do nothing (e.g., ignore the revision if the change is withdrawn). This **Update** process iterates until the CI is no longer required.

Notice that, like the life of a CI, the process diagrammed in Figure 3.23 is quite long; it can extend over years and perhaps decades. Thus it is a *long-lived process*. In software design we are accustomed to think in terms of fast-acting processes such as subroutines. But here we are modeling entities that exist in the environment that our target system will support. Unlike the JSP diagrams of Section 3.3.1, Figure 3.23 does not model the structure of data or a program; rather, it models the behaviors of a real-world object about which a program must manage data. Consequently, if there are 1000 CIs, then there will be 1000 of these structures active during the life of the system. And if the average active life of a CI is five years, then on average each process model will have a life of five years. Obviously, one does not expect a single program to run for five years, but it is reasonable to expect a *system* with a persistent database to run for that period. We use JSD to model the system; once the structure has been defined, JSP can be used to model the programs.

The process in Figure 3.23 is not the only valid representation for the CI management process. In fact, one of the exercises suggests a better solution, and Figure 3.24 contains an alternative process for Update. Which Update description is best? That depends on how the users actually manage the CIs. As with the requirements analysis tasks, there seldom is a right answer; what we are doing is framing an answer to a question in order to create a system that produces the answer. But there is an important difference between the diagrams in Figures 3.23 and 3.24. The first model indicates that, if an Update of the CI is in progress, it would be impossible to Release that CI for modification until the Revise is complete. But the second model is restricted to one Update of a CI; it does not prohibit concurrent updates for a CI. That is, Figure 3.23 models the entire life cycle for a CI, whereas Figure 3.24 models the Update process only. Here is a second question for us: Do we want to allow more than one update to a CI at a time? If the answer is positive, then we probably want two models: an amended model of the CI that does not include the update, and a separate model of Update as shown in Figure 3.23. Obviously, decisions about the best real-world model are independent of the JSD methods we use to represent that model.

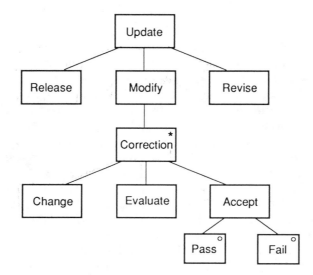

Fig. 3.24. An alternative diagram for Update.

This is a good place to pause. Where have we been and where are we going? We know that before we can build a software product we first must know what it is to do (i.e., its requirements). Once this has been established, we lay out the overall architecture of the system (modeling-in-the-large), and finally we add the details to create an implementation (modeling-in-the-small). When I described structured analysis/structured design, I pointed out that the analysis method models the user environment to create a context diagram, and that diagram defines the system boundary. From that point on, the analysis process both identifies requirements and establishes the system structure; the subsequent structured design activity is concerned with modeling-in-the-small. In this section on composition, I reversed the order of discussion. I began with JSP, which is clearly modeling-in-the-small, and I have just jumped all the way back to the requirements analysis aspects of JSD. Unfortunately, *the world of the software engineer just is not neat.* I could organize the presentation to hide that fact, but sooner or later you would find out. Chapter 6 discusses how management can make software development *seem neat*, but here we ought to examine all those hidden corners (or, to change metaphors, paint the portrait warts and all).

One of the problems with a composition philosophy is that it does not fit neatly into the three-step flow suggested by the titles of Chapters 2 through 4. In our running example, we began with a generic requirement, "Give me a good SCM system." We then studied the problem and produced a software requirements specification (SRS) that details what we are expected to deliver. This serves as the acceptance criteria for what we finally deliver: Does the system manage the CRs and CCB actions as prescribed? Does the system allow the users to access and update CIs as detailed? And so on. But that list does not (and ought not) tell us how to build the system that delivers the enumerated features. Still, it would be nice to know how each requirement was implemented. When we use a decomposition technique, it is not difficult to associate requirements with implementation units. One begins with a decomposition of the entire system into components, and then associates each requirement with the components that implement the behaviors that satisfy it. This linking process can be repeated with each level of decomposition; it is called providing *traceability*. But with composition, we have a different approach. We begin by modeling the universe in which the system will operate, and then we design the software to support that model. The SRS still provides a checklist for the system's mandatory features; each will be provided, but it will be difficult to associate requirements with the implementation units that satisfy them. Of course, in the end the product must comply with the SRS independent of how it was designed. But we should recognize that the SRS plays a very different role when we are designing a system using composition. It serves as a parallel source document rather than a top-level document capable of guiding the design activity.

When we design a system with JSD, we return to the technique that we used in constructing the SRS: We model the environment in which the target system will operate. The SRS identifies the entities to be modeled and their essential interactions with the target system, but it does not provide all the information we need. Therefore, we begin by modeling the real world just as we did when we were conducting requirements analysis. The difference is that the SRS scopes the problem. We already know the events to which the system must respond (actions) and the objects with which it must interact (entities). Therefore, in JSD we can identify the entities of interest to us and their actions. Once this is established, we can model the actions for each entity in the form of a sequential process. In the following example, I limit the scope of the SCM system to the processing of just three entities: the CIs, the two types of change requests (which for the sake of simplicity I shall call CRs), and the designer assignments (tasks).

Given these entities, we now must identify their actions. Each action takes place at one point in time and cannot be extended over a period of time. (In this sense, an action is like an event.) It must take place outside the system itself (i.e., in the real world). Finally, an action must be atomic; it cannot be further decomposed into subactions. What we are about to do is produce a discrete simulation of the entities, and the actions define the granularity of that simulation. The entities chosen for this simulation "must perform or suffer actions[14] in a significant time-ordering" [Jack82, p. 40]. The orderings define what actions are possible and what outcomes are possible when an action occurs. (This description seems to fit that of a state-transition diagram, see Section 2.3.2.) An entity must exist in the real world outside the system, and each entity must be an individual; if there is more than one entity of a type, then it must be uniquely named. Our three entities, CIs, CRs, and tasks, certainly satisfy these criteria.

Again, to simplify things, I shall assume that I am not concerned with what happens before a CI exists or with its retirement. To use one of Jackson's terms, all aspects of the CI other than what happens during

---

[14]I have quoted Jackson directly here because the phrase "suffer or perform actions" often is used in the definition of objects in object-oriented programming. Also, we have seen the term entity used in a slightly different setting in the material on semantic data modeling and the entity-relationship model. The point is that there are a variety of names for the real-world items of interest to the designers, and many (overlapping) paradigms exist for modeling these items and the systems that support them. More on this topic is given in Chapter 4.

an update cycle are considered *Outside the Model Boundary (OMB)*. That being the case, the actions of interest for a CI are

- **Release** The CI is released from configuration control and made available to a designer for change. In this model we shall assume that no CI can be released if it already is in a released status.

- **Change** The CI is in the process of being changed until it is available for reentry to configuration control. Notice that this change action may take a very long period (e.g., months). From the perspective of the CI simulation, however, we are not concerned with anything that happens between the start of change and its conclusion. We will address the real-world aspect of changes when we identify the actions for the task entity.

- **Evaluate** The CI is evaluated to verify that the requested changes have been applied and that the revised item can be returned to configuration control.

- **Pass** The CI passes the acceptance test and can be used to update the revision.

- **Fail** The CI fails the acceptance test and must be returned for an additional correction cycle.

- **Revise** The CI is entered into configuration control and a new revision number is assigned.

Continuing with the CI entity, the next step is to model the CI as a process containing the six actions of interest here. Figure 3.23 models the entire life of a CI from Design to Retire. But we have limited our interest to Maintain, and the Update model in Figure 3.24 has the six terminal nodes whose names are the above actions. Consequently, we will use the alternative Update Jackson diagram for our CI process model. However, this Update allows for concurrent CI updates, which are not permitted according to the description of the Release action. Therefore, to model the entity accurately, we add a CI node and iterate Update as shown in Figure 3.25. Notice that the model describes the orderings of the actions, but it says nothing about how much time elapses between successive actions. Whenever these actions (events) occur, they change the data (state) that we use to keep track of what happens in the model. Our next step, then, is to identify those data and determine where in the model it is used.

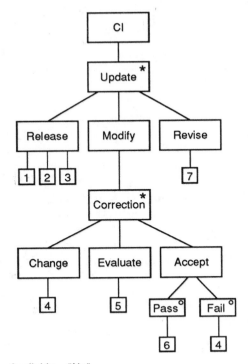

1. Available = "No"
2. Change-for = CR-number
3. Status = "Inactive"
4. Status = "Active"
5. Status = "Complete"
6. Status = "Accept"
7. Available = "Yes"

Fig. 3.25. CI process model.

Figure 3.25 has been augmented to show the *attributes* of a CI that will be modeled in the target system. In other words, the Jackson diagram defines what happens to a CI, and the data (or attributes) define what is to be remembered about the CI. (The notation is similar to that used in JSP.) First the attributes and their data assignments (state changes) are listed, then these changes are associated with actions in the process model. Nine state changes are identified and tied to the diagram. First the CI is initialized. At the time of Release, the CI is marked unavailable for further change, and the associated CR number is logged in. The status is considered active when the change is in progress, and complete during evaluation (i.e., the action of setting

Status="Complete" initiates the evaluation process). If the change is accepted, the CI Status is marked for acceptance; otherwise it is reset as "Active" and another iteration of Correction follows. Revise sets the CI Available flag to "Yes", and the CR field is ignored. This long-lived model can then be expressed as text and *inverted* into suspend-and-resume subprocesses that can be implemented as transactions or subroutines. For example, the text for the diagram in Figure 3.25 is given in Figure 3.26.

```
Q1:    CI   seq
       /*   Some initialization of CI data entry        */
Q2:         Update     iter      until retirement
                 Release   seq
                     Available="No"
                     Change-for=CR-Number
                     Status="Inactive"
                 Release   end
                 Modify seq
                     Correction iter      Status="Accept"
                         Change    seq
                             Status="Active"
                         Change    end
Q3:                      Evaluate   seq
                             Status="Complete"
                         Evaluate   end
Q4:                      Accept     sel Input=Pass
                             Pass       seq
                                 Status="Accept"
                             Pass       end
                                     alt Input=Fail
                             Fail       seq
                                 Status="Active"
                             Fail       end
                         Accept    end
Q5:                  Correction end
                 Modify end
                 Revise seq
                     Available="Yes"
                 Revise end
Q6:         Update     end
       /* Some retirement of the CI entry     */
       CI   end
```

Fig. 3.26. Pseudocode for the CI process.

In this text I have added some labels to indicate where the flow may be broken down into suspend-and-resume subprocesses.

Q1  Here is the start of the processing.

Q2  Once initialization has been performed, here is where an update begins. Although this is shown as an iteration until retirement, there is no attribute that indicates the retirement status. Thus, the data for the iteration predicate is outside this process, and one assumes that the system users will initiate each iteration cycle.

Q3  Here is where processing resumes after change processing returns.

Q4  Here is where processing resumes after evaluate processing returns.

Q5  Here is where processing resumes after the acceptance process has either updated the CI or initiated another iteration of change. This is the end of the Update iteration; because the user is responsible for the iteration, processing also could resume at Q2.

Q6  Here is where the CI retirement processing begins.

The method for introducing the suspend-and-resume mechanism was described with JSP. Notice in this example how each segment can be isolated as an independent subroutine or transaction. If we ignore label Q5, then there are four suspend-and-resume subprocesses for each CI. The flow shown here, of course, was modeled with respect to the input stream. In general, however, the suspend-and-resume process will be more complex in that after resuming $Q_n$ it will not follow that the process will next be suspended at $Q_{n+1}$. As we will see, for this type of application, it is useful to maintain the state in the form of a database. By examining the database state we can determine which suspend-and-resume subprocess is applicable.

We now turn to the other entities we have identified. The actions the CR must address are

- ■  Log  Log in a CR (or SIR) when received.

- ■  Analyze  Analyze the CR and propose action.

- **Cost** Compute the cost to make the necessary change.

- **Propose** Propose the change with the associated cost statement.

- **Assign task** Assign the change task to a designer. (Rejected proposals are assigned the SCM staff.)

- **Distribute** Distribute the modification as appropriate.

For the Task they are

- **Review** Review the proposal and identify the needed CIs.

- **Get CIs** Have the CIs assigned to the developer for update.

- **Work** Perform the task work as broken into work units. (Work units may be defined as a time period, such as a week, or a product deliverable, such as a module change.)

- **Status** Report status at the completion of a work unit.

- **Demonstrate** Demonstrate that the task assignment has been carried out properly.

- **Deliver** Deliver the updated CIs for entry into the SCM system.

In this example we began by identifying the entities and then associating actions with them. One could also begin with a list of activities and then group them to establish the entities. (This approach is similar to the event-list technique described in Section 3.2.3.) The process models for CR and Task are shown in Figures 3.27 and 3.28; the assignment of attributes and the preparation of textual suspend-and-resume subprocesses are left as exercises.

Before going on to the next step in JSD, it will be helpful to review what we have done. We began by identifying the real-world objects of interest to the target system along with the actions that affect the system state. All the actions were atomic; consequently, no state changes could occur without the presence of some action. (Because we are modeling the system as a discrete simulation, the actions define the granularity of our system. Actions thus correspond to the smallest updates that can be made to the database or its equivalent.) We then used the same diagramming technique introduced in JSP to model the entities. Of course, what we modeled in JSP were static data and program structures; in JSD we are modeling sequential processes. In this activity, each process was modeled independently, and the relationships between

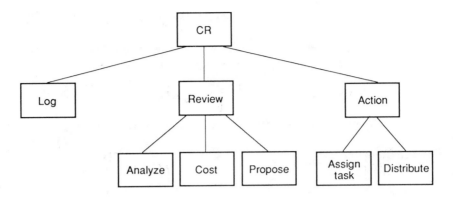

Fig. 3.27. **CR** process model.

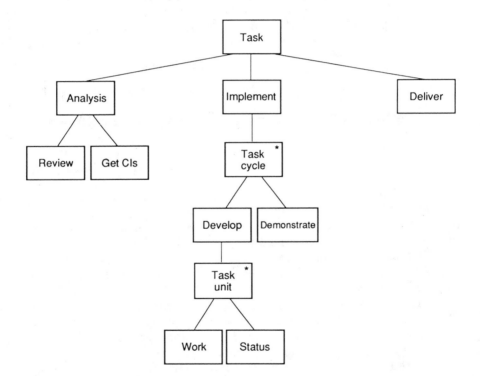

Fig. 3.28. **Task** process model.

process were ignored. For example, we did not try to show that a CR results in both task assignments and the release of CIs. Also we did not indicate restrictions such as that one can assign a task only if the necessary CIs have **Available="Yes"**; we simply record these constraints informally for later use. Our immediate concern has been the definition of the real-world processes, and the data they use. We are composing the system as a set of processes that must communicate with each other.[15]

As we examine the processes that we have defined, we may find that the system model does not support all the desired actions. When this occurs, we must introduce new processes. For example, notice that the Task entity produces some status data for each Task Unit. If we wanted to report on the status of all tasks associated with a given CR, however, we would need another process (CR Progress) that could keep track of the progress of task units by CR. In general, processes are added for three reasons:

- Data collection and error handling processes are added to fit between the reality and the model.

- Output processes are added to extract information from the model, perform calculations, and produce outputs.

- Interactive functions are added to provide feedback into the model.

Thus, the model begins as a description of the real-world that the system is to support, and then additional system-oriented processes are added. As Cameron puts it,

Oversimplifying somewhat, the model processes hold the main data for the system along with its update rules. The other processes contain the algorithms that calculate and format outputs, and that drive the model either by collecting and checking inputs or by generating new actions. [Came86, p. 228]

Now that we have defined a set of processes, we are ready for the next step in JSD: the construction of a network of the process models. By way of introduction, Figure 3.29 contains a fragment of the network that shows how the CR entity releases a CI for Correction. The circle indicates that what is transmitted from the CR entity to the CI entity is a *data stream* (or message). The two processes are shown here at the *network level* as boxes; the boxes can be expanded at the *process level* as the Jackson diagrams in Figures 3.25 and 3.27. For a slightly more complex illustration of a network fragment, consider the CR Progress

[15]The underlying method is similar to that described by Hoare as Communicating Sequential Processes (CSP) [Hoar78, Hoar85].

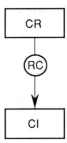

Fig. 3.29.  Network fragment using a data stream.

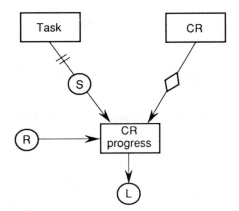

Fig. 3.30.  **CR Program** network fragment.

process, which gets its information from both Task and CR.    Its
processing is contained in the network fragment shown in Figure 3.30.
At the end of each Task Unit the Status data are sent (by the data
stream S) to the process CR Progress; the two lines cutting the upper
line indicate that more than one such data stream may be sent.  The CR
Progress process also receives requests to produce a status listing.  The
request is indicated by the data stream R input to the process, and the
data stream L represents the listing produced by the process.  When the
request is made, information is required about the CR associated with
the task, and that is accessed by examining the CR *state vector*, which is
indicated by the diamond.

In summary, at the modeling level the processes communicate with
each other in two ways.

- *Data stream*, indicated by a circle, which transmits the necessary information in a stream of data. From the perspective of implementation this can be done by parameter or message passing.

- *State vector*, indicated by a diamond, which allows the recipient read-only access to the sender's state vector. From the perspective of implementation, state vector access is normally managed as a database activity.

At the network level, all processes are represented as boxes; at the process level, each box is expanded to its Jackson diagram (i.e., sequential process). During the construction of the network, development proceeds by adding processes for inputs, outputs, and interactions, and by elaborating the processes that are already there. Communications are assumed to be asynchronous, and buffers may be used to ensure the return of coherent states for state vector inspection (e.g., to prohibit the inspection of a state vector when an update is in progress). If there are timing constraints or synchronization requirements, they are noted for implementation at a later time.

We now are ready to build the SCM system network. In addition to the three process models with which we started, I have added three new processes:

- CR Progress This produces progress reports on the status of active CR tasks. Its network fragment has been shown in Figure 3.30.

- Developer Status This lists the status of the developers' assignments. It receives a request for designer status (RDS) and produces a listing (LDS). The data for the output come from the inspection of the Task state vector.

- Manufacture This manufactures configurations from the updated CI. It receives a configuration request (CFR) and outputs a configuration (CF). The data for the output come from the inspection of the CI state vector.

The system network with these six processes is given in Figure 3.31.

The network shows data stream CR input to the process CR. This represents the receipt of the physical change request. In some descriptions of JSD, this input will be expanded into a process CR-0 that sends the data stream CR to the process CR-1. Here CR-0 represents the real-world change request, and CR-1 is its representation within the SCM

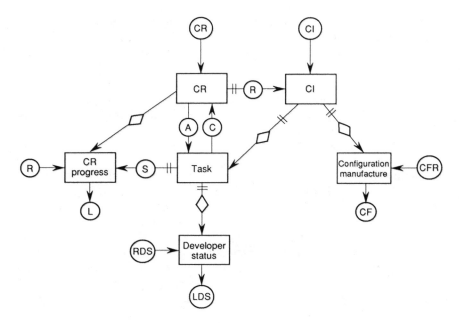

Fig. 3.31.  SCM system network.

system.  In this way, the model is extended to the real-world entities
with which it interacts.  Figure 3.31 ignores this extra level.  A data
stream CI is the input to the process CI; to keep the network simple,
this input method is used for all CIs that are either entered or revised.
(An alternative network in which CIs are revised by means of a data
stream from Task is left as an exercise.)  Tasks have access to available
CIs by inspecting the CI state vector; they also receive assignments (A)
from and return completion notices (C) to CR.  (Actually, I have
simplified the diagram; there are events in Figure 3.28, such as Status
and Demonstrate, that are not indicated in Figure 3.31.)  Despite these
omissions, I now have completed the network phase of JSD.  Each of the
processes has been modeled in detail and broken into suspend-and-
resume fragments, which can be implemented as subroutines.  Separate
(informal) notes have been preserved regarding constraints, timing
demands, synchronization considerations, etc.; these can be used for
scheduling and algorithm refinement.  In short, a discrete simulation of
the target system exists, and we now are ready for the third, and final
phase: implementation.

There are two main issues in the implementation phase: how to
run the processes that comprise the specification, and how to
store the data that they contain.  The first turns out to be

particularly concerned with data streams in the specification, the
second with the state vector inspections.  [Came86, p. 233]

As originally described, JSD offers little assistance in data modeling.
One may view the state vector inspections as relationships between
process entities (in the sense of the ERM described in Section 2.3.1),
but this is only of marginal help.  Once the system framework has been
established (which, of course, is the primary objective of modeling-in-
the-large), the designer must rely on other methods for defining the
database.  The implementation phase, however, does have a technique
for transforming an abstract network of programs into a main program
and a hierarchy of subroutines.  (The method is similar to that we have
used in the transformation of flow diagrams to structure charts.)  I shall
explain this process with the abstract network shown in Figure 3.32.  All
state vector inspections have been removed.  (The data are assumed to
be available through database access, which has no control implications.)
Three external inputs are identified: A, B, and C.  These are included in
one data stream as an input to Main in the subroutine hierarchy shown
in Figure 3.33.  The data flow to produce the output D is then shown in
the form of a control hierarchy.

The example in Figures 3.32 and 3.33 contained no loops.  When
loops exist, a buffer is introduced to ensure synchronization.  For
example, in Figure 3.31 we see that the assign and complete data flows
establish a loop between CR and Task.  Assume that there are a limited
number of changes that can be assigned at one time, and we do not want
to make new assignments if too many assignments are still active.  We
can control this loop by introducing a buffer to contain the completion
notices (C) and have Main process that buffer before processing any new
change requests (CR).  Main can also block the processing of new CRs
until CR is ready to assign them.  (This is not the most satisfying
example for explaining how a buffer can synchronize loop iterations, but
the method should be clear.)  Figure 3.34 contains the hierarchy for the
network shown in Figure 3.31.  It was constructed as follows.  First, the

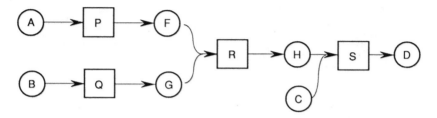

Fig. 3.32.  Abstract network model.
(Adapted from [Came86] with permission, ©1986, IEEE).

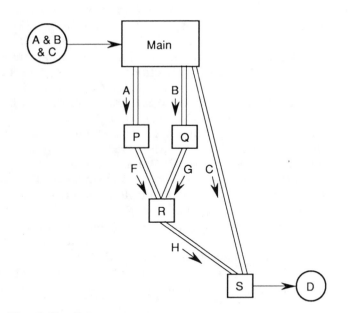

Fig. 3.33.  Subroutine hierarchy for the abstract network.
(Adapted from [Came86] with permission, ©1986, IEEE).

state vector inspections were removed, thereby reducing the network to three units: **Designer Status**, **Configuration Manufacture**, and the rest of the network.  Next, the inputs to these three fragments were identified, and combined as a composite input to **Main**.  Finally, the processes (subroutines), control paths, buffer, and outputs were added. A double line is shown as the control link; the number of lines actually should be the number of inversions plus one (i.e., the number of independent subroutines for a process plus one).

This concludes the overview of JSD.  By way of review, there are three phases in the process:

- *The modeling phase* in which one models the reality that the system is to support.  First the entities and actions are identified, and then the entities are expressed as sequential processes using the Jackson diagram notation.  Data attributes also are identified as the diagrams are augmented and transformed into text.

- *The network phase* in which the processes are joined into a network with communications supported by data stream transfers and state vector inspections.  Additional processes for inputs, outputs, and interactions may be included in this network.

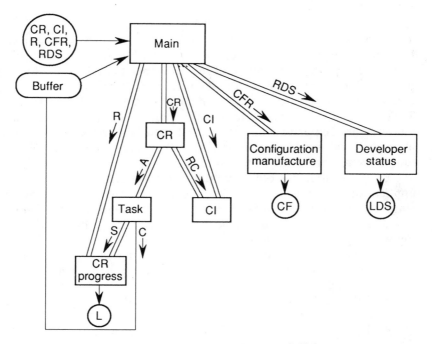

Fig. 3.34. Control hierarchy for the SCM system.

- *The implementation phase* in which the models are decomposed into subroutines, the attributes are used to construct a database model, and a subroutine hierarchy is built.

This scheme is based on Cameron's 1986 description of JSD. In his 1982 book, Jackson offered a slightly different organization of the method. The point is that, like virtually all methods, the method itself is dynamic. It changes as experience is gained and as better explanations evolve. Certainly, this description shows that JSD is no cookbook approach to modeling-in-the-large. Informal techniques are relied on to "remember" important constraints, and the definition of details is left to other methods (i.e., modeling-in-the-small is performed by JSP, database modeling methods, etc.). The method has been used in commercial settings for some time, and—like structured analysis—it also has been applied in real-time projects. Because of its formal foundations, JSD is cited as an example of an operational approach (i.e., one that uses an operational specification that can indicate the system response from a given input at a given state) [Zave84].

### 3.4.    Comparisons and alternatives

The previous sections described two philosophically different approaches to modeling-in-the-large. Moreover, each method was shown to provide a bridge from the earlier phase of requirements analysis to the following phase of modeling-in-the-small. The clear implication is that there are benefits from selecting one family of methods and learning to use it well. There are many reasons to follow this policy. First, I will review why methods are important, and then I will consider why a uniform set of methods is advantageous. Finally, I will consider the alternatives and identify some problems to be avoided.

By definition, a method establishes a systematic process for the application of tools for achieving some objective. In the Software Engineering Hierarchy of Section 1.3.3, the tools include representation schemes and software tools. The method provides guidance in organizing what is known, and it identifies a sequence of actions for obtaining a design goal. If we view software engineering as a problem-solving activity, then the method helps us answer questions such as

- How are these things related to each other?

- How can I explain this to my sponsor or user?

- Were are the areas of greatest uncertainty?

- What should my next step be?

Once these questions are resolved, the software engineer can focus on the problems unique to his assignment:

- What should the software do in this situation?

- What are the design alternatives for satisfying this constraint?

- Will this solution to the problem satisfy the users' needs?

- How can this be organized to maximize reuse, maintainability, reliability, etc.?

Thus, learning a method reduces the software engineer's problem space and frees him to concentrate on the most important issues. Recall from Section 1.3.1, we have a limited short-term memory capacity ($7\pm2$ chunks), and we can understand facts only in some context (mental models). If we become overloaded with too many facts and lack mental models to structure them, then we do one of two things. Either we form naive theories to account for what we find, or we ignore many of the facts and retain only those that conform to some existing model. Although there are no studies to link these human characteristics with common software engineering problems, we all know of examples in which the users' needs were misinterpreted and the delivered system meets its specification but is of little utility. (Is this a naive specification?) Also, we all have seen how programmers, when given a complicated task, will restrict the problem to some understood segment and start coding a solution to that subproblem. (Here modeling-in-the-small clearly is the wrong technique for managing information overload.)

The properties that make humans so intellectually effective mandate the adoption of procedures to decompose large problems into smaller (and therefore manageable) problems. When confronted by a very large problem, we approach it in one of three ways:

- We may interpret this problem in the context of a similar problem that we already have learned. This is how a child learns *hot!* A software engineer reuses experience from previous projects. If one has been implementing SCM systems for a number of years, he will immediately identify flaws in my running example. When one builds C compilers, building another C compiler will be a relatively small problem. But building an Ada compiler, because it introduces new requirements, becomes a more difficult problem. Moreover, the C-compiler expert may have no experience that can be applied to developing an SCM system. Thus, domain experience tends to be relatively narrow.

- We may use a method to decompose the large problem systematically into a series of interrelated smaller problems, each of which can be either solved or decomposed further. In structured analysis, we decomposed the problem into one of identifying functions and their interfaces; in JSD we decomposed our task into identifying entities and modeling them as sequential processes. Thus, the method provides us a two-layered approach to the management of a very large problem: First we determine the most important issues to be addressed, and then we address these issues. Notice that if we have no experience with the method, then we cannot succeed at the first level and we certainly will fail at the second level. The major advantage of a method is that it is relatively domain independent; structured analysis and JSD can be equally effective in the construction of an SCM system or a compiler.

- The final approach to managing a very large problem is to randomly decompose it into related problems whose solutions seem apparent. Without experience or an appropriate method, we have no alternative to this technique. But I do not recommend it. After all, it is the failure of undisciplined decomposition that spawned software engineering.

From a pedagogical perspective, one can be most effective by teaching software engineering methods. Domain-specific experience will be acquired in a professional setting. This setting will adapt the methods to its operational environment, but the method's underlying, domain-independent properties will persevere. Therefore, I have focused here on describing the use of the method and its supporting philosophy. If the method was an algorithmic transformation from one representation to another (e.g., from source to object code), then there would be no need to explore its conceptual foundations. But the methods that we have been discussing in this chapter are all intended to help us model the solution to an essential domain-specific problem. Where SA/SD and JSD/JSP differ is in their *interpretation* of what that essential problem is. It is as if each method were trying to understand some object in n-dimensional space by projecting it onto a plane; different transformations will produce different simplifications, but only selected sets of projections will be complementary.

Two conclusions follow from this discussion. First, it is important to learn the methods and to learn them well. The method structures the users' problem-solving activity; in particular, when the problems require collaboration in arriving at a solution, the method offers a common vocabulary and representation scheme that facilitates cooperation and communication. We have seen, for example, that one of the major benefits of the data flow diagram (DFD) during the early stages of analysis is that it can be readily interpreted by the users. As one who has taught students to draw DFDs, however, I also have seen how syntactically correct organizations of bubbles and arcs can convey absolutely no meaning. Thus, there is a major difference between learning to use a method and learning to use it well. (Because one only learns by making—and correcting—mistakes, an academic setting is a good place to start learning the methods.) The second conclusion is that, as a heuristic for restructuring a problem, methods are subject to variation and change. The tools that they use, however, are far more stable. I have made many references in this chapter to how the methods are evolving. Nevertheless, the DFD and Jackson diagram remain relatively unchanged. This implies that one must *understand* the method, but one can *automate* the tools used by the method. That is, one can separate the diagramming process from the context of the diagram's use. In that way, one may treat the diagram as an independent object. This can be both an advantage and disadvantage. It permits the development of automated tools without insisting that the tool's outputs be used in a reasonable fashion.[16]

As a student of software engineering, I am concerned with how the software process is conducted and the methods that we use to organize it. From that perspective, methods and tools are interesting to me. But most readers will be software engineering practitioners, and their attention will be dominated by the problem domain and the target support environment. Methods and tools are part of their problem-solving armory; serviceability and commonality must be favored over novelty and specialization. Which suggests that each organization probably ought to select one method just as it tries to limit diversity in its programming languages, operating systems, and computers. Naturally, the standards should not be rigid, and every organization should be encouraged to move from one family of methods to another whenever the efficacy of the latter has been demonstrated. Therefore, I think it important for all students of software engineering to understand both the top-down methods that we have traditionally used and the formally based constructive techniques that we are currently adopting.

Given a choice of methods and asked to select one as the standard, which should one choose? The short answer is that this depends on the setting and sponsors. If one method already has been selected and is successful, then one should be careful in making changes. One of the responsibilities of management is to reduce risks, and sometimes there is more risk in moving to a productive, but untried, technology than in continuing along the current path. (More on how to evaluate methods is presented in Chapter 6.) But what if, after reading the first three chapters, management recognizes that what they are doing is so bad that immediate change is necessary? The first criteria is to go with the method that is best understood. If the supervisors are very familiar with one method, then it should be given primary consideration. (Of course, if it is an obsolescent method, then this fact should be considered.)

---

[16]As previously noted, Computer-Aided Software Engineering (CASE) is the generic title for the tools and environments used to manage a project and support product implementation. In one sense, the SCM system that we are using for a case study is considered a CASE tool. There also are CASE tools to draw and maintain many of the diagrams described in this chapter. Most CASE tool vendors offer products to produce DFDs, structure charts, data dictionaries, entity-relationship diagrams, state-transition diagrams, Jackson diagrams, etc. Where validation criteria are well defined (e.g., common spellings for data and correct nesting of DFD bubbles), the tool also can identify potential errors. Obviously, when a method is used, CASE tools reduce errors, facilitate documentation update, improve the quality of the presentations, and enable better collaboration. However, without a commitment to some systematic method (which provide the context for the CASE products), the value of a CASE tool will be marginal. More on this is given in Chapter 6.

Also if there is an organization that can train the staff in a method, that method also should rank high on the list. (Remember, though, that it may take as much as a year before the staff becomes proficient in the method.)

Finally, we get to what you have been waiting for: all things being equal, which method is best? Again, I offer only a soft answer. Yourdon's view of "modern structured analysis" presents a method for combining a variety of modeling tools to produce a design. The structure of the design is top-down, but the method used to construct it is not. Similarly, JSD provides an alternative method for modeling a system. As I have presented the methods here, each begins by examining the external world that the system must support, then turns to issues regarding how the system must be organized to provide the identified services, and finally considers how to program a solution. That is, each guides the problem solving down a path from the domain in which the system will be used, to the structure of the system that implements the solution, down to the details of that implementation. As the problems change, so too do the tools used to resolve them. I am not an ideologue, and would not necessarily choose one as the best, but I can warn the readers of some dangers to be avoided.

- *Premature decisions.* One of the advantages of a method is that it uses earlier decisions to provide a context for future decisions. Thus, once a problem is solved, it need not be revisited. The danger of an early decision is that it may represent an inappropriate solution that will bias the subsequent analysis. For example, a poor allocation of functions early in the design will impact the decisions that follow.

- *Inherent structure clash.* JSD begins by modeling real-world entities so that the structure of the system will reflect the external structure supported by the system. The intent is to facilitate the evolution of the system as the external environment changes. Clearly, this same objective can be achieved with structured analysis. The key for both methods is that we must recognize that we are designing a system that should be adaptive; we seldom are asked to construct a solution to a static problem.

- *Random decomposition.* A poor implementation of a method (or simply the decision to maximize the fun of programming) can lead to a bad decomposition of the problem. Because many managers are taught to measure productivity in lines of code and to view coding as product building, there often is an incentive for an early start to programming. Avoid this temptation. There is, however, one case where early coding should be encouraged:

hacking with a prototype to gain insight into a problem. This, of course, is (in Brooks's words) the one you should plan to throw away.

- *Invalid model.* There is a difference between the model and the objects modeled (i.e., fallacy of identification discussed in Section 1.3.2). Because a method allows us to build on prior decisions systematically, there is the danger that our models will diverge from the reality that they are intended to portray. In modeling-in-the-large virtually all decisions can affect the fidelity of the model, and validation is an essential part of the process.

- *Hawthorne effect benefits.* Frequently, instruction in a method (or the purchase of a CASE tool) will be treated as a low-cost, risk-free investment in productivity improvement. As one would predict, there are benefits. But for a method to be effective it must operate at two levels. At the individual level, it helps the designer organize his activities and structure his problem solving. The method also operates at the project level by laying out a rational plan for developing an effective design, supporting collaborative efforts, integrating the individual design decisions, and establishing a shared vocabulary. Thus, if the use of a method is not vigorously supported by project management, its value is severely diminished.

- *The message becomes medium.* Finally, there is the danger that the method's model becomes viewed as the end product. One must avoid substituting the process of design for the goal of designing a product. In particular, when a design activity takes years, the lack of feedback encourages the design team to divorce their activity from its intended objective. Chapter 6 discusses some alternative project organizations to avoid this problem. Clearly, Yourdon's abandonment of the physical model suggests that this is a common problem.

In conclusion, I have avoided selecting a "best" method or indicating which method would be "best" for some class of application. Each method ignores some aspect of the problem to focus on others. Each is imperfectly integrated and relies on informal techniques to remember the facts discovered along the way. Each of the methods offers a rigid sequence of design activities for separating the design objects from the operational objects (e.g., the source code). Each is inherently a pencil-and-paper process that can be assisted with automated tools. Imperfect as they may be, each is superior to the chaos that preceded its invention.

Drawing by Lorenz; ●1977 The New Yorker Magazine, Inc.

# 4

## MODELING-IN-THE-SMALL

As with any large organization, an ice cream factory must organize its work into small, manageable units. Lorenz offers us one modularization for a company with a large number of flavors. Some very important software engineering principles are employed here. Individual flavors may be added or removed with no impact on the overall system, each flavor has its own operator that hides information from the other flavors, and one can model the whole system as specializations of the FLAVOR_DESK class. I wonder if all ice cream factories have such an elegant architecture.

This chapter on modeling-in-the-small is really a chapter about how to construct software modules. I begin with some generalizations that will be valid for any decomposition philosophy. Documentation is always necessary, and it must be maintained over the life of the module. There are standards for good style, which should become ingrained in all software engineers. Simplicity comes before efficiency; given an efficient design, the transformation of an inefficient module into a more efficient one is a refinement. But I expect the reader knows this already.

The bulk of the chapter is concerned with encapsulation techniques. I introduce this from an historical perspective. Parnas's views on modularization and information hiding are described, and abstract data types are reviewed. After the underlying concepts are presented, Ada is used to illustrate the abstract data type. The next section builds on the abstract data type and describes object-oriented programming. These ideas are expanded to explain object-oriented design and object-oriented analysis. Thus, after starting with an examination of how to define software modules, I end up describing another analysis method.

The final section introduces the program proof. It is pointed out that the proof is not something that one does after the program is written; rather it involves building a program as its proof. In that sense, the proof method is universal; it is not limited to the program-coding activity.

## 4.1.     Implementing the system

This is the third, and final, chapter with modeling in its title. In Chapter 2, we began by analyzing and modeling the features a new system must provide. These essential properties were identified in a Software Requirements Specification (SRS), which became the defining document for the target system. During modeling-in-the-large we used what we had learned from the earlier analysis to establish the system characteristics (e.g., system structure, interface definitions, algorithm descriptions). The result was a preliminary design that determined the target system structure and the functions that it should support. As designers, we had the freedom to do anything so long as the finished system included (and did not conflict with) the features detailed in the SRS.

Now that the modeling-in-the-large is complete, most of the application-specific issues have been resolved. We have descriptions of the key report formats; we may assume that they express the users' desires. We know the principal user interfaces; we need only create the programs that implement them. The critical algorithms are identified in the minispecs and design documents; we now must either find programs to be reused or code the algorithms. In short, modeling-in-the-small begins when most of the application domain uncertainties have been cleared up and a framework for the individual programming units has been established. We are at that point in the essential software process (Fig. 1.5) where we will be concerned with implementation issues. Our problem solving now will be guided by the design requirements and our knowledge of the implementation domain.

### 4.1.1.  Prerequisites to implementation

We begin modeling-in-the-small with a well-defined problem solution (the design specifications) and a target representation scheme (the programming language). The objective is to transform that design into a program that is correct with respect to its specification. But wait, where did the design specification come from? This is one of the problems with the way I have organized this book. If I started with a "document-driven" approach to software engineering, everything would be clear. We would follow the waterfall diagram shown in Figure 1.2 and produce a Design Specification for the system; following a Preliminary Design Review (PDR) and acceptance by the customer, we would produce a Detailed Design Specification for each module or group of modules. Each Detailed Design Specification would then be subjected to a Critical Design Review (CDR), and after acceptance coding would begin. Instead of the generic activity of modeling-in-the-small, there would be a well-defined sequence of phases: Preliminary Design, Detailed Design, and Code and Debug—each with its own end-of-phase certification process. There would be a standard format for each specification type, and management would monitor progress according to the number of accepted specifications (and, later, accepted programs). This is the neat view of the software process, and it is actually how it works in practice.

But I have deferred this neat organization of the software process until the last chapter in order to confront the fuzzy activity of creating the software solution. Obviously, design is carried out in parallel with two other activities: the product's certification (Chapter 5) and the project's management (Chapter 6). Using the principle of separation of concerns, I have left those two issues for later examination. Here I simply assume that we have completed the modeling-in-the-large, and we have a good model for how we want the software to work. We may have arrived at this design by following a document-driven analysis flow in which we used the document's structure to guide our problem solving. Alternatively, we may have used structured analysis/structured design to produce DFDs, structure charts, a data dictionary, and minispecs. Or we may have used JSP/JSD to produce a design (and even program pseudocode). Independent of how we arrived at that design, it is incumbent on us to document that design in a clear and complete fashion, *and then place that document under configuration control.* This is not a management requirement; it is just good engineering practice. Without an authoritative design document, how do we know that all aspects of the problem have been covered? As we make implementation (i.e., low-level design) decisions, how can we determine their impact on the overall design? Remember the problems of information overload, interpretation in context, naive theories, and so on. For the same reasons that we needed an SRS before we started to design, we now need a formal design document before we start to code. Without a specification, there can be no correctness.

There are many formats for a design specification, and often the organization or sponsor provides a standard to be followed. Naturally, the contents of a design specification will reflect the design method used. Nevertheless, the following items should be included in it.

- *Introduction.* This includes a brief statement of purpose and objectives. The text must not just repeat the SRS introduction; it should augment that description from the perspective of design. In particular, one would find sections on

  Interfaces between the target system and users, the hardware, and any external software. Also the definition of any external databases or other implied resources.

- Identification of the principal software functions supported by the target system. If decomposition was used, the functional allocation is preserved in the design; if composition was used, this section will be more descriptive than structural.

- Narrative of the key design constraints or limitations. Because the life of the system is assumed to extend beyond the life of the design team, it is important that the design document identify factors that may be important in its evolution.

- Document references for the system, vendor supplied software, technical reports, etc.

■ *High-Level Design Description.* This effectively provides an overview of and road map for the more detailed design that follows. It describes how the system has been structured, defines the data used and its organization, considers how the interfaces affect the design, and includes much of the documentation produced by modeling-in-the-large (e.g., DFDs). Depending on the size and structure of the system, it may be useful to divide this description into an overview and separate function-specific subsections. This section also may include a data dictionary that defines the file structures and access paths, the global data, and file-data cross references; alternatively, the data definitions can be organized as an independent section.

■ *Detailed Design Specification.* Here we are concerned with specifications in sufficient detail to ensure that computer programs can be written to satisfy them. These specifications need not be in one-to-one correspondence with the implemented programs, but they must be formal enough to guarantee the ability to ascertain correctness. Because each represents a package that can be given to a programmer with little previous experience in this project, each should include a processing narrative, interface descriptions, processing description, data and module interfaces, and any special comments.

Because not all Detailed Design Specifications will be available at the same time, it is common to publish and approve the Design Specification and add the detailed designs as they are approved. Naturally, lessons learned during detailed design will affect the higher level design, and one should expect changes in the design. That is why the document must be placed under configuration control; it is the responsibility of the configuration management team to be certain that all proposed changes are properly reviewed, approved, and—once accepted—entered into the baseline and disseminated to the affected parties.

After the implementation units have been defined in the design specification, it is common to assign each unit to an individual designer who then establishes a *unit development folder* or notebook in which he enters the detailed design specification plus any supporting materials. (If the designer is responsible for preparing the detailed design specification, he can create the unit development folder to assist him in that process.) In any event, the folder becomes the central repository for all information about that product. It contains

- The detailed design plus any appropriate requirements and architectural design information.

- The test plan, test cases, and ultimately, the test results.

- A listing of the source code.

- Change history including all requests, their history, and documentation of revisions.

The folder is retained for the life of the unit, and it serves as the repository for all information regarding that software unit. In time, because the detailed design information is less expensive to maintain in independent folders, the collection of folders replaces the Low-Level Design Specifications of the design specification. As long as the contents of the folder are consistent with the high-level design specification, one can make changes to the former without modifying the latter. From the perspective of configuration management, both the High-Level Design Specification and the unit folders are considered CIs, but only the specification is subject to formal control. That is, the individual designers are responsible for the integrity of the unit folders, and only a subset of their contents (e.g., the source code) is managed by the SCM system. This represents a trade-off between the cost of and the need for formal control.

It is logical to present this discussion of the design specification and the unit folder in one place. This does not imply, however, that documentation is a separate activity; indeed, documents are written and folders are compiled as the design decisions are formalized. For example, it is common to use a *program design language* (PDL) as an intermediate structure between the high-level statement of what a module should do and the operational module code that produces the implementation [CaGo75]. The PDL removes some of the intermediate details to clarify the processing flow. Obviously, the PDL is created before the code, and it becomes a part of the detailed design (and thus the unit folder). If, after the code has been tested, program changes are made by first revising the PDL and then altering the code, then the PDL should be retained as an important component of the unit folder. But if the PDL was simply a device to go from fuzzy to clear thinking (as with the Orr context diagram of Section 2.3.2), then there is little value in retaining the PDL in the unit folder when the code no longer reflects its structure. Thus, the contents of the unit folder may vary over time, and one may archive obsolete documentation when it has no further potential use.

In time, software maintainers will go directly from the high-level design documents to the code.[1] Therefore it is important that the code itself be described with a prologue similar to that outlined in Figure 4.1. This prologue provides a general introduction to the module and also identifies all modifications by date, designer, and purpose. The referenced documents (including the change request, test data, and test results) will be available in the unit folder, and the short prologue description serves as a useful reminder and index of changes.

In this discussion of specifications, I have been very careful to avoid giving detailed document formats. There is a reason for this. I believe that documentation is an integral part of the intellectual process of design. There are two essential reasons for this.

- One cannot create a design without binding the important decisions in writing.

- One cannot detail a design unless there is a reliable source for the accepted decisions.

Thus, we are unable to proceed without some kind of design document. This document will be created as the design proceeds, and its format should be determined by the characteristics of the target system, the tools and methods chosen, the project's reporting responsibilities, and the organization's culture. The process of documentation should never become an end in itself. The documents are containers, and we are interested in their contents. Naturally, good engineering practice demands that we fashion effective containers, but only as the means to

---

[1] If the maintainers reference the code because the high-level documentation serves as a clear road map to the models to be altered, and if the module code employs a style that makes it easy to comprehend, then this referencing of the code is a good thing. But if the maintainers have to rely on the code because all other system documents are of little value, then this is a symptom of poor management.

Module mnemonic and short title
Name of original author
Date of initial compilation†
Date of most recent compilation†
Modification history
    Date, author, change identifier, purpose
    Comment‡
Description of parameters†
Function(s) performed
Definition of modes‡
Exception handling
Description of processing or algorithm
Input assertions
Output assertions
Other assumptions‡
Global variables
Data structure definitions‡
Side effects‡
Timing constraints‡
Calling routines†
Called routines†

Fig. 4.1. Format of a module prologue.
† May be instrumented by the environment, ‡ Only if appropriate.

an end.

    This view contrasts with what I have previously referred to as the "document-driven" approach, in which the design effort is organized around the deliverable documents. Too many people have been taught to conduct software engineering in that manner, and, in that sense, the treatment of documentation in this book is revisionist. We must think of the documents as representing incremental expressions of the problem solution and not as deliverable items. Form must follow function, and if a document has marginal immediate or long-term value, then little effort should be expended on it. Although our documents will be useful for management confidence and sponsor involvement, that always should be a secondary consideration.

### 4.1.2. Elements of style

Typically, computer science training begins with software implementation. We are introduced to a programming language—Pascal, C, FORTRAN, COBOL, Ada, BASIC, LISP, maybe even MUMPS—and eventually we master its commands and syntax. Often we start by finding out how to say "Hello World" and then go on to more complex problems. We are taught good programming habits; for example, we always format the code as structured blocks even when the language does not support those structures directly. From the pedagogical perspective, it is important that we understand how to write clear and effective programs. Programming is a tool for the software engineer just as calculus is a tool for the electrical engineer. We cannot become software engineers until we become proficient in the use of our tools. The computer scientist, of course, has a different view of programming and programming languages, just as the mathematician has his own interpretation of calculus. The computer scientist is concerned with the definition, development, and evaluation of effective tools for practitioners. Software engineers are practitioners, and their focus is not on the programming language but its role in the software process.

From the perspective of software engineering, the programming language is a tool,[2] and the ability to write effective programs is a skill. Obviously, the choice of language will influence the problem solution. If we are working with PROLOG, for example, we will look for rules and facts. That is, we will use the form of solution space to determine the structure of the solution. I shall assume that we are working with an imperative, block-structured language such as Ada, Pascal, or C. I also assume that we have a modern programming language with the following standard characteristics (adopted from [SmMB83]).

- The facilities of a language are simple to understand in all situations where they can be used (*clarity*) and free from unexpected interactions when they are combined (*orthogonality*).

- The notation is easy to understand, and it aids the programmer in the design of his programs (*writability*).

- The meaning of the program is clear from its text without recourse to excessive documentation (*readability*).

- It is difficult to misuse the language (*no tricks*).

With such a language it is possible to translate our design concepts into (writable) easily understood (orthogonal) expressions that perform as expected (without tricks). The result should be a *clear* and *readable* program; if it is not clear and readable, it is the fault of the programmer and not the programming language.

---

[2]Actually, the language is a representation scheme for the computational model, and the compiler (or interpreter) is the tool.

Most readers of this book are either software engineers with the prerequisite skills or persons who have no need to program. Therefore, I need not teach the reader about programming style, and I can presume that if programming is important, the reader's code

- Uses indentation of from tow to four characters to delineate the two basic control structures (i.e., iteration and selection) used in the program.

- Includes a program prologue, such as that described above, to document some essential characteristics of the program.

- Includes inline documentation (plus the use of blank lines, or white space) to complement the program language's readability. (Comments such as "Add 1 to X" are of little value for the statement X := X + 1.)

- Limits the size of a program unit to what can be comprehended as a unit, typically one page. (Old COBOL programmers would measure programs by their finger count: the number of fingers—or pencils—that must be inserted into a listing to trace the processing within a procedure.)

- Relies on descriptive names for the programming units and their variables.

- Avoids the GO TO where appropriate. As an historical note, early interpretations of "structured programming" viewed it as GO-TO-less. Purism did not survive, and there are many situations in which a carefully chosen GO TO (or LEAVE loop) will improve clarity.

These rules simply represent the standards of good programming style, and we assume that everyone who has been taught to write programs in the past decade will conform to these broadly accepted conventions. Naturally, this was not the case in the early 1970s when most programmers were learning their craft on the job. Kernighan and Plauger concluded in their 1974 book, *The Elements of Programming Style*, that "style"

> is not a list of rules so much as an approach and an attitude. "Good programmers" are those who already have learned a set of rules that ensures good style; many of them will read this book and see no reason to change. [KePl74, p.132]

I would hope that no readers would see any reason to change their style on the basis of what I have to say in the next few paragraphs. Nevertheless, it is instructive to review the style elements in the context of problems they address.

*The Elements of Programming Style* consists of an introduction plus six chapters on expression, structure, input and output, common blunders, efficiency and instrumentation, and documentation. In what follows, I have regrouped the style rules[3] according to some attributes of the software process that mandate their adoption.

- *The program code is an expression of a design that is bound to change. Therefore,*

  > Write clearly — don't be too clever.
  > Say what you mean, simply and directly.
  > Use library functions.
  > Avoid temporary variables.
  > Write clearly — don't sacrifice clarity for "efficiency."
  > Replace repetitive expressions by calls to a common function.
  > Parenthesize to avoid ambiguity.
  > Choose variable names that won't be confused.
  > Don't patch bad code — rewrite it.
  > Make sure comments and code agree; don't overcomment.
  > Don't comment bad code — rewrite it.
  > Format a program to help the reader understand it.
  > Document your layouts.

- *The program code is the most detailed representation of the design, and as such it should convey the intellectual clarity that one would expect of a good design (i.e., the program should not be a cobbled artifact that just works). Therefore,*

  > Don't diddle code to make it faster — find a better algorithm.
  > Make it right before you make it faster.
  > Make it fail-safe before you make it faster.
  > Make it clear before you make it faster.
  > Don't sacrifice clarity for small gains in "efficiency."
  > Don't strain to reuse code; reorganize instead.
  > Use data arrays to avoid repetitive control sequences.
  > Choose a data representation that makes the program simple.

---

[3]The indented rules are quoted from the Summary of Rules [KePl74, pp. 135-137]. In all, 63 rules are given in the book, and about half of them are repeated here.

Use recursive procedures for recursively defined data structures.

- *The program code is produced as the result of problem solving, and it will improve if we avoid information overload and learn from past mistakes. Therefore,*

   Write first in an easy-to-understand pseudo-language; then translate into whatever language you have to use.
   If a logical expression is hard to understand, try transforming it.
   Modularize. Use subroutines.
   Write and test a big program in small pieces.
   Instrument your programs. Measure before making "efficiency" changes.
   Use debugging compilers.
   Watch for off-by-one errors.
   Test programs at their boundary values.
   Check some answers by hand.

- *There are program features that are assumed without explicitly specifying them (see Section 2.4). Therefore,*

   Test input for plausibility and validity.
   Identify bad input; recover if possible.
   Make input easy to prepare and output self-explanatory.
   Use self-identifying input. Allow defaults. Echo both on output.
   Make sure your code "does nothing" gracefully.

This listing has emphasized *why* the rules are important, not just *what* the rules are. As we will see, the methods and languages that we use may eliminate the need for some rules, but such improvements will not affect the underlying problems that the rules address.[4]

Notice that many of these rules suggest that correctness should be separated from efficiency. First one should get a program that does the job expected of it, and then one can address its efficiency. (This is the motivation for Balzer's operational approach to the software process discussed in Section 1.2.3.) Bentley warns that "we should almost never consider efficiency in the first design of a module, and rarely make changes for efficiency's sake that convert clean, slow code to messy, fast code" [Bent82, p. 107]. He observes that various studies have shown

---

[4]If, after reading the above list, the reader feels insecure about his programming style, I urge him to read the Kernighan and Plauger book or one of Bentley's programming pearl collections [Bent86, Bent88]. Fairley also provides an effective list of dos and don'ts of good coding style [Fair85].

that about 4% of the code in compute-bound programs accounts for 50% of the run time. Thus, efficiency improvements can be localized. In fact, time devoted to the optimization of program segments that are seldom activated can be counterproductive. Good engineering practice demands that we always get it right, and that we also make it only as efficient as it needs to be. There is a cost-efficiency trade-off, and with software there is also a clarity-efficiency trade-off. Cost and clarity are favored over extra efficiency. Of course, the context of this discussion is programming-in-the-small. It is assumed that we have begun with a sound design, efficient data structures, rational modularization, and so on. Naturally, when we start with an inefficient design, it cannot be improved by efficient programs.

In his *Writing Efficient Programs*, Bentley compiled a set of rules. These are summarized in Figure 4.2, and if the reader is not familiar with them, then Bentley's book is an excellent place to start. The preparation of an efficient program begins with a correct and readily understood solution to the problem. If the resulting program is efficient, the task is complete. If improvement is required, the program should be instrumented and monitored to identify those parts of the code that are executed most frequently. Once this is determined, one should try to improve the processing in those key areas (hot spots). Because we began with a correct program, we must be careful to apply transformations that both preserve correctness and decrease the program's run time. (An example of such a transformation is the movement of a loop-invariant computation from within a loop to a position just before the loop.) Unfortunately, these transformations normally increase the length and decrease the readability of the program, and so some refinement (or documentation) for clarity must follow. This is then followed by a test to see if the performance goals have been reached. If, after several iterations, the requirements have not been satisfied, then another algorithm must be found. Improving efficiency becomes more complex when working with a system. The approach here is to associate the hot spots with programs, and then use the above method to improve the programs. Once the enhanced programs are installed, the process is repeated to identify new resource sinks. After several iterations, only minor improvements will result from continuing this attack. If the required efficiency cannot be achieved, redesign is the only alternative.

In summary, both this and the previous section really have been about documentation. In Section 4.1.1 the documentation was in the form of specifications that defined what the software must do. In this section, the documentation was that of the software. We think of programs as being operational products, and indeed they are. But they are also a readable expression of the computation to be carried out. If we view code as being a document that conveys information to its

## Modifying Data Structures

### Trading Space-For-Time
1. Data structure augmentation
2. Store precompiled results
3. Caching
4. Lazy evaluation

### Trading Time-For-Space
1. Packing
2. Interpreters

## Modifying Code

### Loops
1. Code motion out of loops
2. Combining tests
3. Loop unrolling
4. Transfer-loop unrolling
5. Unconditional branch removal
6. Loop fusion

### Logic
1. Exploit algebraic identities
2. Short-circuiting monotone functions
3. Reordering tests
4. Precompile logical functions
5. Boolean variable elimination

### Procedures
1. Collapsing procedure hierarchies
2. Exploit common cases
3. Coroutines
4. Transformations on recursive procedures
5. Parallelism

### Expressions
1. Compile-time initialization
2. Exploit algebraic identities
3. Common subexpression elimination
4. Pairing computations
5. Exploit word parallelism

Fig. 4.2. Summary of Bentley's rules for improving program efficiency.
(Reprinted from [Bent82] with permission, ©1982, Prentice Hall.)

creator, to other programmers, *and* to the computer, then we will take pride in the form of our programs as well as the effectiveness of their performance. As I have said before, the code is only the most detailed representation of the design, and it ought to be as clear and readable as every other design document.

### 4.1.3. Views of the process

In 1971 Wirth wrote an important paper called "Program Development by Stepwise Refinement." It began as follows.

Programming is usually taught by examples. Experience shows that the success of a programming course critically depends on the choice of these examples. Unfortunately, they

> are too often selected with the prime intent to demonstrate what
> a computer can do.  Instead, a main criterion for selection
> should be their suitability to exhibit certain widely applicable
> *techniques*.  Furthermore, examples of programs are commonly
> presented as finished "products" followed by explanations of
> their purpose and their linguistic details.  But active program-
> ming consists of the design of *new* programs, rather than
> contemplation of old programs.  As a consequence of these
> teaching methods, the student obtains the impression that
> programming consists mainly of mastering a language . . . and
> relying on one's intuition to somehow transform ideas into
> finished programs.  [Wirt71, p. 221]

Software engineering, of course, is concerned with the design of new
products; consequently, software engineers should be most interested in
the *process* of creating the product as opposed to the characteristics of
the resulting *product*.  That is, when we have a disciplined approach to
the process, effective products should be a natural consequence of the
development activity.

Wirth used the eight-queens problem to illustrate his technique.[5]
Briefly, the method establishes a structure for the problem solution,
stops at some point where the solution is not clear, and then—through
a strategy of preselection, stepwise construction of trial solutions,
introduction of auxiliary data, recursion, and so on—refines the solution
through a sequence of refinement steps.

> Every refinement step implies some design decisions.  It is
> important that these decisions be made explicit, and that the
> programmer be aware of the underlying criteria and of the
> existence of alternative solutions.  The possible solutions to a
> given problem emerge as the leaves of a tree, each node to a
> given problem a point of deliberation and decision. . . .
>
> A guide in the process of stepwise refinement should be the
> principle to decompose decisions as much as possible, to
> untangle aspects which are only seemingly interdependent, and
> to defer those decisions which concern details of representation
> as long as possible.  [Wirt71, p. 221]

In this process, both the program and the data specifications are refined
in parallel.  This intertwining of the procedures and the data they use

---

[5]In the eight-queens problem the task is to place eight queens on an $8 \times 8$
board so that no queen can take another queen.  Queens can move any number
of spaces in a row, column, or diagonal.

was emphasized in the title of his book, *Algorithms + Data Structures = Programs* [Wirt76].

In the context of human problem solving (Section 1.3.1), we can explain stepwise refinement in terms of schema refinement. Following some preliminary examination (naive theories), the solution outline (initial schema) is formed, which provides the context for the subsequent refinements. After each refinement has been accepted, the extended solution (more mature schema) expands the context for the resolution (refinement) of another aspect of the solution. The process continues until the solution is complete (schema of the final understanding). This schema analogy is an oversimplification that reeks of misapplied popular psychology, but I have made it for a purpose. In human information processing, the schema represents the structure used for retrieving chunks of information. Given the $7 \pm 2$ limitation, our mental faculties are optimized for pattern recognition and the association of concepts. It is difficult for us to "mentally prove" complex assertions with many interactions. Fortunately, the formal nature of the computer program's representation complements our intellectual strengths. Therefore, we can view program development as the iteration of the recognition of potential (and usually incomplete) problem solutions followed by feedback from an analysis of the solution's formalization.

In other words, modeling-in-the-small employs both models used in the essential software process (Section 1.2.2). The refinements begin as conceptual models, and the formal model is the program that becomes the implementation. Both the conceptual and the formal models use the same representation scheme: that of the target programming language. Conceptual modeling is concerned with using experience in program development to identify solutions (refinements) to a well-defined problem. Formal modeling involves the representation of that solution in a form that is correct and free of potential failures. In the sense of the essential model in Figure 1.5, the application domain is the implementation domain;[6] the conceptual model is that of a computed

---

[6]I have assumed that modeling-in-the-large begins with a design in which the basic application domain issues are resolved and the problems are organized as units that can be understood without the need to refer to the product's potential use. For example, in the eight-queen problem, modeling-in-the-large would have addressed the concerns of why the algorithm was needed, how it interfaced with other parts of the system, what the user interface must be, and so on. In modeling-in-the-small, therefore, we start with a well-defined programming problem, and we need to implement a solution. Although the finished program will be used in the application environment, the definition of the programming problem at this point has abstracted out those concerns that do not contribute to producing an effective program. Thus, my assertion that both the conceptual and formal models deal with objects in the implementation domain.

solution to the target problem, and the formal model is its realization. Naturally, when we are trained to think about our problems in (conceptual) representations that are close to the formalisms of the solution space, it is easier to go from our mental models to the operational models. In fact, this is why the PDL (or pseudocode) is so effective; it provides a bridge from the intended implementation to the product's construction. When using stepwise refinement, the incomplete solution acts as a kind of pseudocode.

Wirth concludes his paper with the following five-point summary.

1. Program construction consists of a sequence of *refinement steps*. In each step a given task is broken up into a number of subtasks. . . . Refinement of the description of program and data structures should proceed in parallel.

2. The degree of *modularity* obtained in this way will determine the ease or difficulty with which a program can be adapted to changes or extensions.

3. During the process of stepwise refinement, a *notation* which is natural to the problem in hand should be used as long as possible.

4. Each refinement implies a number of *design decisions* based on a set of design criteria. Among these criteria are efficiency, storage economy, clarity, and regularity of structure.

5. The detailed elaborations on the development of even a short program form a long story, indicating that careful programming is not a trivial subject. [Wirt71, pp. 226-227]

The orientation of this paper was the teaching of programming, but the method is valid for development by experienced programmers. Wirth's final sentence stated, "If this paper has helped to dispel the widespread belief that programming is easy as long as the programming language is powerful enough and the available computer is fast enough, then it has achieved one of its purposes." Similar comments regarding the limitations of advanced programming languages would be repeated more than a decade later by Brooks in his "No Silver Bullet" paper [Broo87, see Section 1.3.3]. Thus, we cannot avoid confronting the difficulties of creating an implementation.

Wirth presented a top-down, decomposition technique, which borrowed heavily from the earlier work of Hoare and Dijkstra. The problems emerged as the leaves on a tree, and each node represented a decision. (Of course, backtracking might reconfigure the tree.) In the eight-queens example there was sufficient experience so that a known solution could be developed in an intuitively clear fashion. But what if the solution were truly unknown. Consider Jackson's thoughts on this subject. The citation comes from a section that begins with the statement, "JSD is not top-down. This is a proud claim, not an embarrassed confession."

> Top-down is a reasonable way of describing things which are already fully understood. It is usually possible to impose a hierarchial structure for the purposes of description, and it seems reasonable to start a description with the larger, and work towards the smaller aspects of what is to be described. But top-down is not a reasonable way of developing, designing, or discovering anything. There is a close parallel with mathematics. A mathematical textbook describes a branch of mathematics in a logical order: each theorem stated and proved is used in the proofs of subsequent theorems. But the theorems were not developed or discovered in this way, or in this order; the order of description is not the order of development. [Jack82, p. 370]

Again we see the tension between the mind, which is associative and based on judgment, and mathematics, which is hierarchical and precise.

In Chapter 3 I organized modeling-in-the-large into two camps, each of which emphasized the strengths of one of these modeling orientations. Decomposition took the top-down approach, and the nodes in the hierarchy represented refinements and detailing; composition, on the other hand, began by modeling what was best understood and then (with JSD) formally represented that model for conversion into an implementation. In each case, the "possible solutions to a given problem emerge as the leaves of a tree." That tree, of course, represents a trace of the solution process and not the form of the solution. In the context of Wirth's 1971 paper, the solution (i.e., program) also was a tree, but the concept of stepwise refinement need not be restricted to what I have labeled as decomposition methods. It is a general problem-solving paradigm that can be applied to any method that produces a formal solution. It is especially well suited to problem-solving activities that have their expression in formal (provable) representation schemes. Which raises the question, can stepwise refinement be applied to different classes of representation schemes in modeling-in-the-small? The table of contents suggests the answer: Yes, in two ways.

In modeling-in-the-large I pointed out that decomposition evolved from methods concerned with how data were transformed and composition from methods focusing on the structure of data. I can extend that division to modeling-in-the-small by observing that one can look at how abstract algorithms act on particular data structures (i.e., Wirth's view of program design) or one can examine some objects of interest and determine how they may be represented as data structures and what operations are valid for those structures. In the programming-oriented view, the primary concern is the development of a correct model of the specified computation. Here the conceptual models center around representations used in the implementation. Like mathematics, one must learn the notation well and concentrate on the logical implications of the design. (For example, one cannot use algebra until one becomes comfortable with abstracting real-world objects as variables.) In the object-oriented view, on the other hand, the conceptual model first defines the structure of computational objects and then builds the programs around these structures. In both cases the implementations are formal computational models. In the programming-oriented paradigm (which I discuss under the heading of program proofs), one models the solution in a fixed language, whereas in the object-oriented paradigm (which I include in the section on encapsulation techniques), one extends the language to model the problem. As with the division between decomposition and composition, the separation is artificial.

## 4.2.    Encapsulation techniques

Encapsulation involves the packaging of complex concepts in simpler, more directly-comprehensible forms. High-level languages use encapsulation to eliminate the housekeeping demanded by an assembly language program. The WRITE, for example, provides a high-level representation for what otherwise would be a cumbersome sequence of commands. Naturally, this type of encapsulation is fixed by the programming language, and encapsulation extensions to a language can be provided to the developer as I will describe later in this chapter.

A second form of encapsulation is procedural. Subroutines, for instance, are written with fixed (and well-defined) interfaces; they are used to encapsulate processing in the sense that (1) the user need not understand *how the program works*, only *what* it does and *how to use it*, and (2) the procedures may be reused by any program in this (or a similar) system. A library of subroutines allows the designer to draw on processing units as building blocks for the development of his system. Mathematical subroutine libraries are used in this way in scientific computing. These library programs represent computational abstractions similar to the mathematical symbols that the scientist uses in his conceptual modeling. The scientist accepts the processing encapsulated in a library routine just as he accepts his proven theorems.

Harking back to Brooks's "No Silver Bullet" advice, if what we need can be found in a library, we should use it rather than develop our own (i.e., "Buy versus build," see Section 1.3.3 [Broo87]). But what if this is not possible? Can we extend this concept of encapsulation to new developments? Obviously, the answer is yes. One may employ encapsulation in all development activities; also, one may extend the programming languages (and environments) to enlarge the range of encapsulation. In the next section I discuss the first topic, and the following sections describe extensions for abstract data types and object-oriented programming. A final section examines how these concepts have been extended to modeling-in-the-large in the form of object-oriented design and analysis.

### 4.2.1. Some foundations of abstraction

I begin the discussion with a review of a 1968 paper by Dijkstra. I do this, not as an historical exercise, but as a way to fix some basic concepts that have been evolving over the last two decades.[7] Many of the terms introduced in the 1970s have become vapid cliches. It is important that we understand the problems that were being addressed, the solutions that were tried, and how those solutions evolved. In many cases the labels of the past are preserved, but the essence of their meaning has been lost. But that essence is as important today as it was 20 years ago. (For example, before reading on, define *information hiding*.)

In 1968 Dijkstra responded to a call by the *Communication of the ACM* for papers on "timely research and development efforts" and described the structure of the "THE"-Multiprogramming System [Dijk68]. In his paper, he identified two major mistakes in the project. First, they ignored the potential impact of hardware problems and assumed "a perfect installation;" second, they had given only scant thought to debugging tools. As it turned out, however, each of these initial oversights turned out to be a blessing in the long run.

> I knew by bitter experience that as a result of the irreproducibility of the interrupt moments a program error could present itself misleadingly like an occasional machine malfunctioning. As a result I was terribly afraid. Having fears regarding the possibility of debugging, we decided to be as careful as possible and, prevention being better than cure, to try to prevent most bugs from entering the construction. [Dijk68, p. 342]

[7]The reader should be aware that my references to historical documents are selective and often ignore key factors in the intellectual evolution of computing. I exploit these seminal papers to discuss concepts critical to our current understanding of the software process. As a history, my presentation is deeply flawed.

Thus, rather than devote much effort to anticipating equipment "pathologies" or building a debugging environment, the team concentrated on writing programs that were obviously correct.

Essentially what Dijkstra did was to establish a hierarchical structure in which each layer provided an environment for the next. The levels were:

Level 0     Processor allocation to activate one of the processes whose dynamic progress is logically permissible.

Level 1     The segment controller to process memory segments on the drum and in core.

Level 2     The message interpreter to process the console commands. Each process had its private conversational console even though all processes shared the same physical console.

Level 3     The sequential processes associated with buffering and unbuffering of input/output streams.

Level 4     The independent user programs.

Level 5     The operator (not implemented).

As can be seen from this list, the design was built on levels of abstraction. Each level performed services for the functions at the next highest level; each level had exclusive use of certain resources that other levels were not permitted to use. Higher level functions could invoke lower-level functions, but the lower level functions could not invoke higher-level functions. In effect, each level represented a *virtual machine* for the next level functions. Higher level functions need only know what facilities the virtual machine provided, not how they were implemented. Lower level functions need only provide the services specified, they need not know how those services were used. In this way, the system could be reduced to "encapsulated levels" that were both intellectually manageable and verifiable. In the sense of the separation of concerns, given that level $n$ had been verified, one could concentrate on developing level $n+1$ without concern for level $n$'s implementation.

In 1972 Parnas wrote two important papers that showed how to produce a program hierarchy in the sense just described. I begin with a discussion of the second of these papers, "On the Criteria to Be Used in Decomposing Systems into Modules" [Parn72b]. Here Parnas began with the observation that modular programming allows one module to be written without knowledge of the code in another module, and it also permits modules to be reassembled and replaced without the reassembly of the whole system. The benefits of modularization, he continued, include better management of development, improved product flexibility, and enhanced comprehensibility. All these observations are accepted as platitudes today; what is of interest here is his method for modularization, which remains valid but not universally practiced.

Parnas illustrated his method with a keyword-in-context (KWIC) indexing program. In this index, the title of each document is rotated so that each "nonnoise" word (e.g., a, the) heads a string consisting of that word followed by the rest of the title. The entry is sorted by that string, and the result is listed in a form that includes a portion of the title that preceded the keyword followed by the keyword-headed string (truncated), and then the citation. Naturally, each title is listed as many times in the index as there are keywords, and the keyword field is aligned to facilitate alphabetical scanning. A sample KWIC index of three papers is illustrated in Figure 4.3.

Allowing for the technology in use at the time, one way to modularize this program would be to organize it as five modules:

- *Module 1: Input.* This reads in the lines from the input media. (Remember, this was 1972, and one generally used input files rather than databases.)

- *Module 2: Circular Shift.* This would be called after the input was complete; it prepares a two-field index containing the address of the first character of each circular shift and a pointer to the input array where the data are stored.

| | | |
|---|---|---|
| Modules *** On the | Criteria To Be Used in Decomp | Parnas, *CACM*, 1972b |
| To Be Used In | Decomposing Systems into Modules | Parnas, *CACM*, 1972b |
| Specification with | Examples *** A Technique for | Parnas, *CACM*, 1972a |
| into Modules *** | On the Criteria To Be Used in | Parnas, *CACM*, 1972b |
| for Software | Module Specification with | Parnas, *CACM*, 1972a |
| Systems into | Modules *** On the Criteria | Parnas, *CACM*, 1972b |
| A Technique for | Software Module Specification | Parnas, *CACM*, 1972a |
| Software Module | Specification with Examples | Parnas, *CACM*, 1972a |
| System *** The | Structure of the "THE"-Multi | Dijkstra, *CACM*, 1972 |
| Multiprogramming | System *** The Structure of | Dijkstra, *CACM*, 1972 |
| in Decomposing | Systems into Modules *** On | Parnas, *CACM*, 1972b |
| Examples *** A | Technique for Software Module | Parnas, *CACM*, 1972a |
| Structure of the " | THE"-Multiprogramming System | Dijkstra, *CACM*, 1972 |

Fig. 4.3. Sample KWIC index.

- *Module 3: Alphabetizing.* This takes the arrays produced by the first two modules and creates an array similar to that generated by the second module except the index is sorted alphabetically.

- *Module 4: Output.* Using the arrays produced by the first and third module, a neatly formatted listing is produced.

- *Module 5: Master Control.* This simply controls the sequencing of the other modules.

Such an organization, Parnas pointed out, satisfied the criteria of "all proponents of modular programming. The system is divided into a number of modules with well-defined interfaces; each one is small enough and simple enough to be thoroughly understood and well programmed" [Parn72b, p. 1054].

He then proposed a second modularization.

- *Module 1: Line Storage.* This was a collection of low-level routines to be used by the other modules. For example, the function CHAR(r,w,c) returns the value of the cth character in the rth line, wth word, and WORDS(r) returns the number of words in line r. SETCHAR(r,w,c,d) sets the character d (returned by CHAR) in the position r,w,c. DELINE and DELWORD delete portions of lines already stored, and so on. This is the level 0 for the KWIC index; it represents a virtual machine for character string processing.

- *Module 2: Input.* This reads the lines from the input media and calls a procedure to store them internally.

- *Module 3: Circular Shifter.* This module contains functions analogous to those in module 1; it "creates the impression that we have created a line holder containing not all of the lines but all of the circular shifts of the lines." For example, the function CSCHAR(l,w,c) returns the value for the cth character in the wth word of the lth circular shift, with special conditions for wraparound.

- *Module 4: Alphabetizer.* This consists of two functions that generate an alphabetical index.

- *Module 5: Output.* This produces the formatted output.

- *Module 6: Master Control.* As in the first modularization, this sequences the control.

Parnas then went on to compare the two modularizations. In general, both schemes will work. There is, however, a major difference in changeability. If the input format was changed, then both modularizations would limit the modifications to just one module. But if one wanted to change the design so that all lines were not stored in core, then only one module would have to be changed in the second modularization, whereas in the first decomposition *every* module would be affected. Other potential changes shared this characteristic. For example, the internal representation of the way that lines are stored "is entirely hidden from all modules but module 1. Any change in the manner of storage can be confined to that module!" [Parn72b, p. 1055]. He went on to state that the second decomposition also was superior in its support of independent development and comprehensibility.

What was the difference in the criteria between these two decompositions? In the first, the decision was to implement each major step in the processing as a module. The structure of the system followed from the structure of the flowchart.[8] The second decomposition, however, was guided by the principle of *information hiding*. The modules no longer corresponded to steps in the processing. "Every module in the second decomposition is characterized by its knowledge of a design decision which it hides from all others. Its interface or definition was chosen to reveal as little as possible about its inner workings" [Parn72b, p. 1056]. Restating this in the context of the papers just described, stepwise refinement represents a process for development in which one can identify design decisions that can be hidden from the programs relying on them. The result can be levels of abstraction in which each level can access functions developed at lower levels without any knowledge of how they were implemented. Not only would the resulting system be easier to maintain, but it would also be easier to verify. As Dijkstra stated about the T.H.E. system,

> We have found that it is possible to design a refined multiprogramming system in such a way that its logical soundness can be proved a priori and its implementation can admit to exhaustive testing. The only errors that showed up during testing were trivial coding errors. . . . When the system is delivered we shall not live in the perpetual fear that a system derailment may still occur in an unlikely situation, such as might result from an unhappy "coincidence" of two or more critical occurrences, for we shall have proved the correctness of the system with a rigor and explicitness that is unusual for the great majority of mathematical proofs. [Dijk68, p. 432]

---

[8]One could update this by talking of the structure of the DFD. Compare Parnas's observations with those of Jackson and Cameron cited in Chapter 3.

I shall return to this issue of proofs in Section 4.3. Here I shall continue following the (overlapping) path of information hiding.

The other Parnas paper of 1972 explained how to specify modules and provided some examples [Parn72a]. Parnas began with the assertion that the target specification scheme must

- Provide the intended user *all* the information that he will need to use the program, *and nothing more.*

- Provide the intended implementer *all* the information about the intended use that he needs to complete the program, *and no additional information.*

- Be sufficiently formal so that it can conceivably be machine tested for consistency, completeness, and other desirable properties of specifications.

- Discuss the program in the terms used by user and implementer alike (i.e., not some abstract formalism) [From Parn72a, p. 330].

He then defined a module as a collection of subroutines or functions that can make changes to the state and/or give user programs the values of the variables making up that state. For each function one would specify

1. The set of possible values: (integers, reals, truth values, etc.).

2. Initial values: (either "undefined" or a member of the set specified in item 1). "Undefined" is considered a special value, rather than an unpredictable value.

3. Parameters: each parameter is specified as belonging to one of the sets named in item 1.

4. Effect: . . . almost all the information is contained in section 4. . . . If the "effect" section is empty there is absolutely no way to detect that the function has been called [i.e., there are neither state changes nor state values displayed]. [Parn72a, p. 331]

Figure 4.4 contains the specification for a stack. The single quotes identify values before the function is called, the brackets indicate the scope of quantifiers, and = is "equals." What we see here is an example of an abstract data type. In this case the specification is independent of the implementation; the abstract data type extensions described in

Function PUSH(a)
possible values: none
integer: a
effect: call ERR1 if a > p2 ∨ a < 0 ∨ 'DEPTH' = p1
  *else* [VAL = a; DEPTH = 'DEPTH' + 1;]

Function POP
Possible values: none
parameters: none
effect: call ERR2 if 'DEPTH' = 0
  the sequence "PUSH(a); POP" has no net effect if no error calls
  occur.

Function VAL
possible values: integer initial; value undefined
parameters: none
effect: error call if 'DEPTH' = 0

Function DEPTH
possible values: integer; initial value 0
parameters: none
effect: none
  p1 and p2 are parameters. p1 is intended to represent the
  maximum depth of the stack and p2 the maximum width or
  maximum size for each item.

Fig. 4.4. A specification for a stack by Parnas.
(Reprinted from [Parn72a] with permission, ©1972, ACM.)

Section 4.2.1 allow the designer to generate the implementation from its specification. Nevertheless, the principle is the same. As Parnas put it,

> All that you need to know about a stack in order to use it is specified there. There are countless possible implementations (including a large number of sensible ones). The implementation should be free to vary without changing the using programs. If the using programs assume no more about a stack than is stated above, that will be true. [Parn72a, p. 332]

This stack specification would be one of five alternative methods of formally specifying data abstraction reported in a paper by Liskov and Zilles [LiZi75]. Where Parnas was motivated by the need to decompose systems into modules that facilitated change, Liskov and Zilles began with a different orientation.

Of serious concern in software construction are techniques which permit us to recognize whether a given program is correct, i.e., does what it is supposed to do. Although we are coming to realize that correctness is not the only desirable property of reliable software, surely it is the most fundamental. If a program is not correct, then its other properties (e.g., efficiency, fault tolerance) have no meaning since we cannot depend on them. . . . What we are looking for is a process which establishes that a program correctly implements a *concept* which exists in someone's mind. [LiZi75, p. 7]

They went on to define a *specification* in the standard way. "Its purpose is to provide a mathematical description of the concept, and the correctness of a program is established by proving that it is equivalent to the specification" [LiZi75, p. 8]. The proof mechanism, they continued, can fail in two ways. First it may incorrectly establish that a program P is correct with respect to its specification. Second, the methodology can fail if the specification does not correctly capture the meaning of a concept. They concluded, "There is no formal way of establishing that a specification captures a concept, but we expect to have gained from using the proof methodology because (hopefully) a specification is easier to understand than a program, so that 'convincing oneself' that a specification captures a concept is less error prone than a similar process to a program" [LiZi75, p. 8].[9] Naturally, implementers require training in the use of the formalism before it becomes a viable tool for convincing oneself that the specification captures the concept.

Liskov and Zilles presented five models for specifying data abstraction. Their criteria for evaluating these specification methods remain valid. They are

- *Formality*. It should be written in a notation that is mathematically sound. This is a mandatory criterion.

---

[9]This is the tension between conceptual and formal modeling in the essential software process described in Section 1.2.2. Notice that the validity of the method will depend on how well the specification expresses the concept. Parnas's fourth criteria for a specification was that it should discuss the program in terms normally used by the user and implementer. He specifically excluded specifications "in terms of the mappings they provide between large input domains and large output domains or their specification in terms of mappings onto small automata, etc." [Parn72a, p. 330] In general, for a formalism to be effective, the conceptual and formal models must be (in some sense) "close" to each other. For more of the author's views on this topic, see [Blum89].

- *Constructibility.* One should be able to construct specifications with undo difficulty.

- *Comprehensibility.* A trained person should be able to reconstruct the concept by reading the specification.

- *Minimality.* The specification should contain the interesting properties of the concept and *nothing more.*

- *Wide Range of Applicability.* The technique should be able to describe a large number of concept classes easily.

- *Extensibility.* A small change in the concept should produce only a small change to the specification.

I shall not review all specification techniques presented in the paper. As already stated, the Parnas method was one alternative; it was called the *state machine model.* The final two methods discussed in the paper are important because they provide a foundation for the abstract data type mechanisms implemented in some programming languages, and I shall examine them briefly.

One technique was to give a list of the properties possessed by the objects and the operations on them. This could be formalized by expressing the properties as axioms for the data abstraction. Hoare and Wirth had used this method to define the built-in data types in PASCAL [HoWi73], and Liskov and Zilles illustrated how a stack could be specified by a set of axioms. Their 9-axiom specification is shown in Figure 4.5; it assumes that INTEGER has been defined elsewhere. Axioms 1 and 2 define the range of the applicable operations. Axiom 3 is the induction axiom that limits the class of stacks to those that can be constructed with the given operations. Axioms 4 and 5 ensure the distinctness of the results of the PUSH operation. Axioms 6 and 7 define the result of TOP, and Axioms 8 and 9 do the same for POP. Both Axioms 7 and 9 capture the concept that one cannot TOP or POP an empty stack (i.e., the result of CREATE).

Notice that there are many expressions that identify the same stack. For example,

    PUSH (CREATE, 7) and
    POP (PUSH (CREATE, 7), 25))

denote the same stack. Therefore the class of stack objects is represented by *equivalence classes* of the set of all expressions, which are determined by the axioms. If the axioms are well chosen, then the equivalence classes are unique. Liskov and Zilles point out that if

```
1    CREATE(STACK)
2    STACK(S) & INTEGER(I) ⊃ STACK(PUSH(S,I)) &
                 [POP(S) ≠ STACKERROR ⊃ STACK(POP(S))] &
                 [TOP(S) ≠ INTEGERERROR ⊃ INTEGER(TOP(S))]
3    (∀A) [A(CREATE) &
                 (∀S)(∀I) [STACK(S) & INTEGER(I) & A(S)
                     ⊃ A(PUSH(S,I)) & [S ≠ CREATE ⊃ A(POP(S))]
                 ⊃ (∀S) [STACK(S) ⊃ A(S)]]
4    STACK(S) & INTEGER(I) ⊃ PUSH(S,I) ≠ CREATE
5    STACK(S) & STACK(S') & INTEGER(I)
                 ⊃ [PUSH(S,I) = PUSH(S',I) ⊃ S = S']
6    STACK(S) & INTEGER(I) ⊃ TOP(PUSH(S,I)) = I
7    TOP(CREATE) = INTEGERERROR
8    STACK(S) & INTEGER(I) ⊃ POP(PUSH(S,I)) = S
9    POP(CREATE) = STACKERROR
```

Fig. 4.5. Axiomatic specification of the stack abstraction.
(After [LiZi75] with permission, ©1975, IEEE.)

Axiom 4 is omitted, then two distinct equivalence classes would satisfy the axioms: one in which the result of a PUSH is never the empty stack and one in which it can be. "Proving the correctness of an implementation of a data abstraction specified by axioms means showing that the implementation is a model of the axioms" [LiZi75, p. 16]. As readers unfamiliar with axiomatic specifications will surmise from a perusal of Figure 4.5, this is not an intuitively obvious task. Because our goal is to produce a specification that captures a concept, the axiomatic approach must be rejected as a general method on the basis of comprehensibility and constructibility. Fortunately, for finitely constructible, countable domains, which is what we have in the computer, the first three axioms of Figure 4.5 can be omitted, and a better notation can be found.

Figure 4.6 presents an algebraic specification for the stack. Here the algebraic construction technique known as *presentation* is used. The definition of the functionality of the operators replaces Axioms 1-3, and only four axioms (numbered 1'-4' and corresponding to 6-9 in Figure 4.5) are needed. The axioms (*relations* or relation schema) provide a construction in which all expression pairs that cannot be shown to be equivalent must be distinct; thus, Axioms 4 and 5 are not needed, and the concern for multiple equivalence classes has been eliminated. Because we have derived the algebraic specification from the axiomatic specification, it is clear that the two are equally good with regard to the criteria of minimality, wide range of applicability, and extensibility. The algebraic specification is clearly superior with respect to constructibility and comprehensibility. It provides a notation in which a stack can be described by the operators (with their domains and ranges) and the

FUNCTIONALITY
    CREATE:          → STACK
    PUSH:       STACK × INTEGER → STACK
    TOP:        STACK → INTEGER ∪ INTEGERERROR
    POP:        STACK → STACK ∪ STACKERROR

AXIOMS
    1'  TOP(PUSH(S,I)) = I
    2'  TOP(CREATE) = INTEGERERROR
    3'  POP(PUSH(S,I)) = S
    4'  POP(CREATE) = STACKERROR

Fig. 4.6. Algebraic specification of the stack abstraction.
(Reprinted from [ZiLi75] with permission, ©1975, IEEE.)

axioms that affect them. Both the users and implementers can see the interesting properties of the stack, and nothing more. How these operators are implemented and how the stack is structured are hidden from view. Abstract data types and object-oriented programming are but two steps from this algebraic specification in the direction of automated support to improve constructibility and comprehensibility, and it is now time to follow that path.[10]

## 4.2.2. Abstract data types

In the previous section, the concept of an abstract data type (ADT) was presented from the perspectives of both information hiding and formalization of the specification process. There is also a strong intuitive foundation for this concept, which I now shall elaborate. When high-level programming languages were introduced, there was a need to

---

[10]By way of closure, let me point out that Guttag, a colleague of Liskov, pursued the role of abstract data types in verification [Gutt77]. Together they wrote a text on abstraction and specification in program development, which provides an excellent foundation for building insights into this approach [LiGu86]. Parnas also continued his work. An important paper was published in 1979 containing useful rules for easing the extension and contraction of software [Parn79]. He spoke of *program families* and ways to design for change. These methods were adapted for use in specifying the requirements for the A7-E aircraft with the title Software Cost Reduction (SRC) [Heni80, Kmie84, PaCW85]. For a comparison of SCR, structured design and object-oriented design in real-time systems, see [Kell87]. It is interesting to note that a goal of Parnas's early work in data abstraction was to establish mathematical interpretations for specifications. His current research continues in this direction, and the emphasis is placed on making the formal interpretations explicit (e.g., [PaSK90]).

associate each variable name with the format and number of words in storage associated with that name. Thus real and integer were essential identifiers for the compiler. Not only did the data type identify how storage should be managed, but it also specified which computational instructions should be used. One set of arithmetic operators was used for real numbers, and another for integers. The decision regarding the evaluation of mixed expressions was left to the compiler designer. The expression 1.3 + 1 could be evaluated as either the integer 2 or the real numbers 2.0 or 2.3 depending on the method selected for interpreting mixed expressions.

Out of this need to link variables with machine instructions and storage patterns came the recognition that the data type also was an effective tool in software development. It provided a mechanism for establishing a design criterion that could be distributed throughout the system. For example, if one defined CI_No as an integer, then all inputs could automatically be tested for conformance to the defined characteristics of an integer. Letters, special characters (other than an initial + or -), or a decimal point would be rejected as invalid inputs. Of course, defining CI_No to be of type integer also allows one to find the product of two CI identifiers, to increment an identifier by one, and other similarly meaningless operations. One could avoid this by defining CI_No as an alphanumeric data type, but then one would lose the automatic checks for nonnumeric inputs. Ideally, one would like to have a stronger typing mechanism so one could define what was important (e.g., the CI identifier is an unsigned number within a specified range) and rule out what would be inappropriate (e.g., arithmetic on identifiers).

The introduction of strong data typing does have a cost in flexibility, and some programming languages (such as LISP) support only one type. Nevertheless, it is broadly accepted that the benefits of data typing outweigh their limitations, and there has been a trend toward the development of strongly-typed languages and environments (including many written in LISP). Most modern programming languages extend the scope of data types beyond what is required by the compiler. A common feature is the *enumeration* type, with which, for example, SIR_Status can be defined as the set of values {Analysis, Review, Pending acceptance, Not approved (open), Waiting assignment, Changed authorized, Validated change (closed)}. When SIR_Status is defined with that value set, only the specific input values will be accepted. (A specification that is both less verbose and less clear is the set {A, R, P, N, W, C, V}, see Fig. 2.7.)

If we begin with this interpretation of the data type concept, then we recognize that each type establishes a class of objects (e.g., reals, integers, CI identifiers, SIR status indicators) and the valid operations on them (e.g., arithmetic operators, concatenation, input, output). One view of the abstract data type, therefore, is that it is a generalization of the definition of special types and their operations. Naturally, these new definitions hide the implementation just as the double-precision data type hides the internal word formats. When we do double-precision arithmetic, we expect to be told the magnitude ranges and the number of decimal points of accuracy, but there seldom is any reason to know about the internal workings of the computer. Indeed, if we expect our programs to be transportable from one computer to another, then it is essential that these (hardware) implementation details be hidden from us. As system developers, it is important that we limit ourselves to the abstractions of the problem domain and not those of the implementation domain.

Once we accept the fact that we can define new data types, we recognize that we are no longer constrained to defining types constructed of strings of contiguous words in memory. We can extend the advantages of data typing to stacks, queues, matrices, rational numbers, and so on. We can also *overload*[11] operators so that they are valid for more than one type. For example, the plus sign is a valid operator for summing two integers or two reals. Here one symbol has different interpretations depending on the types with which it has been used. We could extend this by defining a data type "rational" with the operator "+" whose result was of type rational. In the functionality notation of Figure 4.6, we have

+: rational × rational → rational
+: real × real → real
+: integer × integer → integer

The programming language implicitly overloaded the plus operator, and in our definition of the rational data type we also chose to overload the plus because *this representation seemed to capture the concept best*. What we are doing is enlarging the programming language to deal with richer representation schemes. The obvious advantage is that the abstracted representations hide from us the housekeeping details that are unimportant in our current level of
problem solving. There is also a danger (to which I will return later): Abstract data type extensions can corrupt the correctness and consistency of the programming language.

---

[11]Overloading is the technique of establishing alternative meanings within the same scope, and it is not limited to operators. For example, the constant Review used in the enumeration of SIR_Status could also be used in other enumerations in the same scope, in which case it would be overloaded.

In what follows, I use Ada as the language to illustrate how to create and use abstract data types.[12] Ada is a *strongly typed* language, which means that objects of a given type may take on only those values defined as valid for that type and use only those operations defined for it. In Ada all typing information is *static*; that is, types must be established prior to compilation time. In contrast, most object-oriented programming languages support *dynamic* typing (i.e., determined at execution time). The *programming units* in Ada are

- *Subprograms.* These executable units are either *procedures* or *functions.* They are defined in two parts. The *declaration* specifies the subprogram name and any parameters; the *body* specifies its execution.

- *Packages.* These units specify a collection of related entities such as constants, types, and subprograms. The *visible part* of a package contains the details necessary to use the package. The *private part* contains the structural details to be hidden from the users. The *package body* contains the implementation (as subprograms, tasks or even further packages) of the visible part.

- *Tasks.* These units may operate in parallel with other tasks. The *task specification* establishes the name and parameters, the *task body* defines its execution, and a *task type* is a specification that permits the subsequent declaration of any number of similar tasks.

Notice that in each case the principle of information hiding relegates the implementation details to a *body* of code; there is always a specification available that simply defines the unit's interface and (with comments) describes its use. Because the abstract data types normally are implemented as packages, I shall discuss only that programming unit.

Let us begin with the construction of a package for the stack abstract data type. Using the algebraic specification described in the previous section (Fig. 4.6), we can see that the functionality of a stack is expressed in the visible part of the STACKS package shown in Figure 4.7. It defines the type STACK and presents the four functions CREATE, PUSH, TOP, and POP that operate on that type. (Ada reserved words are in bold type.) Notice that the type of stack is **limited private**. Both **private** and **limited private** imply that the structure of

---

[12]The following overview draws heavily from Booch's text, which provides an excellent introduction to the use of Ada [Booc83]. Ada, by the way, is a registered trademark of the U. S. Department of Defense.

```
package STACKS is
   type STACK is limited private;
   function CREATE return STACK;
   procedure PUSH(S : in out STACK; I : in INTEGER);
   procedure TOP(S : in STACK; I : out INTEGER);
   procedure POP(S : in out STACK);
   INTEGER_ERROR, STACK_ERROR, OVERFLOW : exception;
```

Fig. 4.7. The visible part of the Ada STACKS package.

the type (in this case the STACK[13]) is hidden from the user. **Private** types allow the use of the assignment and equality/inequality operators as well as the explicitly defined operators; **limited private** is restricted (limited) to only the defined operators. In this definition, one cannot create copies of a stack by using the assignment, and one cannot determine if two stacks are identical without examining their contents. Obviously, this represents an interpretation of the *concept* and not a constraint on its implementation. Continuing with the figure, the **procedure** specifications identify the types for the range and domain, and the errors are reported by **exception**, an Ada feature that I shall not describe. Notice that, in addition to the two error flags identified in the algebraic specification, a third exception has been identified. OVERFLOW is an implementation concern; the overflow flag is raised when the stack is full. The algebraic specification describes the important properties of stacks *independent* of their implementation size. Stacks created with the Ada package, on the other hand, have a finite size, and an exception to avoid adding to a full stack is required. (By way of a side comment, I have adapted the exception names from the algebraic specification; the Ada convention would be to combine the three exceptions into two: OVERFLOW and UNDERFLOW.)

In the private part of the package, shown in Figure 4.8, we identify how the type STACK will be structured internally. This will be hidden from the package's user who can only CREATE, PUSH, TOP, or POP objects that he declares to be of type STACK. In effect, we have the freedom to select any design we consider effective, and change it at will as long as we do not violate the interfaces defined in the visible part.

---

[13]In this example I have chosen to call the data type STACK. This can lead to confusion when distinguishing between the name of the package and the name of the data type. If I chose the data type name STORAGE, the distinction between the package and type names in Figure 4.7 would be quite clear. The result, however, would be a loss in clarity for the package users. The Software Productivity Consortium recommends the use of a suffix to denote the object's class. Using this convention, we would have a package name of STACKS_ PACKAGE and a data type of STACK_TYPE.

```
private
   type STACK is
      record
         STORE : array (1 .. 100) of INTEGER;
         INDEX : NATURAL range 0 .. 100 := 0;
      end record;
```

Fig. 4.8. The private part of the Ada STACKS package.

(Naturally, the cost for changing either the private part or the body will be a recompilation of the affected program units.) The definition shown in Figure 4.8 is one of an array of maximum size 100. The data structure used is the **record**, and a separate variable, INDEX, is maintained as a pointer. The range for the pointer is from 0 to 100; negative values are not permitted. I could have defined INDEX to be of the type INTEGER, but the use of the type NATURAL improves understandability. For each CREATE, a 100-integer array and an integer pointer (initialized to zero) will be allocated. The user will have no access to either component of the record except as defined by PUSH, TOP, and POP. Notice that there is nothing in the algebraic specification of Figure 4.6 that is comparable to the private part shown in Figure 4.8; the former does not address implementation issues, but the latter must.

Finally, there is the package body (also hidden from the user), which implements the STACK operators. Before describing it, however, I will examine some of the potential dangers we face in creating the implementation. Returning to Section 4.2.1, recall that I showed how the algebraic specification of Figure 4.6 was equivalent to the 9 axioms in the axiomatic specification of Figure 4.5. But I never showed how those axioms were selected or proved that they ensured the desired behaviors; I only showed what would happen if one of the axioms was omitted. We are familiar with stacks, and we accept those 9 axioms; there is no need to retrace the steps from the "fuzzy thinking" to the clear thinking that produced them. Yet much of what we will do with encapsulation techniques (and, in general, software engineering) deals with problems for which we must create solutions. We may use techniques such as abstract data types to hide unnecessary details, but the hiding mechanism does not ensure the correctness, consistency, closure, or completeness of what is hidden.

Figure 4.9 contains the body of the package. Notice that the axioms of Figure 4.6 are nowhere to be found. There is a proof obligation to demonstrate that the procedures are models of the theory expressed in those axioms (see the discussion of the LST model in Section 1.3.2). That is, one must prove

```
TOP(PUSH(S,I)) = I
TOP(CREATE) = INTEGER_ERROR
```

```
POP(PUSH(S,I)) = S
POP(CREATE) = STACK_ERROR
```

I leave the proof as an exercise, but it is important to note that the Ada package can provide only a mechanism for the representation of the type's functionality. Verifying that the hidden part does what is implied remains the developer's responsibility. In summary, there is a difference between using a formal representation scheme and using a formal method. Obviously, the scheme provides assistance, but a difficult intellectual task remains.

The package presented in Figures 4.7 through 4.9 encapsulate the concept of a stack as a set of up to 100 integers. This is a very narrow definition. Some stacks will require a greater capacity, others less. Some stacks will be integers, others reals or even characters. Of course, one could simply copy packages and edit them. Ada eliminates the need for this common implementation practice by supporting the generaliza-

```
package body STACKS is
    function CREATE return STACK is
    begin
        STACK.INDEX := 0;
    return STACK;
    end CREATE;
    procedure PUSH(S : in out STACK; I : in INTEGER);
    begin
        if S.INDEX = 100 then raise OVERFLOW;
        end if;
        S.INDEX := S.INDEX + 1;
        S.STORE(S.INDEX) := I;
    end PUSH;
    procedure TOP(S : in STACK; I : out INTEGER);
    begin
        if S.INDEX = 0 then raise INTEGER_ERROR;
        end if;
        I := S.STORE(S.INDEX);
    end TOP;
    procedure POP(S : in out STACK);
    begin
        if S.INDEX = 0 then raise STACK_ERROR;
        end if;
        S.INDEX := S.INDEX - 1;
    end POP;
end STACKS;
```

Fig. 4.9. Package body for STACKS.

tion of a package through *generic* program units. Figure 4.10 contains a generic stack, STACKGEN, in which the maximum capacity of the stack is supplied by the value of SIZE, and the type of element stored in the stack is given by ELEM. (I should point out that a better definition of the original STACKS package would have included in the private part,

STACK_SIZE : CONSTANT POSITIVE := 100;

The test for overflow in the body would then be coded as,

**if** S.INDEX = STACK_SIZE **then raise** OVERFLOW;

Of course, that is just good coding practice, which I ignored to simplify the contents of the private part. The STACKGEN package follows the recommended practice.)

The generic package STACKGEN serves as a template for the generation of packages. For example, the following would instantiate a stack equivalent to that defined in STACKS and a stack with the capacity of 5 boolean values.

```
package STACKS1
   is new STACKGEN(SIZE => 100, ELEM => INTEGER);
package SMALL_BOOL_STACK
   is new STACKGEN(SIZE => 5, ELEM => BOOLEAN);
```

To access the definitions, one *imports* the packages by identifying the encapsulated objects (*library units* in Ada; actually concepts expressed as packages). One method to do this is as follows:

```
with SMALL_BOOL_STACK;
procedure MAIN_PROGRAM is . . .
```

One would then be able to declare S to be of type STACK as defined in the package SMALL_BOOL_STACK with

```
declare
   S :SMALL_BOOL_STACK.STACK;
```

Assuming that there was no ambiguity with the type STACK (i.e., the type name was not used in more that one way in the current program unit), one could eliminate the need for the package prefix with the **use**. Figure 4.11 illustrates how the SMALL_BOOL_STACK might be used. Notice that **use** trades convenience for clarity. A quick glance at the body of Figure 4.11 gives little information about the stack BS. By over-

```
generic
    SIZE : POSITIVE;
    type ELEM is private;

package STACKGEN is
    type STACK is limited private;
    function CREATE return STACK;
    procedure PUSH(S : in out STACK; I : in ELEM);
    procedure TOP(S : in STACK; I : out ELEM);
    procedure POP(S : in out STACK);
    INTEGER_ERROR, STACK_ERROR, OVERFLOW : exception;

private
    type STACK_SIZE is NATURAL range 0 .. SIZE;
    type STACK is
        record
            STORE : array (1 .. SIZE) of ELEM;
            INDEX : STACK_SIZE := 0;
        end record;

package body STACKGEN is
    function CREATE return STACK is
    begin
        STACK.INDEX := 0;
    return STACK;
    end CREATE;
    procedure PUSH(S : in out STACK; I : in ELEM);
    begin
        if S.INDEX = STACK_SIZE then raise OVERFLOW;
        end if;
        S.INDEX := S.INDEX + 1;
        S.STORE(S.INDEX) := I;
    end PUSH;
    procedure TOP(S : in STACK; I : out ELEM);
    begin
        if S.INDEX = 0 then raise INTEGERERROR;
        end if;
        I := S.STORE(S.INDEX);
    end TOP;
    procedure POP(S : in out STACK);
    begin
        if S.INDEX = 0 then raise STACKERROR;
        end if;
        S.INDEX := S.INDEX - 1;
    end POP;
end STACKGEN;
```

Fig. 4.10.   Generic stack package.

```
declare
    use SMALL_BOOL_STACK;
    BS :STACK;
    B :BOOLEAN;
    I, J :INTEGER;
    begin
        . . .
        PUSH (BS, I > J);   -- Enters boolean on stack (True if I > J)
        TOP (BS, B);        -- Gets boolean from top of stack
        POP (BS);           -- Removes top item from stack
    end
```

Fig. 4.11.  Sample use of SMALL_BOOL_STACK.

loading the operators on BS we may end up with unexpected results. Therefore, many organizations do not permit the use of **use**.

Now let us examine how an abstract data type can be used to encapsulate some concepts in the SCM system case study. We know, for example, that we will have to maintain some kind of administrative record for each program maintained under configuration control. At a minimum, that record should contain the CI identifier, the version number, some descriptive information, and the current CI status. Let us define a CI_ID type that maintains this information in some (hidden) structure. Each CI_ID will contain both the CI_No (which is the CI identifier for all versions of that base program) and the version number (which contains both the version and release identifier that distinguishes this CI from the other CIs for the base program). We know from our analysis of HHI's needs that several versions of the same program (i.e., programs with an identical CI_No prefix) can be active at the same time. For example, if CI 12345/4.3 has been installed in several locations and HHI produces a new release, CI 12345/5.1, then it does not necessarily follow that all of HHI's customers will adopt the new version. Thus, HHI must maintain both the *4.3* and *5.1* versions. In this case, therefore, requesting a change to CI 12345 would be ambiguous without specifying the version number; moreover, it is possible to make changes to version *4.3* (thereby producing the version *4.3.1.1* as described in Section 2.2) without making changes to version *5.1* (and vice versa).

Obviously, the management of HHI's configuration can become quite complicated. There are sequences of activities that must be followed and conventions that must be respected. We would like the SCM system to enforce compliance. For instance, it should ensure that

- One cannot create a version *1.1* CI unless no CI with that number already exists.

- One cannot create either a new version or a new release of a CI unless that CI already has been released to be updated.

- One cannot release a CI (of a given version) for modification if its status indicates that it already has been released for a modification.

Let us see how abstract data types can help us structure a solution to this problem.[14]

The classical approach to this problem would be to use a decomposition technique, identify processes called Release_CI and Update_CI, and then write procedural code that incorporates the above conditions. In terms of Parnas's KWIC index problem (Section 4.2.1), this would represent a modularization defined by the flow chart organization. Our goal, of course, is to use the encapsulation property of the abstract data type to create a modularization based on design decisions that can be hidden from the users of the module (i.e., package or object). To illustrate how this may be done, I begin with a package (CI_RECORD) that defines the type CI_ID with the following operations:

- CREATE_CI  This creates a CI_ID entry for a CI_No not already assigned to any CI. It associates the descriptive information with the CI number, and sets the CI_STATUS to Preliminary.

- ACCEPT_CI  This changes the CI_STATUS to Unassigned if the prior status was either Preliminary or Assigned.

- ASSIGN_CI  This changes the CI_STATUS to Assigned if the prior status was Unassigned.

- DELETE_CI  This changes the CI_STATUS to Deleted. Notice that we do not want to delete a CI because we do not want CREATE_ID to reassign the number of a deleted CI. There may be conditions limiting what CIs can be deleted, but we can ignore this issue for now. With the principle of information hiding, we can add those details later without affecting the logic of the programs that use the DELETE_ID operator.

---

[14]The astute reader will recognize that the objects to be defined in the following Ada packages are not persistent (i.e., they cease to exist when the main program terminates). We will ignore that problem by assuming that the package bodies are extended to data stored in files. Because I am less interested in the details of an Ada implementation than I am in explaining how abstract data types are used, I shall ignore the details of ensuring that the stored data persist.

- **EDIT_CI**  This permits the editing of the description contained in the CI_ID type.

- **NEXT_CI**  This returns the version number and description of the next CI (in lexical order) relative to that given as a parameter.  NEXT_CI of a CI_No with a null version number returns with version *1.1*, and NEXT_CI for the last version in a sequence returns a null version number.  Among other things, NEXT_CI can be used to produce a list of the various versions and releases for a specific CI_No.  Notice that NEXT_CI reads the state of CI_ID but must not alter it.

- **STATUS_CI**  This returns a boolean set to true if the identified CI is Unassigned (available for assignment); otherwise it returns false.

A partial implementation of the package is given in Figure 4.12.

This CI_RECORD package with its CI_ID type provides a secure structure for working with the CIs.  We can create CIs with a unique number, and we can assign, unassign, and "delete" created CIs.  But, other than editing the text description, we can only read the CI identification block and test the status of the CI.  In fact, that read-only access will satisfy the needs of most package users; for them, the abstract data type provides only the information that they need and hides the implementation details that they do not require.  In effect, it creates a virtual machine that operates on CI identifiers.  That virtual machine then can be accessed by the next level machine to provide the following operations:

- **NEW_CI**  This enters a new CI with the version number *1.1* and sets the CI_STATUS to Unassigned (i.e., the CI is not currently being modified and is available for assignment to a designer for changes).

- **NEW_VERSION**  This updates the record and computes a new version number [i.e., updates version $r.v$ as $r.(v+1)$] and sets the CI_STATUS to Unassigned.

- **NEW_RELEASE**  This updates the record and computes a new release number [i.e., updates version $r.v$ as $(r+1).1$] and sets the CI_STATUS to Unassigned.

```
package CI_RECORD is
    type CI_ID is limited private;
    function CREATE_CI(CN : in CI_No; D : in Description)
            return CI_ID;
    procedure ACCEPT_CI(C : in out CI_ID);
    procedure ASSIGN_CI(C : in out CI_ID);
    procedure DELETE_CI(C : in out CI_ID);
    procedure EDIT_CI(D : in Description; C : in out CI_ID);
    procedure NEXT_CI(CN : in CI-No; V : in out Version;
            D out Description; S : out Status; C : out CI_ID);
    function STATUS_ID(C : in CI_ID) return BOOLEAN;
    CREATE_ERROR, ASSIGN_ERROR, DELETE_ERROR,
            UNDEFINED_CI : exception;
private
    type CI_ID is
        record
            ID : CI_No;             -- Assume type already defined.
            VER : Version;          -- Assume type already defined.
            DES : Description;      -- Assume type already defined.
            CI_STATUS is (Preliminary, Available, Unavailable,
                Deleted);
        end record;
package body CI_RECORD is
    function CREATE_CI return CI_ID is
    begin
        if [some test to see if CI_No is already assigned to a CI_ID]
            then raise CREATE_ERROR;
        end if;
        CI_ID.ID := CN; CI_ID.VER := ""; CI_ID.DES := D;
        CI_ID.CI_STATUS := Preliminary;
        return CREATE_CI;
    end CREATE_CI;
    . . .
end CI_RECORD;
```

Fig. 4.12. CI_RECORD package that defines the type CI_ID.

- ASSIGN This changes the CI_STATUS to Assigned (i.e., the CI is assigned to a developer for modification and no further assignments are allowed).

Rather than showing the Ada package for this set of operators, Figure 4.13 contains the pre and postconditions for each of the operators. As with the VDM example given in Section 2.3.3, the representation in the figure does not detail how the transformation takes place; it describes

**procedure** NEW_CI(C : **in out** CI_ID);
   **pre** ¬UNDEFINED_CI ∧ CI_ID.STATUS = Preliminary;
   **post** CI_ID.STATUS′ = Unassigned ∧ CI_ID.VER′ = "1.1";

**procedure** NEW_VERSION(C : **in out** CI_ID);
   **pre** ¬UNDEFINED_CI ∧ CI_ID.STATUS = Assigned
          ∧ CI_ID.VER = "r.v";
   **post** CI_ID.STATUS′ = Unassigned ∧ CI_ID.VER′ = "r.(v+1)";

**procedure** NEW_RELEASE(C : **in out** CI_ID);
   **pre** ¬UNDEFINED_CI ∧ CI_ID.STATUS = Assigned
          ∧ CI_ID.VER = "r.v";
   **post** CI_ID.STATUS′ = Unassigned ∧ CI_ID.VER′ = "(r+1).v";

**procedure** ASSIGN(C : **in out** CI_ID);
   **pre** ¬UNDEFINED_CI ∧ CI_ID.STATUS = Unassigned;
   **post** CI_ID.STATUS′ = Assigned;

Fig. 4.13.  Assertions for four CI operations.

only the conditions that must be satisfied for the operation to take place
and the result of that operation (i.e., its behavior).  The prime indicates
the state of an altered variable at the completion of the operation.
Given these sets of conditions and the operators in the CI_RECORD
package, it should not be difficult to convert the specification into
procedural code.  In this example it seems more natural to document
our understanding of the program in terms of the input and output
assertions as opposed to the processing that implements the conditions.
Although the notation used in the figure is not part of the Ada syntax,
assertions like this can be incorporated into the Ada pseudocode.

In this running example, we have used information hiding (in the
sense that Parnas introduced the term) to build a set of operators based
on design decisions regarding the functions that will be useful to the
developers of the system.  The implementors of the CI_ID type need not
know how it is to be used, and the users of the type need not know how
it is implemented.  Can we push this approach too far?  Is there the
potential for introducing faults?  Consider this final ADT example.
Assume that we have defined an ADT called TASK_ID (similar to CI_ID
except that it contains information about each assigned task) and that
the designers are identified by a type called DESIGNER_ID.  We know
that CIs (as identified by CI_ID) are associated with tasks (TASK_ID) and
tasks are assigned to designers (DESIGNER_ID).  Why not define an
ADT that records these associations?  We might define it as follows:

```
type TASK_CI_DESIGNER_TABLE is
    record
        T : TASK_ID;
        C : CI_ID;
        D : DESIGNER_ID;
    end record;
```

Here is a sample instance of TASK_CI_DESIGNER_TABLE:

| TASK_CI_DESIGNER_TABLE | | |
|---|---|---|
| Task | CI | Designer |
| 1 | 12345 | Joe |
| 1 | 23456 | Mary |
| 2 | 34567 | Joe |

So far, so good. Now, we decide that, for the purposes of producing reports and editing the table's contents, it would be useful to have two smaller tables that can be managed separately.

```
type WORK_PACKAGE is         -- CIs affected by a task
    record
        T : TASK_ID;
        C : CI_ID;
    end record;
type TASK_ASSIGNMENT is      -- Designers working on a task
    record
        T : TASK_ID;
        D : DESIGNER_ID;
    end record;
```

We now define the operator (procedure) SPLIT that takes the contents of TASK_CI_DESIGNER_TABLE and creates instances of the ADTs WORK_PACKAGE and TASK_ASSIGNMENT. In this example, the results would be as follows:

| WORK_PACKAGE | | TASK_ASSIGNMENT | |
|---|---|---|---|
| Task | CI | Task | Designer |
| 1 | 12345 | 1 | Joe |
| 1 | 23456 | 1 | Mary |
| 2 | 34567 | 2 | Joe |

To continue with this example, suppose that we then introduce some operators to edit either WORK_PACKAGE or TASK_ASSIGNMENT. Finally, we would like the results of this editing to be combined into an updated TASK_CI_DESIGNER_TABLE, so we define an operator (procedure) COMBINE, which is the inverse of SPLIT. It takes the contents of WORK_PACKAGE and TASK_ASSIGNMENT and creates an updated version of TASK_CI_DESIGNER_TABLE. If we apply COMBINE to the above output of SPLIT, we get the following TASK_CI_ DESIGNER_TABLE:

| TASK_CI_DESIGNER_TABLE | | |
|---|---|---|
| Task | CI | Designer |
| 1 | 12345 | Joe |
| 1 | 12345 | Mary |
| 1 | 23456 | Joe |
| 1 | 23456 | Mary |
| 2 | 34567 | Joe |

What happened? We ignored some underlying theory. This group of ADTs actually consists of relations, and in our definitions we have not applied some knowledge about dependencies and normal forms established by relational database design theory (see Section 2.3.1 or [Kent83, Date86, Ullm88]). What went wrong in this example is that the information in TASK_CI_DESIGNER_TABLE must be expressed as three relations: the two already given plus a third that expresses the multi-valued dependency between designers and CIs (i.e., a designer may be assigned many CIs and a CI may be assigned to more than one designer). Without this third ADT (or relation), we lose information when we use the SPLIT operator. The subsequent use of the COMBINE, therefore, results in a *lossless join*. That is,

$$\text{COMBINE(SPLIT(TASK\_CI\_DESIGNER\_TABLE))} \neq$$
$$\text{TASK\_CI\_DESIGNER\_TABLE}$$

This algebraic notation emphasizes that (as in the case of the algebraic specifications of the stack given in Section 4.2.1) we are defining sets of types and operators on the sets. When we define our operators, we have an obligation to *prove* that they preserve the desired properties of the system we are creating. Using formal tools that hide the unnecessary details becomes a sham unless we apply rigorous tests to ensure that we are using the tools properly. Of course, we were all taught, when we learned to program, that a correct compilation did not imply an error-free program. Encapsulation and abstract data types simply alter how we address the design. They cannot guarantee correctness, closure, consistency, or any of the desirable design properties that we seek. This raises some questions about the validity of the CI_RECORD package. As a pedagogue, I am free to leave the proof to the reader and go on to the next extension of encapsulation: objects in an object-oriented environment. If I were a software engineer, however, I would have some more work to do before I felt comfortable using that package.

### 4.2.3. Object-oriented programming

The previous section on abstract data types showed how one language, Ada, supported encapsulation. The objective, of course, was to demonstrate the ADT and not the features of Ada. I now continue the general discussion of encapsulation techniques with *object-oriented programming* (OOP). Clearly, OOP implies a dependence on a programming language. However, our interest is in the design and implementation *concepts*, and I shall deemphasize language specifics. This section explores encapsulation concepts in the context of modeling-in-the-small; Section 4.2.4 examines the extension of these ideas to modeling-in-the-large.

Smalltalk is accepted as the first language to popularize OOP. Its origins can be traced back to Simula 67, which, as its name suggests, was intended to support simulations [DaMN70].[15] In a discrete simulation one identifies the objects of interest and the events that activate them, terminate them, change their state, etc. In Section 3.3 we used JSD to model the SCM system as a discrete simulation. For example, the life history of a CI shown in Figure 3.23 can be interpreted as a simulation of a CI. For every CI at any point of time, its current status can be associated with exactly one box; the Jackson diagram also indicates the states to which the CI could move next. A common discrete simulation application is the modeling of a factory. There are machines, machine operators, and machine options. Several of the machines may be of the same type or subtype. Both machines and machine operators respond to events that alter the state of his machine. These events (such as, "Set machine X for process Y") may have time delays associated with them, and the simulation reports (for each time slice) the state of each machine, its output items, its production rate, and so on.

In the JSD simulation we modeled every object of interest as a *sequential process* and then combined all the processes as a network. An

[15]Simula 67, simply called Simula since 1986, is actually a general purpose language, and it is still in use [Pool86].

alternative would be to model the objects as independent modules within a simulation (without concern for their sequential processing). Each object would control the information about its status, output items, and production rate. It also would be aware of its options and responses. Thus, an event to set machine X for process Y would be processed as a command sent to the object representing machine X. The effect would be to change its state to one of processing Y. In this case, the object for machine X would need to manage the implications of this state change. Notice that this idea of encapsulating everything known about machine X in one module is conceptually appealing to the simulation designers.

This change in perspective from the algorithm to the object implies a change to the control flow of the simulation program. With a traditional imperative programming language, the control flow is managed by procedure invocations (calls). The scope of the calls is established by some predefined call tree, and each called process or function performs some task as requested by the its invoker. In the simulation machine example, however, it is the machine object that maintains its state. It responds to requests (or messages) by altering its state or reporting on its state. For example, the command to change to process Y will alter its state, and a request for the number and type of items produced in the next time slice returns information derived from its state. Thus, rather than modeling a system in terms of a call hierarchy, the simulation is modeled as a set of modules, each of which responds to asynchronous events (communicated in the form of messages).[16]

One final observation concerning the simulation. Each individual machine may be an instance of some general class of machine. Some machines of the same type (class) may be defined as specializations of a more general class. This allows the designer to specify what is known about the general class and then augment this higher level definition with refinements for the subclass. Continuing with the machine example and using the ISA relationship defined in Section 2.3.1, one might state that a high-speed-lathe ISA lathe. All the attributes of a lathe are valid for a high-speed-lathe, but there may be attributes of the subclass of high-speed-lathes (e.g., their range for production output) that are not valid for the entire class of lathes. In Simula, there is a class SIMULATION with PROCESS classes nested within it; in this way, everything of interest to the simulation is in the class SIMULATION.

In the early 1970s, while still a graduate student, Kay began to

---

[16]This is also how a real-time monitor is constructed; processes are initiated as the result of sensing some external event. Perhaps that is why object-oriented design is so effective for real-time applications.

consider applying some of these ideas in his research. He extended these insights to his work on personal computing environments at Xerox, and in time Smalltalk emerged under the leadership of Kay, Goldberg, and Ingalls [GoRo83, Gold85]. At first only a laboratory system, in 1986 Smalltalk became a commercially supported language and environment. It combines many of the features of Lisp (e.g., its typeless style) with those of Simula. In Smalltalk the processes (routines) are called *methods*, and the application of a routine to an object is accomplished by *sending a message* to the object. Everything in a Smalltalk system is an object. There is a highest level class, called *object*, and the root of the subtree containing only classes is *class*. In this way, Smalltalk has a conceptual unity; all portions of the run-time application are part of the same class hierarchy, and *class methods* within that hierarchy are possible. Thus, for example, if the environment has a class for window objects with methods such as open, close, and move, the developer may define a subclass with some specialized methods or properties and still have the window class methods perform as previously specified.

Before going into further detail, notice that there is no consistent OOP vocabulary. In Smalltalk, a class is an object; in other languages, objects are instances of a class. Therefore it will be best to delay any discussion of individual languages until after reviewing the general concepts. I begin by examining the characteristics of OOP. One widely held definition is that a programming language must incorporate the following four characteristics to qualify as an OOP language [Pasc86].

- *Information hiding.* This is defined as the ability to maintain control over private variables concerning the state of a software module. Manipulation of these variables must be managed by a localized set of procedures. It implies the ability to declare static variables within the scope of a procedure.

- *Data abstraction.* This is presented as a way of using information hiding. A programmer-defined abstract data type includes both an internal representation plus a set of procedures to access and manipulate the data.

- *Dynamic binding.* This defers operational control to run-time rather than requiring all operations to be anticipated at compile-time. That is, instead of building large case statements to respond to all possible conditions, control is decentralized and the module reacts to a message (invocation) based on its current state.

- *Inheritance*. This is the structuring of the abstract data types within a hierarchy or network. Normally, this is expressed as an *ISA* relationship.

The first two items on this list are related. In combination, they imply that each ADT maintains its state. This is a modularization issue. Notice that when we presented the Ada ADT, it was described as a package to be imported by a procedure. The procedure (and not the ADT) maintained the state; the ADT, of course, hid the structural details of that state from the procedure. In Ada, procedures invoke other procedures, and many decisions must be made at compile-time.

Thus, the first difference between OOP and imperative languages such as Pascal and Ada is that they have contrasting philosophies regarding modularization. In Pascal and Ada, the module is a process, and the data structures are used to make that process more efficient. (Review the discussion of stepwise refinement in Section 4.1.3.) With an OOP, however, the module is an object (or abstract data type) and its role is both the management of the object's state and the definition of the processes (methods) that can act on that state. With an imperative language, control paths are predetermined at compile-time, and one module invokes another.[17] With OOP there are no prede-fined control paths. Modules send messages to other modules based on the dynamics of the processing. That is why Smalltalk is so effective for managing interactive displays. The developer need not anticipate all the processing options; he need only define the actions that are valid for an object in a given state.

Given this different view of a module, the second two OOP properties are necessary. Dynamic binding supports decision making based on the state of an object. Clearly, the definition of the process must be supplied before execution, but the determination of the desired action will rely on the state information available at the time of execution. For example, the actions to be taken in moving and clipping a window will depend, in part, on the size and location of the window, and this will have been determined during execution. The final OOP property, inheritance, is useful in generalizing data types. The Ada ADT does not support inheritance, and it is possible to have an object orientation without it. Nevertheless, inheritance is generally considered a prerequisite for OOP.

Now that we have defined four necessary characteristics of an OOP language, let us stop briefly to review where we have been and where we

---

[17]Again, I am simplifying. Modula, for example, supports coroutines, and Ada tasks operate asynchronously. See [Wegn87] for a classification of the language features in the object-oriented paradigm.

are going. Recall that we are still in Section 4.2, entitled Encapsulation Techniques. We are concerned with how we can use software to package complex concepts in simpler, more directly comprehensible forms. In the Parnas definition of information hiding, we seek methods to hide everything about the implementation of a module that the user does not need to know and everything about the use of a module that the implementer does not need to know. Liskov and Zilles showed how to apply this principle by capturing concepts formally. Finally, Section 4.2.2 illustrated these ideas by demonstrating how Ada could express the concepts of a stack or a CI with an ADT. As software engineers, our principal interest is in the identification, representation, and validation of concepts. The implementation language that we use is an important, but secondary detail. Therefore, in the remainder of this section I shall concentrate on the representational and operational concepts behind OOP. The goal is not to introduce the reader to some new programming technique. Rather, it is to describe an important modeling alternative and to show how it can be applied for both implementation (this section) and design (the next section).

To continue. I have introduced the features of an OOP language and observed that the essence of this paradigm stems from a decision regarding modularization. I now reintroduce OOP, but this time I begin from a modularization perspective. Meyer gives five criteria for evaluating design methods with respect to modularity [Meye88].

- *Modular decomposability.* This involves the decomposition of a problem into subproblems. The structured analysis of Section 3.2.1 is an example of a top-down design approach; a collection of many processes with low cohesion and access to many data structures is a counterexample.

- *Modular composability.* This involves the production of software elements that may be composed freely; it enables reuse. Examples include the program library; preprocessors, which cannot be applied serially, represent a counterexample.

- *Modular understandability.* This involves the ability of the designer to express the desired concept and for the maintainer to understand what has been implemented. As stated, the goal of the ADT was to enhance formal understanding; spaghetti code is an obvious counterexample.

- *Modular continuity.* A small change in the problem specification should require only a small change in the module. Liskov and Zilles called this property *extensibility.* The use of symbolic constants is an example; the use of physical representations, on the other hand, is a counterexample.

- *Modular protection.* The effects of abnormal conditions should remain confined to the affected module or, at worst, propagate to a few neighboring modules. In an information system one tests the validity of inputs before accepting them; the use of undisciplined exception conditions is a counterexample.

Notice that the definitions and examples have combined architectural and methodological issues. The first is concerned with what the implementation environment will support, and the second involves how designers use these features. For example, the fact that Ada has powerful exception-handling facilities does not inhibit a programmer from using them poorly. Yet if a language does not support those key features, then it is much more difficult for a programmer to improve the quality of his product.

Meyer uses these criteria to define five principles that must be followed to ensure proper modularity [Meye88, pp. 18-22].

- *Linguistic modular units.* "Modules must correspond to syntactic units in the language used."

- *Few interfaces.* "Every module should communicate with as few others as possible."

- *Small interfaces (weak coupling).* "If any two modules communicate at all, they should exchange as little information as possible."

- *Explicit interfaces.* "Whenever two modules A and B communicate, this must be obvious from the text of A and B or both."

- *Information hiding.* "All information about a module should be private to the module unless it is specifically declared public."

Many of these principles echo what has been said earlier. The section on structured design (3.2.2) addressed the issue of interfaces and coupling, and Meyer supplies this section's third definition of information hiding.

What differentiates Meyer's discussion from those that preceded it is that his goal is the development of a programming language and environment that improves modularization by exploiting these five principles. He concludes his discussion by introducing the *open-closed* principle. A module is said to be open if it is available for modification, and it is closed if it is available for use by other modules. A key problem in software development (and maintenance) is that we would like our modules to be both open and closed at the same time. There always will be changes, and we would like the freedom to make those changes transparently to the module's clients *as long as we do not change the way in which the clients expect the module to act.* In a traditional development environment, a module is either open or closed. When it is stable and ready for use, it is closed. When we need to make a change, we open a copy, implement and test our changes, recertify the module with respect to all its client modules, and then replace the modified (and closed) module with a new (closed) module. The difficulties in managing this process were a major justification for HHI's SCM system.

Object orientedness provides a way to treat modules as both open and closed. The principle of information hiding establishes a fixed interface that guarantees the clients that the module will perform in the specified way. The designers also are free to alter modules on condition that they will not violate the existing client agreement. As long as that interface is preserved, the clients can view the module as closed, and the developers can consider it open. This idea, of course, can be adopted independent of OOP. In fact, the presentation of Parnas's guidelines for modularization given in Section 4.2.1 illustrates how to apply this principle with an imperative language such as FORTRAN. The key issue, therefore, is not if there should be modular units with only a few, small, and explicit interfaces that support information hiding. Virtually all modern programming environments (when employed with modern programming practices) support these principles. Rather, the issue is, "How can we define modules so that these principles are enhanced in a natural way for both the developers and users?"

Debates regarding how to subdivide a system into modular units are not new. Chapter 3 was organized around one such debate: decomposition versus composition. The introduction to Section 3.3 observed that the question originally was phrased in terms of a data flow oriented design (e.g., SA/SD) versus a data structure oriented design (e.g., DSSD and JSP). Which characteristics of the problem space should be used to guide the design activity? Should they be the processes that transform the data or the structures inherent in the data? The same debate continues in this chapter, only here we are concerned with a choice of implementation philosophies. Should we structure our modules to encapsulate algorithms or to encapsulate data structures? Meyer advocates the second alternative. He states,

> *Ask not what the system does;*
> *Ask WHAT it does it to!*

This object orientation offers a different perspective for understanding the problem to be solved, and it is supported by a broad range of implementation tools. Earlier I identified four features necessary for OOP. Naturally, a programming language can apply a subset of these features. Wegner has categorized what he calls *object-based* languages and developed a taxonomy [Wegn87]. For example, in the dimension of classes and inheritance, he identifies three levels:

- *Object-based*. These languages incorporate features to support objects. The object has "operations" and a "state" that remembers the effect of those operations. Ada is an example of an object-based language; it supports the ADT.

- *Class-based*. These are object-based languages in which every object has a class. The class acts as a template for the creation of new objects. This introduces the need for dynamic support. Ada is not class-based because objects are defined at compile-time, whereas in a class-based language new objects can be created at run-time.

- *Object-oriented*. These are class-based languages that support inheritance. That is, there is a class structure that supports a parent-child (superclass-class) relationship. Smalltalk and Simula are object-oriented.

As we will see in Section 4.2.4, one can use *object-oriented design* (OOD) for other than OOP languages. The further one gets from object-oriented languages, however, the greater the burden for the developers. As a general rule, we would like our programming tools to enable the effective expression of our concepts. Therefore, we would expect future development environments to incorporate the object-based features described in this chapter.

There are many object-oriented languages other than Smalltalk and Simula. Three popular languages produce applications coded in C. C++ is a superset of C and includes some features that have little to do with object orientedness [Stro86]. Objective-C grafts some Smalltalk concepts onto a C base [Cox86]. Both C++ and Objective-C use preprocessors to generate the C code. Eiffel is a complete OOP language; the output of its compiler is C code. Several OOPs have been implemented as extensions to a Lisp environment; Loops [BoSt82] and Flavors [Cann80] are the most frequently cited examples. Finally, there are OOP environments that operate in personal computers; the March 1989 *BYTE* contains an overview and summary of object-oriented resources. Eiffel is perhaps the best language for explaining OOP concepts, and I shall use it in the following examples.

Eiffel's developer, Meyer, lists "seven steps towards object-based happiness" [Meye88, pp. 60-62].

- **Level 1** *(Object-based modular structure)*:   Systems are modularized on the basis of their data structures.

- **Level 2** *(Data abstraction)*: Objects should be described as implementations of abstract data types. [This is Wegner's object-based criterion.]

- **Level 3** *(Automatic memory management)*: Unused objects should be deallocated by the underlying language system, without programmer intervention. [This is required for the dynamic creation of objects. The program should be free to create and retire objects without concern for the housekeeping associated with those actions. Therefore, the language environment should manage memory (including garbage collection) as new objects are created, an object's state is modified, and objects are deleted.]

- **Level 4** *(Classes)*: Every non-simple type is a module, and every high-level module is a type. [This is Wegner's class-based criterion. Cox speaks of "factory objects" used to create objects. The factory objects are built at compile-time, and they serve as templates for the instances (i.e., collection of state variables) created at run-time [Cox86]. These factory objects are, of course, classes. One can also think of the class as a kind of database scheme; the database instance represents the object's state. In the relational model, only simple structures (and hence objects) are possible; an *object-oriented database management system* (OODBMS) extends the types of objects that can be maintained in a database. With an OODBMS, relational operators (e.g., project and join) may be unable to deal with an object's inherently more complex structure, and object-specific operators must be supported.]

- **Level 5** *(Inheritance)*: A class may be defined as an extension or restriction of another. [This is Wegner's minimum requirement for object-oriented. In Section 2.3.1 the concepts of extension and restriction were described in terms of *generalization* and *specialization*. In Chapter 2, the focus was on the use of semantic data models to understand what the software should do. Here the concern is for specifying the implementation of that software. Notice how object orientation provides continuity from analysis to realization.]

- **Level 6** *(Polymorphism and dynamic binding)*: Program entities should be permitted to refer to objects of more than one class, and operations should be permitted to have different realizations in different classes. [We have been introduced to the idea of *polymorphism* in the context of overloading the plus sign. The operation "+" has a different realization with different type definitions (classes). Dynamic binding implies that the decision regarding how the operator should act is made at run-time rather than (as in the case of a fixed or float add) at compile-time. Polymorphism implies run-time decisions.]

- **Level 7** *(Multiple and repeated inheritance)*: It should be possible to declare a class as heir to more than one class, and more than once to the same class. [Single inheritance is presented as a tree, with each class belonging to one superclass but perhaps having multiple subclasses dependent on it. For example, a student is a subclass of person. Everything that a program stores about a person (e.g., name and age) also will be true for a student, but the program will maintain additional information about a student (e.g., major and graduation year). The student class, in turn, can be extended to graduate and undergraduate students, and the person class can be given the subclass faculty. The class of teaching assistant, however, would inherit attributes from both the classes of graduate student and faculty. Multiple inheritance allows this.[18]]

As one might expect, Eiffel operates at the seventh level of object-based happiness.

I now will illustrate some of the concepts just presented with some examples. Two points must be kept in mind. First, every module is a class; there is no program called MAIN. Second, objects are the instances of a class; the object *john_smith* is an instance of the class STUDENT. (Eiffel uses upper case for classes, lower case for identifiers, and initial upper case for predefined entities and routines. In what follows, reserve words are in bold and variables are in italics.) Let us now return to the SCM system. Among the objects of primary interest in this system is the CI. It would seem reasonable, therefore, to model CIs as objects with the following operations (to be implemented as *routines* that act on the state of *attributes* in the *class CI*):

---

[18]At the end of Section 2.3.1 a similar example was given with CIs that were classified by both size (small and large) and language (Ada and C).

- *new_ci*. This would initialize a new CI. (In the Ada ADT shown in Fig. 4.12 this was called CREATE_CI, but in Eiffel *Create* has a different meaning. To avoid confusion, *new_ci* is used. In an actual implementation, *new_ci* would probably be replaced by a specific *Create*, but I will use the generic *Create* in this example.)

- *accept_ci*. This would accept a CI after an update.

- *status_ci*. This returns a true if the CI status indicates that it is available for assignment.

- *assign_ci*. This would assign a CI for update.

- *edit_ci_info*. This would edit the CI descriptive information similar to the way EDIT_CI edited it in Figure 4.12.

- *edit_ci_text*. This would edit the text of the CI. Naturally, this editing function will vary according to the type of text. If the text were an Ada program, one would expect one type of editor to be used; if the text were a set of test data, a different editor would be required. (Of course, this process was not included in Fig. 4.12.)

As with the example in Figure 4.12, I shall ignore the fact that we are dealing with persistent objects.

I start with a demonstration of information hiding. Assume that we have created the class *CI* with the above routines (*features* or operations). The code generated from Eiffel will use the class definition as a template for creating instances (objects). To see how this is done, consider the following fragment of some class called *X*. (Remember, all modules are classes.)

    *ci_1: CI*

This declares that the variable (Meyer prefers the term *entity*) *ci_1* is of type *CI*. This is quite similar to the statement in the Ada illustration of Figure 4.11.

    BS :STACK;

In each case, the type has a complex and hidden structure. With the stack example, storage will be allocated to BS by the compiler; for *ci_1*, on the other hand, a type has been associated with a label, but the object does not exist (i.e., it does not yet have state). To create the object, Eiffel supplies the predefined feature *Create*, which is available for all classes.

> *ci_1.Create*

This creates an instance of the object associated with *ci_1*. We now can apply the operations listed above. For example,

> *ci_1.new_ci ("123456", "Square root program", "S", "A");*

declares that the object is a new CI with the attribute values of number "123456", descriptive title "Square root program", category "S" for source code, and language "A" for Ada. Naturally, the user of the feature must know the interface, *but nothing more.*

The feature to accept a program after update might be expressed as

> *ci_1.accept_ci ("123456", "V");*

This interface provides only the CI number ("123456") and the fact that the update represents a version ("V") or release ("R"). Of course, we also could have defined some feature that binds a CI number with an entity (say, *open_ci*). Using that feature would have implied that the CI number of *ci_1* already was bound to "123456", and the first parameter in *accept_ci* would have been unnecessary. Finally, a sequence of code to assign a CI for modification might first test the status of a CI before assigning it to a designer (in this case to Joe) as follows.

> **if** *ci_1.status_ci ("123456")* **then**
>      *ci_1.assign_ci ("123456", "Joe")*
> **else** *print ("Cannot assign")* **end;**

Figure 4.14 displays the class definition for the above features. A few comments are obvious. To begin with, Eiffel does not support the enumerated type that we saw with Ada. There are two reasons for this. First, Eiffel has been designed to be a "small" (Meyer uses the term "ascetic") language; it concentrates on devising powerful notations for the most advanced and common constructs rather than shorthands for all possible cases. Second, as an object-oriented language, the designer is free to define classes for types when that is the best way to express the concept. Another valid comment about the class definition in Figure 4.14 is that it does not seem to do much error checking. In *accept_ci*, for instance, the code allows the processing of CIs that already are in the *Available* status. I omitted that test for a reason. Refer back to Figure 4.13 and observe how preconditions and postconditions were used

**class** *CI* **export**
 *new_ci, accept_ci, status_ci, assign_ci, edit_ci_info, edit_ci_text*
**feature**
 *ci_no: INTEGER ;*
 *ci_name: STRING ;*
 *ci_type: (Source, Object, Test_data, Description)*  [Invalid Eiffel
 *ci_lang: (Ada, C) ;*          syntax, used
 *ci_update: (Version, Release);*       for illustration
 *ci_status: (Available, Unavailable);*    only]
 *ci_developer: STRING ;*

 *new_ci (no: INTEGER, nm: STRING, tp: STRING, lng: STRING)* **is**
  -- This sets the information block in a new CI.
  **do**
   *ci_no := no*
   *ci_name := nm*
   *ci_type := tp*
   *ci_lang := lng*
  **end ;** *-- new_ci*

 *accept_ci (no: INTEGER, up: STRING)* **is**
  -- This accepts an updated CI and modifies the version
  **do**
   *ci_status := Available*
    **if** *up =* "V" **then**
     -- update as $r.(v+1)$
    **else**
     -- update as $(r+1).1$
    **end**
  **end ;** *-- accept_ci*

 *status_ci (no: INTEGER)* **is**
  . . . .

Fig. 4.14. Partial listing of *CI* class in Eiffel.

in the procedures NEW_VERSION and NEW_RELEASE to ensure that
the operation would be performed only if

CI_ID.STATUS = Assigned.

I used this notation because the declarative statement was much more
direct than an equivalent procedural selection (i.e., **if . . . then . . .
else**). Eiffel provides preconditions (called **require**) and postconditions
(called **ensure**).  There also is an **invariants** clause that represents

general consistency constrains that are imposed on all routines of the class. Thus, a better definition of *accept_ci* would begin

```
accept_ci (no: INTEGER, up: STRING) is
                    -- Accepts an updated CI and modify the version
      require
          ci_status = Available
          up = "V" or else up ="R"
      do
          . . . .
```

With a precondition, it also would be possible to eliminate the test using *status_ci* in the previous sample of *assign_ci* use. Of course, the failure to satisfy a precondition implies an exception, which in turn implies exception handling. But I shall not go into that.

When I identified the features of the class *CI*, I included two editing operations: one for the description of the CI (*edit_ci_info*) and the other for the CI contents (*edit_ci_text*). Although I have not yet defined how they are implemented, it should be clear that all CIs probably have the same high-level description. Consequently, one version of *edit_ci_info* should be sufficient for all CIs. However, one would expect to use a different editor if the CI was an Ada program, a C program, a text specification, a set of test data, etc.[19] One of the major advantages of an OOP is that it supports inheritance, which allows us to join these different types of CIs into a hierarchy to customize selected features. For example, consider the following subclasses for *CI*.

- *CI_ADA*. This would be a class with the attributes *package_id*, *s_file*, and *o_file*. (Naturally, all of the attributes of the parent class would remain valid for the descendent classes unless they were **redefined**.) The editor *Ada_editor* would be used for the feature *edit_ci_text*.

- *CI_C*. This would be a class with the attributes *s_file* and *o_file*. It would use the editor *C_editor* for the feature *edit_ci_text*.

- *CI_DOC*. This would be a class with no additional attributes. It would use the editor *vi* for the feature *edit_ci_text*.

---

[19] I am disregarding many implementation details in order to concentrate on the higher level concepts involved. Eiffel generates C programs that operate in a Unix environment. Therefore, in principle, a class definition can have a routine transfer control to an existing Unix-based editor. How that is accomplished and the implications regarding control flow should not concern us here.

These three classes represent specializations of the class *CI*. The definition of *edit_ci_info* in the class *CI* will be valid for each of the three subclasses I have just identified. That is, by indicating that *CI_ADA*, *CI_C*, and *CI_DOC* are all subclasses of *CI*, we can always access the feature *edit_ci_info*. The use of *edit_ci_text*, on the other hand, may be more complex. For example, given the statements

> *ci_1: CI_ADA; ci_2: CI: ci_3: CI_DOC*
> *ci_1.Create(. . . .); ci_2.Create(. . . .); ci_3.Create(. . . .)*

and assuming that a valid CI number was bound to each entity label (e.g., *ci_1* represents the object with CI number "123456"), then the statement

> *ci_1.edit_ci_text*

would cause *Ada_editor* to be invoked, and the statement

> *ci_3.edit_ci_text*

would cause the editor *vi* to be invoked. What would it mean to execute the following statement?

> *ci_2.edit_ci_text*

The feature has been defined for the class, but there is not enough information in the object's state to decide which editor to invoke. Because we would not expect *edit_ci_text* to be valid except for subclasses of *CI*, we ought to define this feature in *CI* as follows:

> *edit_ci_text* **is**
> **require** (the CI number is valid)
> **deferred**
> **end** ; -- *edit_ci_text*

Here, **deferred** implies that the definition of this feature is deferred for definition in descendent classes; the feature will be valid only for those subclasses.

The class hierarchy also controls other operations as well. One can write the statement,

> **if** (some test) **then** *ci_2 := ci_1* **else** *ci_2 := ci_3* **end;**

After execution, $ci\_2$, which was declared to be of class (type) $CI$, will be of either type $CI\_ADA$ or $CI\_DOC$ (depending on the outcome of "some test"). Now, the statement

> $ci\_2.edit\_ci\_text$

will be valid. The type associated with $ci\_2$ was changed during execution (which is an illustration of dynamic binding), and the processing of the edit text feature will be determined by the object's current type (which is an example of polymorphism).

The instances of inheritance presented so far have all been of a hierarchical form. Meyer's seventh level of object happiness requires more. To illustrate this highest level, note that HHI might want two ways of subdividing their program CIs: by language (Ada or C) and by operating environment (Unix or DOS). Some features may vary with language, and others with environment. Multiple inheritance is required. To see how Eiffel supports it, assume that there already is a class called $CI\_UNIX$. The following would then create the class of Ada programs that run under Unix.

```
class CI_ADA_U export . . .
inherit
        CI_ADA;
        CI_UNIX;
feature
        -- Specific features of Ada Unix programs
. . . .
end; -- class CI_ADA_U
```

Because some of the features of $CI\_ADA$ and $CI\_UNIX$ might use identical names for different processes, we will need to be careful that each feature has a unique name. Eiffel employs the **rename** feature to help the developer in accomplishing this. By way of example, let both $CI\_ADA$ and $CI\_UNIX$ have a routine named *save* that performs a slightly different function. The designer could use **rename** to create unique names for them as follows.

```
class CI_ADA_U export . . . inherit
        CI_ADA rename save as save_a;
        CI_UNIX rename save as save_u
feature . . . .
```

In each of the examples of this section I have used domain-specific examples that emphasize application concepts. However, sometimes the OOP examples are clearer when used with familiar data structure examples. Therefore, I close this section by returning to the familiar example of the stack. It is available in the Eiffel Basic Library as STACK[T], where T represents an arbitrary type. The entity x may be declared as a stack of CIs with

x: STACK [CI];

And if we represented a configuration as a list of CIs (e.g., LIST [CI]) and wanted to model the various version changes in the form of a stack of these lists, then the entity y would implement that concept with the declaration

y: STACK [LIST [CI]];

That simple line certainly hides a lot of information from its user.


### 4.2.4.    Object-oriented design and analysis

Object orientation is a relatively new concept, and it is undergoing change [ShWe87, KiLo89]. I have presented the idea as a logical extension of encapsulation's information hiding and abstract data type. One also could present the paradigm as a solution to the reuse problem (e.g., see [Meye87]). Recall that one of Brooks's best hopes for the future was, "Buy rather than build." This can be generalized as, "Reuse rather than program new." The fact that *object-oriented design* (OOD) emphasizes the modularization of general structures together with their operators suggests that OOD offers a path for producing libraries of reusable parts. Cox speaks of a Software-IC library to imply a parallel with building hardware from standard chips [Cox86]. Booch has published a book of reusable Ada packages and parts [Booc87].

In the small, OOD can be interpreted as the design of OOP applications. But this is a rather limiting view; there also is an OOD context that is language independent. Booch initially used the term with Ada implementations [Booc83, Booc86], and his subsequent work extended OOD to other languages. The GE Research and Development Center also has used the Object Modeling Technique (OMT) to develop systems with traditional programming languages [RuBP91]. King suggests that the object is a natural abstraction for system components; indeed, he claims that even his cat is object oriented [King89]. We already have seen some of these design concepts in JSD. As pointed out in Section 3.3.2, JSD begins by identifying entities and actions (classes and methods, objects and operations). In JSD, however, the entities are modeled as sequential processes, whereas in OOD they are modeled as objects to be implemented as modules (or, in an object-based language such as Ada, in the form of ADTs).

It seems clear, then, that composition based on an object orientation is a natural way to design systems. This is especially true when the target environment can support the underlying modeling structures (e.g., the ADT). It is not surprising, therefore, to find a proliferation of object-oriented extensions to our programming environments. There are object-oriented programming languages, design methods, database management systems, and analysis methods. In this section I will consider object orientation only with respect to system design and analysis. Moreover, I will limit myself to just two techniques. First I will describe OOD as Booch currently defines it. For Booch, OOD grew out of his interest in Ada; recently, his methods have been generalized to incorporate a number of object-oriented programming languages as well. My discussion draws primarily from the two previously referenced citations as augmented by a newer book, *Object Oriented Design with Applications* [Booc91]. The second method that I will describe is called *object-oriented analysis* (OOA), which extends OOD into the analysis phase. The particular form of OOA that I will report on was developed by Coad and Yourdon [CoYo91]. It can be viewed as a natural extension of the structured analysis evolution described in Section 3.2.3. One must be aware, however, that—like all methods—the techniques are evolving. For instance, Booch finds his 1983 book on Ada to be out of date and suggests that one begin with his 1991 book. In the case of OOA, although Coad and Yourdon first published their book in 1990, the 1991 edition contains significant notational differences. Nevertheless, although the details change, the elemental concepts persist.

Booch introduced the term object-oriented design in his *Software Engineering with Ada* [Booc83]. He began by reviewing why the primary "conventional software development methodologies" have failed.

> Top-down design techniques are imperative in nature, that is, they force us to concentrate on the operations in the solution space, with little regard for the design of the data structures. Data structure design techniques are at the other end of the spectrum. They concentrate on the objects and treat the operations in global fashion. The Parnas decomposition criterion does allow us to deal with both objects and operations but, because of the limitations of most programming languages, we usually end up with a traditionally functional solution.
>
> Using these design methodologies, we may, on the one hand, have a solution that is totally functional, and thus avoids a reasonable implementation of our real-world object abstractions, or, on the other hand, we may end up with clear data structures, but the operations will be obscure. The effect is somewhat like

trying to communicate in English using just verbs or just nouns. [Booc83, p. 40]

Given an object-based language (in this case Ada), Booch then showed how to design a system with real-world abstractions that map onto implementation representations.

In his current writings, Booch proposes a four-step life cycle for OOD [Booc91, pp. 198-206].

- *Analysis.* This brings together the users and developers of the system to articulate the functions that it should provide. While the boundary between analysis and design is fuzzy, the goal of analysis is "to model the world by identifying the classes and objects that form the vocabulary of the problem domain." In OOD the focus turns to "the abstractions and mechanisms that provide the behavior that this model requires. Stated another way, analysis tells us about the desired behavior of the system we must build, whereas design generates the blueprints for the implementation of that system." The analysis methods he suggests are those already presented in Chapter 2.

- *Design.* Design begins "as soon as we have some (possibly incomplete) formal or informal model of the problem to be solved." Booch suggests a strategy of "analyze a little, design a little." While he recognizes that, in "the real world, analysts and designers may not be tightly coupled," his approach is one of learning from doing. (Cf. Brooks's "No Silver Bullet.") "This process refines a designer's understanding of the requirements, and this improved understanding feeds back into the analysis process."

  He addresses the completion of the design process as follows. "Design only the key abstractions and important mechanisms, so that you have a blueprint that is sufficient for implementation, and defer to a later phase those aspects of the solution that have little or no bearing upon the observable behavior of the system." For large systems, break "the problem into subproblems, so that specialists in that particular problem domain can carry on the design process. . . . The rule of thumb we use is that one can stop designing when key abstractions are simple enough to require no further decomposition, but can be composed from existing reusable software components."

- *Evolution.* This "combines the traditional aspects of coding, testing, and integration." There is never a "big-bang"; instead there is "the incremental production of a series of prototypes, which eventually evolve into the final implementation." Booch defines system development as "trying to satisfy a number of competing constraints, including functionality, time, and space. . . . By evolving the implementation of a software system, we can determine which constraints are really important and which are not."

The kinds of evolutionary changes normally center around the class definitions (e.g., adding a new class, changing the implementation or representation of a class, or reorganizing the class structure). "The key to maintaining sanity during the evolution of a system under development is twofold: focus on building stable interfaces and encapsulate design decisions that are likely to change."

- *Modification.* "Our observation is that modification involves activities that are little different than those required during the evolution of a system. Especially if we have done a good job in the original object-oriented design, adding new functionality or modifying some existing behavior will come naturally."

In allocating effort, more time is spent on design than on analysis, and the design effort and evolution effort are roughly the same.

When he described OOD in 1986, Booch commented that what separates it from other methods is its view of software objects as actors, each with its own set of applicable operations. OOD begins with a system requirement, and—as with JSD—we "structure our system around the objects that exist in our model of reality [Booc86]." Its design philosophy is that

> *Each module in the system denotes an object or class of objects from the problem space.* [Booc86, p. 213]

In his initial work with Ada, the key decisions were related to the identification of classes or objects that could be realized as Ada packages. Booch developed a diagramming convention for Ada packages, subprograms, and tasks that has found widespread acceptance. The basic symbols are shown in Figure 4.15. Objects are indicated by a closed, free-form unit. A subprogram is shown by a rectangle with a small field at the top (representing the subprogram specification) and a larger field at the bottom (for the body). The package has symbols on the left border of the box. Oval symbols indicate abstract data types (data objects), and rectangular symbols name the package's operations. Generic packages and subprograms are shown with dotted lines, and a task (not to be confused with Task in this example) has the basic form of a parallelogram. One may nest symbols (or networks of symbols)

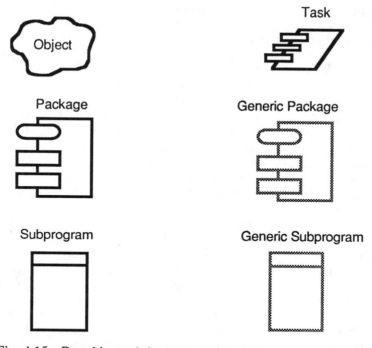

Fig. 4.15.  Booch's module symbols for object-oriented design.
(Reprinted from [Booc86] with permission, ©1986, IEEE.)

within the "body" area of a box to indicate how that body will be implemented.  In his 1991 book, Booch also provides module symbols for subprogram, package, and task bodies; these have shaded interiors. (These diagrams are sometimes called *Boochgrams* or *Gradygrams*; Booch prefers the more benign name of *module diagrams*.)

As Booch's work in OOD expanded beyond the realm of Ada development, he found it necessary to extend his diagramming notation to include classes, class relationships, and class utilities. (He defines a class as a set of objects that share a common structure and a common behavior; a single object is simply an instance of a class.)  The symbol for a class is the cloud-like blob drawn in dashed lines; the symbol for a class utility is a shaded class icon. As one moves from an object-based domain to one that is object oriented, one can model hierarchies of classes to achieve an economy of expression.  Consequently, Booch introduced relationship icons to show inheritance and instantiation as well as the use of one class by another.  To support incompleteness during development, there is also an "undefined" relationship icon. The notation permits object diagrams to display cardinality, labels, and synchronization constraints.  For each object and message there also are templates to define and describe their key properties.  Booch augments the object and module diagrams with state transition diagrams, timing diagrams, and process diagrams. Figure 4.16 contains a simple class diagram that shows the class of **Status Report**, which produces status report objects. Each status report lists out the active CRs and SIRs along with the name of the responsible analyst. The figure displays the inheritance relationship between both **CR** and **SIR** and **Requests for Mods** as well as that between **Analyst** and **Employee**. The class **Status Report** uses **Report Utilities**. The class utility symbol is the shaded class icon, and the relationship is indicated by the double line; the white circle represents the interface. The implementation of **Status Report** uses the three classes connected to it by the double line; the black circle indicates this implementation detail. The solid directed line is used for inherits; a dashed directed line (not shown in the figure) is used for the instantiates relationship.

I conclude this discussion of OOD with an illustration of the module diagramming technique. As befits the title of this chapter, the example is implementation oriented; it reflects Booch's earlier methods. The first step in the process is the identification of the objects and their attributes. In his 1983 book on Ada, Booch adapted a technique developed by Abbott to extract both the objects and their operations from a text description [Abbo83]. Variations of this strategy are used with entity-relationship models and JSD. Here is a brief illustration of the method; I begin with a description of the SCM system processing.

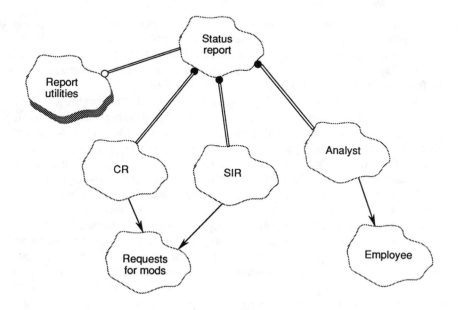

Fig. 4.16. **Status Report** object diagram.

A change request (CR) is received. Either a no action required (NAR) is reported or an engineering change proposal (ECP) is prepared. The ECP is approved or rejected. Tasks are created. Configuration items (CI) and developers are identified with the task. The CIs are assigned and accepted, and the CI files are copied. The status of the CIs is reported. Finally, the tasks are deleted.

This is simply a restatement of the first step used in the JSD example of Section 3.3.2. It really is at too high a level for this illustration, but it facilitates a comparison between OOD and JSD.

With this text description of a process (algorithm), we can proceed by analyzing its contents. We begin by identifying the nouns. These may be classified as *common nouns* (i.e., a class of things such as vehicle or table), *mass nouns and units of measure* (i.e., constraining characteristics or groupings as in the case of "traffic," which refers to a collection of "vehicles"), and *proper names and nouns of direct reference* (i.e., names of specific entities such as Ford truck or a specific table such as Assigned_CI_Table). The first two noun categories define types (classes or ADTs), and the third identifies individual objects within a type. Adjectives indicate attributes. Naturally, the assignment of terms to these categories depends on the semantic context and the level of description. This language analysis, therefore, is not a mechanical way to design a system, but it does provide a way to start. We first underline the nouns.

A <u>change request (CR)</u> is received. Either a <u>no action required (NAR)</u> is reported or an <u>engineering change proposal (ECP)</u> is prepared. The <u>ECP</u> is approved or rejected. <u>Tasks</u> are created. <u>Configuration items (CI)</u> and <u>developers</u> are identified with the <u>task</u>. The <u>CIs</u> are assigned and accepted, and the <u>CI files</u> are copied. The <u>status</u> of the <u>CIs</u> is reported. Finally, the <u>tasks</u> are deleted.

As with the JSD example, there are three primary objects, CRs, CIs, and tasks. I limit myself to those three common nouns because I choose to treat NAR and ECP as attributes of CR, and CI file and status as attributes of CI. Clearly, I am reading between the lines.

The next step is to repeat this process with the verbs to identify the operations on the objects. We speak of operations *suffered by* an object (i.e., those that generally result from the receipt of a message or input by the object) and operations *required of* an object (i.e., those that generally result in the sending of an message or output by the object). Underlining the verbs, we get,

A change request (CR) <u>is received</u>. Either a no action required (NAR) <u>is reported</u> or an engineering change proposal (ECP) <u>is</u>

prepared. The ECP is approved or rejected. Tasks are created. Configuration items (CI) and developers are identified with the task. The CIs are assigned and accepted, and the CI files are copied. The status of the CIs is reported. Finally, the tasks are deleted.

My use of passive verbs has emphasized the actions suffered by the objects of interest; a better style would have been to use active forms of the verbs. Nevertheless, we now can identify the objects and their operations shown on the following page. It is not difficult to see how these objects with their operations can be implemented as packages in Ada.[20]

- CR has the operations
  - Create_CR
  - Report_NAR
  - Create_ECP
  - Approve_ECP
  - Reject_ECP

- CI has the operations
  - Assign_CI
  - Accept_CI
  - Report_Status
  - Copy_File

- Task has the operations
  - Name_CI
  - Name_Developer
  - Create_Task
  - Delete_Task

The next step is to establish the interfaces. This is done by determining the visibility of each object in relation to the other objects. This, of course, simply reflects the object-oriented view of modules. Because the target language here is Ada, we will use Booch's module

---

[20]Now that Booch's primary concern is for objects and classes, he no longer finds this method very helpful. In a personal correspondence, he writes, "The use of identifying nouns and verbs is dated, as it has proved to be of limited utility. As I describe in the OOD book [Booc91], techniques such as CRC cards [class, responsibility, collaboration, see BeCu89], domain analysis, and various classification paradigms, are much more powerful." I include the example here because there are frequent references to it, and the reader should be aware of the concept and—in particular—its limitations.

diagrams, which implies an implementation realization. Figure 4.17 contains a controlling subprogram plus the three objects just defined. Notice that CI shows two data structures, one for the descriptive information (CI_Info) and the other for the text (CI_File), and three operations. Clearly, we have given the design some thought and have added details that were not apparent from the initial identification of objects and operators.

One way of organizing the information about the objects is to build a table and list the objects suffered by and required of each object. These operations may be identified by considering the events that either alter the state of an object, normally as the result of receiving an input, or are the effect of a changed object state, normally causing a message

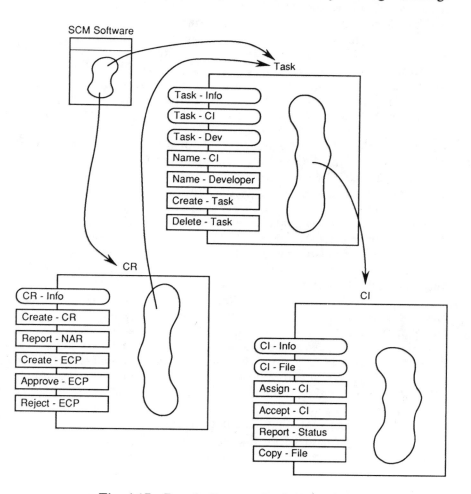

Fig. 4.17. Booch diagram for SCM system.

to be sent to another object. (Notice how OOD expresses concepts associated with the state transition diagram, STD, described in Sections 2.3.2 and 3.2.3. OOD focuses on the structure of the objects, while the STD and related Petri net are neutral with regard to the object's structure. Because OOD is the more general method, the STD can be integrated into its overall framework.) In this simple example, we have only three objects, CR, CI, and Task. When we consider them from the perspective of the operations suffered by and required of them, we see that the catalogue extracted from the text description is incomplete. For example, the four operations on Task are all suffered by that object (i.e., creating a new task, change its state by adding CIs or designers, or deleting a task). As in the case of the DFD process (bubble) with only input data flows, we should be a little suspicious. We certainly ought to add an operator to report the task contents or status (e.g., Report_Task). The hierarchy shown in Figure 4.17 implies that CI is affected by state changes in Task; nevertheless, there are no Task operators that would be suffered by CI (e.g., no Task operation of Authorize_CI_Assignment). Thus, the operations in the module diagram are incomplete, and I leave its completion as an exercise.

Using the same example for both OOD's module diagrams and JSD is, in a sense, unfair. The module diagrams are concerned with the structure of the solution (modeling-in-the-small), and JSD is concerned with the structure of the system (modeling-in-the-large). In 1986, Booch observed that OOD "is a partial-lifecycle method; it focuses upon the design and implementation stages of software development. . . . It is therefore necessary to couple object-oriented development with appropriate requirements and analysis methods in order to help create our model of reality. We have found Jackson Structured Development (JSD) to be a promising match" [Booc86, p. 214]. Thus, at that time, JSD and OOD were considered complementary methods. In his subsequent work in OOD, Booch has extended the scope of his method to address some of the same problems of concern to JSD. Although they now represent alternative approaches, they share a common philosophy. Both begin by identifying the problem space objects. In JSD the problem space is the real world, and the models are defined as sequential processes in a network. The attributes (and states) of those processes are specified, but their internal structures are not. For Booch, OOD begins once the problem space has been established by some preliminary analysis step. The goal is to translate the classes defined in that problem space into implementation objects that operate in the solution space. Of course, Booch's iteration between analysis and design makes it difficult to separate the analysis and OOD activities.

Coad and Yourdon introduced object-oriented analysis (OOA) as the natural successor to the earlier analysis methods [CoYo91].[21] It provides abstraction, encapsulation (which they equate with information hiding), inheritance, and methods for organizing (or classifying). It combines the features of semantic data modeling (e.g., the entity-relationship model) with OOP to provide a systematic method for conducting systems analysis. OOA consists of five major steps, which produces a five-layered model composed of diagrams and textual specifications. The levels are,

- *Subject layer.* A subject is a mechanism for controlling how much of a model is to be considered at one time. It represents a segmentation of concepts and not a decomposition for implementation.

- *Class-&-Object layer.* Class and object here follow the standard definitions. The object is an abstraction that encompasses both data and the exclusive processing on that data. Objects reflect the system's capability to keep information about or interact with something in the real world. The class is a description of one or more objects with a uniform set of attributes and services, and Class-&-Object represents a class and the objects in that class.

- *Structure layer.* Structure represents the complexity of the problem space by means of semantic data modeling. *Gen-Spec Structure* reflects generalization-specialization (*ISA*) and *Whole-Part Structure* expresses the aggregation of components into a whole (*IS_PART_OF*).

- *Attribute layer.* The attribute also uses the standard definition. Attributes are data elements that describe instances of an object or classification structure. They constitute the object state.

- *Service layer.* A service is the processing to be performed on receipt of a message. Services represent the operations on the objects.

[21]The first edition of this book was published in 1990. The second edition changed some of the terminology and notation, and this discussion uses that of the second edition. In some cases I include in parentheses terms used only in the first edition.

One builds this model by first identifying the class-&-objects and then establishing their dependencies using semantic data modeling. Next, the details are reduced by grouping the objects into subjects. Finally, the object data structures (attributes) and operations (services) are defined. Obviously, an example will help.

In what follows I summarize the method presented in [CoYo91]. That book contains sample illustrations and considerable explanation. I have assumed that the reader is familiar with the object-oriented paradigm and the SCM problem; thus my presentation is less complete than that of Coad and Yourdon. Naturally, the interested reader should return to the source. I begin with step 1, *Identifying Class-&-Objects*. From the previous example, the reader knows that I will identify three: CRs, CIs, and Tasks. If I were an analyst starting from scratch, however, how would I determine what the objects were? First I would look at the problem space (real world of HHI in this case) to identify the objects (data and processing), which I would expect to see in the target system, that interact with objects external to the system. I might identify objects by reviewing the work flow, asking questions about the operations, reading the existing documentation, or simply looking at pictures and diagrams. In selecting the objects, I would concern myself with their structure and interactions. For example, Change Requests (CR) and Software Incident Reports (SIR) are both specializations of a generic change request object. A prerequisite for an object is that it must "remember" something of importance to the system (i.e., have state). Other items for consideration include the roles played, the number of attributes, services or attributes shared with other objects, etc. During the process of identifying objects, some will be observed to have marginal value (e.g., they remember nothing of importance, they represent unique instances, or their data can be derived); these potential objects should be eliminated. Finally, we select the objects of interest to our model. They are given names consisting of a singular noun or adjective+noun. We are building a vocabulary for our model, and the names should be readable and clear. Figure 4.18 contains a collection of Class-&-Objects that might be selected after the first iteration of step 1. The symbol for a class-&-object is a three component box inside a shaded box. The name goes into the top section; the next two sections are used to list the attributes and services.

Step 2, *Identifying Structure*, joins the identified objects by either Gen-Spec (*ISA* or inheritance, formerly called classification) or Whole-Part (*IS_PART_OF*, formerly called assembly). During the process of identifying the structure, new objects may be defined. For instance, by generalizing, a new object could be defined that heads a Gen-Spec structure (e.g., Generic CR has been created as a generalization of the two specific change request categories, CR and SIR). Alternatively, one might enumerate a set of objects to create a Whole-Part structure (e.g.,

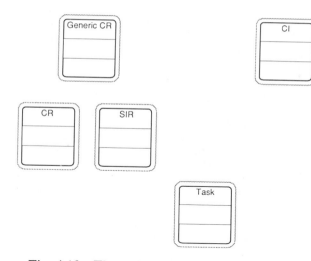

Fig. 4.18.  The objects identified after step 1.

CI is composed of CI-Info and CI-Text).  Figure 4.19 depicts the state of the system model after the structure is established.  Each Gen-Spec structure is shown as an inheritance tree with a semicircular connector. The Whole-Part structure uses a triangle to show the direction of aggregation.  The cardinality and participation constraints are shown numerically.[22]  In this example we see that for every CI there must be exactly one CI-Info and at most one CI-Text.  (Document text is not stored in the SCM database, but surrogates for the accepted documents are mandatory.)  Three specializations of the CI-Text are shown: source, object, and test data.  CI-Version has been elevated to the level of an object because this is important to our SCM system.  Notice that CI-Version is a part of CI-Info, therefore the triangle indicates a Whole-Part structure.  The model indicates that each CI-Version has exactly one CI-Info object identified with it, but there may be zero or many CI-Version objects associated with each CI-Info object.  The Task object has not been elaborated; that is left for an exercise.  The Generic CR is shown as a class (i.e., it has no exterior shaded box).  This implies that every Generic CR is either a CR or an SIR.

Even though Figure 4.19 does not expand the Task object, it is clear that the diagram is getting cluttered.  Step 3, *Identifying Subjects*, collapses the structures and objects into subjects.  The subjects represent a convenient mechanism for collecting conceptual entities.  We define

---

[22]These concepts are described in the discussion of Figure 2.6.  The first edition used the third notation shown in that figure.

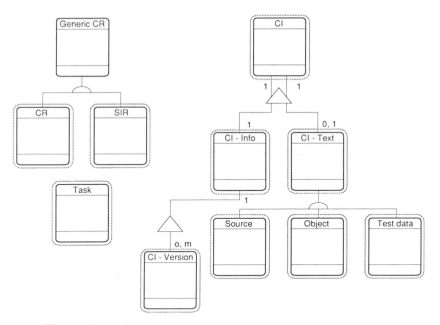

Fig. 4.19.  OOA diagram showing objects and structures.

a subject for each structure.  If objects remain, we add corresponding subjects.  As with the data flow diagram, Coad and Yourdon suggest that we should live within the boundary of $7 \pm 2$ symbols.  Thus, if the number of subjects exceeds 7 or so, they suggest that the subjects be refined further.  Our goal is to control visibility and guide reader attention.  The subjects are a communication convenience; they do not imply a decomposition for implementation.  Once the subjects have been identified, they are numbered and displayed in simple rectangular boxes.  (In the first edition, message connections between subjects were explicitly shown as shaded arrows.)  Figure 4.20 depicts the SCM system as three subjects.

The next two steps fill in the lower two segments of the object symbol.  Step 4, *Defining Attributes*, consists of the following steps.

- *Identify the attributes*.  This involves the identification of the objects that apply to each instance of the object.  For example, CIs have the attributes CI-Number, CI-Name, Version-No, etc.

- *Position the attributes*.  Now that the attributes have been named, they must be positioned within the structure.  For example, CI-Number and CI-Name are attributes at the top-most node in the CI structure, and Version-No and Status are attributes of the CI-Version object.

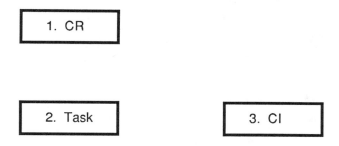

Fig. 4.20. SCM system subjects.

- *Identify instance connections.* The instance connections depict the cardinality and participation constraints among attributes. Again, the entity-relationship model notation is used. Figure 4.21 shows the relationship (connection) between Generic CR (now labeled CR) and Task to be one to many.

- *Revise class-&-objects.* One of the dangers of a textbook is that it contains finished figures that imply a monotonic process. Of course, this is not the case. We learn from errors, and we constantly iterate. We should always question our decisions and be prepared to revise them. For example, what function would the class-&-objects CR and SIR serve that could not be equally well served by an additional attribute (say Type) of Generic CR? I cannot think of any, and I therefore have deleted those two class-&-objects and added the attribute.

- *Specify connection constraints.* This is a documentation activity similar to that of the structured analysis data dictionary. The format for the class-&-object specification is discussed below.

Step 5, *Defining Services*, has a four-step strategy.

- *Identify services (Primary strategy).* This gets the service names onto the diagram. The authors suggest that three fundamental service categories be considered for each object or structure: occur (e.g., add, change, or delete), calculate, and monitor.

- *Identify services (Secondary strategies).* After the obvious services are identified, Coad and Yourdon offer a collection of heuristics to ensure that no important services have been omitted. Examples include a review of the object life history (cf. JSD) and a state-event-response analysis (similar to the use of event tables as described in Section 2.3.2).

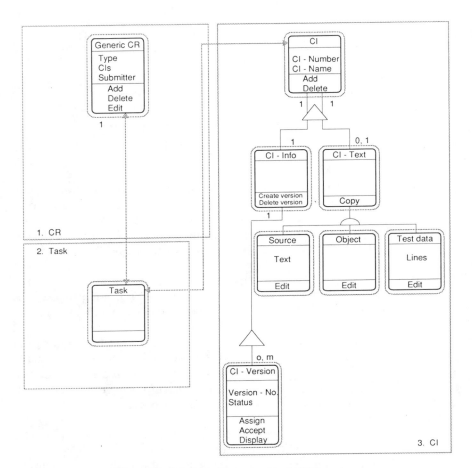

Fig. 4.21.  OOA diagram for SCM system.

- *Identify the message connections.*  Class-&-objects communicate
  with each other by means of messages.  The message connections
  should be identified explicitly with an arrow.

- *Specify the services.*  Again, specification is a documentation
  activity.  Coad and Yourdon suggest the following guidelines.

  - Focus on the required externally observable behavior.
  - Use a template for the specification (see Fig. 4.22).
  - Add diagrams to simplify the service specifications.
  - Add supporting tables.
  - Develop service narratives—if you must.
  - Put the documentation set together.

*specification* <object name>

  *attribute* <...>
  *attribute* <...>
  *attribute* <...>

  *externalInput* <...>
  *externalOutput* <...>

  *objectStateDiagram* <...>

  *additionalConstraints* <...>

  *notes* <...>

  *service* <name & Service Chart>
  *service* <name & Service Chart>
  *service* <name & Service Chart>

and, as needed,

  *traceabilityCodes*
  *applicationStateCodes*
  *timeRequirements*
  *memoryRequirements*

Figure 4.22. Class-&-Object specification template.

Their book contains many illustrations.

Just as the collection of data flow diagrams, data dictionaries, and minispecs provides a system specification for structured analysis, the collection of diagrams and object-oriented specifications comprises the OOA specification. In Section 3.2.3 I reviewed some of Yourdon's evolving views on structured analysis and observed how they were moving from a decomposition to a composition orientation. OOA, I believe, represents his current thinking.

What conclusions can we draw? The growing availability of software tools to manage encapsulation has made it easier for us to express our conceptual models (which normally are object oriented) and transform them into object-based implementations. In earlier times, our code emphasized complex procedures that relied on relatively simple data structures; therefore, it was counterproductive to use analysis and design methods that dealt with a level of complexity that was difficult to program. However, as we have developed more powerful implementation tools, we also have discovered methods to exploit them better.

From the mid-1970s to the mid-1980s, the adjective "structured" was used to imply a modern and productive approach. "Object-oriented" is now the prefix of choice. As the epilogue indicates, object-oriented may not be the ultimate answer. Nevertheless, it is a powerful paradigm that, although it is still in a state of flux, will have a profound impact on the way systems are designed and built throughout the remainder of this century. Today's software engineer is at risk if he does not understand its underlying concepts.

## 4.3.     The program proof

This brief section introduces the concept of *proof of correctness*. Many texts present this material in a chapter on verification and validation. It is as if first we write the program, and then prove it correct. I am discussing the idea here, in the last of the chapters on modeling, because the process of proving correctness is a part of the modeling activity and not a postmodeling verification step. That is, we should prove that our implementation is correct as we develop it. Of course, this is what I have been encouraging throughout this book. Software engineers are constantly solving problems, and they expect their solutions to be correct. Because the cost to repair defects increases with the length of time that the defect remains undiscovered, it is important to verify correctness as early as possible. What better time to ensure correctness than when a decision is formalized?

Correctness is always with respect to some specification. Without a formal specification, no proof of correctness is possible. Indeed, because hackers begin without any specifications and produce syntactically correct formal models (e.g., the compilable source code), they may claim to produce "incestuously provablely correct code" (i.e., the code is its own specification). We would like more than that, and this raises two questions. What do we mean by a specification, and what do we mean by a proof?

The presentations of the LST model (in Section 1.3.2) and formal methods (in Section 2.3.3) provide some answers. The specification is a formal statement about the behavior of the target application that acts as a theory; all models derived from that theory must exhibit those behaviors (i.e., be correct). There is no concept of correctness for the system specification, but it must exhibit certain soundness properties (e.g., be consistent). Once that specification exists, the implementor is obligated to prove that his model (e.g., the program) is correct with respect to its theory (i.e., the defining specification). Perhaps proof is too strong a word. Mathematicians prove theorems, and it may take them months to prove a single theorem. Software engineers, as do all engineers, must take a practical view. Therefore, they cannot *prove* all of their programs, but they should use a *rigorous* approach that implies that they *could complete the proof* if given the time.

If the programmer who wants to prove his programs begins with only a general description of an algorithm (say for the greatest common divisor), what separates him from the hacker? Both begin without a formal specification. The hacker writes a program and uses his interactions with the computer to refine his algorithm. Once finished, he reviews his code and then "proves" to his satisfaction that it is correct. The deliberate programmer, on the other hand, develops a formal specification as he develops his code, and he proves that his code is correct with respect to that specification. That is, the deliberate programmer takes a very different approach to programming. Of course, some things are facilitated by informality. Tailoring a window interface to a particular application benefits from exploratory development. But if you lived next to a nuclear powerplant, how comfortable would you be knowing that a hacker developed the safety system?

In what follows, I first borrow from what Gries calls *The Science of Programming* [Grie81]. I begin with the book's motivating introduction, "Why Use Logic? Why Prove Programs Correct?" The answers are derived from experience with a very simple task: write a program for division by means of repeated subtraction. (The program will be used on a device with no integer division.) Our initial program stores in $r$ and $q$ the remainder and quotient of $x$ divided by $y$:

```
. . .
r := x; q := 0;
while r > y do
    begin r := r-y; q := q+1 end;
. . .
```

We first debug this program by running some test data to see what we find. Of course, if we run the program with a lot of data, we will have to look at a great deal of output. Therefore, we will just check to see if the results are reasonable. We know that there is a precondition that $y$ must be positive, and that after the computation

$$x = y*q + r$$

must hold. We can code these assertions as tests and list the results only when we find a test case that fails.

Success. No failures are listed. Unfortunately, after a while, someone finds a problem: the values

$$x = 6, y = 3, q = 1, r = 3$$

were produced by the program instead of $q = 2$ and $r = 0$. We correct the while statement and add to the postcondition. Placing the assertions in brackets, the revised program is shown in Figure 4.23.

This runs fine for a while until someone else discovers a result of $r = -2$. It turns out that we had a negative value for $x$. Easy to fix, just change the precondition to

$\{x \geq 0 \text{ and } y > 0\}$,

and the postcondition to

$\{x = y*q + r \text{ and } 0 \leq r < y\}$.

Finally we have a correct program. But we did not prove it correct; the discovery of errors forced us to make it correct. As a result of debugging the program, we established the proper assertions. The finished program with the assertions is shown in Figure 4.24. We have made our assertions as *strong* as possible, and we know that if these assertions hold, the output will always be correct. Correct, of course, with respect to our definition of division.

Let us examine what we have done here. The example began with a straightforward solution to the problem. We wrote the code and then, in the implementation domain (the solution space), we proceeded to test if we had a proper solution. Two errors ultimately were discovered, and the result was a correct program. However, there is an alternative. We could have remained in the application domain (the problem space) and sought a solution to the problem. This would force us to think through the algorithm's pre and postconditions rather than discover them after we encountered a problem. Look at the first and last assertion in the final program. They define division. Given this definition, it is not too difficult to find a sequence of state changes that will guarantee that, if the precondition is true, then the postcondition will be true (assuming, of course, that the computer does not fail). And this is what we mean when we speak of proof of correctness. It represents a systematic method for thinking about the problem solution.

```
. . .
{y>0}
r := x; q := 0;
while r ≥ y do
     begin r := r-y; q := q+1 end;
{x = y*q + r and r<y}
. . .
```

Fig. 4.23.  Division program with assertions.

. . .

```
{x≥0 and y>0}
r := x; q := 0;
{r≥0 and y>0 and x = y*q + r}
while r ≥ y do
    begin  {r≥0 and r≥y>0 and x = y*q + r}
           r := r-y; q := q+1
           {r≥0 and y>0 and x = y*q +r}
end;
{x = y*q + r and 0≤r<y}
```

. . .

Fig. 4.24. The correct division program with assertions.

Gries puts it this way:

> . . . the study of program correctness proofs has led to the discovery and elucidation of methods for *developing* programs. Basically, one attempts to develop a program and its proof hand-in-hand, with the proof ideas leading the way! If the methods are practiced with care, they can lead to programs that are free of errors, that take much less time to develop and debug, and that are much more easily understood (by those who have studied the subject). [Grie81, p. 5]

This was Dijkstra's experience with T.H.E. Multiprogramming System in the late 1960s, and the justification for this approach is even more valid today.

It takes time to become proficient in developing programs in this manner, but the general concept is easily understood. The underlying idea carries over into virtually all of software engineering. To link this technique to the previously covered material, recall that JSD models real-world entities as sequential processes using a diagrammatic notation for regular expressions. The JSD diagrams are isomorphic to structured code (such as that used in the above division program), and we can apply assertions to JSD modeling. For example, the life of a CI shown in Figure 3.24 could be given the precondition {Cl-No does not exist} and the postcondition {Cl-No exists ∧ status = retired}. This can be written as follows.

{Cl-No does not exist} CI {Cl-No exists ∧ status = retired}[23]

---

[23] The braces around the predicates indicate *total correctness*; execution is guaranteed to terminate. *Partial correctness* does not require termination.

CI, as depicted in the figure, can be expanded as

**Design; Maintain; Retire.**

The precondition for **CI** is also the precondition for **Design**, and the postcondition for **Design** ({Ci-No exists $\land$ status = active}) serves as the precondition for **Maintain**. Similarly, the postcondition for **Maintain** ({CI-No exists $\land$ status = inactive}) is the precondition for **Retire**. The process can be repeated by expanding the **Design** and **Maintain** sequences until the transition from each pre to postcondition is refined enough to permit the development of routines that guarantee the assertions hold. Reexamine the division program in this context and notice how each statement's postcondition serves as the next statement's precondition. Observe, too, how we have let the proof process help guide the design activity.

Proof of correctness changes our perception of programming. Rather than thinking about *how* the program works, we consider *what* we expect to be true about the program state at each transition. That is, we think about the problem we wish to solve in the mathematical context of the solution space. In the remainder of this section I illustrate this idea with an example taken from a paper by Hoare [Hoar87]. I present only the material that relates to program proofs, and I recommend the paper as an excellent overview of some formal methods for program design. The illustration that Hoare uses is a simple one: writing a greatest common divisor (GCD) program. Although the problem may be considered trivial, it is best to use a simple problem for a complex subject. The methods do scale up. As noted in Section 2.3.3, formal methods are being used effectively for large projects; furthermore, in the next chapter I will discuss the cleanroom technique, which also relies on this proof technique.

The first step in this example is to define what we mean by a GCD. We are free to use any tools for producing a mathematically meaningful definition that enables the reader to understand what a GCD is. Hoare defines the necessary relationship between the parameters $(x,y)$ and their GCD $(z)$ as follows.

D1.1    $z$ divides $x$
D1.2    $z$ divides $y$
D1.3    $z$ is the greatest of the set of numbers satisfying D1.1 and D1.2.
D1.4    [definition of "$p$ divides $q$"]
D1.5    [definition of "$p$ is the greatest member of a set $S$"]

Now that we have a specification, we must perform a consistency check. We need to demonstrate that, for every pair of positive integers $x$ and $y$, there exists a $z$ such that D1.3 holds. The proof is as follows.

P1.1    The number 1 is a divisor of all numbers, so the set of common divisors for any two numbers is nonempty.

P1.2    Each number is its own greatest divisor, so the set of common divisors is both nonempty and finite.

P1.3    Every nonempty set of integers has a greatest number, so the GCD always exists.

Of course, the proof was rigorous but not formal. Nevertheless, the proof has given us confidence that we are pursuing a reasonable goal.

As a rule, there is a tradeoff between generality and efficiency. It would not be difficult to transform the above specification into a logic program, but it would operate very slowly. Because we desire an efficient program, we will use a more restrictive algebraic notation that does not allow disjunction and negation—only conjunction. By reasoning about the problem, we derive the following algebraic equations.

L2.1    $x = gcd(x,x)$                                              for all $x$
        The greatest divisor of $x$ is $x$; therefore it is the GCD of $x$ and $x$.

L2.2    $gcd(x,y) = gcd(x+y,y)$                              for all $x$, $y$
        If $z$ divides $x$ and $y$, then it also divides $x+y$. Therefore, every common divisor of $x$ and $y$ is also a common divisor of $x+y$ and $y$, and the GCD of either pair is the same.

L2.3    $gcd(x,y) = gcd(y,x)$                                  for all $x$, $y$
        Every common divisor of $x$ and $y$ is also a common divisor of $y$ and $x$.

The proofs demonstrate the *consistency* of the specification, but we still must prove *completeness*. That is, we must show that for any positive integers $p$ and $q$, there exists an integer $r$ such that the equation

$r = gcd(p,q)$

can be proved solely from the algebraic specification and the previously known laws of arithmetic. We prove this by induction. Assume that this is true for all $p$ and $q$ strictly less than $N$. From L2.1, this is so for $N = 2$ (i.e., $x = 1$). Then there are four cases.

- Both $p$ and $q$ are less than $N$, in which case we already know it is true.

- Both $p$ and $q$ are equal to $N$, in which case by L2.1 we know it to be true.

- $p = N$ and $q < N$, in which case we note that there is an $r$ such that
$$r = gcd(p\text{-}q,q)$$
is deducible from the algebraic laws. Applying L2.2 we have the desired result.

- $p < N$ and $q = N$, in which case we apply L2.3 and proceed as with the previous case.

We now have two sets of structurally dissimilar specifications. The first describes to the user what a GCD is, and the second defines some rules for the GCD operations. The specifications complement each other, and we need both. (For example, the algebraic specification of a stack would be of little value unless the user had a sound understanding of what a stack was.) We could convert this specification directly into a functional implementation, but it too would be inefficient. We would like to optimize it as a procedural program in a binary arithmetic machine. This suggests that we ought first to develop some very efficient binary-based operations for the GCD. Here are three; I leave their proof to the reader.

L3.1     $2gcd(x,y) = gcd(2x,2y)$

L3.2     $gcd(2x,y) = gcd(x,y)$                              if $y$ odd

L3.3     $gcd(x,y) = gcd((y\text{-}x)/2,x)$          if $x,y$ odd and $x<y$

We have now reduced the basic arithmetic to register shifting. The implementation should be efficient.

I now return to the sequential processes introduced with the JSD model of the CI. We also can model the GCD program as a sequence, say $P; Q$, such that $P$ executes first and $Q$ executes only after $P$ terminates. The precondition for this program is that both $x$ and $y$ are positive.

P4.1     $x>0 \land y>0$

Let $Z$ be the variable introduced to hold the result of the program's execution. The postcondition is

P4.2    $Z = gcd(x,y)$

Clearly, the postcondition of $P$ is the precondition of $Q$. Our strategy, therefore, is to find a postcondition for $P$ that makes $P$ easy to implement and also serves as a good start for the further sequential decomposition of $Q$. Let that postcondition be

P4.3    $2^N gcd(X,Y) = gcd(x,y)$

Notice that the simple assignment statement

$N, X, Y := 0, x, y$

accepts P4.1 as a precondition and satisfies P4.3 as a postcondition. We are chipping away at the problem and have now reduced the unsolved portion to

{P4.3} $Q$ {P4.2}

Again, we will divide to conquer by introducing the intermediate assertion

P4.4    $2^N Z = gcd(x,y)$

to give us

{P4.3} $Q'$ {P4.4}
{P4.4} $Q''$ {P4.2}

which also could be written

{P4.3} $Q'$ {P4.4} $Q''$ {P4.2}

The intermediate assertion was chosen because there is a simple way to go from P4.4 to P4.2; simply reduce $N$ to zero while maintaining P4.4. Therefore, the second of the new tasks, $Q''$, can be accomplished by subtracting one from $N$ and doubling the value of $Z$ until $N = 0$. Of course, we must use the algebraic rules to prove that this preserves the equality of the assertion. The result is a loop that will terminate when $N$, which is nonnegative (how do we know this?), is reduced by 1 to zero. The loop is

**while** $N>0$ **do** $N, Z := N-1, 2Z$

Only the middle task, $Q'$, remains to be developed. Hoare suggests that this be split again into four subtasks in accordance with the following series of intermediate assertions.

| | |
|---|---|
| P4.5 | P4.3 $\wedge$ ($X$ odd $\vee$ $Y$ odd) |
| P4.6 | P4.3 $\wedge$ ($Y$ odd) |
| P4.7 | P4.3 $\wedge$ ($Y$ odd) $\wedge$ $X = Y$ |

He leaves the proof to the reader. Should I do otherwise?

Notice what we have done in this simple example. First we forced ourselves to define formally what was meant by the GCD. Contrast that with the integer division program that opened this section. There we "knew" what we wanted, so we just wrote the code. Another important point is that we actually produced two equivalent specifications for the GCD. One was intended for use in the application (problem) domain, and the second provided insights for the implementation (solution) domain. Indeed, the algebraic specification was even refined to take advantage of the implementation domain's binary organization. Given this set of equivalences, we began with a precondition (P4.1) and a postcondition (P4.2) for the program *GCD*. "Programming" then was accomplished by looking for a trail of assertions that could take us from P4.1 to P4.2. Once we had the assertion, it was a simple matter to write the code that would always be correct with respect to those assertions. Of course, the assertions were *selected* based on our knowledge of programming, but we did not write the program first and then derive the assertions. In this fashion we reduced the original *GCD* program to

$$\{x>0 \wedge y>0\} \ P; \ Q'; \ Q'' \ \{Z = gcd(x,y)\}^{24}$$

The task $Q'$ would, in turn, be expressed as four tasks, but the effect of the program would remain the same. Once the sequential tasks are defined, we will have proven that given P4.1, the result will be P4.2. Moreover, the *annotated program is the proof*. And that is what we mean by proof of correctness.

---

[24]One does not use this kind of notation except for the pedagogic purposes. The subdivision of $Q'$ would present a formidable notational challenge. The normal convention is to integrate the assertions into the structured code, as was done in the integer divide example shown in Figure 4.24.

## 4.4.         Concluding observations on modeling

The three chapters on modeling the software solution for a real-world problem are now finished. There has been a great deal of overlap, but some very important messages have been sent. While this seems obvious to me, I recognize that the wealth of details may have obscured what I wanted to say. So let me tell you what I told you. Everything derives from two simple principles. First, the software process is a transformation from an identified need to an automated response to that need. I said this in Chapter 1 and introduced the essential software process (Fig. 1.5) to clarify the idea. It described two model categories.

- *Conceptual models* focus on the application domain and use a vocabulary (and formalisms) that has meaning in that domain. The conceptual model is concerned with the real-world problem and how automation can produce a solution. Although conceptual models may be used to prove certain facts about the problem and the proposed solutions, these proofs affect the software only to the extent that they are incorporated into the software specification.

- *Formal models* are formal in the context of the implementation domain (i.e., computing), and they rely on logic and mathematics. The software that we deliver is a formal model. There also are higher level formal models, and the concept of correctness depends on the existence of such a formal model. Ideally, the highest level formal model will specify all the essential behaviors of the desired software product. The creation of an implementation always involves formal modeling, but not all development methods exploit this fact.

Thus, the first principle is that software engineering is a modeling activity.

The second basic principle is that software engineering is also a problem-solving activity. It uses models to guide the problem solving and to express the resulting solutions. We begin with conceptual models to understand the problem, and we enhance our confidence in the solution with formal models. During development, the problem-solving concern shifts from the real-world problem solution to the structure of that solution to the solution's implementation. I have labeled this shift as a journey from requirements modeling to modeling-in-the-large to modeling-in-the-small. But as the contents of the modeling chapters make clear, there are few milestones along the way. The kinds of problems that a software engineer solves will depend on the problem and the experience with this class of problem. The nature of the unsolved problems evolves as the project proceeds.  There will always be a problem space and a solution space, but the domains of these two spaces will change as development progresses.  The challenges to the software engineer, therefore, are great.  He must continue to consider each of the visited domains throughout the development.  Validation forces him to examine his solutions in the context of the application problem, and verification demands consideration of his work in the context of the formal models.  Moreover, the tools he uses in this activity have been derived from varied and conflicting methodological foundations; in fact, some may be tailored to a particular problem space. Finally, the problem and the associated solution specification are dynamic; seemingly valid conceptual models are later recognized as flawed.  Thus, it is clear that software engineering is far more complex than the writing of program code.

The difficulty in teaching these principles to new software engineers is further confounded by the fact that the universe of software engineering is itself diversified.  It includes computer science applications (e.g., compilers and operating systems), highly constrained, closed systems (e.g., embedded computers in real-time systems), or under constrained, open systems (e.g., information and knowledge-based medical applications).  The working environments encompass universities, software companies, internal software groups, and very large aerospace organizations.  Clearly, no single modeling or problem-solving paradigm can suit all occasions.  Yet, there are shelves of books that advocate simple solutions.  The software engineer must be wary.  We know that to a five-year-old boy with a hammer, everything looks like a nail.  Similarly, a software engineer with limited experience will be restricted to what he understands.  Like that five-year-old, he too must enlarge his world so that he knows what tools and methods are available and how they should be used.  And that is what I have tried to describe in these last three chapters.

When I choose the title, *Software Engineering: A Holistic View*, I freed myself from the obligation of presenting a neatly organized taxonomy of software engineering modeling methods.  Problem solving is difficult and messy, especially when it involves (at least) two domains and (at least) two categories of modeling tool.  I would have preferred to offer a neater picture; something of the form: for *this* type of problem use *that* type of method.  Unfortunately, I could not.  When solving a problem, one must have the freedom to access any appropriate tool or method.  The key factors remain intellectual honesty and energy.  Tools and methods are necessary but not sufficient.  In the end, the software engineer must rely on his judgment regarding the problem solution and the choice of tools to implement that solution.  He requires tools to help understand the problem to be solved, to organize what has been learned into an effective and maintainable design, and to ensure that the implementation is of high quality (e.g., correct, valid, maintainable). The software engineer's choice of tools will depend on his experience with their use and his awareness of alternatives. No textbook can substitute for that experience; it can offer only a candle to fight the darkness.

I now have said enough about methods and tools for modeling. My advice is that one should learn to use just a few but learn to use them well. The text provides only an introduction to each method; there are references for additional reading. Now that we know the methods and tools to construct the models, we must be certain about the quality of the models—the subject of Chapter 5—and the ability of the project to deliver the desired software on time and within budget—the subject of Chapter 6.

SPEED OF LIGHT IN A VACUUM: 186,000 MILES PER SECOND
SPEED OF LIGHT IN WATER: 139,000 MILES PER SECOND
SPEED OF LIGHT THROUGH A BRICK WALL: 1 INCH PER
843,000 YEARS (DIFFICULT TO PROVE AS THE
LIGHT SOURCE OFTEN MOVES)

# 5

# VERIFICATION AND VALIDATION

As the Harris drawing indicates, some things are more difficult to prove than others. Fortunately, there is an external reality against which this scientist (the one on the right) can test his hypothesis. That is how the figures for the speed of light in a vacuum and in water were verified. I assume that he extrapolated from that model to arrive at the value of 843,000 years per inch for a brick wall. Unless he has an extraordinarily long-lived light bulb, however, he will have trouble with this experiment.

The software engineer has an equally difficult assignment. Wearing his verification and validation (V&V) hat, he is to answer the question, "How good is this software?" Where the modeling of the previous three chapters concerned the forward-looking, problem-solving aspect of software development, this chapter examines V&V—the backward-looking, solution-assessment counterpart to modeling. V&V may be viewed as the shining light that makes the software better by either ensuring that it is right the first time or by removing errors from software perceived to be good. Naturally, it progresses better through a clear medium than a brick wall.

Most errors are made early in the development process, and the most serious of these are those that persist the longest. Therefore, there is an incentive to remove mistakes before the programs are coded. Of course, the only way to identify these defects is by reflection and analysis. When we work with formalisms, they help us identify errors; if the problem or its solution does not have a formal expression, then there is no alternative but to think about the problem and its solution. Reviews, inspections, and walkthroughs are methods for organizing collective thinking about the recognition and removal of errors.

Once the programs exist, they can be tested to see if they are free of bugs. There are two basic approaches to machine testing. We can test programs according to how they have been built. This is structural, or white box testing. Alternatively, we can test programs with respect to what they should do. This is functional, or black box testing. In practice we do both. First with each program and then with components made of programs. In each case we look for errors, and success disappoints us; it comes only when we find a previously undetected error.

## 5.1. On the importance of being ernest

If this book were a symphony, then this chapter would be its third movement. Chapter 1 introduced the theme, and the three modeling chapters could be interpreted as one long, slow movement. This chapter on verification and validation (V&V) would then be presented as a dance, and the book would conclude with a management melody. But, to continue this analogy, the climax comes—as with Beethoven's Ninth—in the longest movement. Problem solving in the construction of the models is really the most important aspect of the software process. V&V and management are supporting activities; isolating them for independent analyses is something of an anticlimax. Nevertheless, each view is an important part of the process, and the principle of separation of concerns permits us to break off parts from the whole to examine them more carefully.

Recall that I described an essential software process in Chapter 1 (Fig. 1.5). It presented the process as a transformation from a need in the application domain into a software solution that executed in the implementation domain. Two categories of model were required. Conceptual models described the problem and its solution in the context of the application domain, and formal models specified the characteristics (e.g., behavior and performance) of the software that would realize the solution. The process had several properties.

- There were no objective criteria for evaluating the conceptual models other than domain-specific formalisms or syntactic tests. Each of these was limited to identifying errors. Thus, decisions regarding if this was the right solution to the problem always relied on human judgment and experience.

- For a model to be formal, it must have the ability to determine without ambiguity when an extension satisfies (or violates) the conditions specified by it. This may be done using logic (e.g., the proof of correctness construction) or an empirical evaluation (e.g., demonstration of explicit usability criteria). Any formal model without this characteristic is, no matter how formal-sounding its title, just another conceptual model.

- Correctness is always with respect to some criteria. Without an initial specification to establish the universe for verification, there is no concept of correctness. Behaviors described in a conceptual model have no impact on the delivered software unless they are incorporated into the formal model.

- For any conceptual model there are many formal models that can produce a desired software solution. Subjective judgment is required to select a formal model that will be, in some sense, the best. Similarly, for any formal model there are many implementations that will be correct with respect to it.

- Every formal model should specify only the essential characteristics of the desired product. The designers are expected to introduce permissive behaviors into the implementation as long as they do not violate the intent of the formal model. This, of course, requires an understanding of the application domain problem.

- The final step in the software process, the transformation of the most detailed expression of the design into an executable product, is always automated. It also always requires a formal model. If this formal model (e.g., the source code) is the only formal model, then no statements can be made about the correctness of the implementation.

Some of these statements may seem counter-intuitive. We know, for example, that finding an error in the software means that it is incorrect. But there are two dimensions of "incorrectness." Is it wrong because it does not do what its users expected of it, or is it wrong because it does not behave as it was expected to? That is, is this not the right system, or is the system not right? These are two different questions with two methods for determining an answer. In the first case, we are concerned with *validation* (from *validus* for strong or worth). This requires a subjective decision based on application domain knowledge. In the second case, the issue is one of *verification* (from *verus* for truth). Given some objective criteria (e.g., a formal specification or a set of axioms), one can always answer true or false.

Notice that validity and correctness are independent of each other. (Examples were given in Chapter 1.) Moreover, the subjective evaluation of design decisions for validity continues throughout the life of the software process. Thus, we are in the unhappy position of having to make insupportable judgments all the time. Furthermore, because correctness is binary (i.e., true or false), finding an error proves the rule to be false, but finding no errors may provide little information. Of course, this is not what we had hoped for. It would be nice if we could just write our programs and then test them to be sure they were correct. Unfortunately, that is just not possible.

The waterfall diagram shown in Chapter 1 (Fig. 1.2) follows the "Code and Debug" phase with one called "Test and Preoperations." Sometimes this organization is naively interpreted to imply that testing is deferred until that later phase.  The principal concern of "Test and Preoperations," however, is integration.  It is assumed that prior to "Code and Debug" we have a correct and valid design and, as a result of debugging, we also have correct program modules.  Thus, in "Test and Preoperations" we really are establishing that our design indeed was correct and valid.  Now that we have finished building the software, we integrate it into its operational environment to certify that the system is right and that this is the right system.  Naturally, this would be a terrible time to find out that we have been wrong; after all, at this point the implementation is complete.

Of course, the waterfall flow does not wait until the product is coded before establishing validity.  Each precoding phase in Figure 1.2 culminates with a validation activity, thereby ensuring that the requirements or design documents are valid before they are passed on to the next phase.  We know that the cost to correct a defect can be 100 times more expensive if it is not discovered until the product has been released.  Thus, the early detection of faults is essential.  Yet the 40-20-40 rule (which provides a guideline for the distribution of effort prior to coding, for coding, and after coding) suggests that a traditional project organization devotes considerable effort to after-the-fact analysis.  Obviously, this allocation of effort indicates that many problems cannot be identified until the software is complete.  But that is not how we build a bridge.  We know the design is correct before construction begins; the first 50 cars to cross it do not constitute a test.  Should software be different?

My prejudice is that software should not be different.  We should solve as many problems as possible as early as possible.  We should never defer an honest appraisal until some later time.  Neither should we assume that some independent group can find or fix our imperfect solutions.  There are some management techniques that can help us get better solutions, and these will be considered in the following chapter.  Nevertheless, the key to quality software is the developers' continuing and serious critiquing of their decisions.  If modeling is the forward-looking aspect of problem solving, then V&V constitutes a backward-looking examination of each solution in its fullest context.  To be effective, all problem solving requires an evaluation that closes the loop, and in this chapter we shall consider evaluation methods.  Because there are many methods for modeling, there also will be many methods for evaluating the decisions expressed in a model.

When the model is formal (as with VDM), methods exist to determine if the design or implementation is correct.  This is the advantage that a formal method offers.  It allows us to reason about concepts in the abstract and have confidence that our products will implement those concepts correctly.  When the model is not formal (as with most requirements documents), then we can find errors only by subjectively examining the products and testing the code. As already noted, testing just finds defects; it cannot guarantee correctness. Before a formal model exists, there is no standard for correctness; before the code exists, there is nothing to test by execution. In both situations, only validation is possible.

Wallace and Fujii observe that while verification and validation have separate definitions, one "can derive the maximum benefit by using them synergistically and treating 'V&V' as an integrated definition" [Wa-Fu89]. They consider V&V to be "a systems-engineering discipline to evaluate software in a systems context." I would refine their definition of V&V as "the evaluation of the existing analysis, design, and implementation decisions in the total problem context;" nevertheless, I find their synergistic view most appropriate. The benefit of defining the two V&V components separately, however, is that the exercise demonstrates the narrow scope of objective correctness and the broad role of subjective judgment and experience. When we have a formal method, we construct correct products using that method; we do not rely on a V&V activity to ascertain correctness. Therefore, V&V is most important when we are unsure of the validity or correctness of our assertions. In effect, the domain of V&V is the set of problem solutions that we have already generated. Evaluating the decisions may be far more difficult than arriving at them. Certainly, one should not hope for a silver bullet here.

The following sections examine V&V in three stages. First I consider validation techniques for use before the code exists. Next I examine methods for testing the code to find defects. Finally, I review some techniques for integrating the tested software. The focus of the presentation is on the technical aspects of V&V; issues concerning the organization of an independent V&V group are discussed in Chapter 6. Some empirical data relating to V&V will be included in this chapter; methods for establishing a measurement program, however, also are deferred until the next chapter. I conclude this introduction with a case study that serves as a warning. Although there are many software examples to choose from, I will illustrate the importance of being ernest about defect identification with a hardware case study.

By way of a long introduction to this vignette, recall that I contrasted the processes of hardware and software development in Section 1.2.1. In both cases, reliability is defined as the product's ability to deliver the same result on different trials. With hardware there is variability among interchangeable components, and parts wear out. Thus, hardware reliability measures properties such as mean time between failures (MTBF) and mean time to repair (MTTR) based on the probability that components will exceed their allowed range of variability and cause the system to fail (i.e., not provide the expected response). This reliability can be computed for both new and used products. More exact component specifications increase reliability and cost. In contrast, software has no variability. Digital systems are uniformly precise, and bits do not wear out. Therefore, unless we change the definition of reliability, every software product will be 100% reliable; it will always yield the same results for exactly the same sequence of events.

Although, in theory, the same inputs should always produce the same outputs, we know that is not always the case. There are indeterminacies in an operation that may not be repeatable. (That is why Dijkstra chose the levels of abstraction model for T.H.E.) Therefore, we have a different definition for software reliability. It measures the probability of an undiscovered defect, and MTTR is an estimate of the time required to code a solution. If the software does not produce identical results for identical inputs it is because there is a failure in either the design or the equipment. In a fault-tolerant system, most failures will be in the design alone. Clearly, the goal of V&V is to eliminate those defects and improve the reliability (and quality) of the software product.

Software engineers often contrast their discipline with the older, more mature hardware engineering disciplines. The complexity of software and the failure of many practitioners to adhere to the principles of software engineering, it is asserted, can result in products that place us at risk.[1]    However, hardware designs are not without faults. I already have cited Petroski's book in which he describes some famous engineering failures [Petr82]. The pattern is one of building confidence in a certain class of problem until the designers assume that instances of this class are quite straightforward. Attention to detail diminishes, and eventually a major error results. A renewed attention to detail follows, and safety is improved—until the next time. He cites the Hyatt walkway as an example of a very simple problem whose careless solution had fatal consequences. In the example that follows, there is a valid design coupled with a misplaced confidence in the implementor's ability to realize it. This combination results in an unhappy outcome.

The case study is that of the main instrument in the Hubble Space Telescope.[2] Its 2.4-meter primary mirror had been roughed into shape and sent to Perkin-Elmer's Danbury plant for final polishing in 1979.

---

[1]The ACM Special Interest Group in Software Engineering (SIGSOFT) publishes the *Software Engineering Notes*, which has a section containing published examples of "risks to the public."

[2]The material in this illustration is taken from a series of occasional articles by M. Mitchell Waldrop in *Science* on this subject. Two key articles were published in Vol. 249, pp.735-736, 17 August 1990 and Vol. 250, p. 1333, 7 December 1990.

Naturally, this was before the Challenger accident that so altered the NASA schedules, and the launch date was less than six years away. Technical and budgetary problems were everywhere. Perkin-Elmer was having trouble with the design of the Fine Guidance Sensors, which would keep the telescopes pointed to celestial targets with high precision; it was not certain that the instrument would be ready for launch. C. Robert O'Dell, the chief scientist, and the astronomers on his science advisory panel felt that they were spending 25 hours per day on budget battles. "I found myself reacting to crises instead of trying to do the job right." In this setting, the task of mirror polishing seemed to require only routine attention. The company already had made a number of mirrors for the intelligence community; moreover, we have been grinding mirrors for more than a century.

The main problem faced by the polishing group was one of precision. To take advantage of the airless clarity of space, the mirror had to be accurate within 1/65 the wavelength of a helium-neon laser. The polishing mechanism used the standard technique, but the device to test the accuracy of the curve would be a variation of the "null corrector" normally used. Whereas the null corrector helped technicians identify surface imperfections by shining light onto the mirror face through a set of lenses, the new "reflective null" used a laser and carefully calibrated mirrors. The reflective null would be capable of identifying Hubble mirror surface imperfections on the order of a thousandth of a wavelength. And so, from 1980 to 1981, the polishing proceeded under the direction of the operations division while the experts, who wrote the proposal and designed the instruments, worked on other tasks.

When the roughly shaped mirror was received, the reflected null indicated that the surface had a spherical aberration of about half a wavelength, which ultimately would be removed. Some minor problems emerged, but they were readily explained away. At the start, when assembling the reflective null corrector, it was found that the adjustment screws would not turn far enough. A 1.3-millimeter-thick spacer was inserted, and the corrector was certified as "correct." Soon thereafter, the opticians tried to double check the alignment of the reflective null with a second device, but when the test failed, the testers accepted the certified device as the more accurate. Finally, after the polishing was complete, a double check was made with a third instrument. Again it failed, and the certified device was trusted once more. In fact, overwhelmed by massive cost overruns and schedule slippages, the Perkin-Elmer technicians did not want to share their results with NASA, and NASA seemed equally content not to ask for them. In this environment, additional confirmatory tests would not be well received; there was neither time nor money for them. The result, as we now know, was a spherical aberration that images each star in a halo of fuzz. From the post facto analysis, we have found out that a crucial lens in the reflective null was 1.308 millimeters out of position. Thus, this lens was polished with the desired degree of precision, but to the wrong curve.

What does this example teach us? Even when we are confident in what we are doing, we still are obliged to test and examine all our decisions as thoroughly as possible. It is NASA policy always to cross check their designs. There appear to have been only two exceptions to that policy. The first was with the O-rings that destroyed Challenger, and the second was with the Hubble Space Telescope mirror. Need I say more about the importance of being ernest?

## 5.2.    Before the programs exist

The most important decisions regarding a software design are made before any programs are written. Undetected faults in the requirements or design will multiply as the designers build on improper assumptions. Therefore, it is essential that we remove errors as early as possible. There are several techniques for defect removal.

- The software requirements specification provides unambiguous criteria for determining if the desired properties are incorporated in the design. With a formal method, such as VDM, one can prove that the product satisfies its specification. At a minimum, however, we must trace the requirements through the design to ensure that each specified function will be delivered.

- The analysis and design decisions can be subjected to syntax tests. At the conceptual level there are tools such as PSL/PSA [TeHe-77] and SREM [Alfo77, Boeh84] that can identify missing or inconsistent definitions. At the implementation level, the compiler rejects syntactically incorrect source programs.

- There are methods for learning more about the application under development and the efficacy of a proposed solution. Particular techniques include the use of simulations and prototypes (both automated and manual).

- Experience from similar applications can be reused through the use of checklists, standards, and formalizations of "lessons learned" from earlier projects (either quantified or descriptive). In the tradition of Brooks's "Buy versus build," the best reuse of experience is that of validated and verified design or program parts.

- Thinking. This may be done independently, or it may be done as part of an organized activity. The teamwork may focus on the views of domain specialists or the experience of other members of the development team. Thinking in the V&V context requires reflection on the *quality* of the design decisions. Obviously, this must be preceded by thinking about what those design decisions should be, but that is not a V&V concern.

The methods and tools that we use will depend on the type of application, the environment in which the product is being developed, and the development stage.

For requirements and design, Boehm suggests the V&V techniques shown in Table 5.1. Notice that, except for common checklists and automated cross-referencing systems, there are no standard tools. The V&V techniques tend to be application specific; each must be tailored to a particular problem. It is assumed that the more one knows about the problem and the proposed solution, the better the quality of that solution will be. In this sense, Table 5.1 does not distinguish between the knowledge necessary to *specify or design* the solution and that needed to *verify and validate* that it is a good solution. The forward-looking

Table 5.1. Verification and validation techniques.

---

Simple manual techniques:
    Reading
    Manual cross-referencing
    Interviews
    Checklists
    Manual models
    Simple scenarios

Simple automated techniques:
    Automated cross-referencing
    Simple automated models

Detailed manual techniques:
    Detailed scenarios
    Mathematical proofs

Detailed automated techniques:
    Detailed automated models
    Prototypes

---

Reprinted from [Boeh84] with permission, ©1984, IEEE.

activity of design and the backward-looking task of V&V are but two perspectives within a single problem-solving process. The advantage of V&V is that it provides respite during which we can examine a stable set of decisions free from other concerns. Without this distinct V&V process, we would accept our decisions solely on the basis of the arguments that induced us to make them.

The techniques in Table 5.1 are quite varied; indeed, we could add to them many of the modeling tools described in Chapter 2. Which tools we choose will depend on the immediate objectives and project constraints. In the cited paper, Boehm presents a table that ranks the listed techniques according to different criteria. For example, he indicates that manual cross-referencing is very effective for completeness, consistency, and traceability for small projects, but it is only moderately effective when the projects are large. Automated cross-referencing, on the other hand, is shown to be very effective for both large and small projects. Reading is more effective for small projects than large projects; checklists are most effective for human engineering, maintainability, and reliability (a fact that suggests that the checklists must be somewhat domain specific); and the two detailed automated techniques are the most effective methods for verifying resource engineering concerns. Clearly, the diversity of software applications leads to an assortment of approaches to V&V.

Figure 5.1 contains a different matrix of tools versus goals, this one prepared by Jones [Jone79]. It is limited to just four categories of technique and five classes of problem. In his experience, machine testing (i.e., testing of the programs) is the least effective method for

|  | Design Reviews | Machine testing | Correctness proofs | Models or prototypes |
|---|---|---|---|---|
| Omitted functions | Good | Fair | Poor | Good |
| Added functions | Good | Poor | Poor | Fair |
| Structural problems | Good | Fair | Poor | Fair |
| Algorithm problems | Fair | Fair | Good | Good |
| Human-factor problems | Fair | Poor | Poor | Good |

Fig. 5.1. Some techniques for defect identification.
(Reprinted from [Jone79] with permission, ©1979, IEEE.)

identifying defects. For algorithms, a formal analysis (which he calls correctness proofs) or modeling is the best way to detect errors. Models and prototypes are shown to be very effective in uncovering omissions and evaluating the human-computer interface. In both these cases the computer provides a more complete expression of the specified solution, thereby allowing the developers and users to examine the design's dynamic implications. Design reviews, however, represent the best technique for uncovering defects in the overall design. (As will be shown in the section on the Cleanroom, correctness proofs also can be conducted as a design review.) I concur with this appraisal. Before the code exists (i.e., that period during which the most critical decisions are made), reviews represent the best mechanism for critiquing the project's working decisions.

There is a very simple rationale behind the review. Prior to a review, the analysts and designers will have used whatever tools and formalisms were available to them to derive the specification of or partial design for the target product. Assuming that there is no formalism to prove correctness and no product to test for errors, the development team has no recourse but to think about the quality of their solutions. This can be accomplished by setting aside some time for each individual to reconsider what he already has done. Naturally, if he has been conscientious and unhurried, he should be satisfied with his work. He will have asked questions as he makes his decisions, he will have used the available tools to test those decisions, and his mental model of the problem will conform to that of his solution. In short, he will have done the best possible job he can. But remember naive theories! Like the Hubble mirror, his product may be polished to the wrong perfection. The only alternative, therefore, is to involve others in a cooperative review of the completed decisions, which is what we mean by a design review.

There are two general categories of review. One has a management or technical orientation. It is concerned with either the status of the project or the quality of the specification and plans. Such reviews are conducted at a relatively high level with limited detail. For example, once the initial design is complete there may be a *preliminary design review (PDR)* in which management and sponsors participate. The objective of this review is to provide confidence that the design is sound; the outcome of a successful review is an authorization to continue on to the detailed design. A *critical design review (CDR)* may be held when the detailed design is complete. Although the material presented is more detailed, the review is intended to justify a decision to start coding. While considerable preparation must go into these reviews, they are not problem-solving activities. The purpose of a technical review is to exhibit confidence in the current work, and it is an inappropriate forum for discovering errors or reworking the design. But to err is human, and errors will be made. Because it is bad software engineering to deliver errors, we must rely on a second category of review to identify and remove them.

The error-detection reviews are usually grouped into two types. The *walkthrough* is the less formal of the two; it also may be used for examining design alternatives and general education. The *structured inspection*, on the other hand, is quite formal, and it concentrates on error detection in the program's design and code. The walkthrough can be traced back to Weinberg's concept of *egoless programming* [Wein71]. Throughout the 1960s, the general feeling was that programming was a personal, creative activity. Although the finished products would be made public, the code and working materials were viewed as private artifacts. The programmer had exposed his innermost creative process, and this must be guarded from the insensitive inspection of others. Weinberg's *The Psychology of Computer Programming* pointed out the fallacies of that view and offered egoless programming as an alternative. We have our good days and bad days, and we work better when we cooperate and share. In this context, the code is part of a collective development, and not a reflection of an individual's persona. The quality of the product improves as the development team turns to supportive assistance instead of isolated problem solving. In this egoless setting, methods were needed to assist in the sharing of ideas; one of these has come to be called the walkthrough.

Freedman and Weinberg have published a *Handbook of Walkthroughs, Inspections, and Technical Reviews* [FrWe90] that serves as an excellent guide to this technique. It describes how reviews may be used for functional specifications, designs, code, documentation, test plans, procedures and standards, and operations and maintenance. I shall use the example of a design review to identify errors. For reasons that I shall explain later, I will avoid the term "walkthrough" in favor of the more general "review." Although the organization of the review is flexible, it normally includes the following participants.

- *The review leader*, whose job is to obtain a good review—or to report the reasons why a good review was not obtained. Notice that this generic task statement allows the review process to be used for virtually any objective.

- *The recorder*, whose job it is to provide information for an accurate report of the review. The review is more than a process for exchanging ideas; it requires the production of a report that documents the important decisions made as a result of the review.

- *The participants*, who must be prepared and must actively engage in the review. Normally either the leader or one of the participants will be the producer of the work being reviewed, and he will be expected to play a major role in the review (e.g., he may be asked to walk through the design). Depending on the objectives, users also may be invited to be participants.

Notice that management was not mentioned. The goal of this kind of review is to examine the technical decisions. The presence of managers, who ultimately will evaluate the participants, is conducive to neither the free exchange of ideas nor the open admission of failure. As I will discuss in the next chapter, management does have important responsibilities in making the reviews work effectively, but attending reviews is not one of them.

An important guideline for the conduct of a review is that the material to be examined must be mature and all the participants must be prepared to discuss it. If both conditions are not satisfied, then the leader should cancel the review and document the reason in the report. The *Handbook* offers considerable advice to the review leader. For example, the following is extracted from a summary checklist [FrWe90, p. 114].

- *Qualifications of the leader.* Do you understand the purpose of reviews in general? Of this particular review? Can you be objective? Have you participated in a review before? Do you have any personal difficulties with the reviewers that might interfere with your ability to lead the review?

- *Before the review.* Is the product ready for review? Are all the relevant materials in your possession? Have they been distributed to the participants? Have the participants confirmed their acceptance? Has the conference room been scheduled?

- *During the review.* Are all participants well prepared? Is there agreement regarding the objectives of the review? Are the participants contributing? Has everyone been heard? Anyone tuned out? Is there agreement on the outcome of the review?

- *After the review.* Was the review successful? Did it reach workable conclusions? Is the report prompt and accurate? Did the product get a fair and adequate treatment? Does the producing group have a reasonable basis for clearing up the issues? What can you do to make the next review better?

The *Handbook* provides useful insight into the problem of starting a review program. It also offers advice on handling interpersonal problems such as habitual tardiness to reviews. (The solution: if a participant is always late, cancel the review and document why; after management reads the report, promptness improves.)

There are also helpful suggestions for the reviewers.

- *Be prepared.* The review typically lasts no more than two hours, and it requires feedback from the participants to be effective. The time to prepare for the review will generally exceed the time spent in the review. It must be kept in mind that the beneficiary of the review is to be the person who already knows the most about the product under review. If all his time is spent in explaining the product, this is not an effective use of anyone's time.

- *Watch your language.* Although we may talk of egoless programming, few of us are egoless. Avoid charged phrases. (Use "I don't understand. . . ." instead of "Why *didn't* you. . . .") For every negative comment find a positive one. Although you may be looking for errors, you are allowed to acknowledge good work.

- *Stick to technical issues.* Do not argue style, and do conform to the agreed standards. Raise issues, but do not try to resolve them; you only have a few hours for the review. Be sure to raise all issues in public, and encourage debate and consensus. Above all, never evaluate the producers; they still will be your colleagues when the review is over.

The outcome of a review requires a consensus regarding subsequent actions. The most severe outcome, of course, would be a decision to *rebuild.* Freedman and Weinberg suggest that the easiest way to get a consensus is to have the committee decision become that of the most severe member. Thus, if three committee members vote to accept the product and one votes to rebuild it, then the consensus is either to rebuild it or to convince the dissenting member. Better safe than sorry. Normally, however, there will be a collection of less dramatic recommendations, and these will be documented in the technical report. This describes what was reviewed, who did the reviewing, and what their conclusions were. The *Handbook* contains a form for a summary report, which is signed by all participants to indicate that they concur with its findings. This report is always sent to management. There is also a more detailed *issues list.* It tells the producers why their work was not fully accepted and provides them with sufficient detail so that they may remedy the situation. Generally, the issues list is a technical document that is not forwarded to management. There is no format for the issues list; it is considered a communication, and any effective organization is appropriate. The examples in the *Handbook* are all in memorandum form.

As this presentation suggests, the actual structure of a review is subject to considerable variation. The use of the review names is also subject to different interpretations. The walkthrough, for example, can represent an informal description of a product by a producer to his unprepared peers, or it can be the name for the kind of review just described. The principal attribute of a walkthrough is that the producer of the reviewed material guides the progression of the review. Freedman and Weinberg define an inspection as "a method for rapidly evaluating material by *confining attention to a few selected aspects, one at a time*" [FrWe90]. Fagan, however, uses the term *inspection* to imply a more formal process; he refers to reviews that do not conform to that particular approach as walkthroughs [Faga76]. Thus, the reader should be aware that not only are the terms poorly defined, but that practitioners use them in different ways. Fortunately, the above observations about reviews are valid for all categories of walkthrough and inspection. In what follows I describe Fagan's method and then summarize some empirical evaluations.

Fagan views the software inspection as the most effective and cost efficient technique for producing zero-defect products [Faga76, Faga86]. His method is to focus on the program design and code before machine testing. Two levels of review are provided for. $I_1$ inspections are concerned with the program design, and $I_2$ inspections deal with the code that implements the design. The differences in these two levels of inspection are found in the materials distributed, the number of participants, and some other minor points. Therefore I will use the term inspection without concern for the type of object being inspected. The distinctions between this form of inspection and the reviews previously described are that they are more formal, they are limited to error detection, and more emphasis is placed on the capture of statistical data.

The inspection team is comprised of members who play particular roles and assume the particular vantage point of those roles. Fagan identifies four roles.

- *Moderator.* Similar to the review leader, the moderator is the key person to a successful inspection. Fagan observes that he must be a competent programmer, but he need not be expert regarding the program under review. In fact, objectivity may be enhanced if the moderator comes from another project. Fagan describes him as the coach and adds that for best results the moderator should be specially trained.

- *Designer*.   The programmer responsible for producing the program design.

- *Coder/Implementor*.  The programmer responsible for translating the design into code.

- *Tester*.  The programmer responsible for writing and/or executing test cases or otherwise testing the product of the designer and coder.

In general, the same team will be formed for both the Design $I_1$ and the Code $I_2$.

The inspection process consists of five steps.

- *Overview*.   This is required for the $I_1$ inspection only.   The objectives are communication and education, and all members of the team participate.  The designer first describes the overall area being addressed and then covers the specifics in some detail. Materials are then distributed for the next step.   The rate of progress is approximately 500 noncommentary source statements (NCSS) per hour for a systems program.   If, as the result of an $I_1$ inspection, errors have been found that require rework, the moderator should flag those changes for special scrutiny.

- *Preparation*.   This is an independent activity performed by all participants.  The material is reviewed *solely* to detect errors.  To improve efficiency, the inspection team should first study the error distributions found in recent inspections.   Checklists are also helpful.  The idea is that the developers may have suffered from information overload and missed some otherwise "obvious" problems.   A systematic review for common faults often will detect such mistakes.  The rate of progress in this step is 100 NCSS per hour for $I_1$ and 125 NCSS per hour for $I_2$ inspections.

- *Inspection*.   This is the inspection or review attended by all participants.  Fagan suggests that a reader (usually the producer of the product being reviewed) be chosen by the moderator. He paraphrases the design; each piece of logic and every branch are considered at least once. *The objective is to find errors*.  Once an error is identified, the fact is recorded, and the process continues. No time should be spent on solving problems.  Each error is noted by the moderator; the type and severity (major or minor) are recorded.  Within a day of the inspection the moderator is expected to issue a written report to ensure that all issues raised in the inspection will be addressed in the following steps.  The rate of coverage for the material is 130 NCSS per hour for $I_1$ and 150 NCSS per hour for $I_2$.

- *Rework.* All errors or problems noted in the inspection report are resolved by the responsible designer or implementor. The Fagan inspection process includes rework as an explicit part of the review. The effort to repair the errors is 20 hours per thousand NCSS at $I_1$ and 16 hours per thousand NCSS at $I_2$.

- *Follow-up.* The final step in the inspection is a follow-up to ensure that all errors have been corrected. This is the responsibility of the moderator. If more than 5% of the material has been reworked, then the team should reconvene for another 100% inspection.

Although Fagan initially defined his inspection method for the design and coding of programs, others have extended the technique to other development activities. Dunn provides extended checklists for requirements and design [Dunn84, pp. 95-98] as well as code [pp. 121-123]. Table 5.2 illustrates a checklist, taken from another source, prepared for a requirements inspection. Examples of $I_1$ and $I_2$ checklists are included in [Faga76]; they contain questions such as, are all constants defined? Clearly, the kinds of questions asked will reflect the kinds of errors most commonly found.

One of the advantages of the formal approach suggested by Fagan is the fact that it collects statistics that can be used both to help in the identification of errors and in the evaluation of the process. For example, a 4,439-NCSS test case that he presented in his 1976 paper showed that an average of 38 errors were found per thousand NCSS during the $I_1$ and $I_2$ inspections, and an additional 8 errors per thousand NCSS were discovered during preparation for acceptance test. No subsequent errors were encountered; that is, the inspection process found 82% of the errors, and the product was delivered defect free. Because the inspection process also retained a record of each type of error found, Fagan was able to compile the distributions summarized in Table 5.3. Although the sample is far too small to make any general observations, notice how many of the errors were related to missing or extra code. The former usually are an indication that some requirements have been omitted; the later represent a maintenance problem (i.e., the delivered product has undocumented and unexpected features).

Not all reviews need be devoted to finding errors. For example, they frequently are used to educate team members new to the project or organization. Naturally, the reviews should be continued after the new members have become indoctrinated; we seldom run out of errors. No matter which form of walkthrough or inspection method is implemented,

Table 5.2.  Sample defects in a requirements-inspection checklist.

---

**Completeness**
1. Are all sources of input identified?
2. What is the total input space?
3. Are there any timing constraints on the inputs?
4. Are all types of outputs identified?
5. What are all the types of runs?
6. What is the input space and output space for each type of run?
7. Is the invocation mechanism for each run type defined?
8. Are all environmental constraints defined?
9. Are all necessary performance requirements defined?

**Ambiguity**
1. Are all special terms clearly defined?
2. Does each sentence have a single interpretation in the proper domain?
3. Is the input-to-output mapping clearly defined for each type of run?

**Consistency**
1. Do any of the designated requirements conflict with the descriptive material?
2. Are there any input states that are mapped to more than one output state?
3. Is a consistent set of quantative units used?  Are all numeric quantities consistent?

---

Extracted from [AcBL89] with permission, © IEEE.

it is important to keep records regarding the utility of the process.  This is not possible when reviews are conducted with such informality that they degenerate into structured bull sessions.  Dunn illustrates this phenomena with a limerick [Dunn84, p. 99].

> There was a young software guru
> Who decided to hold a review.
> So much for intent;
> The time got all spent,
> And he said, "'Twas a lovely walk-through."

Unfortunately, sometimes management takes the guru's position.  They

Table 5.3. Percent distribution of errors reported in [Faga76].

| | Design $I_1$ (%) | Code $I_2$ (%) |
|---|---|---|
| **Name of error** | | |
| Design error | | 24.4 |
| Logic error | 39.8 | 26.4 |
| Prologue/prose error | 17.1 | 14.9 |
| All other errors | 43.1 | 34.3 |
| **Class of error** | | |
| Missing | 57 | 35 |
| Wrong | 32 | 53 |
| Extra | 11 | 12 |

observe that design produces a document, and coding produces a program; therefore, they ask, if no product comes from an inspection, then are they worth the expense? Here are some published data summarized from [Hump89a, pp. 186-187] that demonstrate their value.

- Three experienced programmers inspected the code of a 200-line PL/1 program in 45 minutes and found 25 bugs, 5 of which would not have been found by testing [Your79].

- In another case, 55% of the one-line maintenance changes were in error before inspections were instituted; after inspections the error rate dropped to 2% [FrWe90].

- A study of 6 COBOL programs provided a baseline for error rates; after inspections were instituted, the error rates for the next 5 programs showed an improvement by more than a factor of five [FrWe90].

- An AT&T Bell Laboratory project with approximately 200 professionals found a 14% improvement in productivity. In another AT&T study, the cost of errors was reduced by an order of magnitude. A third study found that inspections were 20 times more effective in finding errors [Fowl86].

- The Aetna Insurance Company reported that inspections found 82% of their errors and increased productivity by 25% [Faga76].

- A TRW study of reported errors found that 63% could have been found by code inspections and that 58% could have been found by design inspections [ThLN78].

The logic behind the utility of inspections is obvious. When the only product the development team has is text, the only way to find errors is to establish an organized method to look for them. Technology can help in removing some of the syntactically identifiable problems, but the hard work still has to be done by us humans.

### 5.3.  After the programs exist

This section is concerned with the testing of debugged programs. The waterfall flow (Fig. 1.2) presents code and debug as one activity. Coding is the formalization of a problem solution as an executable program, and debugging is the identification and removal of the errors from interim solutions. The result, of course, should be an error-free program. The concept of proof of correctness, presented in Section 4.3, illustrated how one could produce programs that were correct and that, therefore, required no testing for errors. Later in this chapter, in the description of the Cleanroom, I shall show how it is possible to produce error-free programs without debugging. Nevertheless, the perception persists that in software development mistakes (or errors, faults, defects, bugs, etc.) are unavoidable and that we require testing to remove them. This section works within that premise and examines the techniques available for finding problems in debugged programs.

A recent survey of V&V and testing of computer software began with this comment.

Programming is an exercise in problem solving. As with any problem-solving activity, determination of the validity of the solution is part of the process. [AdBC82, p. 159]

Each of the three modeling chapters emphasized the role of validation in specification and design. The tools that helped guide the decision making were also used to evaluate the decisions. The reviews described in the previous section defined a process for examining accepted solutions systematically. As the $I_2$ inspections demonstrated, reviews are effective for code. But code also has the property of being executable, and testing takes advantage of that fact. This section, therefore, will concentrate on those techniques that exploit the machine-processible and executable nature of software to identify defects. Still, we ought not assume that bugs are inevitable; error avoidance is always more cost effective than error correction.

I have used the term "bug" several times now. Its use in computing has been traced by Grace Hopper to the final days of the World War II when she was part of a team working to build the Mark II, a large relay computer. One hot summer evening the computer failed, and when they located the defective relay they found a moth in it. The moth and explanation were entered into the logbook (see Fig. 5.2). After then, whenever Howard Aiken asked if the team was "making any numbers," negative responses were given with the explanation, "we were debugging the computer" [Hopp81]. This idea of a bug has a natural appeal. It evokes memories of warm summer evenings with background noises and gnats converging on a cool drink. Benign bugs. Annoying, but unavoidable. Certainly a more forgiving term than error or defect or fault or failure or mistake. Frankly, I find it too forgiving a term, nevertheless, throughout the remainder of this section I will use it. Testing finds the bugs and debugging removes them.

In his *The Art of Software Testing*, Myers describes the objective of testing as follows.

*Testing is the process of executing a program with the intent of finding errors.*

*A good test case is one that has a high probability of detecting an as-yet undiscovered error.*

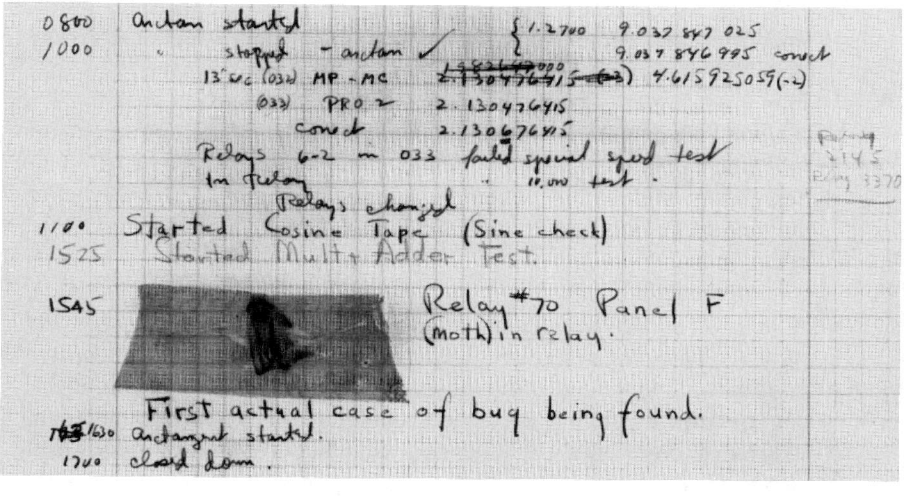

Fig. 5.2. Portion of the log page showing the original bug.
(Photograph curtesy Naval Museum, Naval Surface Weapons Center.)

*A successful test case is one that detects an as-yet undiscovered error.*
[Myer79, p. 16]

Thus, we are now in the business of trying to break things that the programmer believes to be of production quality. We cannot prove correctness; the most that we can hope for is an increased confidence that all the most damaging bugs have been found. Myers describes testing as an extremely creative and intellectually challenging task; just like design, testing is an art.

Adrion, Branstad, and Cherniavsky observe that, before we begin to test, five essential components are required [AdBC82].

- *The program in executable form.* This implies that all syntax errors have been identified and removed, that all project standards have been met, and that all portions of the code can be accessed.

- *A description of the expected behavior.* The goal is to prove that the program is incorrect, therefore we need a specification that establishes the criteria for correctness.

- *A way of observing the program behavior.* The behavior of the program under test must be isolated from the behavior of the other programs in the system. This may be done by inserting special codes (i.e., instrumenting the program), using a test harness to establish the state and then invoke the program, and/or creating stubs that remove potential side effects caused by invoked programs (which will be tested independently).

- *A description of the functional domain.* A part of the specification will define the domain for which the program should work. The test cases should be taken from that domain to demonstrate proper behavior and from outside the domain to demonstrate robustness.

- *A method of determining whether the observed behavior conforms with the expected behavior.* Ideally, we would construct an *oracle* that would, for every input description, describe the corresponding output. Lacking an oracle, we may be forced to perform extensive desk checks. Clearly, we must avoid the beginning-programmer's assumption that the absence of a pathological failure implies the success of a test.

Testing is done at three levels. During debugging each individual programmer tests his programs to be satisfied that they are of operational quality. Once he is satisfied that these conditions have been met, he delivers the program for a more formal test. This normally is conducted by an independent tester. As a general rule, the programmer should avoid testing his own programs. As Myers points out, testing is a destructive process, and the developer may have difficulty in accommodating that orientation for the products he has created. Once the program has been unit tested and accepted, it is placed under configuration control. The tested units then are combined and retested in larger and larger combinations. For each of these tests there is a need to satisfy the above five criteria; given a finished component, we need to know what to test for (the expected behavior and functional domain) and to observe and evaluate the results of the test.

Recall that each step in the waterfall flow produces two categories of output. Specifications and designs are used to initiate the next step; the same material is also used to establish the test criteria for demonstrating a correct implementation (see Fig. 1.3). Thus, we use the systems requirements to create the system acceptance tests, the software requirements for the software acceptance tests, the preliminary design for the software integration tests, the detailed design for the component tests, and the program design for the unit tests. The philosophy is that we first certify the individual units, then we integrate the units and certify the integration. This process iterates until—for the software engineer—the software product satisfies all the properties explicitly called out in the software requirements specification (SRS). Of course, the customer will not be satisfied until the system test has been completed.

In this section I shall concentrate on the techniques used to find bugs in the individual units. These techniques may be used by the implementors during debugging or by the testers during unit test. Later I shall discuss how these and other methods may be applied in integration and testing. In Chapter 6 I will make some comments regarding the organization of the testing effort. For now, however, I shall not distinguish between the testing done by the programmer and that by the tester. (In small projects, these often are the same person.) The process of testing consists of the following steps:

- *Plan the test.* Most software engineering activities begin with a planing activity, and testing is no exception. The objective is to establish a high-level approach to the task, to state the test objectives, and to decide how to meet them. The plans need not be very large—in fact, devoting too much time to the plans can be counterproductive. But good plans ultimately will reduce costs. They offer a roadmap for the testing activity, and they should be as permanent as the software that is being tested.

- *Prepare the test data.* We already know the expected behaviors to be tested and the domain of the data. Most of the succeeding discussion will deal with how to develop a test set that has a high probability of finding an as-yet undetected bug. A great deal of effort goes into creating the test data sets, and they should be maintained under configuration control along with the programs.

- *Identify the bugs.* This step involves the examination of the test outputs and the documentation of the test results. If bugs are detected, then this fact is reported, and the activity reverts to a debugging phase. After debugging, there is an iteration of the present step. All passed tests should be repeated with the revised program. This is called *regression testing*, and it can discover errors introduced during the debugging process. If no bugs are found, then the quality of the test data set should be questioned. If confidence in the product is low, then the test data set will be augmented, and the search for bugs continues. If it is believed that sufficient testing has been conducted, then this fact is reported, and the testing for this particular product is complete.

One could summarize this process as iterations of testing (i.e., bug identification) and debugging (i.e., bug removal) until the project engineers are satisfied that no undiscovered bugs remain. An obvious question is, "When has there been enough testing?" Musa and Ackerman provide some guidelines, and I shall address the topic briefly in the next chapter [MuAc89]. The answer, of course, depends on the reliability required and the previous experience with this class of application.

Because each successful test will cause a return to debugging, I thought it useful to close this introduction to testing with a summary of Myers's debugging principles [Myer79, pp. 141-144].

### Error-Locating Principles
*Think.*
*If you reach an impasse, sleep on it.*
*If you reach an impasse, describe the problem to someone else.*
*Use debugging tools only as a second resort.*
*Avoid experimentation. Use it only as a last resort.*

### Error-Repairing Principles
*Where there is one bug, there is likely to be another.*
*Fix the error, not just the symptom of it.*
*The probability of the fix being correct is not 100%.*
*The probability of the fix being correct drops as the size of the program increases.*

*Beware of the possibility that an error correction creates a new error.*

*The process of error repair should put one back temporarily in the design phase.*

*Change the source code, not the object code.*

Although somewhat out of date, this Myers's book remains one of the most insightful and readable introductions to the art of testing.

### 5.3.1. *Taxonomy of testing*

The discussion of the previous section linked testing with debugging. But testing involves considerably more than finding bugs to be eliminated. Beizer speaks of five phases in the attitudinal progression regarding testing.

**PHASE 0**—There's no difference between testing and debugging. Other than in support of debugging, testing has no purpose.

**PHASE 1**—The purpose of testing is to show that the software works.

**PHASE 2**—The purpose of testing is to show that the software doesn't work.

**PHASE 3**—The purpose of testing is not to prove anything, but to reduce the perceived risk of not working to an acceptable value.

**PHASE 4**—Testing is not an act. It is a mental discipline that results in low-risk software without much testing effort. [Beiz90, p. 4]

While the introduction to this section may have brought the reader to Phase 2, I would hope that the introduction to this chapter is at Phase 4. (Substitute V&V for testing.) In testing we are looking for those persistent errors that remain after inspections, standards, and good design methods and tools. We hope that not too many bugs remain, and we want to develop skills that will eliminate them with as little effort as possible.

When looking for bugs in the program, we have two basic techniques available to us. *Static analysis* examines the program text without execution. A compiler performs some static analysis; it can, for example, identify unreachable statements. *Dynamic analysis* examines the behavior of the program during execution. This is the traditional pattern of program testing. The program is run with some *test data set* (or *test set*), and the results are examined to check whether the program's performance operated as expected. Because it normally is impossible to exhaustively test all cases, we search for a test set that is adequate. Goodenough and Gerhart offered the first formal treatment of this concept [GoGe75]. A criterion $C$ is said to be *reliable* if the test sets $T_1$ and $T_2$ chosen by $C$ are such that all test instances of $T_1$ are successful exactly when all test instances of $T_2$ are successful. A criterion $C$ is said to be *valid* if it can produce test sets that uncover all errors. From these definitions, we can state the fundamental theorem of testing.

> If there exists a consistent, reliable, valid, and complete criterion for test set selection for a program $P$ and if a test set satisfying the criterion is such that all test instances succeed, then the program $P$ is correct.

Unfortunately, it has been shown that there is no algorithm to find consistent, reliable, valid, and complete test criteria [Howd76]. Thus, testing will remain an art.

Inasmuch as there can be no formal methods for establishing test set criteria, perhaps an examination of the kinds of bugs detected will improve our understanding of what we are looking for. Fortunately, Beizer has prepared an extensive taxonomy of bugs [Beiz90]. He groups them into the following nine categories. The category titles are from his book. My descriptions paraphrase his definitions; the titles of selected second-level terms in the taxonomy are given in parentheses.

- *Requirements.* These are bugs having to do with the requirements as specified or implemented. The requirement is incorrect, undesirable, or not needed (requirements incorrect); it is illogical, unreasonable, unachievable, or inconsistent (logic); it is ambiguous, incomplete, overly specified (completeness); it is unverifiable or untestable (verifiability); its presentation is poor or violates standards (presentation); it has changed because features have been added, deleted or changed, or cases within a feature have changed, or the domain or interfaces have changed (requirements changes).

- *Features and functionality.* These are problems with the implementation of correct, implementable, and testable requirements. The feature or its interactions have been misunderstood (feature/function correctness); there are missing, unspecified, or duplicated features (feature completeness); there are missing, extra, or duplicated cases (functional case completeness); the domain is misunderstood or wrong or there are problems with the domain boundary (domain bugs); user messages and diagnostics are incorrect (user messages and diagnostics); the exception conditions are mishandled.

- *Structural bugs.* These are bugs related to the program's code. The general structure may have unachievable paths, unreachable code or dead-end code; the control logic may contain duplicated logic, be illogical, or have other control-flow predicate bugs; there are case selection bugs; the loops have the wrong initial value, terminal value or condition, increment value, or exception condition; the control may be incorrectly initialized or have the wrong state (control flow and sequencing). There also may be problems with the fundamental algorithm; the evaluation of expressions may have arithmetic problems such as the wrong operator, misplaced parentheses, or incorrect sign; the string manipulation may be in error; there are problems in initialization, cleanup, precision, or execution time (processing).

- *Data.* These are bugs in the definition, structure, or use of data. The definition may have the wrong type, dimension, initial or default values, or the aliases may be duplicated; the scope may be global when it should be local, and vice versa; the data may be static when it should be dynamic (or vice versa), there may be insufficient space, or there may be an overlay bug (data definition and structure). The data may be of the wrong type, type transformation, or units; the dimension may have the wrong initialization or constant values, the aliases may be dynamically duplicated; there may be access bugs such as the wrong object is accessed, access rights are violated, there are data-flow anomalies, interlock bugs, saving or protection bugs, restoration bugs, or the object boundary is not properly handled (data access and handling).

- *Implementation and coding.* These bugs have to do with the implementation of the program. There may be typographical errors or the syntax of the language may be misunderstood (coding and typographical); the standards may be violated by the control flow, the complexity may be too great, the loops or calls may be nested too deeply, or there may be standards violations in the data declarations, data access, calling or invocation, mnemonics conventions, format, or comments (style and standards violations); the documentation may be incorrect, inconsistent, incomprehensible, incomplete, or missing (documentation).

- *Integration.* These bugs have to do with the integration of, and interfaces between, components. The internal interfaces may have bugs in the component invocation, interface parameters, or component invocation returns (internal interfaces); there may be problems with the interrupts, the device drivers, or the I/O timing and throughput (external interfaces and timing).

- *System, software architecture.* These are bugs not attributable to a component or to the interfaces between components. There may be an OS bug in invocation, the return of data, or space (OS bug); the software architecture may exhibit problems in interlocks and semaphores, priority, transaction-flow control, resource management and control, recursive calls, or reentrance (software architecture); or there may be bugs related to recovery and accountability, performance, incorrect diagnostics, or the sysgen or environment.

- *Test definition and execution.* These are bugs in the definition, design, or execution of the tests or the data used in the test. The requirements are misunderstood, the incorrect outcome is predicted, the incorrect path is predicted, or there are bugs in the test initialization, test data structure, sequencing, configuration, or verification method (design bugs); for good tests there may have been bugs in the initialization, commands, database, configuration, or verification act (execution bugs); finally, there are problems in the test documentation and text case completeness.

- *Other, unspecified.*

Table 5.4 contains sample statistics accumulated by Beizer from experience reported on projects in 28 different papers.[3] A total of 6,877,000 statements (including comments) were analyzed; 16,209 bugs were identified with an average of 2.36 bugs per 1000 statements of *debugged code.* The table contains the data reported for each major category; significant contributors within a category also are listed.

The data in the table report on the errors found and offer helpful insights into the kinds of problems to expect. First, notice that both the requirements and the implementation bugs represent a small portion of

---

[3]The table was extracted from *Software Testing Techniques*, second edition, by Boris Beizer, copyright Boris Beizer, reprinted with permission of Van Nostrand Reinhold, New York. Percentages of this extracted table may not work out because some of Beizer's low-frequency categories have been deleted.

Table 5.4. Beizer's sample bug statistics.

| Category | Errors | Percent |
|---|---|---|
| Requirements | 1317 | 8.1 |
| Requirements incorrect | 649 | 4.0 |
| Logic | 153 | 0.9 |
| Completeness | 224 | 1.4 |
| Requirements changes | 278 | 1.7 |
| Features and functionality | 2624 | 16.2 |
| Feature/function correctness | 456 | 2.8 |
| Feature completeness | 231 | 1.4 |
| Domain bugs | 778 | 4.8 |
| User messages and diagnostics | 857 | 5.3 |
| Structural bugs | 4082 | 25.2 |
| Control flow and sequencing | 2078 | 12.8 |
| Processing | 2004 | 12.4 |
| Data | 3638 | 22.4 |
| Data definition and structure | 1805 | 11.1 |
| Data access and handling | 1831 | 11.3 |
| Implementation and coding | 1601 | 9.9 |
| Coding and typographical | 322 | 2.0 |
| Style and standards violation | 318 | 2.0 |
| Documentation | 960 | 5.9 |
| Integration | 1455 | 9.0 |
| Internal interfaces | 859 | 5.3 |
| External interfaces and timing | 518 | 3.2 |
| System, software architecture | 282 | 1.7 |
| Test definition and execution | 447 | 2.8 |
| Execution bugs | 355 | 2.2 |
| Other, unspecified | 763 | 4.7 |

Extracted from [Beiz90] with permission, ©1990 by Boris Beizer.

the total bugs reported. Of the requirements bugs, half are due to incorrect requirements; the effect of logic errors in the requirements is negligible. With respect to the implementation and coding errors, most of these can be traced back to problems in the documentation. Approximately two-thirds of the errors, however, are associated with three categories: the improper interpretation of a requirement, or its implementation with a faulty program structure or incorrect data definitions, structure, or declarations. Thus, if we wish to direct our energies to finding the most bugs, then we ought to concentrate on testing for these three categories of bug.

I already have divided testing categories into two groups: the static analysis that tries to detect bugs implicit in the program text, and dynamic analysis that relies on program execution to detect bugs. I now subdivide the latter into two groups.

- *Functional tests*. These are tests to external specifications. They are also called *black box tests* because the tests are conducted without concern for how the programs were implemented. The goal of the black box test is to remove the features and functionality bugs.

- *Structural tests*. These are tests that examine the structure of the program text and its data definitions to identify bugs. They are also called *white box tests* (or sometimes *glass box tests*). The white box tests systematically examine the most detailed design document (i.e., the code) to ensure that no structural or data bugs remain.

There is a certain irony in that half of Beizer's reported errors can be traced to problems with the program text, for which the white box tests are most effective. The white box tests identify problems in the code that may be independent of the function of the program, whereas the black box tests involve the verification of the program with respect to its functional specification. The types of mistakes that white box tests can best discover are those of a random or careless kind. One would hope that better software tools (e.g., improved languages and static analyzers) and development methods (e.g., proofs of correctness and inspections) would eliminate many of these bugs before testing. Yet there is an appeal to white box testing; it can be studied, it deals with the properties of formally defined entities, and there clearly is a need. The message of this book, however, is that we should treat the program as a design and remove all structural errors from the program text before testing it just as we remove the structural errors from the higher levels of design before we detail them. This statement should not be construed to suggest that structural testing is not important. I only suggest that we construct our programs assuming that there will be no subsequent error-identification process and then follow up with machine testing. (More on this is given in Section 5.4.)

Now that the taxonomy for testing has been established, the following sections will discuss static analysis and the two classes of dynamic analysis. The presentation of these techniques focuses on their use with individual programs; a final section considers integration issues. The reader will notice that I borrow heavily from the work of Beizer. His *Software Testing Techniques* is the essential reference and guide for testers.

## 5.3.2.   Static analysis and complexity analysis

Most writers on software testing and quality divide static analysis into two categories. The first involves the extraction of information about the object with nonautomated techniques such as the review or inspection. This was the subject of Section 5.2. The second category takes advantage of the fact that the program is a machine-processible object. It relies on automated techniques to discover real or potential problems. Compilers provide many such facilities; others are supported by commercial tools. Each defect and potential source of a problem identified by a static analyzer represents something that is probably *wrong* with the program. Bugs are not independent events, and where one bug has been found, there is an increased probability that additional bugs remain. Thus, any program that fails any of these tests is likely to be bug prone. Dunn catalogues the capabilities of automated static analysis as shown in Table 5.5.

It follows, therefore, that the automated static analysis techniques can provide three categories of assistance.

- *Bug identification.* The analysis can identify things that are wrong with the program. Some of these bugs may cause immediate failure during execution; others may simply suggest a degree of carelessness that hints at the existence of other, undetected bugs.

- *Supporting information.* Because the implementation can be treated as text, static analysis can produce supporting materials that will be useful in reviews, test case generation, and product maintenance. Some of this information may be limited to the individual units; other outputs (e.g., a call-set matrix, which identifies the interactions among program units) can provide a system view.

Table 5.5.  Dunn's list of automated static analysis capabilities.

---

**Defects likely to be exposed**
   Misuse of variables, both locally and globally
   Mismatched parameter lists
   Improper nesting of loops and branches
   Improper sequencing of processes
   Undefined variables
   Infinite loops
   Unauthorized recursion
   Calls to nonexistent subprograms
   Missing labels or code
   Improper linkages

**Potential sources of problems**
   Unused variables
   Unreachable code
   Unreferenced labels
   Suspicious computations
   Potentially infinite loops

**Outputs not directly related to defects**
   Number of occurrences of each source statement form
   Cross-reference of where variables and constants are used
   Manner of use of identifiers
   Procedures-calling hierarchy
   Violations of coding standards
   Preprocessing for further defect removal
   Selection of test cases

---

Reprinted from [Dunn84] with permission, ©1984 McGraw-Hill.

- *Complexity analysis.*  If we assume that there is a correlation between the complexity of a program and the number of errors in it, then—if we can automatically recognize the properties of programs that correlate with their complexity—we can identify those high-risk programs that either ought to be revised or subjected to additional testing.

Dunn's list contains examples for the first two categories of automated static analysis; the remainder of this section considers the basis for evaluating a program's complexity.

Among the properties of a program that seem to correlate with its complexity are its size (usually measured in lines of code), its interfaces with other modules (usually measured as *fan in*, the number programs invoking the given program, or *fan out*, the number of programs invoked by the given program), the number of parameters passed, etc. There are two special complexity measures—each of which may be calculated automatically—that have received considerable attention, and I shall present them here. In the next chapter I show* how a measurements program can determine their effectiveness within a particular setting.

Halstead sought to establish a *software science* that identifies certain intrinsic, measurable properties embodied in the code of an algorithm [Hals77]. He begins with the following four countable parameters.

$n_1$ = Unique operators used
$n_2$ = Unique operands used
$N_1$ = Total operators used
$N_2$ = Total operands used

For example, in the statement

X := X + 1

the operators are := and +, and the operands are X and 1. He then defines

$$n = n_1 + n_2$$
$$N = N_1 + N_2$$

where $N$ represents the program *length*. It was shown empirically that the length can be approximated by

$$\hat{N} = n_1 \log_2 n_1 + n_2 \log_2 n_2$$

where the $\log_2$ reduces the length value to the number of bits required to express each operator and operand uniquely. From this one can compute the *volume* of the program

$$V = N \log_2 n$$

and approximate $L$, the *program level* as

$$\hat{L} = (1 + M)/n_1 \cdot n_2/N_2$$

where $M$ is the number of modules. The product of the program level ($L$) and volume ($V$) is the *potential volume ($V^*$)*, "which depends only on the algorithm, and is reasonably invariant as the algorithm is translated from one programming language to another" [Hals75]. It is the most compact, or highest level, representation of an algorithm. Depending on the language used, different implementations of the same algorithm will have different volumes. This difference is a function of the *language level*, calculated as

$$\lambda = LV^*;$$

$\lambda$ is viewed as an inherent property of a programming language. The effort required to produce a program is defined as the quotient of volume by the level ($V/L$). Other formulas are provided for computing the time required to implement a program, the number of errors expected in a program, and so on. In short, the theory states that there are some invariant characteristics of a *well-coded* algorithm (e.g., one without redundancies or needless constructs) that can be used to predict other attributes of the program, its implementation, and its maintenance.

There have been numerous empirical studies regarding the accuracy of the Halstead measures, and there is general agreement that the original theory is inadequate but some of its measures have value [FiLo78, ShCD83, Coul83, CaAg87, CaGl90]. Of course, the merit of Halstead measures such as length and volume may simply be the fact that they correlate highly with the number of lines in the program. Nevertheless, Halstead's software science has contributed some very interesting ideas. First, it provides greater granularity than simply the line of code. Second, it introduces a relationship between language choice and its impact on effort and quality. Finally, it illustrates how a decade of empirical studies to confirm (or disconfirm) a software engineering theory may still not produce a consensus.

The second measure for complexity that has received considerable attention is McCabe's complexity measure. Quite simply, McCabe produces a graph of the program's control flow and calculates the *cyclomatic complexity* of that graph. For example, the program shown in Figure 5.3 would produce the graph in Figure 5.4. (All nodes are labeled with the program's line number, and the graph includes only those nodes that affect the flow.) Cyclomatic complexity is computed with the formula

$$V(G) = e - n + 2p$$

where $V(G)$ is the cyclomatic number of a graph $G$ with $n$ vertices, $e$ edges, and $p$ connected components. In a strongly connected graph $G$, the cyclomatic number is equal to the maximum number of linearly independent paths. Clearly, these linearly independent paths can be thought of as independent control flow paths. Therefore, the higher the number of possible control paths, the greater the program's potential complexity.

```
0     ENTRY, Sample program
1     X,A := 1,100
2     DO WHILE (X < A)
3         INPUT Y,Z
4         U := X+Y
5         IF (U <0) THEN DO
6             IF (Z>Y) THEN DO
7                 U := 0
8             END
9             ELSE U := X+Z
10            END
11        END
12        DO WHILE (U > 0)
13            U,X := U-1, X+1
14        END
15    END
16    EXIT
```

Fig. 5.3. Sample program in PDL.

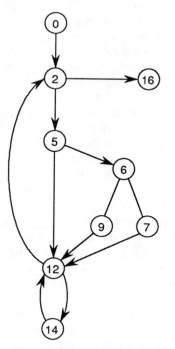

Fig. 5.4. Graph of sample program in Figure 5.2.

If each program has its own graph, then the value of $p$ can be thought of as the number of independent programs.  A structured program will have $p = 1$.  Moreover, it can be shown that the cyclomatic complexity of a structured program equals the number of predicates plus one.  Where there is a compound predicate, such as

IF (X = 0) & (Y > 1) THEN ...,

it should be interpreted as two conditional statements, each with an atomic predicate.  Thus, the statement in this example would be considered to contain two predicates.  One can also think of the cyclomatic complexity number as representing the number of distinct regions in the flow graph.  Euler's formula computes the number of regions $r$ in the graph.  It is

$$n - e + r = 2.$$

For $p = 1$, we have $V(G) = r$, and the cyclomatic number of a structured program equals the number of regions in the graph.

For structured programs it is quite simple to compute the cyclomatic number automatically; one need only identify the predicates, search for connectives to reduce the compound predicates, and then add one.  It is broadly suggested that a number of 11 or greater implies a degree of complexity that will make the program difficult to test or maintain. Hence the term "cyclomatic complexity."  Although there is no theoretical basis for selecting 11 as the boundary between acceptable and excess complexity, it is obvious that excessive complexity is bad.  A cyclomatic complexity measure greater than 10 is one indicator of potential trouble.  There are many other values that can be computed automatically from the program text.  For a period, the identification of new measures (often labeled "metrics") was an area of considerable research interest.  This is the subject of Chapter 7 in [Beiz90]. [CoDS86] offers a comprehensive treatment of software engineering metrics and models; [Weyu88] provides both a formal analysis of axioms for complexity metrics and an evaluation of several popular measures. A good survey of complexity measures useful for program maintenance is contained in [HaMK82], and [McCB89] extends the role of the cyclomatic measure beyond that just presented here.  Although there are many measures in use, practitioners are most familiar with the work of Halstead and McCabe.  However, a careful reading of my description shows that neither measures an invariant property comparable to the speed of light in a vacuum.  Rather, each serves as a predictor of problems in certain situations; understanding which situations is as important as learning to calculate the values.

Chapter 6 discusses how these measures can be applied to meet the needs of a particular organization. In closing this section on static analysis, I simply make the point that we can automatically compute many numbers that provide insight into the quality and maintainability of a program. It would not be difficult, for example, to develop a package for computing the length, fan out, Halstead measures, and cyclomatic complexity for a program. Each number provides a different way of looking at a finished program; properties not obvious during its design may become more visible once the complexity parameters are available. We always benefit from reexamining our work from a new perspective, and these values can help us anticipate operational and maintenance problems. However, the numbers are imperfect predictors. Kafura, for example, advocates the use of multiple measures; only when a program is "out of bounds" for two or more measures should it be considered a candidate for refinement or redesign [KaCa85, KaRe87]. Thus, I conclude the section on static analysis with this observation. Automated processing can find some syntactical errors and warn of potential problems, but there is a limit to what we can expect. We must be careful not to confuse ease of calculation with benefit of use.

### 5.3.3.   White box testing

This section considers how to machine test a program based on the structure of its implementation. As one would expect, some of the same techniques can be used for testing integrated components as well as for testing program functionality (i.e., black box testing). Moreover, the discussion of test set construction presented in the section on black box testing is equally valid for structural (i.e., white box) testing. We begin with the assumption that the program has been subjected to a static analysis and careful review. The tester is familiar with what the program is to do, all the data are of the proper type and dimension, the local standards have been followed in both coding and commenting, and so on. Such problems could not be discovered with white box testing; it is intended to identify the still-overlooked bugs through a systematic examination of the program's control paths and data flows. Assuming that bugs are evenly distributed throughout the program and that the programmer will have tested those functions of the program that he believes to be of the greatest importance, what we now are looking for are bugs that have a low probability of execution, were carelessly implemented, were overlooked by the developer, or reflect fuzzy thinking regarding secondary functions. Naturally, these bugs must be removed.

One common technique is called path testing. We would like to be certain that each path in the program is exercised at least once during testing. This will improve our confidence that no special cases will be exercised for the first time in an operational setting. Unfortunately, this level of path testing is generally impossible to achieve, and we normally must be satisfied with one of two weaker conditions.

- *Statement testing coverage (C1).* Here every statement in the program is executed at least once. Beizer states, "testing less than this for new software is unconscionable and should be criminalized" [Beiz90].

- *Branch testing coverage (C2).* Here there are enough tests to ensure that every branch alternative has been exercised at least once under some test. For structured software, branch testing strictly includes statement coverage.

Because the stronger the test, the more effective it will be, I limit the discussion to branch coverage testing. I also assume that we are working with structured programs with a single entry and exit.

The discussion of cyclomatic complexity in Section 5.3.2 showed how a program's control flow could be represented as a graph. The cyclomatic number counts the number of control paths. If each predicate in the program is based on a single condition, then a systematic test of each path will constitute C2 testing. McCabe observes that the number of test cases to achieve this is equal to the cyclomatic number. Here is the method he uses for establishing a *base set of paths* (or *basis paths*) for *structured testing* [McCa83].

- Draw a control flow graph as shown in Figure 5.4; nodes that are part of a sequential flow are omitted to simplify the graph.

- Select a functional "baseline" path that represents a legitimate function and not just an error exit. Test this baseline; exercise all functional requirements, and look for data that would produce errors in the baseline.

- Identify a second path by locating the first decision in the baseline path and flip that decision while holding the maximum number of baseline decisions the same. Apply the same testing process as above.

- Next return the first decision to its initial state and flip the second decision.

- Continue in this way until every decision has been flipped while all other decisions have been held to the baseline.

Because the choice of the baseline is arbitrary, there may be several sets of data that satisfy this structured-testing criteria. Each application of the method, however, will produce a test set with the following properties:

> *v* distinct independent paths will be generated
> every edge in the program graph will be traversed.

To illustrate the method with the program in Figure 5.3, I select as the baseline path 1-2-5-6-9-12-14-12-2-16. (Note that the DO WHILE iteration is shown as a loop with the branch at the statement with the predicate.) The first decision is at statement 2; flipping it provides the path 1-2-16. The next decision is at statement 5, and flipping it gives the path 1-2-5-12-14-12-2-16. Again returning to the initial baseline for statement 5, we have the next decision to be flipped at statement 6, which produces the path 1-2-5-6-7-12-14-12-2-16. Unflipping the decision at statement 6 brings us to the decision at statement 12 and the path 1-2-5-6-9-12-2-16. Thus, we have 5 test sets for the 5 paths of the program with a cyclomatic complexity of 5. Now to construct the test data. For the baseline path we require

> X < A at statement 2,
> U < 0 at statement 5,
> Z <= Y at statement 6, and
> U > 0 at statement 12.

Two inputs to the program, Y and Z, can be controlled. The first condition will always be true (and hence no input data can be used to test the second path). We can achieve the goal at statement 2 by having the input value of Y less than -1 and the goal at statement 6 by having the input value of Z less than or equal to that of Y; these two inputs will satisfy the goal at statement 12. I leave the construction of the remaining input sets as an exercise. Associated with each input there must also be an output; and I leave that as an exercise as well.

Once it is decided which paths to test, the tester may come to the unhappy realization that either no set of test inputs will result in the desired paths or that additional data (such as a database) are required to carry out the tests. In these cases it may be appropriate to instrument the program either to set variables for tests or to direct control to particular portions of the program. The instrumentation usually prints out intermediate results and the paths taken. Some languages and environments allow the tester to treat these instructions specially; they can be compiled for testing and ignored during the production compilation. Clearly, there is a danger that the instrumentation code will introduce errors. Certainly, it will affect response time and resource utilization. Nevertheless, this may be the only way in which one can test certain flows. It also is the only method for evaluating the loop tests to be described below. Therefore, as its name implies, white box testing may require that the tester do more than just prepare inputs for a run. The tester also should be sensitive to the fact that the program he tests is intended to be a long-lived object. The instrumentation, test sets, and test outcomes should be designed to have a lifetime equal to that of the programs. Thought should be given to the preservation of the test cases and outcomes in a machine processible media that can serve as an oracle for regression testing.

Returning to the topic of path testing,[4] we have seen that McCabe's heuristic is quite effective in producing a test set that covers all branches and paths in the flow. But I have provided a strange program whose function is not clear. Without explaining what that program is to do, it is difficult to determine if its logic is valid. The fact that some paths are never taken may suggest that the program should be reworked, but the basis path selection process can offer us little insight here. Testing each statement at least once has absolved us of criminality. The question now is, was that enough? Beizer states that 65% of all bugs can be caught in unit testing. In practice, about 35% of all bugs are detected by path testing; when these tests are augmented with other methods, the percentage of bugs caught rises to 50 to 60%. Among the limitations of path testing are the following:

- They are more effective for nonstructured than for structured programs.

- Path testing may not cover when there are bugs.

- It cannot reveal wrong or missing functions; neither can it catch specification errors.

- Not all initialization errors are detected.

Therefore, while path testing may establish a minimal standard, it is not sufficient. The remainder of this section presents some structural tests to augment path testing. By way of providing a context for this discussion, I ask the reader to keep in mind the following quotation from Beizer; the italics have not been added.

---

[4]Beizer uses the term "path testing" for a family of testing techniques, of which statement coverage and branch coverage are the first two members. The base-set heuristic just described usually (but not always) provides branch coverage.

Furthermore, *the act of careful, complete, systematic, test design will catch as many bugs as the act of testing.* It's worth repeating here and several times more in this book: *The test design process, at all levels, is at least as effective at catching bugs as is running the test designed by that process.* Personally, I believe that it's far more effective, but I don't have statistics to back that claim. And when you consider the fact that bugs caught during test design cost less to fix than bugs caught during testing, it makes test design bug catching even more attractive. [Beiz90, pp. 90-91]

That is, test design is really a form of static analysis.

Because loops are such a common structure in programs, it is useful to isolate them for some special form of testing. We know that we cannot possibly test all paths; that would require an exhaustive test of all looping combinations. In computing the basis paths using McCabe's method, we insisted that each loop be iterated just once. However, a more comprehensive set of tests may be required to isolate the bugs commonly found in loops. Beizer states that, beyond the single loop, there are only three kinds of loops: *nested, concatenated,* and *horrible.* Most testing books use examples in FORTRAN just so they can illustrate horrible (i.e., nonstructured) loops. Figure 5.5 contains examples of each type. Here are some of the heuristics for generating test sets.

- *Single loops.* If it has a minimum of zero iterations, a maximum of N iterations, and no excluded values, try zero and N iterations. Try N+1 iterations. Have two passes through the loop; some data-flow anomalies such as improper initialization can be found only this way. If the minimum number of iterations is greater than zero, then try 1 less than that minimum. If there are excluded values, make up two sets: one with and one without the excluded values.

- *Nested loops.* Start at the innermost loop, and set the outer loops to their minimum values. Test that loop as a single loop. Continue outward in this manner, but set all but the tested loop to typical values. Repeat the cases for all loops in the nest simultaneously.

- *Concatenated loops.* These loops are structured so that it is possible to reach the second only after completing the first. Therefore, these loops should be tested in combination to uncover interactions. Variations of the single loop tests are used, and special tests may be desired when the loop parameters of the second loop depend on the outcome of the first loop.

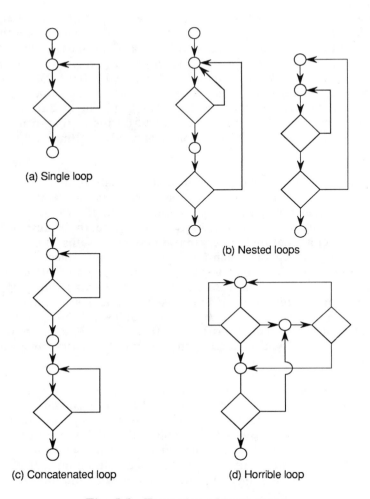

(a) Single loop

(b) Nested loops

(c) Concatenated loop

(d) Horrible loop

Fig. 5.5.  Examples of loop types.

- *Horrible loops*.  Beizer's comment is that the thinking required to check the end points and looping values will be unique for each program.  My comment is that an ounce of prevention is worth a pound of cure.

To close out this discussion of path testing, one must mix thoroughness with thought and practicality.  For every test run there must be an outcome analysis.  Stacks of unread listings violate the intent of testing.  The goal is to find errors, and that requires that we look for them.  Path testing, as usually applied, has a goal of ensuring C1 + C2 coverage; loop testing expands on this basic theme.  Some heuristics can help identify potentially effective test cases. But thought must prevail. Add to the tests by picking additional paths that are slight variations of previous paths. If it is not obvious why some control path exists, question it rather than just test it. Play your hunches and give your intuition free reign. The software is not fragile, and you ought not be able to break it. But go ahead, give it your best shot.

Even when the test sets have been prepared with great care, they still may not detect existing bugs. Among the problems is the possibility that the predicates in the control flow are *correlated* (e.g., we cannot start the loop in the program in Figure 5.3 with $X >= A$). In some cases, we may find that seemingly independent predicates are correlated. For example, consider the following sequence of code.

```
IF A > 0    THEN DO (nothing that changes A)
            ELSE DO (nothing that changes A)

(Some short sequence of code that does not change A)

IF A > 0    THEN DO (something else)
            ELSE DO (something else)
```

Here the program will take the same branch for both selections. The test designer should consider why the program was designed this way. Beizer states that this kind of correlated decision is often associated with the practice of "saving code." Several times I have stressed the importance of reuse, but that is quite different from the practice of creating new programs by combining and editing fragments of old programs. Perhaps the most important quality factor of operational code is its maintainability; code-saving tricks are seldom documented and almost always difficult to maintain. The test designer, therefore, should question whether the program might better be restructured by combining the two selection statements with the predicate $A > 0$ into one.

Another complication is that of *testing blindness* in which the desired path is achieved for the wrong reason. For example, both sets of code will take the same branch, but the code on the right is buggy.

| Correct | Buggy |
| --- | --- |
| X := 7 | X := 7 |
| . . . | . . . |
| IF Y > 0 THEN | IF Y + X > 0 THEN |

Path testing cannot differentiate the buggy from the correct path; only inspection will work here. Related to this is the problem of *coincidental correctness* that results when the presence of a bug is not reflected in the test outcome. For example, one common practice is to instrument the program to print out the path name (and perhaps the state for key variables) each time the path has been taken. The tester then goes through these traces to verify that a test input produced the appropriate trace. If the trace statement is printed only when the program enters the path, however, there may be a bug that causes a change in the control flow without having that change reflected in the trace. To avoid this kind of problem, the trace statements should be placed at both the beginning and end of each traced path.

In addition to examining the control paths, one should also look for *data-flow anomalies*. As Table 5.4 indicates, there are almost as many data bugs as there are structural bugs. Thus, it is prudent to heed the advice of Rapps and Weyuker.

> It is our belief that, just as one would not feel confident about a program without executing every statement in it as part of some test, one should not feel confident about a program without having seen the effect of using the value produced by each and every computation. [RaWe82, p. 272]

What we shall do, then, is assume that the program's control flow is correct and look to see if the data objects are available when they should be, or if silly things are being done to the data objects. Because of the holistic nature of software, such tests will also help us discover previously undetected control-flow bugs.

Beizer defines the following method for data-flow testing. As with control-flow testing, we begin by constructing a graph. Of particular interest will be the state changes for the data. Beizer identifies three possible actions on data objects [Beiz90, pp. 151-153]:

- *Defined (d)*. The object is defined, created, or initialized when it is given a valid state.

- *Killed (k)*. The object is killed, undefined, or released when it ceases to have a state (e.g., a FORTRAN loop variable is undefined when the loop is exited). Note that *d* and *k* are complementary operations; when you see complementary operations, it is a good indication that data-flow analysis may be effective.

- *Used (u)*. The object is used either for *computation (c)* or in a *predicate (p)*.

Given these operators, Beizer uses a two-letter pair or a letter and a dash to denote anomalies, which leads to the following 15 categories.

- *dd* The object is defined twice without an intervening use; probably harmless, but suspicious.

- *dk* The object is defined and killed without ever using it; probably a bug.

- *du* The object is defined and then used; a normal situation.

- *kd* The object is killed and then redefined; normal usage.

- *kk* The object is killed twice; either vindictive or a bug.

- *ku* An attempt to use the object after it has been killed; clearly a bug.

- *ud* The object is defined after a use; a normal situation.

- *uk* The object is killed after a use; a normal situation.

- *uu* Sequential uses; quite normal.

- *—k* Killing an object that has been neither defined nor used; possibly anomalous.

- *—d* This is the first definition in the path; normal.

- *—u* This is the first use in the path, but there is no evidence of definition; possibly anomalous.

- *k—* The last thing done to the object in the path was to kill it; normal.

- *d—* The last thing done to the object in the path was to define it; possibly anomalous.

- *u—* The last thing done to the object was to use it; normal.

In the single-letter combinations, Beizer uses the dash to indicate a sequence of actions without a *d, k,* or *u* for the particular data object being analyzed.

Following Beizer's method, we can now use these combinations as we review the program's control flow with respect to its effect on the data. Figure 5.6a repeats the control flow graph of Figure 5.4 and

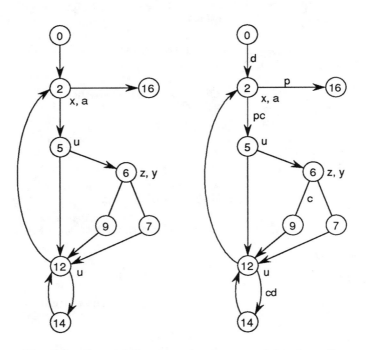

Fig. 5.6.  Control-flow graphs annotated for data flow.

annotates it with the names of the data objects used in the predicates. This graph then can be analyzed for each data object.  For example, Figure 5.6b illustrates the flow for X.  It is defined (*d*) in the link between nodes 0 and 2, used as a predicate and in a calculation (*pc*, which is a detailed form of *uu*) in the link between nodes 2 and 5, and so on.  One can use this flow to identify possible anomalies manually, or one can use it to generate test sets.  It is also possible to develop automated tools that help in the record keeping and reduce the effort. Data-flow testing offers an effective way to identify a relatively large number of bugs.  Moreover, the good coding practices required to support this kind of testability also enhances the quality of the product.

Now that we have identified goals for the test sets, we must prepare the test data.  There are some general rules to follow.  For example, we should test at the boundary of a predicate.  Thus, for the predicate X > 0 the tests should include the case of X = 0.  Often an examination of the outcome will indicate that the predicate was incorrect; it should have been X >= 0.  Of course, this is really not a coding bug; it reflects an inadequate design in which the boundary was not stated clearly.  The next section, on functional or black box testing, deals with these domain issues in a more systematic manner.

## 5.3.4.   Black box testing

In black box testing we are concerned only with the fact that the program or component performs as specified. This introduces a potential problem. The tests can be only as thorough as the specifications. The behaviors of a program can be divided into three categories.

- *Expected*. These are the component's behaviors that are defined as specified outcomes for particular inputs from the input space (i.e., *domain*). That is, for a set of valid inputs, we know what outcome to accept; failure to produce the expected outcome signals the existence of at least one bug.

- *Rejected*. These are the component's behaviors resulting from inputs that are not part of the component's input domain. Clearly we must test to establish that such inputs result in an appropriate response.

- *Rule out*. These are behaviors that are of no concern because they will never occur. For example, if a program expects positive integers and if the system typing ensures that the inputs will be positive integers whenever the program is invoked, then it is not necessary to test the program with nonpositive integer values. In practice, this category consists of the trusted attributes of the software environment; one motivation for more comprehensive environments (e.g., those building on encapsulation techniques or assertion verification) is that they can rule out certain problem states. Those states not ruled out must be tested.

Each of these three categories should be identified and documented; certainly the first two must be defined in the specification (i.e., what to do with valid inputs and what to do if the inputs are invalid). The "rule out" category also should be clearly understood, but it requires no tests.

Consider a test set for a simple program to classify a triangle. Its input is a triple of positive integers, and the data type for the input parameters ensures that they will be integers greater than zero and less than the largest value managed by the computer. The program's output is one of the following words:

[Scalene | Isosceles | Equilateral].

For the expected behaviors, we might try (3,4,5), (4,4,5), and (5,5,5). Each output will be tested. For the rejected behaviors we might try combinations that do not produce triangles such as (1,2,3) or (4,4,100).

The first is a much better test in that it is at the boundary of the domain. It would catch the bug

IF (SIDE1 + SIDE2) < SIDE3 THEN GOTO ERROR,

whereas the second input would not. We need not try combinations with a zero, negative integer values, real values, integer arrays, or character strings; the input data type assures us that we need not care about these situations. We now have the smallest test set we can use. It tests for each expected outcome and one rejected outcome. Do we need more tests? Perhaps there is something about the problem that suggests that the implementation might be dependent on the order of the values in the triple. If so, we should add (4,5,4) and (5,4,4) for the expected outcome and (1,3,2), (2,3,1), (2,1,3), (3,2,1), and (3,1,2) for the rejected outcome. Notice that we have more tests for rejected than for expected outcomes.

The first observation regarding these test cases is that as a result of creating them we have found a bug. (In the previous section, Beizer told us this would happen!) The test cases expect four different outcomes, but the specification defines only three. Therefore, we must alter the output to

[Scalene | Isosceles | Equilateral | Not a triangle].

If this requires a change to the program, we need not run the tests until the program has been corrected; our first test has been successful without ever having been run. A second observation about this example is that if we had thought about the test cases when the program was being designed, then the bug would not have persisted until the time of testing. This, of course, is the message that Gries presented in section 4.3. But, even if one elects not to use proofs of correctness, there are benefits in planning for tests. Bad designs have bugs and are difficult to test; therefore many of their bugs remain undetected until after delivery. Good designs, on the other hand, are testable. Consequently, an early concern for testability can improve the design and reduce the number of bugs to be removed.

Unlike the structural tests of Section 5.3.3, the functional tests are much simpler to set up and run. We seldom have to instrument the software, and we almost always can initiate our tests by invoking a program with a given set of parameters. Thus, the principal function of black box test preparation is the selection of input parameters that will either produce the expected outcome or reject the inputs. Because we cannot exercise the component with every possible combination of input, we seek a more effective method for selecting the tests that will uncover previously undetected bugs. Myers offers the following guidelines for developing those test cases [Myer79].

- The test case should reduce, by more than a count of one, the number of other test cases that must be developed to achieve some predefined goal of "reasonable" testing.

- The test case should cover a large set of other possible test situations. That is, it should tell us something about the presence or absence of errors over and above this specific set of input values.

The most effective way to do this is to identify *equivalence classes* of inputs (or functions) and then test each class. This is called *equivalence partitioning* or *partition testing*.[5] For example, in the triangle problem there were three partitions (the scalene, isosceles, and equilateral triangles), and we selected tests for each partition as well as tests for inputs outside the domain (i.e., the union of all partitions).

Our first objective is to establish which equivalence classes are interesting. If we were testing a program to input telephone numbers, we would find it interesting to establish that it accepted valid numbers with and without an area code. Then we would be interested in the program's ability to recognize area codes with other than a 0 or 1 as the second digit, numbers that were not composed of either 7 or 10 digits, different formatting conventions such as 301-953-5000 and (301) 953-5000, and so on. Uninteresting equivalence classes would be all telephone numbers with an exchange of 792 or all telephones with a 3 in the next-to-last digit. Obviously, separating the interesting from the uninteresting requires an understanding of the program and its intended use. Myers suggests the following method for partitioning.

- Make a list of input conditions. For each, identify at least one valid input and two invalid inputs and describe the expected outcome of the input. Each input represents an equivalence class, and it should be given a label or number.

---

[5] I have chosen to illustrate these concepts using some of Myer's early work, which is both intuitive and easy to explain in a few pages. The approach, however, is dated, and—in that sense—my presentation is distorted. In the past 15 years there has been considerable work in the development of algorithms for producing equivalence classes, and I recommend Beizer's chapter on domain testing for a more thorough and up-to-date discussion.

- First, for the valid equivalence classes, write a new test case that covers as many of the uncovered valid equivalence cases as possible.

- Then, for the invalid equivalence classes, write a test case that covers one, and only one, class.

The reason that we can test more than one valid class at a time is that we are seeking failures. Failure in any one equivalence class will be recognized in the outcome unless there are hidden dependencies among valid classes (which should have been removed during the partitioning process). We must test invalid classes separately, however, because there may be a hierarchy in the program's testing that prohibits the identification of all invalid responses.

In selecting the test cases to be used, Myers notes that we should not rely on arbitrary test data and proposes the method of *boundary-value analysis*. He suggests the following criteria.

- Select one or more elements such that the edge of the equivalence class is the subject of a test. For instance, if the input domain of a computation is defined to be valid for nonnegative values less than or equal to 100, then the valid tests would include the value $10^{-10}$ and 100, and the invalid tests would include the values -1, 0, and 100.001.

- Also consider the *result space* in developing input values. That is, what are the different classes of output, and what inputs are required to produce them. This is the method I used in preparing the test data for the triangle program.

- Try *error guessing* (which Myers lists as a separate technique). Through intuition or experience try to surmise what kinds of errors are probable and then write test cases to expose those errors. Thus, while the methods of equivalence partitioning and boundary analysis may be necessary, they are not sufficient. Sometimes, a good guess will find a bug.

In his section on functional testing, Myers observes, "It is difficult to present a 'cookbook' for boundary-value analysis, since it requires a degree of creativity and a certain amount of specialization toward the problem at hand. (Hence, like many other aspects of testing, it is more a state of mind than anything else.)" [Myer79]

Recognizing that the test will be imperfect, there is the issue of deciding how good a test set is. There are two approaches to this problem. First, we may use historic data that reflect the distribution of errors for this type of product with its required reliability. If the testing has not uncovered the expected number of bugs, then additional testing is suggested. (More on this technique is given in Chapter 6.) The second involves an analysis of the test set. The idea is to calibrate how effective a test set is for a target program with an unknown number of bugs by measuring its performance with the same program and a known set of bugs. The idea of *error seeding*, usually attributed to Mills, is a way to estimate the number of errors in the components being tested [Mill72]. First $S$ errors are seeded into the component so that their placement is statistically similar to that of the actual errors. Prior to the seeding, the test set has been used to discover $I$ errors; when rerun after the seeded errors have been added, $K$ seeded errors will be uncovered. From this we can estimate $E$, the number of errors in the software being tested, as

$$E = IS/K.$$

This estimate of the number of errors originally present can be used to evaluate the effectiveness of the testing and to determine the need for further testing. One criticism of this approach is that the seeded errors are similar to those errors already detected; the kinds are errors that survive the early testing stages tend to be subtle, statistically independent, logical errors, which are not likely to be found in this manner.

*Mutation analysis* is a more scientific extension of this technique [DeML78, DeMM87]. Here a set of mutants of a target program is generated by altering exactly one statement to create each mutant. The alterations reflect the common kinds of program errors found. Two assumptions are used. First, the "competent programmer assumption" states that an incorrect program will not differ very much from the desired program, and second, the "coupling effect" assumes that tests that uncover simple errors will also uncover deeper and more complex errors. The program and its mutants are run against the test set interpretatively. A *mutation score*, $ms(P,T)$ is computed for the program $P$ and test set $T$ as a function of the number of errors found by $T$ in mutants of $P$ that are functionally differentiated from $P$. It has been shown experimentally that mutation scores of .95 or higher provide a very high degree of confidence that the test set will have uncovered all errors and that no errors will be discovered with the program's subsequent use. Because of its heavy computational and data management demands, mutation analysis requires automated support including an interpretative environment.

Most of the methods described in this section have focused on ways of building test sets that will not only exercise the functions of the target components but also uncover bugs in those components. To limit the number of tests to be run, we identify equivalence classes that partition the inputs and select cases from those classes to either produce the expected results or reject the inputs. To maximize the effectiveness of the test cases, we choose values that are on the boundary of the partition where the likelihood of making a mistake is highest. Although this technique has received widespread acceptance, the reader should be aware that some empirical studies are questioning its utility. Hamlet and Taylor report, "comparison between [partition] testing that observes subdomain boundaries and random sampling that ignores the partition gives the counter-intuitive result that partitioning is of little value" [HaTa90]. That is, randomly generated test sets with the same statistical distribution as the data to be processed have been shown to produce better results than partition testing.[6] They assert that partition testing is most effective "when subdomains with a high failure probability can be detected—that is, when the failures are suspected and localized." Naturally, when the prerequisites for random testing have not been met, partition testing is the only option.

Thus, in this imperfect world we must live with uncertainty regarding the validity of the specification, the correctness of the design, the existence of bugs in the implementation, and the strength of the test sets. Errors build on each other, and they become more expensive to remove the later they are detected. Therefore, lacking any foolproof method for identifying bugs, it is far better to avoid their existence than to look for them. This is what Dijkstra set out to do in the T.H.E. system, and another approach is discussed in Section 5.4 on the *cleanroom*. Lacking that discipline, however, there is no alternative to the careful, complete, and systematic act of test design.

### 5.3.5. Integration

The previous three sections described the kinds of tests available for identifying bugs in the software. Static analysis reviews the software text and its surrogates to identify problems, structural testing designs tests based on how the software has been built, and functional testing develops tests using knowledge of what the software is to do. These three techniques are valid for individual programs, units comprised of

---

[6]Notice that the definition of a random sample is quite different from that of an arbitrary test. The random sample is chosen randomly from a statistically valid model, whereas the criterium for an arbitrary test is simply that it satisfy the syntactic constraints. Given a statistically valid model for the functionality (and user profile), random samples are effective in assessing software reliability and detecting some failures. Arbitrary tests at best are inefficient; at worst, they instil a false sense of confidence.

several programs, and complete systems. Each product may be examined with respect to what it is, how it was built, and what it does. For example, we can adapt the white box techniques to a flow graph of a multiprogram component; in fact, such flow graphs can be constructed for components that incorporate both hardware and software. Therefore, integration applies the basic methods just described, but to more complex objects.

Integration can be viewed as the iterative combining of smaller units until a complete system is available for acceptance. Because the full system always includes some hardware (e.g., a computer) and external resources (e.g., users), there is always an evolution from software engineering into system engineering. Depending on the product, the application domain, and the developing organization, the role of the software engineer may be very limited once the software is accepted; in other situations, however, the software engineer may assume the role of the system engineer. For convenience, I assume the latter case in what follows. We begin integration with tested units, accepted and under configuration control; the objective is to culminate with the acceptance of a software system that satisfies its software requirements specification (SRS) and also meets the organization's needs.

Whereas all the tests presented in the previous sections were designed only to identify bugs, we now can think of two types of test.

- *Negative tests*. These are the tests intended to find bugs. In a bug-free system they will always fail; by definition, they are successful only when they find a previously undiscovered bug.

- *Positive tests*. These are designed to demonstrate that the system delivers the services defined in its requirements specification. Some features are functional, others involve performance, user interaction, etc. The tests include the demonstration of expected results and the identification of invalid situations. Although these tests also are designed to find errors, they are positive in the sense that we hope that none will be found.

Naturally the success of a negative test or the failure of a positive test indicates that something is wrong with the system that must be repaired. The objective of the negative tests is to find errors, and that of the positive tests is to certify that the product satisfies the SRS. Because the positive tests come so late in the V&V process, it would be foolish to hope that they would uncover new problems.

How integration is approached depends to a very large extent on how the project has been organized. If this is the $(n+1)$st development of its type and the development team is experienced and there is a thorough and valid SRS, then the team should know how best to integrate and test the components. If, however, this is a system involving hardware and software with a high degree of risk, then a spiral development plan may be appropriate; experience with the prototypes will provide a foundation for anticipating problems in integration. Finally, if the product is being developed incrementally, then the integration plan is predetermined by the sequence of builds.[7] Thus, generalization is difficult. For instance, consider the trade-off between a top-down and a bottom-up approach to testing and integration.

In the top-down method we begin by testing and forming components at the highest level. Programs and components invoked by the "top" are replaced by stubs; once a test has been run successfully, some stubs are replaced by tested programs, and the tests (together with additional tests) are repeated. This continues until the component (which defined the top) has been tested completely. Bottom-up testing, on the other hand, begins by testing the lowest level components first; once they have passed the tests, they will be used in the testing of the next level. (This is the approach advocated by Parnas in Section 4.2.1.) Driver modules (or a test harness) must be prepared to run the tests. Which is better? Myers identifies three advantages for each [Myer79].

- *Advantages of top-down testing.* Best if major flaws occur toward the top of the program. The representation of test cases is easier once the I/O functions are added. The early skeletal program allows an early demonstration, which may boost morale and confidence.

- *Advantages of bottom-up testing.* Best if major flaws occur toward the bottom of the program. The test conditions are easier to create. The observation of test results is easier.

Clearly, the answer must be, "It depends."

In summary, we see that there will be as much variability in integration as there was in design. Once the independent programs are accepted, they will be combined into larger components. Normally, not all the programs will be completed at the same time, and a project will have some development, unit testing, and integration going on at the same time. As shown in Figure 1.3, the criteria for testing is formalized as the software is designed. These criteria are then combined with the

---

[7]Chapter 6 will expand on these concepts further in the context of their management implications. I identify them here only to illustrate how interdependent the technical and management decisions are.

tester's knowledge of the program and application to devise tests intended to break the software. At some point every imaginable problem has been tested for, and there is confidence that no more bugs remain. Although the negative testing will never be complete, we can at this point begin the positive tests. Myers identifies four levels of integration testing [Myer79].

- *Function testing.* This involves negative tests against the program's external specifications. It is intended to find errors, and Myers describes a *cause-effect graphing* technique for exploring the affect of combinations of input circumstances.

- *System testing.* This is a positive test against all the requirements. Clearly, there is no need to rerun all the negative tests because every error that has been uncovered is now corrected, and—through regression testing—we are confident that any bugs introduced during the repair process also have been removed. The definition of "system" is open; all that is required is an SRS against which to test. Myers warns, "of all the testing phases, this is the one that should *definitely* not be performed by the organization responsible for developing the program." After they have completed the testing and integration activities, one would expect the system to conform to the developers' understanding of the SRS. Therefore, it is best to get a different group of testers for the system tests.

  System testing normally is more concerned with validity than with correctness. It addresses the question of, "Is this the right system?" In the sense of the essential software process, most defects will be found in the conceptual model rather than in the implementation of the formal model. Testing uses the formal model to determine incorrectness, and a through testing plan will have removed most of those errors. An evaluation of the software's ability to satisfy the identified need, however, may not be possible until the software system exists—a fact that reinforces the requirement for an independent group of system testers.

- *Acceptance testing.* This test is usually performed by the customer to demonstrate that the system satisfies the contractual requirements. Usually the customer will witness the system testing, and the effort devoted to the acceptance testing will be determined by the resources and knowledge available, the participation in reviewing the V&V activities, and the type of product.

- *Installation testing.* These tests are conducted at the time of installation, and their intent is to determine installation errors. If the software is part of a larger system with hardware, then the installation testing is actually a part of the system integration effort.

Although I have identified system testing as a positive test, this should not be taken to imply that it is a pro forma or casual test. Every system attribute—both functional and nonfunctional, explicit and implicit—must be tested to confirm that proper use provides the desired results and that improper use is not harmful. The definition of the desired results must be predefined in the SRS; without that definition there are no criteria for determining if a test outcome is satisfactory. Depending on the application, the central role of the SRS can present a problem. For instance, in the SCM system case study, the true requirement was to provide automated support to the SCM process. An SRS then was developed that described how that support should be provided, and development of the system was expected to be correct with respect to the SRS. However, during the development of the software much would have been learned about the problem, and some changes will have been made to the SRS to reflect this improved understanding. If the SRS were *not* maintained under configuration control and if the changes were *not* incorporated into a revised SRS, then the system test *should* fail. Yet, given that the SRS has been maintained and that the tests succeed, all that will have been demonstrated is that the finished software operates as the SRS specified. There is no guarantee that the software will be effective in providing "automated support to the SCM process."

Unfortunately, there is no way a tester can validate that the goals of the system (as opposed to its specification) will be met. In situations like this, the developer may augment the testing with two levels of user involvement. In the *alpha tests* a small number of users work with the system at the developer's site, and the developers observe how the system is used. Errors are detected and new test sets are designed. Once the system is shown to perform effectively, a prerelease version of the system is sent to the customer's site for a *beta test*. Again, errors are reported, and new insights into the system's use develop. The results of these tests may lead to the correction of errors, the modification of the SRS, or ideas to be incorporated into the next release. This approach is common with the development of open applications with nonspecific objectives (e.g., an SCM system or a PC-based word processor). For most engineering applications, however, the requirements are exact, and alpha and beta tests are not useful; well-defined criteria exist to establish that the software does precisely what is expected of it.

Myers observes, "Because of the absence of a methodology, system testing requires a substantial amount of creativity; in fact, the design of good system test cases requires more creativity, intelligence, and experience than that required to design the system or program" [Myer-79]. He then goes on to identify 15 categories of test that should be explored when designing test cases.

- *Facility testing.* Does the system provide the expected facilities (i.e., functions)?

- *Volume testing.* Does the system manage large volumes of data in a reasonable way?

- *Stress testing.* Does the system respond in a reasonable way to heavy loads?

- *Usability testing.* Myers describes this as a subjective evaluation of the system's ease of use. A more modern and objective definition of usability for human-computer interaction was given in Section 2.4.1.

- *Security testing.* Does the system satisfy the security and privacy objectives?

- *Performance testing.* Does the system meet its response time or throughput objectives?

- *Storage objectives.* Does the system operate within the available main and secondary storage limitations?

- *Configuration testing.* If the system is to operate on a variety of machine configurations, a representative sample should be tested.

- *Compatibility/conversion testing.* If the system replaces part of some older system, is it compatible with the existing system and can the old system be converted to the new one?

- *Installability testing.* Do the installation procedures (e.g., an operating system sysgen) operate properly?

- *Reliability testing.* This is difficult to test, but there are statistical methods (discussed below in Section 5.4) that provide an estimate for reliability.

- *Recovery testing.* If the system fails, how effective is recovery?

- *Serviceability testing.* How serviceable and maintainable is the system? This is difficult to assess in the abstract, but standards can be developed that facilitate maintainability. Thus, this testing may actually be a review of the product to ensure that the standards are being followed. Of course, this review of the product for conformance to standards is part of the SCM audit process; therefore, an effective SCM system (either automated or manual) enhances serviceability.

- *Documentation testing.* Is the documentation accurate, readable, and complete?

- *Procedure testing.* When a system is to be used by people, then the procedures to be followed by the system's users must be tested.

In describing these tests, Myers points out that the objective should be to find data that will make them fail. This implies an adversarial relationship between the developer and tester. The developer tries to anticipate every problem and make the system correct with respect to the SRS, and the tester uses the same context in order to find fault with the system. Clearly, finding problems before the users do is beneficial to both the developers and testers. I have called the system tests positive in the sense that they are not intended to find bugs; rather, their objective is to exercise the system as severely as possible to certify that it is correct. After the system is accepted and changes have been made, this same certification process must be repeated if we are to maintain confidence in the system. Of course, we can consider the system test positive *only if* we have already run negative tests for each testing category *before* system testing begins. For example, we need to model performance and throughput at an early stage in the design. If these are critical properties of the system, then some prototypes or simulations may be necessary. Key components should be given a performance or throughput budget and tested against that budget as early as possible. Waiting to find that we have failed at the time of system test—when the implementation is complete—is a very poor strategy.

## 5.4.    The cleanroom

This chapter started with a review of the software process and contrasted the building of a bridge with the implementation of software. Whereas the goal of software testing is error discovery, bridge "testing" is seen as a certification process. The engineers are expected to produce a bridge design that will be accepted as correct and valid. After construction begins, changes are expensive; consequently, bridge building (and most hardware manufacture) is optimized for error removal *prior* to implementation. In software, however, there is a perception that errors are inevitable and that debugging and machine testing are the best way to remove them. Justifications for this belief include software's limited experience base and its associated lack of handbooks, the absence of an external constraining reality, and the fact that machine testing is both relatively inexpensive and feasible. As a result, a rationale has been justified that permits developers to defer a complete understanding of the product's behavior until after it has been implemented.

This book has presented several methods for getting it right the first time. Working from formal specifications defines the system's behavior at the outset and ensures that the product satisfies those specifications. Proof of correctness establishes the desired state changes and builds a program that will realize them. There is at least a decade of experience with these methods, and they are successful. There also are demonstrated techniques for refining the specifications when there is uncertainty. The two basic methods cited are prototypes, in which experimentation leads to a specification for the entire system, and incremental development, in which layers of the system are specified and implemented on top of previously defined layers (builds). This ability to develop a system incrementally is a unique property of software. Because software is not bound by an external reality, there are a very large number of ways in which a software system may be layered.

The *cleanroom* approach combines mathematical verification with software's facility for incremental development; the result is an analogue of the hardware development process. Introduced by Mills, Dyer, and Linger in the early 1980s, the intent is to deny entry of defects during software development, hence the term "cleanroom" [MiDL87, SeBB87]. As with bridge building, one produces a design that is correct and valid before implementation begins; incremental development is used to reduce the work tasks to small units whose progress may be tracked easily. If the design is indeed error free, then the traditional error-detection role of testing will not be necessary. Because we expect no errors to be found, a better goal of testing is to measure the probability of the zero-defect assertion. Whenever the desired level of reliability has not been achieved, corrective action can be taken in the next iteration. Thus, the concept of testing as postimplementation bug removal is deemphasized, and the inevitability of software errors can be measured.

The method combines four major characteristics.

- *Software life cycle of executable increments.* The software is developed in increments, and each incremental stage of development is assessed with regard to reliability. Testing results affect subsequent increments; consequently, the cycle involves iterations of development and testing. Both development and testing are guided by a formal specification. Through stepwise refinement, a *structured specification* is decomposed into a nested set of subspecifications that creates the levels of software design.

- *Formal methods for specification and design.* Because the design begins with a formal specification, criteria exist to determine if the resulting program is correct with respect to the specification. (In contrast, the traditional trial-and-error process begins with an incomplete—or informal—specification, and error identification is used to resolve uncertainties.) The method for verification is called *functional verification* (in contrast to axiomatic verification). It reduces software verification to ordinary mathematical reasoning about sets and functions as directly as possible. When a program seems difficult to verify, then it is rewritten into a form that will be easy to verify; in this way, all programs are clear and well understood.

- *Development without program execution.* Because the goal is to get it right the first time, emphasis is placed on comprehension and verification. Developers are denied the ability to machine test (and therefore debug) their programs. An editor provides syntax testing, and there are static analyzers for data flow, type checking, concurrency analysis, etc. The objective, however, is the production of a coherent, readable design. The methods to achieve this goal are called "off-line software review techniques"; they include code reading by stepwise abstraction [LiMW79], code inspections, group walkthroughs, and formal verification. The belief is that problem solving is a human activity that benefits from a mathematical framework for assessing the quality of potential solutions. In this context, observing some of the operational behaviors of an intended solution (i.e., machine testing) is less effective than mathematically reasoning about all behaviors. This reasoning is carried out as both individual and group activities.

- *Statistically based, independent testing.* An independent test team receives the program source code and compiles it for the first time. The programs then are integrated with previous system increments, and the new system is tested with randomly generated data that reflect the statistical distributions of the target system's inputs. The data sets are derived from information in the formal specification; naturally, without a formal specification to define the inputs, statistically based testing would not be possible. Test sets normally emphasize the functions delivered in the most recent increment. A limited number of additional test cases are produced by the testers to ensure correct system operation for situations in which a software failure would be catastrophic. The intent of the test team is to access the reliability of the software [CuDM86]; unlike the testing techniques described in Section 5.3, the goal is not to find errors. If the tests do not indicate that the desired level of quality is being achieved, then earlier increments must be reworked. In this way, testing complements development while providing a better measure of system reliability.

The cleanroom approach has been used in a production setting since the mid-1980s. Among the first systems to be implemented in this way are an IBM COBOL restructuring tool (80K lines), an Air Force helicopter flight program (35K lines), and a NASA system (30K lines). There also has been an empirical evaluation of student experience with the method [SeBB87]. The general conclusion is that the resulting programs are more reliable than programs developed with the traditional life-cycle model, that the time required to produce a verified program is less than or the same as the time necessary to design, code, and debug a program, that the method of functional verification scales up to large programs, and that statistical quality control is superior to the time-honored technique of finding and removing bugs.

To illustrate the benefit of statistical testing, consider Table 5.6 which summarizes data collected by Adams on software failures for nine major IBM projects [Adam84]. It displays the mean time between failures (MTBF) reported for these projects in operational years (i.e., if a product has been installed at 100 sites for one year and only one failure was reported, then the MTBF would be 100 years). Two contrasting measures are shown.

- *Average percentage failures.* This figure accounts for the percentage of the total number of fixes made. For example, 33.4% of the corrections were made to the rare failures whose MTBF was greater than 5000 years.

Table 5.6.  Software failures from nine IBM products.

| MTBF (years) | Over 5000 | 500 - 5000 | 50 - 500 | Under 50 |
|---|---|---|---|---|
| Average percentage failures | 33.4 | 46.9 | 15.8 | 3.9 |
| Probability of a failure for this frequency | 0.008 | 0.065 | 0.202 | 0.724 |

Extracted from [CoMi90], with permission, ©1990, IEEE.

- *Probability of a failure for this frequency.* This figure computes the probability that a user will be affected by a failure in this category. For example, the probability is 0.008 that an individual user will be impacted by a failure that has an MTBF of more than 5000 years.

Thus, the table shows that 33.4% of the fixes were devoted to failures that had a 0.008 probability of being seen by a user, whereas only 3.9% of the fixes were devoted to errors that had a 0.724 probability of impacting the user. If the distribution of effort to repair errors is roughly independent of the MTBF, then this table suggests that IBM spent one-third of its error-correction budget on failures that its customers hardly ever saw and less than 4% of its budget on the failures that represented almost three-quarters of all the failures encountered by its customers! Clearly, this is not an effective allocation of resources.[8]

These data indicate that not all errors are equal; there is a difference between *discoverable* errors and *important* errors. If we spend our V&V budget on just discovering errors, it is not clear that we will find the important errors. To find the important errors we must look for properties of the software that are operationally significant, not just the attributes that are likely to be coded wrong. Cobb and Mills assert that

[8]This may be seen as an illustration of the Pareto 80-20 phenomena in which some 80% of a process can be accounted for by 20% of the population. In this case we find that almost 20% of the effort was devoted to fixes associated with the 80% of the failures most likely to affect users. As will be discussed in Section 6.2.2, the benefit of finding an 80-20 relationship is that it will suggest how a careful analysis of the 20% can yield an 80% improvement. In this case, however, the data imply an inverse-Pareto relationship in which 80% of the effort is devoted to only 20% of the problem.

this may best be done by statistical quality control (i.e., the functional testing of the systems using randomly generated test sets with the same statistical distributions as the specified inputs) [CoMi90]. They present evidence to support their claim from projects developed with and without the cleanroom approach. When the cleanroom is used, of course, there is no need for structural testing; the programs already have been verified with respect to what they are to do, which includes the details of how they do it.

## 5.5. A summing up

The concept of V&V was introduced as a backward-looking activity that provided an independent evaluation of the quality of the forward-directed modeling (i.e., design) process. Sometimes textbooks associate V&V with quality assurance (QA). Both are concerned with properties of the delivered system. V&V is the task of identifying and removing bugs that may inhibit a product from doing its job. QA involves a more complete concern for the product and its mode of implementation; it includes the product's operation plus the ability to revise and transition it [CaMc78]. I have chosen not to address the nature of quality in this chapter. Its dimensions were presented in Section 2.4.2 as implicit requirements. In that sense, I believe that we should treat the quality goals just as we do any other requirements. During V&V we should assure ourselves that the appropriate quality standards have been identified and are being met. That is part of our backward-looking assignment. I think of "quality" as a set of overlapping system properties that is formalized early in the process and is appraised continually. It is an integral part of the product being developed or maintained; it cannot be added at the end.[9]

How do we ensure all the dimensions of quality? The chapter has taken us through a full circle. Figure 5.1, which displays Jones's matrix of methods and defects, indicates that the best way to find errors is through reviews (i.e., thinking about the problem and its solution). The table lists machine testing as the least effective general method.

---

[9]There are many different definitions for quality. Perhaps the most intuitive description is that quality is a measure of the buyer's perception that the software product performs as expected. Notice how this concept incorporates the ideas of validation (the product corresponds to the needs of the environment), verification (the product performs as specified), and the ilities (the product is portable, maintainable, reliable, etc.). Like good art, quality software is difficult to define but—with experience—easy to recognize. The software engineer, lacking a precise definition for quality, must learn to recognize (and to react) when the quality is deficient. Failure to do so will lead to the loss of his customers.

However, most of Section 5.3 was devoted to machine testing. In effect, half of this chapter has focused on what—in some "big-picture" sense—may be considered of secondary importance: the mistakes that we make as a byproduct of realizing the implementation. (Fortunately, the testing research community has been developing automated and semi-automated test design tools that will relegate much of this work to our environments.) The brief section on the cleanroom returned us to the idea of human verification through reviews and effective formalisms. Without a formal statement of what we intend to deliver, there can be neither a concept of correctness nor a standard against which to test. Frequently, projects do not have good specifications, and we must recognize that fact; there are ways of structuring the software process to refine problem understanding. When, on the other hand, we begin with an agreed formal statement of the objectives, we also have the criteria to test the design decisions. We do this by thinking about the correct-ness of the solution and by thinking about the test cases that might find bugs in the solution. This thinking is far more fruitful than the automated tools we employ.

What does that tell us as software engineers? I conclude with two observations.

- First, the software process is basically a human, problem-solving activity in which some of the tasks can be relegated to the computer. Today we expect the system to compile the code automatically; perhaps in a few decades program verification will be supported as well. We require methods that emphasize the human contribution to the process, but we also need conceptual frameworks in which to evaluate the quality of the solutions. All problem solving involves iteration, and this implies errors in the partial solutions. Because the end product of the software process is a mathematically formal object (e.g., source code), an early application of the appropriate mathematical principles improves the evaluation and verification of software.

- Second, the software process is undergoing change. Early researchers focused on the software product (i.e., the program) and its testing. Current research places more emphasis on the system specification. The program can be viewed as the most detailed expression of the specification, and its behavior can be studied independent of its execution. This reorientation (which is not yet fully appreciated) leads us to question other accepted "facts." We find that program bugs are not unavoidable, that not all errors have the same impact, and that different project management paradigms are available. Thus, to help understand why we do what we currently do, today's software engineer must be aware of the state of practice and its historic base. But to evaluate the many alternatives to the present practice, he also needs a holistic view of the software process.

Of course, these observations should come as no surprise. In fact, if this the reader's first book on software engineering, the presentation may have become repetitious. But if the reader is an experienced software engineer, then what I have been saying for so long may just now start to become clear.

Drawing by John O'Brien; ●1989 The New Yorker Magazine, Inc.

# 6

## MANAGING THE PROCESS

We all know about icebergs. The captain of the Titanic taught us a lesson we will never forget. But I think that we have a different perception of seals. Even sealions. Capturing one seems like a reasonable goal to an Eskimo. Still, as O'Brien's drawing shows us, there are risks; we may end up with much more than we expected.

This chapter on management parallels the chapters on modeling. In the earlier chapters, the objective was first to understand a need or a design and then to represent that knowledge in a model. With management the process is reversed. We start with a model (or plan) that describes how we expect the project to turn out, and then we manage the project to make the model come true. Of course, we are never so foolish as to expect our models to be sacred. We must periodically validate the models as we follow them.

The chapter begins with a review of management, management tools, and methods for management modeling. The drawing reminds us that risk management is one of our principal concerns. Methods for instituting a proactive risk management program are presented, and the project organization alternatives that reduce risks are considered. As it turns out, there are a lot of things one can do before feeling a strong tug on the harpoon line.

Several kinds of models are described: for costs and schedule, reliability, and software complexity. The reader is warned, however, that these models are unlike the formulas of physics. We are not measuring invariant phenomena; we are describing *how* we conduct the process. There are strong interactions between the processes and the models, and we must be as careful as that Eskimo.

A major portion of the chapter is devoted to process improvement. How we can make it better. The discussion considers methods for assessment and evaluation. A case study demonstrates that process analysis sometimes yields surprising results. There is also a review of the technologies for reuse, reengineering, and CASE. The bottom line: no silver bullet.

The theme of the chapter is that project management, when done properly, should seem effortless. The manager's job should appear to be trivial. So easy, anyone could do it. Just like capturing a sealion.

## 6.1.   Overview of management

I have described design as forward looking, verification and validation (V&V) as backward looking, and management as downward looking. Although that description may not make immediate sense, it does suggest a perspective that most people share: it places management above the detailed work, looking down. Actually, management has the most difficult of all the jobs in a software development. If they are successful, there will be little evidence that they have done anything. Each designer will be able to point to concepts, documents, and code that he created; each member of the V&V team will have produced products and reports to show for his efforts. But the effective manager will be rewarded only with, "You were lucky, that was a very simple assignment."

Software project management is, like all other activities in the software process, a problem-solving enterprise. As such, it involves a recognition of what is to be done, a decision regarding how to do it, the monitoring of how it is being done, and an evaluation of what was done. The "what" typically takes the form of a plan and the "how" an allocation of resources (e.g., a schedule or budget). Too often, managers stop after these two initial problem-solving steps. Of course, that is an invitation to disaster. The project is dynamic, and the plans will become invalid. More time was required than expected; new requirements were introduced; key personnel were called away. The manager must monitor the activity and adjust the plans and schedules accordingly. He also must evaluate the success of the plans. We learn from the feedback that follows our mistakes. Thus, if management does not exploit postevent evaluations, the process may never improve.

Although management, design, and V&V are all problem-solving activities, each solves a very different kind of problem. At one time we perceived that careers normally progressed from maintenance programmer, to designer, to supervisor, to manager. That is, what one learned doing the job would be used managing the job. But this is not true. Brooks's admonition to develop great designers is based on the fact that design is quite different from management [Broo87]. Skills in one domain may not translate to the other, and excellence in any domain should be rewarded with opportunities for continued growth. Thus, the manager is not a "technical guy who made good"; rather he is a member of the team with a specialized assignment. What kinds of problems does the software project manager solve? Here are a few.

- For a specific task, do we have the necessary resources (e.g., funding, people, time) to achieve the objective?

- How certain are we that the task objective is stated correctly?

- Given certain constraints on resources, how can they be utilized to the best effect?

- How does recent progress on a task alter the validity of the current plan?

- What lessons can be learned from this task that will improve performance in future tasks?

Notice that the manager need not know how to solve the technical problems that he is managing; he need only understand what the technical people are proposing.

Regrettably, empirical evidence suggests that managers are not very effective in this kind of problem solving. In a paper titled "Software Failures Are Management Failures," Wingrove lists the 16 most common reasons given by project management for failure to meet budget, timescale, and specifications [Wing87]. Redmill organizes these reasons as follows [Redm90].

### Perennial software problems
Incomplete and ambiguous requirements
Incomplete and imprecise specifications
Difficulties in modeling systems
Uncertainties in cost and resource estimation

### Symptoms of inadequate management
General lack of visibility
Difficulties with progress monitoring
Complicated error and change control
Lack of agreed metrics
Difficulties in controlling maintenance

### Decisions that need to be made
Lack of common terminology
Uncertainties in software/hardware apportionment
Rapid changes in technology
Determining the suitability of languages

### Other technical issues
Measuring and predicting reliability
Problems with interfacing
Problems with integration

Redmill continues by observing that when audits are conducted, the following shortcomings are common. There is a lack of standards or a failure to comply to existing standards. In particular, the overall project plan (i.e., the life-cycle model) is not adhered to. There are no sign-offs at the end of stages, the project plans are often unavailable, and no project-control statistics are recorded or stored. There is a lack of procedures for quality assurance (QA), change control, and/or configuration control. The records of test data and results are not kept.

Here is a catalogue of management ineptitudes. Can we correct the problem by insisting on the complement of each failed policy? Unfortunately, no. In his research on work motivation, Herzberg identified some factors that served to motivate (such as achievement) and other factors that, if negative, would contribute to dissatisfaction (such as company policy) [HeMS59]. The latter he called *hygiene factors*; they do not motivate when positive, but they inhibit work motivation when negative. Further, he showed that the motivator factors were related to job content, while the hygiene factors are related to job context. Most of the shortcomings listed in the previous paragraphs relate to the context of software development. Clearly, we must correct those deficiencies, but the effect will be only hygienic. We cannot expect rigorous procedures and standards alone to improve project performance. Ultimately, we must consider the content of what we are managing if we are to improve the process. That is, we must restructure the process by both removing what is bad and fostering what is good.

The remainder of this chapter is divided into two main sections. The first describes how we manage software projects. Although it does contain some "how to" information, the emphasis is on understanding and improving the process. It is assumed that this chapter will be read by persons who someday will have the responsibility for project management, and so I stress what Herzberg might call the motivator rather than the hygiene factors. (I also assume that the reader is familiar with what I have written in the earlier chapters.) The second major section is a review of technology improvements. Although it may seem strange to defer this discussion until a nontechnical chapter on management, process improvement is really a management responsibility. Management must expend the resources, train the people, and evaluate the results. Simply buying some CASE tools seldom improves the process, but a process improvement program often involves the buying of CASE tools.

## 6.2.    Principles of software project management

The first question that one should address is how software project management differs from other technical management domains, or indeed from nontechnical management. Each project or organization is identified by a set of goals or objectives, and management's responsibility is to meet those objectives in the most effective manner. The manager can control only three things.

- *Resources.* This can be in the form of dollars, facilities, or personnel. While dollars often are used to purchase other types of resource, sometimes this may not be possible. For example, time on the computer or in a test facility may be limited, or there may be a scarcity of developers with some specialized knowledge.

- *Time.* This, of course, is the schedule. Brooks's Law states that *Adding manpower to a late software project makes it later* [Broo-75]. Thus, the most practical schedule changes are extensions rather than contractions.

- *Product.* Whether the product is software, hardware, or a service, it always is possible to reduce its functionality or quality. Naturally, there is a lower bound below which the product loses its utility.

As it turns out, these three categories are highly interdependent. For example, if a process is out of control and the resources and time are fixed, then the only alternative is to change the product. Of course, that is why software projects are perceived to be so poorly managed. They begin with optimistic assumptions for the resources, time, and product, and then management must make adjustments after the work is underway. As with the repair of software defects, the later the need for an adjustment is discovered, the more costly that adjustment will be.

Here are some general principles for all kinds of management.

- Understand the goals and objectives. Formalize or quantify them as best you can (e.g., the number of customers served per hour in a fast food restaurant or the specification for a software product to be delivered).

- Understand the constraints. Again, formalize or quantify them. Where there is uncertainty, develop a probability estimate and work to refine it (e.g., the likelihood that a necessary piece of equipment will be delivered in time to support the testing of some software modules).

- Plan to meet the objectives within the constraints. Planning is a forward-looking activity, but it is an essential part of all problem solving. If you do not know where you are going, then you will never know how far you still have to go. Note that the plan presupposes knowledge of the objectives and constraints; if you have no idea where you are, a map may be of little help.

■ Monitor and maintain the plan. This is the backward-looking part of problem solving. If the plan were perfect, then no action will be required. This seldom happens. The benefit of a plan is that it provides a mechanism for early problem identification. The earlier a problem is identified and reacted to, the less the impact of that problem on the project. Without monitoring, some problems will go by unnoticed and others will threaten the organization's success.

■ Make adjustments as appropriate. I already mentioned the three dimensions of control available to the manager. These will have to be applied as problems are identified. Naturally, the problems should be ranked, and the most drastic interventions should be reserved only for the most threatening problems. An organization can respond to only a limited number of major changes and still remain efficient.

■ Preserve a calm, productive, and positive work environment. Whether we are serving hamburgers in a fast food restaurant or developing mission-critical software, the role of the individual is central. Good management knows how to protect its key workers from the uncertainties beyond their control and how to maintain an environment in which each contributes his best.

These principles all support the general concept of keeping the project within control. Once it is out of control, the team members tend to react to problems. There is no time to anticipate difficulties, and major defects can develop unnoticed. The problems in the Hubble Space Telescope, described in Section 5.1, resulted from reactive management.

Is there anything special about the management of software projects? Kichenham offers the following observation.

I regard conventional project management techniques as those appropriate to dealing with long-linked technology, i.e., serially independent production in which sequential activities are coordinated by means of a plan. Such techniques are sufficient for dealing with manufacturing processes but are not necessarily sufficient to handle software production, which is a design process.

Walker [Walk81] argues that software production is an "intensive technology," i.e., a process geared to the production of highly dependent components that must be coordinated by mutual adjustment rather than by plan. He suggests that there are two major characteristics of software projects that need to be managed:

- the translation of information from one representation to another
- the ease with which software may be changed.

The first characteristic leads to the need to facilitate communication across translation points, the second to the need to control the change process. [Kitc90, p. 23]

She goes on to add one more characteristic of software, it usually involves novelty, which introduces uncertainty.

This is a very thoughtful and concise description. Nevertheless, the general principles for project management still hold. The properties of what is being managed may be different with software, but the process of its management remains the same. For example, when building a bridge there will be a point when the general architecture is complete and the engineers are ready to begin the detailed design. Before that detailed design can start, however, management must have sufficient confidence in the architecture to warrant the commencement of the next phase. This is typically accomplished with a design review. Software managers have similar responsibilities, which are independent of the project's organization (e.g., waterfall, spiral, or incremental) or product type (e.g., real-time, information, or imaging system). Both the bridge builder and the software manager have a plan composed of a sequence of discrete events, each of which initiates a decision. They manage according to these events, and they monitor performance to predict if the events will take place as expected. The underlying rule is, "No surprises." In that sense, software development is similar to bridge building; it differs, of course, in the nature of the events and the form of the data used to estimate progress.

If the management of a software project is similar to the management of other technical projects, are there special considerations regarding the structure of a software organization? Naturally, this will depend on the size, setting, and mission of the software group. Typically, the following software-related activities must be provided.

- *Software development*, which is the analysis of the software system and its implementation.

- *Software maintenance*, which is the maintenance of existing software products. Most of this work involves enhancements.

- *Verification and validation,* which verifies at each phase that the product satisfies its quality attributes and the requirements of the previous phase.

- *Quality assurance,* which verifies that the development process and the products conform to the established standards and procedures.

- *Configuration management,* which includes monitoring and controlling the program versions and data throughout the product's lifetime.

- *Systems engineering,* which ensures that the software components satisfy the system requirements and objectives.

In very large projects, each activity becomes the responsibility of an independent unit. For organizations with projects of 50 or fewer people, V&V, QA, and CM often are merged into a single group; for smaller organizations it also is common to have the development team assume all responsibilities. As discussed in the previous chapter, there are inherent difficulties in having designers test their own software (e.g., the system test and the cleanroom's independent test team). When the scale of the organization will not permit separate groups for each activity, extra care must be taken to ensure that no ancillary activity tasks are ignored.

Finally, there is the question regarding the nature of software development; is it different from other types of creative technical work? In the 1960s and early 1970s software development was equated with programming, and much effort was expended on trying to identify the characteristics of people who could be trained to be good programmers. With the growth of academic programs, those predictors have become less important. Nevertheless, little was found to separate programmers from other technical specialists (e.g., engineers and accountants) in what motivates them [Wood80] or from all workers in the satisfiers they reported [Fitz78]. In general, therefore, there is nothing to suggest that software development needs to be managed differently from other creative, knowledge-intensive, technical work (which may have been a myth developed during an earlier, supply-restricted, job-hopping era).

Even though we have not been able to differentiate software from other development categories, there have been continuing attempts to do so. For example, the idea of a Chief Programmer Team received considerable attention in the early 1970s [Bake72]. The results of one very successful IBM project were published that suggested a promising new approach for organizing software projects. I mention it here because, even though I doubt that it is widely practiced, references to it are common. In the initial experiment, the team was structured with a Chief Programmer (in this case, Harlan Mills), an assistant (Terry Baker), two to five other programmers, and a librarian who managed the batch computer runs and maintained the system listings as a common, public record. Technical leadership was provided by the Chief Programmer (or the assistant in his absence), and the code was open for all members of the team to examine. In retrospect, we see that the Chief Programmer Team shared some of the ideas of egoless programming and group reviews. When evaluating this type of organization, however, it is difficult to separate the effects of team organization, the principles exploited by the team, and the extraordinary intellectual capacity of the initial team leaders. In any event, software engineering textbooks continue to discuss the advantages and disadvantages of this type of organization, and I felt that I should at least describe it. For a more current view of software teams, see [Rett90].

A second examination of software development organization, which has received considerably less attention, was reported by Licker [Lick83]. By way of background, in 1960 McGregor classified management styles as conforming to either Theory X (authoritarian) or Theory Y (participative and supportive); each theory was based on the perception that the individual may not be or may be responsibility-seeking and eager to work [McGr60]. The result is an ethos for the firm, and an individual—independent of his innate abilities—cannot advance until he becomes accustomed to the style and feeling of the firm. In 1982 Ouchi wrote a book on the Japanese approach to management, and he introduced the next step, *Theory Z* [Ouch82]. A Type Z (American) organization operates in harmony with the Japanese philosophy of life-time employment, slow evaluation and promotion, non-specific career paths, implicit control mechanisms, collective decision-making and responsibility, and holistic concerns. Software-related firms in Ouchi's list of Type Z organizations include IBM, Hewlett-Packard, and Xerox. Briefly, the individual loyalty is to the organization and group, and career paths emphasize cross training over specialization.

In the following extract, Licker first cites some observations made by Kraft [Kraf77], and then comments on the benefit of the holistic approach.

> Instead of a concern with the *total* person and his relationship with to the organization, management offers tit-for-tat paychecks, narrow specialization, and early obsolescence [Kraf77].
>
> With a holistic approach, managers would take a broad view of the work environment rather than focus on specialized tasks such as producing code or debugging. In a holistic environment, a programmer would be responsible for completing programs; the manager for assuring the programmer does this.

> But most programmers work in an environment that is not holistic. And those programmers who don't become obsolete early may opt for the obsolescence of programmer supervision. Still others move into systems analysis. The remainder, suggests Kraft, become a faceless, unpromotable mass of second-class programmers whose sole motivation is to work for money. [Lick83, p. 633]

A dismal picture, and I am not sure I concur with it. But the alternative is certainly worth considering.

> The Type Z firm would not fear rotating prospective programmers into and through marketing, finance, and production areas. Traditionally, our vocational distinctions have set programming apart from occupations in these areas yet this is only partly justified. Each requires technical dexterity, symbolic abilities, task organization, and problem-solving skills. While a programmer may not understand linear programming, price-demand elasticity or consumer behavior, he or she probably did not know CICS until the in-house training program covered it. And if he takes a month to learn a concept in marketing that a marketing graduate picks up in a week, at least when the programmer returns to the data processing shop, he's got some idea of what a marketing analyst brings to the terminal.
> . . . A choice of programming for a vocation shouldn't automatically disqualify a person from working in other areas. [Lick83, p. 634]

The two quotations place different emphases on what the software engineer can do. In the first case, he exploits his current technological knowledge, which has a half-life of five years. In the second case, he develops his problem-solving skills by both building richer conceptual models and expanding his knowledge of the technology for implementing solutions. Clearly the second alternative is the better path for career satisfaction for the individual; it is a motivator. Because a software organization is constrained by the ability of its personnel, such growth also is beneficial to the employer. If one simplifies Theory Z as representing an exchange of job security for a commitment to the class of problem being addressed, then it probably is not very different from Brooks's advice to develop great designers [Broo87]. As software engineers, the experience we gain is a more valuable corporate asset than the technical knowledge we start out with. As managers of software engineers, we need to recognize this fact and encourage the most gifted to experience design, operations, and management and then select the assignments that offer them the greatest professional growth.

Finally, to conclude this alphabet of theories, consider Theory W introduced by Boehm and Ross [BoRo89]. Succinctly stated, Theory W is to *make everybody a winner*. It has two subsidiary principles: *Plan the flight and fly the plan*; and, *Identify and manage your risks*. The software manager's problem stems from his having to respond to many different (and sometimes conflicting) groups, such as those composed of bosses, customers, users, maintainers, and subordinates. In these interactions, he has but three planning alternatives: win-win, win-lose, or lose-lose. The choice should be obvious. In a sense, Theory W builds on what Fisher and Ury label *Getting to Yes* [FiUr81]. One develops a win-win situation by separating the people from the problem, focusing on interests and not positions, inventing options for mutual gain, and insisting on objective criteria. The approach to software project management is summarized in the following three steps.

1. **Establish a set of win-win preconditions.**
   a. Understand how people want to win.
   b. Establish reasonable expectations.
   c. Match people's tasks to their win conditions.
   d. Provide a supportive environment.

2. **Structure a win-win software process.**
   a. Establish a realistic process plan.
   b. Use the plan to control the project.
   c. Identify and manage your win-lose or lose-lose risks.
   d. Keep people involved.

3. **Structure a win-win software product.**
   a. Match product to users', maintainers' win conditions.

Although Theory W is presented in the context of software project management, it is clear that the principles employed are universal.

### 6.2.1.  *Tools for technical management*

We are about to develop a model for the software project to be managed and then validate that model against the actual conduct of the project. If we have a great deal of experience with this type of project, then our model will be valid. All events will occur as predicted. If, as is the general case, the reality of the project's conduct does not conform to the predictive model, then we have two choices: alter the conduct or modify the model. Usually, we will do both. We will recognize that unanticipated events have affected the project in ways that invalidate some of the assumptions on which the model was predicated (e.g., a necessary piece of equipment has not arrived, a proposed solution was flawed, key personnel are unavailable).  In this case the model must be altered to reflect the project's new reality.  Using the model as a guide, we also may notice that planned events will not occur as scheduled (e.g., the development of a module is behind schedule, the users are not available to evaluate a prototype, vacation schedules delay a task's completion).  Here, managers are expected to react to the microproblems before they become macroproblems (i.e., threaten the success of the project).  Using the three dimensions of control at their disposal, managers can modify aspects of local plans without having those changes impact the larger project (or global) plan.  In both situations, the plan (or model) is revised.  In the first case the model was inaccurate; we need to learn from that experience to improve the quality of subsequent models.  In the second case, management is simply exercising the control expected of it.

In this description of what management does, I have used the words model and plan interchangeably.  The model of how a project will be carried out normally is documented as a plan that identifies a sequence of events.  One may think of this plan as a discrete simulation or as a program [Oste87].  Project progress is evaluated with respect to these events.  For each event, management must ask the question, "Have all the criteria for completing this event been satisfied?"  If the answer is positive, then the project moves on to the next events in the plan; if the answer is negative, then management must decide what actions are necessary.  For example, recall the *Preliminary Design Review (PDR)* described in Section 5.2.

Unlike the structured reviews, which are designed to find errors, the PDR is intended to elicit confidence that the preliminary design is sufficiently complete to warrant the initiation of detailed design.  As an activity, the PDR is a "dog and pony show."  Its intent is to demonstrate to the bosses, customers, users, and colleagues that the preliminary design has been thought through thoroughly.  The development team will learn as a result of preparing for the review, and some very useful knowledge will be exchanged during the review.  But this interaction is only a secondary benefit of the PDR.  For management the PDR is one of many events in its plan.  Management must determine if that event has *truly* taken place, and make a decision based on their evaluation.  The PDR is but one of the inputs that they will use in coming to a conclusion regarding the quality of the preliminary design.  The review may have gone well, but the managers may sense that some aspects of the project were not considered in sufficient detail.  Or the review may have gone poorly, but there are other factors that prohibit delaying the detailed design.  (After all, project management does operate in the real world.)  Thus, in the project plan (model), the PDR is an event (node) that represents a decision point (branch).  From the perspective of system design, the PDR could be held a month earlier or later—it would make little difference in the technical outcome. As an event in the (possibly revised) project plan, however, it is essential that the PDR be held as scheduled; its occurrence provides information about *the validity of the current plan*, which is far more important than anything it might tell the technical people about the validity of their design.

From this introduction it is clear that management requires two categories of tool. The first is used to construct the model, and the second is used to evaluate progress with respect to the model. Of course, if all projects were alike, then one model would suffice. Even within a fixed organization, however, this is seldom the case, and project-specific models must be constructed. Notice that I use the word "model" even though its realization will be a "plan." I do this to emphasize that the role of the model (or plan) is twofold. First, it helps the development team organize its thoughts and establishes some necessary baseline documentation, and second, it provides a mechanism for accessing progress and status. Often, plans are treated as *boilerplate* (i.e., documentation to be created, distributed, and filed, but not necessarily read). Obviously, I reject that view. If the plan will not be used and kept current, then management should question if it is worth the effort of its preparation. Software engineering is frequently described as a document-driven discipline, and the many plans—for the project, for QA, for CM, for V&V—are cited as illustrations. I take a pragmatic view. If the plans do not help understand or control the project, then do not write them. Sometimes the activity of planning (and other documentation) becomes an end in and of itself. (Recall Yourdon's criticism of the physical model in Section 3.2.3.) This must be avoided. But without a plan, there is no sense of where one should be. Granularity is reduced to just two events: start and stop. One recognizes trouble only when "stop" never comes.

What tools do we use for constructing a plan? From reading the previous chapters we understand the software process; consequently, we should be able to identify the events that will be of major concern. Early in the project it will be clear that certain project-specific technical issues need additional study. There also will be a group of project-independent events that must be monitored (e.g., QA, CM, and V&V plans, system PDR, system test). Finally, there will be a series of events associated with each system component. These are normally organized in the form of a *work breakdown structure (WBS)* [Taus80]. The WBS is an enumeration of all work activities, structured in a hierarchy, that organizes work into short, manageable tasks. For a task to be manageable, of course, it must have well-defined inputs and outputs, schedules, and assigned responsibilities. Table 6.1 contains the outline of a generic WBS for a software implementation project. Naturally, the lower levels of the WBS will be specific to the project. Each WBS item

**Table 6.1.** Software work breakdown structure.

---

1.1 Software Systems Engineering
  1.1.1 Support to Systems Engineering
  1.1.2 Support to Hardware Engineering
  1.1.5 Software Engineering Trade Studies
  1.1.4 Requirements Analysis (System)
  1.1.5 Requirements Analysis (Software)
  1.1.6 Equations Analysis
  1.1.7 Interface Analysis
  1.1.8 Support to System Test

1.2 Software Development
  1.2.1 Deliverable Software
    1.2.1.1 Requirements Analysis
    1.2.1.2 Architectural Design
    1.2.1.3 Procedural Design
    1.2.1.4 Code
    1.2.1.5 Unit Test
    1.2.1.6 Software Integration Test
    1.2.1.7 Technical Reviews
    1.2.1.8 Technical Training
  1.2.2 Non-Deliverable Software
  1.2.3 Purchased Software
    1.2.3.1 Capabilities Analysis & Specifications
    1.2.3.2 Package Evaluation
    1.2.3.3 Package Acquisition
    1.2.3.4 Package Installation, Demo & Training
  1.2.4 Development Facilities & Tools

1.3 Software Test & Evaluation
  1.3.1 Software Development Test & Evaluation
  1.3.2 End-Product Accept. Test
  1.3.3 Test Bed & Tool Support
  1.3.4 Test Data Management
  1.3.4 Test Data Management

1.4 Management
  1.4.1 Project Management
  1.4.2 Administrative Support
  1.4.3 Management Tools
  1.4.4 Management Reviews
  1.4.5 Management Training

1.5 Product Assurance
  1.5.1 Configuration Management
  1.5.2 Library Operations
  1.5.3 Interface Control
  1.5.4 Data Management
  1.5.5 Quality Assurance
  1.5.6 Quality Control

1.6 Operations & Support
  1.6.1 Software Maintenance
    1.6.1.1 Problem Analysis
    1.6.1.2 Software Repair
    1.6.1.3 Software Modifications
    1.6.1.4 Support Software
    1.6.1.5 Facility & Tool Support
    1.6.1.6 Maintenance Reviews
    1.6.1.7 Training
    1.6.1.8 Document Maintenance
  1.6.2 Support Management
    1.6.2.1 Maintenance Management
    1.6.2.2 Administrative Support
    1.6.2.3 Configuration Management
    1.6.2.4 Data Management
    1.6.2.5 Quality Assurance
    1.6.2.6 Management Reviews
  1.6.3 Test & Operational Support
    1.6.3.1 Initial Operational Test & Evaluation
    1.6.3.2 Operational Test & Evaluation
    1.6.3.3 Version/Release Testing
    1.6.3.4 Test Bed & Tool Support
    1.6.3.5 Test Data Management

---

From [Reif85], © 1985 Texas Instruments, Inc.

438

defines a *milestone* (or event) that will be useful for both decision making and status review. The granularity of the WBS will depend on the number of milestones and the nature of the project. Too few milestones deny management the information necessary to maintain the project under control; too many milestones during a short period may obscure significant trends.

As with design, diagrammatic tools and multiple views aid problem solving. The WBS is an organized list of tasks. Because most of those tasks interact, it is useful to model them as a network using either the *Program Evaluation Review Technique (PERT)* or *Critical Path Method (CPM)*. Figure 6.1 displays a PERT chart (or network) taken from [USAr73]. The first event (0) starts at time $T_E = 0$, and the final event (10) occurs 33 days later ($T_E = 33$). The nodes indicate the day number that each of the nine subtasks is completed, and the $T_E$ value indicates when the event is completed. The edges between nodes indicate the dependencies among the events; they are labeled with the number of days to task completion. The critical path in this network is the longest path through the network between the start and finish nodes. Any schedule slippage on the critical path will cause a project delay. For example, the critical path in Figure 6.1 is 0-2-4-6-9-10. If the completion of any of those events is delayed while all the other events on the path are completed in the scheduled time, then event 10 cannot be finished in 33 days. In contrast, event 3 can be delayed as many as 7 days before the path 0-3-5-8-10 also becomes critical. Boehm provides a useful introduction to PERT methods [Boeh81]. There are many automated tools available for drawing and maintaining these networks.

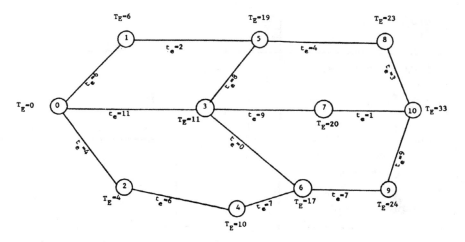

Fig. 6.1. Sample PERT chart from [USAr73].

Schedules also are best presented in a graphic form.  The most common form for displaying schedules is the Gantt chart, named after Henry L. Gantt who developed the technique during World War I.  A sample chart is shown in Figure 6.2.  As one would expect with a 70-year-old diagrammatic technique, there are many variations.  Events are listed in a column on the right, and a time scale is presented across the top.  For each event, a bar is drawn from the start time to the stop time.  Milestones normally are shown as triangles or diamonds, and vertical dashed lines are sometimes used to show the dependency between the completion of one task and the initiation of another.  Again, there are many software tools available for drawing and maintaining Gantt charts.

Other graphic tools include graphs and histograms [Reut79].  Some are used to develop an understanding before the project plan is accepted; others are used to track aspects of the project's progress.  All management tools are designed to support a downward-looking management perspective.  They operate on an abstraction of the software process from which many of the implementation details have been removed.  As with the development tools, management tools cannot substitute for human surveillance and good judgment; they can provide only an environment for the managers to model their projects.  How managers identify the important events in their models and how they react as the models lose their validity are the topics of the next section.

| Project | **SCM system** | | Date | **4/17/1991** |
| Title | **Preliminary studies** | | Author | **B. Blum** |

| Task | May | | | June | | | | | July | |
|---|---|---|---|---|---|---|---|---|---|---|
| | 12 | 19 | 26 | 2 | 9 | 16 | 23 | 30 | 7 | 14 |
| Develop procedures | □——————————————□ - ➤ | | | | | | | | | |
| Perform sizing estimate | | | | □———————□ | | | | | | |
| Analyze special needs | | | | □———————————□ | | | | | | |
| Prepare project plan | | | | | | | | □————□ | | |
| Brief management | | | | | | | | | | □ |

Fig. 6.2.  Portion of a Gantt chart.

## 6.2.2. The risk management process

Earlier I observed that a well-managed project will have seemed easy. Of course, rescuing a project on the brink of disaster is a far more dramatic exhibition of the manager's skills. The distinction is similar to that between a fire department that insists an safety standards and another that expends all its energy in removing people from burning buildings. The first involves *proactive* and the second *reactive* management. With proactive management, the primary goal is to identify potential problem areas and then anticipate them.[1] This may be viewed as *risk management*. The manager's responsibility is to identify risks, prioritize them, and then initiate actions that will reduce them. Risks are precursors to problems. It is always less expensive to deal with risks than to deal with problems. Moreover, when busy confronting a host of immediate problems, it is difficult to find the time and objectivity to evaluate risks. Consequently, once a project is out of control, it tends to stay out of control.

In his tutorial on software risk management, Boehm identifies two main branches of risk management [Boeh89].

- *Risk assessment.* This includes risk identification, risk analysis, and risk prioritization.

- *Risk control.* This includes risk management planning, risk resolution, and risk monitoring.

Risk is defined as the possibility of a loss or injury, and we can extend that definition to include injury to the project's performance or outcome. In some applications, it is possible to compute risks as probabilities. For example, using historical data regarding part failures, one can compute the risk of a device malfunction caused by a part failure. It is much more difficult, however, to compute the risk of a design error. (Recall the difference between hardware and software reliability discussed in Section 5.1.) Consequently, even though it is convenient to speak of risk probabilities, we must recognize that the softness of our numbers will make a mockery of the analysis's suggested precision.

The goal is to evaluate *risk exposure (RE)* and then take actions that provide *risk reduction leverage (RRL)*. RE is a function of an unsatisfactory outcome (UO). Formally, it is defined as the product of the

---

[1]In common American usage, "anticipate" often is equated with the passive act of recognition. It has a much stronger meaning. It implies an action that will counteract some future problem. Naturally, this is how the word is used here.

probability of that outcome and the loss to the parties affected by that outcome. This may be written,

$$RE = Prob(UO) \times Loss(UO).$$

If the RE is perceived to be too high, then it may be reduced at some cost. RRL computes the benefit gained as a ratio of the exposure reduction and the cost to achieve it. It is defined as,

$$RRL = (RE_{BEFORE} - RE_{AFTER}) / \text{Risk Reduction Cost}$$

By estimating RRL, it is possible to evaluate the efficacy of a risk reduction action.

A family of curves for fixed RE values can be plotted with Prob(UO) as the abscissa and Loss(UO) as the ordinate. Each RE curve will associate higher Loss(UO) values with lower Prob(UO) values. If the Loss(UO) value is fixed, one can reduce risk exposure (i.e., RE) only by reducing Prob(UO). However, RE is not an absolute value for decision making; it must be compared with the RE of the alternatives (including not taking any action). For example, consider the risk evaluation for a nuclear powerplant. For a fixed Loss(UO) and RE value, we can compute the necessary Prob(UO). If the current design does not satisfy that Prob(UO), then actions are required to reduce it. A lower Prob(UO) can be achieved by either increasing costs or waiting for newer, lower risk technologies. To evaluate the RE of the nuclear powerplant using the existing technology, one must compare it to the REs of the alternative power technologies plus that of the decision not to increase the power sources. This is a very complex issue; clearly, the most important factors in the equations are subjective. The message here is this: We may be precise in assessing the *risks of the products we implement*, but we require judgment in controlling the *risks of the projects we manage*.

In his *Principles of Software Engineering Management*, Gilb defines a host of principles [Gilb88]. One of these is the "Why not the best?" principle, which states,

The "best imaginable" can be a reality, if you are willing to risk or sacrifice any other planned attributes [p. 78].

This suggests that we can optimize for certain technical aspects at the potential expense of product features, cost, and/or schedule. Naturally, this is what a manager is paid to do. To make risk trade-offs, often in the midst of a project. In most cases, there is a limited window for making a decision. If one does not anticipate risks promptly, problems emerge and an opportunity is lost. In making these trade-offs, the manager can draw on both objective and subjective information. The objective information is formalized in the plans and the metrics used to evaluate status with respect to them. The subjective information is drawn from management's experience and understanding of the project. Some of this can be gained from books, but much of it requires the act of profiting from one's mistakes.

Boehm divides the judgmental information as follows.

- *Generic risks.* These are common to all projects and, therefore, are covered in the basic software development plan. Examples include error-prone products; costly, late fixes; out-of-control projects; and out-of-control products.

- *Project-specific risks.* These must be addressed by a project-specific risk plan. Examples here include user-interface uncertainties; ambitious performance requirements; tight budget and schedule constraints; and reliance on advances in computer science.

These two categories of risk map into the two domains of the essential software process (Section 1.2.2). The generic risks are concerned with the implementation domain and are independent of application domain specifics. In contrast, the project-specific risks are driven by application-domain issues. Naturally, books on software engineering will focus on the methods for reducing generic risks. Management's risk reduction program, however, is expected to build on the lessons learned regarding generic risks and focus on the project-specific risks.

Figure 6.3 depicts Boehm's steps in risk management. First we assess the risks, and then we control them. The former involves identification, analysis, and prioritization; the latter involves planning, resolution, and monitoring. In what follows I review for each step its objectives and tools. Keep in mind that we are operating in two dimensions. One dimension is concerned with generic issues that are valid for all projects of this general class. We expect to develop skills in identifying these risks so that future project plans can anticipate them. The second dimension involves project-specific risks. Here one cannot generalize. Boehm uses case studies to illustrate these risks in [Boeh89]. As with creating a valid requirements specification or developing an effective design, one cannot have a good sense for the risks without also having a solid understanding of the problems to be solved. That is, to become effective in risk management, management must be deeply involved in the project. Management tools without that commitment will not avail.

Obviously, risk assessment begins with risk identification. As with requirements analysis and testing, checklists are helpful. They catalogue

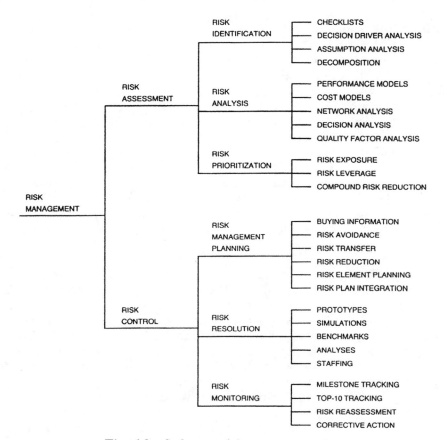

Fig. 6.3. Software risk management steps.
(Reprinted from [Boeh89] with permission, ©1989, IEEE.)

previous experience and serve as a guide to ensure systematic thoroughness. Naturally, most checklist items will be generic. For example, when considering the personnel available for the project, Boehm suggests a checklist with the following questions:

- *Will your project really get all of the best people?* During the period of proposal writing, all the best resumes are used. Now that the work is in hand, are those people really available? Are they even interested in your project?

- *Are there critical skills for which nobody is identified?* This is a project-specific question. Recall that during proposal writing you are expected to be optimistic, but when managing the project Murphy's law requires some pessimism.

- *Are there pressures to staff with available warm bodies?* Within a large organization, one speaks of peaks and valleys, that is labor-intensive periods that require many people followed by periods with limited staffing needs. The organization hopes that the peaks and valleys of many projects will produce a steady average staffing level. Unfortunately, when a new project is identified in an era of valleys, colleagues (i.e., fellow managers) may exert pressures to assign available staff on the basis of warmness of body rather than goodness of fit.

- *Are there pressures to overstaff in the early phases?* A similar problem occurs when a cost-plus-fee contract is initiated. Revenues are a function of expenses, and there are nontechnical incentives for full, early staffing.

- *Are the key people compatible?* In the best of all possible worlds, this is never an issue. This is an example of a hygiene factor.

One should develop these checklists and use them as both reminders and general rules. Each painful mistake should contribute to the list.

Anther technique for risk identification is decision-driver analysis. Here one itemizes the sources of the key decisions about the system. If a decision has been driven by factors other than technical and management achievability, then it may imply a software risk. Examples include politically driven decisions (e.g., choice of a piece of equipment or subcontractor), marketing-driven decisions (e.g., special features or equipment), or short-term versus long-term decisions. One can also identify risks by explicitly examining the assumptions, which tend to be optimistic and hidden. As with error-detection reviews, there is no alternative to thinking about the problem and relying on past experience. Finally, Boehm identifies the technique of decomposition. Basically, this acknowledges that when we deal at a high level of abstraction we hide many of our problems along with the details. One guideline that he offers is the Pareto 80-20 phenomena: 80% of the contribution comes from 20% of the contributors. The examples he lists are:

- 20 percent of the modules contribute 80 percent of the cost.

- 20 percent of the modules contribute 80 percent of the errors (not necessarily the same ones).

- 20 percent of the errors cause 80 percent of the down time.

- 20 percent of the errors consume 80 percent of the cost to fix.

- 20 percent of the modules consume 80 percent of the execution time. [Boeh89, p. 123]

Thus, one aspect of decomposition is to search for that critical 20%. Other identification activities include the use of PERT charts to find task dependencies, and reviews to clarify areas of uncertainty.

Once the risks have been identified, they can be analyzed. I already have defined risk exposure in terms of probability and have pointed out that the numbers that we use will be quite soft. In putting together a successful project proposal (either internal or competitive), one will have come up with values for cost and schedule based on some model derived from previous experience. These models may be repeated with other assumptions; costs and schedules may be derived for these assumptions; and probabilities for the various outcomes may be assigned. Clearly, the goal is to end up with some objective criteria that will allow management to rank and prioritize the risks. For very large projects there are automated tools to support this activity; for small to large projects, however, subjective considerations dominate. That is not a problem. What is desired is a list of the most important *current* risks to the project. (Once these risks are dealt with, new risks will emerge; therefore, risk assessment is an ongoing management activity.) After the risks are known, we can attempt to control them (as opposed to react to the problems that they will generate).

Risk control involves planning, resolution, and monitoring. Like most plans, the risk management plan addresses the following issues for each item of concern.

- *Why?* This is the risk item importance and its relation to the project objectives.

- *What, when?* This identifies the risk resolution deliverables, milestones, activity nets (if PERT charts are used), and so on.

- *Who, where?* This identifies the responsibilities by individual or organization.

- *How?* This describes the approach to be taken. Figure 6.3 identifies prototypes, simulations, benchmarks, analysis, and staffing as the primary techniques for risk resolution.

- *How much?* This identifies the resources (i.e., budget, schedule, key personnel) to be assigned to the planned resolution task.

For each identified risk to be resolved, we get a plan and a task that must be monitored. The outcome of the task tells us something about the project or product and removes some uncertainty. For example, in the SCM system application, we may have detected some risk regarding the ability of the existing hardware configuration to support all the users' files. If this apprehension was justified, then there would be two alternatives. We could alter the system design or enhance the equipment. Once the risk is assessed, we will plan and carry out a task to resolve it. After that task is complete, we will use its findings to adjust either the plan or the design as necessary. If we did not pursue risk management, the alternative might have been the completion of an SCM system that "met specifications" but would not work on the available equipment because we never thought to insist that it should.

I conclude this section on risk management with some more of Gilb's principles; consider them an endorsement for his book [Gilb88].

**The risk principle:**
If you don't actively attack the risks, they will actively attack you.

**The risk sharing principle:**
The real professional is one who knows the risks, their degree, their causes, and the action necessary to counter them, and shares this knowledge with his colleagues and clients.

**The risk prevention principle:**
Risk prevention is more cost-effective than risk detection.

**The principle of risk exposure:**
The degree of risk, and its causes, must never be hidden from the decision makers.

**The asking principle:**
If you don't ask for risk information, you are asking for trouble.

At the level that I have listed these principles, they simply represent sensitivity training. The role of management is to look for risks and anticipate problems. They can assume this proactive assignment, of course, only if they have good models to work from, and this is the topic of Section 6.2.3, which considers how to organize projects to reduce risk, and Section 6.2.4, which addresses the construction and refinement of effective models.

### 6.2.3.  Project organization to reduce risks

Risk management builds on experience.  Just as checklists that catalogue common errors prove helpful in software reviews, an understanding of the most common reasons for project failure can guide in the management of risks.  Boehm provides a list of what he calls the "Top Ten Checklist of Software Risk Items" [Boeh89, p. 117].

- *Personnel shortfalls.*  This can be countered by staffing the project with top talent (if available), improved job matching, teambuilding, agreements with key personnel, training, or the prescheduling of key people.

- *Unrealistic schedules and budgets.*  This can be reduced by the use of detailed multisource cost and estimation schedules, designing to cost, incremental development, software reuse, and requirements scrubbing.

- *Developing the wrong software functions.*  This can be avoided by means of better requirement analysis using techniques such as organizational analysis, mission analysis, operational concept formalization, user surveys, prototyping, and early users' manuals.

- *Developing the wrong user interface.*  This can be averted by means of experimentation with prototypes, scenarios, task analysis, and the characterization of the users with respect to functionality needed, style of interaction, and expected workload.

- *Gold plating.*  This can be controlled by requirements scrubbing, prototyping, cost-benefit analysis, and designing to cost. Remember, good engineering is delivering a sufficient solution rather than the ultimate solution.

- *Continuing stream of requirements changes.*  This can be managed by establishing a high change threshold (which must, of course, allow all the essential changes), information hiding to localize the effects of change, and incremental development (which defers most changes to later increments).

- *Shortfalls in externally furnished components.* This can be mitigated by early and careful benchmarking, inspections, reference checking, and compatibility analysis.

- *Shortfalls in externally performed tasks.* These can be minimized by means of reference checking, preaward audits, award-fee contracts, competitive design or prototyping, and teambuilding.

- *Real-time performance shortfalls.* These can be corrected by targeted analysis using simulations, benchmarks, models, prototypes, instrumentation, and tuning.

- *Straining computer science capabilities.* These can be alleviated by technical analysis, cost-benefit analysis, prototyping, and checking the technical and scientific literature.

Using Boehm's classification, each of the top 10 deals with project-specific risks. Indeed, none is specific to a software project.

We may group this top 10 into three basic categories. The first two items reflect an improper allocation of resources to the project (people in item 1 and time and money in item 2). The eight remaining items are indicative of a poor understanding of the problem to be solved. The first four demonstrate that the desired solution has not been refined, and the last four indicate a mismatch between the solution and its operational environment. From the perspective of the forward-looking activities of this book, 8 of the top 10 software risk items should have been addressed as technical issues in the requirements analysis and modeling stage (i.e., Chapter 2). Looking down, management should have a plan that states when they expect the essential requirements to be complete and a mechanism for establishing if that event has taken place. Failure to produce a solid, stable set of requirements is a signal that some management action is necessary. The current plan may be extended or amended; alternatively, a new plan can be constructed to increase the likelihood of defining effective requirements for the project to meet the overall objectives. (Again, the earlier a risk is anticipated, the less likely that the project will be affected adversely.)

Because the top 10 list suggests problems that should be evident at the beginning of a project, management's first course of action is the choice of project orientation (i.e., the life cycle model to be followed). Much of this material was discussed in a different context in Section 1.2. The traditional waterfall model is based on the development of hardware. It is a convenient method for managing projects in which there is considerable experience [i.e., this is the $(n+1)$st such product] or in which the software must be integrated with hardware that also is under development. The waterfall model assumes that one begins with a complete, valid, and stable set of requirements. The project plan identifies a set of phases with their associated deliverables (i.e., end products). Each deliverable is validated or verified before the subsequent phase can begin. There is also feedback to earlier phases as a better understanding of the problem develops. From the forward-looking modeling perspective, the division between phases is fuzzy. The development team does not rule out design considerations when performing requirements analysis, and they may question the relevance of some requirements as they pursue design trade-offs. From the downward perspective of management, however, the phase boundaries are distinct. Management interprets events in the context of the phase definitions, and they phrase their questions in terms of the deliverables.

- How likely is it that deliverable X will be available on schedule?

- How likely is it that deliverable X will meet the quality standards?

- How likely is it that factors have not been considered that will affect deliverable X?

- Are there changes in other parts of the plan that impact on deliverable X?

To management, the project is an abstract game in which they use their interpretation of the technical staff's inputs to evaluate the current state and to plot their next moves.

There is a subtle tension here that must be examined. The forward-looking development team and the backward-looking V&V team are both concerned with the quality of the software solution to the identified problem. The teams may have opposite orientations, but they rely on a common technical understanding of the problem and solution spaces. From their perspective, there is only one acceptable level of quality: the best. Management, however, has a different responsibility. They must determine if the quality goal will be achieved with the available resources and constraints. If not, they must augment the resources, reduce the constraints, or change the technical problem. Naturally, technical management requires technical understanding to calibrate the technical inputs. But the managers do not make the technical decisions; they help the technical staff define the form of their decisions and the schedule for their delivery. Thus, despite the widespread rejection of the waterfall model, it remains a valid approach to the *management* of a project as long as management recognizes that the conduct of the work may be less rigid than the catalogue of deliverables suggests. Unfortunately, the waterfall flow often reduces to a philosophy of having the work match the deliverables; not one of using the deliverables to evaluate the work's status. It is this kind of document-driven interpretation that has tarnished the waterfall model's reputation. Nevertheless, correctly applied, the model remains an effective way to manage lower-risk projects in which there is considerable experience and/or a need to integrate the development of hardware and software. In fact, most of the alternatives are simply refinements of it.

When the requirements are uncertain, a top-down, requirements-driven project will have a high risk. Brooks suggests two alternatives to the traditional waterfall flow: "requirements refinement and rapid prototyping," and "incremental development—grow, don't build, software" [Broo87]. I see these as contrasting, rather than complementary, approaches. The first, which I shall simply call prototyping, is intended to remove uncertainty from the requirements by means of experimentation with software. To some researchers, rapid prototyping represents a distinct life-cycle model. I do not subscribe to that view. To me, the prototype (which for practical purposes ought to be developed rapidly), is a requirements analysis tool similar to the simulation, scenario, task analysis, and user survey. From a risk-analysis perspective, management identifies project-specific situations that are of high risk, and then defines prototyping tasks to reduce the risk by gaining knowledge. When prototyping is performed during requirements analysis, the results are incorporated in the requirements document. (Prototypes also may be built during design to reduce uncertainty; for instance, most prototypes for real-time performance are intended to test designs.)

Consequently, I see the goal of prototyping as one of supporting a top-down development flow. When there is limited confidence in the top (e.g., the requirements may specify the wrong software functions or the wrong user interface), a prototype (or other analysis tool) is used to gain the insight that improves confidence in that top. The new material then is integrated into the top and the process continues. Boehm describes this flow as representing a spiral development path (see Section 1.2.3) He defines a sequence of *rounds*, each of which has specific objectives, constraints, and alternatives. The risks are identified, and methods are used to resolve them. Because the most frequently used method involves the use of prototypes, the diagram (Fig. 1.6) explicitly associates a prototype with each round in the spiral. The round concludes with the documentation of the risk resolution results, the preparation of a plan for the next phase, and a commitment (e.g., proceed on to the next phase). The spiral is normally depicted as a cycle through a feasibility study, concept of operations, top-level requirements specification, design validation, and implementation. But that is only one representation of the model. This principle of risk reduction through an explicit process is valid throughout the software life cycle, independent of the project orientation. A case can be made for showing that the waterfall flow and the spiral model are isomorphic; the former emphasizes the end-of-phase certification and the feedback from earlier phases but does not depict the risk-reduction activities, whereas the spiral model focuses on risk reduction by hiding the feedback and certification details.

If prototyping is a method for top-down risk reduction, incremental development may be thought of as being bottom up (or outside-in, cf. Section 3.1). The software prototypes are an adaptation of a hardware design validation method. Hardware requires top-down development; the design must be complete before fabrication begins. Incremental development, on the other hand, takes advantage of some features unique to software. Because software possesses conformity and invisibility, it is possible to structure software units to fit arbitrary requirements. Thus there is a far broader range for software increments than would be possible for hardware components. We can think of two classes of software increment. The first is comparable to the hardware unit. It provides its users with some fixed functionality, and the designers can translate operational feedback into product improvements or extensions. This type of incremental development is implicit in Brooks's phrase, "grow, don't build, systems." It is also how Lehman's E-type programs evolve [Lehm80]. This is how PC word processors have moved from file editing tools to desktop publishing systems; it is also how experience with small, stand-alone hospital applications matured as comprehensive hospital information systems [Lind79]. Domain experience accumulates, gold plating is avoided, and symbiotic interactions between the developers and users produces a sound understanding of the requirements. A positive feedback cycle is created. Effective tools help users discover how technology can meet their needs, which leads to more effective tools.

The second form of incremental development focuses on the implementation of a single system. One example of this approach was given in the description of the cleanroom (Section 5.4). Here one begins with a formal specification for the target product; increments then are defined, built, and tested. By keeping the deliverables relatively small, their visibility is enhanced, and their management is easier. The project plan has a fine granularity, and one quickly can tell whenever the schedule is not being met. (In Section 5.4 I emphasized the incremental testing of the product's reliability; naturally, this management-control benefit also was present.) Gilb describes calls his approach to incremental development *evolutionary delivery* or *evo planning* [Gilb88]. It encompasses the following critical concepts.

- *Planning for multiple objectives.* He notes that conventional software planning is overwhelmingly "function" oriented. It concentrates on what the software is to deliver without concern for the control of the critical quality and resource attributes of the system. Gilb proposes iteration towards clear and measurable multidimensional objectives, which include all properties that are essential to the long-term and short-term survival of the system under development (i.e., he offers a holistic view without using that term explicitly).

- *Early, frequent iteration.* Normal planning extends the project plan over an extended period, perhaps years. "Phased planning asks a dangerous question: 'How much can we accomplish within some critical constraint (budget, deadline, storage space)?' Evo planning asks a very different question: 'How little development resource can we expend, and still accomplish something useful in the direction of our ultimate objectives?'" [p. 89]

- *Complete analysis, design, build and test at each step.* Gilb observes the need for effective feedback in the use of today's systems; he believes that it is foolish to spend a great deal of time at the start of a project speculating on the nature of the requirements. Even a large development effort should be viewed as one increment in the extended life of a system. Gilb focuses on small deliveries with measurable objectives. Each has a low risk, and feedback from implementation reduces the risk in subsequent increments. "Start with a basic design which is easy to modify, adapt, port and change; both in the long and short terms. Start using the system, and learn even more, even earlier—while being useful" [p. 92]

- *User orientation.* He observes that with evolutionary delivery the developer is specifically charged with "listening" to user reactions, early and often. Reactions help define the next iteration. In contrast, the prototype establishes the user reaction as part of the requirements analysis process. Clearly, the prototype will be more biased by naive theories than an incrementally produced product.

- *Systems approach, not algorithm orientation.* "Many of our software engineering methods have a common weakness. They are exclusively oriented towards current computer programming languages. They do not even treat software, in the broadest (i.e., non-hardware) sense of that term" [p. 93] He describes evolutionary delivery as involving the developers in a creative process based on early and frequent interaction with the real world.

- *Open ended basic systems architecture.* Because the system evolves in reaction to what is learned from earlier increments, it is essential that it be built with an open-ended structure that can accommodate these changes.

- *Results orientation, not software development process orientation.* By keeping the increments small and measurable, one can manage the project by verifying if the work was done as promised. Thus, the creative developer has the freedom to address the problem without too much concern for intermediate steps, and management has sufficient granularity to avoid any loss of control. This kind of results orientation, of course, would not be possible in a project with a fixed multiyear plan.

The contrast between incremental development and rapid prototyping depends more on philosophy than on the class of product. With incremental development, one begins with an open architecture that can support the full set of potential solutions. The system is then built in layers, learning as one goes. With prototyping, on the other hand, there is a commitment to a top-down approach. One needs a set of requirements for the entire system, and prototypes provide a useful mechanism for establishing validity. In the context of the distinction between composition and decomposition described in Chapter 3, one has the choice of working with what one understands best and then building on it, or working from the top down. As we have seen in Chapter 3, however, even though there may be philosophic distinctions between the two orientations, compromise is possible. For example, the cleanroom was used to develop a COBOL restructuring system that could have been defined in a traditional top-down requirements document. Incremental development, with its many small deliverables, also has been used with very large projects. One 4-year, 200 person-year project was implemented in 45 incremental deliveries, each of which was on time and under budget; a 7000 person-year software development was delivered incrementally with no overruns during the final four years of the project [MiLD80]. TRW also has been using incremental development for some of its large systems coded with Ada [Spri89, Andr90, Royc90]. Thus, having many deliverables does not imply that the development team does not know what it is to implement; rather, it encourages management not to spend too much time planning the activities in which the uncertainties are the greatest.

In conclusion, it is obvious that how we organize a project affects the risk of an undesirable outcome. There are two orientations with a very high degree of built-in risk. The first can be described as the code-first method. Here lines of code are perceived to be a useful product, and management optimizes the process to get the largest number of lines of code as rapidly as possible. This is a programmer's view of progress; it long has been discredited because it does not address the need to which the software is expected to respond. In response to code-first's deficiencies, a specify-everything-first view was proposed. It built on experience with hardware and asserted that we should learn everything about the product before starting to build (i.e., code) it. In practice, however, we found that the requirements were never finished or that the resulting system did not correspond to the environment's needs. The specify-everything-first was associated with the waterfall flow, which led to the latter's discredit. Two project orientations are receiving increasing attention; each avoids the risks inherent in the two extremes just cited. Prototypes increase understanding (in both requirements and implementation concerns), and incremental development focuses on the present—where our knowledge is the greatest. The former gives us a better understanding of the product we are building, and the latter helps us manage that aspect of the project that we can control best: the next deliverables.

For management, the selection of the project orientation represents an early decision point: How should this project be structured to minimize risk? The decision will be affected by both technical and nontechnical concerns. After all, trying a new project orientation is risky in and of itself. Once an orientation is selected, however, changing it invites more risk. Thus, a commitment to a waterfall, spiral, or incremental approach is not a simple decision. Clearly, none offers a silver bullet. Perhaps the best advice to management is to examine what they have been doing that is wrong and consider how they can profit from their mistakes. Are risks assessed routinely and problems anticipated? Does the project plan evolve as the project moves on? Are there distinctions made between the deliverable and what it technically represents? Does the project team routinely evaluate the quality of their estimates? Are the same mistakes repeated project after project? Negative answers to these questions suggest systemic problems that will persist independent of project orientation.

### 6.2.4. Building a management model

I have described project management as the modeling of a project followed by the use of that model to control the project. Naturally, the effectiveness of the project's control will depend on management's ability to conform to the model. DeMarco opens *Controlling Software Projects* with the statement:

*You can't control what you can't measure.* [DeMa82, p. 3]

Thus, a model to support effective control must contain measurable criteria. Examples include deliverables due on specific dates, program units not to exceed a given level of complexity, a certain number of staff available for assignment on a predetermined date, and an established number of errors detected during unit testing. In each case, there is an event paired with a measure that is sufficiently specific to determine if the condition has been met as planned. It should not be difficult to construct a plan (i.e., model) that explicitly defines all the necessary events along with the conditions for their satisfaction. In fact, a plan without this specificity lacks the criteria to confirm that it is being followed. The issue, then, is not what should be measured in a plan, but how to arrive at effective measures. That is the topic of this section.

There are many different metrics that can be used for a model. Conte, Dunsmore, and Shen state,

> We contend that the proper use of *software metrics, measurement, and models* is essential in the successful management of software development and maintenance. Generally, software *metrics* are used to characterize the essential features of software quantitatively, so that classification, comparison, and mathematical analysis can be applied. After a number of useful metrics is identified, it is then important to *measure* software in an algorithmic and objective fashion, so that the values of the selected metrics are consistent among different software products, and are independent of the measurer. In order to control the software development and maintenance processes, it is important to *model* certain interesting factors (metrics), such as effort and defects, based on other metrics that are available. Appropriate management decisions can be made to influence these factors so that management goals can be met. [CoDS86, p. 3]

Notice that this quotation introduces a second definition of model. Up to now, I have used the term to suggest a high-level abstraction of the project's conduct. A PERT chart is a model of the task dependencies; a schedule is a model of the deliverable dates. The second meaning of model implies a mathematical relationship among software metrics. The independent metrics in the relationships are measurable during the development process, and the dependent metrics are important attributes of the project. Thus, when we predict the number of lines of code to be produced, our interest in this metric is predicated on the existence of a mathematical model that computes effort as a function of lines of code. We care about effort, but we can predict lines of code more accurately.

To avoid confusion, I shall now use *plan* when writing of a project abstraction; *model* will be reserved for the relationships among metrics.

Separating these two terms creates a twofold problem for management. Not only must they create a plan, but they must also determine which models are effective in predicting the metrics used by the plan. Software engineering is unlike mechanical engineering just as management is unlike physics. The first in each pair is concerned with a human process and the second with an external reality. The former is adaptive and subjective, and the latter is repeatable and objective. Whereas we can measure the speed of light in a vacuum and know that it is invariant, we cannot expect to find a universal relationship between lines of code and effort. The world of mechanical engineering and physics is external to the practitioner; that of the software engineer and manager is local to his environment. Thus, managers must find *what works best for them*. Handbooks, which catalogue the experience of others, will help, but they cannot suffice.

There are several ways of classifying metrics. They may be algorithmic (i.e., objective and computed precisely independent of changes in time, place, or observer) or subjective (i.e., based on the individual's ideas about what the metric should be). Although we recognize that the interpretation of the measures will be somewhat subjective, we require a common, objective definition for its calculation. A metric can quantify attributes of the process (e.g., schedule) or the product (e.g., lines of code). We also can have *metametrics*, which are measures of a software metric. Conte, Dunsmore, and Shen suggest the following [CoDS86].

- *Simplicity*. It should consist of a simple result, easily interpreted, with a single, intuitive value.

- *Validity*. The metric indeed does measure what it purports to measure.

- *Robustness*. The metric is insensitive to manipulations that do not affect the performance of the software.

- *Prescriptiveness*. The metric should act as a guide to management in predicting; metrics that can be computed only after the project is complete are not prescriptive.

- *Analyzability*. The metrics should be amenable to computation using standard statistical tools.

When identifying the metrics to be used, management must also consider how the data will be obtained. Some are available from static analyzers, others from surveys and interviews. The effort to collect data should be consistent with their utility, and the impact of obtrusive data collection (i.e., that in which the development process is perturbed by the collection activity) must be considered.

By definition, all metrics can be represented as numbers. Four measurement scales establish the valid operations on a metric. They are:

- *Nominal.* This is a determination of equality ($=$, $\neq$). It associates individuals with categories, for example, a documentation or a logic error.

- *Ordinal.* This is a ranking ($<$, $>$). It establishes an order among individuals within a class, for example, a ten-point measure of error severity.

- *Interval.* This refers to numbers with meaningful differences ($+$, $-$). It implies that the differences or intervals between two values have comparable meanings, independent of the initial values. For example, in the Celsius scale for temperature, the difference between 35°C and 70°C is the same as that between 70°C and 105°C, but 70°C is not twice as hot as 35°C.

- *Ratio.* Here ratios are meaningful ($\div$). There is an absolute zero. Thus, for example, we can make statements about being twice as hot when using temperatures in degrees Kelvin.

The four scales are nested, and a ratio scale also has the properties of the other three. Knowing the metric's scale provides information about the allowable operations on it. Of course, the scale may not always be obvious. For example, is an error that takes 8 hours to correct twice as "bad" as one that takes 4 hours to correct? Not if we include cost to recover from, cost to detect, cost to distribute updates for, etc. Thus, the measurement scales warn of some operations that may produce meaningless results (e.g., dividing intervals or subtracting ordinals), but they do not guide us in understanding what our metrics measure.

Because we are not measuring repeatable, objective phenomena, the primary goal in metric identification is to find measurements that will tell us something interesting about the project we are managing. For example, as a metric, lines of code is of little interest. It becomes useful when there is a model that transforms lines of code into effort months or lines of code into an expected number of errors. Given these models, we can estimate lines of code to estimate effort months, or we can count lines of code to estimate the as-yet undetected errors. The problem is, however, that there may not be a model suitable for our specific project. We must either learn to live with an imperfect model or construct a better one. In either case, we begin by examining experience with existing models and then determine how to accommodate local factors.

The remainder of this section reviews the models currently in common use; the next section considers model refinement in the context of process improvement.

There is one area in which virtually all software projects employ modeling: cost projection. At its simplest level, the projection is a back-of-the-envelope calculation. "Based on previous experience with projects of this size and complexity, I sense that the cost for this project will be such and such." This is an expert's judgment. If the expert has been in business for a long time, that judgment is probably good. The more complex the project or the less expert the estimator, the greater the need for a more refined technique. One way of improving the accuracy of the estimate is to find ways to measure product attributes that can be converted into cost and time. Lines of code is the most commonly used independent measure. A second, and complementary, technique is to decompose the product into smaller parts (usually program groups) and estimate the cost for each part; the product cost is the sum of the costs for the parts. This divide-and-conquer approach also can be applied to phases of development, components in a work breakdown structure, and so on.

Here is a method described by Pressman that combines these two methods [Pres87]. First the software is decomposed into its major functional components, and then the size of each component is estimated. For example, in an SCM system the following components might be required.

- User interface and control (UIC)
- File management and security (FMS)
- Version control (VC)
- Change request management (CRM)
- Report generation and query (RGQ)
- Software manufacture (SM)

Each function is given a size estimate in (delivered, noncommentary) lines of code (LOC). Obviously, one can estimate the size only if one has experience in both estimating size and in this type of product. To reduce uncertainty, Pressman suggests 3 estimates. The most likely ($m$) is, as its name suggests, the best guess assuming nothing goes wrong. The other two estimates are an optimistic ($o$) and a pessimistic ($p$) one. The expected ($e$) estimate is computed as

$$e = (o + 4m + p)/6.$$

The formula adjusts the estimate by approximating the fact that, in a normal distribution, one third the points will be more than one standard deviation from the mean.

| Function | Opt. | Most likely | Pess. | Expt. | $/ Line | Line/ mon. | Cost ($K) | Mos. |
|----------|------|-------------|-------|-------|---------|------------|-----------|------|
| UIC | 1800 | 2400 | 2650 | 2340 | | | | |
| FMS | 4100 | 5200 | 7400 | 5380 | | | | |
| VC | 4600 | 6900 | 8600 | 6800 | | | | |
| CRM | 2950 | 3400 | 3600 | 3350 | | | | |
| RGQ | 4050 | 4900 | 6200 | 4950 | | | | |
| SM | 2000 | 2100 | 2450 | 2140 | | | | |
| Total | | | | 24840 | | | | |

Fig. 6.4.  Estimation of project size.

| Function | Opt. | Most likely | Pess. | Expt. | $/ Line | Line/ mon. | Cost ($K) | Mos. |
|----------|------|-------------|-------|-------|---------|------------|-----------|------|
| UIC | 1800 | 2400 | 2650 | 2340 | 14 | 315 | 33 | 7.4 |
| FMS | 4100 | 5200 | 7400 | 5380 | 20 | 220 | 108 | 24.4 |
| VC | 4600 | 6900 | 8600 | 6800 | 20 | 220 | 136 | 30.9 |
| CRM | 2950 | 3400 | 3600 | 3350 | 18 | 240 | 60 | 13.9 |
| RGQ | 4050 | 4900 | 6200 | 4950 | 22 | 200 | 109 | 24.7 |
| SM | 2000 | 2100 | 2450 | 2140 | 28 | 140 | 60 | 15.2 |
| Total | | | | 24960 | | | 506 | 116.5 |

Fig. 6.5.  Estimation of project size with costs.

As the estimates are calculated, they are entered into the first four columns in the table shown in Figure 6.4.   These represent our estimation of the size of the problem to be solved based on our experience with such problems.  The next two columns of the table list the multipliers derived from local experience, and the final two columns contain cost and time as a function of LOC.  Notice that it is assumed that the multipliers vary with the complexity of the software function. The results of the final calculations are shown in Figure 6.5. In this illustration I used a dart-board model for computing cost and effort, and I found that the cost will be $506,000 and that the project will require 116.5 effort months.  Two questions are obvious.  How good is that estimate and is the expenditure reasonable for the project? We can gain some confidence in the estimate by repeating the process using a different project decomposition.  Figure 6.6 shows a decomposition of software components by phase.  Again, historical data are used to convert lines of code into dollars and days.  The totals are within 10% of each other—close enough to suggest that the estimate is reliable.  Now we must address the question of the project's being worth the expenditure.  If it is not, then a design-to-cost philosophy or an incremental-

| | Req. Anl. | Design | Code | Test | Totals |
|---|---|---|---|---|---|
| UIC | 1.0 | 2.0 | 0.5 | 3.5 | 7.0 |
| FMS | 1.5 | 8.0 | 4.5 | 9.5 | 26.0 |
| VC | 2.5 | 10.0 | 6.0 | 11.0 | 31.5 |
| CRM | 1.5 | 6.0 | 3.0 | 4.0 | 15.0 |
| RGQ | 1.5 | 10.0 | 4.0 | 10.5 | 27.0 |
| SM | 1.5 | 6.0 | 3.5 | 5.0 | 16.0 |
| Total (mm) | 9.5 | 42.0 | 21.5 | 43.5 | 120.5 |
| Rate ($) | 5200 | 4800 | 4250 | 4500 | |
| Cost ($K) | 49.4 | 201.6 | 91.4 | 195.8 | 538.2 |

Fig. 6.6.  Effort estimation by phase.

delivery approach may be appropriate.  If one is bidding the job in response to a request for proposal (RFP), then the estimate for development also must be reviewed with respect to a winnable bid price.

In the method just described, the cost model was derived from historical experience and adjusted for a component's complexity or a phase's difficulty.  Without this historic data, the method just described reduces to a reliance on nonspecific project data or—worse yet—back-of-the-envelope calculations.  Clearly, it would be useful to find relationships that were true for all projects.  One then could formalize these relationships in an algorithm and use the resulting model to support planning.  There have been several attempts to identify such process invariants, of which the most important was introduced by Putnam. Here is an overview extracted from his most-cited paper.

This paper will show that software systems follow a life-cycle pattern.  These systems are well described by the Norden/Rayleigh manpower equation, $\dot{y} = 2Kate^{-at^2}$, and its related forms.  The system has two fundamental parameters: the life-cycle effort ($K$), the development time ($t_d$), and a function of these, the difficulty ($K/t_d^2$).  Systems tend to fall on a line normal to a constant gradient.  The magnitude of the difficulty gradient will depend on the inherent entropy of the system, where entropy is used in the thermodynamic sense to connote a measure of disorderedness.  New systems of a given size that interact with other systems will have the greatest entropy and take longer to develop. Rebuilds of old systems, . . . will take the least time to develop. . . .  Other combinations are also possible and will have their own characteristic gradient line. [Putn78, p. 347]

In effect, what Putnam is doing is expressing an invariant relationship between manpower utilization and development time for software projects.

Figure 6.7 displays the Norden/Rayleigh curve's shape; notice how the basic curve can be adjusted as time or effort are altered.   In this model, $K$ is the area under the $y$ curve; it represents the total man-years of effort used by the project over its life cycle.  $t_d$ is the time that the curve reaches its maximum, and it is called the development time.  It is assumed that project cost is directly proportional to people cost (i.e., effort expended), and it is shown that approximately 40% of the cost is expended by the time of $t_d$, which seems to conform to the 40-20-40 rule.
The number of delivered lines of code can be expressed as

$$L = C_k K^{1/3} t_d^{4/3}$$

where $C_k$ is a *state of technology constant* used to adjust the gradients for the environmental and project specifics.  Each fixed value of $C_k$ defines a family of effort-year curves plotted on a graph of development time versus system size.   The values for $C_k$ are computed empirically to reflect experience with the class of problem, development methods used, and so on.  Two sets of $C_k$ curves are displayed in the Putnam paper.  One uses a $C_k$ value of 10040.  Using that curve, one finds that for a system size of 500K lines, development would take 6.5 years if staffed at 25 effort-years and half that time if staffed at 500 effort-years.   The second set of curves is based on a $C_k$ value of 4984.  Here the 25 effort-

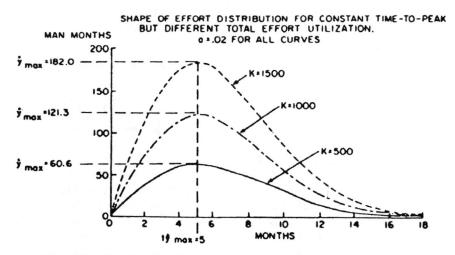

Fig. 6.7.  The Norden/Rayleigh curve with parameter changes.
(Reprinted from [Putn78] with permission, ©1978, IEEE.)

year curve is off the graph for the 500K line system, and a 500 effort-year project requires over 5 years. Naturally, the projects are not as elastic as the curves would suggest. The relationships they define hold true only for larger projects with "reasonable" variations in the scope of the key parameters. Therefore, the model has little utility for the small to large projects that are the focus of this book.

A second class of cost model looks for relationships that will compute cost and time as a function of the number of lines of code. Most such relationships are expressed in the form

$$E = aL^b$$

where $E$ is the effort (or time) and $L$ is the number of lines of code. The models focus on producing families of $(a,b)$ values to account for project-specific factors. The most widely used of these models is the *COnstructive COst MOdel (COCOMO)* developed by Boehm [Boeh81]. It is defined in three levels: basic, intermediate, and detailed. I will describe only the intermediate model.

The first step in using the COCOMO model is to establish the type of project. Boehm defines three modes of development.

- *Organic mode.* This normally involves development by relatively small teams in a highly familiar, in-house environment.

- *Semidetached mode.* This is a combination of the organic and embedded modes; Boehm describes it as an "intermediate stage."

- *Embedded mode.* This implies a need to operate within tight constraints caused by a strongly coupled complex of hardware, software, regulations, and operational procedures.

Different sets of $(a,b)$ values are used for each mode. Once the mode is established, the software components are defined and an initial size estimate in delivered source instructions (DSI) is computed. Unlike the Pressman example, only a most likely value is given for each component. These estimates will now be refined using adaptation and cost-driver data.

The COCOMO adaptation equations first reduce the number of lines by the amount of effort that will be saved through reuse. The equation is based on a 40-30-30 rule, and it accounts for the effort saved in the reuse of designs, code, and/or integration data. The adaptation adjustment factor (AAF) is computed for each component as

AAF = 0.4 (Percent design modified) + 0.3 (Percent code modified) + 0.3 (Percent integration modified).

For new (i.e., 100% modified) components, AAF is 100. The estimated DSI (EDSI) is then calculated as

ESDI = (Adapted DSI)(AAF)/100.

The second adjustment to the EDSI accounts for the attributes of a component that affect the difficulty of its development. These are called the Software Effort Multipliers, and they are grouped into four categories.

- *Product attributes.* These are a function of the product to be implemented. They are the required software reliability, the database size, and the product complexity.

- *Computer attributes.* These are determined by the target environment. They are execution time constraint, main storage constraint, virtual machine volatility, and computer turnaround time.

- *Personnel attributes.* These reflect the experience and ability of the development team. They are analyst capability, applications experience, programmer capability, virtual machine experience, and programming language experience.

- *Project attributes.* These account for the project-specific features. They are the use of modern programming practices, the use of software tools, and the required development schedule.

Each of the 16 effort multipliers is assigned a set of ratings (e.g., very low, low, nominal, high, very high), and each rating is assigned a numeric value. For example, very low complexity has the value 0.70 and very high complexity has the value 1.30. Similarly, a very low analyst capability would have a value greater than 1 (in this case 1.46), and a very high analyst capability a value less than 1 (here 0.71). Nominal values are always 1.00.

The effort multipliers are used to compute an effort adjustment factor (EAF) for each component. Low multiplier values indicate that a component will be less difficult to develop than one with a high value. The product of all the component's effort multipliers therefore indicates how much easier or more difficult it will be to develop that component. The calculation and use of EAF are as follows. First the components are listed on a standard form, and the EDSI is entered. AAF then is computed, and the EDSI is adjusted as necessary. Following this, each of the multipliers is assigned a rating (e.g., VL, LO, N); a table is used to convert the rating into a multiplier value. The product of these 16 values becomes the component's EAF. Next the nominal number of man-months of effort ($(MM)_{NOM}$) for each component is computed using the adjusted component sizes (in thousands of EDSI) with the following ($a,b$) values.

Organic        (3.2, 1.05)
Semidetached   (3.0, 1.12)
Embedded       (2.8, 1.20)

For example, nominal man-months of effort for an organic system is $3.2(KEDSI)^{1.05}$. Once the nominal effort is available, it is adjusted for the difficulty associated with the effort multipliers. This is done by multiplying EAF and $(MM)_{NOM}$; the result is the estimated development effort $(MM)_{DEV}$. Once the development effort is determined, it can be used to calculate the development time by using a formula of the type

$$T = aE^b$$

Three pairs of ($a,b$) values are available to compute the total development time (TDEV) as a function of $(MM)_{DEV}$ and the development mode. Once the total elapsed time is established, it must be distributed into phases (e.g., requirements analysis, product design, programming). Table look-ups are provided to distribute TDEV among the development phases as a function of development mode and project size. The result is a program plan that allocates labor and time by phase.

The basic COCOMO model is similar to the intermediate model except that it does not apply the adaptation and effort multiplier factors. The detailed model extends the analysis to each phase. Naturally, the validity of the model depends on how well the parameters and table values match the realities of a particular project and organization. Boehm's data were derived from numerous studies, and the number of COCOMO users suggests that they provide a useful baseline. Notice how the COCOMO approach differs from that of Putnam. Putnam begins with the assumption that there is something "natural" about the software process, and he sets out to model that property. Boehm, on the other hand, believes that there are many factors that affect productivity in software development, and he sets out to identify and empirically quantify them. In this brief discussion, three factors were identified: the development mode, the degree of reuse (adaptation), and the effort multipliers. Even if one does not use the COCOMO model, an awareness of these factors is important to management. Figure 1.13, presented in a different context in Chapter 1, displays the relative effect of each multiplier. Consistent with my theme of software engineering as problem solving, the range of personnel and team capability is twice as great as that of any other factor. The range suggests that the cost for a project staffed by the least capable personnel will be four times greater than that of a project staffed with the best people. Of course, that is misleading; the least-capable staffing might never get the job done.

One of the problems with models such as COCOMO is that they depend on the number of lines of code to estimate the cost. That is, they assume that the project cost is a function of the size of the delivered product. The use of *fourth generation languages (4GL)* and other productivity-enhancing tools demonstrates that products of different sizes can deliver identical functionality. Naturally, the smaller the product, the lower the development cost. But not all project costs are related to the size of the delivered product. Jones points to the following paradox: for a fixed product, the cost per line of code increases as the total number of lines is reduced [Jone86a]. This is because the fixed costs for requirements analysis, top-level design, integration, training, etc. are independent of the programming language. As the denominator in the cost/line decreases, the ratio increases. Thus, the estimates of the size and effort for atypical development environments present very special problems [VeTa88].

It would be helpful to have a technique that estimates a project's cost as a function of the target system's attributes rather than its predicted size. Such a method would compute the cost of the *problem to be solved* rather than the *product to be delivered*. Function points, initially developed by Albrect for commercial applications, offer an alternative that comes close to this goal [Albr79]. The objective is to characterize the functions to be provided by a system and then to use that characterization for estimating the effort. Five system properties typically are used to compute the function point count (FP).

- *Number of user inputs.* Each user input providing distinct application-oriented data is counted; queries are counted separately.

- *Number of user outputs.* This counts the number of reports, screens, error messages, etc.

- *Number of user inquiries.* Inquiries are defined as an on-line request followed by an immediate response.

- *Number of files.* This is a count of what might be termed master files.

- *Number of external interfaces.* This is a count of the number of machine-readable interfaces (e.g., data files on tape or disk).

FP is the a weighted sum of these five counts. Arthur provides weighting factors for simple, average, and complex systems [Arth85]. A typical formula would be

$$FP = 4 \times inputs + 5 \times outputs + 4 \times inquiries + 10 \times files + 7 \times interfaces$$

Although the definition of function points was motivated by the properties of information systems, the concept has been extended by Reifer to produce estimates in more complex domains [Reif87]. Empirical studies have shown that there is a strong correlation between FP and DSI [AlGa83]. In fact, most users of this costing technique use the FP computation to improve their DSI estimate in the context of a traditional cost model [VeTa87]. That is, function points normally are employed as predictors for the size of the delivered product, which then is used to predict effort and cost.

There are some inherent difficulties in the cost estimation methods just described. First, the models all rely on historic evidence based on variations of the waterfall flow model. If one alters that model, then the database becomes invalid. For example, the cleanroom has a phase distribution that is totally incompatible with that used by the COCOMO model. (Of course, incremental development provides the cleanroom with an alternative means of controlling the project.) A second concern is that the volume of the product depends on the language used (cf. Halstead's concept of volume in Section 5.3.2). An analysis of function points showed that the code to produce one function point required 110 lines of COBOL, 65 lines of PL/1, or 25 lines of a 4GL [AlGa83]. Thus, language choice (or some of the technology improvements to be discussed in Section 6.3) may have an impact that dominates the factors considered by the cost model. Finally, we must be aware that the cost model tends to act as a self-fulfilling prophecy. We use the cost model to construct a project plan that will serve as an abstraction for the project. We then manage according to that plan. Good management is defined as maintaining the project within the plan's parameters. But it has been shown that staffing and costing plans establish how the project will be organized [AbMa86]. The accuracy of an estimate is determined, at the completion of the project, by how closely the project conformed to the estimate. This evaluation of the estimate's accuracy relates only to the effort expected to complete the work; it is independent of the effort required to complete the project using an optimal plan. That is, "more accurate estimates are not necessarily better estimates" [AbMa86].

How discouraging. First I describe three categories of cost and schedule models, and then I throw in a paragraph that details their built-in limitations. How are we to estimate costs for (or anything else about) a project? I offer two pieces of advice. First, use the existing models, but be aware that they have unavoidable flaws. There are many commercial tools for software cost and schedule estimation, and most of them have satisfied and committed users. Find one that works for your organization, and adopt the tool to your environment (but not vice versa). Second, to be done in conjunction with number one, learn how to estimate. If estimation were easy, we would do it instinctively and never make mistakes. But estimation is counterintuitive, and we need to develop the experience that makes it seem instinctive. (Repeat the last sentence with "management," etc. in place of "estimation.") To learn how to estimate we must think of estimating as a continuing process. (Just like planning.)

Figure 6.8 is taken from a paper by Boehm; it shows how cost estimates improve as the project progresses. During the feasibility stage, estimates may be off by as much as a factor of 4. By the time the detailed design specifications have been developed, estimates for the remaining work are quite reliable. Certainly, we should not rely on the least-dependable estimates for planning the project. As we gain more information, we should refine the estimates and adjust the plan.[2] DeMarco suggests that an organization assign a team the sole task of estimating; by staying with this process and refining the estimates, team members become skilled estimators [DeMa82]. (In keeping with Theory Z, one need not stay an estimator forever. In fact, the estimation lessons learned will be very useful in virtually all other assignments.) If an organization is to adopt DeMarco's idea, then it is necessary to understand what estimating is. It is not the default definition of "the most optimistic prediction that has a non-zero probability of coming true." Rather, it is "a prediction that is equally likely to be above or below the actual result." For DeMarco, "Estimates shall be used to create incentives" and not as management-imposed targets to be met. That is, by making the estimate an evolving best guess, it no longer can serve as the abstract event to be managed by. He therefore suggests a restructuring of the software process to create

- *Motivation-free estimates.* These are estimates whose entire purpose is to predict future costs and dates.

- *Estimate-free motivations.* These are motivations that encourage developers to maximize function delivered per dollar of net lifetime cost, which he defines as *Bang Per Buck (BPB)*.

---

[2]Unfortunately, sometimes the prerequisite to being awarded the work is a commitment to an overall cost and schedule that must be made when the understanding of the assignment is weakest. I assign this fact to footnote status and offer no solutions.

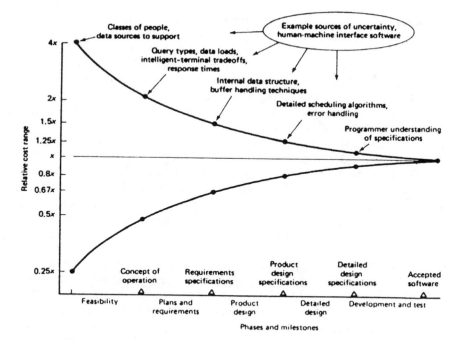

Fig. 6.8. Software cost estimation accuracy versus phase.
(Reprinted from [Boeh84] with permission, ©1984, IEEE.)

His book describes how to define metrics that maximize BPB. As one would expect, the parameters reflect local factors, and they improve as experience accumulates.

A brief reprise. The chapter began with a review of metrics and measurements and then examined three classes of model for estimating time and cost. After considerable build up, the underlying flaw in this process was exposed. We use models to build a plan, and we manage the project with respect to that plan. However, because we are not physicists trying to conform to some external reality, our models (and therefore our plans) are not bound by any external constraints. A poor plan, when well managed, will result in the suboptimal conduct of the project. We have no alternative but to recognize these facts and learn to accommodate these difficulties. We must subjectively define objective criteria for controlling the process; as with other aspects of software development, the fact that our performance is correct with respect to plan offers no assurance that our plan is correct. That important point reiterated, let us continue by examining another category of management model, which addresses the question of how to validate that a piece of software functions as expected. As discussed in the previous chapter, the issue is one of software reliability (i.e., the probability that the software is defect free). Is this a management or a V&V concern? Obviously, both. Management must establish the desired level of reliability and ensure that there is sufficient support for testing; the V&V team, naturally, will be responsible for the conduct of the task and the calculation of the reliability estimates. Both management and V&V must base their decisions using a common set of reliability models.

The field of software reliability is broad, and I cannot hope to cover much of the material here. The standard work is that of Musa, Iannino, and Okumoto [MuIO87]. Shooman covers the topic in some detail in his text [Shoo83]; recent surveys include [Goel85], [Leve91], and [ReVe91]. By way of a short introduction, I review some of the concepts presented in a paper by Musa and Ackerman with the subtitle, "When to stop testing?" [MuAc89]. In it, *failures* are defined as runs in which the outputs do not conform to the requirements, and *faults* are the instructions that underlie the failure. An *operational profile* defines the set of valid inputs with their distribution, and we assume that software failure is a Poisson distribution process. We define $\mu(\tau)$ to be the cumulative number of failures expected to occur by the time that the software has experienced a given amount of execution time, $\tau$. The derivative of $\mu$ represents the instantaneous rate of failure, denoted $\lambda(\tau)$. There are several formulas for computing $\mu(\tau)$. The *static* model assumes that the software is not being changed, and $\lambda(\tau)$ reduces to the constant, $\lambda$. The *basic* model accounts for changes as the software is being debugged; the assumption is that the faults are equally likely to cause failures. In the *logarithmic Poisson* model, some faults are considered more likely to cause failures than others. Figure 6.9 compares these three software reliability models with respect to both failures experienced versus execution time and failure intensity versus execution time.

The preconditions for using one of these reliability models is that the significant failures have been defined, that an operational profile has been specified, and that a failure-intensity objective has been set to some desired level of confidence for the defined failures. The idea is that the model defines the desired reliability property of the software as a function of its testing time. If too many errors are encountered in the specified time, then one may conclude that the desired reliability level has not been achieved. In practice, the process proceeds as follows:

- Select test cases in proportion to the frequencies specified by the operational profile.

- Record, at least approximately, the amount of execution time between failures.

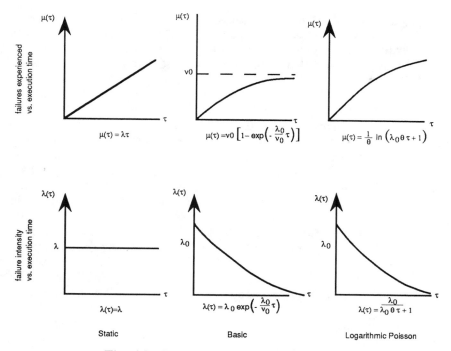

Fig. 6.9.  Three software-reliability models.
(Reprinted from [MuAc89] with permission, ©1989 IEEE.)

- Continue testing until the selected model shows that the required failure-intensity level has been met to the desired level of confidence.  [MuAc89, p. 22]

By selecting test cases that are more likely to fail, testing time may be compressed.  Nevertheless, to provide the necessary confidence for a critical system that will be broadly distributed, considerable testing time must be allocated.  There are two problems with this approach in small to large projects.  First, the reliability models have been validated on very large systems using extensive testing time; it is not certain that the models scale down.  Second, the testing is predicated on the formal definition of the system combined with a solid understanding of its use and the cost of failures.  In effect, what we are doing is using experience with other systems to build general models for software reliability and then fitting one of those models to the target system.  Subjective judgment is used in the selection and parameterizing of the model; once that task is complete, however, decisions regarding the software's reliability become objective.

There is a third category of project attribute that also is frequently modeled to support the planning and control of a project: software complexity. This topic was briefly discussed in Section 5.3.2 with the introduction of the Halstead and McCabe metrics that measure "inherent" properties of the software product. There also are many other metrics that can be used to estimate complexity [McCl78, YaCo80, LiCh87, CaAg88]. The idea is that if we can find properties of the software that correlate with the its complexity, then we use these measurements to predict problems that result from the unit's complexity (e.g., high defect rates or maintenance costs). In my earlier discussion, I observed that the measures were not as precise as many would like, and that they have been used most effectively when used as informal predictors that gain credence when independent predictors complement each other [KaCa85]. In fact, it has been shown that the inappropriate use of software complexity measures can have large, damaging effects by rewarding poor programming practices and demoralizing good programmers [KeST86]. When a metric is defined without a clear understanding of what it measures and why it should be used, using that metric as a guide usually will be counterproductive. For example, there are widely held guidelines regarding module size, coupling, and other desirable properties of software product. How valid are these assumptions? Here is what Card discovered from an analysis of data collected from scientific and satellite-control applications written primarily in FORTRAN [CaGl90].

- *Module size.* The costs for larger modules is relatively lower than that of smaller modules, and there is no difference in fault rate. This suggests that standards limiting the size of software units may be ill advised. However, a subsequent analysis also showed that complexity limits may promote maintainability.

- *Data coupling.* Section 3.2.2 introduced the concepts of coupling (how modules interact with each other) and cohesion (how functions within a module relate to each other). A scale for coupling was introduced in that discussion suggesting that common coupling should be avoided. The use of the copy function, however, has shown that common coupling can beneficial. Indeed, Card found common coupling to be as beneficial as parameter coupling.

- *Span of control (fanout).* Card found a high correlation between the span of control (i.e., the number of modules called by a module) and both the cost per module and the number of errors uncovered. Thus, he suggests minimizing this value by decomposing each function gradually. In particular, he advises against using the 7 ± 2 rule advocated by the structured analysis method.

- *Strength (cohesion).* Here the analysis showed that high strength is beneficial to both cost and quality. In a trade-off between module size and strength, the latter should dominate.

Some of these results confirm existing perceptions while others run counter to the accepted view. This is not to suggest that one view or the other is wrong; rather, the findings show that—for this particular development environment—these relationships define useful heuristics for project control. Thus, while there may be no inherent complexity indicators, there are measures that provide useful predictors for complexity-related difficulties within the current setting. Of course, the process is not stable. As it changes, so too may the validity of the heuristics. In fact, as I discuss in the following section, changes in the heuristics can give us information about how the process is improving.

### 6.2.5. Process improvement

There is very little in the software process that is static. As already observed in this chapter, each project is dynamic, and plans must be adjusted to reflect changing realities. This section begins with the assertion that the organization's processes also are dynamic. Because management and the design team learn from experience, the conduct of subsequent projects should be better than those that preceded them. There are two approaches to process improvement. Default, open-loop learning builds subjective confidence; there is the perception that, having survived $n$ projects, one is prepared for the $(n+1)$st. Because there are no data, there is no way to disconfirm this perception of professional growth. The second alternative, to which this section is devoted, is based on a scientific, closed-loop model. We use our plans as a predictive hypothesis, and then we use the project outcome to evaluate the validity of those predictions. That is, we manage at two levels. First we manage the project, and then we *metamanage* how we manage.[3]

---

[3]Card suggests that what I have called open-loop learning is, in reality, individual learning, which stays with the individual and is not retained as corporate experience. Thus, as individuals move on, their experience base is lost. Process management, however, attempts to share a common process that incorporates the learning; it also provides a foundation for new learning to improve the process. That is, the structure of process improvement should institutionalize the process, the improvements, *and* the improvement process.

Card uses an industrial engineering analogue in which the goal is to analyze and improve the *process* rather than just measure the quality of the *product* [Card90]. He notes that there are three historical levels of quality assurance technology.

- *Product inspection* (c. 1920)—examining intermediate and final products to detect defects.

- *Process control* (c. 1960)—monitoring defect rates to identify defective process elements and control the process.

- *Design improvement* (c. 1980)—engineering the design of the process and the product to minimize the potential for defects. [CaG190, p. 2]

Clearly, our goal as software engineers is to operate at the highest level of design improvement. This implies that we must do more than just follow the practices described in the first five chapters to make our products both correct and valid. We must also examine how we carry out our assignments so that we can do them better, with fewer errors, less expensively, more promptly, and of higher quality. Design improvement is a process, and in DeMarco's words, "You can't control what you can't measure." Therefore, process improvement is based on a measurement activity.

The first task in any measurement program is to determine the baseline (i.e., where we currently are). Humphrey defines five *process maturity levels* that describe the current status of an organization's development process [Hump89a]. Each level assumes a measure of statistical control that permits prediction, and maturity is characterized by improved predictability plus the ability to evaluate the impact of process changes. The levels are

- *Initial.* This implies that the process is not under statistical control and is driven by crisis responses. It is uncontrolled and chaotic; costs, schedule, and quality performance are predicted poorly.

- *Repeatable.* This implies a stable process with a repeatable level of statistical control through management of commitments, costs, schedules, and changes. There is control over the way in which the organization establishes its plans and commitments, and process changes can now be planned without being reaction driven.

- *Defined.* This implies that there exists a defined process that provides consistent implementation. A foundation is now in place for major and continuing progress. While advanced technology can be introduced at each of the previous levels, a defined process is a prerequisite for an effective evaluation.

- *Managed.* This implies that the organization has initiated comprehensive process measurements and analysis. This is when the most significant quality improvements begin.

- *Optimizing.* The organization now has a foundation for continuing improvement and optimization of the process.

The maturity levels are adapted from Deming's concept of statistical process control [Demi82] and Crosby's quality maturity structure [Cros80]. Like the waterfall flow model, the concept has its roots in hardware manufacture. As with that model, there are distinct differences between hardware and software. In Section 5.1 I contrasted hardware and software reliability. The former assumes a correct design and focuses on variations within a product, whereas the latter assumes that there is zero product variation but design errors will persist. Thus, hardware manufacturing samples products coming off the line to predict if the process is under control. The software analogue to this sampling is the comparison of error rates with respect to models of the expected errors, such as those shown in Figure 6.9. Hardware is constrained by the physical universe, but—as Brooks points out—software conforms [Broo87]. In the hierarchy presented by Card, hardware product inspection ensures that the variability among individuals is acceptable, process control uses this variability to ensure that the manufacturing process is under control, and design improvement permits us to evaluate the effect of changes. With software we can only use defects[4] in the product or the management plan to measure the quality of the development process. Still, the basic process improvement concept is the same. One cannot have design improvement without process control; without control there is no way to measure the impact of changes to the process. Therefore,

---

[4]I use a very general definition of defect here. I include failures to meet specified requirements (including both functional and nonfunctional requirements), invalid or inefficient designs (e.g., a cumbersome user interface), and inability to satisfy standards or the ilities. Not all potential defects may be tested for, but if the tests conducted indicate that a relatively large number of defects are present, then flaws in the other, untested quality factors most likely will exist as well. In Chapter 5 I suggested that quality is the customer's perception that the product does what is desired, and here I imply that defects are an indication that the customer's expectations will not be met.

we first must get the process under control so that we can predict outcomes reliably; we then must find ways of improving the process and evaluating those improvements.

The initial chapters in this book discuss how to develop quality software (i.e., software that is delivered on time and within budget, does what is needed, is error free, can be maintained easily, and so on). If it sufficed to follow those practices, management would have little to do. Quality products would result automatically. Conversely, attempts by management to control the process without the commitment of the development and maintenance teams can have limited impact. There is no manufacturing process in software, and the prerequisites for quality improvement are improvements in the analysis, design, and testing of the products. If software development is an intellectual, problem-solving activity, so too is the improvement of that activity. Therefore, process improvement demands the support of both the technical and management staffs, a fact noted throughout Humphrey's six basic principles of software process change.

- *Major changes to the software process must start at the top.* Senior management leadership is required to launch the change effort and to provide continuing resources and priority.

- *Ultimately, everyone must be involved.* Software engineering is a team effort, and anyone who does not participate in improvement will miss the benefits and may even inhibit progress.

- *Effective change requires a goal and knowledge of the current process.* To use a map, you must know where you are.

- *Change is continuous.* Software process improvement is not a one-shot effort; it involves continual learning and growth.

- *Software process changes will not be retained without conscious effort and periodic reinforcement.*

- *Software process improvement requires investment.* It takes planning, dedicated people, management time, and capital investment. [Hump89a, p. 19]

Observe that principles one and six place the primary responsibility for process improvement on management.

Because one cannot evaluate the impact of change unless there is a stable baseline, Humphrey begins with a process assessment designed to learn how the organization works, to identify its major problems, and to enroll its opinion leaders in the change process. This assessment activity requires the support of senior management. The team's assignment is to review the organization's process with respect to some vision of how its processes should be performed. The five-level maturity framework is used as the context for comparison, and one outcome of the assessment is a common view of the desired software process. The objective is to improve how the technical teams operate, and that requires their cooperation. Confidentiality must be preserved, and the assessors should avoid the perception that problems are being reported to management. Honesty and openness are necessary, and the assessment team should avoid presenting itself as knowing all the answers. The focus must be on actions that can produce improvements; general sessions on problems will be limited to a Hawthorne effect. The goal of the assessment process is to establish a baseline and initiate an improvement program. A baseline without the commitment to follow up is a hollow gesture; an attempt to improve the process without a baseline is an open loop.

The thrust of Humphrey's book is a description of the key elements within each improvement phase. Most of this material already has been presented elsewhere in these pages. Nevertheless, it is useful to see how the concepts are organized from the perspective of *Managing the Software Process* [Hump89a]. The tools to achieve the level of a repeatable process include planning, an initial level of configuration control, and a software quality control program. The move up to a defined process requires standards, inspections, testing, extended configuration management, and a definition of the software process. To enable the last activity Humphrey suggests the creation of a Software Engineering Process Group (SEPG) that identifies the key problems, establishes priorities, defines action plans, gets professional and management agreement, assigns people, provides training and guidance, launches implementation, tracks progress, and fixes the inevitable problems. Naturally, the SEPG requires the support of senior management, the line projects, Software Quality Assurance, and the professional staff; it provides a well-staffed, continuing focus for process improvement, which must be integrated into the organization's ongoing activities to succeed. Once a defined process has been established, a baseline exists against which process interventions can be evaluated. This requires data gathering and the management of software quality. Finally, the optimization process emphasizes defect prevention, automated support, and—perhaps—contracting for software.

Notice that process optimization rests on three pillars. The first is the positive removal of errors, which in the software context is the only measure of quality variability. The second is the support of a controlled process using automation to reduce effort or error potential. Notice that the premature introduction of automation may simply institutionalize an out-of-control process. The final suggestion echoes Brooks's advice, "Buy, don't build." Because software quality is a function of persistent defects, I close this overview of Humphrey's book with an examination of his advice regarding defect prevention. He begins with the following, possibly counterintuitive, principle of Deming.

> In the state of statistical control, action initiated on appearance of a defect will be ineffective and will cause more trouble. What is needed is improvement of the process, by reduction of variation, or by change of level, or both. Study of the sources of product, upstream, gives powerful leverage on improvement. [Demi86, cited in Hump89a, p. 367]

That is, when a process is under statistical control, finding results that are outside the expected bounds tells us something about the *process* and not its *control*. If we react to individual out-of-bounds events by adjusting the process's control, we will—by definition—get it out of control. However, if we use the out-of-bounds events to guide an investigation of the process, then we have an opportunity for significant process improvement. The key, therefore, is not to try to correct the statistical control for outliers, but to remove those outliers by means of process changes.

Humphrey's recommendations for the prevention of defects are consistent with the concepts presented throughout this book. They are important enough to bear restatement.

- *The programmers must evaluate their own errors.* They have the greatest interest and will learn the most from the process.

- *Feedback is an essential part of defect prevention.* It represents the learning part of a closed-loop, problem-solving activity.

- *There is no single cure-all that will solve all the problems.* This is implicit in my holistic perspective. Error causes must be removed one at a time; the evaluation of specific interventions requires stability in those aspects not being changed.

- *Process improvement must be an integral part of the process.* Brooks's hope for the future emphasizes the development of great designers; personnel skill improvement is an integral part of the process. Humphrey's principle echoes this idea in a management context. Managers become better managers as they learn to improve the process that they manage.

- *Process improvement takes time to learn.*  Everything is either obvious or counterintuitive.  A baby develops "common sense" during his most intensive learning period: zero to 24 months. Now the difference between "on the table" and "under the table" is apparent, but it did take time to learn.  Our goal is to enhance the development team's intuition regarding defect prevention, and that is a learning process.  Naturally, there are levels in learning, and one progresses from definitions, to logic, to intuition, and finally to an automatic response.

The above principles for defect prevention are free of any measures. Naturally, statistical control implies a measurement system that can indicate when the process is out of control.  In hardware manufacturing, tolerances are computed for the parts; when a sample of parts implies that tolerance is being exceeded, adjustments are made to the production line to bring it back under control.  With software, statistical control is interpreted as the ability to predict with an expected level of certainty. We have seen that management abstracts the project as a plan and then manages that plan.  The plan establishes levels of quality (e.g., reliability and standards) and resource allocations (e.g., effort and schedule).  A project under statistical control will conform to its plan in a predictable way.  Being under statistical control, however, does not imply that the process is in any way optimized; it simply means that we have good models for describing how the processes operate.  Without those models we cannot control the project, but the models themselves are seldom perfect.  They do not model some external, fixed phenomena, and there is no concept of correctness.  Statistical control is equated with the accuracy of prediction, and the process models are best interpreted as stepping stones to better processes (with their models).  All of which raises the following question:  If there is no way of knowing what the process should be, then how do we know when changes improve the process?

The method used to evaluate process changes is based on the experimental paradigm of the scientific method.  We begin with a *null hypothesis ($H_0$)* that states that the change to the system or the event being measured has made no difference (i.e., the magnitude of any effects can be attributed to chance).  An appropriate statistical test for $H_0$ is selected, and a *significance level ($\alpha$)* is specified as the criterion of rejection.  The data are collected, the statistic is computed, and its *p*-value is determined.  The null hypothesis is rejected if and only if the *p*-value is no larger than $\alpha$.  If rejected, we accept the alternative hypothesis $(H_1)$, which is actually the hypothesis we are interested in. Typically, the experimental paradigm is reserved for highly repeatable phenomena, but we have seen that few software processes satisfy such an interpretation.  Basili has adopted the scientific method to software evaluation in his Quality Improvement Paradigm [Basi85]. This is a six-step meta-life-cycle model that aims at improving software quality and productivity based on the measurement and reuse of experience. The steps are

- *Characterize.* First the current environment is characterized. Because Humphrey's focus is project management, statistical control is essential in his approach. For process improvement, however, all that is necessary is an accurate characterization of the existing baseline.

- *Set goals.* Goal improvement must be established in the form of quantifiable questions or metrics. We cannot test hypotheses without appropriate measurements.

- *Choose methods.* Choose the appropriate process models for the project together with the supporting methods and tools.

- *Build.* Using the chosen processes, build the products and collect the prescribed data. Where the processes are closed loop, it is essential that the data be analyzed promptly so that the results can be fed back for process adjustment.

- *Analyze.* After the project has been completed, analyze the data to evaluate the current practices, determine problems, and recommend changes.

- *Feed Back.* Document and make use of the experience gained from the first five steps and repeat the process at step one. As with all applications of the scientific method, the acceptance of one concept suggests new ideas to be tested.

Basili also has defined a *Goal/Question/Metric (GQM)* paradigm for generating measurement in a goal-directed manner [BaWe84]. It establishes a systematic approach for identifying the goals, the questions that determine if the goals are being met, and the metrics necessary to answer the questions. A single question can provide answers for more than one goal, and a single metric can be used to evaluate more than one question. The goals are defined in terms of purpose, perspectives, and environment; their objectives can be to characterize, assess, predict, or motivate. The questions can focus on the product (e.g., physical attributes, cost, changes and defects), aspects of its quality (e.g., functionality, reliability), the process, or aspects of its quality (e.g., reduction of defects, cost effectiveness of use). Clearly, the GQM is not limited to the process improvement approach described by Humphrey (and neither does it include all the aspects discussed by Humphrey). Where the latter is defined for use in an ongoing management context, the former may be used for both process improvement and experimentation in software engineering. There is a growing literature on the GQM paradigm, and it provides a helpful framework for establishing which metrics contribute to answering questions about the goals. Although the approach may seem obvious, it emerged as a response to a heavy reliance on metrics that were used simply because they were there. That is, the availability of measurements defined the questions that could be answered.

We know, of course, that measurement should begin with a theory or model of the object to be measured. For example, we have seen that there are many software complexity metrics, each of which is justified by some model. One can perform empirical studies to determine if such a metric and its model are effective in predicting error rates, effort, maintenance costs, etc. However, even when a model is demonstrated to be valid, it remains narrow in scope. It exists in the context of some much larger model of the software process within the organization. Naturally, the concern should be for that larger model. Despite the early claims of software science, I doubt that we will ever find strong, invariant relationships embedded in our programs. The local, procedural variables will continue to dominate, and therefore we will gain the greatest benefit by modeling those human processes. Although this is a relatively new concept, measurement-based process reviews are proving to be effective [GrCa87, CaMP87, Andr90, Romb90]; indeed, we are to the point that an automated support environment is now under development [BaRo88]. Thus, the collection and utilization of process data for process improvement are not just ideas; they are a validated, operational method.

One center for exploring the effects of process change is the Software Engineering Laboratory (SEL) of the NASA Goddard Space Flight Center. Since the mid-1970s, the SEL has been conducting an extended, and very successful, research program in measurement and evaluation [Card87, SEL90]. The data capture and analysis techniques resulting from that experience have been used to measure design quality and to manage software development in a variety of settings. It is fitting, therefore, that I conclude this section on process improvement with a review of Card's experience, which grew out of his SEL association [CaGl90]. Card proposes a systematic approach to the collection and analysis of software process data, and he begins by identifying four basic uses of software measures.

- *Project estimation.* This involves predicting costs and developing schedules for future projects based on past performance. This is where software engineering has the greatest experience, and

Section 6.2.3 presented several categories of model for producing these measures.

- *Quality control.* This involves assessing quality performance and determining the need for corrective action. The previous section discussed one aspect of this use in the context of reliability. Other common applications are normally presented as part of a quality assurance program [EvMa87, ScMc87].

- *Process analysis.* This involves identifying bottlenecks and leverage points in the software process, as well as evaluating new technology. In Humphrey's scheme, this is difficult to do unless the organization is at maturity level 3 with a defined process.

- *Product engineering.* This involves making engineering decisions and choosing among design alternatives. As with process analysis above, the goal here is one of design improvement. In this case, however, we are concerned with properties of the product and not the process that produces it.

In the GQM paradigm, these uses define goal categories

Card's interest is in the establishment of a basic measurement program that collects the data for use in computing the desired metrics. Obviously, there is a wealth of data produced during a software project. Card presents the following basic software measurement set of "metric primitives."

- *Software design.* These measures are intended to tell us something about the design of the software response to the need to be met. Three measures for complexity are identified. Functional allocation (which can be classified by application type, the number of functions per subsystem, or the number of data sets per subsystem), system design (which can be characterized by the number of units, the sum of fanout squared, or the sum of the number of variables), and unit design (which can be measured with the mean number of decisions per unit). There also are measures for the satisfaction of requirements (the number of design changes and the percent of traceability) and conformance to standards (the number of nonconformances reported).

- *Software product.* These measures provide information about properties of the implementation. Three characteristics are identified: quality (as measured by the number of software errors during unit, integration, and system testing), volume (as indicated by the numbers and sizes of new units, modified units, and reused units), and documentation (measured by the number of pages).

- *Software testing.* Here two measures are discussed that provide insight into the effectiveness of the testing: the percents of testing efficiency (a function of the number of faults found during and after testing) and test coverage (the ratio of the structure tested and the structure available for testing).

- *Resources (cost).* These are the traditional management measures. They include those for the computer (in computer hours), effort (in hours for design, implementation, testing, rework, and other support), and schedule (in the number of elapsed weeks).

Notice that each of these primitives is relatively easy to capture. Figure 6.10 presents Card's model of a software data collection system in which the data are captured routinely. The set can be augmented with more complex measures such as those of Halstead and McCabe. Card makes the point, however, that one should focus on a few key quality characteristics and begin with simple measurements extractable from common design products. Thus, the above measurement set represents a starting point rather than a target objective. There is a trade-off between the cost to collect and analyze data and the benefit gained from their use.

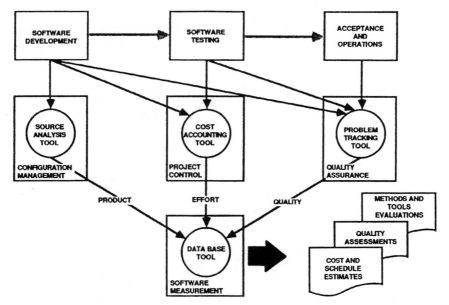

Fig. 6.10. A software data collection system.
(Reprinted from [CaGl90] with permission, ©1990 Prentice Hall, Inc.)

DeMarco estimates the cost of his measurement program is 5 to 10% of the development costs [DeMa82], and experience at SEL puts the costs at 7 to 8% [VaMc88]. The obvious recommendation, therefore, is to begin small and learn by doing. In fact, one of the conclusions of Card's analysis that he labels "surprising" is that a software enterprise can collect too much data.

Once a reliable database has been established, it can be used to support empirical analysis. The results can be unexpected. For example, here are what Card labels his surprise conclusions [CaGl90].

- *Software engineering without measurement is not engineering.* If this comes as a surprise, then I certainly have failed in my presentation.

- *A software enterprise can collect too much data.* There is a natural tendency to collect everything that is easy to collect and then see what it tells us. There is a cost for analyzing data, and the exploitation of already-available data is valuable only for concept formulation. Both the scientific method and the GQM paradigm insist that we know why we need the data before we start collecting them.

- *Software science measures do not appear to have practical usefulness.* There still are practitioners who would disagree with this statement, which tells us more about the difficulty of modeling in software engineering than it does about Halstead's theories.

- *Standards that arbitrarily limit module size seem to be ill-advised.* The SEL data showed that large modules can have relatively lower costs, but they may be harder to maintain.

- *Common coupling is not as bad as we thought.* Coupling was initially described using a linear scale going from best (parameter) to worst (direct). The goal of low coupling, however, was comparable to what we now call information hiding. Keeping that goal in mind removes some of the linear properties from the coupling scale.

- *Fanout should be smaller than we thought.* These data are valid for the FORTRAN programs analyzed. Software engineers would be prudent to test for the importance of fanout in their operational setting. In particular, they should examine the analogue of fanout in object-based environments.

- *Productivity numbers are often crude and may be misleading.* Because the productivities of unnecessary and necessary software are essentially the same, total productivity does not reflect the efficiency of the process. Card concludes, "Identifying and measuring inefficiency is the first step toward correcting it."

- *Delivered source instructions are not always a good measure of work.* The discussion of function points in Section 6.2.3 was motivated by the need to distinguish between the size of the problem to be solved and the realization of that solution as a product.

- *Standards are often too comprehensive.* Too many standards, if not ignored, can be counterproductive. A few standards, understood and broadly accepted, can improve quality and productivity [Glas87].

- *Unique projects can still be measured against themselves.* "Controlling quality means setting quantitative quality objectives, measuring project performance against the objectives, and then taking corrective action as needed to bring performance back into line with the objectives." The difference between the unique and the $(n+1)$st projects is a difference in the precision of (i.e., confidence in) the quality measures.

- *Test coverage is a vital but seldom-used measure.* This, of course, is the thrust of white box testing, described in Section 5.3.3.

- *Unreferenced variables are a good indicator of trouble.* This information, usually provided by the compiler, is an indication that the design expressed in the code is not logical. The Pareto principle suggests that where one defect exists, others may persist.

- *Measurement makes productivity and quality improvement meaningful.* While this may hardly seem like a surprise conclusion, consider how informally many managers approach these improvements (e.g., set up a class, send the staff to meetings, or buy a CASE tool).

One of Card's principal recommendations is the use of statistical process control techniques for software development [Pyzd78]. One prepares a control chart that identifies the historical experience with respect to some key metric (e.g., testing effectiveness, test coverage, error rate as a function of time or release). Each chart includes the historical (or target/expected) rate, upper and lower control limits, and the observed rate from the current project. When the process exceeds a control limit, it is by definition out of control and some management action may be mandated. In this way, the control limits permit normal variability while providing a very early warning of potential problems. The same technique also can be used to evaluate the effect of a technology introduction [Sayw81]. The intervention should produce a new target/expected rate (with its set of control limits) that is in some sense better, and project tracking can assess how well the project conforms to those new limits.

Card's book is clear and concise, and it is recommended reading for both students and practitioners. He offers some very specific conclusions concerning the software he analyzed. However, I have not repeated his results. Unlike physics, with its external universe, the software process is adaptive. There are no universal measures. The *process of modeling* the software process becomes more important than the *form of that perishable process model*. There is an inherent tension between control and improvement. Management needs a fixed model to control software development and maintenance, and process improvements violate the established control limits. Of course, that is an old problem for industrial engineers, but it is still new to software engineers. I let Card have the last word on the subject.

> Software managers, tool vendors, methodologists, and the like do not really want objective measurement. Most of these people are comfortable with a system that puts a premium on presentation rather than performance. Software acquisition managers and software engineers are the ones calling for better measures. The greatest challenge in measurement practice is convincing management to want measurement in the first place. [CaGl90, p. 101]

### 6.3.    Process improvement technologies

The previous section considered how to use models for both management and process improvement. Two complementary modes of improvement are possible. One addresses the hygiene factors that degrade productivity and quality. The first five chapters of this book provide a collection of effective techniques for replacing bad practices. Although many of these methods are philosophically incompatible, there is much to choose from. Each alternative provides the means for avoiding "doing things the wrong way." Thus, in most cases the hygiene factors can be confronted simply by process examination, introduction of refinements and/or education, and then *follow up, follow up, follow up*. The second approach to process improvement derives from the introduction of new concepts or technology. One must be careful, however, when instituting change. Management's responsibility is to reduce risk, and all change involves risk. Therefore, management commitment is a prerequisite; it ensures the necessary resources and training for achieving the expected benefits and evaluating the results. Software improvements not integrated into the process quickly become *shelfware*.

This final section examines some advances in software engineering that currently are receiving considerable attention in both the research and practice communities. In what follows, I describe the basic concepts. If and how an organization (i.e., the organization's management) commits to one or more of these technologies will depend on the local needs, the resources or products available, and the commitment to integrating the change into the environment. But be forewarned, process improvement is not easy. The software process is essentially a thought-intensive, problem-solving activity. For some tasks, such as code syntax testing, automated tool support is a natural extension of the basic process. Here new tools will be quickly accepted and assimilated. For other tasks, such as the machine drawing of data flow diagrams (DFD), automation can replace a manual activity. Benefits will depend on the effectiveness of the tool, its ease of learning and use, and its role in the overall process. For example, if DFDs are drawn only for distribution after the design is complete, then an automated drawing tool can create more attractive deliverables, but it will have no impact on the design activity. Tasks also can be totally changed by the introduction of a new technology. For instance, the adoption of a formal method or a new modeling approach often requires a complete break with current procedures. In such situations, productivity can be expected to degrade during the learning process.

Software technology takes a long time to mature. Redwine and Riddle estimate the time from initial concept to widespread acceptance as 17 ± 3 years [ReRi85]. This long delay time results from the fact that we seldom are dealing with small, incremental improvements to an accepted process. The modifications generally affect how people understand their jobs, and there is a natural resistance to change. A survey by the University of Maryland, conducted in the early 1980s, offers some very interesting insights into the assimilation of software engineering improvements into software production [ZeYH84]. A group of faculty members was invited to assess development practices in 30 organizations: five IBM organizations, 12 other U.S. companies, and 13 Japanese companies. There was a detailed survey, a more complete examination of one project, and—for most organizations—a follow-up site visit. The organizations developed contract software, internal data processing applications, and systems software; their project and team sizes ranged from small to very large. Interestingly, very few companies claimed to be doing typical software.

The reviewers observed that the data collected by each organization were insufficient, and the interpretation of concepts differed markedly among organizations. For example, although many stated that they used chief programmer teams, interviews demonstrated a diversity of approaches, few of which reflected the original organizational intent [Bake72]. "Each company had either written guidelines or unwritten folklore as to how software was developed, and major deviations were rare." Differences among projects within a company were less pronounced than differences between companies. Most companies had a *Software Technology Group* that operated at the same level as the development projects, but there was little transfer from the research to the operational groups. "We found surprisingly little use of software engineering practices across all companies." For instance, although most companies used reviews, newer companies had less commitment to them; often, they were seen as training exercises for junior employees. (In older companies, which had more software to maintain, reviews took on greater significance.) Practices also seemed to vary with the type of product produced. Three types of development environment were identified.

- *Applications software.* This was typically development of new software for a Federal agency in which software "is 'thrown over the wall' to the agency for operation and maintenance." Here the process is optimized for low development costs. "All companies surveyed had a methodology manual; however, they were either out of date, or were just in the process of being updated." Because staff turnover was low, application expertise (i.e., Brooks's great designers) was a major factor in the organization's success.

- *Systems software.* Here they noted a trend away from very large products with most development efforts "limited to no more than two years and 10 programmers on any particular product." Most testing is considered to be part of the development effort, and separate test groups normally report to the development managers. Staff turnover tended to be relatively high, and the software engineering practices varied widely; "the older the system, the fewer software engineering techniques used."

- *Data processing.* These were internal, business-oriented applications, mostly in COBOL. "The success of the project depended on how much the user was involved *before* integration testing."

A phased development approach was common, and the reviewers found quality control to be especially important here.

The results suggest an early move to the idea of incremental delivery with small systems. Ironically, the development environment with the least computer science-derived (i.e., software engineering) discipline was the domain closest to computer science (i.e., systems software); in the application software environments, the contractual framework was the dominant force in distorting the process.

What did they report on tool use? Table 6.1 tabulates the acceptance of various software engineering methods and tools. There was considerable variation in the way a method or tool was used (e.g., reviews), and some tools were used inappropriately. For example, the objective of the program design language (PDL) is to provide a higher level of abstraction for the subsequent development of the code, but the reviewers in one case found the ratio between the lines of PDL and the resulting code to be as high as 1:1.5! "Some produced volumes of PDL with an attitude similar to that for older projects that produced many detailed flowcharts: Nobody cares, but it's in the contract." Companies tended to adopt methods easily because of their low capital costs. Most tools focused on the code development phase, where they served as a natural extension of the essential tools (e.g., compilers and link loaders). Many tools were locally developed and limited to a single project; in fact, in one company three different project managers had each

Table 6.1. Methods or tool use.

| Method or tool | Percentage of companies |
|---|---|
| High-level languages | 100 |
| On-line access | 93 |
| Reviews | 73 |
| Program design languages | 63 |
| Some formal methodology | 41 |
| Some test tools | 27 |
| Code auditors | 18 |
| Chief programmer team | 7 |
| Any formal verification | 0 |
| Formal requirements or specifications | 0 |

developed a text editor. Reporting in the early 1980s, the reviewers wrote, "Tool use generally has the flavor of vintage-1970 timesharing." Thus, using the Redwine and Riddle analysis, it is prudent to base current expectations on a model of early 1980 perceptions.

The reviewers' observations on the difficulty of introducing new tools (independent of their quality and applicability) remain valid today.

- Corporate management typically has a hardware background and is not sympathetic with the need for software tools.

- Tools typically are funded from project budgets, and there are few mechanisms for prorating investment and training across projects.

- When a company works with different hardware, tool transportability is essential. Optimization of a tool for a project limits its portability.

- The need to maintain large existing products constrains the ability to adopt new technologies that are incompatible with those used by the product.

The reviewers also noted that many tools are incomplete or poorly documented. "Because such tools fail to live up to promises, project managers are justifiably reluctant to adopt them or consider subsequently developed tools." One would hope that a new generation of commercially supported software tools would mitigate this problem, but managers (whose primary responsibility is risk reduction) have a long memory for disappointments. Once a tool fails, there is a limited incentive to try another.

The remainder of this section describes three promising technologies, which range in age from 5 to 15 years. Some, therefore, are available for immediate exploitation, others may require a decade of refinement. In making a decision regarding how to implement these technologies, management must understand what is commercially available, how it can be integrated into their organization's operations, and the readiness of their staff to accommodate the changes. It would be foolish for me to offer advice in making that determination. I can, however, explain the technology's underlying concepts, the understanding of which is necessary for an intelligent decision.

### 6.3.1.    Reuse

Reuse is a major topic in software engineering. Selected papers from the Workshop on Reusability in Programming were published in the

September 1984 issue of the *IEEE Transactions on Software Engineering*. The July 1987 issue of *Software* also was devoted to this theme. The IEEE has published two tutorials on the subject [Free87, Trac88], and the ACM has produced a two-volume collection on reusability [BiPe89]. Clearly, it is a major research area with a potential for immediate benefit. Tracz estimates that 40-60% of all code is reusable from one application to another, 60% of the design and code in all business applications is reusable, 75% of the program functions is common to more than one program, and only 15% of the code is unique to a specific application [Trac88]. Obviously, reuse offers a potential for significant productivity improvement.

In its most general form, reuse simply is the exploitation of experience. It often is embodied in the analysts' and designers' understanding of a need and the appropriate responses to it. That level of reuse is the organization's corporate experience; it represents employee domain knowledge. When responding to an RFP, the list of contracts on similar projects is supplied to demonstrate the ability to perform on the proposed contract. The assumption is that what has been done before can be done again. Although there is some research in knowledge-based approaches to capturing this experience (sometimes described under the title *domain analysis* or *domain modeling* [PrAr91]), the most viable method for enhancing reuse still depends on the development of individual skills. Earlier discussion pointed out methods for building and retaining experience through developing great designers [Broo87] or structuring an organization to improve cross training [Lick83]. Perhaps automation will help here, but—for now—it will have only a second order effect.

Another form of reuse focuses on the software artifacts. Program libraries have a long history. Few would want to rewrite the many scientific programs already available from standard libraries. Indeed, who would trust the new programs? Again reverting to Brooks, whenever possible one should buy rather than build; it is the ultimate in reuse. One should also plan to save and reuse the products of previous developments. In his COCOMO model, Boehm adjusts the development costs according to the percentage of design, code, or integration effort that is reused (Section 6.2.3). But Beizer also warns us of the casual reuse of code in the practice of "saving code"; the result can be confusing logic and difficult maintenance (Section 5.3.3). Thus, if we are to reuse program artifacts, we should be controlled and not just opportunistic. That is, we should not simply copy an existing program and tailor it to a new project; we ought to work with tested and certified modular units.

The discussion of encapsulation in Chapter 4 presented ways of modularizing software with a granularity finer than that of the traditional program library. The Ada packages, for example, reduced processes to their specified behaviors and hid information about the implementation. To facilitate reuse, package definitions reinforced common concepts. As Meyer points out [Meye88],

- *Overloading* helps the client programmers develop the same client code when using different implementations of a data structure, and

- *Genericity* helps module implementors write the same module code to describe all instances of the same implementation of a data structure.

Thus, the solution space is smaller, and both concepts and module units can be reused. If management commits to an object-based development environment, the potential for increased reuse is a by-product.

If knowledge-based reuse is not a mature technology and if modular reuse is enhanced with the adoption of an object-based environment, then is there anything that management should do beyond simply promulgating the use of Ada, C++, Eiffel, or Smalltalk? Emphatically, yes. First, management must recognize that simply changing to a new language will not lead to much of a productivity improvement. Recall from Figure 1.13 that the effort multiplier with the least impact is that of language experience. Once one knows how to program in one language, one can quickly learn to program in another. Thus, if one has a decade of experience with FORTRAN programs, it will not take long to learn how to use Ada to write FORTRAN-style programs, which promises no encapsulation payoff. If a new method is to be used, then training is required. There is, however, a corollary to Brooks's law, "Training in a productivity-enhancing technology only reduces near-term productivity." Therefore, a commitment to a new technology without budgeting for both the training and learning costs is really no commitment at all.

Even when the new technology is properly integrated into the environment, reuse benefits will be slow. Because the first projects have no libraries to draw from, little can be reused. In fact, the cost of preparing modules for reuse is greater than the cost for their one-time use. Consequently, one can expect *productivity to decrease* during the first few projects conducted in a reuse context [BaBo91, CaBa91]. Reuse requires a long-term commitment; its benefits may take years to materialize. Furthermore, management would be prudent to follow the risk-reduction principle of starting small and learning by doing. Some researchers are working on environments to maintain and retrieve reusable fragments. In particular, the faceted-retrieval scheme of Prieto-Diaz and Freeman has received considerable attention [PrFr87]. This kind of work focuses on investigations into the management of large bodies of reusable artifacts. For an operational setting, however, the creation of the reusable materials comes first. Methods have to be developed, candidates for reuse have to be identified [CaBa91], and a reuse culture has to be nurtured. Only after this has been accomplished, should the problems of managing reuse libraries be addressed. After all, the library's books are far more important than the elegance of its card catalogue.

### 6.3.2.    Reengineering

Reuse emphasizes a two-pronged approach to implementing new applications. It builds on what has been done already and writes new code fragments to facilitate their reuse. Reengineering, on the other hand, addresses the difficulties of extending or reworking existing systems, usually those created with an older technology. It has become the subject of increasing interest because product longevity is a characteristic of modern systems. Whereas many early applications focused on well-defined objectives with a limited span of utility, most new applications can be thought of as entities within a family. External pressures cause modifications to these families, and—even when individual products within a family are retired—the general family mission persists. Thus, what once was seen as developing discrete, well-specified implementations is becoming recognized as the evolution of products within a family as the missions, external interfaces, platforms, and even programming languages change. In this context, the knowledge embedded in a software product is more long-lived than the software itself.

One may think of this refinement of software families as being maintenance. I have not said very much about software maintenance in this book. Many textbooks devote a chapter to the topic; I restricted my discussion to the few comments in Section 1.4.2, which emphasized that most maintenance is actually product enhancement. I took this nondifferentiating approach because, in the context of the software process, maintenance is just another form of design. Recall that one of Myer's debugging principles was, "The process of error repair should put one back temporarily in the design phase." Similarly, the process of maintenance also puts one back in the design phase. At issue, then, is the difference between a new design and a maintenance redesign. There are two ways of confronting this issue. First, one may examine the staffing philosophy. Should there be a separate maintenance organization, or should the development team retain responsibility? Should maintenance be performed by the junior staff as part of their integration into the organization, or should individuals be encouraged to make a long-term commitment to maintenance activities?

Maintainers need three kinds of knowledge.

- About the problem to be solved (i.e., application domain knowledge).

- About the technology used in to create a solution (i.e., implementation domain knowledge specialized for the target environment).

- About the specific product to be modified.

Designers need to know about only the first two of these; the third is the outcome of their development activity. Clearly, the maintainers must understand what the product does, how it is structured, and what the implications of change are. Prior to structured programming, branching encouraged the distribution of processing throughout the program; after structured programming, the effect of most processing was limited to what could be read on (or evoked from) a single page. Encapsulation, as discussed in Chapter 4, continues this process of localizing concepts and hiding details. Nevertheless, considerable effort is required to gain a sound understanding of the product. The maintenance activity, therefore, should be organized to speed the accumulation of the desired knowledge and maximize its retention.

When a development team follows a throw-it-over-the-wall philosophy, its staff retains the product-specific knowledge only through system acceptance. It is assumed that another contractor will assume maintenance responsibility, which requires an investment in learning the above three categories of knowledge. When, on the other hand, the development team has a mission orientation, the "wall" disappears; team members retain a commitment to the entire product family. In either case a stable, dedicated maintenance staff is desirable. One learns by doing, and in time one gets to be very good at it. Moreover, when maintenance-support tools are used, the training investment also is reduced. Using maintenance as a training ground for new programmers, however, is often inefficient. The important assignments are too difficult for the junior staff, and the knowledge gained from the smaller assignments is seldom developed. When possible, my personal preference is for the mission orientation; here the interest is in the problems and their solutions—not a narrow technology (cf. the above discussion of Theory Z). Knowledge of the problems, technology, and implementation reinforces each other; the potential for reuse and symbiotic transfer grows. The mission orientation is most easily instituted with internal developments.

A second, related aspect of maintenance is the characterization of its process. Basili suggests that we should consider maintenance "reuse-

oriented software development" [Basi90] He identifies three maintenance process models.

- *Quick-fix model.* This is the typical, current approach in which
changes are made at the code level in the fastest and most
expedient manner. (This is why software degrades as described
by Lehman's second law [Lehm80].)

- *Iterative-enhancement model.* This is an evolutionary model in
which, at each step, the process allows the maintainers/developers
to design the system based on an analysis of the existing system.

- *Full-reuse model.* Here one starts with the requirements for the
new systems and reuses as much as possible from the old system.
Because the new system is built from documents and components
in the repository, a mature reuse foundation is a prerequisite.

Today, unfortunately, most maintenance operates at the level of the
quick fix model. In some cases, a team operating in a mission orientation will have developed something close to an iterative-enhancement
model, but this reflects their local commitment rather than the use of
tools or any formal organization.

Notice that if a successful reuse program has been instituted, then
the nature of both development and maintenance will be significantly
altered. The Japanese software factory provides one example of a
process model based on extensive reuse [Mats87]. A specialized family
of products is defined, and a reuse scheme for that family is established.
New products and refinements to existing products draw from and add
to the corporate knowledge of the product family. However, if no such
reuse base exists—and this is currently true for virtually all of our
operational software—is there an alternative to relying on the quick-fix
model until the software has so degraded that it must be retired? That,
of course, is the issue that reengineering and reverse engineering
address.

In the world of hardware, reverse engineering has a sinister
overtone. It implies that one has purchased a competitor's product to
take it apart and see how it works. The goal is to make one's product
better than that of his competition. In software, however, one typically
resorts to the reverse engineering of one's own product simply to find
out what it does. That is, over time the software system has taken on
the quality of a black box. It no longer does what the organization
requires, and changes are necessary. The black box now must be
converted into a white box so the maintainers can get inside and modify
it. A variety of terms are used for this activity, and Chikofsky and Cross
have prepared the taxonomy shown in Figure 6.11. It labels the

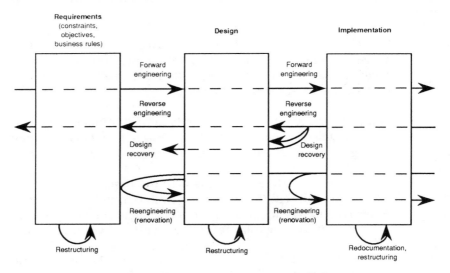

Fig. 6.11. A reengineering taxonomy.
(Reprinted from [ChCr90] with permission, ©1990, IEEE.)

concepts as transformations from one life-cycle phase to another. The
following presents the principal ideas contained in their taxonomy.

- *Forward engineering.* This is the traditional process of moving
  from high-level abstractions and logical, implementation independent designs to the realization of the system as a product.

- *Reverse engineering.* This is the process of analyzing a subject
  system to identify its components and relationships and/or to
  create a representation of the system in another form.

- *Redocumentation.* This is the creation or revision of a semanti-
  cally equivalent representation within the same relative abstraction level. It is the simplest and oldest form of reverse engineering.

- *Design recovery.* This subset of reverse engineering "recreates
  design abstractions from a combination of code, existing design
  documentation (if available), personal experience, and general
  knowledge about problem and application domains" [Bigg89].

- *Restructuring.* This is a transformation from one representation
  to another at the same abstraction level that preserves the

system's behavior. That is, restructuring changes none of the properties of the system other than aspects of its structure.

- *Reengineering.* "Reengineering, also known as both renovation and reclamation, is the examination and alteration of a subject system to reconstitute it in a new form and the subsequent implementation in a new form" [ChCr90].

I have used the term reengineering in the section title; it is the broadest of the concepts defined here.

If an organization is to perform maintenance, then it must engage in design recovery. How else will it know what to change? Naturally, the better the software products conform to modern programming practices, the easier that design recovery should be. Once the software structure has become so degraded that modifications are either very risky, costly, or both, there is no alternative but to freeze or retire the existing programs. Replacement alternatives include a costly new system, a difficult-to-maintain revision of the existing system, or an inexpensive and reliable reengineered system. The adjectives leave little ambiguity about my recommendation. Although reengineering has a clear advantage over the other approaches, in the state of today's practice it is largely an intellectual and manual process. There are some design recovery tools that help designers navigate through the existing programs, and restructuring tools exist to convert operational systems into forms that are more easily maintained [Arno86]. Here is the manager's dilemma. Reuse establishes a foundation for process improvement in later projects, but its immediate impact is increased cost. Until reuse is available, the most cost-effective alternative to new development is reengineering. But, reengineering, without reuse, simply sets the stage for another iteration of reengineering. That is, because there is no repository for the recovered designs, the structure of the newly reengineered system will become obscured during modification, and ultimately another round of design recovery will be needed. Thus, design recovery can never be automated until a reuse scaffolding is in place. And without the ability to reuse, design recovery (which is at the heart of reengineering) will remain a labor-intense, problem-solving activity. No silver bullet.

### 6.3.3. Automated support

Although the title of the overall section is "Process Improvement Technologies," the presentation thus far has not been technological. This section on automated support, I am afraid, will continue to disappoint. Clearly, the reader would welcome a catalog of technologies along with order numbers, purchase costs, mission characteristics, and expected productivity improvements. Unfortunately, that just cannot be done. *Computer-aided software engineering (CASE)* is the catch-all title that we use for automated support. One often thinks of a CASE tool as being able to draw (and perform cross referencing on) DFDs, structure charts, and—perhaps—entity relationship diagrams and Jackson diagrams. But the definition is far more encompassing. CASE includes all the software tools more general than the essential, universal components such as the program editor, compiler, and debugger. There are CASE tools for project control, product design, testing, and requirements analysis. Some rapid prototyping and fourth generation language (4GL) systems are considered CASE technology. COCOMO is a CASE tool. Indeed, the definition is broad enough to have lost its specificity. When we speak of CASE we merely imply an increase in automated assistance to the software process.

Section 1.3.3 introduced the software engineering hierarchy (Fig. 1.10). It described an environment as an integrated collection of tools used to support a cohesive group of methods and practices in carrying out some unifying process description (i.e., process model). The environment represented the unity of the working interface, and tool use was guided by an existing method or practice. Whether or not there is automated assistance, all software development is conducted within an environment. An automated-support environment, naturally, replaces manual tasks with those that can be performed automatically. The objective of CASE technology, therefore, is to identify such tasks and the products that completely or partially automate them. The availability of large markets and open architectures made it possible for a software-tool industry to grow in response to this need.

Each CASE tool is intended to support some method. There can be no "methodology-independent" tools; there are only collections of tools that can support more than one method. Elsewhere in this book I have pointed out that each method institutes a systematic process for achieving some goal. Methods use tools and they define how a tool should support the method's objective. For example, DFDs make sense only in the context of a system decomposition that identifies functions and their interfaces. The DFD represents a natural expression of the system structure when performing analysis in this manner. At the same time, the analysis goals provide the framework for generating a set of DFDs. Having a tool to draw DFDs without a guiding method for their systematic construction would be of little value; it would be equally worthless to rely on a decomposition method while using, say, JSD diagramming tools. Thus, it makes little sense to talk of tools without a commitment to the methods that guide their use.

When an organization already uses the methods the tools facilitate, a context for tool evaluation exists. Often, however, the tool is seen as a catalyst for change. Management hopes that a tool's availability will lead to improvement. This is a common, low-risk strategy. Because change increases risk, management frequently selects strategies that offer the greatest potential with the least disruption. A scale of "interventions" might go from sending people to a course, to buying a few tools, to instituting new methods. The first actions display a response to the need for productivity/quality improvement without having to make difficult, institutional changes. But if the interventions do not reinforce the way the organization currently conducts the software process, then lasting effects will be impossible. This book has described many different and contrasting approaches to software development. One must choose from among the offerings; there must be a commitment. Consequently, it should come as no surprise that, if we are to automate the software process, we must either automate the current practice or adapt the our practices to what has been automated. Of course, that is why Humphrey requires a level 3, defined process before instituting change.

What are the benefits of CASE? Given my vague definition of CASE, one would expect to find a very broad range of benefits. A recent SEI publication "reveals widely divergent claims about the effects of CASE technology on productivity, ranging from negative impacts to 300% increases" [Brid91]. Chikofsky has organized a collection of readings on the topic, but there are few evaluations from which one can generalize [Chik88]. There are many CASE conferences, and the scope and quality of the offerings are continually being improved. One organization, CASE Research Corporation of Bellevue, WA, has started publishing annual surveys. Glass summarized some of their most recent findings.

> According to those who rated themselves as successful [CASE users], keys to their success were
> - using a formal structured method
> - using a formal life-cycle methodology
> - emphasizing quality instead of productivity
> - providing a high degree of training to their software people
> - using both front-end and back-end CASE tools
>
> There seemed to be a large gap between the adoption of new technology and its usage. The survey found such things as
> - Less than 25% of the developers in organizations that have CASE are actually using it.
> - Only 44% of companies that have chosen a primary structured method use that method for more than 50% of new development.

- 76% of respondents have less than half their maintenance supported by a structured method.
- Only 36% of the companies have over half new development supported by a life-cycle methodology. [Glas91, pp. 15-16]

I do not attest to the scientific accuracy of this survey. Nevertheless, the results are consistent with the observation that, if an organization follows good practices, then good tools can be found, but if the practices are imperfect, tools will be of limited help.

I conclude this discussion on automated support with selections from the abstracts of two recent reports.

When evaluating CASE for use, it is important to examine tools that support an organization's existing methods of software development. Support for existing hardware platforms must also be examined. Merely selecting a "good" CASE tool does not insure success. Thorough evaluation of implementing CASE is also critical. Subjects to evaluate for CASE implementation include organization culture, support from management and end users, training resources, and pilot projects. Organizations that benefit most from CASE evaluate CASE features with respect to their needs *and* they properly implement CASE. [Samm90]

Automating a software process both magnifies its strengths and accentuates its weaknesses. Automation can make an effective process more effective, but it can make a chaotic process even worse—and at considerable expense. Anyone who buys expensive tools to solve an ill-defined problem is likely to be disappointed. Unless procuring such tools is part of a thoughtful software process improvement plan, the purchase could be an expensive mistake. [Hump89b]

Clearly, automation can help, but we had better know what we are trying to do before we begin to automate the process.

### 6.4.    Some final observations

The presentation in this chapter has been a "what is" rather than a "how to" description of software project management. I can justify my approach by pointing to all the books that describe the management process. The most widely referenced text on the subject is by Metzger [Metz81]. There also are several books that address the people-oriented aspects of managing software projects [CoZa80, Lick85]. Most software engineering textbooks have sections on management; Sage and Palmer provide detailed coverage from the perspective of systems engineering [SaPa90]. Finally, because the scope of this book is small to large systems, I note that Rakos has a text for the management of such projects [Rako90]. In keeping with my holistic theme, I wanted to emphasize the parallel between the design and management methods. I also decided to tailor the discussion around what I believed would be most important for my readers (even though they might not agree with my assessment).

If the reader is a student, untouched by the harsh realities of a development environment, then I sense he will accept almost any model of project management I propose. While I could have offered one that defines documents, milestones, and reviews, I am sure he will learn about them in his first job. Each new graduate is a potential future manager who's view of the process ought not to be biased by our reactions to the problems of the 1970s. It is important that he recognize technical management as a form of problem solving—not as a career objective with enhanced perks. If he is given Brooks's alternative of continuing on to be come a great designer, then he should choose the management path only if he finds management problem solving more interesting than design problem solving.

The reader who is already a manager, of course, has made a commitment to solving these kinds of problems. He has, by now, developed a style and knows how to manage. I would hope that, after reading this chapter, he will take the time to rethink what he is doing. He should expand his view of the process and seek systematic methods for evaluating and improving what he does. In that sense, this chapter is sensitivity training and a guide to further reading.

Finally, for the practitioner who is not a manager, I hope to have provided a context for understanding his job. The chapter should explain why his management uses tools as they do and how they plan to accomplish their objectives. If his organization operates under Theory X, he has little choice but to follow his instructions to the letter. However, few software (or knowledge-worker-based) organizations succeed in that manner. Therefore, the practitioner should consider sharing his insights with his managers. We tend to operate in hierarchical structures afraid that openness and honesty might be misunderstood. But that is seldom the case. Good managers appreciate feedback and learn from it. With Theory Z all employees have an obligation to the organization to improve productivity, quality, well being, and so forth. If one can help a fellow worker—junior, peer, or manager—one should do so. What a nice, holistic thought with which to end the body of this book.

# EPILOGUE

I now have presented a holistic view of software engineering from the perspective of current practice. As a textbook, it was important that I describe things *as they are* and not *how they ought to be*. The latter is a research issue and of primary interest to researchers. If the practitioner cannot buy it or use it today, then there is little justification for presenting it in a practice-oriented book. Software engineering should be a serious discipline, and there ought to be little encouragement of premature announcements or optimistic speculation. Of course, that is not how software engineering is presented, and I also will describe preoperational concepts. At least, however, I have reserved my discussion for this epilogue.

This paragraph explains what I am about to tell you. If it holds your interest, read on. To begin with, software and software engineering are new. Current processes evolved from experience with hardware, and that orientation has molded our approach. I do not believe that this is a good metaphor. I sense that we have become slaves to invalid perceptions; consequently, a paradigm shift (in the sense of Kuhn) will take place within this millennium. In this book I have described the software process as a formal, problem-solving activity. As it turns out, current practice does not take advantage of the special features of software; neither does it focus on the important problems. This epilogue presents an alternative paradigm that has been validated by a decade of use in the development and maintenance of error-free, life-critical software systems where productivity averages a production program per effort day. What is important in this experience is not how a particular environment works but what that paradigm tells us about the essence of the software process.

In Chapter 1 I pointed out that the waterfall flow was derived from a hardware development model, and in Chapter 6 I suggested that most alternatives to the waterfall model, such as the spiral model, were simply variations of it. Let me restate this by observing that the thrust of the software process is *almost universally* perceived to be a two-step operation. First we decide what is to be done (i.e., analyze and then specify the design) and then we produce the program that realizes the design. Here is how Card puts it.

> Software design is the product engineering part of software develop-
> ment. Programming is in some ways analogous to the manufacturing
> part. [CaG190, p. 13]

Forty years ago, the initial concern in the new discipline was the
creation of high quality programs. It is my thesis that software
engineering is a response to that concern; it focuses on finding better
ways to design and implement programs.

For example, the waterfall model and its variations aim at validating
and refining the design until it is specific enough to be converted into
a set of programs that can be tested individually and then integrated.
The idea is that we cannot create correct programs until we have a valid
design; once that design exists, programs can be coded. The proof of
correctness addresses the issue of algorithm design; it is concerned with
understanding the logic of the computation, which is—of course—a purer
representation for the program. The cleanroom eschews execution-based
testing so that the designers can focus on what the programs should do
rather than how they happen to behave. Emphasis is placed on
reasoning about the program's behavior rather than feedback from
hacking. Formal methods such as VDM use mathematical descriptions
at a higher level. Here the product is a system and not just a program,
and the availability of a formal specification provides a mechanism to
evaluate the correctness of the programs. The debate between followers
of decomposition and composition was motivated, in a large part, by a
concern for the best way to structure a system as program modules. In
fact, programming-in-the-large refers to a module interconnection
language, and—as I have described it—modeling-in-the-small focuses on
modularization techniques for implementation. Have I missed alienating
anyone?

Although the previous paragraph identified many different methods,
the central goal was the same. We need to produce programs, which are
formal models of computation. Therefore, as a prerequisite to producing these programs we must produce a design that specifies what the
programs are to do. Decades of software development have taught us
to believe that our only other choice is to write the programs first and
then produce the design—a universally rejected strategy. Nevertheless,
there is another way of looking at the problem. Revert back to the
essential software process, illustrated in Figure 1.5, and view the
software process as the transformation from a need to an automated
response to that need. As shown in the figure, we begin with subjective,
conceptual models of both the problem and its solution. We next create
a formal model that specifies the desired implementation, and then we
create the implementation. Software engineering thus reduces to the
discipline of combining a group of needs with the understanding of a

technology to develop a product, which in reality is but one of a large number of potentially valid automated responses to that need.

Restating this, the software process can be seen as a transformation from some objectives in a problem space, for which we seldom have precise models, into an implementation in the solution space, for which (at some level of detail) we always have a formal model. During the first decades of software engineering we focused on what then was the most difficult part of the process: the creation and maintenance of high-quality implementations. We had good models for the computations, and the idea of program-as-product fit very well with the hardware metaphor borrowed from the waterfall flow. We *knew* that we needed formal models to define the solution space, and therefore we *assumed* that these formalisms could provide the framework for a discipline. But there is an alternative interpretation.

If we begin with the understanding that our objective is to model a system response to a need rather than a software solution that satisfies that need, then we get a very different paradigm. In the current, *program-as-product* paradigm we require a specification to define the behavior of the product. Prior to the existence of the specification there is no concept of correctness; the specification's validity (as well as that of the products derived from it) is subjective and unprovable. In effect, what we do is select a specification early in the process and then devote our energies to producing a product that is correct with respect to that specification. Where the risk is high, we use prototypes or incremental deliveries to reduce it. Nevertheless, each cycle begins with a specification and ends with a product that has been demonstrated to satisfy its specification. The alternative that I propose is to concentrate on the problem space and recognize the program as what it is: an accidental artifact of the solution.

These are strong words; more explanation is necessary. Table E.1 identifies two paradigms. The *product-oriented* model represents how we now approach software development. At the top is a system specification, and at the bottom is its implementation (normally in the form of a set of programs). I call the proposed alternative a *problem-oriented* paradigm. Here the top is the identification of a solution to the problem and the bottom is the design of that solution. In the product-oriented model, the top and bottom exist in the solution space. That is, for the system specification to be meaningful, it must be as formal as any other object in the solution space. The problem-oriented model, on the other hand, exists in the problem space (as augmented by some solution knowledge). Attention is devoted to the problem solution and not the solution's implementation. Notice that the solution is a function of the problem, and therefore a representation of the solution in the problem space will be more compact than the associated representation of the implementation in the solution space.

Table E.1.  Two software paradigms.

|  | Product oriented | Problem oriented |
| --- | --- | --- |
| Top | System specification | Solution identification |
| Bottom | System implementation | Solution design |

For example, recall the Backus quotation cited in Chapter 1. In it he explained how a task was reduced from about a week to an afternoon by the use of a high-level language (HLL). In his illustration, the 47-line FORTRAN program mirrored the problem-space expression while the 1000 lines of generated assembly language was the equivalent of a pre-FORTRAN solution-space expression. The 1000 minus 47 lines represented housekeeping. They contributed nothing to the solution; they only introduced the potential for additional error. The problem-oriented paradigm assumes that there is a formal representation (i.e., an equivalent to an HLL) that enables us to represent the solution's definition and design. Obviously, this representation will be more compact than one using the product-oriented paradigm. Consequently, it should require less effort to produce, it should be easier to validate, and fewer errors will need to be removed. In effect, I propose that we concentrate on modeling the desired solution and automatically generate the programs from that model.

If the reader has followed this layered argument, then he is probably racing ahead with terms such as program generator and 4GL. Or maybe AI and KBSE. But that is not what about I am about to describe. I am trying to explain a paradigm shift from one that is product oriented to one that is problem oriented. Kuhn observes,

> The transition from a paradigm in crisis to a new one from which a new tradition of normal science can emerge is far from a cumulative process, one achieved by an articulation or extension of the old paradigm. Rather it is a reconstruction of the field from new fundamentals, a reconstruction that changes some of the field's most elementary generalizations as well as many of its paradigm methods and applications. [Kuhn70, pp. 84-85]

That is, one cannot understand the problem-oriented paradigm using the concepts of the product-oriented paradigm. A problem-oriented "program generator" is about as meaningful as a "correct initial specification." There is only an intuitive desire that the term makes sense.

Having rejected the idea that the program is a product to be specified and built, I have emancipated myself from the encumbrances of program development. To address the issue of how to represent the problem to be solved (i.e., the need to be met using automation), I must explore how to exploit the special properties of software. (This pair of complementary sentences expresses the paradigm shift; if that fact is not clear, then reread them before proceeding.) To continue, software has (at least) five characteristics that distinguish it from hardware.

- *Software is a design.* It is wrong to consider the program code a product; it is simply the most detailed expression of the design. Like the rest of the design, the program is only text, and its linkage with higher level text is maintained. When using PDL, for example, one expects the structure of the final program to follow that of the PDL.

- *Software manufacture is cost free.* The conversion of a design in the form of a source program into an implementation in the form of an object program has essentially no cost. Paradoxically, the project structure based on the product-oriented paradigm has been optimized to reduce the cost impact of changes when there is no cost for change.

- *Software design is software.* Virtually all of a software specification and design is expressed in a textual form that can be managed as software. This includes both the design and its realization. Where the text is informal (e.g., text descriptions), it can be treated only as passive knowledge. On the other hand, where the design objects are formally stated, they can be manipulated and transformed by other software.

- *Software can be exercised locally.* Each software module, given the proper context and state, can be exercised independent of the whole. This implies that software can be very tolerant of incompleteness. Moreover, once the desired properties of some software object have been certified, the object is available for use in all settings that conform to its constraints.

- *Software is dynamic.* As a design that expresses a specified problem solution, software evolves with improvements in the knowledge of the problem and the efficacy of the solution. Experience with the software enhances the understanding of the initial problem and sows the seeds for subsequent improvements.

Two important points need to be made before continuing. First, there is a difference between the software design and the software product that represents a correct and valid design. The requirements to which the software responds are dynamic, and so too will be the software design. The software implementation, however, must be a stable instantiation of a tested design; it can be replaced only with other instantiations of a tested design. That is, we must distinguish between a dynamic design (which is incomplete, incorrect, and/or invalid most of the time) and the static operational software system (which should be shown to be correct and valid before it is accepted for operational use). Second, there is a difference between the process of creating a correct and valid implementation and management of that process. For the purposes of management, a waterfall-type flow may be appropriate. Indeed, as I have shown, for projects with both hardware and software it is highly desirable. However, one should be careful to separate the concern for how we carry out the process from how we manage it.

If this analysis is correct, then we should consider software to be a design that captures both what is to be done (i.e., the requirements) plus how the desired goal can be met. This design is subject to constant change as new needs are identified and better methods for achieving the goals are discovered. Fortunately, this design can be inexpensively transformed into a whole or partial implementation, tested and certified incrementally, and managed by an automated environment. In fact, rapid iteration of design decisions improves confidence in the requirements (i.e., the traditional distinction between the "what" and "how" fades). The result is the shift from a sequence of events culminating in code production to an emphasis on the representation and evaluation of the problem solution (i.e., the specification).

Today, few environments take advantage of these special features of software. However, if we were to build environments to exploit these characteristics, the software process would change radically. Design would no longer be considered an activity that culminates in the decision to write code; the code would be part of the design, and the design could be tested operationally. The developers would be free to alter the design as they experimented with the completed code. The fact that there is essentially no cost for manufacture would encourage this kind of exploratory development. Where experience existed, it could be reused; iteration would concentrate on those areas with the greatest uncertainty. Finally, by maintaining the entire design as an integrated knowledge base, designers could access the complete design. Modifications to one portion of the design would be extended automatically to all affected design objects.

Figure E.1 contrasts the alternative software process models. It depicts the amount of knowledge about an application (i.e., system) that is available in machine-sensible form as a function of the development phase. In the standard paradigm, prevalent during the early days of computing when equipment was expensive, only the code—which was necessary—was stored in the computer. As equipment costs fell, the use of tools grew and the tool-enhanced paradigm emerged. Unfortunately, the tools represent a nonintegrated adjunct. One can change the tool database without affecting the code, and vice versa. In keeping with the product-oriented view, most integrated tools support program development activities. The third, fully automated paradigm collects everything known about the application in an integrated database and generates operational products from that knowledge. That is, the fully automated paradigm is problem-oriented; when using such an environment, the developer is as concerned with program design issues as the FORTRAN programmer is aware of assembly-language implications.

This is interesting theory, but how realistic is this paradigm? Since 1980 I have been working with an application development environment (ADE) based on this philosophy. The largest application developed with it is a clinical information system that supports the care of cancer patients at the Johns Hopkins Oncology Center. The Oncology Clinical

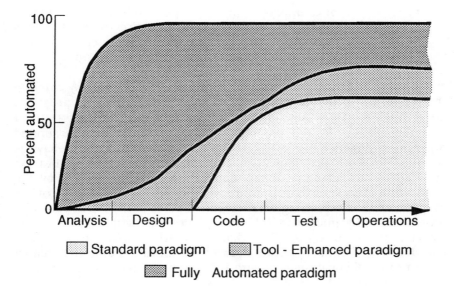

Fig. E.1. Three paradigms for software development.

Information System (OCIS) operates on five networked computers, manages a distributed database containing data from a half-million days of care for 50,000 patients, and supports more than 200 terminals; smaller implementations of this system operate in Australia and Ohio [EnLB89]. Other applications developed with this environment include an intelligent query processor [BlDH87], a clinical system for ambulatory care, and a variety of small systems. TEDIUM,[1] the ADE, is itself a TEDIUM-generated application [Blum90]. It is easiest to describe the environment in terms of the knowledge it utilizes. Three categories of knowledge are identified:

- *Application knowledge.* This is the knowledge of a specific application. In TEDIUM the knowledge is stored in an *application database* (ADB) as a collection of integrated objects including declarative and procedural program specifications, a semantic data model, and descriptive text with links to the associated formal objects.

- *Application-class knowledge.* This is knowledge about all applications of a given class. In the case of TEDIUM, the class is that of interactive information systems, and examples include clinical information systems, software tools, and some knowledge-based applications. Application-class knowledge is represented in a *system style.*

- *Software-tool knowledge.* This is computer science knowledge as applied to software tools for the transformation of specifications into implementations, the creation of a development support environment, the management of the ADB, and so on.

When using TEDIUM, the designer is responsible for *explicitly* entering the properties of the desired application into the ADB. As programs are created, the knowledge in the system style is *implicitly* incorporated into the product by the program generator. Thus, each generated program is functionally complete in that it includes the behaviors specified for both that individual unit (as defined by the application knowledge) and all units of this application class (as defined by the application-class knowledge). Moreover, because the knowledge of the program and the associated data structures exists in the ADB, each new program is fully integrated into the application (with respect to the current contents of the ADB). That is, TEDIUM maintains a holistic knowledge base of the application, and the application units are created as part of a holistic design. Figure E.2 contains a diagram showing the

---

[1]TEDIUM is a registered trademark of Tedious Enterprises, Inc.

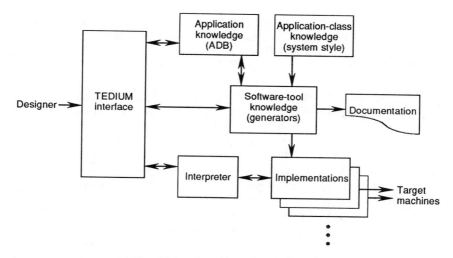

Fig. E.2. Overview of TEDIUM.

interactions of the TEDIUM components.

With this kind of knowledge-based ADE, the software process is affected in the following ways. The approach runs counter to what I previously presented as good software engineering practice.

- Designers do not write specification documents to prescribe the design. Instead, they compose the specification in the ADB by adding fragments of knowledge. When sufficient knowledge exists, implementation units are generated and exercised. The process proceeds iteratively and incrementally. At each step the specification is either modified or the generated product is accepted as complete.

- The existence of implementation units (e.g., programs) is transparent to both the design team and the end users. While some processes (such as process a menu or print a report) are described in a specification unit, each unit is embedded in the whole of the ADB. Thus, there is no concept of module or file except as they may be required for the installed implementation. In other words, the binding of ADE knowledge into modules can be deferred until the delivery of the finished implementation.

- There is no inherent structure for an application. The specification is maintained in a holistic ADB that retains all links among design fragments. One can always produce the listing of a complete specification, but the structure of that specification is determined by the listing format, which imposes a hierarchy by obscuring some of the links among specification objects. (In this sense, the specification listing may be thought of as a projection from some high-dimension holistic specification onto a lower dimension printed specification; information is lost as the number of dimensions is reduced.)

- The distinction between the activities of specification and design is obscured. With a formal approach, the specification captures all the desired behaviors of the target product, and the design adds the details to produce an efficient implementation. The specification must be *valid* with respect to the application need, and the design must be *correct* with respect to the specification. However, in many applications it is not possible to establish a valid specification before design begins. (For example, the requirement for OCIS was to "use automation to improve patient care.") Here the premature freezing of the specification may result in an invalid product, and changing the specification once design begins may destroy the existing design's correctness. In such situations implementation details that affect performance can be embedded in the specification as its validity is evaluated. The resulting specification will be less general than a traditional specification, but the risk of its being invalid will be lower.

It is difficult to reconcile these comments with the product-oriented view that we have come to accept during the past four decades. The thesis of this epilogue, however, is that technology has removed many of the obstacles that constrained us in earlier years. When we channel our energy in avoiding obsolescent difficulties, we fail to recognize the benefits that the special properties of software offer. Of course, this is a research issue. No matter how engrossed the practitioner is in my description, his job remains unaffected until the new paradigm reaches him.

The first step in demonstrating the efficacy of a new approach is to demonstrate its use in an operational setting. Several projects already have been identified that indicate that TEDIUM has been used to produce large-scale, commercial-grade, complex systems. OCIS, the largest of these systems, is widely accepted as the most comprehensive clinical information system used in tertiary care. It is used by 100 people each day to assist in life-threatening medical decision making. The remainder of this section uses data from that project to provide answers to four critical questions regarding application development using the problem-oriented paradigm.

*Can the paradigm support the development of large, complex systems?* Development of OCIS began in 1980, and the complete two-computer system was installed in 1983. By the end of 1989, the ADB specification of OCIS had grown to 13,000 design objects, of which 7500 were program specifications. Because the program specification need not express knowledge maintained elsewhere in the ADB or system style, they are very compact and average 15 lines in length. Thus, the 1989 OCIS specification could be viewed as a 100,000-line "product." By modern standards, this is not a large application. However, every specification requires extensions to produce an implementation. An earlier study of TEDIUM indicated that a 15-line program specification was expanded to a 60-line MUMPS program or a 200-line COBOL program [Blum82]. Thus, if OCIS were implemented in COBOL, the resulting product would be a two-million-line system—clearly, a large-scale application.[2] The difference between the 100K lines of specification and the 2M lines of COBOL represents the difference between the specification of a solution and its implementation. In the case of TEDIUM, the knowledge required to transform a specification into a solution exists, and that transformation can be automated. This frees the designers to concentrate on specifying a response to the application need; implementation issues need be addressed only when confronted by efficiency or operational concerns.

*How effective are designers when using this environment?* There are two measures for designer effectiveness. First, one can compute productivity. One industry guideline is that programs are produced at the rate of two lines per hour over the life of a commercial-grade project. Using this baseline, one would expect OCIS programs to be produced at the rate of one production program per effort day. In 1989 the number of programs in the production system divided by the total number of effort days expended on the project indicated a net rate of 3/4 production program per effort day. When the retired production programs are accounted for, the gross rate becomes approximately one a day. A second dimension of designer effectiveness is the ability of the designer to express his intent effectively. If it can be shown that few edits are required to create and modify programs, then it can be claimed that the holistic environment allows the designers to represent their intent easily. In a 1988 study of a 6500 program baseline, it was shown that—after eight years—half the program specifications were edited 10 or fewer times, and only 10% of the programs were edited more than 33 times. These edits included all debugging, error-correction, and enhancement changes to the specifications. Clearly, once learned, TEDIUM's representation scheme provides an effective means for the designers to model the need and solution.

*How responsive are the applications to changing requirements?* Because the entire design of an application is maintained in an ADB that provides arbitrary local views of the specification, one would expect

---

[2]The version of TEDIUM used for OCIS generates programs in the MUMPS programming language [Lewk89].

it to be relatively easy to adapt the application to the evolving needs of the host environment. The OCIS data confirm this. The first full OCIS application was installed in 1983 as a 3500-program system. During its development, a backlog of requests accumulated. These refinements were addressed, and the system rapidly grew to 5000 programs. Unfortunately, the computer facilities soon became stressed, and further growth was constrained by computer resources. In the next few years, 1200 programs had to be retired to enable system extension; the system size had reached a ceiling of 5500 programs. In 1986 a new software system was installed that removed this limitation, and during the last three years OCIS size has grown by 39%. The limitation on growth now seems to be the ability of the users and developers to define extensions and integrate the changes into an operational setting.

*How deeply integrated are the applications?* An underlying theme in my argument is that every application has a deeply integrated (i.e., holistic) organization; consequently, formulating the implementation as complete modules adds complexity. The previous paragraph indicated that OCIS has been evolving throughout its operational lifetime. At issue, then, is the nature of that evolution. Do the new programs represent separate features that share a common database, or are the system extensions deeply integrated into the OCIS design? A 1988 study of the 6500-program OCIS baseline showed that 1000 new programs had been added in the previous 18 months and another 2000 programs had been edited during the same period. That is, in a year and a half, half of a 6500-program application was either new or had been modified. Many of these edits could be traced to the integration of new features into the existing system. (For a detailed study of the ripple effect in a 100-program application, see [Blum86].) Incidently, all these changes were made by a staff of 4.5 FTEs, and—because OCIS is used in a life-critical setting—the changes were perceived to be free of error. Thus, one can conclude that a holistic design facilitates design comprehension and integration.

I am convinced that environments that share the philosophy of TEDIUM represent the way in which we will develop applications in the twenty-first century. As a researcher, my goal is to work on problems that may take 5 to 10 years before they become the state of practice. Naturally, my ideas will evolve during a decade of adaptation. Therefore, the specifics of TEDIUM are not important to practitioners. But the lesson of this epilogue is significant. We currently address the software process in an archaic fashion; one that is dominated by a false perception of what software is. Most tool and technology refinements aim at automating the manual aspects of the process, an approach that, at best, will have a hygienic effect. In Chapter 6 I indicated that management models how we now conduct the process so that it can predict how future projects will be conducted. This fact, when combined with the principles of risk reduction, fosters the status quo. Evolutionary change.  But, by definition, a paradigm shift is revolutionary, and—as practitioners—you will be caught up in that revolution.

In the era of rare hardware and no experience, knowing how to write a program defined a lucrative profession.  We now are entering an era of ubiquitous computers with widespread computer literacy.  Chapters 1 through 6 were intended to prepare you for today's assignments, which still are defined in terms of the specification, design, and implementation of programs.  This epilogue was added to get you thinking about the changes yet to come.

# Appendix A

## EXERCISES

This appendix contains exercises organized by chapter section. Those exercises flagged with an asterisk are intended for assignment to groups. These assignments are generally small design exercises that build on the illustrations in the text. As with much of software engineering, most of the examples have many correct answers. The student and instructor should be careful, however, to avoid wrong answers.

## 1. The Software Process

### 1.1.1. The Origins of Software Engineering

1.1    In 1957 Backus talked about "one job done with a system." Was this a good evaluation of the system? How could he have made the evaluation better? If one were to evaluate a system today, how should it be done?

1.2    The 1957 Backus quotation showed how FORTRAN changed the problem and reduced the size of the task. Are there systems in the 1990s that apply the same techniques that FORTRAN used in the 1950s? Explain.

1.3    The second NATO Conference identified a lack of communications. Does that problem exist today? Explain.

1.4    Boehm, in his 1976 paper, talked of two problem areas. Where are we today with respect to Area 2? Who are our technicians for Area 2, and what is (or ought to be) their training.

1.5    Mahoney sees software engineering as something primarily of interest to large R&D projects. Debate this observation.

*1.1.2. Some Modern Views of Software Engineering*

1.6     Define software engineering in 25 words or less. Now use 50 words to tell what you left out.

1.7     Belady and Leavenworth talked of two cultures. Is this unique to software engineering? Explain.

1.8     How do you differentiate between a software engineer, a computer engineer, and a computer scientist? How would you characterize your interests? Your training?

1.9     Explain what an engineer (electrical, mechanical, civil, etc.) does and what he needs to learn in his formal education. Compare and contrast this with what a software engineer must know. What are some of the major differences?

*1.2.1. A Traditional Waterfall Model*

1.10     Describe how the simple problem-solving paradigm of Figure 1.1 is used in two different nonsoftware developments.

1.11     In Boehm's 1976 illustration (Fig. 1.2), there are two places where the word "test" appears. Are these the only places that testing is done? Explain.

1.12     Are there other ways to show the flow implied by Figures 1.2 and 1.3? Try your own version of the waterfall flow.

1.13     The waterfall flow was designed for very large projects. Are there problems with its use with small projects? Explain.

1.14     There is a statement that source code is really a detailed design and not a product. Debate this comment. If code were only a design, would it make any difference in how it was created?

*1.2.2. The Essential Software Process*

1.15     Comment on the difference between verification and validation. Is one more important? Give an example of a problem statement that can be validated but not verified; another that can be verified but not validated; and one that must be both validated and verified.

1.16    In Figure 1.4, which shows the essence of the waterfall model, where can computer science improve the process? Explain.

1.17    In the essential software process model (Fig. 1.5), two types of models are identified. From your experience with software, give three examples each of a conceptual and a formal model. In the essential software process, which type of model is of concern to computer scientists? To practicing software engineers?

### 1.2.3.  Some Alternative Models

1.18    What are the advantages of doing it twice? Do you think that this is a common industry practice? Explain.

1.19    Compare and contrast the idea of a hardware and software prototype. How does a software prototype differ from a software simulation?

1.20    Contrast Boehm's spiral model (Figure 1.6) with Brooks's suggestion to throw one away.

1.21    Prototypes can be used to discover what the requirements are or how to build the product. Give some examples of each type of use with software.

1.22    The operational approach treats the specification as a prototype. What are the advantages and disadvantages of this paradigm?

1.23    When is hacking (i.e., improvisation at the keyboard) effective, and when should it be encouraged?

### 1.3.1.  Problem Solving

1.24    Take a computer program you have written and break it down into chunks. Do the chunks map concepts into operational structures (e.g., sequences and loops)? Are the chunks in turn composed of chunks?

1.25    Try this experiment with a colleague: Show him a short program and test his recall; repeat the same experiment with scrambled code. Compare the performance for the two cases.

1.26    "Validation is the elimination of naive theories." Discuss.

1.27    Describe your personal approach to problem solving.  What is the role of your unconscious effort?  Does stopping for a break and relaxing seem to help?

1.28    For the designer of an environment for human users, what clues do the studies of bias in decision making provide?

1.29    Do you agree or disagree with all that has been said about human problem solving?  Explain.

### 1.3.2.  Modeling Concepts

1.30    Give an illustration of the Fallacy of Identification taken from the history of science.  Give an illustration from software.  How does this relate to verification and validation?

1.31    Why do you think that the LST model concentrates on reification rather than abstraction?

1.32    What assumptions must be made if the software process is to become a fully formal activity?

1.33    Give a normative and descriptive model for how to write a computer program.

1.34    Discuss the importance of errors in learning.  What does this suggest about the need to throw one away?

### 1.3.3.  Methods, Tools, and Environments

1.35    Sketch out the contents of a database for the Software Engineering Hierarchy shown in Figure 1.10.  Is your database a hierarchy, or do some of the entries have more than one parent?

1.36    Can you add to or reorganize Brooks's essential difficulties of software?  To what extent do these difficulties deal with design and to what extent with the task of writing code?

1.37    Why do you think that the list of potential improvements that Brooks lists in his "No Silver Bullet" paper can, at best, address only accidental difficulties.

1.38   Comment on this observation, "Brooks most promising attacks on the difficulties of software are to rely on our problem-solving ability."

## *1.4.   Facts, Myths, and Perceptions*

1.39   Add to or dispute the myths listed in Section 1.4.

### *1.4.1.   The Famous GAO Report*

1.40   Cite three lessons from the GAO Report experience.

### *1.4.2.   Software Engineering Findings*

1.41   List five facts that you believe would surprise most noncomputer people.  That would surprise most managers.  Most engineers.

1.42   Identify three factors that most impact productivity.

1.43   If you were to develop a software environment, which three facts would be most important to you in establishing the requirements?

1.44   Comment on this observation, "Development is a special case of software maintenance."

## 2.   Requirements Analysis and Modeling

### *2.1.   Approaching Requirements Analysis*

2.1   Explore the idea that a requirements specification is a contract. How formal must it be?  Are there business situations in which the "sense" of a contract is more important than its "word?"  If so, how does this relate to software requirements?

### *2.1.1.   Distinguishing between the What and How*

2.2   Give an example of some process that can be specified, but that may be difficult to implement as a program.  What are the major implementation difficulties in this example: the functional or nonfunctional requirements?

2.3    Consider the requirements for an automobile that can be designed by a computer for automatic fabrication by a robot.    List some functional requirements for that product.    Some nonfunctional requirements.

### 2.1.2.  The Role of Prototypes

2.4    The quotation on exploratory software development referenced the development of the $(n+1)$st version of a system.   When should exploratory development be used with such applications?

2.5    Distinguish between exploratory development, prototyping, and "hacking."   Which, if any, of these methods is suited to the implementation of production-quality software?

### 2.2.    The Configuration Management Case Study

2.6    Is a formal SCM system required for all projects?   If not, what conditions would justify an informal approach to SCM?

2.7    Identify some of the costs and delays inherent in a formal SCM system.   How can they be reduced?

2.8    Refer to the waterfall diagram in Figure 1.2 and list the CIs that should be maintained under SCM for a large project.   Are there any changes for a small project?

2.9*   Suggest an interface and command parameters for the code management component of the SCM system whose commands are given. Are any commands missing from the list in Section 2.2?

2.10*  Write a short report that defines the method for revision numbering.  Be sure to include sufficient detail so that the report can be referenced as a requirement for the code management component of the SCM system.

## 2.3.1. Data Models

**2.11** Give two examples of systems in which the design of the system can be defined by the data representations it manages. Give two examples in which the data structures are not important. How important are processes that act on the data in these illustrations?

**2.12** Design descriptions are metadata for the implementation. Argue pro or con.

**2.13** Consider the entity-relationship diagram as a knowledge representation scheme (i.e., a formal presentation of what we know). Characterize what knowledge about the SCM it displays. What does it not include? What does it include that a relational scheme does not include?

**2.14*** Modify the ERM in Figure 2.8 to reflect the real-world fact that either customers or developers can submit CRs. (You may have to extend the notation to show this. Does the new notation introduce ambiguity?)

**2.15*** Draw an ERM diagram for a system that makes task assignments, requests the release of CIs, returns CIs, and reports status. Do not try to follow the diagram in Figure 2.8. How does your diagram differ from that in Figure 2.8?

**2.16*** Develop an ERM for the code management system of the SCM system. Assume the external interfaces are messages to copy files to and from the baseline. Obviously, the messages must identify both a designer and an authorized SCM agent.

**2.17** Present a statement using the relational algebra that would list all CIs assigned to designer Jones. Identify the relations, their attributes, and keys. Could you use the algebra without knowing the schema? Now sketch a procedural program to produce the same results from that schema.

**2.18*** Define a relational schema for the code management system. (Hint: use only the names of the files that contain the code, and do not include the code itself in the schema.) Give an example of some relation that is not in third normal form and convert it to third normal form.

**2.19** Inheritance is an *ISA* relationship. Identify some examples of inheritance in the SCM system.

## 2.3.2. Process Descriptions

2.20   Assume that there are two categories of customer.  Some that purchased systems and could not submit CRs and others that could submit both SIRs and CRs.  How would this change the diagram in Figure 2.11?  Why?

2.21*  Assume that only a code management system is required.  Go through the context diagram steps just described and produce a context diagram for that system.

2.22*  Using the context diagram developed in exercise 2.21, describe the sequential flow for the processing of a CI.  Once you have laid out a sequence including both loops and selections (i.e., if ... then ... else), are there any exceptions to this flow?  (Note: in Chapter 3 we will see how Jackson models this kind of sequence.)

2.23*  Expand the Initiate Task box in the SADT diagram shown in Figure 2.18 as a complete SADT diagram.  Be sure that the diagram inputs and outputs match those of the box in its parent diagram.

2.24*  Note that the boxes in Figure 2.18 are actions and the flows are data.  This is sometimes called an "actagram," and it is possible to draw a "datagram" in which the boxes are data and the flows are actions.  Try drawing a datagram for the processing of a CR from receipt to CI update.  What data would be drawn in boxes?  What actions would flow from box to box?  What are the controls and mechanisms?

2.25*  Draw a state-transition diagram for the situation in which a CI can be checked out to more than one designer at a time, but when this happens we are in a "special coordination" state.  (That is, Fig. 2.20 must be extended to include at least three states: not checked out, exclusive update, and special coordination).

2.26*  Define an event list for the condition described in exercise 2.25. Present that event list in the form of a decision table.

2.27*  Draw a Petri net for the state-transition diagram developed in exercise 2.25.  Place the tokens to indicate that the CI has been checked out to just one designer (i.e., exclusive update state).

### 2.3.3. Formal Methods

2.28  Comment on this statement:  CASE tools provide formal representations that eliminate some of the uncertainty found in textual documentation.  What is the limit of these formal representations?

2.29  The operational paradigm as illustrated by the Balzer approach described in Section 1.2.3 is a formal approach.  Explain why you think it is formal.  How does it differ from the mathematical approaches such as VDM?

2.30*  What are the preconditions and postconditions for the two states in the state-transition diagram in Figure 2.20?  For the boxes in the SADT diagram in Figure 2.18?  How formal are your statements?

### 2.3.4. Textual Specifications

2.31  Describe how an SCM requirements specification would vary if the system were to be developed internally, developed as part of a student project, or developed for a customer with a specific application in mind.

2.32  What documents are necessary for developing a system as an internal activity involving one effort year over 6 months?  Involving 10 effort years over 2 years?  Involving 20 people?

2.33*  Write an SRS for the preliminary processing function of the SCM system.  Are some areas unclear?  How can you resolve these issues?  Should you delay the SRS until you have these answers, or should you defer the resolution until design?  Why?

2.34*  Use the various checklists to critique your SRS section.  How much additional effort would be required to get an SRS that satisfies these minimal demands?  Is it possible to produce a good SRS without additional domain knowledge?  Explain.

### 2.4.1. The User Interface

2.35*  Outline the characteristics of the user interface for the code management system.  (See exercise 2.9.)  Critique your design according to the criteria given in the chapter.

2.36    Justify the user interface guidelines by referencing the discussion of human information processing (Section 1.3.1).

### 2.4.2.  The Ilities

2.37*  Which of the ilities are important in the code management system, and how would you ensure their presence?  Would the same ilities be required for the entire SCM system?  Explain.

### 2.5.    The Next Steps

2.38*  Brainstorm:  What we know about the SCM system.  What we do not know.  What is unclear?  If you really had to build a commercial-grade SCM system, describe what you would do in the next 30 days.  How would you use prototypes to help refine your understanding?  For the user interface?  For algorithms?

2.39    How would the emphasis in this chapter change if the case study were a business management system?  An embedded process control device?  The security module of an operating system?

## 3.  Modeling-in-the-Large

### 3.1.    Decomposition and Composition

3.1    Give three examples each of "acceptance" and "validation" criteria for the SCM system.  Could we convert the validation criteria to acceptance criteria?  Explain.

3.2    Distinguish between modeling and programming.  Is programming an example of modeling?  How can modeling be taught in an academic setting?  How do we know when a model is "right?"

3.3    Discuss some aspect of the SCM and examine how it can be implemented.  Does your explanation begin at the top or with some specific characteristic?

3.4    Provide a top-down description of how to use a telephone (e.g., call, answer, call forward).  To what extent did you construct that description by means of composition (i.e., working from the particular details)? To what extent did the top-down approach add to the clarity of your presentation?

## 3.2. Structured Analysis and Structured Design

3.5    Recall that the first conference on software engineering met in 1968 and that the seeds of SA/SD were planted half a decade later. Does SA/SD address current needs? Explain.

### 3.2.1. Structured Analysis and the SCM Case Study

3.6    Describe the current physical and logical models for the way HHI supports SCM. How will the new SCM system alter this (i.e., what is the new logical model)?

3.7*   The context diagram in Figure 3.1 was adapted from the entity diagram developed using Orr's method. In SA one would produce a new physical model in the form of a data flow diagram, draw a boundary around what the system should support, and then reduce what is inside that boundary to a single bubble. Try this as an exercise starting with the current logical model.

3.8*   Complete processes 2 through 5 in the DFD shown in Figure 3.2. Work down as many levels as necessary to define the minispecs; supply minispecs and a data dictionary. Are there problems in the level-1 DFD? Should the first level allocation of processes be changed? Are the levels of DFD expansions uniform across all processes?

3.9*   Assume that the input to a bubble is a sorted file containing all active CRs sorted by Priority, Source, and CR-No. The input file has a header containing its creation date. The output from this process is a report containing a list of active CRs that identifies the source and the number of active CRs for that source. The report starts a new page for each priority category, is headed with the input file creation date, and contains a summary page with the total number of active CRs in each category. Write a minispec for this process (bubble). Write a data dictionary entry for the input file. How would you show the sort order? (Note: there is no standard method.) Write a description of the output file. (Hint: show the report layout and identify the items in the report by their dictionary names, if available.)

3.10* Expand the minispec created in 3.9 into a pseudocode description that displays the detailed structure of the program that will implement the process (bubble). Was there any ambiguity in the minispec?

3.11* Write a data dictionary for the attributes identified in the partial SCM scheme shown in Figure 2.9. Does that scheme match what was produced by completing the DFD? How do you explain the difference?

### 3.2.2. Structured Design

3.12* Discuss the differences between the DFD and the structure chart.

3.13* Draw a structure chart for the process defined in exercise 3.9. Explain where transform analysis was conducted. Was transaction analysis required?

3.14 What insights about the product and its design did you develop as the result of exercise 3.13? After drawing the structure chart, would you change the pseudocode in exercise 3.10?

3.15 Write a descriptive algorithm for transforming a data flow graph into a structured diagram. Can you tell by looking at the data flow graph exactly which bubbles represent transforms and transactions? (Hint: in Fig. 3.10 what are D and F?) If the graph syntax does not capture this information, what does this suggest about the role of analyst understanding?

### 3.2.3. Variations on Structured Analysis

3.16 Make a list of the different application categories (e.g., information system, real-time, operating systems). What attributes of these systems are difficult to model with traditional SA?

3.17 Discuss how (or if) the three phases of the Ward and Mellor book correspond to the titles of Chapters 2 through 4. (Hint: as with much of software engineering, there is no single correct answer.)

3.18* Make an event list for just the code management portion of the SCM. Use the four-step approach suggested by Yourdon and produce a DFD and data dictionary. Is this DFD different from what you described in exercise 3.8? Does a process labeled Source Code Management exist in the earlier DFDs? Should it?

3.19    Yourdon comments on the top-down approach. When does it work well? [Hint: remember the $(n+1)$st version.] Is his modified approach still top down? What difficulties can you detect in "modern systems analysis?" (Note: many people still prefer the more traditional approach to SA.)

### 3.3.1. Jackson Program Design (JSP)

3.20*  Modify the Jackson diagram shown in Figure 3.14 to represent a generic request form (i.e., either a CR or an SIR).

3.21    Because JSP uses a formal notation in which structured programs can be expressed diagrammatically, it should be possible to express any structured program as a Jackson diagram. Draw a Jackson diagram for the pseudocode developed in exercise 3.10.

3.22*  Use JSP to produce the pseudocode for a program that reads in CRs (as structured in Fig. 3.14) and produces a report containing all CRs that are active. It lists the CR number, source, and priority plus a count of the number of CIs and documents affected. A final summary page provides a count of active CRs plus the total number of CIs and documents affected; this is given for each priority, and there is a total.

3.23*  Repeat exercise 3.22 but list only completed CRs. Sort the output by priority and then by date completed (contained in the Status Complete block). List the CR number, source, and counts of CIs and documents affected. Include a final summary page. (Note that this kind of structure clash is easiest to resolve using a sort file as shown in Fig. 3.19.)

3.24*  Assume that each time a CR is completed, a record is entered in an historic file that is sorted by the date an entry is made. Records include the completion date and the CR number. The file containing CRs is accessed directly by CR number. Given these two facts, redo exercise 3.23 using the inversion method shown in Figure 3.20.

### 3.3.2. Jackson System Development (JSD)

3.25*  Figure 3.23 shows the life history of a CI. Draw a similar Jackson diagram for the activities of the CCB.

3.26*  What are the actions of interest to the CCB? How are these actions similar to events as they were discussed in the state-transition model? Are state changes associated with actions? Are state changes associated with moving from box to box in a Jackson diagram?

3.27* Expand the diagram of the CR entity shown in Figure 3.27 to produce a pseudocode description of the process in the form of that for the CI process shown in Figure 3.26.

3.28* Add the suspend-and-resume statements to the pseudocode in Figure 3.26 and as the result of exercise 3.27.

3.29* Produce pseudocode (and the Jackson diagrams) for the three processes introduced in Figure 3.31. Note how each box in the network represents a process diagram that can be converted into pseudocode text.

3.30 Explain the difference between the information contained in Figures 3.31 and 3.34.

3.31* Use the contents of the control hierarchy shown in Figure 3.34 to produce a structure chart for the SCM system. (Treat Task as one module; all the other modules should have been expanded as the result of the above exercises.) Note that one would not normally produce a structure chart using JSD. I offer this as an exercise to show how the information produced by the Jackson method may be represented as a set of interacting modules. The key to JSD is how it helps the designer find the interconnections.

### 3.4.    Comparisons and Alternatives

3.32* Assume that two SCM systems are developed: one from the DFD diagram in Figure 3.5 and the other from the control hierarchy shown in Figure 3.34. How would these two systems differ in their internal structure? The structure of the files on which they operate?

3.33* Assume the two SCM systems were implemented as described in exercise 3.32. Identify a system change that would be easier to implement in the DFD-derived system. One that would be easier to implement in the JSD-derived system.

3.34* Continuing with example 3.33, discuss the effects on both systems if we elected to add the completion file (described in exercise 3.24) and the associated report.

3.35*  Assume that you had to give a presentation to the sponsor about the SCM system that you were about to develop. Which types of diagrams would you find most effective?

3.36  Discuss how you could combine some of the best features of SA/SD and JSD/JSP. What would be the advantages? Disadvantages?


## 4. Modeling-in-the-Small


### 4.1.  Implementing the System

4.1  The general theme of this text is that as the design progresses we go from solving problems defined in the application domain to solving problems in the implementation domain. Using the titles of Chapters 2 through 4 discuss this view. See if you can define the dividing lines between the steps in the overall process.


### 4.1.1.  Prerequisites to Implementation

4.2*  Choose some portion of the SCM design and write a design specification for that set of functions. Include any of the graphic descriptive materials (e.g., DFDs) that you may already have produced.

4.3*  Design a cover sheet for the unit folders to be used by HHI in its development of the SCM system.

4.4*  Select a program module from the detailed design and prepare a sample program prologue for it.


### 4.1.2.  Elements of Style

4.5  Select two programming languages with which you are familiar and rate them according to the characteristics of a modern programming language. Can the languages be improved? If so, how?

4.6*  Prepare your own list of programming style conventions. Document them so that HHI may use them as a company-wide standard. Are there times when this standard should be suspended? If yes, explain.

4.7     Many of the rules in Kernigan and Plauger can be assigned to multiple headings.    Identify these rules and give the alternative heading(s).  Are there headings (i.e., attributes of the software process) that are not included in the discussion?

4.8     Compare and contrast the discussion of specification and optimization as presented by Balzer (Section 1.2.3) and Bently (this section).  How do they differ in the interpretation of the problem?  In the implementation of the solution?

4.9*    Describe some of the rules identified in Figure 4.2.  How many of these rules can be automated and how many rely on human judgment?

### 4.1.3.  Views of the Process

4.10    Try to implement the 8-queens problem using stepwise refinement.  Use an 8 by 8 matrix as the chess board.  Start with a queen in position (1,1), then add a queen to the first available column in the next row, and finally test to see if the position is safe.  If it is safe, move on to the next row until a solution is found.  If it is not safe, then move to the next column in this row.  If no safe position in this row is found, backtrack to the previous row and move that queen to the next column. With this design in mind, keep track of your own backtracking during the design process (i.e., how many times did you find a design decision was faulty and had to be discarded).

4.11    Discuss the advantages and disadvantages of top down as a design philosophy.  As a problem-solving paradigm.  Are top down, functional decomposition, and divide and conquer different names for the same thing?

### 4.2.   Encapsulation Techniques

4.12    Define encapsulation.

### 4.2.1.  Some Foundations of Abstraction

4.13    The design of T.H.E. system could be described as bottom up. Generalize this statement, and define a bottom-up design method.  What are the advantages and disadvantages of this approach.

**4.14\*** Draw a DFD for the KWIC index program. Use JSP to create a program structure diagram for the KWIC index program. How do these designs differ from each other and the two Parnas modularizations?

**4.15\*** Give a "complete" definition of information hiding.

**4.16\*** How does the concept of "program families" relate to encapsulation? To software reuse?

**4.17** Write pre and postconditions assertions for the four stack functions in Figure 4.6. (Use the notation used in the VDM discussion in Section 1.2.3.)

### 4.2.2. Abstract Data Types

**4.18** Explain how the "+" is overloaded in mixed arithmetic expressions. Is the logical and (conjunction or &) ever overloaded? If you were to add the type "matrix" to a language, what operators would you overload? In what cases would you expect mixed expressions? For what operations would the rules of integer arithmetic not be valid?

**4.19** Prove that the procedures in Figure 4.9 satisfy the axioms in Figure 4.6. Is there anything else in Figure 4.9 that requires a proof?

**4.20** The OVERFLOW exception in the Figure 4.7 to 4.9 implementation of the stack points out one difference between a specification and an implementation. Identify some other distinctions.

**4.21\*** Declare S to be of type stack and write some Ada code that uses the operators CREATE, PUSH, TOP, and POP on S. Write some sequences that would raise an exception.

**4.22\*** Define a package for the type LIST with the operations CREATE, HEAD, and TAIL where HEAD returns the first item in the list and TAIL returns the list without the first item. Restrict the list items to the integers, and identify the exceptions.

**4.23\*** Write a generic package for LIST.

**4.24\*** Write a program that uses LIST_CI to list out all versions of a given CI. That is, assume that the program has CI_No as an input. (Use pseudocode and do not be concerned with the exact Ada syntax.) Extend this to a function call SELECT_CI that reads in a value for CI_No, produces the list together with a self-generated sequence number, and once the list is produced prompts the user to select one of the listed items by entering the sequence number. If the entered number is valid, the function returns the CI_ID of the selected item; otherwise it raises a NOT_FOUND exception.

4.25* Augment the definition of the CI_ID record by adding the name of the file in which the CI is actually stored. Explain how this link between the surrogate record that describes the CI and the physical file that stores the CI can be exploited.

4.26* Write the procedure for NEW_VERSION using the CI_RECORD package. Do the same for ASSIGN.

4.27* Define a type CI_ASSIGNMENT and implement the operations (procedures) SPLIT and COMBINE. Do you still get lossless joins? (Note that the three types are in what would be called fifth normal form in relational database theory.)

4.28 Reexamine CI_RECORD and explain why you feel that the design is satisfactory or not satisfactory. Hint: try to determine an invariant and prove that the operators do not affect the invariant.

### 4.2.3. Object-Oriented Programming

4.29 Extend the factory simulation example by identifying a group of machines. Organize that group into a hierarchy, and identify the operations of the machines. Are there operations valid for all machines? Subsets of the machines? Unique to a particular machine? Of no interest to a simulation?

4.30 Compare and contrast the various definitions of information hiding given in this section. Are they all restatements of the same principle?

4.31 Provide more examples and counterexamples for the five criteria for evaluating design methods with respect to modularity. Are there additional criteria?

4.32 Define polymorphism and dynamic binding.

4.33 Meyer states that *overloading* allows client programmers to use the same code for different implementations, and *genericity* allows module designers to write one module for many instances. Explain.

4.34    Eiffel has a predefined feature *Create* that is valid for all classes. Identify some additional predefined features that might be useful. What is the danger of having many predefined features?

4.35*   Based on the discussion in the text, revise and complete the definition of the *CI* class given in Figure 4.14.

4.36*   Define the class *CI-Info*. (Develop your own syntax to show inheritance if necessary.)

4.37*   Define the classes implied by the operations outlined in Figure 4.13. Develop a class hierarchy if appropriate.

4.38*   Define classes for Ada and C programs. Also define classes for Unix and DOS applications. Now define a class for DOS applications in C.

### 4.2.4.   Object-Oriented Design and Analysis

4.39    Explain why an object orientation facilitates reuse. What impact should it have on system maintenance. Why?

4.40    Comment on Booch's evaluation of the current software development methods. Are there alternatives that he did not include?

4.41*   Complete the definition of the Task operations in Figure 4.17.

4.42*   Limit the SCM system to only the CI management functions. Develop a Booch diagram for that system.

4.43*   Complete the definition of the Task object in Figure 4.19. Now complete it in Figure 4.21.

4.44*   Use the template in Figure 4.22 to specify the Task object as defined in exercise 4.43.

4.45*   Critique and complete the diagram in Figure 4.21.

4.46    Summarize the five steps in OOA. How do they differ from SA? JSD? OOD?

### 4.3.    The Program Proof

4.47*   Prove the program shown in Figure 4.24.  How do you know the loop terminates?  Was your proof formal or rigorous?  If you worked in a group, did the group interactions help or slow the process?

4.48    Provide pre and postconditions for Design in the JSD CI example.

4.49*   Prove the L3 statements about the binary properties of the gcd.

4.50*   Complete the proof of $Q'$ using the three intermediate assertions provided by Hoare.

## 5.   Verification and Validation

### 5.1.    On the Importance of Being Ernest

5.1     Provide an example of a product that is valid but incorrect.  Correct but invalid.

5.2     Some methods produce programs that are correct the first time.  The 40-20-40 rule implies that 40% of the total effort will be required for integration and test.  If the programs were already correct before integration, how would the 40-20-40 rule change?  How could you verify this?  (The author cannot supply a suggested answer to the first question, but he has one for the second.)

5.3     Why is it best to combine verification and validation as one integrated process?

5.4     Contrast hardware and software reliability?  If coding were the analogue of hardware manufacturing, how would we test each coded product?

### 5.2.    Before the Programs Exist

5.5*    What software tools would be most helpful in error avoidance or identification before the programs exist?  Can they be integrated with the various design documents and specifications?

5.6 Produce a matrix of defect-identification techniques using column headings taken from the four major categories in Table 5.1 and the rows from Table 5.2. For each cell, rank the effectiveness for a small and a large project.

5.7 Discuss why it is difficult for someone to find his own errors. Are there cases when a person is the best one to identify errors. Recall the discussion of incubation in Section 1.3.1; what is the benefit of having time to think about problems? Recall the situation in the Hubble Space Telescope project in 1980; what are the dangers of a highly stressed environment?

5.8 To what extent do you practice egoless programming?

5.9* Develop a procedure for carrying out the review of a program.

5.10* Using the procedure defined in exercise 5.9, find a program design and conduct a review of it? Was the review a success? If not, were all the necessary materials (and knowledge) available? Were the procedures appropriate? How should the review process be changed?

5.11* Refine the response to exercise 5.9 and repeat exercise 5.10.

5.12* Critique the written report resulting from exercise 5.10.

5.13* Based on the small sample of errors found in exercise 5.10, organize a checklist for errors.

5.14 Share your views on the superiority of Fagan's description of structured inspections. Why do you feel this method is not practiced universally?

5.15* Lay out a plan for reviews from the creation of requirements to the implementation of code. What should be examined, when, how, and by whom?

5.16 Compare Fagan's data in Table 5.4 with Jones's rating of techniques in Table 5.2. Are there any contradictions?

*5.3. After the Programs Exist*

5.17 Discuss the role of evaluation and feedback in problem solving.

5.18   Before reading this chapter, did your view of testing conform to Myers's definition?   Describe your understanding and explain the implications.

5.19   Describe the role of specifications in testing.

5.20   How can one build an oracle?

5.21   Why does Myer suggest that experimentation in debugging should be used only as a last resort?

### 5.3.1.  Taxonomy of Testing

5.22   Compare Fagan's data in Table 5.4 with Beizer's data in Table 5.5.  Are there any contradictions?

5.23*  If one accepts Beizer's data in Table 5.5 as being representative, how should we best allocate our budget for V&V?  What kinds of methods would be most promising?  Are there any automated tools that would be most beneficial?

### 5.3.2.  Static Analysis and Complexity Analysis

5.24*  Which static analysis tools are supported by your compiler?  Within your development environment?   Are there any tools that manage data from a collection of programs?  What static analysis tools would you find most helpful?

5.25*  Find a small program and count its operators and operands.  Compute Halstead length, volume, and program level.  How would you automate this process?

5.26*  Repeat the process using McCabe's cyclomatic complexity measure.  Can you do this with PDL as well as executable code?  With collections of programs?

### 5.3.3.  White Box Testing

5.27*  Construct the test set for path coverage of the program in Figure 5.2.  The test set must include both inputs and expected outcomes.

5.28*  What does the program in Figure 5.2 do?  Should it be recoded to do this better?  Can all paths be tested with the test set?  Is this a problem?

5.29    Observe that exercises 5.27 and 5.28 involve static analysis.  After this analysis are you confident that the program is correct?  What kinds of errors might you find by machine testing?

5.30    Find some programs with examples of each type of structured loop.  Conduct a test of the loops.  How must the program be instrumented to carry out these tests?

5.31*  Test the program in Figure 5.2 for data anomalies.

5.32    Describe an automated tool to identify dataflow anomalies in structured programs with a single entry and exit.  What would be the most difficult part of the program to implement?

### 5.2.4.  Black Box Testing

5.33    Comment on the causes for the following paradox described by Dunn.

> Most of the theory developed for software testing is directed at structural testing.  Most of the advanced tools specific to testing support structural testing.  Most of the software engineering literature that is concerned with testing relates exclusively to structural testing.  Most of the tests actually performed are functional tests without regard to structure.  [Dunn84, p. 193]

5.34*  Using the answer from exercise 5.28, construct a functional test set for the program in Figure 5.2.  What functional tests could be developed using only the program code in Figure 5.2?

5.35*  Assume that there was a program to test for dataflow anomalies by static analysis as suggested in exercise 5.32.  Describe a set of test inputs.

5.36*  Make up a definition for a standard name format and then develop a test set to certify that programs conform to that standard.

5.37*  The program compare(st1,st2,ptr) compares two strings and returns a value, ptr, that counts the number of initial characters that are

identical in each.  Given that the data type for st1 and st2 limits them
to from 0 to 6 characters, develop a test set for this program.

5.38*  Use error guessing to determine the three tests with the highest
probability of finding an error in the program described in exercise 5.37.

### 5.3.5.  Integration

5.39*  Describe an integration plan for the SCM system.

5.40*  Which is a better approach to integration for the SCM system,
top down or bottom up?

5.41*  Describe a system test for the SCM system.  Which of Myers's
test categories are inappropriate for this product?

### 5.3.6.  The Cleanroom

5.42    Describe your initial reaction to the cleanroom approach.  How
would you like to develop applications without program execution?
Why?

5.43*  Contrast the benefits of reviews, automated static analysis and
machine testing.  Are there any kinds of errors that can be found only
with machine testing?

5.44    Compare and contrast the formal methods such as VDM of
Section 2.3.3 with the cleanroom.  How is the cleanroom different from
the idea of program proofs?

5.45*  The cleanroom demonstrates that it is possible to produce very
reliable systems without testing for errors.  Are these systems free of all
errors?  If not, speculate on the types of errors that persist and how they
may be avoided.

## 6.    Managing the Process

### 6.1.    Overview of Management

6.1    List some management problems that are valid for any kind of
project.  List some problems that are unique to a software project.

6.2    Of the 16 problems listed by Wingrove, which can be resolved by using the techniques described in the first five  chapters of this book?

6.3    Use the idea of hygiene factors to evaluate software process activities.   Are there some aspects of the process that we perform poorly, but which—when corrected—will have only a limited impact? What of error reduction methods?

*6.2.    Principles of Software Project Management*

6.4    Management can control only resources, time, and the product. Can a schedule be stretched without affecting the other dimensions?  If so, are there limits?   Do all product changes affect the other two dimensions?  Give examples.

6.5*   Using the general principles for management presented in the text, make up some pithy aphorisms (e.g., Brooks's Law).

6.6    Suggest an organization for software development and maintenance for HHI assuming a total staff of 50 professionals.

6.7    Explain your understanding of Theory Z and share your opinion regarding its applicability in large and small software development companies.

6.8    Explain your understanding of Theory W.  What do you see as its principal contribution?

*6.2.1.   Tools for Technical Management*

6.9*   Develop a work breakdown structure for the HHI SCM project.

6.10*  Develop a PERT chart for the SCM project.

6.11*  Select a well-understood aspect of the SCM project and prepare a schedule.  Use Gantt charts.

*6.2.1   The Risk Management Process*

6.12   Describe how you might estimate risk exposure for the SCM project.  How would you compute risk reduction leverage.

6.13    Plot a family of RE curves on a graph with Prob(UO) and Loss(UO) as the axes.

6.14*   Identify the major risks for the SCM project.  Are they generic or project specific?

6.15    Give some additional examples of the Pareto phenomena outside the domain of software engineering.

6.16*   The outline of a risk management plan follows a general structure common to all plans.  Provide a generic plan organization.

6.17    Add to Gilb's list of principles.  Do not be constrained by limiting yourself to only risk principles.


*6.2.3.  Project Organization to Reduce Risks*

6.18*   Use Boehm's top-10 list and identify specific risk examples that might be expected in the SCM project.

6.19*   What would be the best way for HHI to organize the SCM project.  Explain your recommendation.

6.20    Can one use prototyping with incremental development?

6.21    Can one use incremental development when the project has a fixed requirement specification?


*6.2.4.  Building a Management Model*

6.22    Explain DeMarco's statement, "You can't control what you can't measure."

6.23    Using the metametrics described by Conte, Dunsmore, and Shen, evaluate the metrics of lines of code, McCabe's cyclomatic complexity, and Halstead's volume.

6.24*   Critique the cost estimates shown in Figures 6.5 and 6.6.  Do they seem reasonable?  Is the effort on some modules underestimated? Overestimated?

6.25    How does the Putnam analysis help in planning the SCM project?

6.26* Using the ideas of the COCOMO model, are there any portions of the SCM that could be reused from existing HHI products? What of the effort multipliers; are they all nominal, or are some high? Or low?

6.27* Using the multipliers given in the typical formula, compute the number of function points in the SCM project. If this exercise is being done as part of a group activity, first do the computations individually and then compare results.

6.28 In the context of DeMarco's suggestion of "estimate-free motivations," discuss how to manage a project in this manner. Is this what Gilb would recommend?

6.29* Discuss the reliability of the HHI SCM system. What is the prerequisite to knowing when enough testing has been conducted?

6.30* Assume that you were responsible for estimating the complexity of software. Define three complexity metrics that might be effective in the HHI environment.

### 6.2.5. Process Improvement

6.31 Comment on the following observation, "Metamanagement is the principal challenge to the software industry in the 1990s."

6.32 Explain why we should not institute technological improvements as soon as they become available.

6.33 The software process is a human activity, and therefore it is subject to continuing change. How does this affect the management of the process?

6.34 Describe the scientific method and explain how it is applied in software engineering.

6.35 Given the goal of reducing the number of changes to items under configuration control, use the GQM paradigm to suggest how we might achieve that goal.

6.36* Comment on Card's surprise conclusions. Which might be different in another setting?

6.37* Assume that you are hired as an expert by HHI to improve their process. Draw up a plan for what you would do in the first 30 days given that you have little information about how HHI now conducts its affairs.

### 6.3.   Process Improvement Technologies

6.38   Why does software technology acceptance take so long?   When is technology assimilation very rapid?

6.39*   What do you believe the University of Maryland industry survey would report if it were conducted in 1990?   What methods and tools would be listed in Table 6.1?

6.40*   If HHI were to institute a program to foster reuse, how should they go about doing so?

6.41   Explain why an object-oriented method improves reuse.   Are there dangers in such methods?

6.42   What organizational approach would you recommend for software maintenance in HHI?   Explain.

6.43   Where can automation help in reengineering?   Provide some specific examples of tools that might be useful.   (Commercially supported systems need not be available.)

6.44   Define CASE.   Define Integrated Programming Support Environment (IPSE).

6.45*   Prepare a plan for the introduction of CASE tools into HHI.

# Appendix B

## READINGS

[Abbo83]    R. Abbott, Program Design by Informal English Descriptions, *Commun. ACM*, 26:882-294, 1983.

[AbMa86]    T. K. Abdel-Hamid and S. E. Madnick, Impact of Schedule Estimation on Software Project Behavior, *IEEE Software*, 70-75, July 1986.

[AbMa89]    T. K. Abdel-Hamid and S. E. Madnick, Lessons Learned from Modeling the Dynamics of Software Development, *Commun. ACM*, 32:1426-1438, 1989.

[AcBL89]    A. F. Ackerman, L. S. Buchwald, and F. H. Lewski, Software Inspections: An Effective Verification Process, *Software*, (6,3):31-36, May 1989.

[Adam84]    E. N. Adams, Optimizing Preventative Service of Software Products, *IBM J. Res. Dev.* (28,1):2-14, 1984.

[AdBC82]    W. R. Adrion, M. A. Branstad, and J. C. Cherniavsky, Validation, Verification, and Testing of Computer Software, *Comp. Surveys*, 14:159-192, 1982.

[AdSo85]    B. Adelson and E. Soloway, The Role of Domain Experience in Software Design, *IEEE Trans. S. E.*, SE-11:1351-1360, 1985.

[Ager79]    T. Agerwala, Putting Petri Nets to Work, *Computer*, (12,12):85-94, 1979.

[Agre86]    W. W. Agresti, *New Paradigms for Software Development*, IEEE Computer Society Press, Washington, DC, 1986.

[Albr79]    A. J. Albrecht, Measuring Application Development Productivity, *Proc. IBM Appl. Dev. Symp.*, 14-17, 1979.

[Alfo77]     M. W. Alford, A Requirements Engineering Methodology for Real-Time Processing Requirements, *IEEE Trans. S. E.*, SE-3:60-68, 1977.

[AlGa83]     A. J. Albrecht and J. E. Gaffney, Software Function, Source Lines of Code, and Development Effort Prediction: A Software Science Validation, *IEEE Trans. S. E.*, SE-9:639-648, 1983.

[Ande85]     J. R. Anderson, *Cognitive Psychology and its Implications*, 2nd ed., W. H. Freeman, New York, 1985.

[Andr90]     D. H. Andres, Software Project Management Using Effective Process Metrics: The CCPDS-R Experience, *Proc. AFCEA Mil./Gov. Comp. Conf.*, 1990.

[ArFC91]     K. Araki, Z. Furukawa, and J. Cheng, A General Framework for Debugging, *Software*, 14-20, May 1991.

[Arno86]     R. S. Arnold, *Tutorial on Software Restructuring*, IEEE Computer Society Press, Washington, DC, 1986.

[Arth85]     L. J. Arthur, *Measuring Programmer Productivity and Software Quality*, Wiley-Interscience, New York, 1985.

[AuKe86]     B. Auernheimer and R. A. Kemmerer, RT-ASLAN: A Specification Language for Real-Time Systems, *IEEE Trans. S. E.*, SE-12:879-889, 1986.

[Babi85]     W. A. Babich, *Software Configuration Management: Coordination and Control for Productivity*, Addison-Wesley, Reading, MA, 1985.

[BaBo91]     B. H. Barnes and T. B. Bollonger, Making Reuse Cost-Effective, *Software*, 13-24, January 1991.

[BaBu87]     R. M. Baecker and W. A. S. Buxton (eds.), *Readings in Human-Computer Interaction*, Morgan Kaufmann, Los Altos, CA, 1987.

[BaCG83]     R. Balzer, T. E. Cheatham, Jr., and C. Green, Software Technology in the 1990's: Using a New Paradigm, *Computer*, (16,11):39-45, 1983.

[Back57]     J. Backus, Extract from a 1957 Western Joint Computer Conference paper, cited in J. Bernstein, *The Analytical Engine*, Random House, New York, 1966, p. 74.

[BaGW78] R. Balzer, N. Goldman, and D. Wile, Informality in Program Specifications, *IEEE Trans. S. E.*, SE-4:94-103, 1978.

[Bake72] F. T. Baker, Chief Programmer Team Management of Production Programming, *IBM Sys. J.*, (11,1), 1972.

[Balz85] R. Balzer, A 15 Year Perspective on Automatic Programming, *IEEE Trans. S. E.*, SE-11:1257-1268, 1985.

[BaRo88] V. R. Basili and H. D. Rombach, The TAME Project: Towards Improvement-Oriented Software Environments, *IEEE Trans. S. E.*, SE-14:758-773, 1988.

[Bars84] D. R. Barstow, A Perspective on Automatic Programming, *AI Mag.*, 5-27, Spring 1984.

[Bars85] D. R. Barstow, Domain-Specific Automatic Programming, *IEEE Trans. S. E.*, SE-11:1321-1336, 1985.

[Barw89] J. Barwise, Mathematical Proofs of Computer System Correctness, *Notices Am. Math. Soc.* 36:844-851, 1989.

[BaSH86] V. R. Basili, R. E. Selby, and D. H. Hutchens, Experiments in Software Engineering, *IEEE Trans. S. E.*, SE-12:737-743, 1986.

[Basi80] V. R. Basili, *Tutorial on Models and Metrics for Software Management and Engineering*, IEEE Computer Society Press, Washington, DC, 1980.

[Basi85] V. R. Basili, Quantative Evaluation of Software Engineering Methodology, *Proc. First Pan Pacific Comp. Conf.*, Melbourne, Australia, 1985

[Basi90] V. R. Basili, Viewing Maintenance as Reuse-Oriented Software Development, *Software*, 19-25, January 1990.

[BaSS84] D. R. Barstow, H. E. Shrobe, and E. Sandewall (eds.), *Interactive Programming Environments*, McGraw-Hill, New York, 1984.

[Baue72] F. L. Bauer, Software Engineering, *Information Processing 71*, North Holland, Amsterdam, 1972.

[Baue73] F. L. Bauer, (ed.), *Software Engineering: An Advanced Course*, Springer-Verlag, New York, 1973

[BaWe84]   V. R. Basili and D. M. Weiss, A Methodology for Collecting Valid Software Engineering Data, *IEEE Trans. S. E.*, SE-10:728-738, 1984.

[BeCu89]   K. Beck and W. Cunninham, A Laboratory for Teaching Object-Oriented Thinking, *SIGPLAN Notices*, 24(10), October 1989.

[BeLe76]   L. A. Belady and M. M. Lehman, A Model of Large Program Development, *IBM Sys. J.*, 15:225-252, 1976.

[BeHS79]   E. H. Bersoff, V. D. Henderson, and S. G. Siegel, Software Configuration Management: A Tutorial, *Computer*, 6-14, January 1979.

[BeHS80]   E. H. Bersoff, V. D. Henderson, and S. G. Siegel, *Software Configuration Management: An Investment in Product Integrity*, Prentice-Hall, Englewood Cliffs, NJ, 1980.

[Beiz84]   B. Beizer, *Software System Testing and Quality Assurance*, Van Nostrand Reinhold, New York, 1984.

[Beiz90]   B. Beizer, *Software Testing Techniques*, 2nd ed., Van Nostrand Reinhold, New York, 1990.

[BeLe80]   L. A. Belady and B. Leavenworth, Program Modifiability, in H. Freeman and P.M. Lewis II (eds.), *Software Engineering*, Academic Press, New York, 1980, pp. 25-36.

[Bent82]   J. L. Bentley, *Writing Efficient Programs*, Prentice-Hall, Englewood Cliffs, NJ, 1982.

[Bent86]   J. L. Bentley, *Programming Pearls*, Addison-Wesley, Reading, MA, 1986.

[Bent88]   J. L. Bentley, *More Programming Pearls: Confessions of a Coder*, Addison-Wesley, Reading, MA, 1988.

[BePS87]   W. R. Beam, J. D. Palmer, and A. P. Sage, Systems Engineering for Software Productivity, *IEEE Trans. Sys. Man, Cybernet.*, SMC-17:163-186, 1987.

[Bigg89]   T. J. Biggerstaff, Design Recovery for Maintenance and Reuse, *Computer*, 36-49, July 1989.

[BiPe89]     T. J. Biggerstaff and A. J. Perlis, *Software Reusability*, 2 vols., ACM Press, Addison-Wesley, Reading, MA, 1989.

[BjJo82]     D. Bjørner and C. B. Jones, *Formal Specifications and Software Development*, Prentice-Hall, Englewood Cliffs, NJ, 1982.

[Bjør87]     D. Bjørner, *et al.* (eds.), *VDM'87: VDM—A Formal Method at Work*, Springer-Verlag, Berlin, 1987.

[BlDH87]     B. I. Blum, S. D. Diamond, M. G. Hammond, M. E. Perkins, and R. D. Semmel, An Intelligent Navigational Assistant for a Decision Resource Database, *Proc. Expert Sys. Govern.*, 19-25, 1987.

[Blum82]     B. I. Blum, MUMPS, TEDIUM, and Productivity, *Proc. MEDCOMP*, 200-209, 1982.

[Blum86]     B. I. Blum, Iterative Development of Information Systems: A Case Study, *Software—Practice & Exper.*, 6:503-515, 1986.

[Blum89]     B. I. Blum, Volume, Distance and Productivity, *J. Sys Software*, 10:217-226, 1989.

[Blum90]     B. I. Blum, *TEDIUM and the Software Process*, MIT Press, Cambridge, MA, 1990.

[BoBK78]     B. W. Boehm, J. R. Brown, H. Kaspar, M. Lipow, G. Macleod, and M. Merrit, *Characteristics of Software Quality*, TRW Series on Software Technology, North Holland, Amsterdam, 1978.

[Bødk89]     S. Bødker, A Human Activity Approach to User Interfaces, *Human-Comp. Interact.*, 4:171-195, 1989.

[Boeh76]     B. W. Boehm, Software Engineering, *IEEE Trans. Comp.*, C-25:1226-1241, 1975.

[Boeh81]     B. W. Boehm, *Software Engineering Economics*, Prentice-Hall, Englewood Cliffs, NJ, 1981.

[Boeh84]     B. W. Boehm, Verifying and Validating Software Requirements and Design Specifications, *Software*, 75-88, January 1984.

[Boeh87]     B. W. Boehm, Improving Software Productivity, *Computer*, (20,9):43-58, 1987.

[Boeh88]   B. W. Boehm, A Spiral Model of Software Development and Enhancement, *Computer*, (21,5):61-72, 1988.

[Boeh89]   B. W. Boehm, *Software Risk Management*, IEEE Computer Society Press, Washington, DC, 1989.

[BoJa66]   C. Bohm and G. Jacopini, Flow Diagrams, Turing Machines, and Languages with Only Two Formation Rules, *Commun. ACM*, 9, 1966.

[Booc83]   G. Booch, *Software Engineering With Ada*, Benjamin/Cummings, Menlo Park, CA, 1983.

[Booc86]   G. Booch, Object-Oriented Development, *IEEE Trans. S. E.*, SE-12:211-221, 1986.

[Booc87]   G. Booch, *Software Components with Ada-Structures, Tools, and Subsystems*, Benjamin/Cummings, Menlo Park, CA, 1987.

[Booc91]   G. Booch, *Object-Oriented Design with Applications*, Benjamin/Cummings, Menlo Park, CA, 1991.

[Boot89]   P. Booth, *An Introduction to Human-Computer Interaction*, Lawrence Erlbaum, Hillsdale, NJ, 1989.

[BoRo89]   B. W. Boehm and R. Ross, Theory-W Software Project Management: Principles and Examples, *IEEE Trans. S. E.*, SE-15:902-916, 1989.

[BoSt82]   D. G. Bobrow and M. J. Stefik, *LOOPS: An Object-Oriented Programming System for INTERLISP*, Xerox PARC, 1982.

[BoSt83]   B. W. Boehm and T. A. Standish, Software Technology in the 1990's: Using an Evolutionary Paradigm, *Computer*, (16,11):30-38, 1983.

[Brid91]   There is No Best CASE, *Bridge*, Software Engineering Institute, 4-5, March 1991.

[Brit88]   R. N. Britcher, Using Inspections to Investigate Program Correctness, *Computer*, 38-44, November 1988.

[Broo75]   F. P. Brooks, Jr., *The Mythical Man-Month*, Addison-Wesley, Reading, MA, 1975.

[Broo87]   F. P. Brooks, Jr., No Silver Bullet, *Computer*, (20,4):10-19, 1987.

[BrSt84]   J. D. Bransford and B. S. Stein, *The IDEAL Problem Solver*, Freeman, New York, 1984.

[Buch53]   W. Buchholz, Editor's Introduction, "Computer Issue," *IRE Proc.*, 41, October 1953.

[BuRa70]   J. N. Buxton and B. Randell (eds.), *Software Engineering Techniques: Report on a Conference Sponsored by the NATO Science Committee, Rome, Italy, 27th to 31st October 1969*, Scientific Affairs Division, NATO, Brussels, 1970.

[CaAg87]   D. N. Card and W. W. Agresti, Resolving the Software Science Anomaly, *J. Sys. Software*, 7:29-35, 1987.

[CaAg88]   D. N. Card and W. W. Agresti, Measuring Software Design Complexity, *J. Sys. Software*, 8:185-198, 1988.

[CaBa91]   G. Caldiera and V. R. Basili, Identifying and Qualifying Reusable Software Components, *Computer*, 61-70, February 1991.

[CaCA86]   D. N. Card, V. E. Church, and W. W. Agresti, An Empirical Study of Software Design Practices, *IEEE Trans. S. E.*, SE-12:264-271, 1986.

[CaGl90]   D. N. Card with R. L. Glass, *Measuring Software Design Quality*, Prentice-Hall, Englewood Cliffs, NJ, 1990.

[CaGo75]   S. Caine and K. Gordon, PDL—A Tool for Software Design, *Proc. Nat'l. Comp. Conf.*, 271-276, 1975.

[CaMc78]   J. P. Cavano and J. A. McCall, A Framework for the Measurement of Software Quality, *Proc. Software Qual. Assur. Workshop*, 133-139, 1978.

[Came86]   J. R. Cameron, An Overview of JSD, *IEEE Trans. S. E.*, SE-12:222-240, 1986.

[Came89]   J. R. Cameron, (ed.), *JSP & JSD*, 2nd ed., IEEE Computer Society Press, Washington, DC, 1989.

[CaMN83]   S. K. Card, T. P. Moran and A. Newell, *The Psychology of Human-Computer Interaction*, Lawrence Erlbaum, Hillside, NJ, 1983.

[CaMP87]  D. N. Card, F. E. McGarry, and G. T. Page, Evaluating Software Engineering Technologies, *IEEE Trans. S. E.*, SE-13:845-851, 1987.

[Cann80]  H. I. Cannon, Flavors, Tech. Report, MIT Artificial Intelligence Laboratory, Cambridge, MA, 1980.

[CaOl87]  J. M. Carrol and J. R. Olson (eds.), *Mental Models in Human-Computer Interaction*, National Academy Press, Washington, DC, 1987.

[Card87]  D. N. Card, A Software Technology Evaluation Program, *Info. Sci. Technol.*, 29:291-300, 1987.

[Card90]  D. N. Card, Software Quality Engineering, *Inform. Software Technol.*, 32:3-10, 1990.

[Ceru89]  P. Ceruzzi, Electronics Technology and Computer Science, 1940-1975: A Coevolution, *Ann. History Comp.*, 10:257-275, 1989.

[ChCr90]  E. J. Chikofsky and J. H. Cross II, Reverse Engineering and Design Recovery: A Taxonomy, *Software*, 13-17, January 1990.

[Chen76]  P. S. Chen, The Entity-Relationship Model: Toward a Unifying View of Data, *TODS*, 1:9-36, 1976.

[Chen85]  P. S. Chen, Database Design Based on Entity and Relationship, in S. B. Yao (ed.), *Principles of Database Design*, Prentice-Hall, Englewood Cliffs, NJ, 1985, pp. 174-210.

[Chik88]  E. J. Chikofsky (ed.), *Computer-Aided Software Engineering (CASE)*, IEEE Computer Society Press, Washington, DC, 1988.

[Chow85]  T. S. Chow (ed), *Tutorial on Software Quality Assurance*, IEEE Computer Society Press, Washington, DC, 1985.

[Chri84]  J. M. Christensen, The Nature of Systems Development, in R. W. Pew, and P. Green (eds.), *Human Factors Engineering*, University of Michigan College of Engineering, Ann Arbor, MI, 1984.

[ChSi73]  W. G. Chase and H. A. Simon, The Mind's Eye in Chess, *Visual Information Processing*, Academic Press, New York, 1973.

[CMS82]  *Code Management System*, Digital Equipment Corporation, Document No. EA-23134-82, 1982.

[Codd70]   E. F. Codd, A Relational Model of Data for Large Shared Data Banks, *Commun. ACM*, 13:377-87, 1970.

[CoDS86]   S. D. Conte, H. E. Dunsmore, and V. Y. Shen, *Software Engineering Metrics and Models*, Benjamin/Cummings, Menlo Park, CA, 1986.

[Cohe81]   L. J. Cohen, Can Human Irrationality Be Experimentally Demonstrated?, *Behav. Brain Sci.*, 4:317-370, 1981.

[Cohe89]   G. Cohen, *Memory in the Real World*, Lawrence Erlbaum, Hillsdale, NJ, 1989.

[CoHJ86]   B. Cohen, W. T. Harwood, and M. I. Jackson, *The Specification of Complex Systems*, Addison Wesley, Reading, MA, 1986.

[CoMi90]   R. H. Cobb and H. D. Mills, Engineering Software under Statistical Quality Control, *Software*, (7,6):44-54, November 1990.

[Conk87]   J. Conklin, Hypertext: An Introduction and Survey, *Software*, (4,9):17-42, 1987.

[CoRo83]   J. E. Coolahan, Jr. and N. Roussopoules, Timing Requirements for Time-Driven Systems Using Augmented Petri Nets, *IEEE Trans. S. E.*, SE-13:603-616, 1983.

[Coul83]   N. S. Coulter, Software Science and Cognitive Psychology, *IEEE Trans. S. E.*, SE-9:166-171, 1983.

[Cox86]    B. J. Cox, *Object-Oriented Programming*, Addison-Wesley, Reading, MA, 1986.

[CoYo91]   P. Coad and E. Yourdon, *Object-Oriented Analysis*, 2nd ed., Yourdon Press, Prentice-Hall, Englewood Cliffs, NJ, 1991.

[CoZa80]   D. Cougar and R. Zawacki, *Motivating and Managing Computer Personnel*, Wiley, New York, 1980.

[Cros80]   P. B. Crosby, *Quality Is Free: The Art of Making Quality Certain*, Mentor, New York, 1980.

[CuDM86]   P. A. Currit, M. Dyer, and H. D. Mills, Certifying the Reliability of Software, *IEEE Trans. S. E.*, SE-12:3-11, 1986.

[CuKI88]   B. Curtis, H. Krasner, and N. Iscoe, A Field Study of the Software Design Process for Large Systems, *Commun. ACM*, 31:1268-1287, 1988.

[Curt80]   B. Curtis, Measurement and Experimentation in Software Engineering, *Proc. IEEE*, 68:1144-1157, 1980.

[Curt81]   B. Curtis, Substantiating Programmer Variability, *Proc. IEEE*, 69:846, 1981.

[Curt84]   B. Curtis, Fifteen Years of Psychology in Software Engineering: Individual Differences and Cognitive Science, *Proc. 7th Int. Conf. S. E.*, 97-106, 1984.

[Curt85]   B. Curtis, *Tutorial: Human Factors in Software Development*, 2nd ed., IEEE Computer Society Press, Washington, DC, 1985.

[DaMN70]   O.-J. Dahl, B. Myhaug, and K. Nygaard, (Simula 67) Common Base Language, Publication N. S-22, Norwegian Computing Center, Oslo, October 1970.

[Date86]   C. J. Date, *An Introduction to Database Systems,* 2 vols., Addison-Wesley, Reading, MA, 1986.

[deGr65]   A. de Groot, *Thought and Choice in Chess*, Mouton, The Hague, 1965.

[DeMa78]   T. DeMarco, *Structured Analysis and System Specification*, Yourdon Press, New York, 1978.

[DeMa82]   T. DeMarco, *Controlling Software Projects*, Yourdon Press, New York, 1982.

[Demi82]   W. E. Deming, *Quality, Productivity, and Competitive Position*, MIT Center for Advanced Engineering, Cambridge, MA, 1982.

[Demi86]   W. E. Deming, *Out of the Crisis*, MIT Center for Advanced Engineering, Cambridge, MA, 1986.

[DeML78]   R. A. DeMillo, R. J. Lipton, and F. G. Sayward, Hints on Test Data Selection: Help for the Practicing Programmer, *Computer*, (11,4):34-43, 1978.

[DeMM87]  R. A. DeMillo, W. M. McCracken, R. J. Martin, and J. F. Passafiume, *Software Testing and Evaluation*, Benjamin/Cummings, Menlo Park, CA, 1987.

[DeRK76]  F. DeRemer and H. H. Kron, Programming-in-the-Large versus Programming-in-the-Small, *IEEE Trans. S. E.*, SE-2:80-86, 1976.

[Dijk68]  E. W. Dijkstra, Go To Statement Considered Harmful, *Commun. ACM*, 11:147-148, 1968.

[Dijk68]  E. W. Dijkstra, The Structure of "THE"-Multiprogramming System, *Commun. ACM*, 11:341-346, 1968.

[Dijk76]  E. W. Dijkstra, *A Discipline of Programming*, Prentice Hall, Englewood Cliffs, NJ, 1976.

[Dunn84]  R. Dunn, *Software Defect Removal*, McGraw-Hill, New York, 1984.

[DuUl82]  R. Dunn and R. Ullman, *Quality Assurance for Computer Software*, McGraw-Hill, New York, 1982.

[Dyer82]  M. Dyer, Cleanroom Software Development Method, IBM Federal Systems Division, Bethesda, MD, October 14, 1982.

[Edit89]  Editorial Process Verification, ACM Forum, *Commun. ACM*, 32:287-290, 1989.

[Ehn88]  P. Ehn, *Work-Oriented Design of Computer Artifacts*, Arbetslivscentrum, Stockholm, 1988.

[ElNa89]  R. Elmasri and S. B. Navathe, *Fundamentals of Database Systems*, Benjamin/Cummings, Menlo Park, CA, 1989.

[ElSS78]  A. Elstein, L. S. Shulman and S. A. Sparafka, et al., *Medical Problem Solving*, Harvard University Press, Cambridge, MA, 1978.

[EnLB89]  J. P. Enterline, R. E. Lenhard and B. I. Blum (eds.), *A Clinical Information System for Oncology*, Springer-Verlag, New York, 1989.

[ErSi84]  K. A. Ericsson and H. A. Simon, *Protocol Analysis: Verbal Reports as Data*, MIT Press, Cambridge, MA, 1984.

[Evan89]    J. St. B. T. Evans, *Bias in Human Reasoning*, Lawrence Erlbaum, Hillsdale, NJ, 1989.

[EvMa87]    M. W. Evans and J. J. Marciniak, *Software Quality Assurance and Management*, Wiley, New York, 1987.

[Faga76]    M. E. Fagan, Design and Code Inspection to Reduce Errors in Program Development, *IBM Sys. J.*, (15,3):182-211, 1976.

[Faga86]    M. E. Fagan, Advances in Software Inspections, *IEEE Trans. S. E.*, SE-12:744-751, 1986.

[Fair85]    R. E. Fairley, *Software Engineering Concepts*, McGraw-Hill, New York, 1985.

[Feld79]    S. I. Feldman, Make — A Program for Maintaining Computer Programs, *Software—Practice & Exper.*, 9:255-265, 1979.

[Fetz88]    J. H. Fetzer, Program Verification: The Very Idea, *Commun. ACM*, 31:1048-1063, 1988.

[Ferr78]    D. Ferrari, *Computer Systems Performance Evaluation*, Prentice-Hall, Englewood Cliffs, NJ, 1978.

[FiLo78]    A. Fitzsimmons and T. Love, A Review and Evaluation of Software Science, *ACM Comp. Surveys*, 10:3-18, 1978.

[Fitz78]    J. Fitz-Enz, Who Is the DP Professional?, *Datamation*, 9:125-128, September 1978.

[FiUr81]    R. Fisher and W. Ury, *Getting to Yes*, Houghton-Mifflin, New York, 1981.

[Floy67]    R. W. Floyd, Assigning Meanings to Programs, *Proc. Symp. Appl. Math.*, 19-32, 1967.

[FoGi89]    G. A. Ford and N. E. Gibbs, A Master of Software Engineering Curriculum, *Computer*, (22,9):59-71, 1989.

[Fowl86]    P. J. Fowler, In-Process Inspections of Work Products at AT&T, *AT&T Technical Journal*, 102-112, March-April 1986.

[Free80]    P. Freeman, The Central Role of Design in Software Engineering: Implications for Research, in H. Freeman and P. M. Lewis II, (eds.), *Software Engineering*, Academic Press, New York, 1980.

[Free87a]   P. Freeman, *Tutorial on Software Reusability*, IEEE Computer Society Press, Washington, DC, 1987.

[Free87b]   P. Freeman, *Software Perspectives*, Addison-Wesley, Reading, MA, 1987.

[FrWa83]   P. Freeman and A. Wasserman, *Tutorial on Software Design Techniques*, IEEE Computer Society Press, Washington, DC, 1983.

[FrWe90]   D. P. Freedman and G. M. Weinberg, *Handbook of Walkthroughs, Inspections, and Technical Reviews*, 3rd ed., Dorset House Publishing, New York, 1990.

[FuNe86]   A. L. Furtado and E. J. Neuhold, *Formal Techniques for Data Base Design*, Springer-Verlag, Berlin, 1986.

[Gall88]   J. Gall, *Systemantics*, 2nd ed., General Systemantics Press, 1988.

[GAO79]   *Contracting for Computer Software Development—Serious Problems Require Management Attention to Avoid Wasting Additional Millions*, GAO Report FGMSD-80-4, November 9, 1979.

[Gard85]   H. Gardner, *The Mind's New Science*, Basic Books, New York, 1985.

[GaSa79]   C. Gane and T. Sarson, *Structured Systems Analysis*, Prentice-Hall, Englewood Cliffs, NJ, 1979.

[GeHe88]   D. Gelperin and B. Hetzel, The Growth of Software Testing, *Commun. ACM*, 31:687-695, 1988.

[GeMc86]   N. Gehani and A. McGettrick, *Software Specification Techniques*, Addison Wesley, Reading, MA, 1986.

[Gerh90]   S. L. Gerhart, Application of Formal Methods: Developing Virtuoso Software, *Software*, (7,5):6-10, 1990.

[GeSt83]   D. Gentner and A. L. Stevens (eds.), *Mental Models*, Lawrence Erlbaum, Hillsdale, NJ, 1983.

[GhJM91]   C. Ghezzi, M. Jazayeri, and D. Mandrioli, *Fundamentals of Software Engineering*, Prentice-Hall, Englewood Cliffs, NJ, 1991.

[Gilb77]   T. Gilb, *Software Metrics*, Winthrop, 1977.

[Gilb88]     T. Gilb, *Principles of Software Engineering Management*, Addison Wesley, Reading, MA, 1988.

[Gilh88]     K. J. Gilhooly, *Thinking: Directed, Undirected and Creative*, Academic Press, New York, 1988.

[Glas81]     R. L. Glass, Persistent Software Errors, *IEEE Trans. S. E.*, SE-7:162-168, 1981.

[Glas83]     R. L. Glass, *Real-Time Software*, Prentice-Hall, Englewood Cliffs, NJ, 1983.

[Glas87]     R. L. Glass, Standards and Enforcers: Do They Really Achieve Software Quality, *J. Sys. Software*, 7:87-88, 1987.

[Glas91]     R. L. Glass, CASE Survey, *Software Practitioner*, 15-16, May-August 1991.

[GlNo81]     R. L. Glass and R. A. Noiseux, *Software Maintenance Guidebook*, Prentice-Hall, Englewood Cliffs, NJ, 1981.

[Goel85]     A. L. Goel, Software Reliability Models: Assumptions, Limitations, and Applicability, *IEEE Trans. S. E.*, SE-11:1411-1423, 1985.

[GoGe75]     J. B. Goodenough and S. L. Gerhart, Toward a Theory of Test Data Selection, *IEEE Trans. S. E.*, SE-1:156-173, 1975.

[Gold85]     A. Goldberg, *Smalltalk-80: The Interactive Programming Environment*, Addison-Wesley, Reading, MA, 1985.

[Gold88]     A. Goldberg, *A History of Personal Workstations*, ACM Press/Addison-Wesley, Reading, MA, 1988.

[Goma84]     H. Gomaa, A Software Design Method for Real-Time Systems, *Commun. ACM*, 29:938-949, 1984.

[Goma86]     H. Gomaa, Software Development of Real-Time Systems, *Commun. ACM*, 29:657-668, 1986.

[GoRo83]     A. Goldberg and D. Robson, *Smalltalk-80: The Language and Its Implementation*, Addison-Wesley, Reading, MA, 1983.

[GoSc81]   H. Gomaa and D. B. H. Scott, Prototyping as a Tool in the Specification of User Requirements, *Proc. Intl. Conf. S.E.*, 333-342, 1981.

[Grad87]   R. B. Grady, Measuring and Managing Software Maintenance, *Software*, 35-45, September 1987.

[GrCa87]   R. B. Grady and D. L. Caswell, *Software Metrics: Establishing a Company-Wide Program*, Prentice-Hall, Englewood Cliffs, NJ, 1987.

[Grie81]   D. Gries, *The Science of Programming*, Springer-Verlag, New York, 1981.

[GrLP86]   A. G. Greenwald, M. R. Leippe, A. R. Pratkanis, and M. H. Baumgardner, Under What Conditions Does Theory Obstruct Research Progress?, *Psychol. Rev.*, 93:216-229, 1986.

[Grud89]   J. Grudin, The Case against User Interface Consistency. *Commun. ACM*, 32:1164-1173, 1989.

[Grud91]   J. Grudin, Interactive Systems: Bridging the Gaps between Developers and Users, *Computer*, 59-69, April 1991.

[Guin90]   R. Guindon, Designing the Design Process: Exploiting Opportunistic Thoughts, *Human-Computer Interact.*, 5:305-344, 1990.

[Gutt77]   J. Guttag, Abstract Data Types and the Development of Data Structures, *Commun. ACM*, 20:396-405, 1977.

[HaHi89]   H. R. Hartson and D. Hix, Human-Computer Interface Development: Concepts and Systems, *ACM Comp. Surveys*, 21:5-92, 1989.

[Hals75]   M. H. Halstead, A Method of Programming Measurement and Estimation, *Proc. ACM Conf.*, 222-24, 1975.

[Hals77]   M. H. Halstead, *Elements of Software Science*, North Holland, Amsterdam, 1977.

[HaMK82]   W. Harrison, K. Magel, R. Kluczny, and A. DeKock, Applying Software Metrics to Program Maintenance, *Computer*, 65-79, September 1982.

[Haml88]     R. Hamlet, Introduction to Special Section on Software Testing, *Commun. ACM*, 31:662-667, 1988.

[Hans83]     K. Hansen, *Data Structured Program Design*, Kenn Orr & Associates, Topeka, KS, 1983.

[HaPi87]     D. J. Hatley and I. A. Pirbhai, *Strategies for Real-Time System Specification*, Dorset House, New York, 1987.

[HaTa90]     D. Hamlet and R. Taylor, Partition Testing Does Not Inspire Confidence, *IEEE Trans. S. E.*, SE-16:1402-1411, 1990.

[Haye87]     I. Hayes (ed.), *Specification Case Studies*, Prentice-Hall, London, 1987.

[HeIn88]     S. Hekmatpour and D. Ince, *Software Prototyping, Formal Methods and VDM*, Addison-Wesley, Workingham, England, 1988.

[HeKa81]     S. M. Henry and D. G. Kafura, Software Structure Metrics Based in Information Flow, *IEEE Trans. S. E.*, SE-7:510-518, 1981.

[HeMS59]     F. Herzberg, B. Mausner, and B. B. Sayderman, *The Motivation to Work*, 2nd ed, Wiley, London, 1959.

[Heni80]     K. Heninger, Specifying Software Requirements for Complex Systems: New Techniques and Their Application, *IEEE Trans. S. E.*, SE-6:2-13, 1980.

[Hoar69]     C. A. R. Hoare, An Axiomatic Basis for Computer Programming, *Commun. ACM*, 12:576-583, 1969.

[Hoar78]     C. A. R. Hoare, Communicating Sequential Processes, *Commun. ACM*, 21:666-677, 1978.

[Hoar85]     C. A. R. Hoare, *Communicating Sequential Processes*, Prentice-Hall, Englewood Cliffs, NJ, 1985.

[Hoar87]     C. A. R. Hoare, An Overview of Some Formal Methods for Program Design, *Computer*, 85-91, September 1987.

[HoMu84]     E. Horowitz and J. B. Munson, An Expansive View of Reusable Software, *IEEE Trans. S. E.*, SE-10:477-487, 1984.

[Hopp81]     G. M. Hopper, The First Bug, *Ann. History Comp.*, 3:285-286, 1981.

[Howd76]   W. E. Howden, Reliability of the Path Analysis Testing Strategy, *IEEE Trans. S. E.*, SE-2:208-215, 1976.

[Howd86]   W. E. Howden, A Functional Approach to Program Testing and Analysis, *IEEE Trans. S. E.*, SE-12:997-1005, 1986.

[HoWi73]   C. A. R. Hoare and N. Wirth, An Axiomatic Definition of the Language PASCAL, *Acta Inform.*, 2:335-355, 1973.

[HuKi87]   R. Hull and R. King, Semantic Database Modeling: Survey, Applications, and Research Issues, *ACM Comp. Surveys*, 19:201-260, 1987.

[Hump89a]  W. S. Humphrey, *Managing the Software Process*, Addison-Wesley, Reading, MA, 1989.

[Hump89b]  W. S. Humphrey, CASE Planning and the Software Process, Software Engineering Institute Technical Report CMU/SEI-89-TR-26, May 1989.

[Jack75]   M. A. Jackson, *Principles of Program Design*, Academic Press, New York, 1975.

[Jack82]   M. A. Jackson, *System Development*, Prentice-Hall, Englewood Cliffs, NJ, 1982.

[JeTo79]   R. W. Jensen and C. C. Tonies, *Software Engineering*, Prentice-Hall, Englewood Cliffs, NJ, 1979.

[John83]   P. N. Johnson-Laird, *Mental Models*, Cambridge University Press, Cambridge, 1983.

[Jone79]   T. C. Jones, A Survey of Programming Design and Specification Techniques, *Proc. Specifications Reliable Software*, 1979.

[Jone80]   C. B. Jones, *Software Development, A Rigorous Approach*, Prentice-Hall, Englewood Cliffs, NJ, 1980.

[Jone86a]  T. C. Jones, *Programmer Productivity*, McGraw-Hill, New York, 1986.

[Jone86b]  C. B. Jones, *Systematic Software Development Using VDM*, Prentice-Hall, Englewood Cliffs, NJ, 1986.

[JRVS89]  J. Johnson, T. L. Roberts, W. Verplank, D. C. Smith, C. H. Irby, M. Beard, and K. Mackey, The Xerox Star: A Retrospective, *Computer*, (22,9):11-29, 1989.

[KaCa85]  D. Kafura and J. Canning, A Validation of Software Metrics Using Many Metrics and Many Resources, Computer Science Report TR-85-6, Virginia Tech, Blacksberg, VA, 1985.

[KaHe81]  D. G. Kafura and S. M. Henry, Software Quality Metrics Based on Interconnectivity, *J. Sys. Software*, 2:121-131, 1981.

[KaRe87]  D. G. Kafura and G. R. Reddy, The Use of Software Complexity Metrics in Software Maintenance, *IEEE Trans. S. E.*, SE-13:335-343, 1987.

[Katz90]  R. H. Katz, Toward a Unified Framework for Version Modeling in Engineering Databases, *ACM Comp. Surveys*, 4:375-408, 1990.

[Kell87]  J. C. Kelly, A Comparison of Four Design Methods for Real-Time Systems, *Proc. 9th Int. Conf. S. E.*, 238-252, 1987.

[Kent83]  W. Kent, A Simple Guide to Five Normal Forms in Relational Database Theory, *Commun. ACM*, 26:120-125, 1983.

[KePl74]  B. W. Kernighan and P.J. Plauger, *The Elements of Programming Style*, McGraw-Hill, New York, 1974.

[KeST86]  J. K. Kearney, R. L. Sedlmeyer, W. B. Thompson, M. A. Gray and M. A. Adler, Software Complexity Measurement, *Commun. ACM*, 29:1044-1050, 1986.

[KiCN90]  A. Kierulf, K. Chen, and J. Nievergelt, Smart Game Board and Go Explorer: A Study in Software and Knowledge Engineering, *Commun. ACM*, 33:152-166, 1990.

[KiLo89]  W. Kim and F. H. Lochovsky (eds.), *Object-Oriented Concepts, Databases, and Applications*, ACM Press, New York, 1989.

[Kim90]  S. H. Kim, *Essence of Creativity*, Oxford University Press, New York, 1990.

[King88]  D. King, *Creating Effective Software*, Yourdon Press, Englewood Cliffs, NJ, 1988.

[King89]     R. King, My Cat is Object-Oriented, in W. Kim and F. H. Lochovsky (eds.), *Object-Oriented Concepts, Databases, and Applications*, ACM Press, New York, 1989, pp. 23-30.

[Kitc90]     B. Kitchenham, Comments on "Considering Quality in the Management of Software-Based Development Projects," *Inform. Software Technol.*, 32:23-25, 1990.

[Kmie84]     J. Kmiecik, et al., Software Cost Reduction Guideline, Grumman Aerospace Corporation, Report #SRSR-NRL-84-001, August 1984.

[Kowa88]     J. A. Kowal, *Analyzing Systems*, Prentice-Hall, Englewood Cliffs, 1988.

[Kraf77]     P. Kraft, *Programmers and Managers: The Routinization of Computer Programming in the United States*, Springer-Verlag, New York, 1977.

[KuAO88]    D. Kuhn, E. Amsel, M. O'Loughlin, et al., *The Development of Scientific Thinking Skills*, Academic Press, San Diego, CA, 1988.

[Kuhn70]     T. S. Kuhn, *The Structure of Scientific Revolutions*, 2nd ed., University of Chicago Press, Chicago, 1970.

[Lamp84]     B. W. Lampson, Hints for Computer System Design, *Software*, 11-28, January, 1984.

[LeBe85]     M. M. Lehman and L. A. Belady, *Program Evolution Processes and Software Change*, Academic Press, New York, 1985.

[Lehm80]     M. M. Lehman, Life Cycles and Laws of Program Evolution, *Proc. IEEE*, 68:1060-1076, 1980.

[LeST84]     M. M. Lehman, V. Stenning, and W. M. Turski, Another Look at Software Design Methodology, *ACM SIGSOFT SEN*, (9,3), 1984.

[Leve86]     N. G. Leveson, Software Safety: What, Why and How, *ACM Comp. Surveys*, 18:125-164, 1986.

[Leve91]     Y. Levendel, Improving Quality with a Manufacturing Process, *Software*, 13-25, March 1991.

[Lewk89]     J. Lewkowicz, *The Complete MUMPS*, Prentice-Hall, Englewood Cliffs, NJ, 1989.

[LiCh87]   H. F. Li and W. K. Cheung, An Empirical Study of Software Metrics, *IEEE Trans. S. E.*, SE-13:697-708, 1987.

[Lick83]   P. S. Licker, The Japanese Approach: A Better Way to Manage Programmers?, *Commun. ACM*, 26:631-636, 1983.

[Lick85]   P. S. Licker, *The Art of Managing Software Development People*, Wiley, New York, 1985.

[Lien83]   B. P. Lientz, Issues in Software Maintenance, *ACM Comp. Surveys*, 15:271-278, 1983.

[LiGu86]   B. Liskov and J. Guttag, *Abstraction and Specification in Program Development*, MIT Press, Cambridge, MA, 1986

[LiLe89]   C. Y. Lin and R. R. Levary, Computer-Aided Software Development Process Design, *IEEE Trans. S. E.*, SE-15:1025-1037, 1989.

[LiMW79]   R. C. Linger, H. D. Mills, and B. I. Witt, *Structured Programming — Theory and Practice*, Addison-Wesley, Reading, MA, 1979.

[Lind79]   D. A. B. Lindberg, *The Growth of Medical Information Systems in the United States*, Lexington Books, Lexington, MA, 1979.

[LiSw80]   B. P. Lientz and E. G. Swanson, *Software Maintenance Management*, Addison-Wesley, Reading, MA, 1980.

[LiZi75]   B. H. Liskov and S. N. Zilles, Specification Techniques for Data Abstraction, *IEEE Trans. S. E.*, SE-1:7-19, 1975.

[MaBu87]   A. Macro and J. Buxton, *The Craft of Software Engineering*, Addison-Wesley, Reading, MA, 1987.

[Maho76]   M. J. Mahoney, *Scientist as Subject: The Psychological Imperative*, Ballinger, Cambridge, MA, 1976.

[Maho88]   M. S. Mahoney, The History of Computing in the History of Technology, *Ann. History Comp.*, 10:113-125, 1988.

[MaMc88]   D. A. Marca and C. L. McGowan, *SADT, Structured Analysis and Design Technique*, McGraw-Hill, New York, 1988.

[Mart82]   J. Martin, *Application Development without Programmers*, Prentice-Hall, Englewood Cliffs, NJ, 1982.

[Mats87]  Y. Matsumoto, A Software Factory: An Overall Approach to Software Production, in P. Freeman (ed.), *Tutorial: Software Reusability*, IEEE Computer Science Press, Washington, DC, 1987, pp. 155-177.

[MaTu84]  T. S. E. Maibaum and W. M. Turski, On What Exactly Is Going On When Software Is Developed Step-by-Step, *Seventh Int. Conf. S.E.*, 528-533, 1984.

[Maye83]  R. E. Mayer, *Thinking, Problem Solving, Cognition*, W. H. Freeman, New York, 1983.

[Mayr90]  A. von Mayrhauser, *Software Engineering Methods and Management*, Academic Press, Boston, MA, 1990.

[McCa76]  T. J. McCabe, A Complexity Measure, *IEEE Trans. S. E.*, SE-2:308-320, 1976.

[McCa83]  T. J. McCabe, *Structured Testing*, IEEE Computer Society Press, Washington, DC, 1983.

[McCB89]  T. J. McCabe and C. W. Butler, Design Complexity Measurement and Testing, *Commun. ACM*, 32:1415-1425, 1989.

[McCl78]  C. McClure, A Model for Program Complexity Analysis, *Proc. Int. Conf. S. E.*, 149-157, 1978.

[McDo76]  C. J. McDonald, Computer Reminders, the Quality of Care, and the Nonperfectability of Man, *N. Engl. J. Med.*, 295:1351-1355, 1976.

[McGr60]  D. M. McGregor, *The Human Side of Enterprise*, McGraw-Hill, New York, 1960.

[McIl69]  M.D. McIlroy, Mass Produced Software Components, in P. Naur and B. Randell (eds.), *Software Engineering: Report on a Conference Sponsored by the NATO Science Committee*, Scientific Affairs Division, Brussels, 1969.

[McMP84]  S. McMenamin and J. Palmer, *Essential Systems Analysis*, Yourdon Press, New York, 1984.

[McRW77]  J. A. McCall, P. K. Richards, and G. F. Walters, *Factors in Software Quality* (Tech. Rep. 77CISO2), General Electric, Command and Information Systems, Sunnyvale, CA, 1977.

[Mell83]     D. A. Mellichamp (ed.), *Real Time Computing*, Van Nostrand Reinhold, New York, 1983.

[Metz81]     P. W. Metzger, *Managing a Programming Project*, (2nd ed.), Prentice-Hall, Englewood Cliffs, NJ, 1981.

[MeWa85]     S. J. Mellor and P. T. Ward, *Structured Development for Real-Time Systems*, 3 vols., Yourdon Press, New York, 1985, 1986.

[Meye85]     B. Meyer, On Formalism in Specifications, *Software*, 6-26, January 1985.

[Meye87]     B. Meyer, Reusability: The Case for Object-Oriented Design, *Software*, (4,2):50-64, March 1987.

[Meye88]     B. Meyer, *Object-oriented Software Construction*, Prentice-Hall, New York, 1988.

[Meye91]     B. Meyer, *Eiffel: The Language*, Prentice -Englewood Cliffs, NJ, 1991.

[MiDL87]     H. D. Mills, M. Dyer, and R. Linger, Cleanroom Software Engineering, *Software*, (4,5):19-25, 1987.

[MiLD80]     H. D. Mills, R. C. Linger, M. Dyer, and R. E. Quinnan, The Management of Software Engineering, *IBM Sys. J.*, (24,2):414-477, 1980.

[MiLi86]     H. D. Mills and R.C. Linger, Data Structured Programming: Program Design without Arrays and Pointers, *IEEE Trans. S. E.*, SE-12:192-197, 1986.

[Mill56]     G. A. Miller, The Magical Number Seven Plus or Minus Two: Some Limits on Our Capacity for Processing Information, *Psychol. Rev.*, 63:81-97, 1956.

[Mill72]     H. D. Mills, On Statistical Validation of Computer Programs, IBM Report FSC72-6015, FSD, Gaithersburg, MD, 1972.

[Mill86]     H. D. Mills, Structured Programming, *Software*, 58-66, November 1986.

[MoNi90]     R. Molich and J. Nielsen, Improving a Human-Computer Dialogue, *Commun. ACM*, 33:338-348, 1990.

[MoSu84]   C. Morgan and B. A. Sufrin, Specification of the UNIX File System, *IEEE Trans. S. E.*, SE-10:128-142, 1984.

[MuAc89]   J. D. Musa and A. F. Ackerman, Quantifying Software Validation: When to Stop Testing?, *Software*, (6,3):19-27, May 1989.

[MuIO87]   J. D. Musa, A. Iannino, and K. Okumoto, *Software Reliability: Measurement, Prediction, Application*, McGraw-Hill, New York, 1987.

[Mura84]   T. Murata, Modeling and Analysis of Concurrent Systems, in C. R. Vick and C. V. Ramamoorthy (eds.), *Handbook of Software Engineering*, Van Nostrand Reinhold, New York, 1984, pp. 39-63.

[Mura89]   T. Murata, Petri Nets: Properties, Analysis and Applications, *Proc. IEEE*, 77:541-580, 1989.

[Musa80]   J. Musa, The Measurement and Management of Software Reliability, *Proc. IEEE*, 68:1131-1143, 1980.

[Musa83]   J. Musa (ed.), Stimulating Software Engineering Progress, A Report of the Software Engineering Planning Group, *ACM SIGSOFT SEN*, (8,2):29-54, 1983.

[Myer75]   G. J. Myers, *Reliable Software Through Composite Design*, Petrocelli/Charter, New York, 1975.

[Myer78]   G. J. Myers, *Composite/Structured Design*, Van Nostrand Reinhold, New York, 1978.

[Myer79]   G. J. Myers, *The Art of Software Testing*, Wiley, New York, 1979.

[NaRa69]   P. Naur and B. Randell (eds.), *Software Engineering: Report on a Conference Sponsored by the NATO Science Committee, Garmisch, Germany, 7th to 11th October 1968*, Scientific Affairs Division, NATO, Brussels, 1969.

[Neum89]   P. G. Neumann, RISKS: Cumulative Index of Software Engineering Notes, *ACM SIGSOFT SEN*, 22-26, January 1989.

[NeSi72]   A. Newell and H. A. Simon, *Human Problem Solving*, Prentice-Hall, Englewood Cliffs, NJ, 1972.

[NiSh88]   K. Nielsen and K. Shumate, *Designing Large Real-Time Systems with Ada*, Multiscience Press, New York, 1988.

[NoDr86]    D. A. Norman and S. W. Draper (eds.), *User Centered System Design*, Lawrence Erlbaum, Hillsdale, NJ, 1986.

[Norm82]    D. A. Norman, *Learning and Memory*, W. H. Freeman, New York, 1982.

[NoSt89]    A. F. Norcio and J. Stanley, Adaptive Human-Computer Interfaces: A Literature Survey and Perspective, *IEEE Trans. Sys., Man Cybernet.*, SMC-19:399-408, 1989.

[OlJo76]    R. M. Olton and D. M. Johnson, Mechanisms of Incubation in Creative Problem Solving, *Am. J. Psychol.*, 89:617-630, 1976.

[OlSS87]    G. M. Olson, S. Sheppard, and E. Soloway (eds.), *Empirical Studies of Programmers: Second Workshop*, Ablex, Norwood, NJ, 1987.

[Orr81]     K. Orr, *Structured Requirements Definition*, Ken Orr and Associates, Topeka, KS, 1981.

[Oste87]    L. Osterweil, Software Processes Are Software Too, *Proc. 9th Int. Conf. S. E.*, 2-13, 1987.

[Ouch82]    W. Ouchi, *Theory Z*, Avon, New York, 1982.

[PaCl86]    D. L. Parnas and P. C. Clements, A Rational Design Process: How and Why to Fake It, *IEEE Tans. S. E.*, SE-12:251-257, 1986.

[PaCW85]    D. L. Parnas, P. C. Clements, and D. M. Weiss, The Modular Structure of Complex Systems, *IEEE Trans. S. E.*, SE-11:259-266, 1985.

[Page88]    M. Page-Jones, *The Practical Guide to Structured Systems Design*, 2nd ed., Prentice-Hall, Englewood Cliffs, NJ, 1988.

[Parn72a]   D. L. Parnas, A Technique for Software Module Specification with Examples, *Commun. ACM*, 15:330-336, 1972.

[Parn72b]   D. L. Parnas, On Criteria to Be Used in Decomposing Systems into Modules, *Commun. ACM*, 15:1053-1058, 1972.

[Parn79]    D. L. Parnas, Designing Software for Ease of Extension and Contraction, *IEEE Trans. S. E.*, SE-5:128-138, 1979.

[Pasc86]    G. A. Pascoe, Elements of Object-Oriented Programming, *Byte*, 139-144, August 1986.

[PaSK90]   D. L. Parnas, A. J. van Schouwen, and S. P. Kwan, Evaluation of Safety-Critical Software, *Commun. ACM*, 33:636-648, 1990.

[PeKa91]   D. E. Perry and G. E. Kaiser, Models of Software Development Environments, *IEEE Trans. S. E.*, 17:283-295, 1991.

[PeMa88]   J. Peckham and F. Maryanski, Semantic Data Models, *ACM Comp. Surveys*, 20:153-189, 1988.

[Pete81]    J. L. Peterson, *Petri Net Theory and the Modeling of Systems*, Prentice-Hall, Englewood Cliffs, NJ, 1981.

[Pete87]    L. Peters, *Advanced Structured Analysis and Design*, Prentice-Hall, Englewood Cliffs, NJ, 1987.

[Petr82]    H. Petroski, *To Engineer Is Human*, St. Martins Press, New York, 1982.

[Pool86]    R. J. Pooley, *An Introduction to Programming in SIMULA*, Blackwell Scientific, Oxford, 1986.

[Popp59]   K. R. Popper, *The Logic of Scientific Discovery*, Harper & Row, New York, 1959.

[Popp62]   K. R. Popper, *Conjectures and Refutations: The Growth of Scientific Knowledge*, Basic Books, New York, 1962.

[Post85]    R. M. Poston, Software Standards, *Software*, 83-86, January 1985.

[PrAr91]    R. Prieto-Diaz and G. Arango, *Tutorial: Domain Analysis and Software Systems Modeling*, IEEE Computer Society Press, Washington, DC, 1991.

[Pres87]    R. S. Pressman, *Software Engineering: A Practitioner's Approach*, 2nd ed., McGraw-Hill, New York, 1987.

[PrFr87]    R. Prieto-Diaz and P. Freeman, Classifying Software for Reusability, *Software*, (4,1):6-16, 1987.

[Prie91]    R. Prieto-Diaz, Implementing Faceted Classification for Software Reuse, *Commun. ACM*, 34:88-97, 1991.

[Putn78]    L. H. Putnam, A General Empirical Solution to the Macro Software Sizing and Estimating Problem, *IEEE Trans. S. E.*, SE-4:345-361, 1978.

[Pyzd78]    T. Pyzdek, *An SPC (Statistical Process Control) Primer*, Quality America, Tuscon, AZ, 1978.

[Rako90]    J. J. Rakos, *Software Project Management for Small to Medium Sized Projects*, Prentice-Hall, Englewood Cliffs, NY, 1990.

[RaWe82]    S. Rapps and E. J. Weyuker, Data Flow Analysis Techniques for Test Data Selection, *Proc. 6th Int. Conf. S. E.*, 272-278, 1982.

[Redm90]    F. J. Redmill, Considering Quality in the Management of Software-Based Development Projects, *Inform. Software Technol.*, 32:18-22, 1990.

[Reif85]    D. J. Reifer, A Poor Man's Guide to Estimating Software Costs, RCI-TR-012, Texas Instruments, Inc., Lewisville, TX 75067, Reprinted in D. J. Reifer, *Tutorial: Software Management*, 3rd ed., IEEE Computer Science Press, Washington, DC, 1986.

[Reif86]    D. J. Reifer, *Tutorial: Software Management*, 3rd ed., IEEE Computer Society Press, Washington, DC, 1986.

[Reif87]    D. J. Reifer, ASSET-R: A Function Point Sizing Tool for Scientific and Real-Time Systems, Reifer Consultants, Inc. Report RCI-TN-299, 1987.

[ReRi85]    S. T. Redwine and W. E. Riddle, Software Technology Maturation, *Proc. Intl. Conf. S. E.*, 189-200, 1985.

[Resn83]    B. Resnick, Mathematics and Science Learning: A New Conception, *Science*, 220:477-478, 1983.

[Rett90]    M. Rettig, Software Teams, *Commun. ACM*, 33:23-27, 1990.

[Reut79]    V. G. Reuter, Using Graphic Management Tools, *J. Sys. Manage.*, 30:6-17, 1979.

[ReVe91]    A. L. Reibman and M. Veeraraghavan, Reliability Modeling: An Overview for System Designers, *Computer*, 49-57, April 1991.

[RoAl90]   M. B. Rosson and S. R. Alpert, The Cognitive Consequences of Object-OrientedDesign,*Human-ComputerInteraction*,5:415-444, 1990.

[Roch75]   M. J. Rochkind, The Source Code Control System, *IEEE Trans. S. E.*, SE-1:364-370, 1975.

[Romb90]   H. D. Rombach, Design Measurement: Some Lessons Learned, *Software*, 17-25, March 1990.

[RoSc77]   D. T. Ross and K. E. Schoman, Jr., Structured Analysis for Requirements Definition, *IEEE Trans. S.E.*, SE-3:6-15, 1977.

[Ross77]   D. T. Ross, Structured Analysis (SA): A Language for Communicating Ideas, *IEEE Trans. S. E.*, SE-3:16-34, 1977.

[Ross88]   D. T. Ross, Foreword, in D. A. Marca and C. L. McGowan, *SADT, Structured Analysis and Design Technique*, McGraw-Hill, New York, NY, 1988, pp. xi-viv.

[Royc70]   W. W. Royce, Managing the Development of Large Software Systems, *IEEE WESCON*, 1-9, 1970.

[Royc89]   W. Royce, Reliable, Reusable Ada Components for Constructing Large, Distributed Multi-Task Networks: Network Architectural Services (NAS), *TRI-Ada Proc.*, 1989.

[Royc90]   W. Royce, TRW's Ada Process Model for Incremental Development of Large Software Systems, *Proc. Int. Conf. S. E.*, 1990.

[RuBP91]   J. Rumbaugh, M. Blaha, W. Premerlani, F. Eddy, and W. Lorensen, *Object-Oriented Modeling and Design*, Prentice-Hall, Englewood Cliffs, NJ, 1991.

[SaEG68]   H. Sackman, W. J. Erickson, and E. E. Grant, Exploratory Experimental Studies Comparing Online and Offline Programmers, *Commun. ACM*, 11:3-11, 1968.

[Sage87]   A. P. Sage (ed.), *System Design for Human Interaction*, IEEE Press, New York, 1987.

[Samm90]   J. J. Sammarco, Computer-Aided Software Engineering (CASE) for Software Automation, Bureau of Mines Information Circular 9265, 1990.

[SaPa90]    A. P. Sage and J. D. Palmer, *Software Systems Engineering*, Wiley, New York, 1990.

[Sayw81]    F. G. Sayward, Design of Software Experiments, in A. J. Perlis, et al., eds., *Software Metrics: An Analysis and Evaluation*, MIT Press, Cambridge, MA, 1981, pp. 43-57.

[ScMc87]    G. G. Schulmeyer and J. I. McManus, *Handbook of Software Quality Assurance*, Van Nostrand Reinhold, New York, 1987.

[SeBa91]    R. W. Selby and V. R. Basili, Analyzing Error-Prone System Structure, *IEEE Trans. S. E.*, SE-17:141-152, 1991.

[SeBB87]    R. W. Selby, V. R. Basili and F. T. Baker, Cleanroom Software Development: An Empirical Evaluation, *IEEE Trans S. E.*, SE-13:1027-1037, 1987.

[SEL90]     *Annotated Bibliography of Software Engineering Laboratory Literature*, NASA Goddard Space Flight Center, Greenbelt, MD, 1990.

[Shaw90]    M. Shaw, Prospects for an Engineering Discipline of Software, *Software*, 15-24, November 1990.

[ShCD83]    V. Y. Shen, S. D., Conte, and H. E. Dunsmore, Software Science —A Critical Examination, *IEEE Trans. S. E.*, SE-9:155-165, 1983.

[ShMe88]    S. Shlaer and S. J. Mellor, *Object-Oriented Systems Analysis*, Yourdon Press, Englewood Cliffs, NJ, 1988.

[Shne80]    B. Shneiderman, *Software Psychology*, Winthrop, Cambridge, MA, 1980.

[Shne83]    B. Shneiderman, Direct Manipulation: A Step Beyond Programming Languages, *Computer*, (16,8):57-69, August 1983.

[Shne87]    B. Shneiderman, *Designing the User Interface: Strategies for Effective Human-Computer Interaction*, Addison-Wesley, Reading, MA, 1987.

[Shoo83]    M. L. Shooman, *Software Engineering*, McGraw-Hill, New York, 1983.

[ShWe87]    B. Shriver and P. Wegner (eds.), *Research Directions in Object-Oriented Programming*, MIT Press, Cambridge, MA, 1987.

[ShYT85]  V. Y. Shen, T.-J. Yu, S. M. Thebaut, and L. R. Paulsen, Identifying Error-Prone Software — An Empirical Approach, *IEEE Trans. S. E.*, SE-11:317-323, 1985.

[Simo69]  H. A. Simon, *The Sciences of the Artificial*, MIT Press, Cambridge, MA, 1969.

[SmMB83]  C. H. Smedema, P. Medema, and M. Boasson, *The Programming Languages Pascal, Modula, Chill, and Ada*, Prentice-Hall, Englewood Cliffs, NJ, 1983.

[SmSm77]  J. M. Smith and D. C. P. Smith, Database Abstractions: Aggregation and Generalization, *ACM Trans. Database Sys.*, 2:105-133, 1977.

[SoEh84]  E. Soloway and K. Ehrlich, Empirical Studies of Programming Knowledge, *IEEE Trans. S. E.*, SE-10:595-609, 1984.

[SoIy86]  E. Soloway and S. Iyengar (eds.), *Empirical Studies of Programmers*, Ablex, Norwood, NJ, 1986.

[SoJo85]  E. Soloway and W. L. Johnson, PROUST: Knowledge-Based Program Understanding, *IEEE Trans. S. E.*, SE-11:267-275, 1985.

[Somm89]  I. Sommerville, *Software Engineering*, 3rd ed., Addison-Wesley, Reading, MA, 1989.

[SpDe81]  S. P. Springer and G. Deutch, *Left Brain, Right Brain*, W.H. Freeman, New York, 1981.

[Spiv89]  J. M. Spivey, *The Z Notation: A Reference Manual*, Prentice-Hall, Englewood Cliffs, NJ, 1989.

[Spri89]  M. C. Springman, Incremental Software Test Methodology for a Major Government Ada Project, *TRI-Ada Proc.*, 1989.

[StCo78]  A. Stevens and P. Coupe, Distortions in Judged Spatial Relations, *Cog. Psychol.*, 10:422-437, 1978.

[StMC74]  W. Stevens, G. Myers and L. Constantine, Structured Design, *IBM Sys. J.*, 13:115-139, 1974.

[StRa88]  J. A. Stankovic and K. Ramamritham (eds.), *Hard Real-Time Systems* (Tutorial), IEEE Computer Society Press, Washington, DC, 1988.

[Stro86]    B. Stroustrup, *The C++ Programming Language*, Addison-Wesley, Reading, MA, 1986.

[Sutc88]    A. Sutcliffe, *Jackson System Development*, Prentice-Hall, Englewood Cliffs, NJ, 1988.

[Taus80]    R. C. Tausworth, The Work Breakdown Structure in Software Project Management, *J. Sys. Software*, 3:181-186, 1980.

[TeHe77]    D. Teichroew and E. A. Hershey III, PSL/PSA: A Computer-Aided Technique for Structured Documentation and Analysis of Information Processing Systems, *IEEE Trans. S. E.*, SE-3:41-48, 1977.

[ThLN78]    T. A. Thayer, M. Lipow, and E. C. Nelson, *Software Reliability, A Study of Large Project Reality*, vol. 2, TRW Series of Software Technology, North-Holland, Amsterdam, 1978.

[Tich84]    W. F. Tichy, The String-to-String Correction Problem with Block Moves, *ACM Trans. Comp. Sys.*, 2:309-321, 1984.

[Tich85]    W. F. Tichy, RCS — A System for Version Control, *Software—Practice & Exper.*, 15:637-654, 1985.

[Tich86]    W. F. Tichy, Smart Recompilation, *ACM Trans. Prog. Lang. Sys.*, 8:273-291, 1986.

[Trac88]    W. Tracz, *Software Reuse — Emerging Technologies*, IEEE Computer Society Press, Washington, DC, 1988.

[TsKl78]    D. Tsichritzis and A. Klug (eds.), *The ANSI/X3/SPACRC Framework*, AFIPS Press, Montvale, NJ, 1978.

[TuMa87]    W. M. Turski and T. S. E. Maibaum, *The Specification of Computer Programs*, Addison-Wesley, Wokingham, England, 1987.

[Turs85]    W. M. Turski, The Role of Logic in Software Enterprise, *Proc. Int. Conf. S.E.*, 400, 1985.

[TvKa74]    A. Tversky and D. Kahneman, Judgment under Uncertainty: Heuristics and Biases, *Science*, 185:1124-1131, September 1974.

[Ullm88]    J. D. Ullman, *Principles of Database and Knowledge-Based Systems*, Computer Science Press, Rockville, MD, vol. I, 1988, vol. II, 1989.

[USAr73]    *Program Evaluation and Review Technique*, United States Army Management Engineering Training Agency, Rock Island, IL, 1973.

[VaMc88]    J. D. Valett and F. E. McGarry, A Summary of Software Measurement Experience in the Software Engineering Laboratory, *Proc. Hawaii Int. Conf. Sys. Sci.*, 1988.

[VeTa87]    J. M. Verner and G. Tate, A Model for Software Sizing, *J. Sys. Software*, 7:173-177, 1987.

[VeTa88]    J. M. Verner and G. Tate, Estimating Size and Effort in Fourth-Generation Development, *IEEE Software*, 15-22, July 1988.

[VGHM88]   G. van der Veer, T. R. G. Green, J.-M. Hoc, and D. M. Murray (eds.), *Working with Computers: Theory versus Outcome*, Academic Press, New York, 1988.

[ViRa84]    C. R. Vick and C. V. Ramamoorthy (eds.), *Handbook of Software Engineering*, Van Nostrand Reinhold, New York, 1984.

[WaFe77]    C. E. Walston and C. P. Felix, A Method of Programming Measurement and Estimation, *IBM Sys. J.*, 16:54-73, 1977.

[WaFu89]    D. R. Wallace and R. U. Fujii, Software Verification and Validation: An Overview, *Software*, (6,3):10-17, May 1989.

[WaGa82]    A. I. Wasserman and S. Gatz, The Future of Programming, *Commun. ACM*, 25:196-206, 1982.

[Walk81]    M. G. Walker, *Managing Software Reliability. The Paradigmatic Approach*, North Holland, Amsterdam, 1981.

[Wall26]    G. Wallas, *The Art of Thought*, Harcourt, Brace, New York, 1926.

[WaMe85]    P. T. Ward and S. J. Mellor, *Structured Development for Real-Time Systems*, 3 vols., Yourdon Press, Englewood-Cliffs, vols. 1 and 2, 1985, vol. 3, 1986.

[Warn75]    J. D. Warnier, *Logical Construction of Programs*, Van Nostrand, New York, 1975.

[Warn81]    J. D. Warnier, *Logical Construction of Systems*, Van Nostrand, New York, 1981.

[WeBa85]    D. M. Weiss and V. R. Basili, Evaluating Software Development by Analysis of Changes: Some Data from the Software Engineering Laboratory, *IEEE Trans. S. E.*, SE-11:157-168, 1985.

[Wegn76]    P. Wegner, Programming Languages — The First 25 Years, *IEEE Trans. on Comp.*, C-25:1207-1225, 1976.

[Wegn87]    P. Wegner, Dimensions of Object-Based Language Design, *Proc. OOPSLA '87*, 168-182, 1987.

[Wein71]    G. M. Weinberg, *The Psychology of Computer Programming*, Van Nostrand Reinhold, New York, 1971.

[Wein86]    G. M. Weinberg, *Becoming a Technical Leader*, Dorset House, New York, 1986.

[Weis80]    R. W. Weisberg, *Memory, Thought, and Behavior*, Oxford University Press, New York, 1980.

[Weis86]    R. W. Weisberg, *Creativity and Other Myths*, W. H. Freeman, New York, 1986.

[WeKe89]    J. R. Weitzel and L. Kerschberg, Developing Knowledge-Based Systems: Reorganizing the System Development Life Cycle, *Commun. ACM*, 32:482-488, 1989.

[WeSc74]    G. M. Weinberg and E. L. Schulman, Goals and Performance in Computer Programming, *Human Factors*, 16:70-77, 1974.

[Weyu88]    E. J. Weyuker, Evaluating Software Complexity Measures, *IEEE Trans. S. E.*, SE-14:1357-1365, 1988.

[WiFl86]    T. Winograd and F. Flores, *Understanding Computers and Cognition*, Ablex, Norwood, NJ, 1986.

[Wile82]    D. S. Wile, *Program Developments: Formal Explanations of Implementations*, USC Information Sciences Institute, RR-82-99, 1982.

[Wilk85]    M. V. Wilkes, *Memoirs of a Computer Pioneer*, MIT Press, Cambridge, MA, 1985.

[Wing87]  A. Wingrove, Software Failures Are Management Failures, in B. Littlewood (ed.), *Software Reliability Achievement and Assessment*, Blackwell, Oxford, 1987.

[Wing90]  J. M. Wing, A Specifier's Introduction to Formal Methods, *Computer*, (23,9):8-24, 1990.

[WiNi89]  J. M. Wing and M. R. Nixon, Extending Ina Jo with Temporal Logic, *IEEE Trans. S. E.*, SE-15:181-197, 1989.

[Wink87]  J. F. H. Winkler, Version Control in Families of Large Programs, *9th Int. Conf. S. E.*, 150-161, 1987.

[Wino79]  T. Winograd, Beyond Programming Languages, *Commun. ACM*, 22:391-401, 1979.

[Wirt71]  N. Wirth, Program Development by Stepwise Refinement, *Commun. ACM*, 14:221-227, 1971.

[Wirt76]  N. Wirth, *Algorithms + Data Structures = Programs*, Prentice Hall, Englewood Cliffs, NJ, 1976.

[Wolv74]  R. Wolverton, The Cost of Developing Large-Scale Software, *IEEE Trans. Compt.*, C-23:615-636, 1974.

[Wood80]  C. K. Woodruff, Data Processing People—Are They Satisfied/Dissatisfied with Their Jobs?, *Inform. Manage.*, 3:219-225, 1980.

[YaCo80]  S. Yau and J. Collofello, Some Stability Measures for Software Maintenance, *IEEE Trans. S. E.*, SE-6, 1980.

[YaNT88]  S. S. Yau, R. A. Nicoll, J. J.-P. Tsai, and S.-S. Liu, An Integrated Life-Cycle Model for Software Maintenance, *IEEE Trans. S. E.*, SE-14:1128-1144, 1988.

[YeZa80]  R. T. Yeh and P. Zave, Specifying Software Requirements, *Proc. IEEE*, 68:1077-1085, 1980.

[YoCo79]  E. Yourdon and L. L. Constantine, *Structured Design*, Prentice-Hall, Englewood Cliffs, NJ, 1979.

[Your79]  E. Yourdon, *Structured Walkthroughs*, second edition, Prentice-Hall, Englewood Cliffs, NJ, 1979.

[Your89]    E. Yourdon, *Modern Structured Analysis*, Prentice Hall, Englewood Cliffs, NJ, 1989.

[ZaSc86]    P. Zave and W. Schell, Salient Features of an Executable Language and Its Environment, *IEEE Trans. S. E.*, SE-12:312-325, 1986.

[Zave84]    P. Zave, The Operational versus the Conventional Approach to Software Development, *Commun. ACM*, 27:104-118, 1984.

[ZeYH84]    M. V. Zelkowitz, R. T. Yeh, R. G. Hamlet, J. D. Gannon, and V. R. Basili, Software Engineering Practices in the US and Japan, *Computer*, 57-66, June 1984.

[ZvPa83]    N. Zvegintzov and G. Parikh, *Tutorial on Software Maintenance*, IEEE Computer Society Press, Washington, DC, 1983.

# INDEX